Fundamentals of Multimedia

Ze-Nian Li and Mark S. Drew

School of Computing Science
Simon Fraser University

PEARSON
Prentice
Hall

Upper Saddle River, NJ 07458

Library of Congress Cataloging-in-Publication Data

CIP DATA AVAILABLE.

Vice President and Editorial Director, ECS: *Marcia J. Horton*
Senior Acquisitions Editor: *Kate Hargett*
Editorial Assistant: *Michael Giacobbe*
Vice President and Director of Production and Manufacturing, ESM: *David W. Riccardi*
Executive Managing Editor: *Vince O'Brien*
Managing Editor: *Camille Trentacoste*
Production Editor: *Irwin Zucker*
Director of Creative Services: *Paul Belfanti*
Art Director and Cover Manager: *Jayne Conte*
Cover Designer: *Suzanne Behnke*
Managing Editor, AV Management and Production: *Patricia Burns*
Art Editor: *Gregory Dulles*
Manufacturing Manager: *Trudy Pisciotti*
Manufacturing Buyer: *Lisa McDowell*
Marketing Manager: *Pamela Shaffer*

© 2004 by Pearson Education, Inc.
Pearson Prentice Hall
Pearson Education, Inc.
Upper Saddle River, NJ 07458

All rights reserved. No part of this book may be reproduced in any format or by any means, without permission in writing from the publisher.

Images of Lena that appear in Figures 3.1, 3.3, 3.4, 3.10, 8.20, 9.2, and 9.3, are reproduced by special permission of *Playboy* magazine. Copyright 1972 by Playboy.

The author and publisher of this book have used their best efforts in preparing this book. These efforts include the development, research, and testing of the theories and programs to determine their effectiveness. The author and publisher make no warranty of any kind, expressed or implied, with regard to these programs or the documentation contained in this book. The author and publisher shall not be liable in any event for incidental or consequential damages in connection with, or arising out of, the furnishing, performance, or use of these programs.

Printed in the United States of America

10 9 8 7 6 5 4 3 2 1

ISBN 0-13-061872-1

Pearson Education Ltd., *London*
Pearson Education Australia Pty., *Sydney*
Pearson Education Singapore, Pte. Ltd.
Pearson Education North Asia Ltd., *Hong Kong*
Pearson Education Canada, Inc., *Toronto*
Pearson Educación de Mexico, S.A. de C.V.
Pearson Education—Japan, *Tokyo*
Pearson Education Malaysia, Pte. Ltd.
Pearson Education Inc., *Upper Saddle River, New Jersey*

To my mom, and my wife Yansin.

Ze-Nian

To Noah, James (Ira), Eva, and, especially, to Jenna.

Mark

List of Trademarks

The following is a list of products noted in this text that are trademarks or registered trademarks their associated companies.

3D Studio Max is a registered trademark of Autodesk, Inc.

After Effects, Illustrator, Photoshop, Premiere, and Cool Edit are registered trademarks of Adobe Systems, Inc.

Authorware, Director, Dreamweaver, Fireworks, and Freehand are registered trademarks, and Flash and Soundedit are trademarks of Macromedia, Inc., in the United States and/or other countries.

Cakewalk Pro Audio is a trademark of Twelve Tone Systems, Inc.

CorelDRAW is a registered trademark of Corel and/or its subsidiaries in Canada, the United States and/or other countries.

Cubase is a registered trademark of Pinnacle Systems.

DirectX, Internet Explorer, PowerPoint, Windows, Word, Visual Basic, and Visual C++ are registered trademarks of Microsoft Corporation in the United States and/or other countries.

Gifcon is a trademark of Alchemy Mindworks Corporation.

HyperCard and Final Cut Pro are registered trademarks of Apple Computer, Inc.

HyperStudio is a registered trademark of Sunburst Technology.

Java Media Framework and Java 3D are trademarks of Sun Microsystems, Inc., in the United States and other countries.

Jell-O is a registered trademark of Kraft Foods Incorporated.

MATLAB is a trademark of The MathWorks, Inc.

Maya and OpenGL are registered trademarks of Silicon Graphics Inc.

Mosaic is a registered trademark of National Center for Supercomputing Applications (NCSA).

Netscape is a registered trademark of Netscape Communications Corporation in the U.S. and other countries.

Playstation is a registered trademark of Sony Corporation.

Pro Tools is a registered trademark of Avid Technology, Inc.

Quest Multimedia Authoring System is a registered trademark of Allen Communication Learning Services.

RenderMan is a registered trademark of Pixar Animation Studios.

Slinky is a registered trademark of Slinky Toys.

Softimage XSI is a registered trademark of Avid Technology Inc.

Sound Forge is a registered trademark of Sonic Foundry.

WinZip is a registered trademark WinZip Computing, Inc.

Contents

Preface

A course in multimedia is rapidly becoming a necessity in computer science and engineering curricula, especially now that multimedia touches most aspects of these fields. Multimedia was originally seen as a vertical application area; that is, a niche application with methods that belong only to itself. However, like pervasive computing, multimedia is now essentially a horizontal application area and forms an important component of the study of computer graphics, image processing, databases, real-time systems, operating systems, information retrieval, computer networks, computer vision, and so on. Multimedia is no longer just a toy but forms part of the technological environment in which we work and think. This book fills the need for a university-level text that examines a good deal of the core agenda computer science sees as belonging to this subject area. Multimedia has become associated with a certain set of issues in computer science and engineering, and we address those here.

The book is not an introduction to simple design issues—it serves a more advanced audience than that. On the other hand, it is not a reference work — it is more a traditional textbook. While we perforce discuss multimedia tools, we would like to give a sense of the underlying principles in the tasks those tools carry out. Students who undertake and succeed in a course based on this text can be said to really understand fundamental matters in regard to this material; hence the title of the text.

In conjunction with this text, a full-fledged course should also allow students to make use of this knowledge to carry out interesting or even wonderful practical projects in multimedia, interactive projects that engage and sometimes amuse and, perhaps, even teach these same concepts.

Who Should Read This Book?

This text aims at introducing the basic ideas in multimedia to an audience comfortable with technical applications—that is, computer science and engineering students. It aims to cover an upper-level undergraduate multimedia course but could also be used in more advanced courses and would be a good reference for anyone, including those in industry, interested in current multimedia technologies. Graduate students needing a solid grounding in materials they may not have seen before would undoubtedly benefit from reading it.

The text mainly presents concepts, not applications. A multimedia course, on the other hand, teaches these concepts and tests them but also allows students to use coding and presentation skills they already know to address problems in multimedia. The accompanying web site shows some of the code for multimedia applications, along with some of the better projects students have developed in such a course and other useful materials best presented electronically.

The ideas in the text drive the results shown in student projects. We assume the reader knows how to program and is also completely comfortable learning yet another tool. Instead of concentrating on tools, however, we emphasize what students do not already know.

Using the methods and ideas collected here, students are also able to learn more themselves, sometimes in a job setting. It is not unusual for students who take the type of multimedia course this text aims at to go on to jobs in a multimedia-related industry immediately after their senior year, and sometimes before.

The selection of material in the text addresses real issues these learners will face as soon as they show up in the workplace. Some topics are simple but new to the students; some are more complex but unavoidable in this emerging area.

Have the Authors Used This Material in a Real Class?

Since 1996, we have taught a third-year undergraduate course in multimedia systems based on the introductory materials set out in this book. A one-semester course could very likely not include all the material covered in this text, but we have usually managed to consider a good many of the topics addressed and to mention a select number of issues in Part III within that time frame.

Over the same time period as an introduction to more advanced materials, we have also taught a one-semester graduate-level course using notes covering topics similar to the ground covered by this text. A fourth-year or graduate course would do well to consider material from Parts I and II of the book and then some material from Part III, perhaps in conjunction with some of the original research references included here and results presented at topical conferences.

We have attempted to fill both needs, concentrating on an undergraduate audience but including more advanced material as well. Sections that can safely be omitted on a first reading are marked with an asterisk.

What is Covered in This Text?

In Part I, Multimedia Authoring and Data Representations, we introduce some of the notions included in the term *multimedia* and look at its history as well as its present. Practically speaking, we carry out multimedia projects using software tools, so in addition to an overview of these tools, we get down to some of the nuts and bolts of multimedia authoring. Representing data is critical in multimedia, and we look at the most important data representations for multimedia applications, examining image data, video data, and audio data in detail. Since color is vitally important in multimedia programs, we see how this important area impacts multimedia issues.

In Part II, Multimedia Data Compression, we consider how we can make all this data fly onto the screen and speakers. Data compression turns out to be an important enabling technology that makes modern multimedia systems possible, so we look at lossless and lossy compression methods. For the latter category, JPEG still-image compression standards, including JPEG2000, are arguably the most important, so we consider these in detail. But since a picture is worth a thousand words and video is worth more than a million words per minute, we examine the ideas behind MPEG standards MPEG-1, MPEG-2, MPEG-4, MPEG-7, and beyond. Separately, we consider some basic audio compression techniques and take a look at MPEG Audio, including MP3.

In Part III, Multimedia Communication and Retrieval, we consider the great demands multimedia places on networks and systems. We go on to consider network technologies and protocols that make interactive multimedia possible. Some of the applications discussed include multimedia on demand, multimedia over IP, multimedia over ATM, and multimedia over wireless networks. Content-based retrieval is a particularly important issue in digital libraries and interactive multimedia, so we examine ideas and systems for this application in some detail.

Textbook Web Site

The book's web site is www.cs.sfu.ca/mmbook. There, you will find copies of figures from the book, an errata sheet updated regularly, programs that help demonstrate concepts in the text, and a dynamic set of links for the Further Exploration section of each chapter. Since these links are regularly updated (and of course URLs change often) they are mostly online rather than in the text.

Instructors' Resources

The main text web site has no ID and password, but access to sample student projects is at the instructor's discretion and is password-protected. Prentice Hall also hosts a web site containing Course Instructor resources for adopters of the text. These include an extensive collection of online course notes, a one-semester course syllabus and calendar of events, solutions for the exercises in the text, sample assignments and solutions, sample exams, and extra exam questions.

Acknowledgements

We are most grateful to colleagues who generously gave of their time to review this text, and we wish to express our thanks to Shu-Ching Chen, Edward Chang, Qianping Gu, Rachelle S. Heller, Gongzhu Hu, S. N. Jayaram, Tiko Kameda, Xiaobo Li, Siwei Lu, Dennis Richards, and Jacques Vaisey.

The writing of this text has been greatly aided by a number of suggestions from present and former colleagues and students. We would like to thank James Au, Chad Ciavarro, Hao Jiang, Steven Kilthau, Michael King, Cheng Lu, Yi Sun, Dominic Szopa, Zinovi Tauber, Malte von Ruden, Jian Wang, Jie Wei, Edward Yan, Yingchen Yang, Osmar Zaïane, Wenbiao Zhang, and William Zhong for their assistance. As well, Mr. Ye Lu made great contributions to Chapters 8 and 9 and his valiant efforts are particularly appreciated. We are also most grateful for the students who generously made their course projects available for instructional use for this book.

PART ONE

MULTIMEDIA AUTHORING AND DATA REPRESENTATIONS

Introduction to Multimedia

As an introduction to multimedia, in Chapter 1 we consider the question of just what multimedia is. We examine its history and the development of hypertext and hypermedia. We then get down to practical matters with an overview of multimedia software tools. These are the basic means we use to develop multimedia content. But a multimedia production is much more than the sum of its parts, so Chapter 2 looks at the nuts and bolts of multimedia authoring design and a taxonomy of authoring metaphors. The chapter also sets out a list of important contemporary multimedia authoring tools in current use.

Multimedia Data Representations

As in many fields, the issue of how to best represent the data is of crucial importance in the study of multimedia. Chapters 3 through 6 consider how this is addressed in this field, setting out the most important data representations in multimedia applications. Because the main areas of concern are images, moving pictures, and audio, we begin investigating these in Chapter 3, Graphics and Image Data Representations, then look at Basics of Video in Chapter 5. Before going on to Chapter 6, Basics of Digital Audio, we take a side trip in Chapter 4 to explore several issues on the use of color, since color is vitally important in multimedia programs.

CHAPTER 1

Introduction to Multimedia

1.1 WHAT IS MULTIMEDIA?

People who use the term "multimedia" often seem to have quite different, even opposing, viewpoints. A PC vendor would like us to think of multimedia as a PC that has sound capability, a DVD-ROM drive, and perhaps the superiority of multimedia-enabled micro-processors that understand additional multimedia instructions. A consumer entertainment vendor may think of multimedia as interactive cable TV with hundreds of digital channels, or a cable-TV-like service delivered over a high-speed Internet connection.

A computer science student reading this book likely has a more application-oriented view of what multimedia consists of: applications that use multiple modalities to their advantage, including text, images, drawings (graphics), animation, video, sound (including speech), and, most likely, interactivity of some kind. The popular notion of "convergence" is one that inhabits the college campus as it does the culture at large. In this scenario, PCs, DVDs, games, digital TV, set-top web surfing, wireless, and so on are converging in technology, presumably to arrive in the near future at a final all-around, multimedia-enabled product. While hardware may indeed involve such devices, the present is already exciting — multimedia is part of some of the most interesting projects underway in computer science. The convergence going on in this field is in fact a convergence of areas that have in the past been separated but are now finding much to share in this new application area. Graphics, visualization, HCI, computer vision, data compression, graph theory, networking, database systems — all have important contributions to make in multimedia at the present time.

1.1.1 Components of Multimedia

The multiple modalities of text, audio, images, drawings, animation, and video in multimedia are put to use in ways as diverse as

- Video teleconferencing

- Distributed lectures for higher education

- Telemedicine

- Cooperative work environments that allow business people to edit a shared document or schoolchildren to share a single game using two mice that pass control back and forth

- Searching (very) large video and image databases for target visual objects

- "Augmented" reality: placing real-appearing computer graphics and video objects into scenes so as to take the physics of objects and lights (e.g., shadows) into account

- Audio cues for where video-conference participants are seated, as well as taking into account gaze direction and attention of participants

- Building searchable features into new video and enabling very high to very low bitrate use of new, scalable multimedia products

- Making multimedia components *editable* — allowing the user side to decide what components, video, graphics, and so on are actually viewed and allowing the client to move components around or delete them — making components distributed

- Building "inverse-Hollywood" applications that can re-create the process by which a video was made, allowing storyboard pruning and concise video summarization

- Using voice recognition to build an interactive environment — say a kitchen-wall web browser

From the computer science student's point of view, what makes multimedia interesting is that so much of the material covered in traditional computer science areas bears on the multimedia enterprise: networks, operating systems, real-time systems, vision, information retrieval. Like databases, multimedia touches on many traditional areas.

1.1.2 Multimedia Research Topics and Projects

To the computer science researcher, multimedia consists of a wide variety of topics [1]:

- **Multimedia processing and coding.** This includes multimedia content analysis, content-based multimedia retrieval, multimedia security, audio/image/video processing, compression, and so on.

- **Multimedia system support and networking.** People look at such topics as network protocols, Internet, operating systems, servers and clients, quality of service (QoS), and databases.

- **Multimedia tools, end systems, and applications.** These include hypermedia systems, user interfaces, authoring systems, multimodal interaction, and integration: "ubiquity" — web-everywhere devices, multimedia education, including computer supported collaborative learning and design, and applications of virtual environments.

The concerns of multimedia researchers also impact researchers in almost every other branch of computer science. For example, data mining is an important current research area, and a large database of multimedia data objects is a good example of just what we may be interested in mining. Telemedicine applications, such as "telemedical patient consultative encounters," are multimedia applications that place a heavy burden on existing network architectures.

Current Multimedia Projects   Many exciting research projects are currently underway in multimedia, and we'd like to introduce a few of them here.

For example, researchers are interested in camera-based object tracking technology. One aim is to develop control systems for industrial control, gaming, and so on that rely on moving scale models (toys) around a real environment (a board game, say). Tracking the control objects (toys) provides user control of the process.

3D motion capture can also be used for multiple actor capture, so that multiple *real* actors in a *virtual* studio can be used to automatically produce realistic *animated* models with natural movement.

Multiple views from several cameras or from a single camera under differing lighting can accurately acquire data that gives both the shape and surface properties of materials, thus automatically generating synthetic graphics models. This allows photo-realistic (video-quality) synthesis of virtual actors.

3D capture technology is next to fast enough now to allow acquiring dynamic characteristics of human facial expression during speech, to synthesize highly realistic facial animation from speech.

Multimedia applications aimed at handicapped persons, particularly those with poor vision and the elderly, are a rich field of endeavor in current research.

"Digital fashion" aims to develop smart clothing that can communicate with other such enhanced clothing using wireless communication, so as to artificially enhance human interaction in a social setting. The vision here is to use technology to allow individuals to allow certain thoughts and feelings to be broadcast automatically, for exchange with others equipped with similar technology.

Georgia Tech's Electronic Housecall system, an initiative for providing interactive health monitoring services to patients in their homes, relies on networks for delivery, challenging current capabilities.

Behavioral science models can be brought into play to model interaction between people, which can then be extended to enable natural interaction by virtual characters. Such "augmented interaction" applications can be used to develop interfaces between real and virtual humans for tasks such as augmented storytelling.

Each of these application areas pushes the development of computer science generally, stimulates new applications, and fascinates practitioners.

1.2   MULTIMEDIA AND HYPERMEDIA

To place multimedia in its proper context, in this section we briefly consider the history of multimedia, a recent part of which is the connection between multimedia and hypermedia. We go on to a quick overview of multimedia software tools available for creation of multimedia content, which prepares us to examine, in Chapter 2, the larger issue of integrating this content into full-blown multimedia productions.

1.2.1   History of Multimedia

A brief history of the use of multimedia to communicate ideas might begin with newspapers, which were perhaps the *first* mass communication medium, using text, graphics, and images.

Motion pictures were originally conceived of in the 1830s to observe motion too rapid for perception by the human eye. Thomas Alva Edison commissioned the invention of a motion picture camera in 1887. Silent feature films appeared from 1910 to 1927; the silent era effectively ended with the release of *The Jazz Singer* in 1927.

In 1895, Guglielmo Marconi sent his first wireless radio transmission at Pontecchio, Italy. A few years later (1901), he detected radio waves beamed across the Atlantic. Initially invented for telegraph, radio is now a major medium for audio broadcasting. In 1909, Marconi shared the Nobel Prize for physics. (Reginald A. Fessenden, of Quebec, beat Marconi to human voice transmission by several years, but not all inventors receive due credit. Nevertheless, Fessenden was paid $2.5 million in 1928 for his purloined patents.)

Television was the new medium for the twentieth century. It established video as a commonly available medium and has since changed the world of mass communication.

The connection between *computers* and ideas about multimedia covers what is actually only a short period:

1945 As part of MIT's postwar deliberations on what to do with all those scientists employed on the war effort, Vannevar Bush (1890–1974) wrote a landmark article [2] describing what amounts to a hypermedia system, called "Memex." Memex was meant to be a universally useful and personalized memory device that even included the concept of associative links — it really is the forerunner of the World Wide Web. After World War II, 6,000 scientists who had been hard at work on the war effort suddenly found themselves with time to consider other issues, and the Memex idea was one fruit of that new freedom.

1960s Ted Nelson started the Xanadu project and coined the term "hypertext." Xanadu was the first attempt at a hypertext system — Nelson called it a "magic place of literary memory."

1967 Nicholas Negroponte formed the Architecture Machine Group at MIT.

1968 Douglas Engelbart, greatly influenced by Vannevar Bush's "As We May Think," demonstrated the "On-Line System" (NLS), another early hypertext program. Engelbart's group at Stanford Research Institute aimed at "augmentation, not automation," to enhance human abilities through computer technology. NLS consisted of such critical ideas as an outline editor for idea development, hypertext links, teleconferencing, word processing, and e-mail, and made use of the mouse pointing device, windowing software, and help systems [3].

1969 Nelson and van Dam at Brown University created an early hypertext editor called FRESS [4]. The present-day Intermedia project by the Institute for Research in Information and Scholarship (IRIS) at Brown is the descendant of that early system.

1976 The MIT Architecture Machine Group proposed a project entitled "Multiple Media." This resulted in the *Aspen Movie Map*, the first hypermedia videodisc, in 1978.

1985 Negroponte and Wiesner cofounded the MIT Media Lab, a leading research institution investigating digital video and multimedia.

1989 Tim Berners-Lee proposed the World Wide Web to the European Council for Nuclear Research (CERN).

1990 Kristina Hooper Woolsey headed the Apple Multimedia Lab, with a staff of 100. Education was a chief goal.

1991 MPEG-1 was approved as an international standard for digital video. Its further development led to newer standards, MPEG-2, MPEG-4, and further MPEGs, in the 1990s.

1991 The introduction of PDAs in 1991 began a new period in the use of computers in general and multimedia in particular. This development continued in 1996 with the marketing of the first PDA with no keyboard.

1992 JPEG was accepted as the international standard for digital image compression. Its further development has now led to the new JPEG2000 standard.

1992 The first MBone audio multicast on the Net was made.

1993 The University of Illinois National Center for Supercomputing Applications produced NCSA Mosaic, the first full-fledged browser, launching a new era in Internet information access.

1994 Jim Clark and Marc Andreessen created the Netscape program.

1995 The JAVA language was created for platform-independent application development.

1996 DVD video was introduced; high-quality, full-length movies were distributed on a single disk. The DVD format promised to transform the music, gaming and computer industries.

1998 XML 1.0 was announced as a W3C Recommendation.

1998 Handheld MP3 devices first made inroads into consumer tastes in the fall, with the introduction of devices holding 32 MB of flash memory.

2000 World Wide Web (WWW) size was estimated at over 1 billion pages.

1.2.2 Hypermedia and Multimedia

Ted Nelson invented the term "HyperText" around 1965. Whereas we may think of a book as a *linear* medium, basically meant to be read from beginning to end, a hypertext system is meant to be read nonlinearly, by following links that point to other parts of the document, or indeed to other documents. Figure 1.1 illustrates this idea.

Hypermedia is not constrained to be text-based. It can include other media, such as graphics, images, and especially the continuous media — sound and video. Apparently Ted Nelson was also the first to use this term. The World Wide Web (WWW) is the best example of a hypermedia application.

As we have seen, *multimedia* fundamentally means that computer information can be represented through audio, graphics, images, video, and animation in addition to traditional media (text and graphics). Hypermedia can be considered one particular multimedia application.

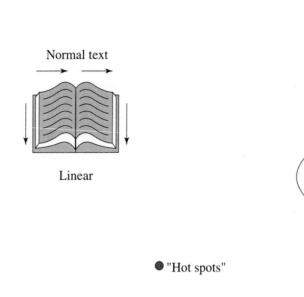

FIGURE 1.1: Hypertext is nonlinear.

Examples of typical multimedia applications include: digital video editing and production systems; electronic newspapers and magazines; the World Wide Web; online reference works, such as encyclopedias; games; groupware; home shopping; interactive TV; multimedia courseware; video conferencing; video-on-demand; and interactive movies.

1.3 WORLD WIDE WEB

The World Wide Web is the largest and most commonly used hypermedia application. Its popularity is due to the amount of information available from web servers, the capacity to post such information, and the ease of navigating such information with a web browser. WWW technology is maintained and developed by the World Wide Web Consortium (W3C), although the Internet Engineering Task Force (IETF) standardizes the technologies. The W3C has listed the following three goals for the WWW: universal access of web resources (by everyone everywhere), effectiveness of navigating available information, and responsible use of posted material.

1.3.1 History of the WWW

Amazingly, one of the most predominant networked multimedia applications has its roots in nuclear physics! As noted in the previous section, Tim Berners-Lee proposed the World Wide Web to CERN (European Center for Nuclear Research) as a means for organizing and sharing their work and experimental results. The following is a short list of important dates in the creation of the WWW:

1960s It is recognized that documents need to have formats that are human-readable and that identify structure and elements. Charles Goldfarb, Edward Mosher, and Raymond Lorie developed the Generalized Markup Language (GML) for IBM.

1986 The ISO released a final version of the Standard Generalized Markup Language (SGML), mostly based on the earlier GML.

1990 With approval from CERN, Tim Berners-Lee started developing a hypertext server, browser, and editor on a NeXTStep workstation. He invented hypertext markup language (HTML) and the hypertext transfer protocol (HTTP) for this purpose.

1993 NCSA released an alpha version of Mosaic based on the version by Marc Andreessen for the X Windows System. This was the first popular browser. Microsoft's Internet Explorer is based on Mosaic.

1994 Marc Andreessen and some colleagues from NCSA joined Dr. James H. Clark (also the founder of Silicon Graphics Inc.) to form Mosaic Communications Corporation. In November, the company changed its name to Netscape Communications Corporation.

1998 The W3C accepted XML version 1.0 specifications as a Recommendation. XML is the main focus of the W3C and supersedes HTML.

1.3.2   HyperText Transfer Protocol (HTTP)

HTTP is a protocol that was originally designed for transmitting hypermedia, but it also supports transmission of any file type. HTTP is a "stateless" request/response protocol, in the sense that a client typically opens a connection to the HTTP server, requests information, the server responds, and the connection is terminated — no information is carried over for the next request.

The basic request format is

```
Method URI Version
Additional-Headers

Message-body
```

The Uniform Resource Identifier (URI) identifies the resource accessed, such as the host name, always preceded by the token "http://". A URI could be a Uniform Resource Locator (URL), for example. Here, the URI can also include query strings (some interactions require submitting data). Method is a way of exchanging information or performing tasks on the URI. Two popular methods are GET and POST. GET specifies that the information requested is in the request string itself, while the POST method specifies that the resource pointed to in the URI should consider the message body. POST is generally used for submitting HTML forms. Additional-Headers specifies additional parameters about the client. For example, to request access to this textbook's web site, the following HTTP message might be generated:

```
GET http://www.cs.sfu.ca/mmbook/ HTTP/1.1
```

The basic response format is

```
Version Status-Code Status-Phrase
Additional-Headers

Message-body
```

Status-Code is a number that identifies the response type (or error that occurs), and Status-Phrase is a textual description of it. Two commonly seen status codes and phrases are 200 OK when the request was processed successfully and 404 Not Found when the URI does not exist. For example, in response to the example request above for this textbook's URL, the web server may return something like

```
HTTP/1.1 200 OK Server:
[No-plugs-here-please] Date: Wed, 25 July 2002
20:04:30 GMT
Content-Length: 1045 Content-Type: text/html

<HTML>
...
</HTML>
```

1.3.3   HyperText Markup Language (HTML)

HTML is a language for publishing hypermedia on the World Wide Web. It is defined using SGML and derives elements that describe generic document structure and formatting. Since it uses ASCII, it is portable to all different (even binary-incompatible) computer hardware, which allows for global exchange of information. The current version of HTML is version 4.01, specified in 1999. The next generation of HTML is XHTML, a reformulation of HTML using XML.

HTML uses tags to describe document elements. The tags are in the format <token params> to define the start point of a document element and </token> to define the end of the element. Some elements have only inline parameters and don't require ending tags. HTML divides the document into a HEAD and a BODY part as follows:

```
<HTML>
<HEAD>
...
</HEAD>
<BODY>
...
</BODY>
</HTML>
```

The HEAD describes document definitions, which are parsed before any document rendering is done. These include page title, resource links, and meta-information the author decides to specify. The BODY part describes the document structure and content. Common structure elements are paragraphs, tables, forms, links, item lists, and buttons.

A very simple HTML page is as follows:

```
<HTML>
<HEAD>
  <TITLE>
  A sample web page.
  </TITLE>
  <META NAME = "Author" CONTENT = "Cranky Professor">
</HEAD> <BODY>
  <P>
  We can put any text we like here, since this is
  a paragraph element.
  </P>
</BODY>
</HTML>
```

Naturally, HTML has more complex structures and can be mixed with other standards. The standard has evolved to allow integration with script languages, dynamic manipulation of almost all elements and properties after display on the client side (*dynamic HTML*), and modular customization of all rendering parameters using a markup language called *Cascading Style Sheets* (CSS). Nonetheless, HTML has rigid, nondescriptive structure elements, and modularity is hard to achieve.

1.3.4 Extensible Markup Language (XML)

There is a need for a markup language for the WWW that has modularity of data, structure, and view. That is, we would like a user or an application to be able to *define* the tags (structure) allowed in a document and their relationship to each other, in one place, then define data using these tags in another place (the XML file) and, finally, define in yet another document how to render the tags.

Suppose you wanted to have stock information retrieved from a database according to a user query. Using XML, you would use a global *Document Type Definition* (DTD) you have already defined for stock data. Your server-side script will abide by the DTD rules to generate an XML document according to the query, using data from your database. Finally, you will send users your *XML Style Sheet* (XSL), depending on the type of device they use to display the information, so that your document looks best both on a computer with a 21-inch CRT monitor and on a cellphone.

The current XML version is XML 1.0, approved by the W3C in February 1998. XML syntax looks like HTML syntax, although it is much stricter. All tags are lowercase, and a tag that has only inline data has to terminate itself, for example, `<token params />`. XML also uses namespaces, so that multiple DTDs declaring different elements but with similar tag names can have their elements distinguished. DTDs can be imported from URIs as well. As an example of an XML document structure, here is the definition for a small XHTML document:

```
<?xml version="1.0" encoding="iso-8859-1"?>
<!DOCTYPE html PUBLIC "-//W3C//DTD XHTML 1.0"
 "http://www.w3.org/TR/xhtml1/DTD/xhtml1-transition.dtd">
<html xmlns="http://www.w3.org/1999/xhtml">
... [html that follows
    the above mentioned
    XML rules]
</html>
```

All XML documents start with `<?xml version="ver"?>`. `<!DOCTYPE ...>` is a special tag used for importing DTDs. Since it is a DTD definition, it does not adhere to XML rules. `xmlns` defines a unique XML namespace for the document elements. In this case, the namespace is the XHTML specifications web site.

In addition to XML specifications, the following XML-related specifications are standardized:

- **XML Protocol**. Used to exchange XML information between processes. It is meant to supersede HTTP and extend it as well as to allow interprocess communications across networks.

- **XML Schema**. A more structured and powerful language for defining XML data types (tags). Unlike a DTD, XML Schema uses XML tags for type definitions.

- **XSL**. This is basically CSS for XML. On the other hand, XSL is much more complex, having three parts: *XSL Transformations* (XSLT), *XML Path Language* (XPath), and *XSL Formatting Objects*.

- **SMIL: Synchronized Multimedia Integration Language, pronounced "smile"**. This is a particular application of XML (globally predefined DTD) that permits specifying temporally scripted interaction among any media types and user input. For example, it can be used to show a streaming video synchronized with a slide show presentation, both reacting to user navigation through the slide show or video.

1.3.5   Synchronized Multimedia Integration Language (SMIL)

Just as it was beneficial to have HTML provide text-document publishing using a readable markup language, it is also desirable to be able to publish multimedia presentations using a markup language. Multimedia presentations have additional characteristics: whereas in text documents the text is read sequentially and displayed all at once (at the same time), multimedia presentations can include many elements, such as video and audio, that have content changing through time. Thus, a multimedia markup language must enable scheduling and synchronization of different multimedia elements and define these elements' interactivity with the user.

The W3C established a Working Group in 1997 to come up with specifications for a multimedia synchronization language. That group produced specifications for SMIL 1.0 that became a Recommendation in June 1998. As HTML was being redefined in XML (XHTML specifications), so too did SMIL 1.0, with some enhancements. SMIL 2.0, which also provides integration with HTML, was accepted as a Recommendation in August 2001.

SMIL 2.0 is specified in XML using a *modularization* approach similar to the one used in XHTML. All SMIL elements are divided into modules — sets of XML elements, attributes, and values that define one conceptual functionality. In the interest of modularization, not all available modules must be included for all applications. For that reason, *Language Profiles* are defined, specifying a particular grouping of modules. Particular modules may have integration requirements a profile must follow. SMIL 2.0 has a main language profile that includes almost all SMIL modules, a Basic profile that includes only modules necessary to support basic functionality, and an XHTML+SMIL profile designed to integrate HTML and SMIL. The latter includes most of the XHTML modules, with only the SMIL timing modules (but not structure modules — XHTML has its own structure modules) added.

The SMIL language structure is similar to XHTML. The root element is `smil`, which contains the two elements `head` and `body`. `head` contains information not used for synchronization — metainformation, layout information, and content control, such as media bitrate. `body` contains all the information relating to which resources to present, and when.

Three types of resource synchronization (grouping) are available: `seq`, `par`, and `excl`. `seq` specifies that the elements grouped are to be presented in the specified order (sequentially). Alternatively, `par` specifies that all the elements grouped are to be presented at the same time (in parallel). `excl` specifies that only one of the grouped elements can be presented at a time (exclusively); order does not matter.

Let's look at an example of SMIL code:

```
<!DOCTYPE smil PUBLIC "-//W3C//DTD SMIL 2.0"
"http://www.w3.org/2001/SMIL20/SMIL20.dtd">
<smil xmlns=
 "http://www.w3.org/2001/SMIL20/Language">
 <head>
    <meta name="Author" content="Some Professor" />
 </head>
 <body>
    <par id="MakingOfABook">
       <seq>
          <video src="authorview.mpg" />
          <img src="onagoodday.jpg" />
       </seq>

       <audio src="authorview.wav" />
       <text src="http://www.cs.sfu.ca/mmbook/" />
    </par>
 </body>
</smil>
```

A SMIL document can optionally use the `<!DOCTYPE...>` directive to import the SMIL DTD, which will force the interpreter to verify the document against the DTD. A SMIL document starts with `<smil>` and specifies the default namespace, using the `xmlns` attribute. The `<head>` section specifies the author of the document. The `body` element contains the synchronization information and resources we wish to present.

In the example given, a video source called `"authorview.mpg"`, an audio source, `"authorview.wav"`, and an HTML document at `"http://booksite.html"` are presented simultaneously at the beginning.   When the video ends, the image `"onagoodday.jpg"` is shown, while the audio and the HTML document are still presented. At this point, the audio will thank the listeners and conclude the interview.

Additional information on SMIL specifications and available modules is available on the W3C web site.

1.4   OVERVIEW OF MULTIMEDIA SOFTWARE TOOLS

In this subsection, we look briefly at some of the software tools available for carrying out tasks in multimedia. These tools are really only the beginning — a fully functional multimedia project can also call for stand-alone programming as well as just the use of predefined tools to fully exercise the capabilities of machines and the Net.[1]

The categories of software tools we examine here are

- Music sequencing and notation

- Digital audio

- Graphics and image editing

- Video editing

- Animation

- Multimedia authoring

1.4.1   Music Sequencing and Notation

Cakewalk   Cakewalk is a well known older name for what is now called Pro Audio. The firm producing this *sequencing* and editing software, Twelve Tone Systems, also sells an introductory version of their software, "Cakewalk Express", over the Internet for a low price.

The term *sequencer* comes from older devices that stored sequences of notes in the MIDI music language (*events*, in MIDI; see Section 6.2). It is also possible to insert WAV files and Windows MCI commands (for animation and video) into music tracks. (MCI is a ubiquitous component of the Windows API.)

Cubase   Cubase is another sequencing/editing program, with capabilities similar to those of Cakewalk. It includes some digital audio editing tools (see below).

---

[1] See the accompanying web site for several interesting uses of software tools. In a typical computer science course in multimedia, the tools described here might be used to create a small multimedia production as a first assignment. Some of the tools are powerful enough that they might also form part of a course project.

Macromedia Soundedit   Soundedit is a mature program for creating audio for multimedia projects and the web that integrates well with other Macromedia products such as Flash and Director.

1.4.2 Digital Audio

Digital Audio tools deal with accessing and editing the actual sampled sounds that make up audio.

Cool Edit   Cool Edit is a powerful, popular digital audio toolkit with capabilities (for PC users, at least) that emulate a professional audio studio, including multitrack productions and sound file editing, along with digital signal processing effects.

Sound Forge   Sound Forge is a sophisticated PC-based program for editing WAV files. Sound can be captured from a CD-ROM drive or from tape or microphone through the sound card, then mixed and edited. It also permits adding complex special effects.

Pro Tools   Pro Tools is a high-end integrated audio production and editing environment that runs on Macintosh computers as well as Windows. Pro Tools offers easy MIDI creation and manipulation as well as powerful audio mixing, recording, and editing software.

1.4.3 Graphics and Image Editing

Adobe Illustrator   Illustrator is a powerful publishing tool for creating and editing vector graphics, which can easily be exported to use on the web.

Adobe Photoshop   Photoshop is the standard in a tool for graphics, image processing, and image manipulation. Layers of images, graphics, and text can be separately manipulated for maximum flexibility, and its "filter factory" permits creation of sophisticated lighting effects.

Macromedia Fireworks   Fireworks is software for making graphics specifically for the web. It includes a bitmap editor, a vector graphics editor, and a JavaScript generator for buttons and rollovers.

Macromedia Freehand   Freehand is a text and web graphics editing tool that supports many bitmap formats, such as GIF, PNG, and JPEG. These are *pixel-based* formats, in that each pixel is specified. It also supports *vector-based* formats, in which endpoints of lines are specified instead of the pixels themselves, such as SWF (Macromedia Flash) and FHC (Shockwave Freehand). It can also read Photoshop format.

1.4.4 Video Editing

Adobe Premiere   Premiere is a simple, intuitive video editing tool for *nonlinear* editing — putting video clips into any order. Video and audio are arranged in *tracks*, like a musical score. It provides a large number of video and audio tracks, superimpositions, and virtual clips. A large library of built-in transitions, filters, and motions for clips allows easy creation of effective multimedia productions.

Adobe After Effects   After Effects is a powerful video editing tool that enables users to add and change existing movies with effects such as lighting, shadows, and motion blurring. It also allows layers, as in Photoshop, to permit manipulating objects independently.

Final Cut Pro   Final Cut Pro is a video editing tool offered by Apple for the Macintosh platform. It allows the capture of video and audio from numerous sources, such as film and DV. It provides a complete environment, from capturing the video to editing and color correction and finally output to a video file or broadcast from the computer.

1.4.5   Animation

Multimedia APIs

Java3D is an API used by Java to construct and render 3D graphics, similar to the way Java Media Framework handles media files. It provides a basic set of object primitives (cube, splines, etc.) upon which the developer can build scenes. It is an abstraction layer built on top of OpenGL or DirectX (the user can select which), so the graphics are accelerated.

DirectX, a Windows API that supports video, images, audio, and 3D animation, is the most common API used to develop modern multimedia Windows applications, such as computer games.

OpenGL was created in 1992 and has become the most popular 3D API in use today. OpenGL is highly portable and will run on all popular modern operating systems, such as UNIX, Linux, Windows, and Macintosh.

Rendering Tools

3D Studio Max includes a number of high-end professional tools for character animation, game development, and visual effects production. Models produced using this tool can be seen in several consumer games, such as for the Sony Playstation.

Softimage XSI (previously called Softimage 3D) is a powerful modeling, animation, and rendering package for animation and special effects in films and games.

Maya, a competing product to Softimage, is a complete modeling package. It features a wide variety of modeling and animation tools, such as to create realistic clothes and fur.

RenderMan is a rendering package created by Pixar. It excels in creating complex surface appearances and images and has been used in numerous movies, such as *Monsters Inc.* and *Final Fantasy: The Spirits Within*. It is also capable of importing models from Maya.

GIF Animation Packages   For a simpler approach to animation that also allows quick development of effective small animations for the web, many shareware and other programs permit creating animated GIF images. GIFs can contain several images, and looping through them creates a simple animation. Gifcon and GifBuilder are two of these. Linux also provides some simple animation tools, such as `animate`.

1.4.6   Multimedia Authoring

Tools that provide the capability for creating a complete multimedia presentation, including interactive user control, are called *authoring* programs.

Macromedia Flash   Flash allows users to create interactive movies by using the score metaphor — a timeline arranged in parallel event sequences, much like a musical score consisting of musical notes. Elements in the movie are called *symbols* in Flash. Symbols are added to a central repository, called a library, and can be added to the movie's timeline. Once the symbols are present at a specific time, they appear on the Stage, which represents what the movie looks like at a certain time, and can be manipulated and moved by the tools built into Flash. Finished Flash movies are commonly used to show movies or games on the web.

Macromedia Director   Director uses a movie metaphor to create interactive presentations. This powerful program includes a built-in scripting language, Lingo, that allows creation of complex interactive movies.[2] The "cast" of characters in Director includes bitmapped sprites, scripts, music, sounds, and palettes. Director can read many bitmapped file formats. The program itself allows a good deal of interactivity, and Lingo, with its own debugger, allows more control, including control over external devices, such as VCRs and videodisc players. Director also has web authoring features available, for creation of fully interactive Shockwave movies playable over the web.

Authorware   Authorware is a mature, well-supported authoring product that has an easy learning curve for computer science students because it is based on the idea of flowcharts (the so-called *iconic/flow-control* metaphor). It allows hyperlinks to link text, digital movies, graphics, and sound. It also provides compatibility between files produced in PC and Mac versions. Shockwave Authorware applications can incorporate Shockwave files, including Director movies, Flash animations, and audio.

Quest   Quest, which uses a type of flowcharting metaphor, is similar to Authorware in many ways. However, the flowchart nodes can encapsulate information in a more abstract way (called "frames") than simply subroutine levels. As a result, connections between icons are more conceptual and do not always represent flow of control in the program.

1.5   FURTHER EXPLORATION

Chapters 1 and 2 of Steinmetz and Nahrstedt [5] provide a good overview of multimedia concepts.

The web site for this text is kept current on new developments. Chapter 1 of the Further Exploration directory on the web site provides links to much of the history of multimedia. As a start, the complete Vannevar Bush article on the Memex system conception is online. This article was and still is considered seminal. Although written over 50 years ago, it adumbrates many current developments, including fax machines and the associative memory model that underlies the development of the web. Nielsen's book [6] is a good overview of hypertext

---

[2]Therefore, Director is often a popular choice with students for creating a final project in multimedia courses — it provides the desired power without the inevitable pain of using a full-blown C++ program.

and hypermedia. For more advanced reading, the collection of survey papers by Jeffay and Zhang [1] provides in-depth background as well as future directions of research.

Other links in the text web site include information on

- Ted Nelson and the Xanadu project

- Nicholas Negroponte's work at the MIT Media Lab. Negroponte's small book on multimedia [7] has become a much-quoted classic.

- Douglas Engelbart and the history of the "On-Line System"

- The MIT Media Lab. Negroponte and Wiesner cofounded the MIT Media Lab, which is still going strong and is arguably the most influential idea factory in the world.

- Client-side execution. Java and client-side execution started in 1995; "Duke", the first JAVA applet, is also on the textbook's web site.

Chapter 12 of Buford's book [8] provides a detailed introduction to authoring. Neuschotz's introductory text [9] gives step-by-step instructions for creating simple Lingo-based interactive Director movies.

Other links include

- Digital Audio. This web page includes a link to the Sonic Foundry company for information on Sound Forge, a sample Sound Forge file, and the resulting output WAV file. The example combines left and right channel information in a complex fashion. Little effort is required to produce sophisticated special effects with this tool. Digidesign is one firm offering high-end Macintosh software, which can even involve purchasing extra boards for specialized processing.

- Music sequencing and notation

- Graphics and image editing information

- Video editing products and information

- Animation sites

- Multimedia authoring tools

- XML

1.6 EXERCISES

1. Identify three novel applications of the Internet or multimedia applications. Discuss why you think these are novel.
2. Briefly explain, in your own words, "Memex" and its role regarding hypertext. Could we carry out the Memex task today? How do you use Memex ideas in your own work?

3. Your task is to think about the transmission of smell over the Internet. Suppose we have a smell sensor at one location and wish to transmit the *Aroma Vector* (say) to a receiver to reproduce the same sensation. You are asked to design such a system. List three key issues to consider and two applications of such a delivery system. *Hint*: Think about medical applications.

4. Tracking objects or people can be done by both sight and sound. While vision systems are precise, they are relatively expensive; on the other hand, a pair of microphones can detect a person's *bearing* inaccurately but cheaply. Sensor *fusion* of sound and vision is thus useful. Surf the web to find out who is developing tools for video conferencing using this kind of multimedia idea.

5. *Non-photorealistic* graphics means computer graphics that do well enough without attempting to make images that look like camera images. An example is conferencing (let's look at this cutting-edge application again). For example, if we track lip movements, we can generate the right animation to fit our face. If we don't much like our own face, we can substitute another one — facial-feature modeling can map correct lip movements onto another model. See if you can find out who is carrying out research on generating avatars to represent conference participants' bodies.

6. Watermarking is a means of embedding a hidden message in data. This could have important legal implications: Is this image copied? Is this image doctored? Who took it? Where? Think of "messages" that could be sensed while capturing an image and secretly embedded in the image, so as to answer these questions. (A similar question derives from the use of cell phones. What could we use to determine who is putting this phone to use, and where, and when? This could eliminate the need for passwords.)

1.7   REFERENCES

1 K. Jeffay and H. Zhang, *Readings in Multimedia Computing and Networking*, San Francisco: Morgan Kaufmann, CA, 2002.

2 Vannevar Bush, "As We May Think," *The Atlantic Monthly*, Jul. 1945.

3 D. Engelbart and H. Lehtman, "Working Together," *BYTE Magazine*, Dec. 1998, 245–252.

4 N. Yankelovitch, N. Meyrowitz, and A. van Dam, "Reading and Writing the Electronic Book," in *Hypermedia and Literary Studies*, ed. P. Delany and G.P. Landow, Cambridge, MA: MIT Press, 1991.

5 R. Steinmetz and K. Nahrstedt, *Multimedia: Computing, Communications and Applications*, Upper Saddle River, NJ: Prentice Hall PTR, 1995.

6 J. Nielsen, *Multimedia and Hypertext: The Internet and Beyond*, San Diego: AP Professional, 1995.

7 N. Negroponte, *Being Digital*, New York: Vintage Books, 1995.

8 J.F.K. Buford, *Multimedia Systems*, Reading, MA: Addison Wesley, 1994.

9 N. Neuschotz, *Introduction to Director and Lingo: Multimedia and Internet Applications*, Upper Saddle River, NJ: Prentice Hall, 2000.

CHAPTER 2

Multimedia Authoring and Tools

2.1 MULTIMEDIA AUTHORING

Multimedia authoring is the creation of multimedia productions, sometimes called "movies" or "presentations". Since we are interested in this subject from a computer science point of view, we are mostly interested in *interactive* applications. Also, we need to consider still-image editors, such as Adobe Photoshop, and simple video editors, such as Adobe Premiere, because these applications help us create interactive multimedia projects.

How much interaction is necessary or meaningful depends on the application. The spectrum runs from almost no interactivity, as in a slide show, to full-immersion virtual reality.

In a slide show, interactivity generally consists of being able to control the pace (e.g., click to advance to the next slide). The next level of interactivity is being able to control the sequence and choose where to go next. Next is media control: start/stop video, search text, scroll the view, zoom. More control is available if we can control variables, such as changing a database search query.

The level of control is substantially higher if we can control objects — say, moving objects around a screen, playing interactive games, and so on. Finally, we can control an entire simulation: move our perspective in the scene, control scene objects.

For some time, people have indeed considered what should go into a multimedia project; references are given at the end of this chapter.

In this section, we shall look at

- Multimedia authoring metaphors

- Multimedia production

- Multimedia presentation

- Automatic authoring

The final item deals with general authoring issues and what benefit automated tools, using some artificial intelligence techniques, for example, can bring to the authoring task. As a first step, we consider programs that carry out automatic linking for legacy documents.

After an introduction to multimedia paradigms, we present some of the practical tools of multimedia content production — software tools that form the arsenal of multimedia production. Here we go through the nuts and bolts of a number of standard programs currently in use.

2.1.1 Multimedia Authoring Metaphors

Authoring is the process of creating multimedia applications. Most authoring programs use one of several *authoring metaphors*, also known as *authoring paradigms*: metaphors for easier understanding of the methodology employed to create multimedia applications [1].

Some common authoring metaphors are as follows:

- **Scripting language metaphor**
  The idea here is to use a special language to enable interactivity (buttons, mouse, etc.) and allow conditionals, jumps, loops, functions/macros, and so on. An example is the OpenScript language in Asymetrix Learning Systems' Toolbook program. Open-Script looks like a standard object-oriented, event-driven programming language. For example, a small Toolbook program is shown below. Such a language has a learning curve associated with it, as do all authoring tools — even those that use the standard C programming language as their scripting language — because of the object libraries that must be learned.

```
-- load an MPEG file
extFileName of MediaPlayer "theMpegPath" =
        "c:\windows\media\home33.mpg";
-- play
extPlayCount of MediaPlayer "theMpegPath" = 1;
-- put the MediaPlayer in frames mode (not time mode)
extDisplayMode of MediaPlayer "theMpegPath" = 1;
-- if want to start and end at specific frames:
extSelectionStart of MediaPlayer "theMpegPath" = 103;
extSelectionEnd of MediaPlayer "theMpegPath" = 1997;
-- start playback
get extPlay() of MediaPlayer "theMpegPath";
```

- **Slide show metaphor**
  Slide shows are by default a linear presentation. Although tools exist to perform jumps in slide shows, few practitioners use them. Example programs are PowerPoint or ImageQ.

- **Hierarchical metaphor**
  Here, user-controllable elements are organized into a tree structure. Such a metaphor is often used in menu-driven applications.

- **Iconic/flow-control metaphor**
  Graphical icons are available in a toolbox, and authoring proceeds by creating a flowchart with icons attached. The standard example of such a metaphor is Author-ware, by Macromedia. Figure 2.1 shows an example flowchart. As well as simple flowchart elements, such as an IF statement, a CASE statement, and so on, we can

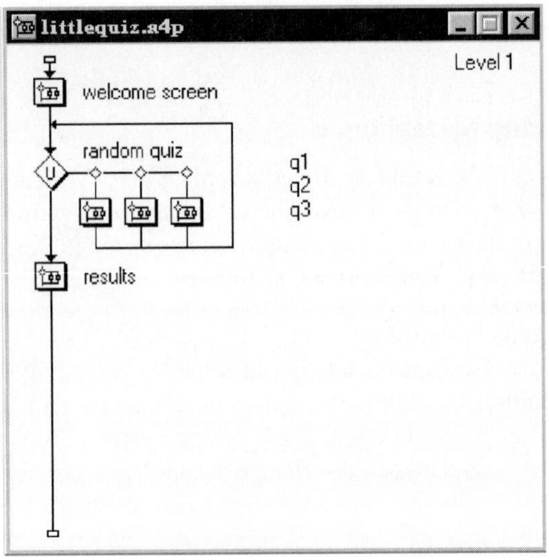

FIGURE 2.1: Authorware flowchart.

group elements using a Map (i.e., a subroutine) icon. With little effort, simple animation is also possible.

- **Frames metaphor**
  As in the iconic/flow-control metaphor, graphical icons are again available in a toolbox, and authoring proceeds by creating a flowchart with icons attached. However, rather than representing the actual flow of the program, links between icons are more conceptual. Therefore, "frames" of icon designs represent more abstraction than in the simpler iconic/flow-control metaphor. An example of such a program is Quest, by Allen Communication. The flowchart consists of "modules" composed of "frames". Frames are constructed from objects, such as text, graphics, audio, animations, and video, all of which can respond to events. A real benefit is that the scripting language here is the widely used programming language C. Figure 2.2 shows a Quest frame.

- **Card/scripting metaphor**
  This metaphor uses a simple index-card structure to produce multimedia productions. Since links are available, this is an easy route to producing applications that use hypertext or hypermedia. The original of this metaphor was HyperCard by Apple. Another example is HyperStudio by Knowledge Adventure. The latter program is now used in many schools. Figure 2.3 shows two cards in a HyperStudio stack.

- **Cast/score/scripting metaphor**
  In this metaphor, time is shown horizontally in a type of spreadsheet fashion, where rows, or tracks, represent instantiations of characters in a multimedia production. Since these tracks control synchronous behavior, this metaphor somewhat parallels a music score. Multimedia elements are drawn from a "cast" of characters, and "scripts"

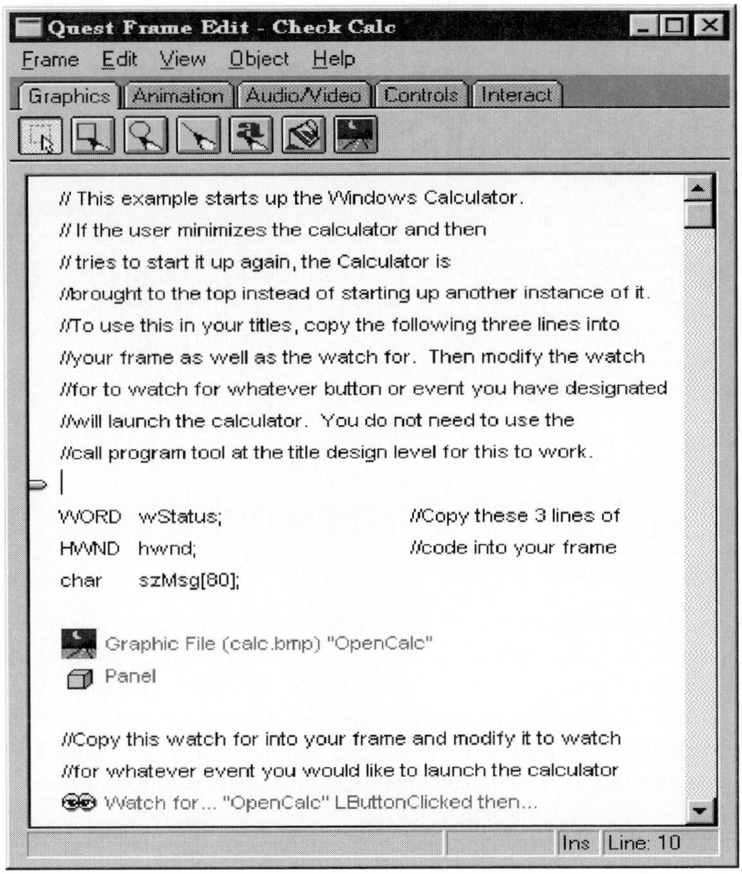

FIGURE 2.2: Quest frame.

are basically event procedures or procedures triggered by timer events. Usually, you can write your own scripts. In a sense, this is similar to the conventional use of the term "scripting language" — one that is concise and invokes lower-level abstractions, since that is just what one's own scripts do. Director, by Macromedia, is the chief example of this metaphor. Director uses the Lingo scripting language, an object-oriented, event-driven language.

2.1.2 Multimedia Production

A multimedia project can involve a host of people with specialized skills. In this book we focus on more technical aspects, but multimedia production can easily involve an art director, graphic designer, production artist, producer, project manager, writer, user interface designer, sound designer, videographer, and 3D and 2D animators, as well as programmers.

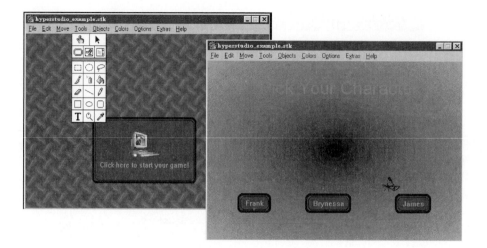

FIGURE 2.3: Two cards in a HyperStudio stack.

The production timeline would likely only involve programming when the project is about 40% complete, with a reasonable target for an alpha version (an early version that does not contain all planned features) being perhaps 65–70% complete. Typically, the design phase consists of storyboarding, flowcharting, prototyping, and user testing, as well as a parallel production of media. Programming and debugging phases would be carried out in consultation with marketing, and the distribution phase would follow.

A storyboard depicts the initial idea content of a multimedia concept in a series of sketches. These are like "keyframes" in a video — the story hangs from these "stopping places". A flowchart organizes the storyboards by inserting navigation information — the multimedia concept's structure and user interaction. The most reliable approach for planning navigation is to pick a traditional data structure. A hierarchical system is perhaps one of the simplest organizational strategies.

Multimedia is not really like other presentations, in that careful thought must be given to organization of movement between the "rooms" in the production. For example, suppose we are navigating an African safari, but we also need to bring specimens back to our museum for close examination — just how do we effect the transition from one locale to the other? A flowchart helps imagine the solution.

The flowchart phase is followed by development of a detailed functional specification. This consists of a walk-through of each scenario of the presentation, frame by frame, including all screen action and user interaction. For example, during a mouseover for a character, the character reacts, or a user clicking on a character results in an action.

The final part of the design phase is prototyping and testing. Some multimedia designers use an authoring tool at this stage already, even if the intermediate prototype will not be used in the final product or continued in another tool. User testing is, of course, extremely important before the final development phase.

2.1.3   Multimedia Presentation

In this section, we briefly outline some effects to keep in mind for presenting multimedia content as well as some useful guidelines for content design.

Graphics Styles   Careful thought has gone into combinations of color schemes and how lettering is perceived in a presentation. Many presentations are meant for business displays, rather than appearing on a screen. Human visual dynamics are considered in regard to how such presentations must be constructed. Most of the observations here are drawn from Vetter et al. [2], as is Figure 2.4.

Color Principles and Guidelines   Some *color schemes* and *art styles* are best combined with a certain theme or style. Color schemes could be, for example, natural and floral for outdoor scenes and solid colors for indoor scenes. Examples of art styles are oil paints, watercolors, colored pencils, and pastels.

A general hint is to not use too many colors, as this can be distracting. It helps to be consistent with the use of color — then color can be used to signal changes in theme.

Fonts   For effective visual communication, large fonts (18 to 36 points) are best, with no more than six to eight lines per screen. As shown in Figure 2.4, sans serif fonts work better than serif fonts (serif fonts are those with short lines stemming from and at an angle to the upper and lower ends of a letter's strokes). Figure 2.4 shows a comparison of two screen projections, (Figure 2 and 3 from Vetter, Ward and Shapiro [2]).

The top figure shows *good* use of color and fonts. It has a consistent color scheme, uses large and all sans-serif (Arial) fonts. The bottom figure is *poor*, in that too many colors are used, and they are inconsistent. The red adjacent to the blue is hard to focus on, because the human retina cannot focus on these colors simultaneously. The serif (Times New Roman) font is said to be hard to read in a darkened, projection setting. Finally, the lower right panel does not have enough contrast — pretty pastel colors are often usable only if their background is sufficiently different.

A Color Contrast Program   Seeing the results of Vetter et al.'s research, we constructed a small Visual Basic program to investigate how readability of text colors depends on color and the color of the background (see the Further Exploration section at the end of this chapter for a pointer to this program on the text web site. There, both the executable and the program source are given).

The simplest approach to making readable colors on a screen is to use the principal complementary color as the background for text. For color values in the range 0 to 1 (or, effectively, 0 to 255), if the text color is some triple (R, G, B), a legible color for the background is likely given by that color subtracted from the maximum:

$$(R, G, B) \Rightarrow (1 - R, 1 - G, 1 - B) \tag{2.1}$$

That is, not only is the color "opposite" in some sense (not the same sense as artists use), but if the text is bright, the background is dark, and vice versa.

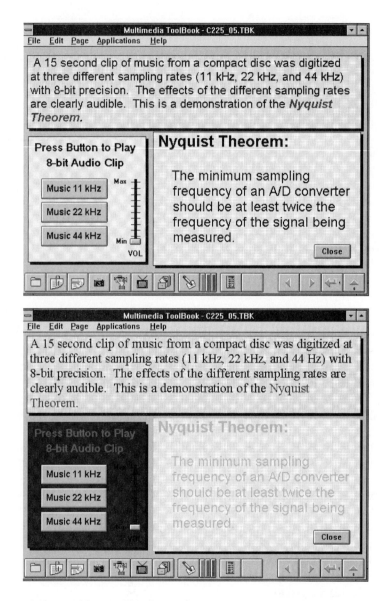

FIGURE 2.4: Colors and fonts. (This figure also appears in the color insert section.) *Courtesy of Ron Vetter.*

In the Visual Basic program given, sliders can be used to change the background color. As the background changes, the text changes to equal the principal complementary color. Clicking on the background brings up a color-picker as an alternative to the sliders.

If you feel you can choose a better color combination, click on the text. This brings up a color picker not tied to the background color, so you can experiment. (The text itself can also be edited.) A little experimentation shows that some color combinations are more

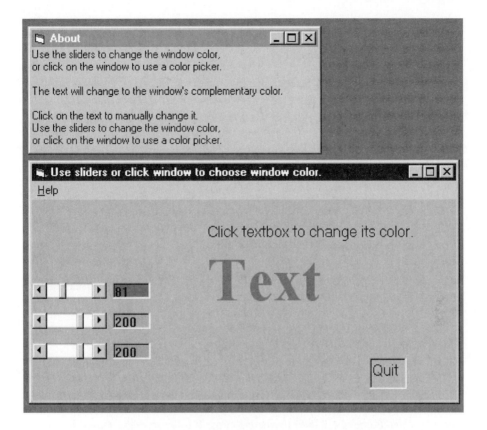

FIGURE 2.5: Program to investigate colors and readability.

pleasing than others — for example, a pink background and forest green foreground, or a green background and mauve foreground. Figure 2.5 shows this small program in operation.

Figure 2.6 shows a "color wheel", with opposite colors equal to $(1-R, 1-G, 1-B)$. An artist's color wheel will not look the same, as it is based on feel rather than on an algorithm. In the traditional artist's wheel, for example, yellow is opposite magenta, instead of opposite blue as in Figure 2.6, and blue is instead opposite orange.

Sprite Animation   *Sprites* are often used in animation. For example, in Macromedia Director, the notion of a sprite is expanded to an instantiation of any resource. However, the basic idea of sprite animation is simple. Suppose we have produced an animation figure, as in Figure 2.7(a). Then it is a simple matter to create a 1-bit mask M, as in Figure 2.7(b), black on white, and the accompanying sprite S, as in Figure 2.7(c).

Now we can overlay the sprite on a colored background B, as in Figure 2.8(a), by first ANDing B and M, then ORing the result with S, with the final result as in Figure 2.8(e). Operations are available to carry out these simple compositing manipulations at frame rate and so produce a simple 2D animation that moves the sprite around the frame but does not change the way it looks.

FIGURE 2.6: Color wheel. (This figure also appears in the color insert section.)

Video Transitions Video transitions can be an effective way to indicate a change to the next section. Video transitions are syntactic means to signal "scene changes" and often carry semantic meaning. Many different types of transitions exist; the main types are *cuts, wipes, dissolves, fade-ins* and *fade-outs*.

A cut, as the name suggests, carries out an abrupt change of image contents in two consecutive video frames from their respective clips. It is the simplest and most frequently used video transition.

A wipe is a replacement of the pixels in a region of the viewport with those from another video. If the boundary line between the two videos moves slowly across the screen, the second video gradually replaces the first. Wipes can be left-to-right, right-to-left, vertical, horizontal, like an iris opening, swept out like the hands of a clock, and so on.

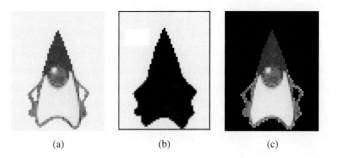

(a)   (b)   (c)

FIGURE 2.7: Sprite creation: (a) original; (b) mask image M; and (c) sprite S. *"Duke" figure courtesy of Sun Microsystems.*

(a)   (b)   (c)

(d)   (e)

FIGURE 2.8: Sprite animation: (a) Background B; (b) Mask M; (c) B AND M; (d) Sprite S; (e) B AND M OR S.

A dissolve replaces every pixel with a mixture over time of the two videos, gradually changing the first to the second. A fade-out is the replacement of a video by black (or white), and fade-in is its reverse. Most dissolves can be classified into two types, corresponding, for example, to *cross dissolve* and *dither dissolve* in Adobe Premiere video editing software.

In type I (cross dissolve), every pixel is affected gradually. It can be defined by

$$\mathbf{D} = (1 - \alpha(t)) \cdot \mathbf{A} + \alpha(t) \cdot \mathbf{B} \qquad (2.2)$$

where $\mathbf{A}$ and $\mathbf{B}$ are the color 3-vectors for video A and video B. Here, $\alpha(t)$ is a transition function, which is often linear with time t:

$$\alpha(t) = kt, \quad \text{with} \quad kt_{max} \equiv 1 \qquad (2.3)$$

Type II (dither dissolve) is entirely different. Determined by $\alpha(t)$, increasingly more and more pixels in video A will abruptly (instead of gradually, as in Type I) change to video B. The positions of the pixels subjected to the change can be random or sometimes follow a particular pattern.

Obviously, fade-in and fade-out are special types of a Type I dissolve, in which video A or B is black (or white). Wipes are special forms of a Type II dissolve, in which changing pixels follow a particular geometric pattern.

FIGURE 2.9: (a) Video$_L$; (b) Video$_R$; (c) Video$_L$ sliding into place and pushing out Video$_R$.

Despite the fact that many digital video editors include a preset number of video transitions, we may also be interested in building our own. For example, suppose we wish to build a special type of wipe that slides one video out while another video slides in to replace it. The usual type of wipe does not do this. Instead, each video stays in place, and the transition line moves across each "stationary" video, so that the left part of the viewport shows pixels from the left video, and the right part shows pixels from the right video (for a wipe moving horizontally from left to right).

Suppose we would like to have each video frame not held in place, but instead move progressively farther into (out of) the viewport: we wish to slide Video$_L$ in from the left and push out Video$_R$. Figure 2.9 shows this process. Each of Video$_L$ and Video$_R$ has its own values of R, G, and B. Note that R is a function of position in the frame, (x, y), as well as of time t. Since this is video and not a collection of images of various sizes, each of the two videos has the same maximum extent, x_{max}. (Premiere actually makes all videos the same size — the one chosen in the preset selection — so there is no cause to worry about different sizes.)

As time goes by, the horizontal location x_T for the transition boundary moves across the viewport from $x_T = 0$ at $t = 0$ to $x_T = x_{max}$ at $t = t_{max}$. Therefore, for a transition that is linear in time, $x_T = (t/t_{max})x_{max}$.

So for any time t, the situation is as shown in Figure 2.10(a). The viewport, in which we shall be writing pixels, has its own coordinate system, with the x-axis from 0 to x_{max}. For each x (and y) we must determine (a) from which video we take RGB values, and (b) from what x position in the *unmoving* video we take pixel values — that is, from what position x from the left video, say, in its own coordinate system. It is a video, so of course the image in the left video frame is changing in time.

Let's assume that dependence on y is implicit. In any event, we use the same y as in the source video. Then for the red channel (and similarly for the green and blue), $R = R(x, t)$. Suppose we have determined that pixels should come from Video$_L$. Then the x-position x_L in the *unmoving* video should be $x_L = x + (x_{max} - x_T)$, where x is the position we are trying to fill in the viewport, x_T is the position in the viewport that the transition boundary has reached, and x_{max} is the maximum pixel position for any frame.

To see this, we note from Figure 2.10(b) that we can calculate the position x_L in Video$_L$'s coordinate system as the sum of the distance x, in the viewport, and the difference $x_{max} - x_T$.

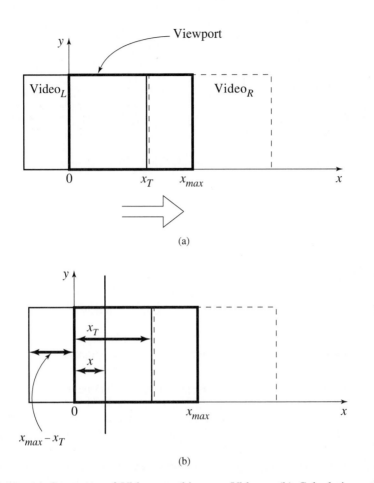

FIGURE 2.10: (a) Geometry of Video$_L$ pushing out Video$_R$; (b) Calculating position in Video$_L$ from where pixels are copied to the viewport.

Substituting the fact that the transition moves linearly with time, $x_T = x_{max}(t/t_{max})$, we can set up a pseudocode solution as in Figure 2.11. In Figure 2.11, the slight change in formula if pixels are actually coming from Video$_R$ instead of from Video$_L$ is easy to derive.

Some Technical Design Issues   Technical parameters that affect the design and delivery of multimedia applications include computer platform, video format and resolution, memory and disk space, delivery methods.

- **Computer Platform.** Usually we deal with machines that are either some type of UNIX box (such as a Sun) or else a PC or Macintosh. While a good deal of software is ostensibly "portable", much cross-platform software relies on runtime modules that may not work well across systems.

```
for  t  in  0.. t_max
     for  x  in  0.. x_max
          if  (  ────  <  ────)
               R = R_L  (  x + x_max * [1 − ────],  t)
          else
               R = R_R  (  x − x_max * ────,  t)
```

$$\text{for } t \text{ in } 0..t_{max}$$
$$\quad \text{for } x \text{ in } 0..x_{max}$$
$$\quad\quad \text{if } \left(\frac{x}{x_{max}} < \frac{t}{t_{max}} \right)$$
$$\quad\quad\quad R = R_L \left(x + x_{max} * [1 - \frac{t}{t_{max}}], \ t \right)$$
$$\quad\quad \text{else}$$
$$\quad\quad\quad R = R_R \left(x - x_{max} * \frac{t}{t_{max}}, \ t \right)$$

FIGURE 2.11: Pseudocode for slide video transition.

- **Video Format and Resolution.** The most popular video formats are NTSC, PAL, and SECAM. They are not compatible, so conversion is required to play a video in a different format.

  The graphics card, which displays pixels on the screen, is sometimes referred to as a "video card". In fact, some cards are able to perform "frame grabbing", to change analog signals to digital for video. This kind of card is called a "video capture card".

  The graphics card's capacity depends on its price. An old standard for the capacity of a card is S-VGA, which allows for a resolution of $1,280 \times 1,024$ pixels in a displayed image and as many as 65,536 colors using 16-bit pixels or 16.7 million colors using 24-bit pixels. Nowadays, graphics cards that support higher resolution, such as $1,600 \times 1,200$, and 32-bit pixels or more are common.

- **Memory and Disk Space Requirement.** Rapid progress in hardware alleviates the problem, but multimedia software is generally greedy. Nowadays, at least 128 megabytes of RAM and 20 gigabytes of hard-disk space should be available for acceptable performance and storage for multimedia programs.

- **Delivery Methods.** Once coding and all other work is finished, how shall we present our clever work? Since we have presumably purchased a large disk, so that performance is good and storage is not an issue, we could simply bring along our machine and show the work that way. However, we likely wish to distribute the work as a product. Presently, rewritable DVD drives are not the norm, and CD-ROMs may lack sufficient storage capacity to hold the presentation. Also, access time for CD-ROM drives is longer than for hard-disk drives.

  Electronic delivery is an option, but this depends on network bandwidth at the user side (and at our server). A streaming option may be available, depending on the presentation.

No perfect mechanism currently exists to distribute large multimedia projects. Nevertheless, using such tools as PowerPoint or Director, it is possible to create acceptable presentations that fit on a single CD-ROM.

2.1.4 Automatic Authoring

Thus far, we have considered notions developed for authoring new multimedia. Nevertheless, a tremendous amount of legacy multimedia documents exists, and researchers have been interested in methods to facilitate *automatic authoring*. By this term is meant either an advanced helper for creating new multimedia presentations or a mechanism to facilitate automatic creation of more useful multimedia documents from existing sources.

Hypermedia Documents   Let us start by considering hypermedia documents. Generally, three steps are involved in producing documents meant to be viewed nonlinearly: information generation or capture, authoring, and publication. A question that can be asked is, how much of this process can be automated?

The first step, capture of media, be it from text or using an audio digitizer or video frame-grabber, is highly developed and well automated. The final step, presentation, is the objective of the multimedia tools we have been considering. But the middle step (authoring) is most under consideration here.

Essentially, we wish to structure information to support access and manipulation of the available media. Clearly, we would be well advised to consider the standard computing science data structures in structuring this information: lists, trees, or networks (graphs). However, here we would like to consider how best to structure the data to support multiple views, rather than a single, static view.

Externalization versus Linearization   Figure 2.12 shows the essential problem involved in communicating ideas without using a hypermedia mechanism: the author's ideas are "linearized" by setting them down in linear order on paper. In contrast, hyperlinks allow us the freedom to partially mimic the author's thought process (i.e., externalization). After all, the essence of Bush's Memex idea in Section 1.2.1 involves associative links in human memory.

Now, using Microsoft Word, say, it is trivial to create a hypertext version of one's document, as Word simply follows the layout already set up in chapters, headings, and so on. But problems arise when we wish to extract semantic content and find links and anchors, even considering just text and not images. Figure 2.13 displays the problem: while it is feasible to mentally manage a few information nodes, once the problem becomes large, we need automatic assistants.

Once a dataset becomes large, we should employ database methods. The issues become focused on scalability (to a large dataset), maintainability, addition of material, and reusability. The database information must be set up in such a way that the "publishing" stage, presentation to the user, can be carried out just-in-time, presenting information in a user-defined view from an intermediate information structure.

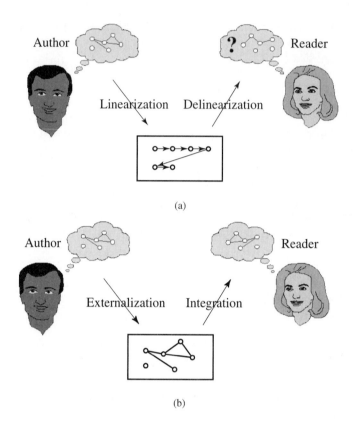

FIGURE 2.12: Communication using hyperlinks. *Courtesy of David Lowe; (©1995 IEEE).* [5]

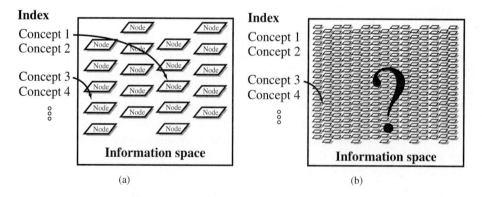

FIGURE 2.13: Complex information space: (a) complexity: manageable; (b) complexity: overwhelming. *Courtesy of David Lowe; (©1995 IEEE).* [5]

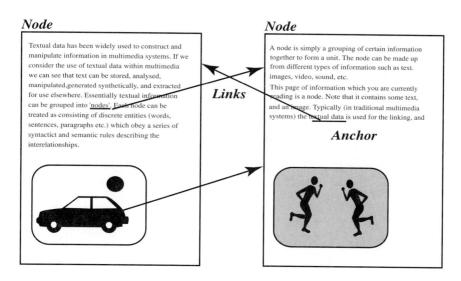

FIGURE 2.14: Nodes and anchors in hypertext. *Courtesy of David Lowe.* [6]

Semiautomatic Migration of Hypertext   The structure of hyperlinks for text information is simple: "nodes" represent semantic information and are anchors for links to other pages. Figure 2.14 illustrates these concepts.

For *text*, the first step for migrating paper-based information to hypertext is to automatically convert the format used to HTML. Then, sections and chapters can be placed in a database. Simple versions of data mining techniques, such as word stemming, can easily be used to parse titles and captions for keywords — for example, by frequency counting. Keywords found can be added to the database being built. Then a helper program can automatically generate additional hyperlinks between related concepts.

A semiautomatic version of such a program is most likely to be successful, making suggestions that can be accepted or rejected and manually added to. A database management system can maintain the integrity of links when new nodes are inserted. For the publishing stage, since it may be impractical to re-create the underlying information structures, it is best to delay imposing a *viewpoint* on the data until as late as possible.

Hyperimages   Matters are not nearly so straightforward when considering image or other multimedia data. To treat an image in the same way as text, we would wish to consider an image to be a node that contains objects and other anchors, for which we need to determine image entities and rules. What we desire is an automated method to help us produce true hypermedia, as in Figure 2.15.

It is possible to manually delineate syntactic image elements by masking image areas. These can be tagged with text, so that previous text-based methods can be brought into play. Figure 2.16 shows a "hyperimage", with image areas identified and automatically linked to other parts of a document.

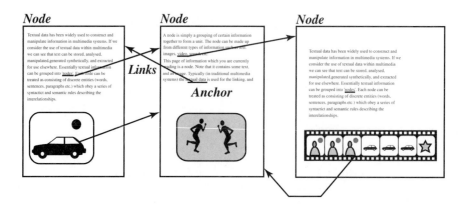

FIGURE 2.15: Structure of hypermedia. *Courtesy of David Lowe.* [6]

Such methods are certainly in their infancy but provide a fascinating view of what is to come in authoring automation. Naturally, we are also interested in what tools from database systems, data mining, artificial intelligence, and so on can be brought to bear to assist production of full-blown multimedia systems, not just hypermedia systems. The above discussion shows that we are indeed at the start of such work.

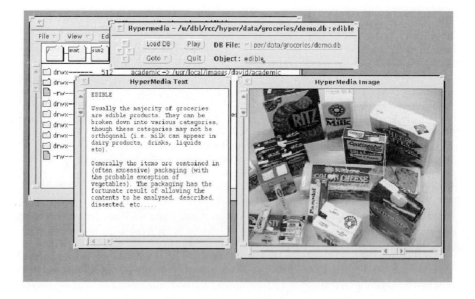

FIGURE 2.16: Hyperimage. *Courtesy of David Lowe.* [6]

2.2   SOME USEFUL EDITING AND AUTHORING TOOLS

This text is primarily concerned with principles of multimedia — the fundamentals to be grasped for a real understanding of this subject. Nonetheless, we need real vehicles for showing this understanding, and straight programming in C++ or Java is not always the best way of showing your knowledge. Most introductory multimedia courses ask you to at least start off delivering some multimedia product (e.g., see Exercise 11). So we need a jump-start to help you learn "yet another software tool." This section aims to give you that jump-start.

Therefore, we'll consider some popular authoring tools. Since the first step in creating a multimedia application is probably creation of interesting video clips, we start off looking at a video editing tool. This is not really an authoring tool, but video creation is so important that we include a small introduction to one such program.

The tools we look at are the following:

- Adobe Premiere 6

- Macromedia Director 8 and MX

- Flash 5 and MX

- Dreamweaver MX

While this is not an exhaustive list, these tools are often used in creating multimedia content.

2.2.1   Adobe Premiere

Premiere Basics   Adobe Premiere is a very simple video editing program that allows you to quickly create a simple digital video by assembling and merging multimedia components. It effectively uses the score authoring metaphor, in that components are placed in "tracks" horizontally, in a Timeline window.

The `File > New Project` command opens a window that displays a series of "presets" — assemblies of values for frame resolution, compression method, and frame rate. There are many preset options, most of which conform to some NTSC or PAL video standard.

Start by importing resources, such as AVI (Audio Video Interleave) video files and WAV sound files and dragging them from the Project window onto tracks 1 or 2. (In fact, you can use up to 99 video and 99 audio tracks!)

Video 1 is actually made up of three tracks: Video 1A, Video 1B and Transitions. Transitions can be applied only to Video 1. Transitions are dragged into the Transitions track from the Transition window, such as a gradual replacement of Video 1A by Video 1B (a dissolve), sudden replacement of random pixels in a checkerboard (a dither dissolve), or a wipe, with one video sliding over another. There are many transitions to choose from, but you can also design an original transition, using Premiere's Transition Factory.

You can import WAV sound files by dragging them to Audio 1 or Audio 2 of the Timeline window or to any additional sound tracks. You can edit the properties of any sound track by right-clicking on it.

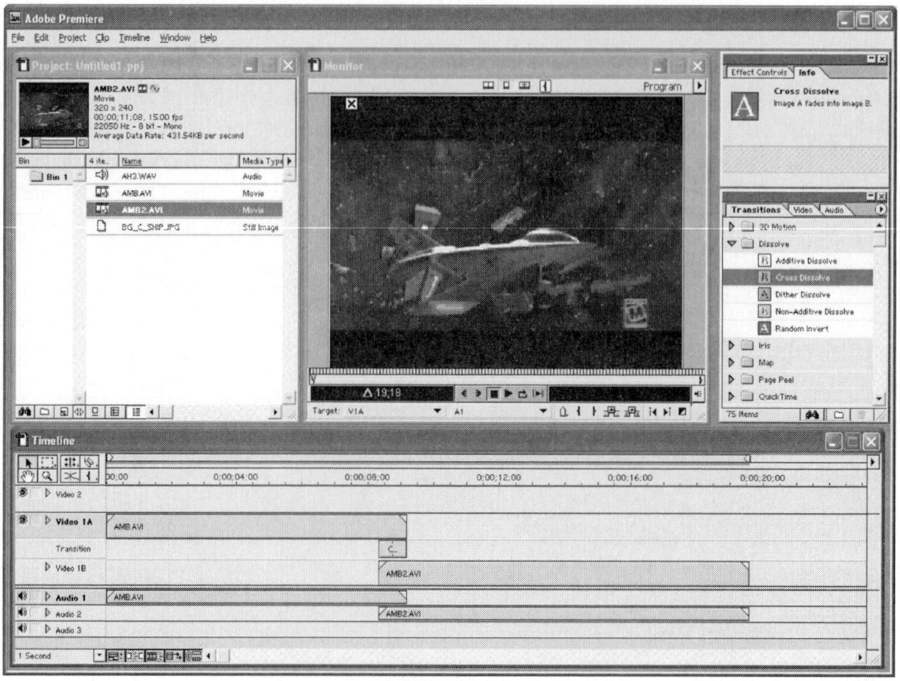

FIGURE 2.17: Adobe Premiere screen.

Figure 2.17 shows what a typical Premiere screen might look like. The yellow ruler at the top of the Timeline window delineates the working timeline — drag it to the right amount of time. The 1 Second dropdown box at the bottom represents showing one video keyframe per 1 second.

To "compile" the video, go to `Timeline > Render Work Area` and save the project as a `.ppj` file. Now it gets interesting, because you must make some choices here, involving how and in what format the movie is to be saved. Figure 2.18 shows the project options. The dialogs that tweak each codec are provided by the codec manufacturer; bring these up by clicking on the Configure button. Compression codecs (compression-decompression protocols) are often in hardware on the video capture card. If you choose a codec that requires hardware assistance, someone else's system may not be able to play your brilliant digital video, and all is in vain!

Images can also be inserted into tracks. We can use transitions to make the images gradually appear or disappear in the final video window. To do so, set up a "mask" image, as in Figure 2.19. Here, we have imported an Adobe Photoshop 6.0 layered image, with accompanying alpha channel made in Photoshop.

Then in Premiere, we click on the image, which has been placed in its own video track, and use `Clip > Video Options > Transparency` to set the Key (which triggers transparency) to Alpha Channel. It is also simple to use `Clip > Video Options > Motion` to have the image fly in and out of the frame.

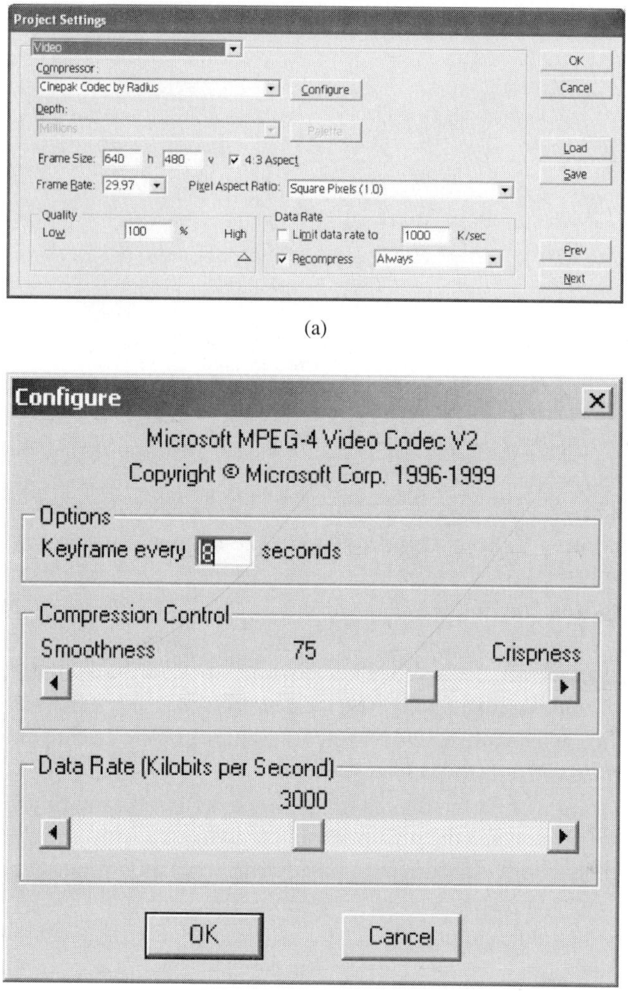

(a)

(b)

FIGURE 2.18: (a) output options; (b) compression options.

In Photoshop, we set up an alpha channel as follows:

1. Use an image you like — a .JPG, say.
2. Make the background some solid color — white, say.
3. Make sure you have chosen Image > Mode > RGB Color.
4. Select that background area (you want it to remain opaque in Premiere) — use the magic wand tool.
5. Go to Select > Save Selection....
6. Ensure that Channel = New. Press OK.

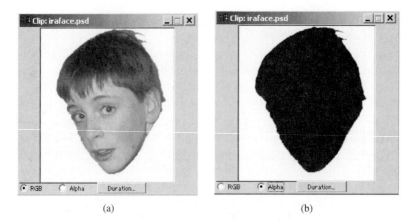

(a)   (b)

FIGURE 2.19: (a): RGB channels. (b): Alpha channel.

7. Go to `Window > Show Channels`, double-click the new channel, and rename it Alpha; make its color (0, 0, 0).

8. Save the file as a `PSD`.

If the alpha channel you created in Photoshop has a white background, you'll need to choose Reverse Key in Premiere when you choose `Alpha`.

Premiere has its own simple method of creating titles (to give credit where credit is due) for your digital video.

Another nice feature of Premiere is that it is simple to use in capturing video. To form a digital video from a videotape or camcorder input, go to `File > Capture > Movie Capture`. (The menu for video/audio capture options appears by right-clicking the capture window.) Similarly, saving to analog tape format is also simple.

Premiere Transitions   Premiere offers an interesting assortment of video transitions. However, examining the resulting video frame by frame reveals that the built-in transitions do not work quite as "advertised". For example, on close examination, what purports to be a wipe that is linear with time turns out to have a nonlinear dip as it begins — the video transition line moves at not quite constant speed.

The Premiere Transition Factory provides a good many functions for building our own transitions, if we are interested in doing so. Since we are actually in an `int` regime, these functions, such as `sin` and `cos`, have both domain and range in the `ints` rather than `floats`. Therefore, some care is required in using them. Exercise 9 gives some of these details in a realistic problem setting.

2.2.2 Macromedia Director

Director Windows   Director is a complete environment (see Figure 2.20) for creating interactive "movies". The movie metaphor is used throughout Director, and the windows

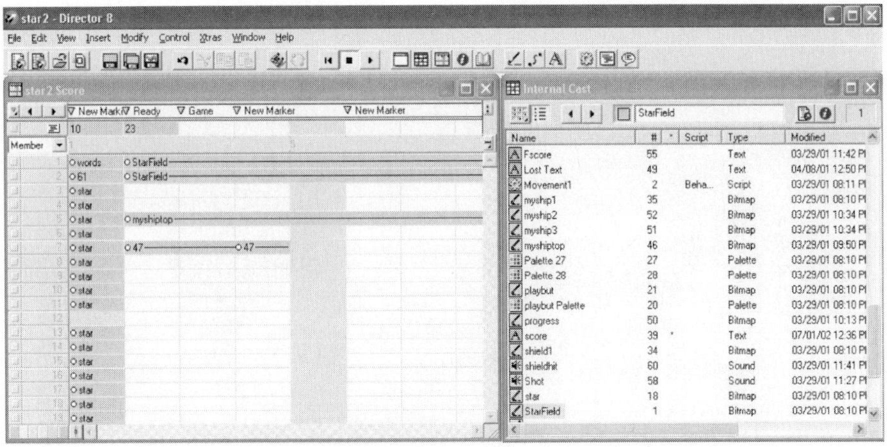

FIGURE 2.20: Director: main windows.

used in the program reflect this. The main window, on which the action takes place, is the Stage. Explicitly opening the Stage automatically closes the other windows. (A useful shortcut is Shift + Keypad-Enter (the Enter key next to the numeric keypad, not the usual Enter key); this clears all windows except the Stage and plays the movie.)

The other two main windows are Cast and Score. A Cast consists of resources a movie may use, such as bitmaps, sounds, vector-graphics shapes, Flash movies, digital videos, and scripts. Cast members can be created directly or simply imported. Typically you create several casts, to better organize the parts of a movie. Cast members are placed on the Stage by dragging them there from the Cast window. Because several instances may be used for a single cast member, each instance is called a sprite. Typically, cast members are raw media, whereas sprites are objects that control where, when, and how cast members appear on the stage and in the movie.

Sprites can become interactive by attaching "behaviors" to them (for example, make the sprite follow the mouse) either prewritten or specially created. Behaviors are in the internal script language of Director, called Lingo. Director is a standard event-driven program that allows easy positioning of objects and attachment of event procedures to objects.

The set of predefined events is rich and includes mouse events as well as network events (an example of the latter would be testing whether cast members are downloaded yet). The type of control achievable might be to loop part of a presentation until a video is downloaded, then continue or jump to another frame. Bitmaps are used for buttons, and the most typical use would be to jump to a frame in the movie after a button-click event.

The Score window is organized in horizontal lines, each for one of the sprites, and vertical frames. Thus the Score looks somewhat like a musical score, in that time is from left to right, but it more resembles the list of events in a MIDI file (see Chapter 6.)

Both types of behaviors, prewritten and user-defined, are in Lingo. The Library palette provides access to all prewritten behavior scripts. You can drop a behavior onto a sprite or attach behaviors to a whole frame.

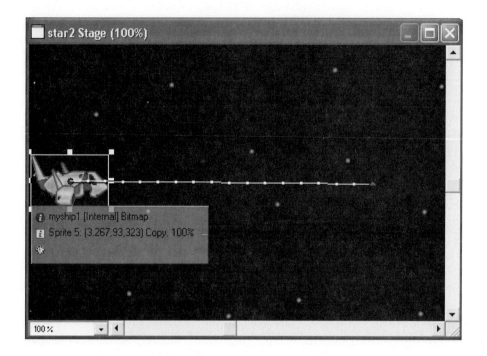

FIGURE 2.21: A tweened sprite.

If a behavior includes parameters, a dialog box appears. For example, navigation behaviors must have a specified frame to jump to. You can attach the same behavior to many
sprites or frames and use different parameters for each instance. Most behaviors respond to
simple events, such as a click on a sprite or the event triggered when the "playback head"
enters a frame. Most basic functions, such as playing a sound, come prepackaged. Writing
your own user-defined Lingo scripts provides more flexibility. Behaviors are modified using
Inspector windows: the Behavior Inspector, or Property Inspector.

Animation   Traditional animation (cel animation) is created by showing slightly different images over time. In Director, this approach amounts to using different cast members in
different frames. To control this process more easily, Director permits combining many cast
members into a single sprite. (To place on the score, select all the images to be combined,
then use the Cast To Time menu item to place them in the current score location.) A useful
feature is that expanding the time used on the score for such an animation slows the playback
time for each image, so the whole animation takes the required amount of time.

A less sophisticated-looking but simple animation is available with the *tweening* feature
of Director. Here, you specify a particular image and move it around the stage without
altering the original image. "Tweening" refers to the job of minor animators, who used to
have to fill in between the keyframes produced by more experienced animators — a role
Director fulfills automatically.

To prepare such an animation, specify the path on the stage for the tweened frames to
take. You can also specify several keyframes and the kind of curve for the animation to

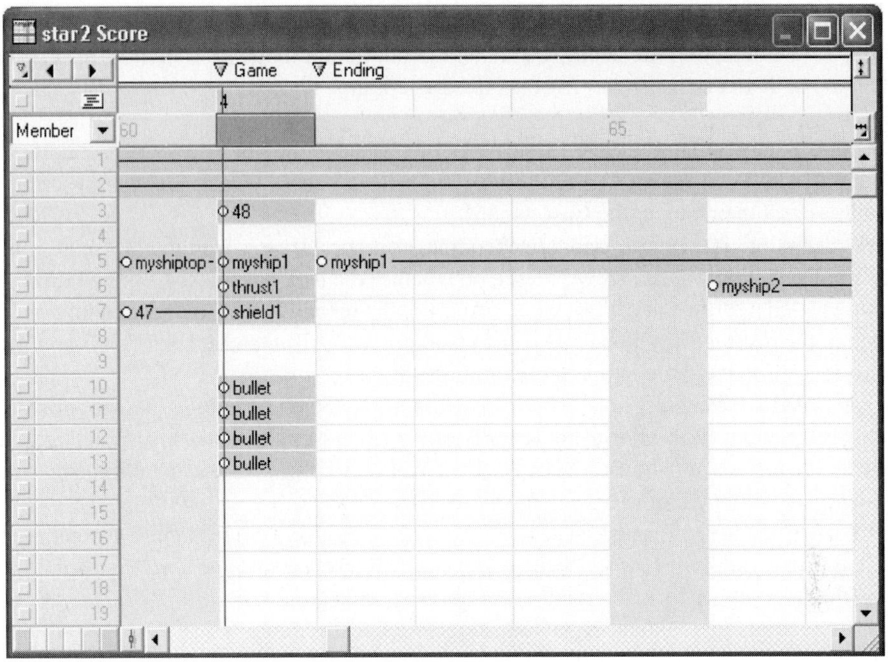

FIGURE 2.22: Score window.

follow between keyframes. You also specify how the image should accelerate and decelerate at the beginning and end of the movement ("ease-in" and "ease-out"). Figure 2.21 shows a tweened sprite.

A simple kind of animation called *palette animation* is also widely used. If images are 8-bit, cycling through the color lookup table or systematically replacing lookup table entries produces interesting (or strange) effects.

The Score window's important features are channels, frames, and the playback head. The latter shows where we are in the score; clicking anywhere in the score repositions the playback head. Channels are the rows in the Score and can contain sprite instances of visible media. Therefore, these numbered channels are called Sprite channels.

At the top of the Score window are Special Effects channels for controlling the palettes, tempo, transitions, and sounds. Figure 2.22 shows these channels in the Score window. Frames are numbered horizontally in the Sprite and Special Effects channels. A frame is a single step in the movie, as in a traditional film. The movie's playback speed can be modified by resetting the number of frames per second.

Control   You can place named markers at any frame. Then the simplest type of control event would be to jump to a marker. In Director parlance, each marker begins a Scene. Events triggered for frame navigation are Go To Frame, Go To Marker, or Hold on Current Frame, which stops the movie at that frame. Behaviors for frames appear in a Script Channel in the score window.

Buttons are simply bitmaps with behaviors attached. You usually make use of two bitmaps, one depicting the depressed state of the button and one for the undepressed state. Then the built-in event on mouseUp effects the jump.

Lingo Scripts   Director uses four types of scripts: behaviors, scripts attached to cast members, movie scripts, and parent scripts. Behaviors, movie scripts, and parent scripts all appear as cast members in the Cast window.

A "behavior" is a Lingo script attached to a sprite or a frame. You might use a script to determine whether a sprite moves, based on whether the user has clicked a button. A useful feature is that a script can control when a multimedia resource is played, depending on how much of the resource has already streamed from the web. To attach a behavior, drag it from a cast to a sprite or frame in the Score or on the Stage.

Also used are Movie scripts, which are available to the entire movie. Movie scripts can control event responses when a movie starts, stops, or pauses and can also respond to events, such as key presses and mouse clicks. Parent scripts can be used to create multiple instances of an object without adding cast members to the score.

User-written Lingo scripts can be used to create animation or to respond to typical events, such as user actions with the keyboard and mouse. Scripts can also be used to stream videos from the Internet, perform navigation, format text, and so on.

Lingo scripts also extend behaviors beyond what the Score alone can do. The basic data type is a list, which is of course the fundamental data structure. Using lists, you can manipulate arrays as well. Math operations and string handling are also available. Lists are of two types: *linear* and *property*.

A linear list is simply a list as in LISP, such as [32,43,12]. A property list is an association list, again as in LISP: each element contains two values separated by a colon. Each property is preceded by a number sign. For example, statements to create two different property lists to specify the Stage coordinates of two sprites are as follows:

```
sprite1Location = [#left:100, #top:150, #right:300, #bottom:350]
sprite2Location = [#left:400, #top:550, #right:500, #bottom:750]
```

Lingo has many functions that operate on lists, such as append to add an element to the end of a list and deleteOne to delete a value from a list.

Lingo Specifics

- The function the frame refers to the current frame.

- Special markers next or previous refer to adjacent *markers* (not adjacent frames).

- Function marker(-1) returns the identifier for the previous marker. If the frame is marked and has a marker name, marker(0) returns the name of the current frame; otherwise, it returns the name of the previous marker.

- movie ''Jaws'' refers to the start frame of the global movie named ''Jaws''. This would typically be the name of another Director movie. The reference frame 100 of movie ''Jaws'' points into that movie.

These details are well outlined in the Lingo Help portion of the online help. The Help directory `Learning > Lingo_Examples` has many DIR files that detail the basics of Lingo use.

Lingo Movie-in-a-Window   For an excellent example of Lingo usage, the Lingo Help article on creating a movie-in-a-window shows a good overview of how to attach a script.

Lingo is a standard, event-driven programming language. Event handlers are attached to specific events, such as a `mouseDown` message. Scripts contain event handlers. You attach a set of event handlers to an object by attaching the script to the object.

3D Sprites   A new feature recently added to Director is the ability to create, import, and manipulate 3D objects on the stage. A simple 3D object that can be added in Director is 3D text. To create 3D text, select any regular text, then in the Property Inspector click on the Text tab and set the display mode to 3D. Other options, such as text depth and texture, can be changed from the 3D Extruder tab in the Property Inspector window. These properties can also be dynamically set in Lingo as well, to change the text as the movie progresses.

3D objects other than text can be formed only using Lingo or imported from 3D Studio Max. Director supports many basic elements of 3D animation, including basic shapes such as spheres and user-definable meshes. The basic shapes can have textures and shaders added to them; textures are 2D images drawn onto the 3D models, while shaders define how the basic model looks. Lights can also be added to the scene; by default, one light provides ambient lighting to the whole scene. Four types of lights can be added: ambient, directional, point, and a spotlight. The strength and color of the light can also be specified.

The viewpoint of the user, called the *camera*, can be moved around to show the 3D objects from any angle. Movement of the camera, such as panning and tilting, can be controlled using built-in scripts in the Library window.

Properties and Parameters   Lingo behaviors can be created with more flexibility by specifying behavior parameters. Parameters can change a behavior by supplying input to the behavior when it is created. If no parameters are specified, a default value will be used. Parameters can be easily changed for a particular behavior by double-clicking on the name of the behavior while it is attached to another cast member, with dialog-driven parameter change as shown in Figure 2.23.

A behavior can have a special handler called `getPropertyDescriptionList` that is run when a sprite attached to the behavior is created. The handler returns a list of parameters that can be added by the `addProp` function. For example, if a movement behavior is made in Lingo, parameters can be added to specify the direction and speed of the movement. The behavior can then be attached to many cast members for a variety of movements.

The parameters defined in the `getPropertyDescriptionList` handler are properties of the behavior that can be accessed within any handle of that behavior. Defining a property in a behavior can be done by simply using the `property` keyword outside any handler and listing all the properties, separated by commas. Global variables can be

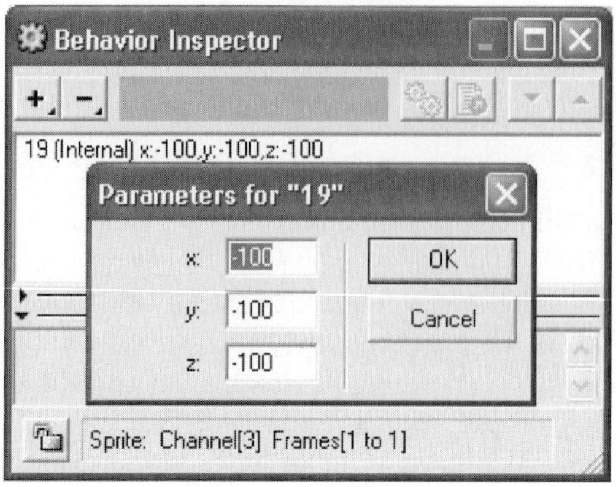

FIGURE 2.23: Parameters dialog box.

accessed across behaviors; they can be declared like a property, except that the `global` keyword is used instead. Each behavior that needs to access a global variable must declare it with the `global` keyword.

Director Objects   Director has two main types of objects: those created in Lingo and those on the Score. Parent scripts are used to create a new object in Lingo. A behavior can be transformed into a parent script by changing the script type in the Property Inspector. Parent scripts are different from other behaviors, in that parameters are passed into the object when it is created in Lingo script.

Parent scripts can be created and changed only in Lingo, while objects in the Score can only be manipulated. The most common objects used are the sprites in the Score. Sprites can be used only in the same time period as the Lingo script referencing them. Reference the sprite at the channel using the `Sprite` keyword followed by the sprite channel number.

A sprite has many properties that perform a variety of actions. The location of the sprite can be changed by the `locv` and `loch` properties to change the vertical and horizontal position, respectively. The `member` property specifies the sprite's cast member and can be used to change the cast member attached to that behavior. This can be useful in animation — instead of changing the sprite in the Score to reflect a small change, it can be done in Lingo.

2.2.3 Macromedia Flash

Flash is a simple authoring tool that facilitates the creation of interactive movies. Flash follows the score metaphor in the way the movie is created and the windows are organized. Here we give a brief introduction to Flash and provide some examples of its use.

Windows   A movie is composed of one or more scenes, each a distinct part of the movie. The command `Insert > Scene` creates a new scene for the current movie.

In Flash, components such as images and sound that make up a movie are called *symbols*, which can be included in the movie by placing them on the Stage. The stage is always visible as a large, white rectangle in the center window of the screen. Three other important windows in Flash are the Timeline, Library, and Tools.

Library Window   The Library window shows all the current symbols in the scene and can be toggled by the `Window > Library` command. A symbol can be edited by double-clicking its name in the library, which causes it to appear on the stage. Symbols can also be added to a scene by simply dragging the symbol from the Library onto the stage.

Timeline Window   The Timeline window manages the layers and timelines of the scene. The left portion of the Timeline window consists of one or more layers of the Stage, which enables you to easily organize the Stage's contents. Symbols from the Library can be dragged onto the Stage, into a particular layer. For example, a simple movie could have two layers, the background and foreground. The background graphic from the library can be dragged onto the stage when the background layer is selected.

Another useful function for layering is the ability to lock or hide a layer. Pressing the circular buttons next to the layer name can toggle their hidden/locked state. Hiding a layer can be useful while positioning or editing a symbol on a different layer. Locking a layer can prevent accidental changes to its symbols once the layer has been completed.

The right side of the Timeline window consists of a horizontal bar for each layer in the scene, similar to a musical score. This represents the passage of time in the movie. The Timeline is composed of a number of keyframes in different layers. A new keyframe can be inserted into the current layer by pressing `F6`. An event such as the start of an animation or the appearance of a new symbol must be in a keyframe. Clicking on the timeline changes the current time in the movie being edited.

Tools Window   The Tools window, which allows the creation and manipulation of images, is composed of four main sections: *Tools*, *View*, *Colors*, and *Options*. Tools consists of selection tools that can be used to demarcate existing images, along with several simple drawing tools, such as the pencil and paint bucket. View consists of a zoom tool and a hand tool, which allow navigation on the Stage. Colors allows foreground and background colors to be chosen, and symbol colors to be manipulated. Options allows additional options when a tool is selected.

Many other windows are useful in manipulating symbols. With the exception of the Timeline window, which can be toggled with the `View > Timeline` command, all other windows can be toggled under the `Window` menu. Figure 2.24 shows the basic Flash screen.

Symbols   Symbols can be either composed from other symbols, drawn, or imported into Flash. Flash is able to import several audio, image, and video formats into the symbol library. A symbol can be imported by using the command `File > Import`, which automatically adds it to the current library. To create a new symbol for the movie, press `ctrl + F8`. A pop-up dialog box will appear in which you can specify the name and behavior of the symbol. Symbols can take on one of three behaviors: a *button*, a *graphic*, or a *movie*. Symbols, such as a button, can be drawn using the Tools window.

FIGURE 2.24: Macromedia Flash.

Buttons   To create a simple button, create a new symbol with the button behavior. The Timeline window should have four keyframes: up, down, over, and hit. These keyframes show different images of the button when the specified action is taken. Only the up keyframe is required and is the default; all others are optional. A button can be drawn by selecting the rectangular tool in the Tools window and then dragging a rectangle onto the Stage.

To add images, so that the button's appearance will change when an event is triggered, click on the appropriate keyframe and create the button image. After at least one keyframe is defined, the basic button is complete, although no action is yet attached to it. Actions are discussed further in the action scripts section below.

Creating a symbol from other symbols is similar to creating a scene: drag the desired symbols from the Library onto the Stage. This allows the creation of complex symbols by combining simpler symbols. Figure 2.25 shows a dialog box for symbol creation.

Animation in Flash   Animation can be accomplished by creating subtle differences in each keyframe of a symbol. In the first keyframe, the symbol to be animated can be dragged onto the stage from the Library. Then another keyframe can be inserted, and the symbol changed. This can be repeated as often as needed. Although this process is time-consuming, it offers more flexibility than any other technique for animation. Flash also allows specific animations to be more easily created in several other ways. *Tweening* can produce simple animations, with changes automatically created between keyframes.

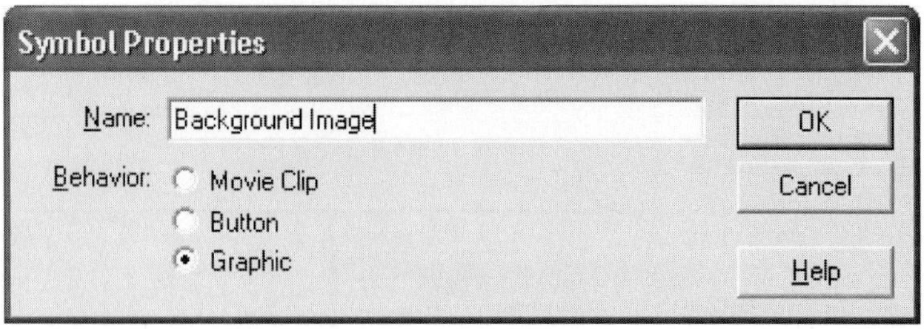

Symbol Properties

Name: Background Image

Behavior: ○ Movie Clip
○ Button
● Graphic

OK

Cancel

Help

FIGURE 2.25: Create symbol dialog.

Tweening   There are two types of tweening: *shape* and *movement* tweening. Shape tweening allows you to create a shape that continuously changes to a different shape over time. Movement tweening allows you to place a symbol in different places on the Stage in different keyframes. Flash automatically fills in the keyframes along a path between the start and finish. To carry out movement tweening, select the symbol to be tweened, choose `Insert > Create Motion Tween`, and select the end frame. Then use the command `Insert > Frame` and move the symbol to the desired position. More advanced tweening allows control of the path as well as of acceleration. Movement and shape tweenings can be combined for additional effect.

Mask animation involves the manipulation of a layer mask — a layer that selectively hides portions of another layer. For example, to create an explosion effect, you could use a mask to cover all but the center of the explosion. Shape tweening could then expand the mask, so that eventually the whole explosion is seen to take place. Figure 2.26 shows a scene before and after a tweening effect is added.

Action Scripts   Action scripts allow you to trigger events such as moving to a different keyframe or requiring the movie to stop. Action scripts can be attached to a keyframe or symbols in a keyframe. Right-clicking on the symbol and pressing `Actions` in the list can modify the actions of a symbol. Similarly, by right-clicking on the keyframe and pressing `Actions` in the pop-up, you can apply actions to a keyframe. A Frame Actions window will come up, with a list of available actions on the left and the current actions being applied symbol on the right. Action scripts are broken into six categories: *Basic*

FIGURE 2.26: Before and after tweening letters.

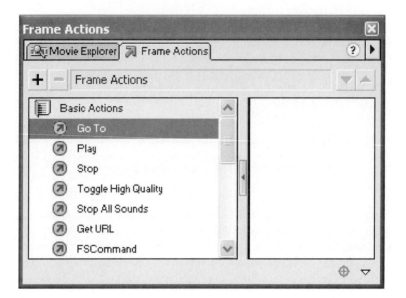

FIGURE 2.27: Action scripts window.

Actions, *Actions*, *Operators*, *Functions*, *Properties*, and *Objects*. Figure 2.27 shows the Frame Actions window.

Basic Actions allow you to attach many simple actions to the movie. Some common actions are

- Goto. Moves the movie to the keyframe specified and can optionally stop. The stop action is commonly used to stop interactive movies when the user is given an option.

- Play. Resumes the movie if the movie is stopped.

- Stop. Stops the movie if it is playing.

- Tell Target. Sends messages to different symbols and keyframes in Flash. It is commonly used to start or stop an action on a different symbol or keyframe.

The *Actions* category contains many programming constructs, such as Loops and Goto statements. Other actions are also included, similar to those in typical high-level, event-driven programming languages, such as Visual Basic. The *Operators* category includes many comparison and assignment operators for variables. This allows you to perform operations on variables in the action script.

The *Functions* category contains built-in functions included in Flash that are not specific to a Flash object. The *Properties* section includes all the global variables predefined in Flash. For example, to refer to the current frame, the variable _currentframe is defined. The *Objects* section lists all objects, such as movie clips or strings and their associated functions.

Buttons need action scripts — event procedures — so that pressing the button will cause an effect. It is straightforward to attach a simple action, such as replaying the Flash movie, to a button. Select the button and click to launch the action script window, located at the bottom right of the screen. Then click on `Basic Actions`, which generates a drop-down list of actions. Double-clicking on the `Play` action automatically adds it to the right side of the window. This button now replays the movie when clicked.

2.2.4   Dreamweaver

Dreamweaver is quite a popular Macromedia product (Dreamweaver MX is the current version) for building multimedia-enabled web sites as well as Internet applications in HTML, XML, and other formats. It provides visual layout tools and code-editing capability for file types such as JavaScript, Active Server Pages, PHP, and XML. The product is integrated with other Macromedia products such as Flash MX and Fireworks MX.

Along with its use as basically a WYSIWYG web development tool, an interesting part of Dreamweaver that relates more directly to authoring is the fact that it comes with a prepackaged set of behaviors and is also extensible. The behaviors are essentially event procedures, responding to events such as mouseover — the set of possible events is different for each target browser and is reconfigurable for each browser and version number. Computer Science students can write their own Javascript code, say, and attach this to events.

2.3   VRML

2.3.1   Overview

VRML, which stands for *Virtual Reality Modeling Language*, was conceived at the first international conference of the World Wide Web. Mark Pesce, Tony Parisi, and David Ragget outlined the structure of VRML at the conference and specified that it would be a platform-independent language that would be viewed on the Internet. The objective of VRML was to have the capability to put colored objects into a 3D environment.

VRML is an interpreted language, which can be seen as a disadvantage, because it runs slowly on many computers today. However, it has been influential, because it was the first method available for displaying a 3D world on the World Wide Web.

Strictly speaking, VRML is not a "tool," like Premiere or Director. In fact, the only piece of software needed to create VRML content is a text editor. Nonetheless, VRML is a tool used to create 3D environments on the web, much like Flash is a tool used to create interactive movies.

History   VRML 1.0 was created in May 1995, with a revision for clarification called VRML 1.0C in January 1996. VRML is based on a subset of the file inventor format created by Silicon Graphics Inc. VRML 1.0 allowed for the creation of many simple 3D objects, such as a cube, sphere, and user-defined polygons. Materials and textures can be specified for objects to make the objects more realistic.

The last major revision of VRML was VRML 2.0. This revision added the ability to create an interactive world. VRML 2.0, also called "Moving Worlds", allows for animation and sound in an interactive virtual world. New objects were added to make the creation of virtual worlds easier. Java and Javascript have been included in VRML, to allow for interactive

FIGURE 2.28: Basic VRML shapes.

objects and user-defined actions. VRML 2.0 was a major change from VRML 1.0, and the two versions are not compatible. However, utilities are available to convert VRML 1.0 to VRML 2.0.

VRML 2.0 was submitted for standardization to the International Organization for Standardization (ISO), and as a result, VRML97 was specified. VRML97 is virtually identical to VRML 2.0 — only minor documentation changes and clarifications were added. VRML97 is an ISO/IEC standard.

VRML Shapes   VRML is made up of nodes put into a hierarchy that describe a scene of one or more objects. VRML contains basic geometric shapes that can be combined to create more complex objects. The Shape node is a generic node for all objects in VRML. The Box, Cylinder, Cone, and Sphere are geometry nodes that place basic objects in the virtual world.

VRML allows for the definition of complex shapes that include IndexedFaceSet and Extrusion. An IndexedFaceSet is a set of faces that make up an object. This allows for the creation of complex shapes, since an arbitrary number of faces is allowed. An Extrusion is a 2D cross-section extruded along a spine and is useful in creating a simple curved surface, such as a flower petal.

An object's shape, size, color, and reflective properties can be specified in VRML. The Appearance node controls the way a shape looks and can contain a Material node and texture nodes. Figure 2.28 displays some of these shapes.

A Material node specifies an object's surface properties. It can control what color the object is by specifying the red, green, and blue values of the object. The specular and emissive colors can be specified similarly. Other attributes, such as how much the object reflects direct and indirect light, can also be controlled. Objects in VRML can be transparent or partially transparent. This is also included in the Material node.

Three kinds of texture nodes can be used to map textures onto any object. The most common one is the ImageTexture, which can take an external JPEG or PNG image file and map it onto the shape. The way the image is textured can be specified — that is, the way the image should be tiled onto the object is editable.

A MovieTexture node allows mapping an MPEG movie onto an object; the starting and stopping time can also be specified.

FIGURE 2.29: A simple VRML scene.

The final texture-mapping node is called a `PixelTexture`, which simply means creating an image to use with `ImageTexture` VRML. Although it is more inefficient than an `ImageTexture` node, it is still useful for simple textures.

Text can be put into a VRML world using the `Text` node. You can specify the text to be included, as well as the font, alignment, and size. By default, the text faces in the positive Y direction, or "up".

All shapes and text start in the middle of the VRML world. To arrange the shapes, `Transform` nodes must be wrapped around the shape nodes. The `Transform` node can contain `Translation`, `Scale`, and `Rotation` nodes. `Translation` simply moves the object a specific distance from its current location, which is by default the center of the world. `Scale` increases or decreases the size of the object, while `Rotation` rotates the object around its center.

VRML World   A virtual world needs more than just shapes to be realistic; it needs cameras to view the objects, as well as backgrounds and lighting. The default camera is aligned with the negative z-axis, a few meters from the center of the scene. Using `Viewpoint` nodes, the default camera position can be changed and other cameras added. Figure 2.29 displays a simple VRML scene from one viewpoint.

The viewpoint can be specified with the `position` node and can be rotated from the default view with the `orientation` node. The camera's angle for its field of view can be changed from its default 0.78 radians with the `fieldOfView` node. Changing the field of view can create a telephoto effect.

Three types of lighting can be used in a VRML world. A `DirectionalLight` node shines a light across the whole world in a certain direction, similar to the light from the sun — it is from one direction and affects all objects in the scene. A `PointLight` shines a light in all directions from a certain point in space. A `SpotLight` shines a light in a certain direction from a point. Proper lighting is important in adding realism to a world. Many parameters, such as the color and strength of the light, can be specified for every type of light.

The background of the VRML world can also be specified using the `Background` node. The background color, black by default, as well as the sky color can be changed. A `Panorama` node can map a texture to the sides of the world. A panorama is mapped onto a large cube surrounding the VRML world. If a panorama is used, the user can never approach the texture, because the panorama is centered on the user. It is also possible to add fog in VRML using the `Fog` node, where the color and density of the fog can be specified. Fog can increase the frame rate of a world, since objects hidden by the fog are not rendered.

2.3.2 Animation and Interactions

An advantage of VRML97 over the original VRML 1.0 is that the VRML world can be interactive. The only method of animation in VRML is tweening, which can be done by slowly changing an object specified in an interpolator node. This node will modify an object over time, based on the type of interpolator.

There are six interpolators: *color*, *coordinate*, *normal*, *orientation*, *position*, and *scalar*. All interpolators have two nodes that must be specified: the `key` and `keyValue`. The `key` consists of a list of two or more numbers, starting with 0 and ending with 1. Each `key` element must be complemented with a `keyValue` element. The `key` defines how far along the animation is, and the `keyValue` defines what values should change. For example, a `key` element of 0.5 and its matching `keyvalue` define what the object should look like at the middle of the animation.

A `TimeSensor` node times an animation, so that the interpolator knows what stage the object should be in. A `TimeSensor` has no physical form in the VRML world and just keeps time. To notify an interpolator of a time change, a `ROUTE` is needed to connect two nodes. One is needed between the `TimeSensor` and the interpolator and another between the interpolator and the object to be animated. Most animation can be accomplished this way. Chaining `ROUTE` commands so that one event triggers many others can accomplish complex animations.

Two categories of sensors can be used in VRML to obtain input from a user. The first is *environment* sensors. There are three kinds of environment sensor nodes: `VisibilitySensor`, `ProximitySensor`, and `Collision`. A `VisibilitySensor` is activated when a user's field of view enters an invisible box. A `ProximitySensor` is activated when a user enters or leaves an area. A `Collision` is activated when the user hits the node.

The second category of sensors is called *pointing device* sensors. The first pointing device sensor is a *touch* sensor, activated when an object is clicked with the mouse. Three other sensors are called *drag* sensors. These sensors allow the rotation of spheres, cylinders, and planes when a mouse is dragging the object.

2.3.3 VRML Specifics

A VRML file is simply a text file with a `.wrl` extension. VRML97 must include the line `#VRML V2.0 UTF8` in the first line of the file. A # denotes a comment anywhere in the file except for the first line. The first line of a VRML file tells the VRML client what version of VRML to use. VRML nodes are case sensitive and are usually built hierarchically.

Although only a simple text editor such as notepad is needed, VRML-specific text editors are available, such as VRMLpad. They aid in creating VRML objects by providing different colors and collapsing or expanding nodes.

All nodes begin with "{" and end with "}" and most can contain nodes inside nodes. Special nodes, called group nodes, can cluster multiple nodes. The keyword children followed by "[" begins the list of children nodes, which ends with "]". A "Transform" node is an example of a group node.

Nodes can be named using DEF and can be used again later by using the keyword USE. This allows for creation of complex objects using many simple objects.

To create a simple box in VRML

```
Shape {
      Geometry Box{}
      }
```

The box defaults to a 2-meter-long cube in the center of the screen. Putting it into a Transform node can move this box to a different part of the scene. We can also give the box a different color, such as red:

```
Transform { translation 0 10 0 children [
   Shape {
     Geometry Box{}
     appearance Appearance {
       material Material {
         diffuseColor 1 0 0
       }
     }
   }
]}
```

This VRML fragment puts a red box centered in the +10 Y direction. The box can be reused if DEF mybox is put in front of the Transform. Now, whenever the box needs to be used again, simply putting USE mybox will make a copy.

2.4 FURTHER EXPLORATION

Good general references for multimedia authoring are introductory books [3, 1] and Chapters 5–8 in [4]. Material on automatic authoring is fully expanded in [7].

A link to the overall, very useful FAQ file for multimedia authoring is in the textbook web site's Further Exploration section for this chapter.

Our TextColor.exe program for investigating complementary colors, as in Figure 2.5, is on the textbook web site as well.

We also include a link to a good FAQ collection on Director. A simple Director movie demonstrating the ideas set out in Section 2.2.2 may be downloaded from the web site, along with information on Dreamweaver, VRML, and a small demo VRML world.

2.5 EXERCISES

1. What extra information is multimedia good at conveying?

   (a) What can spoken text convey that written text cannot?
   (b) When might written text be better than spoken text?

2. Find and learn 3D Studio Max in your local lab software. Read the online tutorials to see this software's approach to a 3D modeling technique. Learn texture mapping and animation using this product. Make a 3D model after carrying out these steps.

3. Design an interactive web page using Dreamweaver. HTML 4 provides layer functionality, as in Adobe Photoshop. Each layer represents an HTML object, such as text, an image, or a simple HTML page. In Dreamweaver, each layer has a marker associated with it. Therefore, highlighting the layer marker selects the entire layer, to which you can apply any desired effect. As in Flash, you can add buttons and behaviors for navigation and control. You can create animations using the Timeline behavior.

4. In regard to automatic authoring,

   (a) What would you suppose is meant by the term "active images"?
   (b) What are the problems associated with moving text-based techniques to the realm of image-based automatic authoring?
   (c) What is the single most important problem associated with automatic authoring using legacy (already written) text documents?

5. Suppose we wish to create a simple animation, as in Figure 2.30. Note that this image is exactly what the animation looks like at some time, not a figurative representation of the *process* of moving the fish; the fish is repeated as it moves. State what we need to carry out this objective, and give a simple pseudocode solution for the problem.

FIGURE 2.30: Sprite, progressively taking up more space.

Assume we already have a list of (x, y) coordinates for the fish path, that we have available a procedure for centering images on path positions, and that the movement takes place on top of a video.

6. For the slide transition in Figure 2.11, explain how we arrive at the formula for x in the unmoving right video R_R.

7. Suppose we wish to create a video transition such that the second video appears under the first video through an opening circle (like a camera iris opening), as in Figure 2.31. Write a formula to use the correct pixels from the two videos to achieve this special effect. Just write your answer for the red channel.

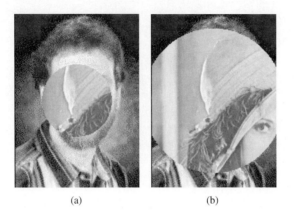

(a)   (b)

FIGURE 2.31: Iris wipe: (a) iris is opening; (b) at a later moment.

8. Now suppose we wish to create a video transition such that the second video appears under the first video through a moving radius (like a clock hand), as in Figure 2.32. Write a formula to use the correct pixels from the two videos to achieve this special effect for the red channel.

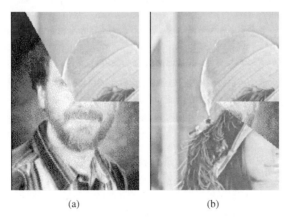

(a)   (b)

FIGURE 2.32: Clock wipe: (a) clock hand is sweeping out; (b) at a later moment.

FIGURE 2.33: Filter applied to video.

9. Suppose you wish to create a wavy effect, as in Figure 2.33. This effect comes from replacing the image x value by an x value offset by a small amount. Suppose the image size is 160 rows $\times$ 120 columns of pixels.

  (a) Using float arithmetic, add a sine component to the x value of the pixel such that the pixel takes on an RGB value equal to that of a different pixel in the original image. Make the maximum shift in x equal to 16 pixels.

  (b) In Premiere and other packages, only integer arithmetic is provided. Functions such as `sin` are redefined so as to take an `int` argument and return an `int`. The argument to the `sin` function must be in $0..1{,}024$, and the value of `sin` is in $-512..512$: `sin(0)` returns 0, `sin(256)` returns 512, `sin(512)` returns 0, `sin(768)` returns -512 and `sin(1,024)` returns 0.

    Rewrite your expression in part (a) using integer arithmetic.

  (c) How could you change your answer to make the waving time-dependent?

10. How would you create the image in Figure 2.6? Write a small program to make such an image. *Hint:* Place R, G, and B at the corners of an equilateral triangle inside the circle. It's best to go over all columns and rows in the output image rather than simply going around the disk and trying to map results back to (x, y) pixel positions.

11. As a longer exercise for learning existing software for manipulating images, video, and music, make a 1-minute digital video. By the end of this exercise, you should be familiar with PC-based equipment and know how to use Adobe Premiere, Photoshop,

Cakewalk Pro Audio, and other multimedia software.

(a) Capture (or find) at least three video files. You can use a camcorder or VCR to make your own (through Premiere or the like) or find some on the Net.

(b) Compose (or edit) a small MIDI file with Cakewalk Pro Audio.

(c) Create (or find) at least one WAV file. You may either digitize your own or download some from the net.

(d) Use Photoshop to create a title and an ending.

(e) Combine all of the above to produce a movie about 60 seconds long, including a title, some credits, some soundtracks, and at least three transitions. Experiment with different compression methods; you are encouraged to use MPEG for your final product.

(f) The above constitutes a minimum statement of the exercise. You may be tempted to get very creative, and that's fine, but don't go overboard and take too much time away from the rest of your life!

2.6   REFERENCES

1 A.C. Luther, *Authoring Interactive Multimedia*, The IBM Tools Series, San Diego: AP Professional, 1994.

2 R. Vetter, C. Ward, and S. Shapiro, "Using Color and Text in Multimedia Projections," *IEEE Multimedia*, 2(4): 46–54, 1995.

3 J.C. Shepherd and D. Colaizzi, *Authoring Authorware: A Practical Guide*, Upper Saddle River, NJ: Prentice Hall, 1998.

4 D.E. Wolfgram, *Creating Multimedia Presentations*, Indianapolis: Que Publishing, 1994.

5 A. Ginige, D. Lowe, and J. Robertson, "Hypermedia Authoring," *IEEE Multimedia*, 2: 24–35, 1995.

6 A. Ginige and D. Lowe, "Next Generation Hypermedia Authoring Systems," In *Proceedings of Multimedia Information Systems and Hypermedia*, 1995, 1–11.

7 D. Lowe and W. Hall, *Hypermedia and the Web: An Engineering Approach*, New York: Wiley, 1999.

CHAPTER 3

Graphics and Image Data Representations

In this chapter we look at images, starting with 1-bit images, then 8-bit gray images and how to print them, then 24-bit color images and 8-bit versions of color images. The specifics of file formats for storing such images will also be discussed.

We consider the following topics:

- Graphics/image data types

- Popular file formats

3.1 GRAPHICS/IMAGE DATA TYPES

The number of file formats used in multimedia continues to proliferate [1]. For example, Table 3.1 shows a list of file formats used in the popular product Macromedia Director. In this text, we shall study just a few popular file formats, to develop a sense of how they operate. We shall concentrate on GIF and JPG image file formats, since these two formats are distinguished by the fact that most web browsers can decompress and display them.

To begin, we shall discuss the features of file formats in general.

TABLE 3.1: Macromedia Director file formats.

File import					File export		Native
Image	Palette	Sound	Video	Animation	Image	Video	
BMP, DIB,	PAL	AIFF	AVI	DIR	BMP	AVI	DIR
GIF, JPG,	ACT	AU	MOV	FLA		MOV	DXR
PICT, PNG,		MP3		FLC			EXE
PNT, PSD,		WAV		FLI			
TGA, TIFF,				GIF			
WMF				PPT			

FIGURE 3.1: Monochrome 1-bit Lena image.

3.1.1 1-Bit Images

Images consist of *pixels*, or *pels* — picture elements in digital images. A 1-bit image consists of on and off bits only and thus is the simplest type of image. Each pixel is stored as a single bit (0 or 1). Hence, such an image is also referred to as a *binary image*.

It is also called a 1-bit *monochrome* image, since it contains no color. Figure 3.1 shows a 1-bit monochrome image (called "Lena" by multimedia scientists — this is a standard image used to illustrate many algorithms). A 640 × 480 monochrome image requires 38.4 kilobytes of storage (= 640 × 480/8). Monochrome 1-bit images can be satisfactory for pictures containing only simple graphics and text.

3.1.2 8-Bit Gray-Level Images

Now consider an 8-bit image — that is, one for which each pixel has a *gray value* between 0 and 255. Each pixel is represented by a single byte — for example, a dark pixel might have a value of 10, and a bright one might be 230.

The entire image can be thought of as a two-dimensional array of pixel values. We refer to such an array as a *bitmap*, — a representation of the graphics/image data that parallels the manner in which it is stored in video memory.

Image resolution refers to the number of pixels in a digital image (higher resolution always yields better quality). Fairly high resolution for such an image might be 1,600 × 1,200, whereas lower resolution might be 640 × 480. Notice that here we are using an *aspect ratio* of 4:3. We don't have to adopt this ratio, but it has been found to look natural.

Such an array must be stored in hardware; we call this hardware a *frame buffer*. Special (relatively expensive) hardware called a "video" card (actually a graphics card) is used for this purpose. The resolution of the video card does not have to match the desired resolution of the image, but if not enough video card memory is available, the data has to be shifted around in RAM for display.

We can think of the 8-bit image as a set of 1-bit *bitplanes*, where each plane consists of a 1-bit representation of the image at higher and higher levels of "elevation": a bit is turned on if the image pixel has a nonzero value at or above that bit level.

Figure 3.2 displays the concept of bitplanes graphically. Each bit-plane can have a value of 0 or 1 at each pixel but, together, all the bitplanes make up a single byte that stores

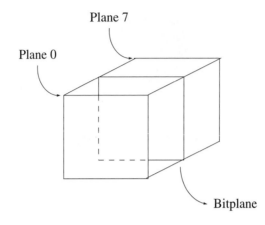

FIGURE 3.2: Bitplanes for 8-bit grayscale image.

values between 0 and 255 (in this 8-bit situation). For the least significant bit, the bit value translates to 0 or 1 in the final numeric sum of the binary number. Positional arithmetic implies that for the next, second, bit each 0 or 1 makes a contribution of 0 or 2 to the final sum. The next bits stand for 0 or 4, 0 or 8, and so on, up to 0 or 128 for the most significant bit. Video cards can refresh bitplane data at video rate but, unlike RAM, do not hold the data well. Raster fields are refreshed at 60 cycles per second in North America.

Each pixel is usually stored as a byte (a value between 0 to 255), so a 640×480 grayscale image requires 300 kilobytes of storage ($640 \times 480 = 307,200$). Figure 3.3 shows the Lena image again, this time in grayscale.

If we wish to *print* such an image, things become more complex. Suppose we have available a 600 dot-per-inch (dpi) laser printer. Such a device can usually only print a dot or not print it. However, a 600×600 image will be printed in a 1-inch space and will thus not be very pleasing. Instead, *dithering* is used. The basic strategy of dithering is to trade *intensity resolution* for *spatial resolution*. (See [2], p. 568, for a good discussion of dithering).

FIGURE 3.3: Grayscale image of Lena.

Dithering   For printing on a 1-bit printer, dithering is used to calculate larger patterns of dots, such that values from 0 to 255 correspond to pleasing patterns that correctly represent darker and brighter pixel values. The main strategy is to replace a pixel value by a larger pattern, say 2×2 or 4×4, such that the number of printed dots approximates the varying-sized disks of ink used in *halftone printing*. Half-tone printing is an analog process that uses smaller or larger filled circles of black ink to represent shading, for newspaper printing, say.

If instead we use an $n \times n$ matrix of on-off 1-bit dots, we can represent $n^2 + 1$ levels of intensity resolution — since, for example, three dots filled in any way counts as one intensity level. The dot patterns are created heuristically. For example, if we use a 2×2 "dither matrix":

$$\begin{pmatrix} 0 & 2 \\ 3 & 1 \end{pmatrix}$$

we can first remap image values in $0 .. 255$ into the new range $0 .. 4$ by (integer) dividing by $256/5$. Then, for example, if the pixel value is 0, we print nothing in a 2×2 area of printer output. But if the pixel value is 4, we print all four dots. So the rule is

> If the intensity is greater than the dither matrix entry, print an on dot at that entry location: replace each pixel by an $n \times n$ matrix of dots.

However, we notice that the number of levels is small for this type of printing. If we increase the number of effective intensity levels by increasing the dither matrix size, we also increase the size of the output image. This reduces the amount of detail in any small part of the image, effectively reducing the spatial resolution.

Note that the image size may be much larger for a dithered image, since replacing each pixel by a 4×4 array of dots, say, makes an image 16 times as large. However, a clever trick can get around this problem. Suppose we wish to use a larger, 4×4 dither matrix, such as

$$\begin{pmatrix} 0 & 8 & 2 & 10 \\ 12 & 4 & 14 & 6 \\ 3 & 11 & 1 & 9 \\ 15 & 7 & 13 & 5 \end{pmatrix}$$

Then suppose we slide the dither matrix over the image four pixels in the horizontal and vertical directions at a time (where image values have been reduced to the range $0 .. 16$). An "ordered dither" consists of turning on the printer output bit for a pixel if the intensity level is greater than the particular matrix element just at that pixel position. Figure 3.4(a) shows a grayscale image of Lena. The ordered-dither version is shown as Figure 3.4(b), with a detail of Lena's right eye in Figure 3.4(c).

FIGURE 3.4: Dithering of grayscale images.   (a) 8-bit gray image `lenagray.bmp`; (b) dithered version of the image; (c) detail of dithered version. (This figure also appears in the color insert section.)

An algorithm for ordered dither, with $n \times n$ dither matrix, is as follows:

ALGORITHM 3.1   ORDERED DITHER

begin
    for $x = 0$ to x_{max} // columns
        for $y = 0$ to y_{max} // rows
            $i = x \bmod n$
            $j = y \bmod n$
            // $I(x, y)$ is the input, $O(x, y)$ is the output, D is the dither matrix.
            if $I(x, y) > D(i, j)$
                $O(x, y) = 1;$
            else
                $O(x, y) = 0;$
end

Foley, et al. [2] provides more details on ordered dithering.

3.1.3   Image Data Types

The next sections introduce some of the most common data types for graphics and image file formats: 24-bit color and 8-bit color. We then discuss file formats. Some formats are restricted to particular hardware/operating system platforms, while others are *platform-independent*, or *cross-platform*, formats. Even if some formats are not cross-platform, conversion applications can recognize and translate formats from one system to another.

Most image formats incorporate some variation of a *compression* technique due to the large storage size of image files. Compression techniques can be classified as either *lossless* or *lossy*. We will study various image, video, and audio compression techniques in Chapters 7 through 14.

3.1.4   24-Bit Color Images

In a color 24-bit image, each pixel is represented by three bytes, usually representing RGB. Since each value is in the range 0–255, this format supports $256 \times 256 \times 256$, or a total

(a)

(b)

(c)

(d)

FIGURE 3.5: High-resolution color and separate R, G, B color channel images. (a) example of 24-bit color image `forestfire.bmp`; (b, c, d) R, G, and B color channels for this image. (This figure also appears in the color insert section.)

of 16,777,216, possible combined colors. However, such flexibility does result in a storage penalty: a 640 × 480 24-bit color image would require 921.6 kilobytes of storage without any compression.

An important point to note is that many 24-bit color images are actually stored as 32-bit images, with the extra byte of data for each pixel storing an α (*alpha*) value representing special-effect information. (See [2], p. 835, for an introduction to use of the α-channel for compositing several overlapping objects in a graphics image. The simplest use is as a transparency flag.)

Figure 3.5 shows the image `forestfire.bmp`, a 24-bit image in Microsoft Windows BMP format (discussed later in the chapter). Also shown are the grayscale images for just the red, green, and blue channels, for this image. Taking the byte values $0..255$ in each color channel to represent intensity, we can display a gray image for each color separately.

3.1.5   8-Bit Color Images

If space is a concern (and it almost always is), reasonably accurate color images can be obtained by quantizing the color information to collapse it. Many systems can make use of only 8 bits of color information (the so-called "256 colors") in producing a screen image. Even if a system has the electronics to actually use 24-bit information, backward compatibility demands that we understand 8-bit color image files.

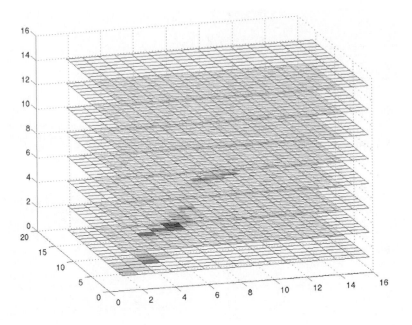

FIGURE 3.6: Three-dimensional histogram of RGB colors in `forestfire.bmp`.

Such image files use the concept of a *lookup table* to store color information. Basically, the image stores not color but instead just a set of bytes, each of which is an index into a table with 3-byte values that specify the color for a pixel with that lookup table index. In a way, it's a bit like a paint-by-number children's art set, with number 1 perhaps standing for orange, number 2 for green, and so on — there is no inherent pattern to the set of actual colors.

It makes sense to carefully choose just which colors to represent best in the image: if an image is mostly red sunset, it's reasonable to represent red with precision and store only a few greens.

Suppose all the colors in a 24-bit image were collected in a $256 \times 256 \times 256$ set of cells, along with the count of how many pixels belong to each of these colors stored in that cell. For example, if exactly 23 pixels have RGB values (45, 200, 91) then store the value 23 in a three-dimensional array, at the element indexed by the index values [45, 200, 91]. This data structure is called a *color histogram* (see, e.g., [3, 4]).

Figure 3.6 shows a 3D histogram of the RGB values of the pixels in `forestfire.bmp`. The histogram has $16 \times 16 \times 16$ bins and shows the count in each bin in terms of intensity and pseudocolor. We can see a few important clusters of color information, corresponding to the reds, yellows, greens, and so on, of the `forestfire` image. Clustering in this way allows us to pick the most important 256 groups of color.

Basically, large populations in 3D histogram bins can be subjected to a split-and-merge algorithm to determine the "best" 256 colors. Figure 3.7 shows the resulting 8-bit image in GIF format (discussed later in this chapter). Notice that it is difficult to discern the difference between Figure 3.5(a), the 24-bit image, and Figure 3.7, the 8-bit image. This is

FIGURE 3.7: Example of 8-bit color image. (This figure also appears in the color insert section.)

not always the case. Consider the field of medical imaging: would you be satisfied with only a "reasonably accurate" image of your brain for potential laser surgery? Likely not — and that is why consideration of 64-bit imaging for medical applications is not out of the question.

Note the great savings in space for 8-bit images over 24-bit ones: a 640×480 8-bit color image requires only 300 kilobytes of storage, compared to 921.6 kilobytes for a color image (again, without any compression applied).

3.1.6 Color Lookup Tables (LUTs)

Again, the idea used in 8-bit color images is to store only the index, or code value, for each pixel. Then, if a pixel stores, say, the value 25, the meaning is to go to row 25 in a color lookup table (LUT). While images are displayed as two-dimensional arrays of values, they are usually *stored* in row-column order as simply a long series of values. For an 8-bit image, the image file can store in the file header information just what 8-bit values for R, G, and B correspond to each index. Figure 3.8 displays this idea. The LUT is often called a *palette*.

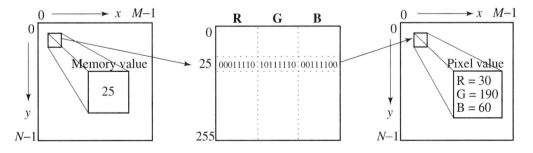

FIGURE 3.8: Color LUT for 8-bit color images.

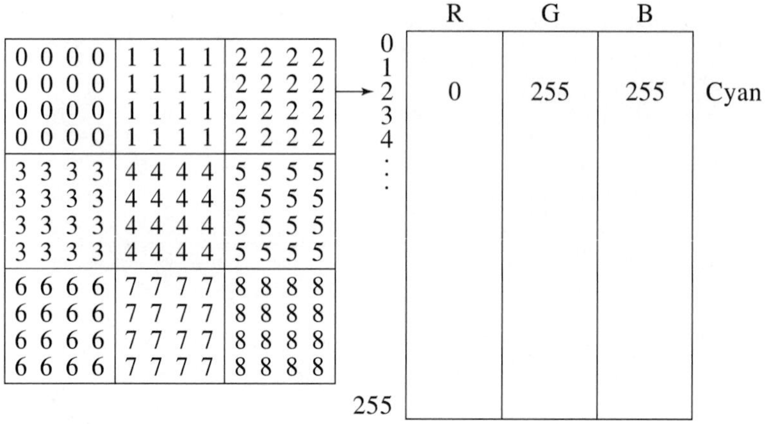

```
                                                    R      G      B
0 0 0 0  1 1 1 1  2 2 2 2      0
0 0 0 0  1 1 1 1  2 2 2 2      1
0 0 0 0  1 1 1 1  2 2 2 2  →   2    0     255    255    Cyan
0 0 0 0  1 1 1 1  2 2 2 2      3
                              4
3 3 3 3  4 4 4 4  5 5 5 5      :
3 3 3 3  4 4 4 4  5 5 5 5
3 3 3 3  4 4 4 4  5 5 5 5
3 3 3 3  4 4 4 4  5 5 5 5

6 6 6 6  7 7 7 7  8 8 8 8
6 6 6 6  7 7 7 7  8 8 8 8
6 6 6 6  7 7 7 7  8 8 8 8
6 6 6 6  7 7 7 7  8 8 8 8      255
```

FIGURE 3.9: Color picker for 8-bit color: each block of the color picker corresponds to one row of the color LUT.

A *color picker* consists of an array of fairly large blocks of color (or a semicontinuous range of colors) such that a mouse click will select the color indicated. In reality, a color picker displays the palette colors associated with index values from 0 to 255. Figure 3.9 displays the concept of a color picker: if the user selects the color block with index value 2, then the color meant is cyan, with RGB values (0, 255, 255).

A simple animation process is possible via simply changing the color table: this is called *color cycling* or *palette animation*. Since updates from the color table are fast, this can result in a simple, pleasing effect.

Dithering can also be carried out for color printers, using 1 bit per color channel and spacing out the color with R, G, and B dots. Alternatively, if the printer or screen can print only a limited number of colors, say using 8 bits instead of 24, color can be made to seem printable, even if it is not available in the color LUT. The apparent color resolution of a display can be increased without reducing spatial resolution by averaging the intensities of neighboring pixels. Then it is possible to trick the eye into perceiving colors that are not available, because it carries out a spatial blending that can be put to good use. Figure 3.10(a) shows a 24-bit color image of Lena, and Figure 3.10(b) shows the same image reduced to only 5 bits via dithering. Figure 3.10(c) shows a detail of the left eye.

How to Devise a Color Lookup Table In Section 3.1.5, we briefly discussed the idea of *clustering* to generate the most important 256 colors from a 24-bit color image. However, in general, clustering is an expensive and slow process. But we need to devise color LUTs somehow — how shall we accomplish this?

The most straightforward way to make 8-bit lookup color out of 24-bit color would be to divide the RGB cube into equal slices in each dimension. Then the centers of each of the resulting cubes would serve as the entries in the color LUT, while simply scaling the RGB ranges 0 .. 255 into the appropriate ranges would generate the 8-bit codes.

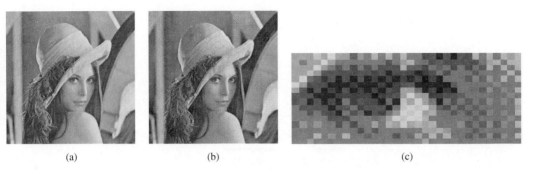

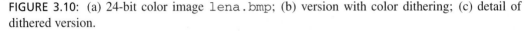

FIGURE 3.10: (a) 24-bit color image `lena.bmp`; (b) version with color dithering; (c) detail of dithered version.

Since humans are more sensitive to R and G than to B, we could shrink the R range and G range $0..255$ into the 3-bit range $0..7$ and shrink the B range down to the 2-bit range $0..3$, making a total of 8 bits. To shrink R and G, we could simply divide the R or G byte value by $(256/8 =) 32$ and then truncate. Then each pixel in the image gets replaced by its 8-bit index, and the color LUT serves to generate 24-bit color.

However, what tends to happen with this simple scheme is that edge artifacts appear in the image. The reason is that if a slight change in RGB results in shifting to a new code, an edge appears, and this can be quite annoying perceptually.

A simple alternate solution for this color reduction problem called the *median-cut algorithm* does a better job (and several other competing methods do as well or better). This approach derives from computer graphics [5]; here, we show a much simplified version. The method is a type of adaptive partitioning scheme that tries to put the most bits, the most discrimination power, where colors are most clustered.

The idea is to sort the R byte values and find their median. Then values smaller than the median are labeled with a 0 bit and values larger than the median are labeled with a 1 bit. The median is the point where half the pixels are smaller and half are larger.

Suppose we are imaging some apples, and most pixels are reddish. Then the median R byte value might fall fairly high on the red $0..255$ scale. Next, we consider only pixels with a 0 label from the first step and sort their G values. Again, we label image pixels with another bit, 0 for those less than the median in the greens and 1 for those greater. Now applying the same scheme to pixels that received a 1 bit for the red step, we have arrived at 2-bit labeling for all pixels.

Carrying on to the blue channel, we have a 3-bit scheme. Repeating all steps, R, G, and B, results in a 6-bit scheme, and cycling through R and G once more results in 8 bits. These bits form our 8-bit color index value for pixels, and corresponding 24-bit colors can be the centers of the resulting small color cubes.

You can see that in fact this type of scheme will indeed concentrate bits where they most need to differentiate between high populations of close colors. We can most easily visualize finding the median by using a histogram showing counts at position $0..255$. Figure 3.11 shows a histogram of the R byte values for the `forestfire.bmp` image along with the median of these values, depicted as a vertical line.

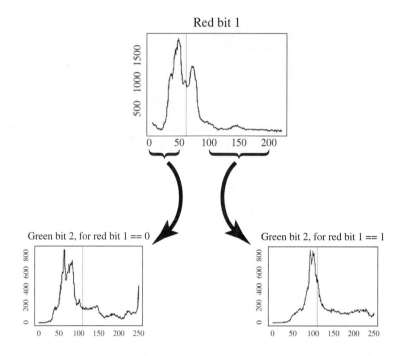

FIGURE 3.11: Histogram of R bytes for the 24-bit color image `forestfire.bmp` results in a 0 or 1 bit label for every pixel. For the second bit of the color table index being built, we take R values less than the R median and label just those pixels as 0 or 1 according as their G value is less or greater than the median of the G value. Continuing over R, G, B for 8 bits gives a color LUT 8-bit index.

The 24-bit color image resulting from replacing every pixel by its corresponding color LUT 24-bit color is only an approximation to the original 24-bit image, of course, but the above algorithm does a reasonable job of putting most discriminatory power where it is most needed — where small color shading differences will be most noticeable. It should also be mentioned that several methods exist for distributing the approximation errors from one pixel to the next. This has the effect of smoothing out problems in the 8-bit approximation.

The more accurate version of the median-cut algorithm proceeds via the following steps:

1. Find the smallest box that contains all the colors in the image.
2. Sort the enclosed colors along the longest dimension of the box.
3. Split the box into two regions at the median of the sorted list.
4. Repeat the above process in steps (2) and (3) until the original color space has been divided into, say, 256 regions.
5. For every box, call the mean of R, G, and B in that box the representative (the center) color for the box.
6. Based on the Euclidean distance between a pixel RGB value and the box centers, assign every pixel to one of the representative colors. Replace the pixel by the code

in a lookup table that indexes representative colors (in the table, each representative color is 24-bits — 8 bits each for R, G, and B.)

This way, we might have a table of 256 rows, each containing three 8-bit values. The row indices are the codes for the lookup table, and these indices are what are stored in pixel values of the new, *color quantized* or *palettized* image.

3.2 POPULAR FILE FORMATS

Some popular file formats for information exchange are described below. One of the most important is the 8-bit GIF format, because of its historical connection to the WWW and HTML markup language as the first image type recognized by net browsers. However, currently the most important common file format is JPEG, which will be explored in great depth in Chapter 9.

3.2.1 GIF

Graphics Interchange Format (GIF) was devised by UNISYS Corporation and Compuserve, initially for transmitting graphical images over phone lines via modems. The GIF standard uses the Lempel-Ziv-Welch algorithm (a form of compression — see Chapter 7), modified slightly for image scanline packets to use the line grouping of pixels effectively.

The GIF standard is limited to 8-bit (256) color images only. While this produces acceptable color, it is best suited for images with few distinctive colors (e.g., graphics or drawing).

The GIF image format has a few interesting features, notwithstanding the fact that it has been largely supplanted. The standard supports *interlacing* — the successive display of pixels in widely spaced rows by a four-pass display process.

In fact, GIF comes in two flavors. The original specification is GIF87a. The later version, GIF89a, supports simple *animation* via a Graphics Control Extension block in the data. This provides simple control over *delay time*, a *transparency index*, and so on. Software such as Corel Draw allows access to and editing of GIF images.

It is worthwhile examining the file format for GIF87 in more detail, since many such formats bear a resemblance to it but have grown a good deal more complex than this "simple" standard. For the standard specification, the general file format is as in Figure 3.12. The *Signature* is 6 bytes: GIF87a; the *Screen Descriptor* is a 7-byte set of flags. A GIF87 file can contain more than one image definition, usually to fit on several different parts of the screen. Therefore each image can contain its own color lookup table, a *Local Color Map*, for mapping 8 bits into 24-bit RGB values. However, it need not, and a global color map can instead be defined to take the place of a local table if the latter is not included.

The Screen Descriptor comprises a set of attributes that belong to every image in the file. According to the GIF87 standard, it is defined as in Figure 3.13. *Screen Width* is given in the first 2 bytes. Since some machines invert the order MSB/LSB (most significant byte/least significant byte — i.e., byte order), this order is specified. *Screen Height* is the next 2 bytes. The "m" in byte 5 is 0 if no global color map is given. Color resolution, "cr", is 3 bits in 0 .. 7. Since this is an old standard meant to operate on a variety of low-end hardware, "cr" is *requesting* this much color resolution.

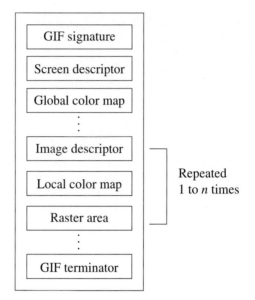

FIGURE 3.12: GIF file format.

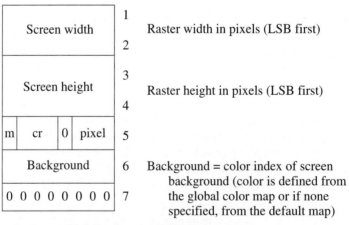

FIGURE 3.13: GIF screen descriptor.

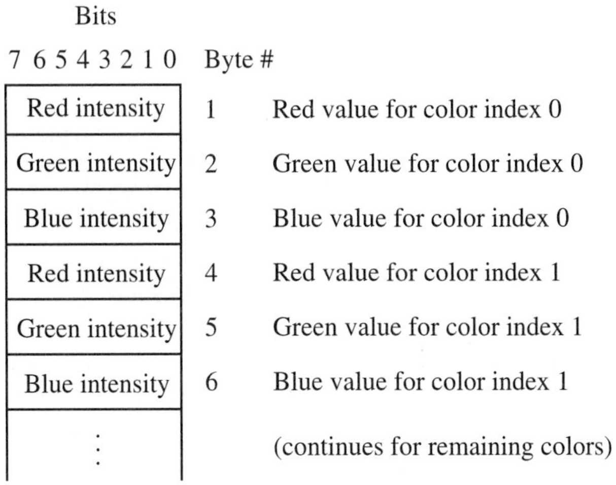

Bits

7 6 5 4 3 2 1 0   Byte #

Red intensity	1	Red value for color index 0
Green intensity	2	Green value for color index 0
Blue intensity	3	Blue value for color index 0
Red intensity	4	Red value for color index 1
Green intensity	5	Green value for color index 1
Blue intensity	6	Blue value for color index 1
⋮		(continues for remaining colors)

FIGURE 3.14: GIF color map.

The next bit, shown as "0", is extra and is not used in this standard. "Pixel" is another 3 bits, indicating the number of bits per pixel in the image, as stored in the file. Although "cr" usually equals "pixel", it need not. Byte 6 gives the color table index byte for the background color, and byte 7 is filled with zeros. For present usage, the ability to use a small color resolution is a good feature, since we may be interested in very low-end devices such as web-enabled wristwatches, say.

A *color map* is set up in a simple fashion, as in Figure 3.14. However, the actual length of the table equals $2^{pixel+1}$ as given in the screen descriptor.

Each image in the file has its own Image Descriptor, defined as in Figure 3.15. Interestingly, the developers of this standard allowed for future extensions by ignoring any bytes between the end of one image and the beginning of the next, identified by a comma character. In this way, future enhancements could have been simply inserted in a backward-compatible fashion.

If the *interlace* bit is set in the local Image Descriptor, the rows of the image are displayed in a four-pass sequence, as in Figure 3.16. Here, the first pass displays rows 0 and 8, the second pass displays rows 4 and 12, and so on. This allows for a quick sketch to appear when a web browser displays the image, followed by more detailed fill-ins. The JPEG standard (below) has a similar display mode, denoted *progressive mode*.

The *actual raster data* itself is first compressed using the LZW compression scheme (see Chapter 7) before being stored.

The GIF87 standard also set out, for future use, how Extension Blocks could be defined. Even in GIF87, simple animations can be achieved, but no delay was defined between images, and multiple images simply overwrite each other with no screen clears.

GIF89 introduced a number of Extension Block definitions, especially those to assist animation: transparency and delay between images. A quite useful feature introduced in GIF89 is the idea of a sorted color table. The most important colors appear first, so that if

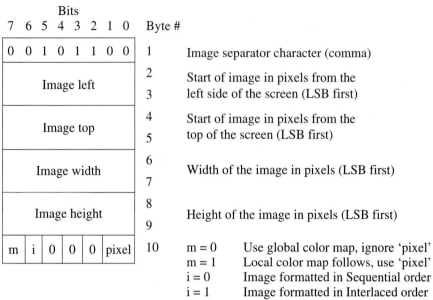

FIGURE 3.15: GIF image descriptor.

Image row	Pass 1	Pass 2	Pass 3	Pass 4	Result
0	*1a*				*1a*
1				*4a*	*4a*
2			*3a*		*3a*
3				*4b*	*4b*
4		*2a*			*2a*
5				*4c*	*4c*
6			*3b*		*3b*
7				*4d*	*4d*
8	*1b*				*1b*
9				*4e*	*4e*
10			*3c*		*3c*
11				*4f*	*4f*
12		*2b*			*2b*
⋮					

FIGURE 3.16: GIF four-pass interlace display row order.

a decoder has fewer colors available, the most important ones are chosen. That is, only a segment of the color lookup table is used, and nearby colors are mapped as well as possible into the colors available.

We can investigate how the file header works in practice by having a look at a particular GIF image. Figure 3.7 is an 8-bit color GIF image. To see how the file header looks, we can simply use everyone's favorite command in the UNIX operating system: od (octal dump). In UNIX,[1] then, we issue the command

```
od -c forestfire.gif | head -2
```

and we see the first 32 bytes interpreted as characters:

```
G   I   F   8   7   a   \208 \2   \188 \1   \247 \0   \0   \6   \3 \5
J \132 \24 |   )   \7  \198 \195 \   \128 U   \27 \196 \166 &   T
```

To decipher the remainder of the file header (after GIF87a), we use hexadecimal:

```
od -x forestfire.gif | head -2
```

with the result

```
4749 4638 3761 d002 bc01 f700 0006 0305
ae84 187c 2907 c6c3 5c80 551b c4a6 2654
```

The d002 bc01 following the Signature are Screen Width and Height; these are given in least-significant-byte-first order, so for this file in decimal the Screen Width is $0 + 13 \times 16 + 2 \times 16^2 = 720$, and Screen Height is $11 \times 16 + 12 + 1 \times 16^2 = 444$. Then the f7 (which is 247 in decimal) is the fifth byte in the Screen Descriptor, followed by the background color index, 00, and the 00 delimiter. The set of flags, f7, in bits, reads 1, 111, 0, 111, or in other words: global color map is used, 8-bit color resolution, 0 separator, 8-bit pixel data.

3.2.2 JPEG

The most important current standard for image compression is JPEG [6]. This standard was created by a working group of the International Organization for Standardization (ISO) that was informally called the Joint Photographic Experts Group and is therefore so named. We shall study JPEG in a good deal more detail in Chapter 9, but a few salient features of this compression standard can be mentioned here.

The human vision system has some specific limitations, which JPEG takes advantage of to achieve high rates of compression. The eye–brain system cannot see extremely fine detail. If many changes occur within a few pixels, we refer to that image segment as having *high spatial frequency* — that is, a great deal of change in (x, y) space. This limitation is even more conspicuous for color vision than for grayscale (black and white). Therefore, color information in JPEG is *decimated* (partially dropped, or averaged) and then small blocks of an image are represented in the spatial frequency domain (u, v), rather than in (x, y). That is, the speed of changes in x and y is evaluated, from low to high, and a new "image" is formed by grouping the coefficients or weights of these speeds.

---

[1] Solaris version; older versions use slightly different syntax.

FIGURE 3.17: JPEG image with low quality specified by user. (This figure also appears in the color insert section.)

Weights that correspond to slow changes are then favored, using a simple trick: values are divided by some large integer and truncated. In this way, small values are zeroed out. Then a scheme for representing long runs of zeros efficiently is applied, and *voila!* — the image is greatly compressed.

Since we effectively throw away a lot of information by the division and truncation step, this compression scheme is "lossy" (although a lossless mode exists). What's more, since it is straightforward to allow the user to choose how large a denominator to use and hence how much information to discard, JPEG allows the user to set a desired level of quality, or compression ratio (input divided by output).

As an example, Figure 3.17 shows our `forestfire` image with a quality factor $Q = 10\%$. (The usual default quality factor is $Q = 75\%$.)

This image is a mere 1.5% of the original size. In comparison, a JPEG image with $Q = 75\%$ yields an image size 5.6% of the original, whereas a GIF version of this image compresses down to 23.0% of the uncompressed image size.

3.2.3 PNG

One interesting development stemming from the popularity of the Internet is efforts toward more system-independent image formats. One such format is *Portable Network Graphics* (PNG). This standard is meant to supersede the GIF standard and extends it in important ways. The motivation for a new standard was in part the patent held by UNISYS and Compuserve on the LZW compression method. (Interestingly, the patent covers only compression, not decompression: this is why the UNIX `gunzip` utility can decompress LZW-compressed files.)

Special features of PNG files include support for up to 48 bits of color information — a large increase. Files may also contain gamma-correction information (see Section 4.1.6) for correct display of color images and alpha-channel information for such uses as control of transparency. Instead of a progressive display based on widely separated rows, as in GIF images, the display progressively displays pixels in a two-dimensional fashion a few at a time over seven passes through each 8×8 block of an image.

3.2.4   TIFF

Tagged Image File Format (TIFF) is another popular image file format. Developed by the Aldus Corporation in the 1980s, it was later supported by Microsoft. Its support for attachment of additional information (referred to as "tags") provides a great deal of flexibility. The most important tag is a format signifier: what type of compression etc. is in use in the stored image. For example, TIFF can store many different types of images: 1-bit, grayscale, 8-bit, 24-bit RGB, and so on. TIFF was originally a lossless format, but a new JPEG tag allows you to opt for JPEG compression. Since TIFF is not as user-controllable as JPEG, it does not provide any major advantages over the latter.

3.2.5   EXIF

Exchange Image File (EXIF) is an image format for digital cameras. Initially developed in 1995, its current version (2.2) was published in 2002 by the Japan Electronics and Information Technology Industries Association (JEITA). Compressed EXIF files use the baseline JPEG format. A variety of tags (many more than in TIFF) is available to facilitate higher-quality printing, since information about the camera and picture-taking conditions (flash, exposure, light source, white balance, type of scene) can be stored and used by printers for possible color-correction algorithms. The EXIF standard also includes specification of file format for audio that accompanies digital images. It also supports tags for information needed for conversion to FlashPix (initially developed by Kodak).

3.2.6   Graphics Animation Files

A few dominant formats are aimed at storing graphics animations (i.e., series of drawings or graphic illustrations) as opposed to video (i.e., series of images). The difference is that animations are considerably less demanding of resources than video files. However, animation file formats can be used to store video information and indeed are sometimes used for such.

FLC is an important animation or moving picture file format; it was originally created by Animation Pro. Another format, FLI, is similar to FLC.

GL produces somewhat better quality moving pictures. GL animations can also usually handle larger file sizes.

Many older formats are used for animation, such as DL and Amiga IFF, as well as alternates such as Apple Quicktime. And, of course, there are also animated GIF89 files.

3.2.7   PS and PDF

PostScript is an important language for typesetting, and many high-end printers have a PostScript interpreter built into them. PostScript is a vector-based, rather than pixel-based, picture language: page elements are essentially defined in terms of vectors. With fonts defined this way, PostScript includes text as well as vector/structured graphics; bit-mapped images can also be included in output files. Encapsulated PostScript files add some information for including PostScript files in another document.

Several popular graphics programs, such as Illustrator and FreeHand, use PostScript. However, the PostScript page description language itself does not provide compression; in fact, PostScript files are just stored as ASCII. Therefore files are often large, and in academic settings, it is common for such files to be made available only after compression by some UNIX utility, such as `compress` or `gzip`.

Therefore, another text + figures language has begun to supersede PostScript: Adobe Systems Inc. includes LZW (see Chapter 7) compression in its *Portable Document Format* (PDF) file format. As a consequence, PDF files that do not include images have about the same compression ratio, 2:1 or 3:1, as do files compressed with other LZW-based compression tools, such as UNIX `compress` or `gzip` on PC-based `winzip` (a variety of `pkzip`). For files containing images, PDF may achieve higher compression ratios by using separate JPEG compression for the image content (depending on the tools used to create original and compressed versions). The Adobe Acrobat PDF reader can also be configured to read documents structured as linked elements, with clickable content and handy summary tree-structured link diagrams provided.

3.2.8   Windows WMF

Windows MetaFile (WMF) is the native vector file format for the Microsoft Windows operating environment. WMF files actually consist of a collection of *Graphics Device Interface* (GDI) function calls, also native to the Windows environment. When a WMF file is "played" (typically using the Windows `PlayMetaFile()` function) the described graphic is rendered. WMF files are ostensibly device-independent and unlimited in size.

3.2.9   Windows BMP

BitMap (BMP) is the major system standard graphics file format for Microsoft Windows, used in Microsoft Paint and other programs. It makes use of run-length encoding compression (see Chapter 7) and can fairly efficiently store 24-bit bitmap images. Note, however, that BMP has many different modes, including uncompressed 24-bit images.

3.2.10   Macintosh PAINT and PICT

PAINT was originally used in the MacPaint program, initially only for 1-bit monochrome images.

PICT is used in MacDraw (a vector-based drawing program) for storing structured graphics.

3.2.11   X Windows PPM

This is the graphics format for the X Windows System. Portable PixMap (PPM) supports 24-bit color bitmaps and can be manipulated using many public domain graphic editors, such as *xv*. It is used in the X Windows System for storing icons, pixmaps, backdrops, and so on.

3.3   FURTHER EXPLORATION

Foley et al. [2] provide an excellent introduction to computer graphics. For a good discussion on issues involving image processing, see Gonzalez and Woods [7]. More information including a complete up-to-date list of current file formats can be viewed on the textbook web site, in Chapter 3 of the Further Exploration directory.

Other links include

- GIF87 and GIF89 details. Although these file formats are not so interesting in themselves, they have the virtue of being simple and are a useful introduction to how such bitstreams are set out.

- A popular shareware program for developing GIF animations

- JPEG considered in detail

- PNG details

- The PDF file format

- The ubiquitous BMP file format

In terms of actual input/output of such file formats, code for simple 24-bit BMP file reading and manipulation is given on the web site.

3.4   EXERCISES

1. Briefly explain why we need to be able to have less than 24-bit color and why this makes for a problem. Generally, what do we need to do to adaptively transform 24-bit color values to 8-bit ones?

2. Suppose we decide to quantize an 8-bit grayscale image down to just 2 bits of accuracy. What is the simplest way to do so? What ranges of byte values in the original image are mapped to what quantized values?

3. Suppose we have a 5-bit grayscale image. What size of ordered dither matrix do we need to display the image on a 1-bit printer?

4. Suppose we have available 24 bits per pixel for a color image. However, we notice that humans are more sensitive to R and G than to B — in fact, 1.5 times more sensitive to R or G than to B. How could we best make use of the bits available?

5. At your job, you have decided to impress the boss by using up more disk space for the company's grayscale images. Instead of using 8 bits per pixel, you'd like to use 48 bits per pixel in RGB. How could you store the original grayscale images so that in the new format they would appear the same as they used to, visually?

6. Sometimes bitplanes of an image are characterized using an analogy from mapmaking called "elevations". Figure 3.18 shows some elevations.

   Suppose we describe an 8-bit image using 8 bitplanes. Briefly discuss how you could view each bitplane in terms of geographical concepts.

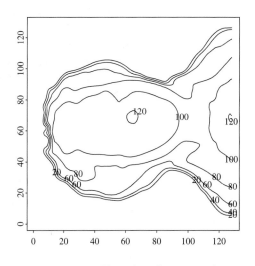

FIGURE 3.18: Elevations in geography.

7. For the color LUT problem, try out the median-cut algorithm on a sample image. Explain briefly why it is that this algorithm, carried out on an image of red apples, puts more color gradation in the resulting 24-bit color image where it is needed, among the reds.

8. In regard to nonordered dithering, a standard graphics text [2] states, "Even larger patterns can be used, but the spatial versus intensity resolution trade-off is limited by our visual acuity (about one minute of arc in normal lighting)."

   (a) What does this sentence mean?

   (b) If we hold a piece of paper out at a distance of 1 foot, what is the approximate linear distance between dots? (*Information*: One minute of arc is 1/60 of one degree of angle. Arc length on a circle equals angle (in radians) times radius.) Could we see the gap between dots on a 300 dpi printer?

   (c) Write down an algorithm (pseudocode) for calculating a color histogram for RGB data.

3.5 REFERENCES

1 J. Miano, *Compressed Image File Formats: JPEG, PNG, GIF, XBM, BMP*, Reading, MA: Addison-Wesley, 1999.

2 J. D. Foley, A. van Dam, S. K. Feiner, and J. F. Hughes, *Computer Graphics: Principles and Practice in C*, 2nd ed., Reading, MA: Addison-Wesley, 1996.

3 M. Sonka, V. Hlavac, and R. Boyle, *Image Processing, Analysis, and Machine Vision*, Boston: PWS Publishing, 1999.

4 L.G. Shapiro and G.C. Stockman, *Computer Vision*, Upper Saddle River, NJ: Prentice Hall, 2001.

5 P. Heckbert, "Color Image Quantization for Frame Buffer Display," in *SIGGRAPH Proceedings*, vol. 16, p. 297–307, 1982.

6 W.B. Pennebaker and J.L. Mitchell, *The JPEG Still Image Data Compression Standard*, New York: Van Nostrand Reinhold, 1993.

7 R.C. Gonzalez and R.E. Woods, *Digital Image Processing*, 2nd ed., Upper Saddle River, NJ: Prentice Hall, 2002.

CHAPTER 4

Color in Image and Video

Color images and videos are ubiquitous on the web and in multimedia productions. Increasingly, we are becoming aware of the discrepancies between color as seen by people and the sometimes very different color displayed on our screens. The latest version of the HTML standard attempts to address this issue by specifying color in terms of a standard, "sRGB", arrived at by color scientists.

To become aware of the simple yet strangely involved world of color, in this chapter we shall consider the following topics:

- Color science

- Color models in images

- Color models in video

4.1 COLOR SCIENCE

4.1.1 Light and Spectra

Recall from high school that light is an electromagnetic wave and that its color is characterized by the wavelength of the wave. Laser light consists of a single wavelength — for example, a ruby laser produces a bright, scarlet beam. So if we were to plot the light intensity versus wavelength, we would see a spike at the appropriate red wavelength and no other contribution to the light.

In contrast, most light sources produce contributions over many wavelengths. Humans cannot detect all light — just contributions that fall in the visible wavelength. Short wavelengths produce a blue sensation, and long wavelengths produce a red one.

We measure visible light using a device called a *spectrophotometer*, by reflecting light from a diffraction grating (a ruled surface) that spreads out the different wavelengths, much as a prism does. Figure 4.1 shows the phenomenon that white light contains all the colors of a rainbow. If you have ever looked through a prism, you will have noticed that it generates a rainbow effect, due to a natural phenomenon called *dispersion*. You see a similar effect on the surface of a soap bubble.

Visible light is an electromagnetic wave in the range 400–700 nm (where nm stands for *nanometer*, or 10^{-9} meter). Figure 4.2 shows the relative power in each wavelength interval for typical outdoor light on a sunny day. This type of curve, called a spectral power distribution (SPD), or *spectrum*, shows the relative amount of light energy (electromagnetic signal) at each wavelength. The symbol for wavelength is λ, so this type of curve might be called $E(\lambda)$.

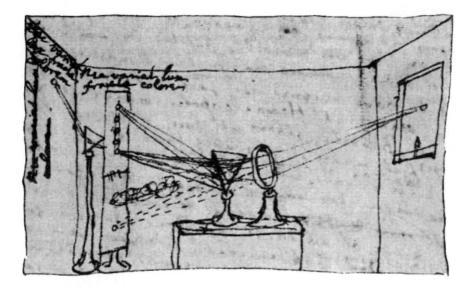

FIGURE 4.1: Sir Isaac Newton's experiments. *By permission of the Warden and Fellows, New College, Oxford.*

In practice, measurements are used that effectively sum up voltage in a small wavelength range, say 5 or 10 nanometers, so such plots usually consist of segments joining function values every 10 nanometers. This means also that such profiles are actually stored as vectors. Below, however, we show equations that treat $E(\lambda)$ as a continuous function, although in reality, integrals are calculated using sums.

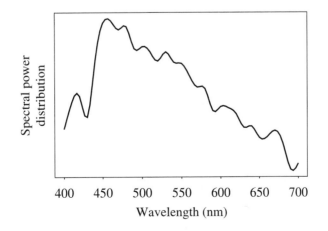

FIGURE 4.2: Spectral power distribution of daylight.

4.1.2 Human Vision

The eye works like a camera, with the lens focusing an image onto the retina (upside-down and left-right reversed). The retina consists of an array of *rods* and three kinds of *cones*, so named because of their shape. The rods come into play when light levels are low and produce an image in shades of gray ("At night, all cats are gray!"). For higher light levels, the cones each produce a signal. Because of their differing pigments, the three kinds of cones are most sensitive to red (*R*), green (*G*), and blue (*B*) light.

Higher light levels result in more neurons firing, but just what happens in the brain further down the pipeline is the subject of much debate. However, it seems likely that the brain makes use of *differences R–G, G–B*, and *B–R*, as well as combining all of *R*, *G*, and *B* into a high-light-level achromatic channel (and thus we can say that the brain is good at algebra).

4.1.3 Spectral Sensitivity of the Eye

The eye is most sensitive to light in the middle of the visible spectrum. Like the SPD profile of a light source, as in Figure 4.2, for receptors we show the relative sensitivity as a function of wavelength. The blue receptor sensitivity is not shown to scale, because it is much smaller than the curves for red or green. Blue is a late addition in evolution (and, statistically, is the favorite color of humans, regardless of nationality — perhaps for this reason: blue is a bit surprising!). Figure 4.3 shows the overall sensitivity as a dashed line, called the luminous-efficiency function. It is usually denoted $V(\lambda)$ and is the sum of the response curves to red, green, and blue [1, 2].

The rods are sensitive to a broad range of wavelengths, but produce a signal that generates the perception of the black–white scale only. The rod sensitivity curve looks like the luminous-efficiency function $V(\lambda)$ but is shifted somewhat to the red end of the spectrum [1].

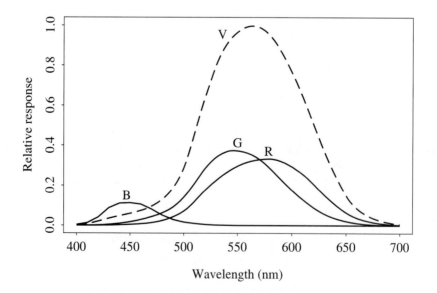

FIGURE 4.3: Cone sensitivities: R, G, and B cones, and luminous-efficiency curve V(λ).

The eye has about 6 million cones, but the proportions of R, G, and B cones are different. They likely are present in the ratios 40:20:1 (see [3] for a complete explanation). So the achromatic channel produced by the cones is thus something like $2R + G + B/20$.

These spectral sensitivity functions are usually denoted by some other letters than R, G, and B, so here let us denote them by the vector function $q(\lambda)$, with components

$$q(\lambda) = [q_R(\lambda), q_G(\lambda), q_B(\lambda)]^T \tag{4.1}$$

That is, there are three sensors (a vector index $k = 1..3$ therefore applies), and each is a function of wavelength.

The response in each color channel in the eye is proportional to the number of neurons firing. For the red channel, any light falling anywhere in the nonzero part of the red cone function in Figure 4.3 will generate some response. So the total response of the red channel is the sum over all the light falling on the retina to which the red cone is sensitive, weighted by the sensitivity at that wavelength. Again thinking of these sensitivities as continuous functions, we can succinctly write down this idea in the form of an integral:

$$
\begin{aligned}
R &= \int E(\lambda)\, q_R(\lambda)\, d\lambda \\
G &= \int E(\lambda)\, q_G(\lambda)\, d\lambda \\
B &= \int E(\lambda)\, q_B(\lambda)\, d\lambda
\end{aligned}
\tag{4.2}
$$

Since the signal transmitted consists of three numbers, colors form a three-dimensional vector space.

4.1.4 Image Formation

Equation (4.2) above actually applies only when we view a self-luminous object (i.e., a light). In most situations, we image light reflected from a surface. Surfaces reflect different amounts of light at different wavelengths, and dark surfaces reflect less energy than light surfaces. Figure 4.4 shows the surface spectral reflectance from orange sneakers and faded bluejeans [4]. The reflectance function is denoted $S(\lambda)$.

The image formation situation is thus as follows: light from the illuminant with SPD $E(\lambda)$ impinges on a surface, with surface spectral reflectance function $S(\lambda)$, is reflected, and is then filtered by the eye's cone functions $q(\lambda)$. The basic arrangement is as shown in Figure 4.5. The function $C(\lambda)$ is called the *color signal* and is the product of the illuminant $E(\lambda)$ and the reflectance $S(\lambda)$: $C(\lambda) = E(\lambda)\, S(\lambda)$.

The equations similar to Eqs. (4.2) that take into account the image formation model are

$$
\begin{aligned}
R &= \int E(\lambda)\, S(\lambda)\, q_R(\lambda)\, d\lambda \\
G &= \int E(\lambda)\, S(\lambda)\, q_G(\lambda)\, d\lambda \\
B &= \int E(\lambda)\, S(\lambda)\, q_B(\lambda)\, d\lambda
\end{aligned}
\tag{4.3}
$$

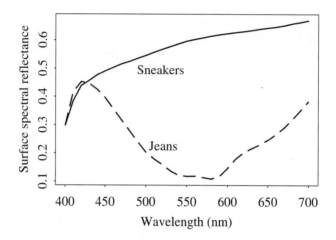

FIGURE 4.4: Surface spectral reflectance functions S(λ) for two objects.

4.1.5 Camera Systems

Now, we humans develop camera systems in a similar fashion. A good camera has three signals produced at each pixel location (corresponding to a retinal position). Analog signals are converted to digital, truncated to integers, and stored. If the precision used is 8-bit, the maximum value for any of R, G, B is 255, and the minimum is 0.

However, the light entering the eye of the computer user is what the screen emits — the screen is essentially a self-luminous source. Therefore, we need to know the light $E(\lambda)$ entering the eye.

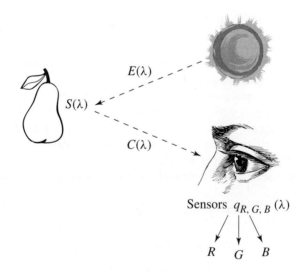

FIGURE 4.5: Image formation model.

4.1.6   Gamma Correction

The RGB numbers in an image file are converted back to analog and drive the electron guns in the cathode ray tube (CRT). Electrons are emitted proportional to the driving voltage, and we would like to have the CRT system produce light linearly related to the voltage. Unfortunately, it turns out that this is not the case. The light emitted is actually roughly proportional to the voltage raised to a power; this power is called "gamma", with symbol γ.

Thus, if the file value in the red channel is R, the screen emits light proportional to R^γ, with SPD equal to that of the red phosphor paint on the screen that is the target of the red-channel electron gun. The value of gamma is around 2.2.

Since the mechanics of a television receiver are the same as those for a computer CRT, TV systems precorrect for this situation by applying the inverse transformation before transmitting TV voltage signals. It is customary to append a prime to signals that are "gamma-corrected" by raising to the power $(1/\gamma)$ before transmission. Thus we have

$$R \rightarrow R' = R^{1/\gamma} \Rightarrow (R')^\gamma \rightarrow R \tag{4.4}$$

and we arrive at "linear signals".

Voltage is often normalized to maximum 1, and it is interesting to see what effect these gamma transformations have on signals. Figure 4.6(a) shows the light output with no gamma correction applied. We see that darker values are displayed too dark. This is also shown in Figure 4.7(a), which displays a linear ramp from left to right.

Figure 4.6(b) shows the effect of precorrecting signals by applying the power law $R^{1/\gamma}$, where it is customary to normalize voltage to the range 0 to 1. We see that applying first the correction in Figure 4.6(b), followed by the effect of the CRT system in Figure 4.6(a),

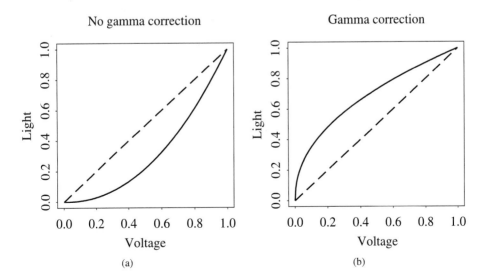

FIGURE 4.6: Effect of gamma correction: (a) no gamma correction — effect of CRT on light emitted from screen (voltage is normalized to range 0 .. 1); (b) gamma correction of signal.

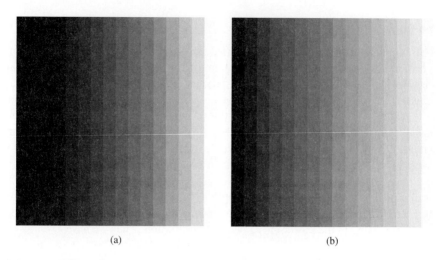

(a)
(b)

FIGURE 4.7: Effect of gamma correction: (a) display of ramp from 0 to 255, with no gamma correction; (b) image with gamma correction applied.

would result in linear signals. Figure 4.7(b) shows the combined effect. Here, a ramp is shown in 16 steps, from gray level 0 to gray level 255.

A more careful definition of gamma recognizes that a simple power law would result in an infinite derivative at zero voltage — which makes constructing a circuit to accomplish gamma correction difficult to devise in analog. In practice a more general transform, such as $R \rightarrow R' = a \times R^{1/\gamma} + b$ is used, along with special care at the origin:

$$
V_{out} = \begin{cases} 4.5 \times V_{in} & V_{in} < 0.018 \\ 1.099 \times (V_{in} - 0.099) & V_{in} \geq 0.018 \end{cases}
\tag{4.5}
$$

This is called a *camera transfer function*, and the above law is recommended by the Society of Motion Picture and Television Engineers (SMPTE) as standard SMPTE–170M.

Why a gamma of 2.2? In fact, this value does *not* produce a final power law of 1.0. The history of this number is buried in decisions of the National Television System Committee of the U.S.A. (NTSC) when TV was invented. The power law for color receivers may in actuality be closer to 2.8. However, if we compensate for only about 2.2 of this power law, we arrive at an overall value of about 1.25 instead of 1.0. The idea was that in viewing conditions with a dim surround, such an overall gamma produces more pleasing images, albeit with color errors — darker colors are made even darker, and also the eye–brain system changes the relative contrast of light and dark colors [5].

With the advent of CRT-based computer systems, the situation has become even more interesting. The camera may or may not have inserted gamma correction; software may write the image file using some gamma; software may decode expecting some (other) gamma; the image is stored in a frame buffer, and it is common to provide a lookup table for gamma in the frame buffer. After all, if we generate images using computer graphics, no gamma is applied, but a gamma is still necessary to precompensate for the display.

It makes sense, then, to define an overall "system" gamma that takes into account all such transformations. Unfortunately, we must often simply guess at the overall gamma. Adobe Photoshop allows us to try different gamma values. For WWW publishing, it is important to know that a Macintosh does gamma correction in its graphics card, with a gamma of 1.8. SGI machines expect a gamma of 1.4, and most PCs or Suns do no extra gamma correction and likely have a display gamma of about 2.5. Therefore, for the most common machines, it might make sense to gamma-correct images at the average of Macintosh and PC values, or about 2.1.

However, most practitioners might use a value of 2.4, adopted by the sRGB group. A new "standard" RGB for WWW applications called sRGB, to be included in all future HTML standards, defines a standard modeling of typical light levels and monitor conditions and is (more or less) "device-independent color space for the Internet".

An issue related to gamma correction is the decision of just what intensity levels will be represented by what bit patterns in the pixel values in a file. The eye is most sensitive to *ratios* of intensity levels rather than absolute intensities. This means that the brighter the light, the greater must be the change in light level for the change to be perceived.

If we had precise control over what bits represented what intensities, it would make sense to code intensities logarithmically for maximum usage of the bits available. Then we could include that coding in an inverse of the $(1/\gamma)$ power law transform, as in Equation (4.4), or perhaps a lookup table implementation of such an inverse function (see [6], p. 564).

However, it is most likely that images or videos we encounter have no nonlinear encoding of bit levels but have indeed been produced by a camcorder or are for broadcast TV. These images will have been gamma corrected according to Equation (4.4). The CIE-sponsored CIELAB perceptually based color-difference metric discussed in Section 4.1.14 provides a careful algorithm for including the nonlinear aspect of human brightness perception.

4.1.7   Color-Matching Functions

Practically speaking, many color applications involve specifying and re-creating a particular desired color. Suppose you wish to duplicate a particular shade on the screen, or a particular shade of dyed cloth. Over many years, even before the eye-sensitivity curves of Figure 4.3 were known, a technique evolved in psychology for matching a combination of basic R, G, and B lights to a given shade. A particular set of three basic lights was available, called the set of *color primaries*. To match a given shade, a set of observers was asked to separately adjust the brightness of the three primaries using a set of controls, until the resulting spot of light most closely matched the desired color. Figure 4.8 shows the basic situation. A device for carrying out such an experiment is called a *colorimeter*.

The international standards body for color, the Commission Internationale de L'Eclairage (CIE), pooled all such data in 1931, in a set of curves called the *color-matching functions*. They used color primaries with peaks at 440, 545, and 580 nanometers. Suppose, instead of a swatch of cloth, you were interested in matching a given wavelength of laser (i.e., monochromatic) light. Then the color-matching experiments are summarized by a statement of the proportion of the color primaries needed for each individual narrow-band wavelength of light. General lights are then matched by a linear combination of single wavelength results.

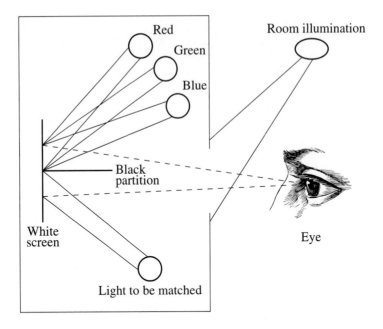

FIGURE 4.8: Colorimeter experiment.

Figure 4.9 shows the CIE color-matching curves, denoted $\bar{r}(\lambda)$, $\bar{g}(\lambda)$, $\bar{b}(\lambda)$. In fact, such curves are a linear matrix-multiplication away from the eye sensitivities in Figure 4.3.

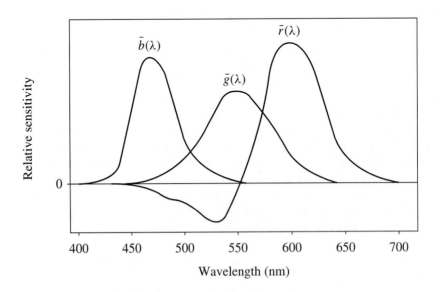

FIGURE 4.9: CIE color-matching functions $\bar{r}(\lambda)$, $\bar{g}(\lambda)$, $\bar{b}(\lambda)$.

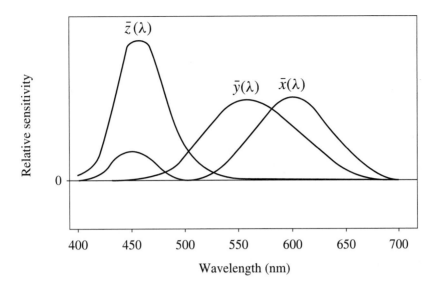

FIGURE 4.10: CIE standard color-matching functions $\bar{x}(\lambda)$, $\bar{y}(\lambda)$, $\bar{z}(\lambda)$.

Why are some parts of the curves negative? This indicates that some colors cannot be reproduced by a linear combination of the primaries. For such colors, one or more of the primary lights has to be shifted from one side of the black partition in Figure 4.8 to the other, so they illuminate the sample to be matched instead of the white screen. Thus, in a sense, such samples are being matched by negative lights.

4.1.8   CIE Chromaticity Diagram

In times long past, engineers found it upsetting that one CIE color-matching curve in Figure 4.9 has a negative lobe. Therefore, a set of fictitious primaries was devised that led to color-matching functions with only positives values. Figure 4.10 shows the resulting curves; these are usually referred to as *the* color-matching functions. They result from a linear (3 × 3 matrix) transform from the $\bar{r}$, $\bar{g}$, $\bar{b}$ curves, and are denoted $\bar{x}(\lambda)$, $\bar{y}(\lambda)$, $\bar{z}(\lambda)$. The matrix is chosen such that the middle standard color-matching function $\bar{y}(\lambda)$ exactly equals the luminous-efficiency curve $V(\lambda)$ shown in Figure 4.3.

For a general SPD $E(\lambda)$, the essential "colorimetric" information required to characterize a color is the set of *tristimulus values* X, Y, Z, defined in analogy to Equation (4.1) as

$$X = \int E(\lambda)\, \bar{x}(\lambda)\, d\lambda$$

$$Y = \int E(\lambda)\, \bar{y}(\lambda)\, d\lambda \qquad (4.6)$$

$$Z = \int E(\lambda)\, \bar{z}(\lambda)\, d\lambda$$

The middle value, Y, is called the *luminance*. All color information and transforms are tied to these special values, which incorporate substantial information about the human visual system. However, 3D data is difficult to visualize, and consequently, the CIE devised a 2D diagram based on the values of (X, Y, Z) triples implied by the curves in Figure 4.10. For each wavelength in the visible, the values of X, Y, Z given by the three curve values form the limits of what humans can see. However, from Equation (4.6) we observe that increasing the brightness of illumination (turning up the light bulb's wattage) increases the tristimulus values by a scalar multiple. Therefore, it makes sense to devise a 2D diagram by somehow factoring out the magnitude of vectors (X, Y, Z). In the CIE system, this is accomplished by dividing by the sum $X + Y + Z$:

$$
\begin{aligned}
x &= X/(X + Y + Z) \\
y &= Y/(X + Y + Z) \\
z &= Z/(X + Y + Z)
\end{aligned}
\tag{4.7}
$$

This effectively means that one value out of the set (x, y, z) is redundant, since we have

$$
x + y + z = \frac{X + Y + Z}{X + Y + Z} \equiv 1
\tag{4.8}
$$

so that

$$
z = 1 - x - y
\tag{4.9}
$$

Values x, y are called *chromaticities*.

Effectively, we are projecting each tristimulus vector (X, Y, Z) onto the plane connecting points $(1, 0, 0)$, $(0, 1, 0)$, and $(0, 0, 1)$. Usually, this plane is viewed projected onto the $z = 0$ plane, as a set of points inside the triangle with vertices having (x, y) values $(0, 0)$, $(1, 0)$, and $(0, 1)$.

Figure 4.11 shows the locus of points for monochromatic light, drawn on this CIE "chromaticity diagram". The straight line along the bottom of the "horseshoe" joins points at the extremities of the visible spectrum, 400 and 700 nanometers (from blue through green to red). That straight line is called the *line of purples*. The horseshoe itself is called the *spectrum locus* and shows the (x, y) chromaticity values of monochromatic light at each of the visible wavelengths.

The color-matching curves are devised so as to add up to the same value [the area under each curve is the same for each of $\bar{x}(\lambda)$, $\bar{y}(\lambda)$, $\bar{z}(\lambda)$]. Therefore for a white illuminant with all SPD values equal to 1 — an "equi-energy white light" — the chromaticity values are $(1/3, 1/3)$. Figure 4.11 displays this white point in the middle of the diagram. Finally, since we must have $x, y \leq 1$ and $x + y \leq 1$, all possible chromaticity values must necessarily lie below the dashed diagonal line in Figure 4.11.

Note that one may choose different "white" spectra as the standard illuminant. The CIE defines several of these, such as illuminant A, illuminant C, and standard daylights D65 and D100. Each of these will display as a somewhat different white spot on the CIE diagram: D65 has a chromaticity equal to $(0.312713, 0.329016)$, and illuminant C has chromaticity

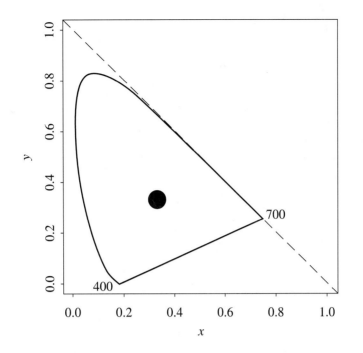

FIGURE 4.11: CIE chromaticity diagram.

(0.310063, 0.316158). Figure 4.12 displays the SPD curves for each of these standard lights. Illuminant A is characteristic of incandescent lighting, with an SPD typical of a tungsten bulb, and is quite red. Illuminant C is an early attempt to characterize daylight, while D65 and D100 are respectively a midrange and a bluish commonly used daylight. Figure 4.12 also shows the much more spiky SPD for a standard fluorescent illumination, called F2 [2].

Colors with chromaticities on the spectrum locus represent "pure" colors. These are the most "saturated": think of paper becoming more and more saturated with ink. In contrast, colors closer to the white point are more unsaturated.

The chromaticity diagram has the nice property that, for a mixture of two lights, the resulting chromaticity lies on the straight line joining the chromaticities of the two lights. Here we are being slightly cagey in not saying that this is the case for *colors* in general, just for "lights". The reason is that so far we have been adhering to an *additive* model of color mixing. This model holds good for lights or, as a special case, for monitor colors. However, as we shall see below, it does not hold for printer colors (see p. 102).

For any chromaticity on the CIE diagram, the "dominant wavelength" is the position on the spectrum locus intersected by a line joining the white point to the given color and extended through it. (For colors that give an intersection on the line of purples, a complementary dominant wavelength is defined by extending the line backward through the white point.) Another useful definition is the set of complementary colors for some given color, which is given by all the colors on the line through the white spot. Finally, the *excitation purity* is the

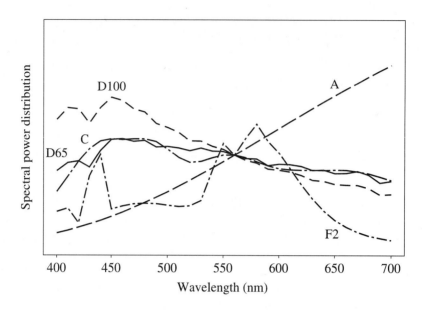

FIGURE 4.12: Standard illuminant SPDs

ratio of distances from the white spot to the given color and to the dominant wavelength, expressed as a percentage.

4.1.9 Color Monitor Specifications

Color monitors are specified in part by the white point chromaticity desired if the RGB electron guns are all activated at their highest power. Actually, we are likely using gamma-corrected values R', G', B'. If we normalize voltage to the range 0 to 1, then we wish to specify a monitor such that it displays the desired white point when $R' = G' = B' = 1$ (abbreviating the transform from file value to voltage by simply stating the pixel color values, normalized to maximum 1).

However, the phosphorescent paints used on the inside of the monitor screen have their own chromaticities, so at first glance it would appear that we cannot independently control the monitor white point. However, this is remedied by setting the gain control for each electron gun such that at maximum voltages the desired white appears.

Several monitor specifications are in current use. Monitor specifications consist of the fixed, manufacturer-specified chromaticities for the monitor phosphors, along with the standard white point needed. Table 4.1 shows these values for three common specification statements. NTSC is the standard North American and Japanese specification. SMPTE is a more modern version of this, wherein the standard illuminant is changed from illuminant C to illuminant D65 and the phosphor chromaticities are more in line with modern machines. Digital video specifications use a similar specification in North America. The EBU system derives from the European Broadcasting Union and is used in PAL and SECAM video systems.

TABLE 4.1: Chromaticities and white points for monitor specifications.

System	Red		Green		Blue		White Point	
	x_r	y_r	x_g	y_g	x_b	y_b	x_W	y_W
NTSC	0.67	0.33	0.21	0.71	0.14	0.08	0.3101	0.3162
SMPTE	0.630	0.340	0.310	0.595	0.155	0.070	0.3127	0.3291
EBU	0.64	0.33	0.29	0.60	0.15	0.06	0.3127	0.3291

4.1.10 Out-of-Gamut Colors

For the moment, let's not worry about gamma correction. Then the really basic problem for displaying color is how to generate *device-independent* color, by agreement taken to be specified by (x, y) chromaticity values, using *device-dependent* color values RGB.

For any (x, y) pair we wish to find that RGB triple giving the specified (x, y, z): therefore, we form the z values for the phosphors via $z = 1 - x - y$ and solve for RGB from the manufacturer-specified chromaticities. Since, if we had no green or blue value (i.e., file values of zero) we would simply see the red-phosphor chromaticities, we combine nonzero values of R, G, and B via

$$\begin{bmatrix} x_r & x_g & x_b \\ y_r & y_g & y_b \\ z_r & z_g & z_b \end{bmatrix} \begin{bmatrix} R \\ G \\ B \end{bmatrix} = \begin{bmatrix} x \\ y \\ z \end{bmatrix} \tag{4.10}$$

If (x, y) is *specified* instead of derived from the above, we have to invert the matrix of phosphor (x, y, z) values to obtain the correct RGB values to use to obtain the desired chromaticity.

But what if any of the RGB numbers is *negative*? The problem in this case is that while humans are able to perceive the color, it is not representable on the device being used. We say in that case the color is *out of gamut*, since the set of all possible displayable colors constitutes the gamut of the device.

One method used to deal with this situation is to simply use the closest in-gamut color available. Another common approach is to select the closest complementary color.

For a monitor, every displayable color is within a *triangle*. This follows from so-called *Grassman's Law*, describing human vision, stating that "color matching is linear". This means that linear combinations of lights made up of three primaries are just the linear set of weights used to make the combination times those primaries. That is, if we compose colors from a linear combination of the three "lights" available from the three phosphors, we can create colors only from the convex set derived from the lights — in this case, a triangle. (We'll see below that for printers, this convexity no longer holds.)

Figure 4.13 shows the triangular gamut for the NTSC system drawn on the CIE diagram. Suppose the small triangle represents a given desired color. Then the in-gamut point on the boundary of the NTSC monitor gamut is taken to be the intersection of (a) the line connecting the desired color to the white point with (b) the nearest line forming the boundary of the gamut triangle.

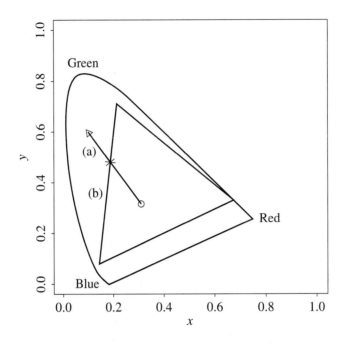

FIGURE 4.13: Approximating an out-of-gamut color by an in-gamut one. The out-of-gamut color shown by a triangle is approximated by the intersection of (a) the line from that color to the white point with (b) the boundary of the device color gamut.

4.1.11 White-Point Correction

One deficiency in what we have done so far is that we need to be able to map tristimulus values XYZ to device RGBs, and not just deal with chromaticity xyz. The difference is that XYZ values include the magnitude of the color. We also need to be able to alter matters such that when each of R, G, B is at maximum value, we obtain the white point.

But so far, Table 4.1 would produce incorrect values. Consider the SMPTE specifications. Setting $R = G = B = 1$ results in a value of X that equals the sum of the x values, or $0.630 + 0.310 + 0.155$, which is 1.095. Similarly, the Y and Z values come out to 1.005 and 0.9. Dividing by $(X + Y + Z)$ results in a chromaticity of $(0.365, 0.335)$ rather than the desired values of $(0.3127, 0.3291)$.

The method used to correct both deficiencies is to first take the white-point magnitude of Y as unity:

$$Y \text{ (white point)} = 1 \tag{4.11}$$

Now we need to find a set of three correction factors such that if the gains of the three electron guns are multiplied by these values, we get exactly the white point XYZ value at $R = G = B = 1$. Suppose the matrix of phosphor chromaticities $x_r, x_g, \ldots$ in Equation (4.10) is called $\boldsymbol{M}$. We can express the correction as a diagonal matrix $\boldsymbol{D} = diag(d_1, d_2, d_3)$ such that

$$XYZ_{\text{white}} \equiv \boldsymbol{M}\boldsymbol{D}(1, 1, 1)^T \tag{4.12}$$

where $(\ )^T$ means transpose.

For the SMPTE specification, we have $(x, y, z) = (0.3127, 0.3291, 0.3582)$ or, dividing by the middle value, $XYZ_{white} = (0.95045,\ 1,\ 1.08892)$. We note that multiplying D by $(1, 1, 1)^T$ just gives $(d_1, d_2, d_3)^T$, and we end up with an equation *specifying* $(d_1, d_2, d_3)^T$:

$$\begin{bmatrix} X \\ Y \\ Z \end{bmatrix}_{white} = \begin{bmatrix} 0.630 & 0.310 & 0.155 \\ 0.340 & 0.595 & 0.070 \\ 0.03 & 0.095 & 0.775 \end{bmatrix} \begin{bmatrix} d_1 \\ d_2 \\ d_3 \end{bmatrix} \tag{4.13}$$

Inverting, with the new values XYZ_{white} specified as above, we arrive at

$$(d_1, d_2, d_3) = (0.6247, 1.1783, 1.2364) \tag{4.14}$$

4.1.12   XYZ to RGB Transform

Now the 3×3 transform matrix from XYZ to RGB is taken to be

$$T = MD \tag{4.15}$$

even for points other than the white point:

$$\begin{bmatrix} X \\ Y \\ Z \end{bmatrix} = T \begin{bmatrix} R \\ G \\ B \end{bmatrix} \tag{4.16}$$

For the SMPTE specification, we arrive at

$$T = \begin{bmatrix} 0.3935 & 0.3653 & 0.1916 \\ 0.2124 & 0.7011 & 0.0866 \\ 0.0187 & 0.1119 & 0.9582 \end{bmatrix} \tag{4.17}$$

Written out, this reads

$$\begin{aligned} X &= 0.3935 \cdot R + 0.3653 \cdot G + 0.1916 \cdot B \\ Y &= 0.2124 \cdot R + 0.7011 \cdot G + 0.0866 \cdot B \\ Z &= 0.0187 \cdot R + 0.1119 \cdot G + 0.9582 \cdot B \end{aligned} \tag{4.18}$$

4.1.13   Transform with Gamma Correction

The above calculations assume we are dealing with linear signals. However, instead of linear R, G, B, we most likely have nonlinear, gamma-corrected R', G', B'.

The best way of carrying out an XYZ-to-RGB transform is to calculate the linear RGB required by inverting Equation (4.16), then create nonlinear signals via gamma correction.

Nevertheless, this is not usually done as stated. Instead, the equation for the Y value is used as is but is applied to nonlinear signals. This does not imply much error, in fact, for colors near the white point. The only concession to accuracy is to give the new name Y' to this new Y value created from R', G', B'. The significance of Y' is that it codes a descriptor of brightness for the pixel in question.[1]

---

[1] In the Color FAQ file on the text web site, this new value Y' is called "luma".

The most-used transform equations are those for the original NTSC system, based upon an illuminant C white point, even though these are outdated. Following the procedure outlined above but with the values in Table 4.1, we arrive at the following transform:

$$
\begin{aligned}
X &= 0.607 \cdot R + 0.174 \cdot G + 0.200 \cdot B \\
Y &= 0.299 \cdot R + 0.587 \cdot G + 0.114 \cdot B \\
Z &= 0.000 \cdot R + 0.066 \cdot G + 1.116 \cdot B
\end{aligned}
\tag{4.19}
$$

Thus, coding for nonlinear signals begins with encoding the nonlinear-signal correlate of luminance:

$$
Y' = 0.299 \cdot R' + 0.587 \cdot G' + 0.114 \cdot B'
\tag{4.20}
$$

(See Section 4.3 below for more discussion on encoding of nonlinear signals.)

4.1.14   L*a*b* (CIELAB) Color Model

The discussion above of how best to make use of the bits available to us touched on the issue of how well human vision sees changes in light levels. This subject is actually an example of *Weber's Law*, from psychology: the more there is of a quantity, the more change there must be to perceive a difference. For example, it's relatively easy to tell the difference in weight between your 4-year-old sister and your 5-year-old brother when you pick them up. However, it is more difficult to tell the difference in weight between two heavy objects. Another example is that to see a change in a bright light, the difference must be much larger than to see a change in a dim light. A rule of thumb for this phenomenon states that equally perceived changes must be relative. Changes are about equally perceived if the ratio of the change is the same, whether for dark or bright lights, and so on. After some thought, this idea leads to a logarithmic approximation to perceptually equally spaced units.

For human vision, however, CIE arrived at a somewhat more involved version of this kind of rule, called the CIELAB space. What is being quantified in this space is, again, *differences* perceived in color and brightness. This makes sense because, practically speaking, color differences are most useful for comparing source and target colors. You would be interested, for example, in whether a particular batch of dyed cloth has the same color as an original swatch. Figure 4.14 shows a cutaway into a 3D solid of the coordinate space associated with this color difference metric.

CIELAB (also known as L*a*b*) uses a power law of 1/3 instead of a logarithm. CIELAB uses three values that correspond roughly to luminance and a pair that combine to make colorfulness and hue (variables have an asterisk to differentiate them from previous versions devised by the CIE). The color difference is defined as

$$
\Delta E = \sqrt{(L^*)^2 + (a^*)^2 + (b^*)^2}
\tag{4.21}
$$

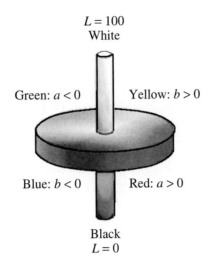

$L = 100$
White

Green: $a < 0$ Yellow: $b > 0$

Blue: $b < 0$ Red: $a > 0$

Black
$L = 0$

FIGURE 4.14: CIELAB model. (This figure also appears in the color insert section.)

where

$$L^* = 116 \left(\frac{Y}{Y_n} \right)^{(1/3)} - 16$$

$$a^* = 500 \left[\left(\frac{X}{X_n} \right)^{(1/3)} - \left(\frac{Y}{Y_n} \right)^{(1/3)} \right] \qquad (4.22)$$

$$b^* = 200 \left[\left(\frac{Y}{Y_n} \right)^{(1/3)} - \left(\frac{Z}{Z_n} \right)^{(1/3)} \right]$$

with X_n, Y_n, Z_n the XYZ values of the white point. Auxiliary definitions are

$$\text{chroma} = c^* = \sqrt{(a^*)^2 + (b^*)^2}$$

$$\text{hue angle} = h^* = \arctan \frac{b^*}{a^*} \qquad (4.23)$$

Roughly, the maximum and minimum of value a^* correspond to red and green, while b^* ranges from yellow to blue. The *chroma* is a scale of colorfulness, with more colorful (more saturated) colors occupying the outside of the CIELAB solid at each L^* brightness level, and more washed-out (desaturated) colors nearer the central achromatic axis. The hue angle expresses more or less what most people mean by "the color" — that is, you would describe it as red or orange.

The development of such color-differences models is an active field of research, and there is a plethora of other human-perception-based formulas (the other competitor of the same vintage as CIELAB is called CIELUV — both were devised in 1976). The interest is generated partly because such color metrics impact how we model differences in lighting and viewing across device and/or network boundaries [7]. Several high-end products, including Adobe Photoshop, use the CIELAB model.

4.1.15   More Color-Coordinate Schemes

There are several other coordinate schemes in use to describe color as humans perceive it, with some confusion in the field as to whether gamma correction should or should not be applied. Here we are describing device-independent color — based on XYZ and correlated to what humans see. However, generally users make free use of RGB or R', G', B'.

Other schemes include: CMY (described on p. 101); HSL — Hue, Saturation and Lightness; HSV — Hue, Saturation and Value; HSI — and Intensity; HCI — C=Chroma; HVC — V=Value; HSD — D=Darkness; the beat goes on!

4.1.16   Munsell Color Naming System

Accurate *naming* of colors is also an important consideration. One time-tested standard system was devised by Munsell in the early 1900's and revised many times (the last one is called the *Munsell renotation*) [8]. The idea is to set up (yet another) approximately perceptually uniform system of three axes to discuss and specify color. The axes are value (black-white), hue, and chroma. Value is divided into 9 steps, hue is in 40 steps around a circle, and chroma (saturation) has a maximum of 16 levels. The circle's radius varies with value.

The main idea is a fairly invariant specification of color for any user, including artists. The Munsell corporation therefore sells books of all these patches of paint, made up with proprietary paint formulas (the book is quite expensive). It has been asserted that this is the most often used uniform scale.

4.2   COLOR MODELS IN IMAGES

We now have had an introduction to color science and some of the problems that crop up with respect to color for image displays. But how are color models and coordinates systems really used for stored, displayed, and printed images?

4.2.1   RGB Color Model for CRT Displays

According to Chapter 3, we usually store color information directly in RGB form. However, we note from the previous section that such a coordinate system is in fact device-dependent.

We expect to be able to use 8 bits per color channel for color that is accurate enough. In fact, we have to use about 12 bits per channel to avoid an aliasing effect in dark image areas — contour bands that result from gamma correction, since gamma correction results in many fewer available integer levels (see Exercise 7).

For images produced from computer graphics, we store integers proportional to intensity in the frame buffer. Then we should have a gamma correction LUT between the frame buffer and the CRT. If gamma correction is applied to floats before quantizing to integers, before storage in the frame buffer, then we can use only 8 bits per channel and still avoid contouring artifacts.

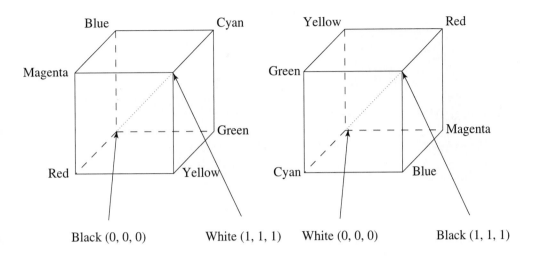

FIGURE 4.15: RGB and CMY color cubes. (This figure also appears in the color insert section.)

4.2.2 Subtractive Color: CMY Color Model

So far, we have effectively been dealing only with *additive color*. Namely, when two light beams impinge on a target, their colors add; when two phosphors on a CRT screen are turned on, their colors add. So, for example, red phosphor + green phosphor makes yellow light.

But for ink deposited on paper, in essence the opposite situation holds: yellow ink *subtracts* blue from white illumination but reflects red and green; which is why it appears yellow!

So, instead of red, green, and blue primaries, we need primaries that amount to −red, −green, and −blue; we need to *subtract* R, G, or B. These subtractive color primaries are cyan (C), magenta (M), and yellow (Y) inks. Figure 4.15 shows how the two systems, RGB and CMY, are connected. In the additive (RGB) system, black is "no light", $RGB = (0, 0, 0)$. In the subtractive CMY system, black arises from subtracting all the light by laying down inks with $C = M = Y = 1$.

4.2.3 Transformation from RGB to CMY

Given our identification of the role of inks in subtractive systems, the simplest model we can invent to specify what ink density to lay down on paper, to make a certain desired RGB color, is as follows:

$$\begin{bmatrix} C \\ M \\ Y \end{bmatrix} = \begin{bmatrix} 1 \\ 1 \\ 1 \end{bmatrix} - \begin{bmatrix} R \\ G \\ B \end{bmatrix} \tag{4.24}$$

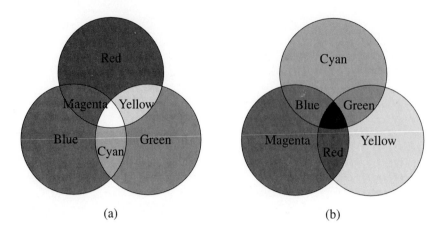

(a) (b)

FIGURE 4.16: Additive and subtractive color: (a) RGB is used to specify additive color; (b) CMY is used to specify subtractive color. (This figure also appears in the color insert section.)

Then the inverse transform is

$$
\begin{bmatrix} R \\ G \\ B \end{bmatrix} = \begin{bmatrix} 1 \\ 1 \\ 1 \end{bmatrix} - \begin{bmatrix} C \\ M \\ Y \end{bmatrix} \tag{4.25}
$$

4.2.4 Undercolor Removal: CMYK System

C, M, and Y are supposed to mix to black. However, more often they mix to a muddy brown (we all know this from kindergarten). Truly "black" black ink is in fact cheaper than mixing colored inks to make black, so a simple approach to producing sharper printer colors is to calculate that part of the three-color mix that would be black, remove it from the color proportions, and add it back as real black. This is called "undercolor removal".

The new specification of inks is thus

$$
K \equiv min\{C, M, Y\}
$$

$$
\begin{bmatrix} C \\ M \\ Y \end{bmatrix} \Rightarrow \begin{bmatrix} C - K \\ M - K \\ Y - K \end{bmatrix} \tag{4.26}
$$

Figure 4.16 depicts the color combinations that result from combining primary colors available in the two situations: additive color, in which we usually specify color using RGB, and subtractive color, in which we usually specify color using CMY or CMYK.

4.2.5 Printer Gamuts

In a common model of the printing process, printers lay down transparent layers of ink onto a (generally white) substrate. If we wish to have a cyan printing ink truly equal to minus-red,

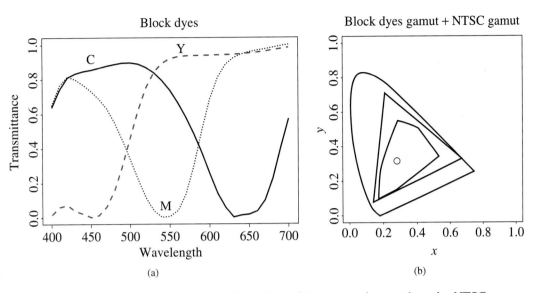

FIGURE 4.17: (a) transmission curves for block dyes; (b) spectrum locus, triangular NTSC gamut, and six-vertex printer gamut.

our objective is to produce a cyan ink that completely blocks red light but also completely passes all green and blue light. Unfortunately, such "block dyes" are only approximated in industry. In reality, transmission curves overlap for the C, M, and Y inks. This leads to "crosstalk" between the color channels and difficulties in predicting colors achievable in printing.

Figure 4.17(a) shows typical transmission curves for real block dyes, and Figure 4.17(b) shows the resulting color gamut for a color printer that uses such inks. We see that the gamut is smaller than that of an NTSC monitor and can overlap it.

Such a gamut arises from the model used for printer inks. Transmittances are related to *optical density* D via a logarithm: $D = -\ln T$, where T is one of the curves in Figure 4.17(a). A color is formed by a linear combination D of inks, with D a combination of the three densities weighted by weights w_i, $i = 1..3$, and w_i can be in the range from zero to the maximum allowable without smearing.

So the overall transmittance T is formed as a product of exponentials of the three weighted densities — light is extinguished exponentially as it travels through a "sandwich" of transparent dyes. The light reflected from paper (or through a piece of slide film) is $TE = e^{-D}E$, where E is the illuminating light. Forming colors XYZ with Equation (4.6) leads to the printer gamut in Figure 4.17(b).

The center of the printer gamut is the white-black axis, and the six boundary vertices correspond to C, M, Y, and the three combinations CM, CY, and MY laid down at full density. Lesser ink densities lie more in the middle of the diagram. Full density for all inks corresponds to the black/white point, which lies in the center of the diagram, at the point marked "o". For these particular inks, that point has chromaticity $(x, y) = (0.276, 0.308)$.

4.3 COLOR MODELS IN VIDEO

4.3.1 Video Color Transforms

Methods of dealing with color in digital video derive largely from older analog methods of coding color for TV. Typically, some version of the luminance is combined with color information in a single signal. For example, a matrix transform method similar to Equation (4.19) called YIQ is used to transmit TV signals in North America and Japan. This coding also makes its way into VHS videotape coding in these countries, since video tape technologies also use YIQ.

In Europe, videotape uses the PAL or SECAM codings, which are based on TV that uses a matrix transform called YUV.

Finally, digital video mostly uses a matrix transform called YCbCr that is closely related to YUV.[2]

4.3.2 YUV Color Model

Initially, YUV coding was used for PAL analog video. A version of YUV is now also used in the CCIR 601 standard for digital video.

First, it codes a luminance signal (for gamma-corrected signals) equal to Y' in Equation (4.20). (Recall that Y' is often called the "luma.") The luma Y' is similar to, but not exactly the same as, the CIE luminance value Y, gamma-corrected. In multimedia, practitioners often blur the difference and simply refer to both as the luminance.

As well as magnitude or brightness we need a colorfulness scale, and to this end *chrominance* refers to the difference between a color and a reference white at the same luminance. It can be represented by the color *differences* U, V:

$$
\begin{aligned}
U &= B' - Y' \\
V &= R' - Y'
\end{aligned}
\tag{4.27}
$$

From Equation (4.20), Equation (4.27) reads

$$
\begin{bmatrix} Y' \\ U \\ V \end{bmatrix} = \begin{bmatrix} 0.299 & 0.587 & 0.144 \\ -0.299 & -0.587 & 0.886 \\ 0.701 & -0.587 & -0.114 \end{bmatrix} \begin{bmatrix} R' \\ G' \\ B' \end{bmatrix}
\tag{4.28}
$$

We go backward, from (Y', U, V) to (R', G', B'), by inverting the matrix in Equation (4.28).

Note that for a gray pixel, with $R' = G' = B'$, the luminance Y' is equal to that same gray value, R', say, since the sum of the coefficients in Equation (4.20) is $0.299 + 0.587 + 0.114 = 1.0$. So for a gray ("black-and-white") image, the *chrominance* (U, V) is zero, since the sum of coefficients in each of the lower two equations in (4.28) is zero. Color TV can be displayed on a black-and-white television by just using the Y' signal.[3] For backward compatibility, color TV uses old black-and-white signals with no color information by identifying the signal with Y'.

---

[2] The luminance-chrominance color models (YIQ, YUV, YCbCr) are proven effective. Hence, they are also adopted in image-compression standards such as JPEG and JPEG2000.

[3] It should be noted that many authors and users simply use these letters with no primes and (perhaps) mean them as if they were with primes!

Finally, in the actual implementation, U and V are rescaled for purposes of having a more convenient maximum and minimum. For analog video, the scales are chosen such that each of U or V is limited to the range between ± 0.5 times the maximum of Y' [9]. (Note that actual voltages are in another, non-normalized range — for analog, Y' is often in the range 0 to 700 mV, so rescaled U and V, called P_B and P_R in that context, range over ± 350 mV.)

Such scaling reflects how to deal with component video — three separate signals. However, for dealing with *composite* video, in which we want to compose a single signal out of Y', U, and V at once, it turns out to be convenient to contain the composite signal magnitude $Y' \pm \sqrt{U^2 + V^2}$ within the range $-1/3$ to $+4/3$, so that it will remain within the amplitude limits of the recording equipment. For this purpose, U and V are rescaled as follows:

$$
\begin{aligned}
U &= 0.492111(B' - Y') \\
V &= 0.877283(R' - Y')
\end{aligned}
\tag{4.29}
$$

(with multipliers sometimes rounded to three significant digits). Then the chrominance signal is composed from U and V as the composite signal

$$
C = U \cdot \cos(\omega t) + V \cdot \sin(\omega t)
\tag{4.30}
$$

where ω represents the NTSC color frequency.

From equations (4.29) we note that zero is not the minimum value for U, V. In terms of real, positive colors, U is approximately from blue ($U > 0$) to yellow ($U < 0$) in the RGB cube; V is approximately from red ($V > 0$) to cyan ($V < 0$).

Figure 4.18 shows the decomposition of a typical color image into its Y', U, V components. Since both U and V go negative, the images are in fact shifted, rescaled versions of the actual signals.

Because the eye is most sensitive to black-and-white variations, in terms of spatial frequency (e.g., the eye can see a grid of fine gray lines more clearly than fine colored lines), in the analog PAL signal a bandwidth of only 1.3 MHz is allocated to each of U and V, while 5.5 MHz is reserved for the Y' signal. In fact, color information transmitted for color TV is actually very blocky.

4.3.3 YIQ Color Model

YIQ (actually, $Y' I Q$) is used in NTSC color TV broadcasting. Again, gray pixels generate zero (I, Q) chrominance signal. The original meanings of these names came from combinations of analog signals — I for *in-phase chrominance*, and Q for *quadrature chrominance* — and can now be safely ignored.

It is thought that, although U and V are more simply defined, they do not capture the most-to-least hierarchy of human vision sensitivity. Although they nicely define the color differences, they do not best correspond to actual human perceptual color sensitivities. NTSC uses I and Q instead.

YIQ is just a version of YUV, with the same Y' but with U and V rotated by $33°$:

$$
\begin{aligned}
I &= 0.877283(R' - Y')\cos 33° - 0.492111(B' - Y')\sin 33° \\
Q &= 0.877283(R' - Y')\sin 33° + 0.492111(B' - Y')\cos 33°
\end{aligned}
\tag{4.31}
$$

(a)

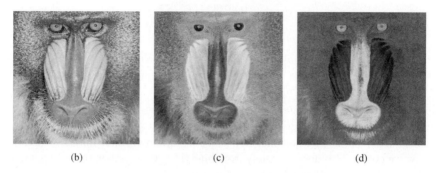

(b)   (c)   (d)

FIGURE 4.18: $Y'UV$ decomposition of color image: (a) original color image; (b) Y'; (c) U; (d) V. (This figure also appears in the color insert section.)

This leads to the following matrix transform:

$$
\begin{bmatrix} Y' \\ I \\ Q \end{bmatrix} = \begin{bmatrix} 0.299 & 0.587 & 0.144 \\ 0.595879 & -0.274133 & -0.321746 \\ 0.211205 & -0.523083 & 0.311878 \end{bmatrix} = \begin{bmatrix} R' \\ G' \\ B' \end{bmatrix} \tag{4.32}
$$

I is roughly the orange-blue direction, and Q roughly corresponds to the purple-green direction.

Figure 4.19 shows the decomposition of the same color image as above into YIQ components. Only the I and Q components are shown, since the original image and the Y' component are the same as in Figure 4.19.

For this particular image, most of the energy is captured in the Y' component, which is typical. However, in this case the YIQ decomposition does a better of job of forming a hierarchical sequence of images: for the 8-bit Y' component, the root-mean-square (RMS) value is 137 (with 255 the maximum possible). The U, V components have RMS values 43 and 44. For the YIQ decomposition, the I and Q components have RMS values 42 and 14, so they better prioritize color values. Originally, NTSC allocated 4.2 MHz to Y, 1.5 MHz to I, and 0.6 MHz to Q. Today, both I and Q are each allocated 1.0 MHz.

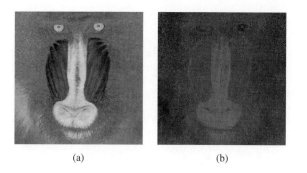

(a)   (b)

FIGURE 4.19: (a) I and (b) Q components of color image.

4.3.4 YCbCr Color Model

The international standard for component (three-signal, studio quality) *digital* video is officially Recommendation ITU-R BT.601-4 (known as "Rec. 601"). This standard uses another color space, YC_bC_r, often simply written *YCbCr*. The YCbCr transform is used in JPEG image compression and MPEG video compression and is closely related to the YUV transform. YUV is changed by scaling such that C_b is U, but with a coefficient of 0.5 multiplying B'. In some software systems, C_b and C_r are also shifted such that values are between 0 and 1. This makes the equations as follows:

$$
\begin{aligned}
C_b &= ((B' - Y')/1.772) + 0.5 \\
C_r &= ((R' - Y')/1.402) + 0.5
\end{aligned}
\tag{4.33}
$$

Written out, we then have

$$
\begin{bmatrix} Y' \\ C_b \\ C_r \end{bmatrix}
=
\begin{bmatrix}
0.299 & 0.587 & 0.144 \\
-0.168736 & -0.331264 & 0.5 \\
0.5 & -0.418688 & -0.081312
\end{bmatrix}
\begin{bmatrix} R' \\ G' \\ B' \end{bmatrix}
+
\begin{bmatrix} 0 \\ 0.5 \\ 0.5 \end{bmatrix}
\tag{4.34}
$$

In practice, however, Rec. 601 specifies 8-bit coding, with a maximum Y' value of only 219 and a minimum of $+16$. Values below 16 and above 235, denoted *headroom* and *footroom*, are reserved for other processing. C_b and C_r have a range of ±112 and offset of $+128$ (in other words, a maximum of 240 and a minimum of 16). If R', G', B' are floats in $[0.. + 1]$, we obtain Y', C_b, C_r in $[0..255]$ via the transform [9]

$$
\begin{bmatrix} Y' \\ C_b \\ C_r \end{bmatrix}
=
\begin{bmatrix}
65.481 & 128.553 & 24.966 \\
-37.797 & -74.203 & 112 \\
112 & -93.786 & -18.214
\end{bmatrix}
\begin{bmatrix} R' \\ G' \\ B' \end{bmatrix}
+
\begin{bmatrix} 16 \\ 128 \\ 128 \end{bmatrix}
\tag{4.35}
$$

In fact, the output range is also clamped to $[1..254]$, since the Rec. 601 synchronization signals are given by codes 0 and 255.

4.4 FURTHER EXPLORATION

In a deep way, color is one of our favorite pleasures as humans and arguably is one of the chief attributes that makes multimedia so compelling. The most-used reference on color in general is the classic handbook [2]. A compendium of important techniques used today is the collection [10].

Links in the Chapter 4 section of the Further Exploration directory on the text web site include

- More details on gamma correction for publication on the WWW

- The full specification of the new sRGB standard color space for WWW applications

- An excellent review of color transforms and a standard color FAQ

- A MATLAB script to exercise (and expand upon) the color transform functions that are part of the Image Toolbox in MATLAB: the standard Lena image is transformed to YIQ and to YCbCr

- A new color space. The new MPEG standard, MPEG-7, (discussed in Chapter 12) somewhat sidesteps the thorny question of whose favorite color space to use in a standard definition by including six color spaces. One of them is a new variant on HSV space, *HMMD color space*, that purports to allow a simple color quantization — from 24-bit down to 8-bit color, say, — that is effectively equivalent to a complex vector color quantization (i.e., considering a more careful but also more expensive mapping of the colors in an image into the color LUT). This new color space may indeed become important.

4.5 EXERCISES

1. Consider the following set of color-related terms:

    (a) Wavelength
    (b) Color level
    (c) Brightness
    (d) Whiteness

    How would you match each of the following (more vaguely stated) characteristics to each of the above terms?

    (e) Luminance
    (f) Hue
    (g) Saturation
    (h) Chrominance

2. What color is outdoor light? For example, around what wavelength would you guess the peak power is for a red sunset? For blue sky light?

3. "The LAB gamut covers all colors in the visible spectrum."

    (a) What does this statement mean? Briefly, how does LAB relate to color? Just be descriptive.

(b) What are (roughly) the relative sizes of the LAB gamut, the CMYK gamut, and a monitor gamut?

4. Where does the chromaticity "horseshoe" shape in Figure 4.11 come from? Can we calculate it? Write a small pseudocode solution for the problem of finding this so-called "spectrum locus". *Hint*: Figure 4.20(a) shows the color-matching functions in Figure 4.10 drawn as a set of points in three-space. Figure 4.20(b) shows these points mapped into another 3D set of points. *Another hint*: Try a programming solution for this problem, to help you answer it more explicitly.

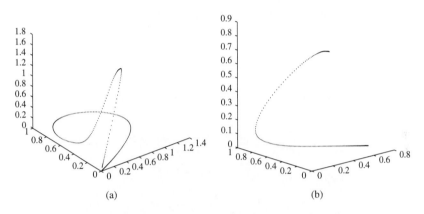

(a)   (b)

FIGURE 4.20: (a) color-matching functions; (b) transformed color matching functions.

5. Suppose we use a new set of color-matching functions $\bar{x}^{new}(\lambda)$, $\bar{y}^{new}(\lambda)$, $\bar{z}^{new}(\lambda)$ with values

λ (nm)	$\bar{x}^{new}(\lambda)$	$\bar{y}^{new}(\lambda)$	$\bar{z}^{new}(\lambda)$
450	0.2	0.1	0.5
500	0.1	0.4	0.3
600	0.1	0.4	0.2
700	0.6	0.1	0.0

In this system, what are the chromaticity values (x, y) of equi-energy white light $E(\lambda)$ where $E(\lambda) \equiv 1$ for all wavelengths λ? Explain.

6. **(a)** Suppose images are *not* gamma corrected by a camcorder. Generally, how would they appear on a screen?

    (b) What happens if we artificially increase the output gamma for stored image pixels? (We can do this in Photoshop.) What is the effect on the image?

7. Suppose image file values are in $0..255$ in each color channel. If we define $\bar{R} = R/255$ for the red channel, we wish to carry out gamma correction by passing a new value $\bar{R}'$ to the display device, with $\bar{R}' \simeq \bar{R}^{1/2.0}$.

It is common to carry out this operation using integer math. Suppose we approximate the calculation as creating new integer values in $0..255$ via

$$(int)\,(255\cdot(\overline{R}^{1/2.0}))$$

(a) Comment (very roughly) on the effect of this operation on the number of actually available levels for display. *Hint*: Coding this up in any language will help you understand the mechanism at work better — and will allow you to simply count the output levels.

(b) Which end of the levels $0..255$ is affected most by gamma correction — the low end (near 0) or the high end (near 255)? Why? How much at each end?

8. In many computer graphics applications, γ-correction is performed only in color LUT (lookup table). Show the first five entries of a color LUT meant for use in γ-correction. *Hint*: Coding this up saves you the trouble of using a calculator.

9. Devise a program to produce Figure 4.21, showing the color gamut of a monitor that adheres to SMPTE specifications.

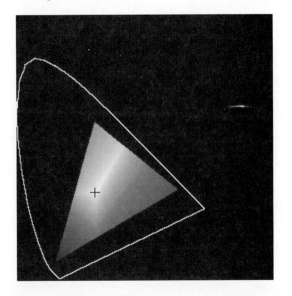

FIGURE 4.21: SMPTE Monitor Gamut. (This figure also appears in the color insert section.)

10. Hue is the color, independent of brightness and how much pure white has been added to it. We can make a *simple* definition of hue as the set of ratios R:G:B. Suppose a color (i.e., an RGB) is divided by 2.0, so that the RGB triple now has values 0.5 times its former values. Explain, using numerical values:

(a) If gamma correction is applied after the division by 2.0 and before the color is stored, does the darker RGB have the same hue as the original, in the sense of having the same ratios R:G:B of *light* emanating from the CRT display device?

(We're not discussing any psychophysical effects that change our perception —
here we're just worried about the machine itself).

    (b) If gamma correction is *not* applied, does the second RGB have the same hue as
the first, when displayed?

    (c) For what color triples is the hue always unchanged?

11. We wish to produce a graphic that is pleasing and easily readable. Suppose we make
the background color `pink`. What color text font should we use to make the text
most readable? Justify your answer.

12. To make matters simpler for eventual printing, we buy a camera equipped with CMY
sensors, as opposed to RGB sensors (CMY cameras are in fact available).

    (a) Draw spectral curves roughly depicting what such a camera's sensitivity to
frequency might look like.

    (b) Could the output of a CMY camera be used to produce ordinary RGB pictures?
How?

13. Color inkjet printers use the CMY model. When the cyan ink color is sprayed onto a
sheet of white paper,

    (a) Why does it look cyan under daylight?

    (b) What color would it appear under a blue light? Why?

4.6 REFERENCES

1 D.H. Pritchard, "U.S. Color Television Fundamentals — A Review," *IEEE Trans. Consumer
Electronics* 23(4): p. 467–478, 1977.

2 G. Wyszecki and W.S. Stiles, *Color Science: Concepts and Methods, Quantitative Data and
Formulas*, 2nd ed., New York: Wiley, 1982.

3 R.W.G. Hunt, "Color Reproduction and Color Vision Modeling," in *1st Color Imaging Conference: Transforms & Transportability of Color*, Society for Imaging Science & Technology
(IS&T)/Society for Information Display (SID) joint conference, 1993, 1–5.

4 M.J. Vrhel, R. Gershon, and L.S. Iwan, "Measurement and Analysis of Object Reflectance
Spectra," *Color Research and Application*, 19: 4–9, 1994.

5 R.W.G. Hunt. *The Reproduction of Color*, 5th ed., Tolworth, Surry, U.K.: Fountain Press, 1995.

6 J. D. Foley, A. van Dam, S. K. Feiner, and J. F. Hughes, *Computer Graphics: Principles and
Practice in C*, 2nd ed., Reading MA: Addison-Wesley, 1996.

7 Mark D. Fairchild, *Color Appearance Models*, Reading MA: Addison-Wesley, 1998.

8 D. Travis, *Effective Color Displays*, San Diego: Academic Press, 1991.

9 C.A. Poynton, *A Technical Introduction to Digital Video*, New York: Wiley, 1996.

10 P. Green and L. MacDonald, eds., *Colour Engineering: Achieving Device Independent Colour*,
New York: Wiley, 2002.

CHAPTER 5

Fundamental Concepts in Video

In this chapter, we introduce the principal notions needed to understand video. Digital video compression is explored separately, in Chapters 10 through 12.

Here we consider the following aspects of video and how they impact multimedia applications:

- Types of video signals

- Analog video

- Digital video

Since video is created from a variety of sources, we begin with the signals themselves. Analog video is represented as a continuous (time-varying) signal, and the first part of this chapter discusses how it is measured. Digital video is represented as a sequence of digital images, and the second part of the chapter discusses standards and definitions such as HDTV.

5.1 TYPES OF VIDEO SIGNALS

Video signals can be organized in three different ways: *Component video*, *Composite video*, and *S-video*.

5.1.1 Component Video

Higher-end video systems, such as for studios, make use of three separate video signals for the red, green, and blue image planes. This is referred to as *component video*. This kind of system has three wires (and connectors) connecting the camera or other devices to a TV or monitor.

Color signals are not restricted to always being RGB separations. Instead, as we saw in Chapter 4 on color models for images and video, we can form three signals via a luminance-chrominance transformation of the RGB signals — for example, YIQ or YUV. In contrast, most computer systems use component video, with separate signals for R, G, and B signals.

For any color separation scheme, component video gives the best color reproduction, since there is no "crosstalk" between the three different channels, unlike composite video or S-video. Component video, however, requires more bandwidth and good synchronization of the three components.

5.1.2   Composite Video

In *composite video*, color ("chrominance") and intensity ("luminance") signals are mixed into a *single* carrier wave. Chrominance is a composite of two color components (I and Q, or U and V). This is the type of signal used by broadcast color TVs; it is downward compatible with black-and-white TV.

In NTSC TV, for example [1], I and Q are combined into a chroma signal, and a color subcarrier then puts the chroma signal at the higher frequency end of the channel shared with the luminance signal. The chrominance and luminance components can be separated at the receiver end, and the two color components can be further recovered.

When connecting to TVs or VCRs, composite video uses only one wire (and hence one connector, such as a BNC connector at each end of a coaxial cable or an RCA plug at each end of an ordinary wire), and video color signals are mixed, not sent separately. The audio signal is another addition to this one signal. Since color information is mixed and both color and intensity are wrapped into the same signal, some interference between the luminance and chrominance signals is inevitable.

5.1.3   S-Video

As a compromise, *S-video* (separated video, or super-video, e.g., in S-VHS) uses two wires: one for luminance and another for a composite chrominance signal. As a result, there is less crosstalk between the color information and the crucial gray-scale information.

The reason for placing luminance into its own part of the signal is that black-and-white information is crucial for visual perception. As noted in the previous chapter, humans are able to differentiate spatial resolution in grayscale images much better than for the color part of color images (as opposed to the "black-and-white" part). Therefore, color information sent can be much less accurate than intensity information. We can see only fairly large blobs of color, so it makes sense to send less color detail.

5.2   ANALOG VIDEO

Most TV is still sent and received as an analog signal. Once the electrical signal is received, we may assume that brightness is at least a monotonic function of voltage, if not necessarily linear, because of gamma correction (see Section 4.1.6).

An analog signal $f(t)$ samples a time-varying image. So-called *progressive* scanning traces through a complete picture (a frame) row-wise for each time interval. A high-resolution computer monitor typically uses a time interval of 1/72 second.

In TV and in some monitors and multimedia standards, another system, *interlaced* scanning, is used. Here, the odd-numbered lines are traced first, then the even-numbered lines. This results in "odd" and "even" *fields* — two fields make up one frame.

In fact, the odd lines (starting from 1) end up at the middle of a line at the end of the odd field, and the even scan starts at a half-way point. Figure 5.1 shows the scheme used. First the solid (odd) lines are traced — P to Q, then R to S, and so on, ending at T — then the even field starts at U and ends at V. The scan lines are not horizontal because a small voltage is applied, moving the electron beam down over time.

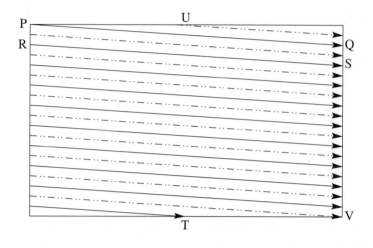

FIGURE 5.1: Interlaced raster scan.

Interlacing was invented because, when standards were being defined, it was difficult to transmit the amount of information in a full frame quickly enough to avoid flicker. The double number of fields presented to the eye reduces perceived flicker.

Because of interlacing, the odd and even lines are displaced in time from each other. This is generally not noticeable except when fast action is taking place onscreen, when blurring may occur. For example, in the video in Figure 5.2, the moving helicopter is blurred more than the still background.

Since it is sometimes necessary to change the frame rate, resize, or even produce stills from an interlaced source video, various schemes are used to *de-interlace* it. The simplest de-interlacing method consists of discarding one field and duplicating the scan lines of the other field, which results in the information in one field being lost completely. Other, more complicated methods retain information from both fields.

CRT displays are built like fluorescent lights and must flash 50 to 70 times per second to appear smooth. In Europe, this fact is conveniently tied to their 50 Hz electrical system, and they use video digitized at 25 frames per second (fps); in North America, the 60 Hz electric system dictates 30 fps.

The jump from Q to R and so on in Figure 5.1 is called the *horizontal retrace*, during which the electronic beam in the CRT is blanked. The jump from T to U or V to P is called the *vertical retrace*.

Since voltage is one-dimensional — it is simply a signal that varies with time — how do we know when a new video line begins? That is, what part of an electrical signal tells us that we have to restart at the left side of the screen?

The solution used in analog video is a small voltage offset from zero to indicate black and another value, such as zero, to indicate the start of a line. Namely, we could use a "blacker-than-black" zero signal to indicate the beginning of a line.

Figure 5.3 shows a typical electronic signal for one scan line of NTSC composite video. 'White' has a peak value of 0.714 V; 'Black' is slightly above zero at 0.055 V; whereas

(a)

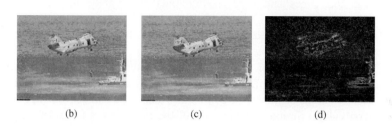

(b)   (c)   (d)

FIGURE 5.2: Interlaced scan produces two fields for each frame: (a) the video frame; (b) Field 1; (c) Field 2; (d) difference of Fields.

Blank is at zero volts. As shown, the time duration for blanking pulses in the signal is used for synchronization as well, with the tip of the Sync signal at approximately -0.286 V. In fact, the problem of reliable synchronization is so important that special signals to control sync take up about 30% of the signal!

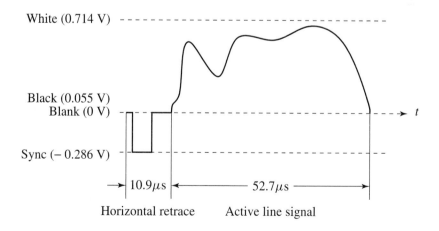

FIGURE 5.3: Electronic signal for one NTSC scan line.

The vertical retrace and sync ideas are similar to the horizontal one, except that they happen only once per field. Tekalp [2] presents a good discussion of the details of analog (and digital) video. The handbook [3] considers many fundamental problems in video processing in great depth.

5.2.1 NTSC Video

The NTSC TV standard is mostly used in North America and Japan. It uses a familiar 4:3 *aspect ratio* (i.e., the ratio of picture width to height) and 525 scan lines per frame at 30 frames per second.

More exactly, for historical reasons NTSC uses 29.97 fps — or, in other words, 33.37 msec per frame. NTSC follows the interlaced scanning system, and each frame is divided into two fields, with 262.5 lines/field. Thus the horizontal sweep frequency is $525 \times 29.97 \approx 15,734$ lines/sec, so that each line is swept out in $1/15,734$ sec ≈ 63.6 μsec. Since the horizontal retrace takes 10.9 μsec, this leaves 52.7 μsec for the active line signal, during which image data is displayed (see Figure 5.3).

Figure 5.4 shows the effect of "vertical retrace and sync" and "horizontal retrace and sync" on the NTSC video raster. Blanking information is placed into 20 lines reserved for control information at the beginning of each field. Hence, the number of *active video lines* per frame is only 485. Similarly, almost 1/6 of the raster at the left side is blanked for horizontal retrace and sync. The nonblanking pixels are called *active pixels*.

Pixels often fall between scanlines. Therefore, even with noninterlaced scan, NTSC TV is capable of showing only about 340 (visually distinct) lines, — about 70% of the 485 specified active lines. With interlaced scan, it could be as low as 50%.

Image data is not encoded in the blanking regions, but other information can be placed there, such as V-chip information, stereo audio channel data, and subtitles in many languages.

NTSC video is an analog signal with no fixed horizontal resolution. Therefore, we must decide how many times to sample the signal for display. Each sample corresponds to one pixel output. A *pixel clock* divides each horizontal line of video into samples. The higher the frequency of the pixel clock, the more samples per line.

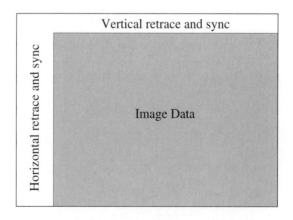

FIGURE 5.4: Video raster, including retrace and sync data.

TABLE 5.1: Samples per line for various analog video formats.

Format	Samples per line
VHS	240
S-VHS	400–425
Beta-SP	500
Standard 8 mm	300
Hi-8 mm	425

Different video formats provide different numbers of samples per line, as listed in Table 5.1. Laser disks have about the same resolution as Hi-8. (In comparison, miniDV 1/4-inch tapes for digital video are 480 lines by 720 samples per line.)

NTSC uses the YIQ color model. We employ the technique of *quadrature modulation* to combine (the spectrally overlapped part of) I (in-phase) and Q (quadrature) signals into a single chroma signal C [1, 2]:

$$C = I \cos(F_{sc}t) + Q \sin(F_{sc}t) \qquad (5.1)$$

This modulated chroma signal is also known as the *color subcarrier*, whose magnitude is $\sqrt{I^2 + Q^2}$ and phase is $\tan^{-1}(Q/I)$. The frequency of C is $F_{sc} \approx 3.58$ MHz.

The I and Q signals are multiplied in the time domain by cosine and sine functions with the frequency F_{sc} [Equation (5.1)]. This is equivalent to convolving their Fourier transforms in the frequency domain with two impulse functions at F_{sc} and $-F_{sc}$. As a result, a copy of I and Q frequency spectra are made which are centered at F_{sc} and $-F_{sc}$, respectively.[1]

The NTSC composite signal is a further composition of the luminance signal Y and the chroma signal, as defined below:

$$\text{composite} = Y + C = Y + I \cos(F_{sc}t) + Q \sin(F_{sc}t) \qquad (5.2)$$

NTSC assigned a bandwidth of 4.2 MHz to Y but only 1.6 MHz to I and 0.6 MHz to Q, due to humans' insensitivity to color details (high-frequency color changes). As Figure 5.5 shows, the picture carrier is at 1.25 MHz in the NTSC video channel, which has a total bandwidth of 6 MHz. The chroma signal is being "carried" by $F_{sc} \approx 3.58$ MHz towards the higher end of the channel and is thus centered at $1.25 + 3.58 = 4.83$ MHz. This greatly reduces the potential interference between the Y (luminance) and C (chrominance) signals, since the magnitudes of higher-frequency components of Y are significantly smaller than their lower frequency counterparts.

Moreover, as Blinn[1] explains, great care is taken to interleave the discrete Y and C spectra so as to further reduce the interference between them. The "interleaving" is illustrated in Figure 5.5, where the frequency components for Y (from the discrete Fourier transform) are shown as solid lines, and those for I and Q are shown as dashed lines. As

---

[1] Negative frequency $(-F_{sc})$ is a mathematical notion needed in the Fourier transform. In the physical spectrum, only positive frequency is used.

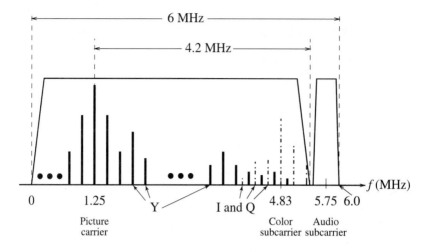

FIGURE 5.5: Interleaving Y and C signals in the NTSC spectrum.

a result, the 4.2 MHz band of Y is overlapped and interleaved with the 1.6 MHz to I and 0.6 MHz to Q.

The first step in decoding the composite signal at the receiver side is to separate Y and C. Generally, low-pass filters can be used to extract Y, which is located at the lower end of the channel. TV sets with higher quality also use comb filters [1] to exploit the fact that Y and C are interleaved.

After separation from Y, the chroma signal C can be demodulated to extract I and Q separately.

To extract I:

1. Multiply the signal C by $2\cos(F_{sc}t)$

$$
\begin{aligned}
C \cdot 2\cos(F_{sc}t) &= I \cdot 2\cos^2(F_{sc}t) + Q \cdot 2\sin(F_{sc}t)\cos(F_{sc}t) \\
&= I \cdot (1 + \cos(2F_{sc}t)) + Q \cdot 2\sin(F_{sc}t)\cos(F_{sc}t) \\
&= I + I \cdot \cos(2F_{sc}t) + Q \cdot \sin(2F_{sc}t)
\end{aligned}
$$

2. Apply a low-pass filter to obtain I and discard the two higher-frequency ($2F_{sc}$) terms.

Similarly, extract Q by first multiplying C by $2\sin(F_{sc}t)$ and then applying low-pass filtering.

The NTSC bandwidth of 6 MHz is tight. Its audio subcarrier frequency is 4.5 MHz, which places the center of the audio band at $1.25 + 4.5 = 5.75$ MHz in the channel (Figure 5.5). This would actually be a bit too close to the color subcarrier — a cause for potential interference between the audio and color signals. It was due largely to this reason that NTSC color TV slowed its frame rate to $30 \times 1,000/1,001 \approx 29.97$ fps [4]. As a result, the adopted NTSC color subcarrier frequency is slightly lowered, to

$$f_{sc} = 30 \times 1,000/1,001 \times 525 \times 227.5 \approx 3.579545 \text{ MHz}$$

where 227.5 is the number of color samples per scan line in NTSC broadcast TV.

5.2.2 PAL Video

PAL (Phase Alternating Line) is a TV standard originally invented by German scientists. It uses 625 scan lines per frame, at 25 frames per second (or 40 msec/frame), with a 4:3 aspect ratio and interlaced fields. Its broadcast TV signals are also used in composite video. This important standard is widely used in Western Europe, China, India and many other parts of the world.

PAL uses the YUV color model with an 8 MHz channel, allocating a bandwidth of 5.5 MHz to Y and 1.8 MHz each to U and V. The color subcarrier frequency is $f_{sc} \approx$ 4.43 MHz. To improve picture quality, chroma signals have alternate signs (e.g., +U and −U) in successive scan lines; hence the name "Phase Alternating Line."[2] This facilitates the use of a (line-rate) comb filter at the receiver — the signals in consecutive lines are averaged so as to cancel the chroma signals (which always carry opposite signs) for separating Y and C and obtain high-quality Y signals.

5.2.3 SECAM Video

SECAM, which was invented by the French, is the third major broadcast TV standard. SECAM stands for *Systeme Electronique Couleur Avec Memoire*. SECAM also uses 625 scan lines per frame, at 25 frames per second, with a 4:3 aspect ratio and interlaced fields. The original design called for a higher number of scan lines (over 800), but the final version settled for 625.

SECAM and PAL are similar, differing slightly in their color coding scheme. In SECAM, U and V signals are modulated using separate color subcarriers at 4.25 MHz and 4.41 MHz, respectively. They are sent in alternate lines — that is, only one of the U or V signals will be sent on each scan line.

Table 5.2 gives a comparison of the three major analog broadcast TV systems.

5.3 DIGITAL VIDEO

The advantages of digital representation for video are many. It permits

- Storing video on digital devices or in memory, ready to be processed (noise removal, cut and paste, and so on) and integrated into various multimedia applications

- Direct access, which makes nonlinear video editing simple

- Repeated recording without degradation of image quality

- Ease of encryption and better tolerance to channel noise

---

[2] According to Blinn [1], NTSC selects a half integer (227.5) number of color samples for each scan line. Hence, its chroma signal also switches sign in successive scan lines.

TABLE 5.2: Comparison of analog broadcast TV systems.

TV system	Frame rate (fps)	Number of scan lines	Total channel width (MHz)	Bandwidth allocation (MHz)		
				Y	I or U	Q or V
NTSC	29.97	525	6.0	4.2	1.6	0.6
PAL	25	625	8.0	5.5	1.8	1.8
SECAM	25	625	8.0	6.0	2.0	2.0

In earlier Sony or Panasonic recorders, digital video was in the form of composite video. Modern digital video generally uses component video, although RGB signals are first converted into a certain type of color opponent space, such as YUV. The usual color space is YCbCr [5].

5.3.1 Chroma Subsampling

Since humans see color with much less spatial resolution than black and white, it makes sense to decimate the chrominance signal. Interesting but not necessarily informative names have arisen to label the different schemes used. To begin with, numbers are given stating how many pixel values, per four original pixels, are actually sent. Thus the chroma subsampling scheme "4:4:4" indicates that no chroma subsampling is used. Each pixel's Y, Cb, and Cr values are transmitted, four for each of Y, Cb, and Cr.

The scheme "4:2:2" indicates horizontal subsampling of the Cb and Cr signals by a factor of 2. That is, of four pixels horizontally labeled 0 to 3, all four Ys are sent, and every two Cbs and two Crs are sent, as $(Cb0, Y0)(Cr0, Y1)(Cb2, Y2)(Cr2, Y3)(Cb4, Y4)$, and so on.

The scheme "4:1:1" subsamples horizontally by a factor of 4. The scheme "4:2:0" subsamples in both the horizontal and vertical dimensions by a factor of 2. Theoretically, an average chroma pixel is positioned between the rows and columns, as shown in Figure 5.6. We can see that the scheme 4:2:0 is in fact another kind of 4:1:1 sampling, in the sense that we send 4, 1, and 1 values per 4 pixels. Therefore, the labeling scheme is not a very reliable mnemonic!

Scheme 4:2:0, along with others, is commonly used in JPEG and MPEG (see later chapters in Part II).

5.3.2 CCIR Standards for Digital Video

The CCIR is the *Consultative Committee for International Radio*. One of the most important standards it has produced is CCIR-601, for component digital video (introduced in Section 4.3.4). This standard has since become standard ITU-R-601, an international standard for professional video applications. It is adopted by certain digital video formats, including the popular DV video.

The NTSC version has 525 scan lines, each having 858 pixels (with 720 of them visible, not in the blanking period). Because the NTSC version uses 4:2:2, each pixel can be

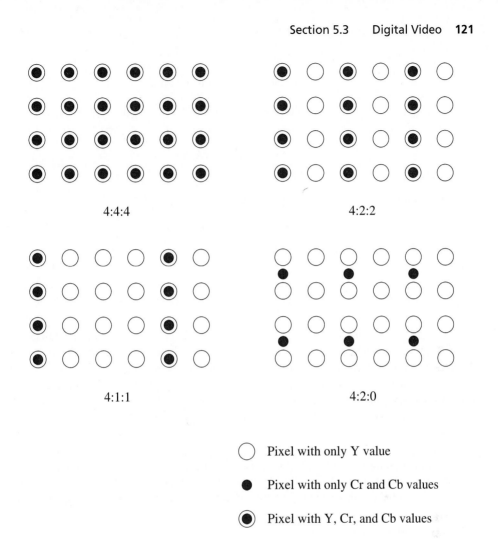

4:4:4

4:2:2

4:1:1

4:2:0

○ Pixel with only Y value

● Pixel with only Cr and Cb values

◉ Pixel with Y, Cr, and Cb values

FIGURE 5.6: Chroma subsampling.

represented with two bytes (8 bits for Y and 8 bits alternating between Cb and Cr). The CCIR 601 (NTSC) data rate (including blanking and sync but excluding audio) is thus approximately 216 Mbps (megabits per second):

$$525 \times 858 \times 30 \times 2 \text{ bytes} \times 8 \frac{\text{bits}}{\text{byte}} \approx 216 \text{ Mbps}$$

During blanking, digital video systems may make use of the extra data capacity to carry audio signals, translations into foreign languages, or error-correction information.

Table 5.3 shows some of the digital video specifications, all with an aspect ratio of 4:3. The CCIR 601 standard uses an interlaced scan, so each field has only half as much vertical resolution (e.g., 240 lines in NTSC).

TABLE 5.3: Digital video specifications.

	CCIR 601 525/60 NTSC	CCIR 601 625/50 PAL/SECAM	CIF	QCIF
Luminance resolution	720 × 480	720 × 576	352 × 288	176 × 144
Chrominance resolution	360 × 480	360 × 576	176 × 144	88 × 72
Color subsampling	4:2:2	4:2:2	4:2:0	4:2:0
Aspect ratio	4:3	4:3	4:3	4:3
Fields/sec	60	50	30	30
Interlaced	Yes	Yes	No	No

CIF stands for *Common Intermediate Format*, specified by the International Telegraph and Telephone Consultative Committee (CCITT), now superseded by the International Telecommunication Union, which oversees both telecommunications (ITU-T) and radio frequency matters (ITU-R) under one United Nations body. The idea of CIF, which is about the same as VHS quality, is to specify a format for lower bitrate. CIF uses a progressive (noninterlaced) scan. QCIF stands for Quarter-CIF, and is for even lower bitrate. All the CIF/QCIF resolutions are evenly divisible by 8, and all except 88 are divisible by 16; this is convenient for block-based video coding in H.261 and H.263, discussed in Chapter 10.

CIF is a compromise between NTSC and PAL, in that it adopts the NTSC frame rate and half the number of active lines in PAL. When played on existing TV sets, NTSC TV will first need to convert the number of lines, whereas PAL TV will require frame-rate conversion.

5.3.3 High Definition TV (HDTV)

The introduction of wide-screen movies brought the discovery that viewers seated near the screen enjoyed a level of participation (sensation of immersion) not experienced with conventional movies. Apparently the exposure to a greater field of view, especially the involvement of peripheral vision, contributes to the sense of "being there". The main thrust of High Definition TV (HDTV) is not to increase the "definition" in each unit area, but rather to increase the visual field, especially its width.

First-generation HDTV was based on an analog technology developed by Sony and NHK in Japan in the late 1970s. HDTV successfully broadcast the 1984 Los Angeles Olympic Games in Japan. MUltiple sub-Nyquist Sampling Encoding (MUSE) was an improved NHK HDTV with hybrid analog/digital technologies that was put in use in the 1990s. It has 1,125 scan lines, interlaced (60 fields per second), and a 16:9 aspect ratio. It uses satellite to broadcast — quite appropriate for Japan, which can be covered with one or two satellites. The Direct Broadcast Satellite (DBS) channels used have a bandwidth of 24 MHz.

In general, terrestrial broadcast, satellite broadcast, cable, and broadband networks are all feasible means for transmitting HDTV as well as conventional TV. Since uncompressed

TABLE 5.4: Advanced Digital TV Formats Supported by ATSC.

Number of active pixels per line	Number of active lines	Aspect ratio	Picture rate
1,920	1,080	16:9	60I 30P 24P
1,280	720	16:9	60P 30P 24P
704	480	16:9 and 4:3	60I 60P 30P 24P
640	480	4:3	60I 60P 30P 24P

HDTV will easily demand more than 20 MHz bandwidth, which will not fit in the current 6 MHz or 8 MHz channels, various compression techniques are being investigated. It is also anticipated that high-quality HDTV signals will be transmitted using more than one channel, even after compression.

In 1987, the FCC decided that HDTV standards must be compatible with the existing NTSC standard and must be confined to the existing Very High Frequency (VHF) and Ultra High Frequency (UHF) bands. This prompted a number of proposals in North America by the end of 1988, all of them analog or mixed analog/digital.

In 1990, the FCC announced a different initiative — its preference for full-resolution HDTV. They decided that HDTV would be simultaneously broadcast with existing NTSC TV and eventually replace it. The development of digital HDTV immediately took off in North America.

Witnessing a boom of proposals for digital HDTV, the FCC made a key decision to go all digital in 1993. A "grand alliance" was formed that included four main proposals, by General Instruments, MIT, Zenith, and AT&T, and by Thomson, Philips, Sarnoff and others. This eventually led to the formation of the Advanced Television Systems Committee (ATSC), which was responsible for the standard for TV broadcasting of HDTV. In 1995, the U.S. FCC Advisory Committee on Advanced Television Service recommended that the ATSC digital television standard be adopted.

The standard supports video scanning formats shown in Table 5.4. In the table, "I" means interlaced scan and "P" means progressive (noninterlaced) scan. The frame rates supported are both integer rates and the NTSC rates — that is, 60.00 or 59.94, 30.00 or 29.97, 24.00 or 23.98 fps.

For video, MPEG-2 is chosen as the compression standard. As will be seen in Chapter 11, it uses Main Level to High Level of the Main Profile of MPEG-2. For audio, AC-3 is the standard. It supports the so-called 5.1 channel Dolby surround sound — five surround channels plus a subwoofer channel.

The salient difference between conventional TV and HDTV [4, 6] is that the latter has a much wider aspect ratio of 16:9 instead of 4:3. (Actually, it works out to be exactly one-third wider than current TV.) Another feature of HDTV is its move toward progressive (noninterlaced) scan. The rationale is that interlacing introduces serrated edges to moving objects and flickers along horizontal edges.

The FCC has planned to replace all analog broadcast services with digital TV broadcasting by the year 2006. Consumers with analog TV sets will still be able to receive signals via an 8-VSB (8-level vestigial sideband) demodulation box. The services provided will include

- **Standard Definition TV (SDTV)** — the current NTSC TV or higher

- **Enhanced Definition TV (EDTV)** — 480 active lines or higher — the third and fourth rows in Table 5.4

- **High Definition TV (HDTV)** — 720 active lines or higher. So far, the popular choices are 720P (720 lines, progressive, 30 fps) and 1080I (1,080 lines, interlaced, 30 fps or 60 fields per second). The latter provides slightly better picture quality but requires much higher bandwidth.

5.4 FURTHER EXPLORATION

Tekalp [2] covers various important issues for digital video processing. Chapter 5 of Steinmetz and Nahrstedt [7] provides detailed discussions of video and television systems. Poynton [6] provides an extensive and updated review of digital video and HDTV.

Links given for this chapter on the text web site include:

- Tutorials on NTSC television

- The official ATSC home page

- The latest news on the digital TV front

- Introduction to HDTV

- The official FCC home page

5.5 EXERCISES

1. NTSC video has 525 lines per frame and 63.6 μsec per line, with 20 lines per field of vertical retrace and 10.9 μsec horizontal retrace.

   (a) Where does the 63.6 μsec come from?
   (b) Which takes more time, horizontal retrace or vertical retrace? How much more time?

2. Which do you think has less detectable flicker, PAL in Europe or NTSC in North America? Justify your conclusion.

3. Sometimes the signals for television are combined into fewer than all the parts required for TV transmission.

   (a) Altogether, how many and what are the signals used for studio broadcast TV?
   (b) How many and what signals are used in S-video? What does S-video stand for?
   (c) How many signals are actually broadcast for standard analog TV reception? What kind of video is that called?

4. Show how the Q signal can be extracted from the NTSC chroma signal C [Equation (5.1)] during demodulation.

5. One sometimes hears that the old Betamax format for videotape, which competed with VHS and lost, was actually a better format. How would such a statement be justified?

6. We don't see flicker on a workstation screen when displaying video at NTSC frame rate. Why do you think this might be?

7. Digital video uses *chroma subsampling*. What is the purpose of this? Why is it feasible?

8. What are the most salient differences between ordinary TV and HDTV? What was the main impetus for the development of HDTV?

9. What is the advantage of interlaced video? What are some of its problems?

10. One solution that removes the problems of interlaced video is to de-interlace it. Why can we not just overlay the two fields to obtain a de-interlaced image? Suggest some simple de-interlacing algorithms that retain information from both fields.

5.6 REFERENCES

1 J.F. Blinn, "NTSC: Nice Technology, Super Color," *IEEE Computer Graphics and Applications*, 13(2): 17–23, 1993.

2 A.M. Tekalp, *Digital Video Processing*, Upper Saddle River, NJ: Prentice Hall PTR, 1995.

3 A. Bovik, editor, *Handbook of Image and Video Processing*, San Diego: Academic Press, 2000.

4 C.A. Poynton, *A Technical Introduction to Digital Video*, New York: Wiley, 1996.

5 J.F. Blinn, "The World of Digital Video." *IEEE Computer Graphics and Applications*, 12(5): 106–112, 1992.

6 C.A. Poynton, *Digital Video and HDTV Algorithms and Interfaces*, San Francisco: Morgan Kaufmann, 2003.

7 R. Steinmetz and K. Nahrstedt. *Multimedia: Computing, Communications and Applications*, Upper Saddle River, NJ: Prentice Hall PTR, 1995.

CHAPTER 6

Basics of Digital Audio

Audio information is crucial for multimedia presentations and, in a sense, is the simplest type of multimedia data. However, some important differences between audio and image information cannot be ignored. For example, while it is customary and useful to occasionally drop a video frame from a video stream, to facilitate viewing speed, we simply cannot do the same with sound information or all sense will be lost from that dimension. We introduce basic concepts for sound in multimedia in this chapter and examine the arcane details of compression of sound information in Chapters 13 and 14. The digitization of sound necessarily implies sampling and quantization of signals, so we introduce these topics here.

We begin with a discussion of just what makes up sound information, then we go on to examine the use of MIDI as an enabling technology to capture, store, and play back digital audio. We go on to look at some details of audio quantization, for transmission and give some introductory information on how digital audio is dealt with for storage or transmission. This entails a first discussion of how subtraction of signals from predicted values yields numbers that are close to zero, and hence easier to deal with.

6.1 DIGITIZATION OF SOUND

6.1.1 What Is Sound?

Sound is a wave phenomenon like light, but it is macroscopic and involves molecules of air being compressed and expanded under the action of some physical device. For example, a speaker in an audio system vibrates back and forth and produces a longitudinal pressure wave that we perceive as sound. (As an example, we get a longitudinal wave by vibrating a Slinky along its length; in contrast, we get a transverse wave by waving the Slinky back and forth perpendicular to its length.)

Without air there is no sound — for example, in space. Since sound is a pressure wave, it takes on continuous values, as opposed to digitized ones with a finite range. Nevertheless, if we wish to use a digital version of sound waves, we must form digitized representations of audio information.

Even though such pressure waves are longitudinal, they still have ordinary wave properties and behaviors, such as reflection (bouncing), refraction (change of angle when entering a medium with a different density), and diffraction (bending around an obstacle). This makes the design of "surround sound" possible.

Since sound consists of measurable pressures at any 3D point, we can detect it by measuring the pressure level at a location, using a transducer to convert pressure to voltage levels.

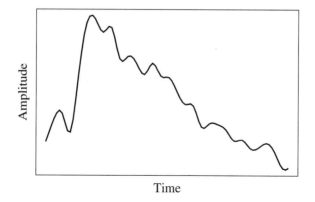

FIGURE 6.1: An analog signal: continuous measurement of pressure wave.

6.1.2 Digitization

Figure 6.1 shows the one-dimensional nature of sound. Values change over time in *ampli-tude*: the pressure increases or decreases with time [1]. The amplitude value is a continuous quantity. Since we are interested in working with such data in computer storage, we must *digitize* the *analog signals* (i.e., continuous-valued voltages) produced by microphones. For image data, we must likewise digitize the time-dependent analog signals produced by typical videocameras. Digitization means conversion to a stream of numbers — preferably *integers* for efficiency.

Since the graph in Figure 6.1 is two-dimensional, to fully digitize the signal shown we have to *sample* in each dimension — in time and in amplitude. Sampling means measur-ing the quantity we are interested in, usually at evenly spaced intervals. The first kind of sampling — using measurements only at evenly spaced time intervals — is simply called *sampling* (surprisingly), and the rate at which it is performed is called the *sampling fre-quency*. Figure 6.2(a) shows this type of digitization.

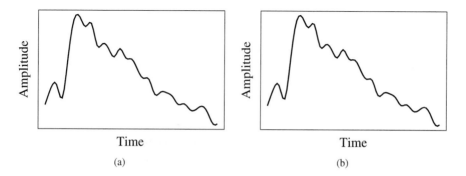

FIGURE 6.2: Sampling and quantization: (a) sampling the analog signal in the time dimen-sion; (b) quantization is sampling the analog signal in the amplitude dimension.

For audio, typical sampling rates are from 8 kHz (8,000 samples per second) to 48 kHz. The human ear can hear from about 20 Hz (a very deep rumble) to as much as 20 kHz; above this level, we enter the range of ultrasound. The human voice can reach approximately 4 kHz and we need to bound our sampling rate from below by at least double this frequency (see the discussion of the Nyquist sampling rate, below). Thus we arrive at the useful range about 8 to 40 or so kHz.

Sampling in the amplitude or voltage dimension is called *quantization*, shown in Figure 6.2(b). While we have discussed only uniform sampling, with equally spaced sampling intervals, nonuniform sampling is possible. This is not used for sampling in time but is used for quantization (see the μ-law rule, below). Typical uniform quantization rates are 8-bit and 16-bit; 8-bit quantization divides the vertical axis into 256 levels, and 16-bit divides it into 65,536 levels.

To decide how to digitize audio data, we need to answer the following questions:

1. What is the sampling rate?
2. How finely is the data to be quantized, and is the quantization uniform?
3. How is audio data formatted (i.e., what is the file format)?

6.1.3   Nyquist Theorem

Signals can be decomposed into a sum of sinusoids, if we are willing to use enough sinusoids. Figure 6.3 shows how weighted sinusoids can build up quite a complex signal. Whereas frequency is an absolute measure, pitch is a perceptual, subjective quality of sound — generally, pitch is relative. Pitch and frequency are linked by setting the note A above middle C to exactly 440 Hz. An *octave* above that note corresponds to doubling the frequency and takes us to another A note. Thus, with the middle A on a piano ("A4" or "A440") set to 440 Hz, the next A up is 880 Hz, one octave above.

Here, we define *harmonics* as any series of musical tones whose frequencies are integral multiples of the frequency of a fundamental tone. Figure 6.3 shows the appearance of these harmonics.

Now, if we allow noninteger multiples of the base frequency, we allow non-A notes and have a complex resulting sound. Nevertheless, each sound is just made from sinusoids. Figure 6.4(a) shows a single sinusoid: it is a single, pure, frequency (only electronic instruments can create such boring sounds).

Now if the sampling rate just equals the actual frequency, we can see from Figure 6.4(b) that a false signal is detected: it is simply a constant, with zero frequency. If, on the other hand, we sample at 1.5 times the frequency, Figure 6.4(c) shows that we obtain an incorrect (*alias*) frequency that is lower than the correct one — it is half the correct one (the wavelength, from peak to peak, is double that of the actual signal). In computer graphics, much effort is aimed at masking such alias effects by various methods of antialiasing. An alias is any artifact that does not belong to the original signal. Thus, for correct sampling we must use a sampling rate equal to at least twice the maximum frequency content in the signal. This is called the *Nyquist rate*.

The Nyquist Theorem is named after Harry Nyquist, a famous mathematician who worked at Bell Labs. More generally, if a signal is *band-limited* — that is, if it has a lower limit f_1

Fundamental
frequency

$+ 0.5 \times$
$2 \times$ fundamental

$+ 0.33 \times$
$3 \times$ fundamental

$+ 0.25 \times$
$4 \times$ fundamental

$+ 0.5 \times$
$5 \times$ fundamental

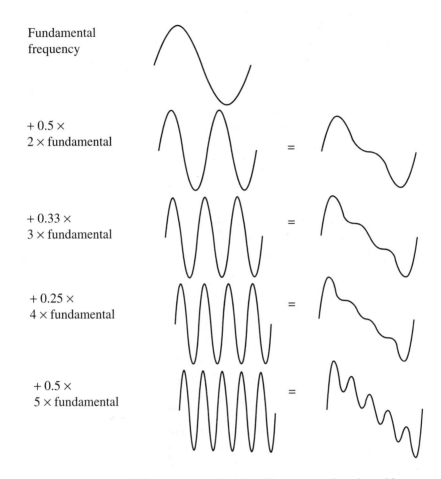

FIGURE 6.3: Building up a complex signal by superposing sinusoids.

and an upper limit f_2 of frequency components in the signal — then we need a sampling rate of at least $2(f_2 - f_1)$.

Suppose we have a *fixed* sampling rate. Since it would be impossible to recover frequencies higher than half the sampling rate in any event, most systems have an *antialiasing filter* that restricts the frequency content of the sampler's input to a range at or below half the sampling frequency. Confusingly, the frequency equal to half the Nyquist rate is called the *Nyquist frequency*. Then for our fixed sampling rate, the Nyquist frequency is half the sampling rate. The highest possible signal frequency component has frequency equal to that of the sampling itself.

Note that the true frequency and its alias are located symmetrically on the frequency axis with respect to the Nyquist frequency pertaining to the sampling rate used. For this reason, the Nyquist frequency associated with the sampling frequency is often called the "folding" frequency. That is to say, if the sampling frequency is less than twice the true frequency, and is greater than the true frequency, then the alias frequency equals the sampling frequency

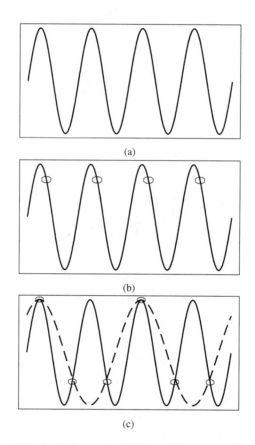

FIGURE 6.4: Aliasing: (a) a single frequency; (b) sampling at exactly the frequency produces a constant; (c) sampling at 1.5 times per cycle produces an *alias* frequency that is perceived.

minus the true frequency. For example, if the true frequency is 5.5 kHz and the sampling frequency is 8 kHz, then the alias frequency is 2.5 kHz:

$$f_{alias} = f_{sampling} - f_{true}, \quad \text{for} \quad f_{true} < f_{sampling} < 2 \times f_{true}. \tag{6.1}$$

As well, a frequency at double any frequency could also fit sample points. In fact, adding any positive or negative multiple of the sampling frequency to the true frequency always gives another possible alias frequency, in that such an alias gives the same set of samples when sampled at the sampling frequency.

So, if again the sampling frequency is less than twice the true frequency and is less than the true frequency, then the alias frequency equals n times the sampling frequency minus the true frequency, where the n is the lowest integer that makes n times the sampling frequency larger than the true frequency. For example, when the true frequency is between 1.0 and 1.5 times the sampling frequency, the alias frequency equals the true frequency minus the sampling frequency.

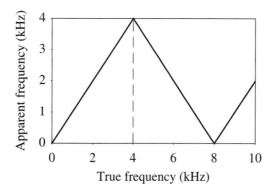

FIGURE 6.5: Folding of sinusoid frequency sampled at 8,000 Hz. The folding frequency, shown dashed, is 4,000 Hz.

In general, the apparent frequency of a sinusoid is the lowest frequency of a sinusoid that has exactly the same samples as the input sinusoid. Figure 6.5 shows the relationship of the apparent frequency to the input (true) frequency.

6.1.4 Signal-to-Noise Ratio (SNR)

In any analog system, random fluctuations produce *noise* added to the signal, and the measured voltage is thus incorrect. The ratio of the power of the correct signal to the noise is called the *signal-to-noise ratio* (*SNR*). Therefore, the SNR is a measure of the quality of the signal.

The SNR is usually measured in *decibels* (*dB*), where 1 dB is a tenth of a *bel*. The SNR value, in units of dB, is defined in terms of base-10 logarithms of squared voltages:

$$SNR = 10 \log_{10} \frac{V_{signal}^2}{V_{noise}^2} = 20 \log_{10} \frac{V_{signal}}{V_{noise}} \tag{6.2}$$

The power in a signal is proportional to the square of the voltage. For example, if the signal voltage V_{signal} is 10 times the noise, the SNR is $20 \times \log_{10}(10) = 20$ dB.

In terms of power, if the squeaking we hear from ten violins playing is ten times the squeaking we hear from one violin playing, then the ratio of power is given in terms of decibels as 10 dB, or, in other words, 1 Bel. Notice that decibels are always defined in terms of a ratio. The term "decibels" as applied to sounds in our environment usually is in comparison to a just-audible sound with frequency 1 kHz. The levels of sound we hear around us are described in terms of decibels, as a ratio to the quietest sound we are capable of hearing. Table 6.1 shows approximate levels for these sounds.

6.1.5 Signal-to-Quantization-Noise Ratio (SQNR)

For digital signals, we must take into account the fact that only quantized values are stored. For a digital audio signal, the precision of each sample is determined by the number of bits per sample, typically 8 or 16.

TABLE 6.1: Magnitudes of common sounds, in decibels

Threshold of hearing	0
Rustle of leaves	10
Very quiet room	20
Average room	40
Conversation	60
Busy street	70
Loud radio	80
Train through station	90
Riveter	100
Threshold of discomfort	120
Threshold of pain	140
Damage to eardrum	160

Aside from any noise that may have been present in the original analog signal, additional error results from quantization. That is, if voltages are in the range of 0 to 1 but we have only 8 bits in which to store values, we effectively force all continuous values of voltage into only 256 different values. Inevitably, this introduces a roundoff error. Although it is not really "noise," it is called *quantization noise* (or *quantization error*). The association with the concept of noise is that such errors will essentially occur randomly from sample to sample.

The quality of the quantization is characterized by the *signal-to-quantization-noise ratio (SQNR)*. Quantization noise is defined as the difference between the value of the analog signal, for the particular sampling time, and the nearest quantization interval value. At most, this error can be as much as half of the interval.

For a quantization accuracy of N bits per sample, the range of the digital signal is -2^{N-1} to $2^{N-1} - 1$. Thus, if the actual analog signal is in the range from $-V_{max}$ to $+V_{max}$, each quantization level represents a voltage of $2V_{max}/2^N$, or $V_{max}/2^{N-1}$. SQNR can be simply expressed in terms of the peak signal, which is mapped to the level V_{signal} of about 2^{N-1}, and the SQNR has as denominator the maximum V_{quan_noise} of 1/2. The ratio of the two is a simple definition of the SQNR:[1]

$$
\begin{aligned}
SQNR &= 20\log_{10}\frac{V_{signal}}{V_{quan\_noise}} = 20\log_{10}\frac{2^{N-1}}{\frac{1}{2}} \\
&= 20 \times N \times \log 2 = 6.02N \, (\text{dB})
\end{aligned}
\tag{6.3}
$$

In other words, each bit adds about 6 dB of resolution, so 16 bits provide a maximum SQNR of 96 dB.

---

[1]This ratio is actually the *peak* signal-to-quantization-noise ratio, or PSQNR.

We have examined the worst case. If, on the other hand, we assume that the input signal is sinusoidal, that quantization error is statistically independent, and that its magnitude is uniformly distributed between 0 and half the interval, we can show ([2], p. 37) that the expression for the SQNR becomes

$$SQNR = 6.02N + 1.76(dB) \tag{6.4}$$

Since larger is better, this shows that a more realistic approximation gives a better characterization number for the quality of a system.

Typical digital audio sample precision is either 8 bits per sample, equivalent to about telephone quality, or 16 bits, for CD quality. In fact, 12 bits or so would likely do fine for adequate sound reproduction.

6.1.6   Linear and Nonlinear Quantization

We mentioned above that samples are typically stored as uniformly quantized values. This is called *linear format*. However, with a limited number of bits available, it may be more sensible to try to take into account the properties of human perception and set up nonuniform quantization levels that pay more attention to the frequency range over which humans hear best.

Remember that here we are quantizing magnitude, or amplitude — how loud the signal is. In Chapter 4, we discussed an interesting feature of many human perception subsystems (as it were) — Weber's Law — which states that the more there is, proportionately more must be added to discern a difference. Stated formally, Weber's Law says that equally perceived differences have values proportional to absolute levels:

$$\Delta\text{Response} \propto \Delta\text{Stimulus}/\text{Stimulus} \tag{6.5}$$

This means that, for example, if we can feel an increase in weight from 10 to 11 pounds, then if instead we start at 20 pounds, it would take 22 pounds for us to feel an increase in weight.

Inserting a constant of proportionality k, we have a differential equation that states

$$dr = k(1/s)\,ds \tag{6.6}$$

with response r and stimulus s. Integrating, we arrive at a solution

$$r = k \ln s + C \tag{6.7}$$

with constant of integration C. Stated differently, the solution is

$$r = k \ln(s/s_0) \tag{6.8}$$

where s_0 is the lowest level of stimulus that causes a response ($r = 0$ when $s = s_0$).

Thus, nonuniform quantization schemes that take advantage of this perceptual characteristic make use of logarithms. The idea is that in a log plot derived from Equation (6.8), if we simply take uniform steps along the s axis, we are not mirroring the nonlinear response along the r axis.

Instead, we would like to take uniform steps along the r axis. Thus, nonlinear quantization works by first transforming an analog signal from the raw s space into the theoretical r space, then uniformly quantizing the resulting values. The result is that for steps near the low end of the signal, quantization steps are effectively more concentrated on the s axis, whereas for large values of s, one quantization step in r encompasses a wide range of s values.

Such a law for audio is called μ-*law* encoding, or *u-law*, since it's easier to write. A very similar rule, called *A-law*, is used in telephony in Europe.

The equations for these similar encodings are as follows:

μ-law:

$$r = \frac{\text{sgn}(s)}{\ln(1 + \mu)} \ln \left\{ 1 + \mu \left| \frac{s}{s_p} \right| \right\}, \qquad \left| \frac{s}{s_p} \right| \leq 1 \tag{6.9}$$

A-law:

$$r = \begin{cases} \frac{A}{1+\ln A} \left(\frac{s}{s_p} \right), & \left| \frac{s}{s_p} \right| \leq \frac{1}{A} \\[3mm] \frac{\text{sgn}(s)}{1+\ln A} \left[1 + \ln A \left| \frac{s}{s_p} \right| \right], & \frac{1}{A} \leq \left| \frac{s}{s_p} \right| \leq 1 \end{cases} \tag{6.10}$$

$$\text{where } \text{sgn}(s) = \begin{cases} 1 & \text{if } s > 0, \\ -1 & \text{otherwise} \end{cases}$$

Figure 6.6 depicts these curves. The parameter of the μ-law encoder is usually set to $\mu = 100$ or $\mu = 255$, while the parameter for the A-law encoder is usually set to $A = 87.6$.

Here, s_p is the *peak signal value* and s is the current signal value. So far, this simply means that we wish to deal with s/s_p, in the range -1 to 1.

The idea of using this type of law is that if s/s_p is first transformed to values r as above and then r is quantized uniformly before transmitting or storing the signal, most of the available bits will be used to store information where changes in the signal are most apparent to a human listener, because of our perceptual nonuniformity.

To see this, consider a small change in $|s/s_p|$ near the value 1.0, where the curve in Figure 6.6 is flattest. Clearly, the change in s has to be much larger in the flat area than near the origin to be registered by a change in the quantized r value. And it is at the quiet, low end of our hearing that we can best discern small changes in s. The μ-law transform concentrates the available information at that end.

First we carry out the μ-law transformation, then we quantize the resulting value, which is a nonlinear transform away from the input. The logarithmic steps represent low-amplitude, quiet signals with more accuracy than loud, high-amplitude ones. What this means for signals that are then encoded as a fixed number of bits is that for low-amplitude, quiet signals, the amount of noise — the error in representing the signal — is a smaller number than for high-amplitude signals. Therefore, the μ-law transform effectively makes the signal-to-noise ratio more uniform across the range of input signals.

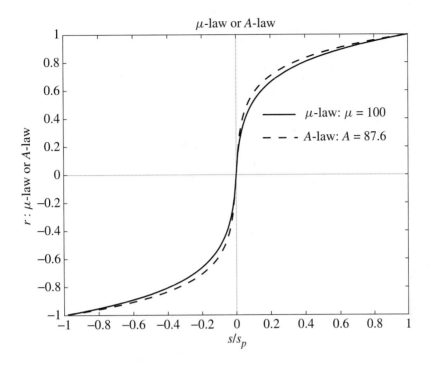

FIGURE 6.6: Nonlinear transform for audio signals.

This technique is based on human perception — a simple form of "perceptual coder". Interestingly, we have in effect also made use of the statistics of sounds we are likely to hear, which are generally in the low-volume range. In effect, we are asking for most bits to be assigned where most sounds occur — where the probability density is highest. So this type of coder is also one that is driven by statistics.

In summary, a logarithmic transform, called a "compressor" in the parlance of telephony, is applied to the analog signal before it is sampled and converted to digital (by an analog-to-digital, or AD, converter). The amount of compression increases as the amplitude of the input signal increases. The AD converter carries out a uniform quantization on the "compressed" signal. After transmission, since we need analog to hear sound, the signal is converted back, using a digital-to-analog (DA) converter, then passed through an "expander" circuit that reverses the logarithm. The overall transformation is called *companding*. Nowadays, companding can also be carried out in the digital domain.

The μ-law in audio is used to develop a nonuniform quantization rule for sound. In general, we would like to put the available bits where the most perceptual acuity (sensitivity to small changes) is. Ideally, bit allocation occurs by examining a curve of stimulus versus response for humans. Then we try to allocate bit levels to intervals for which a small change in stimulus produces a large change in response.

That is, the idea of companding reflects a less specific idea used in assigning bits to signals: put the bits where they are most needed to deliver finer resolution where the result can be perceived. This idea militates against simply using uniform quantization schemes, instead favoring nonuniform schemes for quantization. The μ-law (or A-law) for audio is an application of this idea.

6.1.7   Audio Filtering

Prior to sampling and AD conversion, the audio signal is also usually *filtered* to remove unwanted frequencies. The frequencies kept depend on the application. For speech, typically from 50 Hz to 10 kHz is retained. Other frequencies are blocked by a *band-pass filter*, also called a *band-limiting* filter, which screens out lower and higher frequencies.

An audio music signal will typically contain from about 20 Hz up to 20 kHz. (Twenty Hz is the low rumble produced by an upset elephant. Twenty kHz is about the highest squeak we can hear.) So the band-pass filter for music will screen out frequencies outside this range.

At the DA converter end, even though we have removed high frequencies that are likely just noise in any event, they reappear in the output. The reason is that because of sampling and then quantization, we have effectively replaced a perhaps smooth input signal by a series of step functions. In theory, such a discontinuous signal contains all possible frequencies. Therefore, at the decoder side, a *low-pass* filter is used after the DA circuit, making use of the same cutoff as at the high-frequency end of the coder's band-pass filter.

We have still somewhat sidestepped the issue of just how many bits are required for speech or audio application. Some of the exercises at the end of the chapter will address this issue.

Some important audio file formats include AU (for UNIX workstations), AIFF (for MAC and SGI machines), and WAV (for PCs and DEC workstations). The MP3 compressed file format is discussed in Chapter 14.

6.1.8   Audio Quality versus Data Rate

The uncompressed data rate increases as more bits are used for quantization. Stereo information, as opposed to mono, doubles the amount of bandwidth (in bits per second) needed to transmit a digital audio signal. Table 6.2 shows how audio quality is related to data rate and bandwidth.

The term *bandwidth*, in analog devices, refers to the part of the response or transfer function of a device that is approximately constant, or flat, with the x-axis being the frequency and the y-axis equal to the transfer function. *Half-power bandwidth* (*HPBW*) refers to the bandwidth between points when the power falls to half the maximum power. Since $10 \log_{10}(0.5) \approx -3.0$, the term -3 dB bandwidth is also used to refer to the HPBW.

So for analog devices, the bandwidth is expressed in frequency units, called *Hertz* (Hz), which is cycles per second. For digital devices, on the other hand, the amount of data that can be transmitted in a fixed bandwidth is usually expressed in bits per second (bps) or bytes per amount of time. For either analog or digital, the term expresses the amount of data that can be transmitted in a fixed amount of time.

TABLE 6.2: Data rate and bandwidth in sample audio applications

Quality	Sample rate (kHz)	Bits per sample	Mono/ stereo	Data rate (if uncompressed) (kB/sec)	Frequency band (Hz)
Telephone	8	8	Mono	8	200–3,400
AM radio	11.025	8	Mono	11.0	100–5,500
FM radio	22.05	16	Stereo	88.2	20–11,000
CD	44.1	16	Stereo	176.4	5–20,000
DAT	48	16	Stereo	192.0	5–20,000
DVD audio	192 (max)	24 (max)	Up to 6 channels	1,200.0 (max)	0–96,000 (max)

Telephony uses μ-law (or u-law) encoding, or A-law in Europe. The other formats use linear quantization. Using the μ-law rule shown in Equation (6.9), the dynamic range of digital telephone signals is effectively improved from 8 bits to 12 or 13.

Sometimes it is useful to remember the kinds of data rates in Table 6.2 in terms of bytes per minute. For example, the uncompressed digital audio signal for CD-quality stereo sound is 10.6 megabytes per minute — roughly 10 megabytes — per minute.

6.1.9 Synthetic Sounds

Digitized sound must still be converted to analog, for us to hear it. There are two fundamentally different approaches to handling stored sampled audio. The first is termed *FM*, for *frequency modulation*. The second is called *Wave Table*, or just *Wave*, sound.

In the first approach, a carrier sinusoid is changed by adding another term involving a second, modulating frequency. A more interesting sound is created by changing the argument of the main cosine term, putting the second cosine inside the argument itself — then we have a cosine of a cosine. A time-varying amplitude "envelope" function multiplies the whole signal, and another time-varying function multiplies the inner cosine, to account for overtones. Adding a couple of extra constants, the resulting function is complex indeed.

For example, Figure 6.7(a) shows the function $\cos(2\pi t)$, and Figure 6.7(b) is another sinusoid at twice the frequency. A cosine of a cosine is the more interesting function Figure 6.7(c), and finally, with carrier frequency 2 and modulating frequency 4, we have the much more interesting curve Figure 6.7(d). Obviously, once we consider a more complex signal, such as the following [3],

$$x(t) = A(t) \cos[\omega_c \pi t + I(t) \cos(\omega_m \pi t + \phi_m) + \phi_c] \quad (6.11)$$

we can create a most complicated signal.

This FM synthesis equation states that we make a signal using a basic carrier frequency ω_c and also use an additional, modulating frequency ω_m. In Figure 6.7(d), these values were $\omega_c = 2$ and $\omega_m = 4$. The *phase* constants ϕ_m and ϕ_c create time-shifts for a more interesting sound. The time-dependent function $A(t)$ is called the *envelope* — it specifies

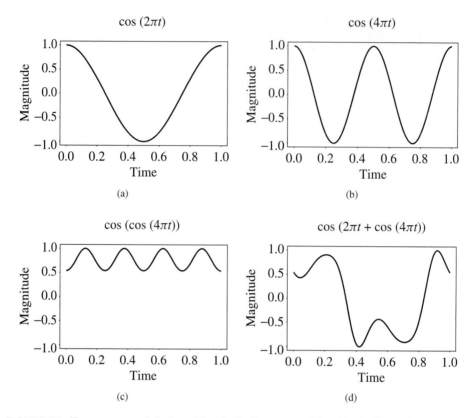

FIGURE 6.7: Frequency modulation: (a) a single frequency; (b) twice the frequency; (c) usually, FM is carried out using a sinusoid argument to a sinusoid; (d) a more complex form arises from a carrier frequency $2\pi t$ and a modulating frequency $4\pi t$ cosine inside the sinusoid.

overall loudness over time and is used to fade in and fade out the sound. A guitar string has an *attack* period, then a *decay* period, a *sustain* period, and finally a *release* period.

Finally, the time-dependent function $I(t)$ is used to produce a feeling of *harmonics* ("overtones") by changing the amount of modulation frequency heard. When $I(t)$ is small, we hear mainly low frequencies, and when $I(t)$ is larger, we hear higher frequencies as well. FM synthesis is used in low-end versions of the ubiquitous Creative Labs Sound Blaster PC sound card.

A more accurate way of generating sounds from digital signals is called *wave-table synthesis*. In this technique, digital samples are stored sounds from real instruments. Since wave tables are stored in memory on the sound card, they can be manipulated by software so that sounds can be combined, edited, and enhanced. Sound reproduction is a good deal better with wave tables than with FM synthesis. To save memory space, a variety of special techniques, such as sample looping, pitch shifting, mathematical interpolation, and polyphonic digital filtering, can be applied [4, 5].

For example, it is useful to be able to change the key — suppose a song is a bit too high for your voice. A wave table can be mathematically shifted so that it produces lower-pitched sounds. However, this kind of extrapolation can be used only just so far without sounding wrong. Wave tables often include sampling at various notes of the instrument, so that a key change need not be stretched too far. Wave table synthesis is more expensive than FM synthesis, partly because the data storage needed is much larger.

6.2   MIDI: MUSICAL INSTRUMENT DIGITAL INTERFACE

Wave-table files provide an accurate rendering of real instrument sounds but are quite large. For simple music, we might be satisfied with FM synthesis versions of audio signals that could easily be generated by a sound card. A sound card is added to a PC expansion board and is capable of manipulating and outputting sounds through speakers connected to the board, recording sound input from a microphone connected to the computer, and manipulating sound stored on a disk.

If we are willing to be satisfied with the sound card's defaults for many of the sounds we wish to include in a multimedia project, we can use a simple scripting language and hardware setup called MIDI.

6.2.1   MIDI Overview

MIDI, which dates from the early 1980s, is an acronym that stands for *Musical Instrument Digital Interface*. It forms a protocol adopted by the electronic music industry that enables computers, synthesizers, keyboards, and other musical devices to communicate with each other. A synthesizer produces synthetic music and is included on sound cards, using one of the two methods discussed above. The MIDI standard is supported by most synthesizers, so sounds created on one can be played and manipulated on another and sound reasonably close. Computers must have a special MIDI interface, but this is incorporated into most sound cards. The sound card must also have both DA and AD converters.

MIDI is a scripting language — it codes "events" that stand for the production of certain sounds. Therefore, MIDI files are generally very small. For example, a MIDI event might include values for the pitch of a single note, its duration, and its volume.

Terminology.   A *synthesizer* was, and still may be, a stand-alone sound generator that can vary pitch, loudness, and tone color. (The pitch is the musical note the instrument plays — a C, as opposed to a G, say.) It can also change additional music characteristics, such as attack and delay time. A good (musician's) synthesizer often has a microprocessor, keyboard, control panels, memory, and so on. However, inexpensive synthesizers are now included on PC sound cards. Units that generate sound are referred to as tone modules or sound modules.

A *sequencer* started off as a special hardware device for storing and editing a *sequence* of musical events, in the form of MIDI data. Now it is more often a software *music editor* on the computer.

A *MIDI keyboard* produces no sound, instead generating sequences of MIDI instructions, called MIDI messages. These are rather like assembler code and usually consist of just a few bytes. You might have 3 minutes of music, say, stored in only 3 kB. In comparison, a wave-table file (WAV) stores 1 minute of music in about 10 MB. In MIDI parlance, the keyboard is referred to as a *keyboard controller*.

MIDI Concepts.   Music is organized into *tracks* in a sequencer. Each track can be turned on or off on recording or playing back. Usually, a particular instrument is associated with a MIDI *channel*. MIDI channels are used to separate messages. There are 16 channels, numbered from 0 to 15. The channel forms the last four bits (the least significant bits) of the message. The idea is that each channel is associated with a particular instrument — for example, channel 1 is the piano, channel 10 is the drums. Nevertheless, you can switch instruments midstream, if desired, and associate another instrument with any channel.

The channel can also be used as a placeholder in a message. If the first four bits are all ones, the message is interpreted as a *system common* message.

Along with *channel messages* (which include a channel number), several other types of messages are sent, such as a general message for all instruments indicating a change in tuning or timing; these are called *system messages*. It is also possible to send a special message to an instrument's channel that allows sending many notes without a channel specified. We will describe these messages in detail later.

The way a synthetic musical instrument responds to a MIDI message is usually by simply ignoring any "play sound" message that is not for its channel. If several messages are for its channel, say several simultaneous notes being played on a piano, then the instrument responds, provided it is *multi-voice* — that is, can play more than a single note at once.

It is easy to confuse the term *voice* with the term *timbre*. The latter is MIDI terminology for just what instrument we are trying to emulate — for example, a piano as opposed to a violin. It is the quality of the sound. An instrument (or sound card) that is *multi-timbral* is capable of playing many different sounds at the same time, (e.g., piano, brass, drums)

On the other hand, the term "voice", while sometimes used by musicians to mean the same thing as timbre, is used in MIDI to mean every different timbre and pitch that the tone module can produce at the same time. Synthesizers can have many (typically 16, 32, 64, 256, etc.) voices. Each voice works independently and simultaneously to produce sounds of different timbre and pitch.

The term *polyphony* refers to the number of voices that can be produced at the same time. So a typical tone module may be able to produce "64 voices of polyphony" (64 different notes at once) and be "16-part multi-timbral" (can produce sounds like 16 different instruments at once).

How different timbres are produced digitally is by using a *patch*, which is the set of control settings that define a particular timbre. Patches are often organized into databases, called *banks*. For true aficionados, software patch editors are available.

A standard mapping specifying just what instruments (patches) will be associated with what channels has been agreed on and is called *General MIDI*. In General MIDI, there are 128 patches are associated with standard instruments, and channel 10 is reserved for percussion instruments.

For most instruments, a typical message might be Note On (meaning, e.g., a keypress), consisting of what channel, what pitch, and what *velocity* (i.e., volume). For percussion instruments, the pitch data means which kind of drum. A Note On message thus consists of a *status* byte — which channel, what pitch — followed by two data bytes. It is followed

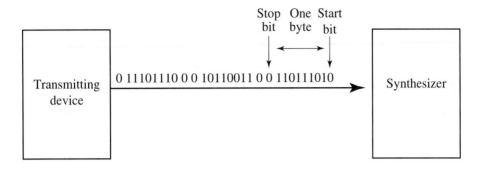

FIGURE 6.8: Stream of 10-bit bytes; for typical MIDI messages, these consist of {status byte, data byte, data byte} = {Note On, Note Number, Note Velocity}.

by a Note Off message (key release), which also has a pitch (which note to turn off) and — for consistency, one supposes — a velocity (often set to zero and ignored).

The data in a MIDI status byte is between 128 and 255; each of the data bytes is between 0 and 127. Actual MIDI bytes are 8 bit, plus a 0 start and stop bit, making them 10-bit "bytes". Figure 6.8 shows the MIDI datastream.

A MIDI device often is capable of *programmability*, which means it has filters available for changing the bass and treble response and can also change the "envelope" describing how the amplitude of a sound changes over time. Figure 6.9 shows a model of a digital instrument's response to Note On/Note Off messages.

MIDI sequencers (editors) allow you to work with standard music notation or get right into the data, if desired. MIDI files can also store wave-table data. The advantage of wave-

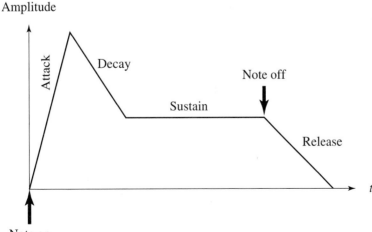

FIGURE 6.9: Stages of amplitude versus time for a music note.

table data (WAV files) is that it much more precisely stores the exact sound of an instrument. A sampler is used to sample the audio data — for example, a "drum machine" always stores wave-table data of real drums.

Sequencers employ several techniques for producing more music from what is actually available. For example, looping over (repeating) a few bars can be more or less convincing. Volume can be easily controlled over time — this is called *time-varying amplitude modulation*. More interestingly, sequencers can also accomplish time compression or expansion with no pitch change.

While it is possible to change the pitch of a sampled instrument, if the key change is large, the resulting sound begins to sound displeasing. For this reason, samplers employ *multi-sampling*. A sound is recorded using several band-pass filters, and the resulting recordings are assigned to different keyboard keys. This makes frequency shifting for a change of key more reliable, since less shift is involved for each note.

6.2.2 Hardware Aspects of MIDI

The MIDI hardware setup consists of a 31.25 kbps (kilobits per second) serial connection, with the 10-bit bytes including a 0 start and stop bit. Usually, MIDI-capable units are either input devices or output devices, not both.

Figure 6.10 shows a traditional synthesizer. The modulation wheel adds vibrato. Pitch bend alters the frequency, much like pulling a guitar string over slightly. There are often other controls, such as foots pedals, sliders, and so on.

The physical MIDI ports consist of 5-pin connectors labeled IN and OUT and a third connector, THRU. This last data channel simply copies data entering the IN channel. MIDI communication is half-duplex. MIDI IN is the connector via which the device receives all MIDI data. MIDI OUT is the connector through which the device transmits all the MIDI data it generates itself. MIDI THRU is the connector by which the device echoes the data it receives from MIDI IN (and only that — all the data generated by the device itself is sent via MIDI OUT). These ports are on the sound card or interface externally, either on a separate card on a PC expansion card slot or using a special interface to a serial or parallel port.

Keyboard

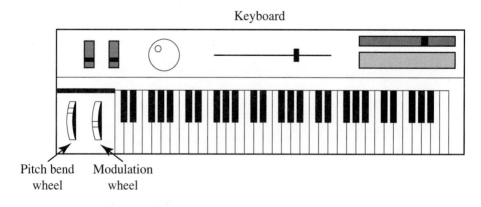

Pitch bend   Modulation
wheel   wheel

FIGURE 6.10: A MIDI synthesizer.

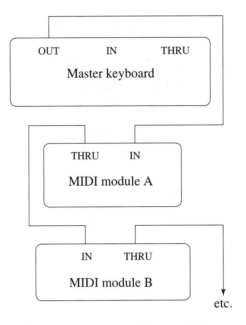

FIGURE 6.11: A typical MIDI setup.

Figure 6.11 shows a typical MIDI sequencer setup. Here, the MIDI OUT of the keyboard is connected to the MIDI IN of a synthesizer and then THRU to each of the additional sound modules. During recording, a keyboard-equipped synthesizer sends MIDI messages to a sequencer, which records them. During playback, messages are sent from the sequencer to all the sound modules and the synthesizer, which play the music.

6.2.3 Structure of MIDI Messages

MIDI messages can be classified into two types, as in Figure 6.12 — channel messages and system messages — and further classified as shown. Each type of message will be examined below.

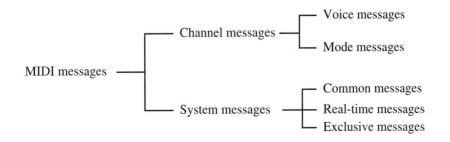

FIGURE 6.12: MIDI message taxonomy.

TABLE 6.3: MIDI voice messages

Voice message	Status byte	Data byte1	Data byte2
Note Off	&H8n	Key number	Note Off velocity
Note On	&H9n	Key number	Note On velocity
Polyphonic Key Pressure	&HAn	Key number	Amount
Control Change	&HBn	Controller number	Controller value
Program Change	&HCn	Program number	None
Channel Pressure	&HDn	Pressure value	None
Pitch Bend	&HEn	MSB	LSB

&H indicates hexadecimal, and *n* in the Status byte hex value stands for a channel number. All values are in 0 .. 127 except Controller number, which is in 0 .. 120.

Channel Messages.   A channel message can have up to 3 bytes; the first is the status byte (the opcode, as it were), and has its most significant bit set to 1. The four low-order bits identify which of the 16 possible channels this message belongs to, with the three remaining bits holding the message. For a data byte, the most significant bit is set to zero.

Voice Messages.   This type of channel message controls a voice — that is, sends information specifying which note to play or to turn off — and encodes key pressure. Voice messages are also used to specify controller effects, such as sustain, vibrato, tremolo, and the pitch wheel. Table 6.3 lists these operations.

For *Note On* and *Note Off* messages, the *velocity* is how quickly the key is played. Typically, a synthesizer responds to a higher velocity by making the note louder or brighter. Note On makes a note occur, and the synthesizer also attempts to make the note sound like the real instrument while the note is playing. *Pressure* messages can be used to alter the sound of notes while they are playing. The *Channel Pressure* message is a force measure for the keys on a specific channel (instrument) and has an identical effect on all notes playing on that channel. The other pressure message, *Polyphonic Key Pressure* (also called *Key Pressure*), specifies how much volume keys played together are to have and can be different for each note in a chord. Pressure is also called *aftertouch*.

The Control Change instruction sets various controllers (faders, vibrato, etc.). Each manufacturer may make use of different controller numbers for different tasks. However, controller 1 is likely the modulation wheel (for vibrato).

For example, a Note On message is followed by two bytes, one to identify the note and one to specify the velocity. Therefore, to play note number 80 with maximum velocity on channel 13, the MIDI device would send the following three hex byte values: &H9C &H50 &H7F. (A hexadecimal number has a range 0 .. 15. Since it is used to denote channels 1 to 16, "&HC" refers to channel 13). Notes are numbered such that middle C has number 60.

To play two notes simultaneously (effectively), first we would send a Program Change message for each of two channels. Recall that Program Change means to load a particular

TABLE 6.4: MIDI mode messages

1st data byte	Description	Meaning of 2nd data byte
&H79	Reset all controllers	None; set to 0
&H7A	Local control	0 = off; 127 = on
&H7B	All notes off	None; set to 0
&H7C	Omni mode off	None; set to 0
&H7D	Omni mode on	None; set to 0
&H7E	Mono mode on (Poly mode off)	Controller number
&H7F	Poly mode on (Mono mode off)	None; set to 0

patch for that channel. So far, we have attached two timbres to two different channels. Then sending two Note On messages (in serial) would turn on both channels. Alternatively, we could also send a Note On message for a particular channel and then another Note On message, with another pitch, before sending the Note Off message for the first note. Then we would be playing two notes effectively at the same time on the same instrument.

Polyphonic Pressure refers to how much force simultaneous notes have on several instruments. Channel Pressure refers to how much force a single note has on one instrument.

Channel Mode Messages.   Channel mode messages form a special case of the Control Change message, and therefore all mode messages have opcode B (so the message is "&HBn," or 1011nnnn). However, a Channel Mode message has its first data byte in 121 through 127 (&H79–7F).

Channel mode messages determine how an instrument processes MIDI voice messages. Some examples include respond to all messages, respond just to the correct channel, don't respond at all, or go over to local control of the instrument.

Recall that the status byte is "&HBn," where n is the channel. The data bytes have meanings as shown in Table 6.4. *Local Control Off* means that the keyboard should be disconnected from the synthesizer (and another, external, device will be used to control the sound). *All Notes Off* is a handy command, especially if, as sometimes happens, a bug arises such that a note is left playing inadvertently. *Omni* means that devices respond to messages from all channels. The usual mode is OMNI OFF — pay attention to your own messages only, and do not respond to every message regardless of what channel it is on. *Poly* means a device will play back several notes at once if requested to do so. The usual mode is POLY ON.

In POLY OFF — monophonic mode — the argument that represents the number of monophonic channels can have a value of zero, in which case it defaults to the number of voices the receiver can play; or it may set to a specific number of channels. However, the exact meaning of the combination of OMNI ON/OFF and *Mono/Poly* depends on the specific combination, with four possibilities. Suffice it to say that the usual combination is OMNI OFF, POLY ON.

TABLE 6.5: MIDI System Common messages

System common message	Status byte	Number of data bytes
MIDI Timing Code	&HF1	1
Song Position Pointer	&HF2	2
Song Select	&HF3	1
Tune Request	&HF6	None
EOX (terminator)	&HF7	None

System Messages.   System messages have no channel number and are meant for commands that are not channel-specific, such as timing signals for synchronization, positioning information in prerecorded MIDI sequences, and detailed setup information for the destination device. Opcodes for all system messages start with "&HF." System messages are divided into three classifications, according to their use.

System Common Messages.   Table 6.5 sets out these messages, which relate to timing or positioning. Song Position is measured in beats. The messages determine what is to be played upon receipt of a "start" real-time message (see below).

System Real-Time Messages.   Table 6.6 sets out system real-time messages, which are related to synchronization.

System Exclusive Message.   The final type of system message, *System Exclusive* messages, is included so that manufacturers can extend the MIDI standard. After the initial code, they can insert a stream of any specific messages that apply to their own product. A System Exclusive message is supposed to be terminated by a terminator byte "&HF7," as specified in Table 6.5. However, the terminator is optional, and the datastream may simply be ended by sending the status byte of the next message.

TABLE 6.6: MIDI System Real-Time messages

System real-time message	Status byte
Timing Clock	&HF8
Start Sequence	&HFA
Continue Sequence	&HFB
Stop Sequence	&HFC
Active Sensing	&HFE
System Reset	&HFF

6.2.4 General MIDI

For MIDI music to sound more or less the same on every machine, we would at least like to have the same patch numbers associated with the same instruments — for example, patch 1 should always be a piano, not a flugelhorn. To this end, General MIDI [5] is a scheme for assigning instruments to patch numbers. A standard percussion map also specifies 47 percussion sounds. Where a "note" appears on a musical score determines just what percussion element is being struck. This book's web site includes both the General MIDI Instrument Path Map and the Percussion Key map.

Other requirements for General MIDI compatibility are that a MIDI device must support all 16 channels; must be multi-timbral (i.e., each channel can play a different instrument/program); must be polyphonic (i.e., each channel is able to play many voices); and must have a minimum of 24 dynamically allocated voices.

General MIDI Level2.   An extended General MIDI has recently been defined, with a standard SMF *Standard MIDI File* format defined. A nice extension is the inclusion of extra character information, such as karaoke lyrics, which can be displayed on a good sequencer.

6.2.5 MIDI-to-WAV Conversion

Some programs, such as early versions of Premiere, cannot include MIDI files — instead, they insist on WAV format files. Various shareware programs can approximate a reasonable conversion between these formats. The programs essentially consist of large lookup files that try to do a reasonable job of substituting predefined or shifted WAV output for some MIDI messages, with inconsistent success.

6.3 QUANTIZATION AND TRANSMISSION OF AUDIO

To be transmitted, sampled audio information must be digitized, and here we look at some of the details of this process. Once the information has been quantized, it can then be transmitted or stored. We go through a few examples in complete detail, which helps in understanding what is being discussed.

6.3.1 Coding of Audio

Quantization and transformation of data are collectively known as *coding* of the data. For audio, the μ-law technique for companding audio signals is usually combined with a simple algorithm that exploits the temporal redundancy present in audio signals. Differences in signals between the present and a previous time can effectively reduce the size of signal values and, most important, concentrate the histogram of pixel values (differences, now) into a much smaller range. The result of reducing the variance of values is that lossless compression methods that produce a bitstream with shorter bit lengths for more likely values, introduced in Chapter 7, fare much better and produce a greatly compressed bitstream.

In general, producing quantized sampled output for audio is called *Pulse Code Modulation*, or *PCM*. The differences version is called *DPCM* (and a crude but efficient variant is called *DM*). The adaptive version is called *ADPCM*, and variants that take into account speech properties follow from these. More complex models for audio are outlined in Chapter 13.

6.3.2 Pulse Code Modulation

PCM in General.   Audio is analog — the waves we hear travel through the air to reach our eardrums. We know that the basic techniques for creating digital signals from analog ones consist of *sampling* and *quantization*. Sampling is invariably done uniformly — we select a sampling rate and produce one value for each sampling time.

In the magnitude direction, we digitize by quantization, selecting breakpoints in magnitude and remapping any value within an interval to one representative output level. The set of interval boundaries is sometimes called *decision boundaries*, and the representative values are called *reconstruction levels*.

We say that the boundaries for quantizer input intervals that will all be mapped into the same output level form a *coder mapping*, and the representative values that are the output values from a quantizer are a *decoder mapping*. Since we quantize, we may choose to create either an accurate or less accurate representation of sound magnitude values. Finally, we may wish to *compress* the data, by assigning a bitstream that uses fewer bits for the most prevalent signal values.

Every compression scheme has three stages:

1. **Transformation.** The input data is *transformed* to a new representation that is easier or more efficient to compress. For example, in Predictive Coding, (discussed later in the chapter) we predict the next signal from previous ones and transmit the prediction error.

2. **Loss.** We may introduce *loss* of information. Quantization is the main lossy step. Here we use a limited number of reconstruction levels, fewer than in the original signal. Therefore, quantization necessitates some loss of information.

3. **Coding.** Here, we assign a *codeword* (thus forming a binary bitstream) to each output level or symbol. This could be a fixed-length code or a variable-length code, such as Huffman coding (discussed in Chapter 7).

For audio signals, we first consider PCM, the digitization method. That enables us to consider Lossless Predictive Coding as well as the DPCM scheme; these methods use *differential coding*. We also look at the adaptive version, ADPCM, which is meant to provide better compression.

Pulse Code Modulation, is a formal term for the sampling and quantization we have already been using. *Pulse* comes from an engineer's point of view that the resulting digital signals can be thought of as infinitely narrow vertical "pulses". As an example of PCM, audio samples on a CD might be sampled at a rate of 44.1 kHz, with 16 bits per sample. For stereo sound, with two channels, this amounts to a data rate of about 1,400 kbps.

PCM in Speech Compression.   Recall that in Section 6.1.6 we considered *companding*: the so-called compressor and expander stages for speech signal processing, for telephony. For this application, signals are first transformed using the μ-law (or A-law for Europe) rule into what is essentially a logarithmic scale. Only then is PCM, using uniform quantization, applied. The result is that finer increments in sound volume are used at the low-volume end of speech rather than at the high-volume end, where we can't discern small changes in any event.

Assuming a bandwidth for speech from about 50 Hz to about 10 kHz, the Nyquist rate would dictate a sampling rate of 20 kHz. Using uniform quantization without companding, the minimum sample size we could get away with would likely be about 12 bits. Hence, for mono speech transmission the bitrate would be 240 kbps. With companding, we can safely reduce the sample size to 8 bits with the same perceived level of quality and thus reduce the bitrate to 160 kbps. However, the standard approach to telephony assumes that the highest-frequency audio signal we want to reproduce is about 4 kHz. Therefore, the sampling rate is only 8 kHz, and the companded bitrate thus reduces to only 64 kbps.

We must also address two small wrinkles to get this comparatively simple form of speech compression right. First because only sounds up to 4 kHz are to be considered, all other frequency content must be noise. Therefore, we should remove this high-frequency content from the analog input signal. This is done using a band-limiting filter that blocks out high frequencies as well as very low ones. The "band" of not-removed ("passed") frequencies are what we wish to keep. This type of filter is therefore also called a band-pass filter.

Second, once we arrive at a pulse signal, such as the one in Figure 6.13(a), we must still perform digital-to-analog conversion and then construct an output analog signal. But

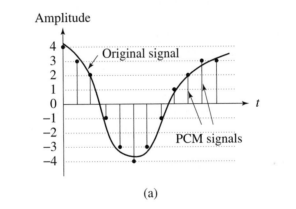

(a)

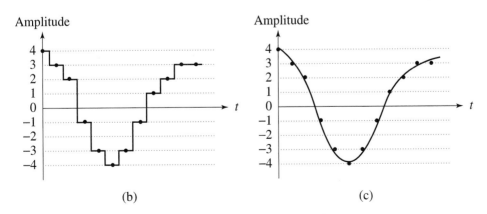

(b)   (c)

FIGURE 6.13: Pulse code modulation (PCM): (a) original analog signal and its corresponding PCM signals; (b) decoded staircase signal; (c) reconstructed signal after low-pass filtering.

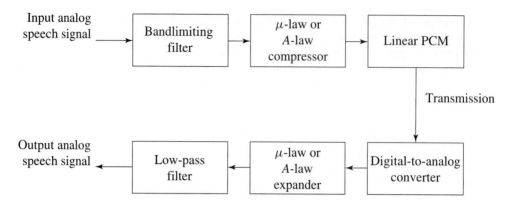

FIGURE 6.14: PCM signal encoding and decoding.

the signal we arrive at is effectively the staircase shown in Figure 6.13(b). This type of discontinuous signal contains not just frequency components due to the original signal but, because of the sharp corners, also a theoretically infinite set of higher-frequency components (from the theory of Fourier analysis, in signal processing). We know these higher frequencies are extraneous. Therefore, the output of the digital-to-analog converter is in turn passed to a *low-pass filter*, which allows only frequencies up to the original maximum to be retained. Figure 6.14 shows the complete scheme for encoding and decoding telephony signals as a schematic. As a result of the low-pass filtering, the output becomes smoothed, as Figure 6.13(c) shows. For simplicity, Figure 6.13 does not show the effect of companding.

A-law or μ-law PCM coding is used in the older International Telegraph and Telephone Consultative Committee (CCITT) standard G.711, for digital telephony. This CCITT standard is now subsumed into standards promulgated by a newer organization, the International Telecommunication Union (ITU).

6.3.3   Differential Coding of Audio

Audio is often stored not in simple PCM but in a form that exploits differences. For a start, differences will generally be smaller numbers and hence offer the possibility of using fewer bits to store.

An advantage of forming differences is that the histogram of a difference signal is usually considerably more peaked than the histogram for the original signal. For example, as an extreme case, the histogram for a linear ramp signal that has constant slope is uniform, whereas the histogram for the derivative of the signal (i.e., the differences, from sampling point to sampling point) consists of a spike at the slope value.

Generally, if a time-dependent signal has some consistency over time (*temporal redundancy*), the difference signal — subtracting the current sample from the previous one — will have a more peaked histogram, with a maximum around zero. Consequently, if we then go on to assign bitstring codewords to differences, we can assign short codes to prevalent values and long codewords to rarely occurring ones.

To begin with, consider a lossless version of this scheme. Loss arises when we quantize. If we apply no quantization, we can still have compression — via the decrease in the variance of values that occurs in differences, compared to the original signal. Chapter 7 introduces more sophisticated versions of lossless compression methods, but it helps to see a simple version here as well. With quantization, Predictive Coding becomes DPCM, a lossy method; we'll also try out that scheme.

6.3.4 Lossless Predictive Coding

Predictive coding simply means transmitting differences — we predict the next sample as being equal to the current sample and send not the sample itself but the error involved in making this assumption. That is, if we predict that the next sample equals the previous one, then the error is just the difference between previous and next. Our prediction scheme could also be more complex.

However, we do note one problem. Suppose our integer sample values are in the range $0..255$. Then differences could be as much as $-255..255$. So we have unfortunately increased our *dynamic range* (ratio of maximum to minimum) by a factor of two: we may well need more bits than we needed before to transmit some differences. Fortunately, we can use a trick to get around this problem, as we shall see.

So, basically, predictive coding consists of finding differences and transmitting them, using a PCM system such as the one introduced in Section 6.3.2. First, note that differences of integers will at least be integers. Let's formalize our statement of what we are doing by defining the integer signal as the set of values f_n. Then we *predict* values $\hat{f}_n$ as simply the previous value, and we define the error e_n as the difference between the actual and predicted signals:

$$\begin{aligned} \hat{f}_n &= f_{n-1} \\ e_n &= f_n - \hat{f}_n \end{aligned} \qquad (6.12)$$

We certainly would like our error value e_n to be as small as possible. Therefore, we would wish our prediction $\hat{f}_n$ to be as close as possible to the actual signal f_n. But for a particular sequence of signal values, some *function* of a few of the previous values, $f_{n-1}, f_{n-2}, f_{n-3}$, etc., may provide a better prediction of f_n. Typically, a linear *predictor* function is used:

$$\hat{f}_n = \sum_{k=1}^{2 \text{ to } 4} a_{n-k} f_{n-k} \qquad (6.13)$$

Such a predictor can be followed by a truncating or rounding operation to result in integer values. In fact, since now we have such coefficients a_{n-k} available, we can even change them adaptively (see Section 6.3.7 below).

The idea of forming differences is to make the histogram of sample values more peaked. For example, Figure 6.15(a) plots 1 second of sampled speech at 8 kHz, with magnitude resolution of 8 bits per sample.

A histogram of these values is centered around zero, as in Figure 6.15(b). Figure 6.15(c) shows the histogram for corresponding speech signal *differences*: difference values are much more clustered around zero than are sample values themselves. As a result, a method that

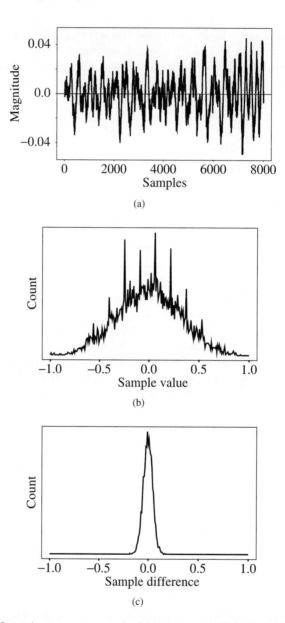

FIGURE 6.15: Differencing concentrates the histogram: (a) digital speech signal; (b) histogram of digital speech signal values; (c) histogram of digital speech signal differences.

assigns short codewords to frequently occurring symbols will assign a short code to *zero* and do rather well. Such a coding scheme will much more efficiently code sample differences than samples themselves, and a similar statement applies if we use a more sophisticated predictor than simply the previous signal value.

However, we are still left with the problem of what to do if, for some reason, a particular set of difference values does indeed consist of some exceptional large differences. A clever solution to this difficulty involves defining two new codes to add to our list of difference values, denoted SU and SD, standing for Shift-Up and Shift-Down. Some special values will be reserved for them.

Suppose samples are in the range $0..255$, and differences are in $-255..255$. Define SU and SD as shifts by 32. Then we could in fact produce codewords for a limited set of signal differences, say only the range $-15..16$. Differences (that inherently are in the range $-255..255$) lying in the limited range can be coded as is, but if we add the extra two values for SU, SD, a value outside the range $-15..16$ can be transmitted as a series of shifts, followed by a value that is indeed inside the range $-15..16$. For example, 100 is transmitted as SU, SU, SU, 4, where (the codes for) SU and for 4 are what are sent.

Lossless Predictive Coding is ... lossless! That is, the decoder produces the same signals as the original. It is helpful to consider an explicit scheme for such coding considerations, so let's do that here (we won't use the most complicated scheme, but we'll try to carry out an entire calculation). As a simple example, suppose we devise a predictor for $\hat{f}_n$ as follows:

$$
\begin{aligned}
\hat{f}_n &= \lfloor \frac{1}{2}(f_{n-1} + f_{n-2}) \rfloor \\
e_n &= f_n - \hat{f}_n
\end{aligned}
\tag{6.14}
$$

Then the error e_n (or a codeword for it) is what is actually transmitted.

Let's consider an explicit example. Suppose we wish to code the sequence f_1, f_2, f_3, f_4, $f_5 = 21, 22, 27, 25, 22$. For the purposes of the predictor, we'll invent an extra signal value f_0, equal to $f_1 = 21$, and first transmit this initial value, uncoded; after all, every coding scheme has the extra expense of some header information.

Then the first error, e_1, is zero, and subsequently

$$
\hat{f}_2 = 21, \quad e_2 = 22 - 21 = 1
$$

$$
\begin{aligned}
\hat{f}_3 &= \lfloor \frac{1}{2}(f_2 + f_1) \rfloor = \lfloor \frac{1}{2}(22 + 21) \rfloor = 21 \\
e_3 &= 27 - 21 = 6
\end{aligned}
$$

$$
\begin{aligned}
\hat{f}_4 &= \lfloor \frac{1}{2}(f_3 + f_2) \rfloor = \lfloor \frac{1}{2}(27 + 22) \rfloor = 24 \\
e_4 &= 25 - 24 = 1
\end{aligned}
$$

$$
\begin{aligned}
\hat{f}_5 &= \lfloor \frac{1}{2}(f_4 + f_3) \rfloor = \lfloor \frac{1}{2}(25 + 27) \rfloor = 26 \\
e_5 &= 22 - 26 = -4
\end{aligned}
\tag{6.15}
$$

The error does center around zero, we see, and coding (assigning bitstring codewords) will be efficient. Figure 6.16 shows a typical schematic diagram used to encapsulate this type of system. Notice that the Predictor emits the predicted value $\hat{f}_n$. What is invariably (and annoyingly) left out of such schematics is the fact that the predictor is based on f_{n-1}, f_{n-2}, $\ldots$.

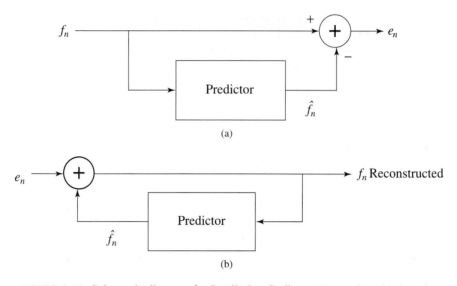

FIGURE 6.16: Schematic diagram for Predictive Coding: (a) encoder; (b) decoder.

Therefore, the predictor must involve a memory. At the least, the predictor includes a circuit for incorporating a delay in the signal, to store f_{n-1}.

6.3.5 DPCM

Differential Pulse Code Modulation is exactly the same as Predictive Coding, except that it incorporates a quantizer step. Quantization is as in PCM and can be uniform or nonuniform. One scheme for analytically determining the best set of nonuniform quantizer steps is the *Lloyd-Max* quantizer, named for Stuart Lloyd and Joel Max, which is based on a least-squares minimization of the error term.

Here we should adopt some nomenclature for signal values. We shall call the original signal f_n, the predicted signal $\hat{f}_n$, and the quantized, reconstructed signal $\tilde{f}_n$. How DPCM operates is to form the prediction, form an error e_n by subtracting the prediction from the actual signal, then quantize the error to a quantized version, $\tilde{e}_n$. The equations that describe DPCM are as follows:

$$
\begin{aligned}
\hat{f}_n &= function\_of \, (\tilde{f}_{n-1}, \, \tilde{f}_{n-2}, \, \tilde{f}_{n-3}, \dots) \\
e_n &= f_n - \hat{f}_n \\
\tilde{e}_n &= Q[e_n] \\
&\quad \text{transmit } codeword(\tilde{e}_n) \\
&\quad \text{reconstruct: } \tilde{f}_n = \hat{f}_n + \tilde{e}_n
\end{aligned}
\tag{6.16}
$$

Codewords for quantized error values $\tilde{e}_n$ are produced using entropy coding, such as Huffman coding (discussed in Chapter 7).

Notice that the predictor is always based on the reconstructed, quantized version of the signal: the reason for this is that then the encoder side is not using any information not available to the decoder side. Generally, if by mistake we made use of the *actual* signals f_n in the predictor instead of the reconstructed ones $\tilde{f}_n$, quantization error would tend to accumulate and could get worse rather than being centered on zero.

The main effect of the coder-decoder process is to produce reconstructed, quantized signal values $\tilde{f}_n = \hat{f}_n + \tilde{e}_n$. The "distortion" is the average squared error $[\sum_{n=1}^{N}(\tilde{f}_n - f_n)^2]/N$, and one often sees diagrams of distortion versus the number of bit levels used. A Lloyd-Max quantizer will do better (have less distortion) than a uniform quantizer.

For any signal, we want to choose the size of quantization steps so that they correspond to the range (the maximum and minimum) of the signal. Even using a uniform, equal-step quantization will naturally do better if we follow such a practice. For speech, we could modify quantization steps as we go, by estimating the mean and variance of a patch of signal values and shifting quantization steps accordingly, for every block of signal values. That is, starting at time i we could take a block of N values f_n and try to minimize the quantization error:

$$\min \sum_{n=i}^{i+N-1} (f_n - Q[f_n])^2 \tag{6.17}$$

Since signal *differences* are very peaked, we could model them using a Laplacian probability distribution function, which is also strongly peaked at zero [6]: it looks like $l(x) = (1/\sqrt{2\sigma^2})exp(-\sqrt{2}|x|/\sigma)$, for variance σ^2. So typically, we assign quantization steps for a quantizer with nonuniform steps by assuming that signal differences, d_n, say, are drawn from such a distribution and then choosing steps to minimize

$$\min \sum_{n=i}^{i+N-1} (d_n - Q[d_n])^2\, l(d_n) \tag{6.18}$$

This is a least-squares problem and can be solved iteratively using the Lloyd-Max quantizer.

Figure 6.17 shows a schematic diagram for the DPCM coder and decoder. As is common in such diagrams, several interesting features are more or less not indicated. First, we notice that the predictor makes use of the reconstructed, quantized signal values $\tilde{f}_n$, not actual signal values f_n — that is, the encoder simulates the decoder in the predictor path. The quantizer can be uniform or non-uniform.

The box labeled "Symbol coder" in the block diagram simply means a Huffman coder — the details of this step are set out in Chapter 7. The prediction value $\hat{f}_n$ is based on however much history the prediction scheme requires: we need to buffer previous values of $\tilde{f}$ to form the prediction. Notice that the quantization noise, $f_n - \tilde{f}_n$, is equal to the quantization effect on the error term, $e_n - \tilde{e}_n$.

It helps us explicitly understand the process of coding to look at actual numbers. Suppose we adopt a particular predictor as follows:

$$\hat{f}_n = \text{trunc}\left[\left(\tilde{f}_{n-1} + \tilde{f}_{n-2}\right)/2\right]$$

so that $e_n = f_n - \hat{f}_n$ is an integer. $\tag{6.19}$

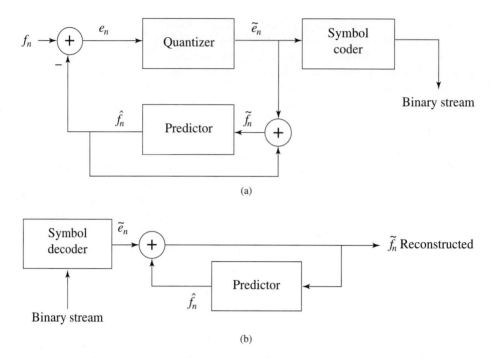

FIGURE 6.17: Schematic diagram for DPCM: (a) encoder; (b) decoder.

Let us use the particular quantization scheme

$$
\begin{aligned}
\tilde{e}_n &= Q[e_n] = 16 * \text{trunc}\left[(255 + e_n)/16\right] - 256 + 8 \\
\tilde{f}_n &= \hat{f}_n + \tilde{e}_n
\end{aligned}
\tag{6.20}
$$

First, we note that the error is in the range $-255 \, .. \, 255$ — that is, 511 levels are possible for the error term. The quantizer takes the simple course of dividing the error range into 32 patches of about 16 levels each. It also makes the representative reconstructed value for each patch equal to the midway point for each group of 16 levels.

Table 6.7 gives output values for any of the input codes: 4-bit codes are mapped to 32 reconstruction levels in a staircase fashion. (Notice that the final range includes only 15 levels, not 16.)

As an example stream of signal values, consider the set of values

f_1	f_2	f_3	f_4	f_5
130	150	140	200	230

We prepend extra values $f = 130$ in the datastream that replicate the first value, f_1, and initialize with quantized error $\tilde{e}_1 \equiv 0$, so that we ensure the first reconstructed value is

TABLE 6.7: DPCM quantizer reconstruction levels

e_n in range	Quantized to value
$-255 .. -240$	-248
$-239 .. -224$	-232
$\vdots$	$\vdots$
$-31 .. -16$	-24
$-15 .. 0$	-8
$1 .. 16$	8
$17 .. 32$	24
$\vdots$	$\vdots$
$225 .. 240$	232
$241 .. 255$	248

exact: $\tilde{f}_1 = 130$. Then subsequent values calculated are as follows (with prepended values in a box):

$$\hat{f} = \boxed{130}, \quad 130, \quad 142, \quad 144, \quad 167$$
$$e = \boxed{0}, \quad 20, \quad -2, \quad 56, \quad 63$$
$$\tilde{e} = \boxed{0}, \quad 24, \quad -8, \quad 56, \quad 56$$
$$\tilde{f} = \boxed{130}, \quad 154, \quad 134, \quad 200, \quad 223$$

On the decoder side, we again assume extra values $\tilde{f}$ equal to the correct value $\tilde{f}_1$, so that the first reconstructed value $\tilde{f}_1$ is correct. What is received is $\tilde{e}_n$, and the reconstructed $\tilde{f}_n$ is identical to the one on the encoder side, provided we use exactly the same prediction rule.

6.3.6 DM

DM stands for *Delta Modulation*, a much-simplified version of DPCM often used as a quick analog-to-digital converter. We include this scheme here for completeness.

Uniform-Delta DM.   The idea in DM is to use only a *single* quantized error value, either positive or negative. Such a 1-bit coder thus produces coded output that follows the original signal in a staircase fashion. The relevant set of equations is as follows:

$$\hat{f}_n = \tilde{f}_{n-1}$$
$$e_n = f_n - \hat{f}_n = f_n - \tilde{f}_{n-1}$$
$$\tilde{e}_n = \begin{cases} +k & \text{if } e_n > 0, \text{ where } k \text{ is a constant} \\ -k & otherwise, \end{cases} \quad (6.21)$$
$$\tilde{f}_n = \hat{f}_n + \tilde{e}_n$$

Note that the prediction simply involves a delay.

Again, let's consider actual numbers. Suppose signal values are as follows:

$$
\begin{array}{cccc}
f_1 & f_2 & f_3 & f_4 \\
10 & 11 & 13 & 15
\end{array}
$$

We also define an exact reconstructed value $\tilde{f}_1 = f_1 = 10$.

Suppose we use a step value $k = 4$. Then we arrive at the following values:

$$
\begin{array}{llll}
\hat{f}_2 = 10, & e_2 = 11 - 10 = 1, & \tilde{e}_2 = 4, & \tilde{f}_2 = 10 + 4 = 14 \\
\hat{f}_3 = 14, & e_3 = 13 - 14 = -1, & \tilde{e}_3 = -4, & \tilde{f}_3 = 14 - 4 = 10 \\
\hat{f}_4 = 10, & e_4 = 15 - 10 = 5, & \tilde{e}_4 = 4, & \tilde{f}_4 = 10 + 4 = 14
\end{array}
$$

We see that the reconstructed set of values 10, 14, 10, 14 never strays far from the correct set 10, 11, 13, 15.

Nevertheless, it is not difficult to discover that DM copes well with more or less constant signals, but not as well with rapidly changing signals. One approach to mitigating this problem is to simply increase the sampling, perhaps to many times the Nyquist rate. This scheme can work well and makes DM a very simple yet effective analog-to-digital converter.

Adaptive DM. However, if the slope of the actual signal curve is high, the staircase approximation cannot keep up. A straightforward approach to dealing with a steep curve is to simply change the step size k *adaptively* — that is, in response to the signal's current properties.

6.3.7 ADPCM

Adaptive DPCM takes the idea of adapting the coder to suit the input much further. Basically, two pieces make up a DPCM coder: the quantizer and the predictor. Above, in Adaptive DM, we adapted the quantizer step size to suit the input. In DPCM, we can *adaptively modify the quantizer*, by changing the step size as well as decision boundaries in a nonuniform quantizer.

We can carry this out in two ways: using the properties of the input signal (called *forward adaptive quantization*), or the properties of the quantized output. For if quantized errors become too large, we should change the nonuniform Lloyd-Max quantizer (this is called *backward adaptive quantization*).

We can also *adapt the predictor*, again using forward or backward adaptation. Generally, making the predictor coefficients adaptive is called *Adaptive Predictive Coding* (APC). It is interesting to see how this is done. Recall that the predictor is usually taken to be a linear function of previously reconstructed quantized values, $\tilde{f}_n$. The number of previous values used is called the *order* of the predictor. For example, if we use M previous values, we need M coefficients a_i, $i = 1..M$ in a predictor

$$
\hat{f}_n = \sum_{i=1}^{M} a_i \tilde{f}_{n-i} \tag{6.22}
$$

However we can get into a difficult situation if we try to *change* the prediction coefficients that multiply previous quantized values, because that makes a complicated set of equations to solve for these coefficients. Suppose we decide to use a least-squares approach to solving a minimization, trying to find the best values of the a_i:

$$\min \sum_{n=1}^{N} (f_n - \hat{f}_n)^2 \tag{6.23}$$

where here we would sum over a large number of samples f_n for the current patch of speech, say. But because $\hat{f}_n$ depends on the quantization, we have a difficult problem to solve. Also, we should really be changing the fineness of the quantization at the same time, to suit the signal's changing nature; this makes things problematical.

Instead, we usually resort to solving the simpler problem that results from using not $\tilde{f}_n$ in the prediction but simply the signal f_n itself. This is indeed simply solved, since, explicitly writing in terms of the coefficients a_i, we wish to solve

$$\min \sum_{n=1}^{N} \left(f_n - \sum_{i=1}^{M} a_i f_{n-i} \right)^2 \tag{6.24}$$

Differentiation with respect to each of the a_i and setting to zero produces a linear system of M equations that is easy to solve. (The set of equations is called the Wiener-Hopf equations.)

Thus we indeed find a simple way to adaptively change the predictor as we go. For speech signals, it is common to consider *blocks* of signal values, just as for image coding, and adaptively change the predictor, quantizer, or both. If we sample at 8 kHz, a common block size is 128 samples — 16 msec of speech. Figure 6.18 shows a schematic diagram for the ADPCM coder and decoder [7].

6.4 FURTHER EXPLORATION

Fascinating work is ongoing in the use of audio to help sight-impaired persons. One technique is presenting HTML structure by means of audio cues, using creative thinking as in the papers [8, 9, 10].

An excellent resource for digitization and SNR, SQNR, and so on is the book by Pohlmann [2]. The audio quantization μ-law is described in the Chapter 6 web page in the *Further Exploration* section of the text web site. Other useful links included are

- An excellent discussion of the use of FM to create synthetic sound

- An extensive list of audio file formats

- A good description of various CD audio file formats, which are somewhat different. The main music format is called *red book audio*.

- A General MIDI Instrument Patch Map, along with a General MIDI Percussion Key Map

- A link to a good tutorial on MIDI and wave-table music synthesis

- A link to a Java program for decoding MIDI streams

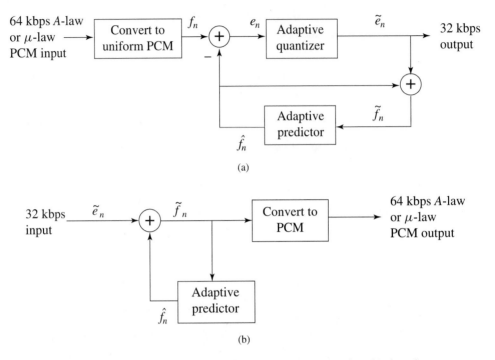

FIGURE 6.18: Schematic diagram for: (a) ADPCM encoder; (b) decoder.

- A good multimedia/sound page, including a source for locating Internet sound/music materials

- A performing-arts-oriented site that is an excellent all-around resource on sound generally, including a great deal of information on definitions of terms, signal processing, and sound perception.

6.5 EXERCISES

1. My old SoundBlaster card is an 8-bit card.

    (a) What is it 8 bits of?
    (b) What is the best SQNR it can achieve?

2. If a set of ear protectors reduces the noise level by 30 dB, how much do they reduce the intensity (the power)?

3. A loss of audio output at both ends of the audible frequency range is inevitable, due to the frequency response function of an audio amplifier and the medium (e.g., tape).

    (a) If the output was 1 volt for frequencies at midrange, what is the output voltage after a loss of -3 dB at 18 kHz?

(b) To compensate for the loss, a listener can adjust the gain (and hence the output) on an equalizer at different frequencies. If the loss remains -3 dB and a gain through the equalizer is 6 dB at 18 kHz, what is the output voltage now? *Hint:* Assume $\log_{10} 2 = 0.3$.

4. Suppose the sampling frequency is 1.5 times the true frequency. What is the alias frequency?

5. In a crowded room, we can still pick out and understand a nearby speaker's voice, notwithstanding the fact that general noise levels may be high. This is known as the *cocktail-party effect*. The way it operates is that our hearing can localize a sound source by taking advantage of the difference in phase between the two signals entering our left and right ears (*binaural auditory perception*). In mono, we could not hear our neighbor's conversation well if the noise level were at all high. State how you think a karaoke machine works. *Hint:* The mix for commercial music recordings is such that the "pan" parameter is different going to the left and right channels for each instrument. That is, for an instrument, either the left or right channel is emphasized. How would the singer's track timing have to be recorded to make it easy to subtract the sound of the singer (which is typically done)?

6. The *dynamic range* of a signal V is the ratio of the maximum to the minimum absolute value, expressed in decibels. The dynamic range expected in a signal is to some extent an expression of the signal quality. It also dictates the number of bits per sample needed to reduce the quantization noise to an acceptable level. For example, we may want to reduce the noise to at least an order of magnitude below V_{min}. Suppose the dynamic range for a signal is 60 dB. Can we use 10 bits for this signal? Can we use 16 bits?

7. Suppose the dynamic range of speech in telephony implies a ratio V_{max}/V_{min} of about 256. Using uniform quantization, how many bits should we use to encode speech to make the quantization noise at least an order of magnitude less than the smallest detectable telephonic sound?

8. *Perceptual nonuniformity* is a general term for describing the nonlinearity of human perception. That is, when a certain parameter of an audio signal varies, humans do not necessarily perceive the difference in proportion to the amount of change.

(a) Briefly describe at least two types of perceptual nonuniformities in human auditory perception.

(b) Which one of them does A-law (or μ-law) attempt to approximate? Why could it improve quantization?

9. Draw a diagram showing a sinusoid at 5.5 kHz and sampling at 8 kHz (show eight intervals between samples in your plot). Draw the alias at 2.5 kHz and show that in the eight sample intervals, exactly 5.5 cycles of the true signal fit into 2.5 cycles of the alias signal.

10. Suppose a signal contains tones at 1, 10, and 21 kHz and is sampled at the rate 12 kHz (and then processed with an antialiasing filter limiting output to 6 kHz). What tones are included in the output? *Hint:* Most of the output consists of aliasing.

11. (a) Can a single MIDI message produce more than one note sounding?

(b) Is it possible for more than one note to sound at once on a particular instrument? If so, how is it done in MIDI?

(c) Is the Program Change MIDI message a Channel Message? What does this message accomplish? Based on the Program Change message, how many different instruments are there in General MIDI? Why?

(d) In general, what are the two main kinds of MIDI messages? In terms of data, what is the main difference between the two types of messages? Within those two categories, list the different subtypes.

12. (a) Give an example (in English, not hex) of a MIDI voice message.

(b) Describe the parts of the "assembler" statement for the message.

(c) What does a Program Change message do? Suppose Program change is hex "&HC1." What does the instruction "&HC103" do?

13. In PCM, what is the *delay*, assuming 8 kHz sampling? Generally, delay is the time penalty associated with any algorithm due to sampling, processing, and analysis.

14. (a) Suppose we use a predictor as follows:

$$\hat{f}_n = \text{trunc}\left[\frac{1}{2}(\tilde{f}_{n-1} + \tilde{f}_{n-2})\right]$$

$$e_n = f_n - \hat{f}_n \tag{6.25}$$

Also, suppose we adopt the quantizer Equation (6.20). If the input signal has values as follows:

20 38 56 74 92 110 128 146 164 182 200 218 236 254

show that the output from a DPCM coder (without entropy coding) is as follows:

20 44 56 74 89 105 121 153 161 181 195 212 243 251

Figure 6.19(a) shows how the quantized reconstructed signal tracks the input signal. As a programming project, write a small piece of code to verify your results.

(b) Suppose by mistake on the coder side we inadvertently use the predictor for *lossless coding*, Equation (6.14), using original values f_n instead of quantized ones, $\tilde{f}_n$. Show that on the decoder side we end up with reconstructed signal values as follows:

20 44 56 74 89 105 121 137 153 169 185 201 217 233

so that the error gets progressively worse.

Figure 6.19(b) shows how this appears: the reconstructed signal gets progressively worse. Modify your code from above to verify this statement.

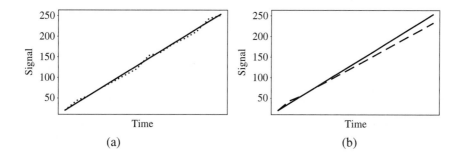

FIGURE 6.19: (a) DPCM reconstructed signal (dotted line) tracks the input signal (solid line); (b) DPCM reconstructed signal (dashed line) steers farther and farther from the input signal (solid line).

6.6 REFERENCES

1 B. Truax, *Handbook for Acoustic Ecology*, 2nd ed., Burnaby, BC, Canada: Cambridge Street Publishing, 1999.

2 K.C. Pohlmann, *Principles of Digital Audio*, 4th ed., New York: McGraw-Hill, 2000.

3 J.H. McClellan, R.W. Schafer, and M.A. Yoder, *DSP First: A Multimedia Approach*, Upper Saddle River, NJ: Prentice-Hall PTR, 1998.

4 J. Heckroth, *Tutorial on MIDI and Music Synthesis*, La Habra, CA: The MIDI Manufacturers Association, 1995, www.harmony-central.com/MIDI/Doc/tutorial.html.

5 P.K. Andleigh and K. Thakrar, *Multimedia Systems Design*, Upper Saddle River, NJ: Prentice-Hall PTR, 1984.

6 K. Sayood, *Introduction to Data Compression*, 2nd ed., San Francisco: Morgan Kaufmann, 2000.

7 Roger L. Freeman, *Reference Manual for Telecommunications Engineering*, 2nd ed., New York: Wiley, 1997.

8 M.M. Blattner, D.A. Sumikawa, and R. Greenberg, "Earcons and Icons: Their Structure and Common Design Principles," *Human-Computer Interaction*, 4: 11–44, 1989.

9 M.M. Blattner, "Multimedia Interfaces: Designing for Diversity," *Multimedia Tools and Applications*, 3: 87–122, 1996.

10 W.W. Gaver and R. Smith, "Auditory Icons in Large-Scale Collaborative Environments," in *Readings in Human-Computer Interaction: Toward the Year 2000*, ed. R. Baecker, J. Grudin, W. Buxton, and S. Greenberg, San Francisco: Morgan-Kaufman, 1990, pp. 564–569.

PART TWO

MULTIMEDIA DATA COMPRESSION

In this part, we examine the role played by data compression, perhaps the most important enabling technology that makes modern multimedia systems possible.

We start off in Chapter 7 looking at lossless data compression — that is, involving no distortion of the original signal once it is decompressed or reconstituted. So much data exists, in archives and elsewhere, that it has become critical to compress this information. Lossless compression is one way to proceed.

For example, suppose we decide to spend our savings on a whole-body MRI scan, looking for trouble. Then we certainly want this costly medical information to remain pristine, with no loss of information. This example of *volume data* forms a simply huge dataset, but we can't afford to lose any of it, so we'd best use lossless compression. WinZip, for example, is a ubiquitous tool that uses lossless compression.

Another good example is archival storage of precious artworks. Here, we may go to the trouble of imaging an Old Master's painting using a high-powered camera mounted on a dolly, to avoid parallax. Certainly we do not wish to lose any of this hard-won information, so again we'll use lossless compression.

On the other hand, when it comes to home movies, we're more willing to lose some information. If we have a choice between losing some information anyway, because our PC cannot handle all the data we want to push through it, or losing some information on purpose, using a *lossy* compression method, we'll choose the latter. Nowadays, almost all video you see is compressed in some way, and the compression used is mostly lossy. Almost every image on the web is in the standard JPEG format, which is usually lossy.

So in Chapter 8 we go on to look at lossy methods of compression, mainly focusing on the Discrete Cosine Transform and the Discrete Wavelet Transform. The major applications of these important methods is in the set of JPEG still image compression standards, including JPEG2000, examined in Chapter 9.

We then go on to look at how data compression methods can be applied to moving images — videos. We start with basic video compression techniques in Chapter 10. We examine the ideas behind the MPEG standard, starting with MPEG-1 and 2 in Chapter 11 and MPEG-4, 7, and beyond in Chapter 12. Audio compression in a sense stands by itself, and we consider some basic audio compression techniques in Chapter 13, while in Chapter 14 we look at MPEG Audio, including MP3.

CHAPTER 7

Lossless Compression Algorithms

7.1 INTRODUCTION

The emergence of multimedia technologies has made *digital libraries* a reality. Nowadays, libraries, museums, film studios, and governments are converting more and more data and archives into digital form. Some of the data (e.g., precious books and paintings) indeed need to be stored without any loss.

As a start, suppose we want to encode the call numbers of the 120 million or so items in the Library of Congress (a mere 20 million, if we consider just books). Why don't we just transmit each item as a 27-bit number, giving each item a unique binary code (since $2^{27} > 120,000,000$)?

The main problem is that this "great idea" requires too many bits. And in fact there exist many coding techniques that will effectively reduce the total number of bits needed to represent the above information. The process involved is generally referred to as *compression* [1, 2].

In Chapter 6, we had a beginning look at compression schemes aimed at audio. There, we had to first consider the complexity of transforming analog signals to digital ones, whereas here, we shall consider that we at least start with digital signals. For example, even though we know an image is captured using analog signals, the file produced by a digital camera is indeed digital. The more general problem of coding (compressing) a set of any symbols, not just byte values, say, has been studied for a long time.

Getting back to our Library of Congress problem, it is well known that certain parts of call numbers appear more frequently than others, so it would be more economic to assign fewer bits as their codes. This is known as *variable-length coding (VLC)* — the more frequently-appearing symbols are coded with fewer bits per symbol, and vice versa. As a result, fewer bits are usually needed to represent the whole collection.

In this chapter we study the basics of information theory and several popular lossless compression techniques. Figure 7.1 depicts a general data compression scheme, in which compression is performed by an encoder and decompression is performed by a decoder.

We call the output of the encoder *codes* or *codewords*. The intermediate medium could either be data storage or a communication/computer network. If the compression and decompression processes induce no information loss, the compression scheme is *lossless*; otherwise, it is *lossy*. The next several chapters deal with lossy compression algorithms as they are commonly used for image, video, and audio compression. Here, we concentrate on lossless compression.

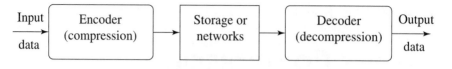

FIGURE 7.1: A general data compression scheme.

If the total number of bits required to represent the data before compression is B_0 and the total number of bits required to represent the data after compression is B_1, then we define the *compression ratio* as

$$compression\ ratio = \frac{B_0}{B_1} \qquad (7.1)$$

In general, we would desire any *codec* (encoder/decoder scheme) to have a *compression ratio* much larger than 1.0. The higher the *compression ratio*, the better the lossless compression scheme, as long as it is computationally feasible.

7.2 BASICS OF INFORMATION THEORY

According to the famous scientist Claude E. Shannon, of Bell Labs [3, 4], the *entropy* η of an information *source* with alphabet $S = \{s_1, s_2, \ldots, s_n\}$ is defined as:

$$\eta = H(S) \quad = \quad \sum_{i=1}^{n} p_i \log_2 \frac{1}{p_i} \qquad (7.2)$$

$$= \quad -\sum_{i=1}^{n} p_i \log_2 p_i \qquad (7.3)$$

where p_i is the probability that symbol s_i in S will occur.

The term $\log_2 \frac{1}{p_i}$ indicates the amount of information (the so-called *self-information* defined by Shannon [3]) contained in s_i, which corresponds to the number of bits[1] needed to encode s_i. For example, if the probability of having the character n in a manuscript is $1/32$, the amount of information associated with receiving this character is 5 bits. In other words, a character string nnn will require 15 bits to code. This is the basis for possible data reduction in text compression, since it will lead to character coding schemes different from the ASCII representation, in which each character is always represented with 8 bits.

What is the entropy? In science, entropy is a measure of the *disorder* of a system — the more entropy, the more disorder. Typically, we add *negative* entropy to a system when we impart more order to it. For example, suppose we sort a deck of cards. (Think of a bubble sort for the deck — perhaps this is not the usual way you actually sort cards, though.) For

---

[1] Since we have chosen 2 as the base for logarithms in the above definition, the unit of information is *bit* — naturally also most appropriate for the binary code representation used in digital computers. If the log base is 10, the unit is the *hartley*; if the base is e, the unit is the *nat*.

every decision to swap or not, we impart 1 bit of information to the card system and transfer 1 bit of negative entropy to the card deck.

The definition of entropy includes the idea that two decisions means the transfer of twice the negative entropy in its use of the log base 2. A two-bit vector can have 2^2 states, and the logarithm takes this value into 2 bits of negative entropy. Twice as many sorting decisions impart twice the entropy change.

Now suppose we wish to *communicate* those swapping decisions, via a network, say. Then for our two decisions we'd have to send 2 bits. If we had a two-decision system, then of course the average number of bits for all such communications would also be 2 bits. If we like, we can think of the possible number of states in our 2-bit system as four outcomes. Each outcome has probability 1/4. So on average, the number of bits to send per outcome is $4 \times (1/4) \times \log((1/(1/4))) = 2$ bits — no surprise here. To communicate (transmit) the results of our two decisions, we would need to transmit 2 bits.

But if the probability for one of the outcomes were higher than the others, the average number of bits we'd send would be different. (This situation might occur if the deck were already partially ordered, so that the probability of a not-swap were higher than for a swap.) Suppose the probabilities of one of our four states were 1/2, and the other three states each had probability 1/6 of occurring. To extend our modeling of how many bits to send on average, we need to go to noninteger powers of 2 for probabilities. Then we can use a logarithm to ask how many (float) bits of information must be sent to transmit the information content. Equation (7.3) says that in this case, we'd have to send just $(1/2) \times \log_2(2) + 3 \times (1/6) \times \log_2(6) = 1.7925$ bits, a value less than 2. This reflects the idea that if we could somehow *encode* our four states, such that the most-occurring one means fewer bits to send, we'd do better (fewer bits) on average.

The definition of entropy is aimed at identifying often-occurring symbols in the data-stream as good candidates for *short* codewords in the compressed bitstream. As described earlier, we use a *variable-length coding* scheme for entropy coding — frequently-occurring symbols are given codes that are quickly transmitted, while infrequently-occurring ones are given longer codes. For example, E occurs frequently in English, so we should give it a shorter code than Q, say.

This aspect of "surprise" in receiving an infrequent symbol in the datastream is reflected in the definition (7.3). For if a symbol occurs rarely, its probability p_i is low (e.g., 1/100), and thus its logarithm is a large negative number. This reflects the fact that it takes a longer bitstring to encode it. The probabilities p_i sitting outside the logarithm in Eq. (7.3) say that over a long stream, the symbols come by with an average frequency equal to the probability of their occurrence. This weighting should multiply the long or short information content given by the element of "surprise" in seeing a particular symbol.

As another concrete example, if the information source S is a gray-level digital image, each s_i is a gray-level intensity ranging from 0 to $(2^k - 1)$, where k is the number of bits used to represent each pixel in an uncompressed image. The range is often [0, 255], since 8 bits are typically used: this makes a convenient one byte per pixel. The image histogram (as discussed in Chapter 3) is a way of calculating the probability p_i of having pixels with gray-level intensity i in the image.

One wrinkle in the algorithm implied by Eq. (7.3) is that if a symbol occurs with zero frequency, we simply don't count it into the entropy: we cannot take a log of zero.

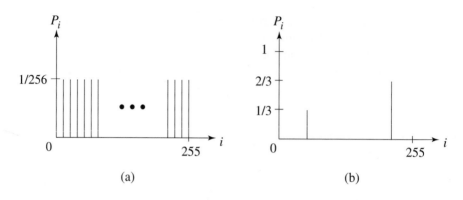

FIGURE 7.2: Histograms for two gray-level images.

Figure 7.2(a) shows the histogram of an image with *uniform* distribution of gray-level intensities, — that is, $\forall i \; p_i = 1/256$. Hence, the entropy of this image is

$$\eta = \sum_{i=0}^{255} \frac{1}{256} \cdot \log_2 256 = 8 \tag{7.4}$$

As can be seen in Eq. (7.3), the entropy η is a weighted sum of terms $\log_2 \frac{1}{p_i}$; hence it represents the *average* amount of information contained per symbol in the source S. For a memoryless source[2] S, the entropy η represents the minimum average number of bits required to represent each symbol in S. In other words, it specifies the lower bound for the average number of bits to code each symbol in S.

If we use $\bar{l}$ to denote the average length (measured in bits) of the codewords produced by the encoder, the Shannon Coding Theorem states that the entropy is the *best* we can do (under certain conditions):

$$\eta \leq \bar{l} \tag{7.5}$$

Coding schemes aim to get as close as possible to this theoretical lower bound.

It is interesting to observe that in the above uniform-distribution example we found that $\eta = 8$ — the minimum average number of bits to represent each gray-level intensity is at least 8. No compression is possible for this image! In the context of imaging, this will correspond to the "worst case," where neighboring pixel values have no similarity.

Figure 7.2(b) shows the histogram of another image, in which 1/3 of the pixels are rather dark and 2/3 of them are rather bright. The entropy of this image is

$$\begin{aligned}
\eta &= \frac{1}{3} \cdot \log_2 3 + \frac{2}{3} \cdot \log_2 \frac{3}{2} \\
&= 0.33 \times 1.59 + 0.67 \times 0.59 = 0.52 + 0.40 = 0.92
\end{aligned}$$

In general, the entropy is greater when the probability distribution is flat and smaller when it is more peaked.

---

[2]An information source that is independently distributed, meaning that the value of the current symbol does not depend on the values of the previously appeared symbols.

7.3 RUN-LENGTH CODING

Instead of assuming a memoryless source, *run-length coding* (RLC) exploits memory present in the information source. It is one of the simplest forms of data compression. The basic idea is that if the information source we wish to compress has the property that symbols tend to form continuous groups, instead of coding each symbol in the group individually, we can code one such symbol and the length of the group.

As an example, consider a bilevel image (one with only 1-bit black and white pixels) with monotone regions. This information source can be efficiently coded using run-length coding. In fact, since there are only two symbols, we do not even need to code any symbol at the start of each run. Instead, we can assume that the starting run is always of a particular color (either black or white) and simply code the length of each run.

The above description is the one-dimensional run-length coding algorithm. A two-dimensional variant of it is usually used to code bilevel images. This algorithm uses the coded run information in the previous row of the image to code the run in the current row. A full description of this algorithm can be found in [5].

7.4 VARIABLE-LENGTH CODING (VLC)

Since the entropy indicates the information content in an information source S, it leads to a family of coding methods commonly known as *entropy coding* methods. As described earlier, *variable-length coding* (VLC) is one of the best-known such methods. Here, we will study the Shannon–Fano algorithm, Huffman coding, and adaptive Huffman coding.

7.4.1 Shannon–Fano Algorithm

The Shannon–Fano algorithm was independently developed by Shannon at Bell Labs and Robert Fano at MIT [6]. To illustrate the algorithm, let's suppose the symbols to be coded are the characters in the word HELLO. The frequency count of the symbols is

Symbol	H	E	L	O
Count	1	1	2	1

The encoding steps of the Shannon–Fano algorithm can be presented in the following *top-down* manner:

1. Sort the symbols according to the frequency count of their occurrences.
2. Recursively divide the symbols into two parts, each with approximately the same number of counts, until all parts contain only one symbol.

A natural way of implementing the above procedure is to build a binary tree. As a convention, let's assign bit 0 to its left branches and 1 to the right branches.

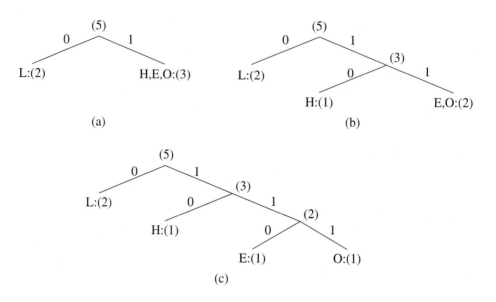

FIGURE 7.3: Coding tree for HELLO by the Shannon–Fano algorithm.

Initially, the symbols are sorted as LHEO. As Figure 7.3 shows, the first division yields two parts: (a) L with a count of 2, denoted as L:(2); and (b) H, E and O with a total count of 3, denoted as H,E,O:(3). The second division yields H:(1) and E,O:(2). The last division is E:(1) and O:(1).

Table 7.1 summarizes the result, showing each symbol, its frequency count, information content $\left(\log_2 \frac{1}{p_i} \right)$, resulting codeword, and the number of bits needed to encode each symbol in the word HELLO. The total number of bits used is shown at the bottom.

To revisit the previous discussion on entropy, in this case,

$$
\begin{aligned}
\eta &= p_L \cdot \log_2 \frac{1}{p_L} + p_H \cdot \log_2 \frac{1}{p_H} + p_E \cdot \log_2 \frac{1}{p_E} + p_O \cdot \log_2 \frac{1}{p_O} \\
&= 0.4 \times 1.32 + 0.2 \times 2.32 + 0.2 \times 2.32 + 0.2 \times 2.32 = 1.92
\end{aligned}
$$

TABLE 7.1: One result of performing the Shannon–Fano algorithm on HELLO.

Symbol	Count	$\log_2 \frac{1}{p_i}$	Code	Number of bits used
L	2	1.32	0	2
H	1	2.32	10	2
E	1	2.32	110	3
O	1	2.32	111	3
TOTAL number of bits:				10

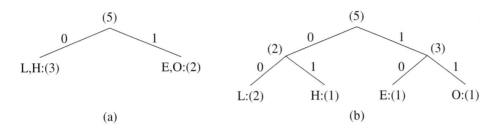

FIGURE 7.4: Another coding tree for HELLO by the Shannon–Fano algorithm.

This suggests that the minimum average number of bits to code each character in the word HELLO would be at least 1.92. In this example, the Shannon–Fano algorithm uses an average of $10/5 = 2$ bits to code each symbol, which is fairly close to the lower bound of 1.92. Apparently, the result is satisfactory.

It should be pointed out that the outcome of the Shannon–Fano algorithm is not necessarily unique. For instance, at the first division in the above example, it would be equally valid to divide into the two parts L,H:(3) and E,O:(2). This would result in the coding in Figure 7.4. Table 7.2 shows the codewords are different now. Also, these two sets of codewords may behave differently when errors are present. Coincidentally, the total number of bits required to encode the world HELLO remains at 10.

The Shannon–Fano algorithm delivers satisfactory coding results for data compression, but it was soon outperformed and overtaken by the Huffman coding method.

7.4.2 Huffman Coding

First presented by David A. Huffman in a 1952 paper [7], this method attracted an overwhelming amount of research and has been adopted in many important and/or commercial applications, such as fax machines, JPEG, and MPEG.

In contradistinction to Shannon–Fano, which is top-down, the encoding steps of the Huffman algorithm are described in the following *bottom-up* manner. Let's use the same example word, HELLO. A similar binary coding tree will be used as above, in which the left branches are coded 0 and right branches 1. A simple list data structure is also used.

TABLE 7.2: Another result of performing the Shannon–Fano algorithm on HELLO.

Symbol	Count	$\log_2 \frac{1}{p_i}$	Code	Number of bits used
L	2	1.32	00	4
H	1	2.32	01	2
E	1	2.32	10	2
O	1	2.32	11	2
		TOTAL number of bits:		10

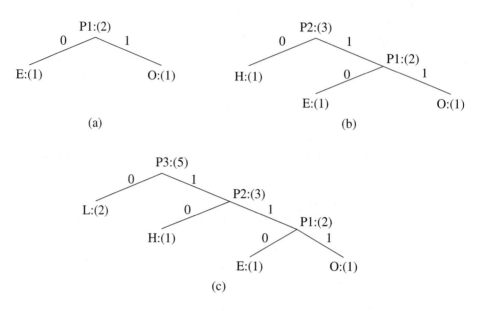

FIGURE 7.5: Coding tree for HELLO using the Huffman algorithm.

ALGORITHM 7.1   HUFFMAN CODING

1. Initialization: put all symbols on the list sorted according to their frequency counts.
2. Repeat until the list has only one symbol left.

    (a) From the list, pick two symbols with the lowest frequency counts. Form a Huffman subtree that has these two symbols as child nodes and create a parent node for them.
    (b) Assign the sum of the children's frequency counts to the parent and insert it into the list, such that the order is maintained.
    (c) Delete the children from the list.

3. Assign a codeword for each leaf based on the path from the root.

In the above figure, new symbols P1, P2, P3 are created to refer to the parent nodes in the Huffman coding tree. The contents in the list are illustrated below:

After initialization:	L H E O
After iteration (a):	L P1 H
After iteration (b):	L P2
After iteration (c):	P3

For this simple example, the Huffman algorithm apparently generated the same coding result as one of the Shannon–Fano results shown in Figure 7.3, although the results are usually better. The average number of bits used to code each character is also 2, (i.e., $(1 + 1 + 2 + 3 + 3)/5 = 2$). As another simple example, consider a text string containing a set of characters and their frequency counts as follows: A:(15), B:(7), C:(6), D:(6) and E:(5). It is easy to show that the Shannon–Fano algorithm needs a total of 89 bits to encode this string, whereas the Huffman algorithm needs only 87.

As shown above, if correct probabilities ("prior statistics") are available and accurate, the Huffman coding method produces good compression results. Decoding for the Huffman coding is trivial as long as the statistics and/or coding tree are sent before the data to be compressed (in the file header, say). This overhead becomes negligible if the data file is sufficiently large.

The following are important properties of Huffman coding:

- **Unique prefix property**. No Huffman code is a prefix of any other Huffman code. For instance, the code 0 assigned to L in Figure 7.5(c) is not a prefix of the code 10 for H or 110 for E or 111 for O; nor is the code 10 for H a prefix of the code 110 for E or 111 for O. It turns out that the unique prefix property is guaranteed by the above Huffman algorithm, since it always places all input symbols at the leaf nodes of the Huffman tree. The Huffman code is one of the *prefix codes* for which the unique prefix property holds. The code generated by the Shannon–Fano algorithm is another such example.

  This property is essential and also makes for an efficient decoder, since it precludes any ambiguity in decoding. In the above example, if a bit 0 is received, the decoder can immediately produce a symbol L without waiting for any more bits to be transmitted.

- **Optimality**. The Huffman code is a *minimum-redundancy code*, as shown in Huffman's 1952 paper [7]. It has been proven [8, 2] that the Huffman code is *optimal* for a given data model (i.e., a given, accurate, probability distribution):

  - The two least frequent symbols will have the same length for their Huffman codes, differing only at the last bit. This should be obvious from the above algorithm.

  - Symbols that occur more frequently will have shorter Huffman codes than symbols that occur less frequently. Namely, for symbols s_i and s_j, if $p_i \geq p_j$ then $l_i \leq l_j$, where l_i is the number of bits in the codeword for s_i.

  - It has been shown (see [2]) that the average code length for an information source S is strictly less than $\eta + 1$. Combined with Eq.(7.5), we have

$$\eta \leq \bar{l} < \eta + 1 \qquad (7.6)$$

Extended Huffman Coding.   The discussion of Huffman coding so far assigns each symbol a codeword that has an *integer* bit length. As stated earlier, $\log_2 \frac{1}{p_i}$ indicates the amount of information contained in the information source s_i, which corresponds to the number of bits needed to represent it. When a particular symbol s_i has a large probability (close to 1.0), $\log_2 \frac{1}{p_i}$ will be close to 0, and assigning one bit to represent that symbol will be costly. Only when the probabilities of all symbols can be expressed as 2^{-k}, where k is a positive integer, would the average length of codewords be truly optimal — that is, $\bar{l} \equiv \eta$. Clearly, $\bar{l} > \eta$ in most cases.

One way to address the problem of integral codeword length is to group several symbols and assign a single codeword to the group. Huffman coding of this type is called *Extended Huffman Coding* [2]. Assume an information source has alphabet $S = \{s_1, s_2, \dots, s_n\}$. If k symbols are grouped together, then the *extended alphabet* is

$$S^{(k)} = \{\overbrace{s_1 s_1 \dots s_1}^{k\ symbols}, s_1 s_1 \dots s_2, \dots, s_1 s_1 \dots s_n, s_1 s_1 \dots s_2 s_1, \dots, s_n s_n \dots s_n\}$$

Note that the size of the new alphabet $S^{(k)}$ is n^k. If k is relatively large (e.g., $k \geq 3$), then for most practical applications where $n \gg 1$, n^k would be a very large number, implying a huge symbol table. This overhead makes Extended Huffman Coding impractical.

As shown in [2], if the entropy of S is η, then the average number of bits needed for each symbol in S is now

$$\eta \leq \bar{l} < \eta + \frac{1}{k} \tag{7.7}$$

so we have shaved quite a bit from the coding schemes' bracketing of the theoretical best limit. Nevertheless, this is not as much of an improvement over the original Huffman coding (where group size is 1) as one might have hoped for.

7.4.3 Adaptive Huffman Coding

The Huffman algorithm requires prior statistical knowledge about the information source, and such information is often not available. This is particularly true in multimedia applications, where future data is unknown before its arrival, as for example in live (or streaming) audio and video. Even when the statistics are available, the transmission of the symbol table could represent heavy overhead.

For the non-extended version of Huffman coding, the above discussion assumes a so-called *order-0* model — that is, symbols/characters were treated singly, without any context or history maintained. One possible way to include contextual information is to examine k preceding (or succeeding) symbols each time; this is known as an *order-k* model. For example, an order-1 model can incorporate such statistics as the probability of "qu" in addition to the individual probabilities of "q" and "u". Nevertheless, this again implies that much more statistical data has to be stored and sent for the order-k model when $k \geq 1$.

The solution is to use *adaptive* compression algorithms, in which statistics are gathered and updated dynamically as the datastream arrives. The probabilities are no longer based on prior knowledge but on the actual data received so far. The new coding methods are "adaptive" because, as the probability distribution of the received symbols changes, symbols will be given new (longer or shorter) codes. This is especially desirable for multimedia data, when the content (the music or the color of the scene) and hence the statistics can change rapidly.

As an example, we introduce the *Adaptive Huffman Coding* algorithm in this section. Many ideas, however, are also applicable to other adaptive compression algorithms.

PROCEDURE 7.1   Procedures for Adaptive Huffman Coding

```
ENCODER                          DECODER
-------                          -------

Initial_code();                  Initial_code();
while not EOF                    while not EOF
   {                                {
      get(c);                          decode(c);
      encode(c);                       output(c);
      update_tree(c);                  update_tree(c);
   }                                }
```

- `Initial_code` assigns symbols with some initially agreed-upon codes, without any prior knowledge of the frequency counts for them. For example, some conventional code such as ASCII may be used for coding character symbols.

- `update_tree` is a procedure for constructing an adaptive Huffman tree. It basically does two things: it increments the frequency counts for the symbols (including any new ones), and updates the configuration of the tree.

  - The Huffman tree must always maintain its *sibling property* — that is, all nodes (internal and leaf) are arranged in the order of increasing counts. Nodes are numbered in order from left to right, bottom to top. (See Figure 7.6, in which the first node is 1.A:(1), the second node is 2.B:(1), and so on, where the numbers in parentheses indicates the count.) If the sibling property is about to be violated, a *swap* procedure is invoked to update the tree by rearranging the nodes.

  - When a swap is necessary, the farthest node with count N is swapped with the node whose count has just been increased to $N + 1$. Note that if the node with count N is not a leaf-node — it is the root of a subtree — the entire subtree will go with it during the swap.

- The encoder and decoder must use exactly the same `Initial_code` and `update_tree` routines.

Figure 7.6(a) depicts a Huffman tree with some symbols already received. Figure 7.6(b) shows the updated tree after an additional A (i.e., the second A) was received. This increased the count of As to $N + 1 = 2$ and triggered a swap. In this case, the farthest node with count $N = 1$ was D:(1). Hence, A:(2) and D:(1) were swapped.

Apparently, the same result could also be obtained by first swapping A:(2) with B:(1), then with C:(1), and finally with D:(1). The problem is that such a procedure would take three swaps; the rule of swapping with "the farthest node with count N" helps avoid such unnecessary swaps.

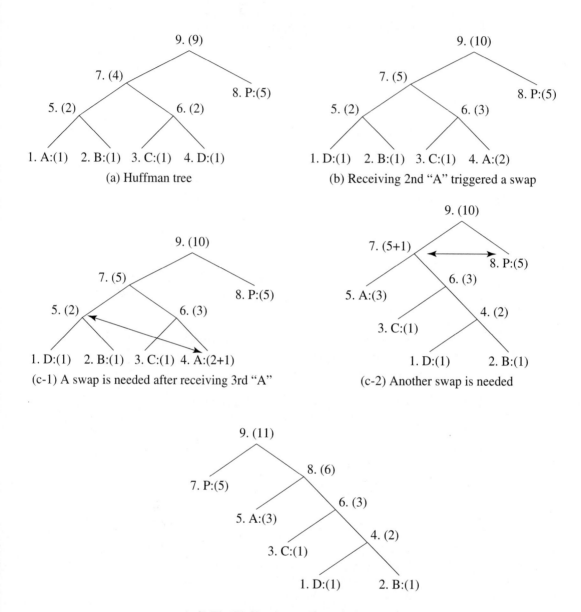

(a) Huffman tree

(b) Receiving 2nd "A" triggered a swap

(c-1) A swap is needed after receiving 3rd "A"

(c-2) Another swap is needed

(c-3) The Huffman tree after receiving 3rd "A"

FIGURE 7.6: Node swapping for updating an adaptive Huffman tree: (a) a Huffman tree; (b) receiving 2nd "A" triggered a swap; (c-1) a swap is needed after receiving 3rd "A"; (c-2) another swap is needed; (c-3) the Huffman tree after receiving 3rd "A".

The update of the Huffman tree after receiving the third A is more involved and is illustrated in the three steps shown in Figure 7.6(c-1) to (c-3). Since A:(2) will become A:(3) (temporarily denoted as A:(2+1)), it is now necessary to swap A:(2+1) with the fifth node. This is illustrated with an arrow in Figure 7.6(c-1).

Since the fifth node is a non-leaf node, the subtree with nodes 1. D:(1), 2. B:(1), and 5. (2) is swapped as a whole with A:(3). Figure 7.6(c-2) shows the tree after this first swap. Now the seventh node will become (5+1), which triggers another swap with the eighth node. Figure 7.6(c-3) shows the Huffman tree after this second swap.

The above example shows an update process that aims to maintain the sibling property of the adaptive Huffman tree — the update of the tree sometimes requires more than one swap. When this occurs, the swaps should be executed in multiple steps in a "bottom-up" manner, starting from the lowest level where a swap is needed. In other words, the update is carried out sequentially: tree nodes are examined in order, and swaps are made whenever necessary.

To clearly illustrate more implementation details, let's examine another example. Here, we show exactly what *bits* are sent, as opposed to simply stating how the tree is updated.

EXAMPLE 7.1   Adaptive Huffman Coding for Symbol String AADCCDD

Let's assume that the initial code assignment for both the encoder and decoder simply follows the ASCII order for the 26 symbols in an alphabet, A through Z, as Table 7.3 shows. To improve the implementation of the algorithm, we adopt an additional rule: if any character/symbol is to be sent the first time, it must be preceded by a special symbol, NEW. The initial code for NEW is 0. The *count* for NEW is always kept as 0 (the count is never increased); hence it is always denoted as NEW:(0) in Figure 7.7.

Figure 7.7 shows the Huffman tree after each step. Initially, there is no tree. For the first A, 0 for NEW and the initial code 00001 for A are sent. Afterward, the tree is built and shown as the first one, labeled A. Now both the encoder and decoder have constructed the same first tree, from which it can be seen that the code for the second A is 1. The code sent is thus 1.

After the second A, the tree is updated, shown labeled as AA. The updates after receiving D and C are similar. More subtrees are spawned, and the code for NEW is getting longer — from 0 to 00 to 000.

TABLE 7.3: Initial code assignment for AADCCDD using adaptive Huffman coding.

	Initial Code
NEW:	0
A:	00001
B:	00010
C:	00011
D:	00100
.	.
.	.
.	.

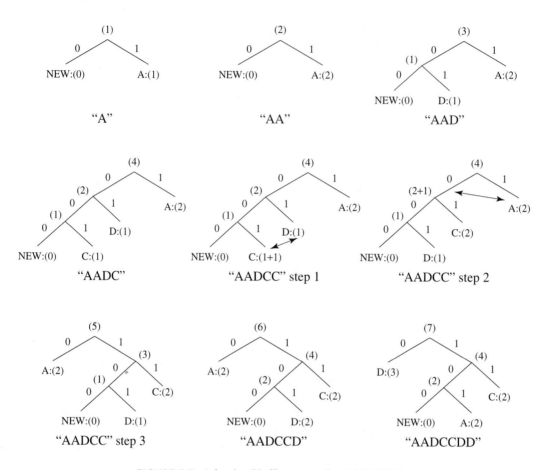

FIGURE 7.7: Adaptive Huffman tree for AADCCDD.

From AADC to AADCC takes two swaps. To illustrate the update process clearly, this is shown in three steps, with the required swaps again indicated by arrows.

- **AADCC Step 1**. The frequency count for C is increased from 1 to $1 + 1 = 2$; this necessitates its swap with D:(1).

- **AADCC Step 2**. After the swap between C and D, the count of the parent node of C:(2) will be increased from 2 to $2 + 1 = 3$; this requires its swap with A:(2).

- **AADCC Step 3**. The swap between A and the parent of C is completed.

Table 7.4 summarizes the sequence of symbols and code (zeros and ones) being sent to the decoder.

TABLE 7.4: Sequence of symbols and codes sent to the decoder

Symbol	NEW	A	A	NEW	D	NEW	C	C	D	D
Code	0	00001	1	0	00100	00	00011	001	101	101

It is important to emphasize that the code for a particular symbol often changes during the adaptive Huffman coding process. The more frequent the symbol up to the moment, the shorter the code. For example, after AADCCDD, when the character D overtakes A as the most frequent symbol, its code changes from 101 to 0. This is of course fundamental for the adaptive algorithm — codes are reassigned dynamically according to the new probability distribution of the symbols.

The "Squeeze Page" on this book's web site provides a Java applet for adaptive Huffman coding that should aid you in learning this algorithm.

7.5 DICTIONARY-BASED CODING

The Lempel-Ziv-Welch (LZW) algorithm employs an adaptive, dictionary-based compression technique. Unlike variable-length coding, in which the lengths of the codewords are different, LZW uses fixed-length codewords to represent variable-length strings of symbols/characters that commonly occur together, such as words in English text.

As in the other adaptive compression techniques, the LZW encoder and decoder builds up the same dictionary dynamically while receiving the data — the encoder and the decoder both develop the same dictionary. Since a single code can now represent more than one symbol/character, data compression is realized.

LZW proceeds by placing longer and longer repeated entries into a dictionary, then emitting the *code* for an element rather than the string itself, if the element has already been placed in the dictionary. The predecessors of LZW are LZ77 [9] and LZ78 [10], due to Jacob Ziv and Abraham Lempel in 1977 and 1978. Terry Welch [11] improved the technique in 1984. LZW is used in many applications, such as UNIX compress, GIF for images, V.42 bis for modems, and others.

ALGORITHM 7.2   LZW COMPRESSION

```
BEGIN
    s = next input character;
    while not EOF
        {
            c = next input character;

            if s + c exists in the dictionary
                s = s + c;
```

```
      else
        {
        output the code for s;
        add string s + c to the dictionary with a new code;
        s = c;
        }
      }
  output the code for s;
END
```

EXAMPLE 7.2 LZW Compression for String ABABBABCABABBA

Let's start with a very simple dictionary (also referred to as a *string table*), initially containing only three characters, with codes as follows:

```
code      string
---------------
  1         A
  2         B
  3         C
```

Now if the input string is ABABBABCABABBA, the LZW compression algorithm works as follows:

s	c	output	code	string
			1	A
			2	B
			3	C
A	B	1	4	AB
B	A	2	5	BA
A	B			
AB	B	4	6	ABB
B	A			
BA	B	5	7	BAB
B	C	2	8	BC
C	A	3	9	CA
A	B			
AB	A	4	10	ABA
A	B			
AB	B			
ABB	A	6	11	ABBA
A	EOF	1		

The output codes are 1 2 4 5 2 3 4 6 1. Instead of 14 characters, only 9 codes need to be sent. If we assume each character or code is transmitted as a byte, that is quite a saving (the compression ratio would be $14/9 = 1.56$). (Remember, the LZW is an adaptive algorithm, in which the encoder and decoder independently build their own string tables. Hence, there is no overhead involving transmitting the string table.)

Obviously, for our illustration the above example is replete with a great deal of redundancy in the input string, which is why it achieves compression so quickly. In general, savings for LZW would not come until the text is more than a few hundred bytes long.

The above LZW algorithm is simple, and it makes no effort in selecting optimal new strings to enter into its dictionary. As a result, its string table grows rapidly, as illustrated above. A typical LZW implementation for textual data uses a 12-bit codelength. Hence, its dictionary can contain up to 4,096 entries, with the first 256 (0–255) entries being ASCII codes. If we take this into account, the above compression ratio is reduced to $(14 \times 8)/(9 \times 12) = 1.04$.

ALGORITHM 7.3   LZW DECOMPRESSION (SIMPLE VERSION)

```
BEGIN
    s = NIL;
    while not EOF
        {
            k = next input code;
            entry = dictionary entry for k;
            output entry;
            if (s != NIL)
                add string s + entry[0] to dictionary
                with a new code;
            s = entry;
        }
END
```

EXAMPLE 7.3   LZW decompression for string ABABBABCABABBA

Input codes to the decoder are 1 2 4 5 2 3 4 6 1. The initial string table is identical to what is used by the encoder.

The LZW decompression algorithm then works as follows:

s	k	entry/output	code	string
			1	A
			2	B
			3	C
NIL	1	A		

A	2	B	4	AB
B	4	AB	5	BA
AB	5	BA	6	ABB
BA	2	B	7	BAB
B	3	C	8	BC
C	4	AB	9	CA
AB	6	ABB	10	ABA
ABB	1	A	11	ABBA
A	EOF			

Apparently the output string is ABABBABCABABBA — a truly lossless result!

LZW Algorithm Details   A more careful examination of the above simple version of the LZW decompression algorithm will reveal a potential problem. In adaptively updating the dictionaries, the encoder is sometimes ahead of the decoder. For example, after the sequence ABABB, the encoder will output code 4 and create a dictionary entry with code 6 for the new string ABB.

On the decoder side, after receiving the code 4, the output will be AB, and the dictionary is updated with code 5 for a new string, BA. This occurs several times in the above example, such as after the encoder outputs another code 4, code 6. In a way, this is anticipated — after all, it is a sequential process, and the encoder had to be ahead. In this example, this did not cause problem.

Welch [11] points out that the simple version of the LZW decompression algorithm will break down when the following scenario occurs. Assume that the input string is ABAB-BABCABBABBAX....

The LZW encoder:

s	c	output	code	string
			1	A
			2	B
			3	C
A	B	1	4	AB
B	A	2	5	BA
A	B			
AB	B	4	6	ABB
B	A			
BA	B	5	7	BAB
B	C	2	8	BC
C	A	3	9	CA
A	B			
AB	B			

ABB	A	6	10	ABBA
A	B			
AB	B			
ABB	A			
ABBA	X	10	11	ABBAX
		.		
		.		
		.		

The sequence of output codes from the encoder (and hence the input codes for the decoder) is 1 2 4 5 2 3 6 10....

The simple LZW decoder:

s	k	entry/output	code	string
			1	A
			2	B
			3	C
NIL	1	A		
A	2	B	4	AB
B	4	AB	5	BA
AB	5	BA	6	ABB
BA	2	B	7	BAB
B	3	C	8	BC
C	6	ABB	9	CA
ABB	10	???		

"???" indicates that the decoder has encountered a difficulty: no dictionary entry exists for the last input code, 10. A closer examination reveals that code 10 was most recently created at the encoder side, formed by a concatenation of Character, String, Character. In this case, the character is A, and string is BB — that is, A + BB + A. Meanwhile, the sequence of the output symbols from the encoder are A, BB, A, BB, A.

This example illustrates that whenever the sequence of symbols to be coded is Character, String, Character, String, Character, and so on, the encoder will create a new code to represent Character + String + Character and use it right away, before the decoder has had a chance to create it!

Fortunately, this is the only case in which the above simple LZW decompression algorithm will fail. Also, when this occurs, the variable s = Character + String. A modified version of the algorithm can handle this exceptional case by checking whether the input code has been defined in the decoder's dictionary. If not, it will simply assume that the code represents the symbols $s + s[0]$; that is Character + String + Character.

ALGORITHM 7.4   LZW DECOMPRESSION (MODIFIED)

```
BEGIN
    s = NIL;
    while not EOF
        {
            k = next input code;
            entry = dictionary entry for k;

            /* exception handler */
            if (entry == NULL)
                entry = s + s[0];

            output entry;
            if (s != NIL)
                add string s + entry[0] to dictionary
                with a new code;
            s = entry;
        }
END
```

Implementation requires some practical limit for the dictionary size — for example, a maximum of 4,096 entries for GIF and 2,048 entries for V.42 bis. Nevertheless, this still yields a 12-bit or 11-bit code length for LZW codes, which is longer than the word length for the original data — 8-bit for ASCII.

In real applications, the code length l is kept in the range of $[l_0, l_{max}]$. For the UNIX compress command, $l_0 = 9$ and l_{max} is by default 16. The dictionary initially has a size of 2^{l_0}. When it is filled up, the code length will be increased by 1; this is allowed to repeat until $l = l_{max}$.

If the data to be compressed lacks any repetitive structure, the chance of using the new codes in the dictionary entries could be low. Sometimes, this will lead to *data expansion* instead of data reduction, since the code length is often longer than the word length of the original data. To deal with this, V.42 bis, for example, has built in two modes: *compressed* and *transparent*. The latter turns off compression and is invoked when data expansion is detected.

Since the dictionary has a maximum size, once it reaches $2^{l_{max}}$ entries, LZW loses its adaptive power and becomes a static, dictionary-based technique. UNIX compress, for example, will monitor its own performance at this point. It will simply flush and re-initialize the dictionary when the compression ratio falls below a threshold. A better dictionary management is perhaps to remove the LRU (least recently used) entries. V.42 bis will look for any entry that is not a prefix to any other dictionary entry, because this indicates that the code has not been used since its creation.

7.6   ARITHMETIC CODING

Arithmetic coding is a more modern coding method that usually outperforms Huffman coding in practice. It was fully developed in the late 1970s and 1980s [12, 13, 14]. The initial idea of arithmetic coding was introduced in Shannon's 1948 work [3]. Peter Elias developed its first recursive implementation (which was not published but was mentioned in Abramson's 1963 book [15]). The method was further developed and described in Jelinek's 1968 book [16]. Modern arithmetic coding can be attributed to Pasco (1976) [17] and Rissanen and Langdon (1979) [12].

Normally (in its non-extended mode), Huffman coding assigns each symbol a codeword that has an integral bit length. As stated earlier, $\log_2 \frac{1}{p_i}$ indicates the amount of information contained in the information source s_i, which corresponds to the number of bits needed to represent it.

For example, when a particular symbol s_i has a large probability (close to 1.0), $\log_2 \frac{1}{p_i}$ will be close to 0, and assigning one bit to represent that symbol will be very costly. Only when the probabilities of all symbols can be expressed as 2^{-k}, where k is a positive integer, would the average length of codewords be truly optimal — that is, $\bar{l} = \eta$ (with η the entropy of the information source, as defined in Eq. (7.3)). Apparently, $\bar{l} > \eta$ in most cases.

Although it is possible to group symbols into metasymbols for codeword assignment (as in extended Huffman coding) to overcome the limitation of integral number of bits per symbol, the increase in the resultant symbol table required by the Huffman encoder and decoder would be formidable.

Arithmetic coding can treat the whole message as one unit. In practice, the input data is usually broken up into chunks to avoid error propagation. However, in our presentation below, we take a simplistic approach and include a terminator symbol.

A message is represented by a half-open interval $[a, b)$ where a and b are real numbers between 0 and 1. Initially, the interval is $[0, 1)$. When the message becomes longer, the length of the interval shortens, and the number of bits needed to represent the interval increases. Suppose the alphabet is $[A, B, C, D, E, F, \$]$, in which $\$$ is a special symbol used to terminate the message, and the known probability distribution is as shown in Figure 7.8(a).

ALGORITHM 7.5   ARITHMETIC CODING ENCODER

```
BEGIN
    low = 0.0;    high = 1.0;    range = 1.0;

    while (symbol != terminator)
        {
            get (symbol);
            low =   low + range * Range_low(symbol);
            high = low + range * Range_high(symbol);
            range = high - low;
        }

    output a code so that low <= code < high;
END
```

Symbol	Probability	Range
A	0.2	[0, 0.2)
B	0.1	[0.2, 0.3)
C	0.2	[0.3, 0.5)
D	0.05	[0.5, 0.55)
E	0.3	[0.55, 0.85)
F	0.05	[0.85, 0.9)
$	0.1	[0.9, 1.0)

(a)

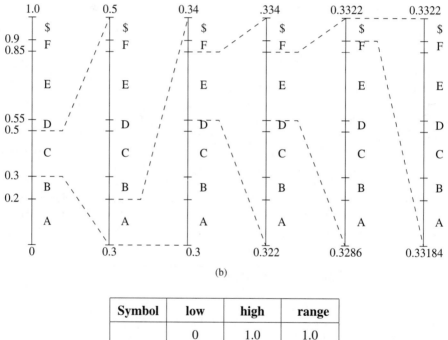

(b)

Symbol	low	high	range
	0	1.0	1.0
C	0.3	0.5	0.2
A	0.30	0.34	0.04
E	0.322	0.334	0.012
E	0.3286	0.3322	0.0036
$	0.33184	0.33220	0.00036

(c)

FIGURE 7.8: Arithmetic coding: encode symbols CAEE$: (a) probability distribution of symbols; (b) graphical display of shrinking ranges; (c) new *low*, *high*, and *range* generated.

The encoding process is illustrated in Figure 7.8(b) and (c), in which a string of symbols CAEE\$ is encoded. Initially, $low = 0$, $high = 1.0$, and $range = 1.0$. After the first symbol C, $Range\_low(C) = 0.3$, $Range\_high(C) = 0.5$; so $low = 0 + 1.0 \times 0.3 = 0.3$, $high = 0 + 1.0 \times 0.5 = 0.5$. The new $range$ is now reduced to 0.2.

For clarity of illustration, the ever-shrinking ranges are enlarged in each step (indicated by dashed lines) in Figure 7.8(b). After the second symbol A, low, $high$, and $range$ are 0.30, 0.34, and 0.04. The process repeats itself until after the terminating symbol \$ is received. By then low and $high$ are 0.33184 and 0.33220, respectively. It is apparent that finally we have

$$range = P_C \times P_A \times P_E \times P_E \times P_\$ = 0.2 \times 0.2 \times 0.3 \times 0.3 \times 0.1 = 0.00036$$

The final step in encoding calls for generation of a number that falls within the range $[low, high)$. Although it is trivial to pick such a number in decimal, such as 0.33184, 0.33185, or 0.332 in the above example, it is less obvious how to do it with a binary fractional number. The following algorithm will ensure that the shortest binary codeword is found if low and $high$ are the two ends of the range and $low < high$.

PROCEDURE 7.2   Generating Codeword for Encoder

```
BEGIN
    code = 0;
    k = 1;
    while (value(code) < low)
        {
            assign 1 to the kth binary fraction bit;
            if (value(code) > high)
                replace the kth bit by 0;
            k = k + 1;
        }
END
```

For the above example, $low = 0.33184$, $high = 0.3322$. If we assign 1 to the first binary fraction bit, it would be 0.1 in binary, and its decimal $value(code) = value(0.1) = 0.5 > high$. Hence, we assign 0 to the first bit. Since $value(0.0) = 0 < low$, the `while` loop continues.

Assigning 1 to the second bit makes a binary $code$ 0.01 and $value(0.01) = 0.25$, which is less than $high$, so it is accepted. Since it is still true that $value(0.01) < low$, the iteration continues. Eventually, the binary codeword generated is 0.01010101, which is $2^{-2} + 2^{-4} + 2^{-6} + 2^{-8} = 0.33203125$.

It must be pointed out that we were lucky to have found a codeword of only 8 bits to represent this sequence of symbols CAEE\$. In this case, $\log_2 \frac{1}{P_C} + \log_2 \frac{1}{P_A} + \log_2 \frac{1}{P_E} + \log_2 \frac{1}{P_E} + \log_2 \frac{1}{P_\$} = \log_2 \frac{1}{range} = \log_2 \frac{1}{0.00036} \approx 11.44$, which would suggest that it could take 12 bits to encode a string of symbols like this.

It can be proven [2] that $\lceil \log_2(1/\prod_i P_i) \rceil$ is the upper bound. Namely, in the worst case, the shortest codeword in arithmetic coding will require k bits to encode a sequence of symbols, and

$$k = \lceil \log_2 \frac{1}{range} \rceil = \lceil \log_2 \frac{1}{\prod_i P_i} \rceil \tag{7.8}$$

where P_i is the probability for symbol i and *range* is the final range generated by the encoder.

Apparently, when the length of the message is long, its *range* quickly becomes very small, and hence $\log_2 \frac{1}{range}$ becomes very large; the difference between $\log_2 \frac{1}{range}$ and $\lceil \log_2 \frac{1}{range} \rceil$ is negligible.

Generally, Arithmetic Coding achieves better performance than Huffman coding, because the former treats an entire sequence of symbols as one unit, whereas the latter has the restriction of assigning an integral number of bits to each symbol. For example, Huffman coding would require 12 bits for CAEE$, equaling the worst-case performance of Arithmetic Coding.

Moreover, Huffman coding cannot always attain the upper bound illustrated in Eq. (7.8). It can be shown (see Exercise 5) that if the alphabet is $[A, B, C]$ and the known probability distribution is $P_A = 0.5$, $P_B = 0.4$, $P_C = 0.1$, then for sending BBB, Huffman coding will require 6 bits, which is more than $\lceil \log_2(1/\prod_i P_B) \rceil = 4$, whereas arithmetic coding will need only 4 bits.

ALGORITHM 7.6   ARITHMETIC CODING DECODER

```
BEGIN
   get binary code and convert to decimal value = value(code);
   Do
      {
        find a symbol s so that
             Range_low(s) <= value < Range_high(s);
        output s;
        low = Rang_low(s);
        high = Range_high(s);
        range = high - low;
        value = [value - low] / range;
      }
   Until symbol s is a terminator
END
```

Table 7.5 illustrates the decoding process for the above example. Initially, *value* = 0.33203125. Since *Range_low(C)* = 0.3 $\leq$ 0.33203125 < 0.5 = *Range_high(C)*, the first output symbol is C. This yields *value* = [0.33203125 − 0.3]/0.2 = 0.16015625, which in turn determines that the second symbol is A. Eventually, *value* is 0.953125, which falls in the range [0.9, 1.0) of the terminator $.

TABLE 7.5: Arithmetic coding: decode symbols CAEE$

Value	Output symbol	Low	High	Range
0.33203125	C	0.3	0.5	0.2
0.16015625	A	0.0	0.2	0.2
0.80078125	E	0.55	0.85	0.3
0.8359375	E	0.55	0.85	0.3
0.953125	$	0.9	1.0	0.1

The algorithm described previously has a subtle implementation difficulty. When the intervals shrink, we need to use very high-precision numbers to do encoding. This makes practical implementation of this algorithm infeasible. Fortunately, it is possible to rescale the intervals and use only integer arithmetic for a practical implementation [18].

In the above discussion, a special symbol, $, is used as a terminator of the string of symbols. This is analogous to sending *end-of-line* (EOL) in image transmission. In conventional compression applications, no terminator symbol is needed, as the encoder simply codes all symbols from the input. However, if the transmission channel/network is noisy (lossy), the protection of having a terminator (or EOL) symbol is crucial for the decoder to regain synchronization with the encoder.

The coding of the EOL symbol itself is an interesting problem. Usually, EOL ends up being relatively long. Lei et al. [19] address some of these issues and propose an algorithm that controls the length of the EOL codeword it generates.

7.7   LOSSLESS IMAGE COMPRESSION

One of the most commonly used compression techniques in multimedia data compression is *differential coding*. The basis of data reduction in differential coding is the redundancy in consecutive symbols in a datastream. Recall that we considered lossless differential coding in Chapter 6, when we examined how audio must be dealt with via subtraction from predicted values. Audio is a signal indexed by one dimension, time. Here we consider how to apply the lessons learned from audio to the context of digital image signals that are indexed by two, spatial, dimensions (x, y).

7.7.1   Differential Coding of Images

Let's consider differential coding in the context of digital images. In a sense, we move from signals with domain in one dimension to signals indexed by numbers in two dimensions (x, y) — the rows and columns of an image. Later, we'll look at video signals. These are even more complex, in that they are indexed by space and time (x, y, t).

Because of the continuity of the physical world, the gray-level intensities (or color) of background and foreground objects in images tend to change relatively slowly across the image frame. Since we were dealing with signals in the time domain for audio, practitioners generally refer to images as signals in the *spatial domain*. The generally slowly changing

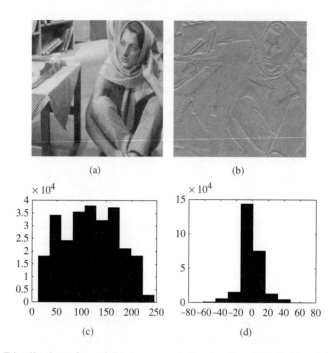

FIGURE 7.9: Distributions for original versus derivative images. (a,b) original gray-level image and its partial derivative image; (c,d) histograms for original and derivative images. This figure uses a commonly employed image called Barb.

nature of imagery spatially produces a high likelihood that neighboring pixels will have similar intensity values. Given an original image $I(x, y)$, using a simple difference operator we can define a difference image $d(x, y)$ as follows:

$$d(x, y) = I(x, y) - I(x - 1, y) \qquad (7.9)$$

This is a simple approximation of a partial differential operator $\partial/\partial x$ applied to an image defined in terms of integer values of x and y.

Another approach is to use the discrete version of the 2D Laplacian operator to define a difference image $d(x, y)$ as

$$d(x, y) = 4 I(x, y) - I(x, y - 1) - I(x, y + 1) - I(x + 1, y) - I(x - 1, y) \qquad (7.10)$$

In both cases, the difference image will have a histogram as in Figure 7.9(d), derived from the $d(x, y)$ partial derivative image in Figure 7.9(b) for the original image I in Figure 7.9(a). Notice that the histogram for I is much broader, as in Figure 7.9(c). It can be shown that image I has larger entropy than image d, since it has a more even distribution in its intensity values. Consequently, Huffman coding or some other variable-length coding scheme will produce shorter bit-length codewords for the difference image. Compression will work better on a difference image.

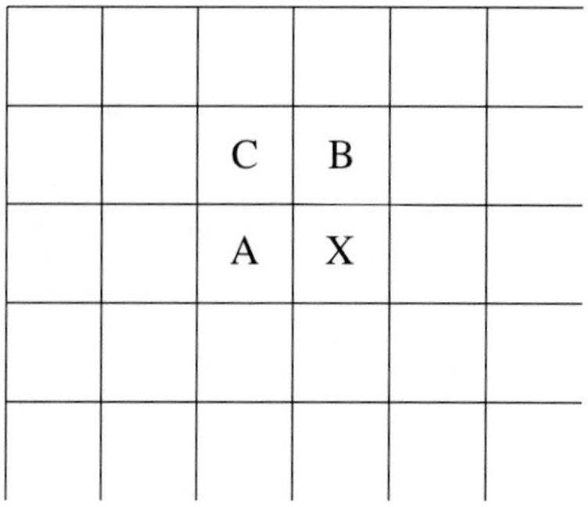

FIGURE 7.10: Neighboring pixels for predictors in lossless JPEG. Note that any of A, B, or C has already been decoded before it is used in the predictor, on the decoder side of an encode/decode cycle.

7.7.2 Lossless JPEG

Lossless JPEG is a special case of the JPEG image compression. It differs drastically from other JPEG modes in that the algorithm has no lossy steps. Thus we treat it here and consider the more used JPEG methods in Chapter 9. Lossless JPEG is invoked when the user selects a 100% *quality factor* in an image tool. Essentially, lossless JPEG is included in the JPEG compression standard simply for completeness.

The following predictive method is applied on the unprocessed original image (or each color band of the original color image). It essentially involves two steps: forming a differential prediction and encoding.

1. A predictor combines the values of up to three neighboring pixels as the predicted value for the current pixel, indicated by X in Figure 7.10. The predictor can use any one of the seven schemes listed in Table 7.6. If predictor P1 is used, the neighboring intensity value A will be adopted as the predicted intensity of the current pixel; if

TABLE 7.6: Predictors for lossless JPEG

Predictor	Prediction
P1	A
P2	B
P3	C
P4	$A + B - C$
P5	$A + (B - C) / 2$
P6	$B + (A - C) / 2$
P7	$(A + B) / 2$

TABLE 7.7: Comparison of lossless JPEG with other lossless compression programs

Compression program	Compression ratio			
	Lena	**Football**	**F-18**	**Flowers**
Lossless JPEG	1.45	1.54	2.29	1.26
Optimal lossless JPEG	1.49	1.67	2.71	1.33
compress (LZW)	0.86	1.24	2.21	0.87
gzip (LZ77)	1.08	1.36	3.10	1.05
gzip-9 (optimal LZ77)	1.08	1.36	3.13	1.05
pack (Huffman coding)	1.02	1.12	1.19	1.00

predictor P4 is used, the current pixel value is derived from the three neighboring pixels as $A + B - C$; and so on.

2. The encoder compares the prediction with the actual pixel value at position X and encodes the difference using one of the lossless compression techniques we have discussed, such as the Huffman coding scheme.

Since prediction must be based on previously encoded neighbors, the very first pixel in the image $I(0, 0)$ will have to simply use its own value. The pixels in the first row always use predictor P1, and those in the first column always use P2.

Lossless JPEG usually yields a relatively low compression ratio, which renders it impractical for most multimedia applications. An empirical comparison using some 20 images indicates that the compression ratio for lossless JPEG with any one of the seven predictors ranges from 1.0 to 3.0, with an average of around 2.0. Predictors 4 to 7 that consider neighboring nodes in both horizontal and vertical dimensions offer slightly better compression (approximately 0.2 to 0.5 higher) than predictors 1 to 3.

Table 7.7 shows a comparison of the compression ratio for several lossless compression techniques using test images Lena, football, F-18, and flowers. These standard images used for many purposes in imaging work are shown on the textbook web site in the Further Exploration section for this chapter.

This chapter has been devoted to the discussion of lossless compression algorithms. It should be apparent that their *compression ratio* is generally limited (with a maximum at about 2 to 3). However, many of the multimedia applications we will address in the next several chapters require a much higher compression ratio. This is accomplished by *lossy* compression schemes.

7.8   FURTHER EXPLORATION

Mark Nelson's book [1] is a standard reference on data compression, as is the text by Khalid Sayood [2].

The Further Exploration section of the text web site for this chapter provides a set of web resources for lossless compression, including

- An excellent resource for data compression compiled by Mark Nelson that includes libraries, documentations, and source code for Huffman Coding, Adaptive Huffman Coding, LZW, Arithmetic Coding, and so on.

- Source code for Adaptive Arithmetic Coding

- The Theory of Data Compression web page, which introduces basic theories behind both lossless and lossy data compression. Shannon's original 1948 paper on information theory can be downloaded from this site as well.

- The FAQ for the `comp.compression` and `comp.compression.research` groups. This FAQ answers most of the commonly asked questions about data compression in general.

- A set of applets for lossless compression that effectively show interactive demonstrations of Adaptive Huffman, LZW, and so on. (Impressively, this web page is the fruit of a student's final project in a third-year undergraduate multimedia course based on the material in this text.)

- A good introduction to Arithmetic Coding.

- Grayscale test images `f-18.bmp, flowers.bmp, football.bmp, lena.bmp`.

7.9 EXERCISES

1. Suppose eight characters have a distribution A:(1), B:(1), C:(1), D:(2), E:(3), F:(5), G:(5), H:(10). Draw a Huffman tree for this distribution. (Because the algorithm may group subtrees with equal probability in a different order, your answer is not strictly unique.)

2. **(a)** What is the entropy (η) of the image below, where numbers (0, 20, 50, 99) denote the gray-level intensities?

99	99	99	99	99	99	99	99
20	20	20	20	20	20	20	20
0	0	0	0	0	0	0	0
0	0	50	50	50	50	0	0
0	0	50	50	50	50	0	0
0	0	50	50	50	50	0	0
0	0	50	50	50	50	0	0
0	0	0	0	0	0	0	0

   (b) Show step by step how to construct the Huffman tree to encode the above four intensity values in this image. Show the resulting code for each intensity value.

   (c) What is the average number of bits needed for each pixel, using your Huffman code? How does it compare to η?

3. Consider an alphabet with two symbols A, B, with probability $P(A) = x$ and $P(B) = 1 - x$.

   (a) Plot the entropy as a function of x. You might want to use $\log_2(3) = 1.6$, $\log_2(7) = 2.8$.

   (b) Discuss why it must be the case that if the probability of the two symbols is $1/2 + \epsilon$ and $1/2 - \epsilon$, with small ϵ, the entropy is less than the maximum.

   (c) Generalize the above result by showing that, for a source generating N symbols, the entropy is maximum when the symbols are all equiprobable.

   (d) As a small programming project, write code to verify the conclusions above.

4. Extended Huffman Coding assigns one codeword to each group of k symbols. Why is *average*(l) (the average number of bits for each symbol) still no less than the entropy η as indicated in equation (7.7)?

5. (a) What are the advantages and disadvantages of Arithmetic Coding as compared to Huffman Coding?

   (b) Suppose the alphabet is $[A, B, C]$, and the known probability distribution is $P_A = 0.5$, $P_B = 0.4$, $P_C = 0.1$. For simplicity, let's also assume that both encoder and decoder know that the length of the messages is always 3, so there is no need for a terminator.

      i. How many bits are needed to encode the message BBB by Huffman coding?

      ii. How many bits are needed to encode the message BBB by arithmetic coding?

6. (a) What are the advantages of Adaptive Huffman Coding compared to the original Huffman Coding algorithm?

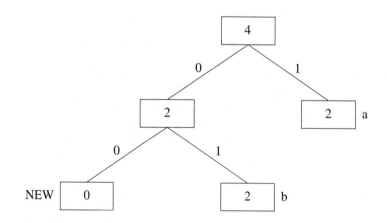

FIGURE 7.11: Adaptive Huffman tree.

(b) Assume that Adaptive Huffman Coding is used to code an information source S with a vocabulary of four letters (a, b, c, d). Before any transmission, the initial coding is a = 00, b = 01, c = 10, d = 11. As in the example illustrated in Figure 7.7, a special symbol NEW will be sent before any letter if it is to be sent the first time.

Figure 7.11 is the Adaptive Huffman tree after sending letters **aabb**. After that, the additional bitstream received by the decoder for the next few letters is 01010010101.

    i. What are the additional letters received?

    ii. Draw the adaptive Huffman trees after each of the additional letters is received.

7. Compare the rate of adaptation of adaptive Huffman coding and adaptive arithmetic coding (see the textbbook web site for the latter). What prevents each method from adapting to quick changes in source statistics?

8. Consider the dictionary-based LZW compression algorithm. Suppose the alphabet is the set of symbols {0,1}. Show the dictionary (symbol sets plus associated codes) and output for LZW compression of the input

$$0\ 1\ 1\ 0\ 0\ 1\ 1$$

9. Implement Huffman coding, adaptive Huffman, arithmetic coding, and the LZW coding algorithms using your favorite programming language. Generate at least three types of statistically different artificial data sources to test your implementation of these algorithms. Compare and comment on each algorithm's performance in terms of compression ratio for each type of data source.

7.10 REFERENCES

1 M. Nelson, *The Data Compression Book*, 2nd ed., New York: M&T Books, 1995.

2 K. Sayood, *Introduction to Data Compression*, 2nd ed., San Francisco: Morgan Kaufmann, 2000.

3 C.E. Shannon, "A Mathematical Theory of Communication," *Bell System Technical Journal*, 27: 379–423 and 623–656, 1948.

4 C.E. Shannon and W. Weaver, *The Mathematical Theory of Communication*, Champaign, IL: University of Illinois Press, 1949.

5 R.C. Gonzalez and R.E. Woods, *Digital Image Processing*, 2nd ed., Upper Saddle River, NJ: Prentice Hall, 2002.

6 R. Fano, *Transmission of Information*, Cambridge, MA: MIT Press, 1961.

7 D.A. Huffman, "A Method for the Construction of Minimum-Redundancy Codes," *Proceedings of the IRE* [Institute of Radio Engineers, now the IEEE], 40(9): 1098–1101, 1952.

8 T.H. Cormen, C.E. Leiserson, and R.L. Rivest, *Introduction to Algorithms*, Cambridge, MA: MIT Press, 1992.

9 J. Ziv and A. Lempel, "A Universal Algorithm for Sequential Data Compression," *IEEE Transactions on Information Theory*, 23(3): 337–343, 1977.

10 J. Ziv and A. Lempel, "Compression of Individual Sequences Via Variable-Rate Coding," *IEEE Transactions on Information Theory*, 24(5): 530–536, 1978.

11 T.A. Welch, "A Technique for High Performance Data Compression," *IEEE Computer*, 17(6): 8–19, 1984.

12 J. Rissanen and G.G. Langdon, "Arithmetic Coding," *IBM Journal of Research and Development*, 23(2): 149–162, 1979.

13 I.H. Witten, R.M. Neal, and J.G. Cleary, "Arithmetic Coding for Data Compression," *Communications of the ACM*, 30(6): 520–540, 1987.

14 T.C. Bell, J.G. Cleary, and I.H. Witten, *Text Compression*, Englewood Cliffs, NJ, Prentice Hall, 1990.

15 N. Abramson, *Information Theory and Coding*, New York: McGraw-Hill, 1963.

16 F. Jelinek, *Probabilistic Information Theory*, New York: McGraw-Hill, 1968.

17 R. Pasco, "Source Coding Algorithms for Data Compression," Ph.D. diss., Department of Electrical Engineering, Stanford University, 1976.

18 P. G. Howard and J. S. Vitter, "Practical Implementation of Arithmetic Coding," *Image and Text Compression*, ed. J. A. Storer, Boston: Kluwer Academic Publishers, 1992, 85–112.

19 S.M. Lei and M.T. Sun, "An Entropy Coding System for Digital HDTV Applications," *IEEE Transactions on Circuits and Systems for Video Technology*, 1(1): 147–154, 1991.

C H A P T E R 8

Lossy Compression Algorithms

In this chapter, we consider *lossy* compression methods. Since information loss implies some tradeoff between error and bitrate, we first consider measures of *distortion* — e.g., squared error. Different quantizers are introduced, each of which has a different distortion behavior. A discussion of transform coding leads into an introduction to the Discrete Cosine Transform used in JPEG compression (see Chapter 9) and the Karhunen Loève transform. Another transform scheme, wavelet based coding, is then set out.

8.1 INTRODUCTION

As discussed in Chapter 7, the *compression ratio* for image data using lossless compression techniques (e.g., Huffman Coding, Arithmetic Coding, LZW) is low when the image histogram is relatively flat. For image compression in multimedia applications, where a higher compression ratio is required, lossy methods are usually adopted. In lossy compression, the compressed image is usually not the same as the original image but is meant to form a close approximation to the original image *perceptually*. To quantitatively describe how close the approximation is to the original data, some form of distortion measure is required.

8.2 DISTORTION MEASURES

A *distortion measure* is a mathematical quantity that specifies how close an approximation is to its original, using some distortion criteria. When looking at compressed data, it is natural to think of the distortion in terms of the numerical difference between the original data and the reconstructed data. However, when the data to be compressed is an image, such a measure may not yield the intended result.

For example, if the reconstructed image is the same as original image except that it is shifted to the right by one vertical scan line, an average human observer would have a hard time distinguishing it from the original and would therefore conclude that the distortion is small. However, when the calculation is carried out numerically, we find a large distortion, because of the large changes in individual pixels of the reconstructed image. The problem is that we need a measure of *perceptual distortion*, not a more naive numerical approach. However, the study of perceptual distortions is beyond the scope of this book.

Of the many numerical distortion measures that have been defined, we present the three most commonly used in image compression. If we are interested in the average pixel difference, the *mean square error* (MSE) σ^2 is often used. It is defined as

$$\sigma^2 = \frac{1}{N} \sum_{n=1}^{N} (x_n - y_n)^2 \tag{8.1}$$

where x_n, y_n, and N are the input data sequence, reconstructed data sequence, and length of the data sequence, respectively.

If we are interested in the size of the error relative to the signal, we can measure the signal-to-noise ratio (SNR) by taking the ratio of the average square of the original data sequence and the mean square error (MSE), as discussed in Chapter 6. In decibel units (dB), it is defined as

$$SNR = 10 \log_{10} \frac{\sigma_x^2}{\sigma_d^2} \tag{8.2}$$

where σ_x^2 is the average square value of the original data sequence and σ_d^2 is the MSE. Another commonly used measure for distortion is the *peak-signal-to-noise ratio* (PSNR), which measures the size of the error relative to the peak value of the signal x_{peak}. It is given by

$$PSNR = 10 \log_{10} \frac{x_{peak}^2}{\sigma_d^2} \tag{8.3}$$

8.3   THE RATE-DISTORTION THEORY

Lossy compression always involves a tradeoff between rate and distortion. Rate is the average number of bits required to represent each source symbol. Within this framework, the tradeoff between rate and distortion is represented in the form of a rate-distortion function $R(D)$.

Intuitively, for a given source and a given distortion measure, if D is a tolerable amount of distortion, $R(D)$ specifies the lowest rate at which the source data can be encoded while keeping the distortion bounded above by D. It is easy to see that when $D = 0$, we have a lossless compression of the source. The rate-distortion function is meant to describe a fundamental limit for the performance of a coding algorithm and so can be used to evaluate the performance of different algorithms.

Figure 8.1 shows a typical rate-distortion function. Notice that the minimum possible rate at $D = 0$, no loss, is the entropy of the source data. The distortion corresponding to a rate $R(D) \equiv 0$ is the maximum amount of distortion incurred when "nothing" is coded.

Finding a closed-form analytic description of the rate-distortion function for a given source is difficult, if not impossible. Gyorgy [1] presents analytic expressions of the rate-distortion function for various sources. For sources for which an analytic solution cannot be readily obtained, the rate-distortion function can be calculated numerically, using algorithms developed by Arimoto [2] and Blahut [3].

8.4   QUANTIZATION

Quantization in some form is the heart of any lossy scheme. Without quantization, we would indeed be losing little information. Here, we embark on a more detailed discussion of quantization than in Section 6.3.2.

The source we are interested in compressing may contain a large number of distinct output values (or even infinite, if analog). To efficiently represent the source output, we have to reduce the number of distinct values to a much smaller set, via quantization.

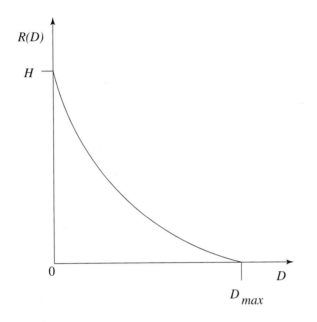

FIGURE 8.1: Typical rate-distortion function.

Each algorithm (each *quantizer*) can be uniquely determined by its partition of the input range, on the encoder side, and the set of output values, on the decoder side. The input and output of each quantizer can be either scalar values or vector values, thus leading to *scalar quantizers* and *vector quantizers*. In this section, we examine the design of both uniform and nonuniform scalar quantizers and briefly introduce the topic of *vector quantization* (VQ).

8.4.1 Uniform Scalar Quantization

A uniform scalar quantizer partitions the domain of input values into equally spaced intervals, except possibly at the two outer intervals. The endpoints of partition intervals are called the quantizer's *decision boundaries*. The output or reconstruction value corresponding to each interval is taken to be the midpoint of the interval. The length of each interval is referred to as the *step size*, denoted by the symbol Δ. Uniform scalar quantizers are of two types: *midrise* and *midtread*. A midtread quantizer has zero as one of its output values, whereas the midrise quantizer has a partition interval that brackets zero (see Figure 8.2). A midrise quantizer is used with an even number of output levels, and a midtread quantizer with an odd number.

A midtread quantizer is important when source data represents the zero value by fluctuating between small positive and negative numbers. Applying the midtread quantizer in this case would produce an accurate and steady representation of the value zero. For the special case $\Delta = 1$, we can simply compute the output values for these quantizers as

$$Q_{midrise}(x) = \lceil x \rceil - 0.5 \qquad (8.4)$$
$$Q_{midtread}(x) = \lfloor x + 0.5 \rfloor \qquad (8.5)$$

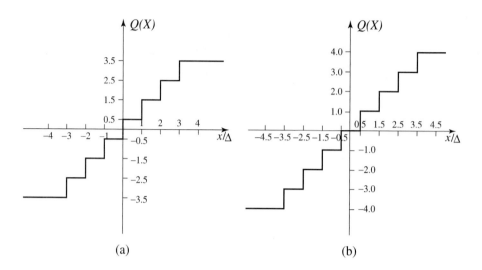

FIGURE 8.2: Uniform scalar quantizers: (a) midrise; (b) midtread.

The goal for the design of a successful uniform quantizer is to minimize the distortion for a given source input with a desired number of output values. This can be done by adjusting the step size Δ to match the input statistics.

Let's examine the performance of an M level quantizer. Let $B = \{b_0, b_1, \ldots, b_M\}$ be the set of decision boundaries and $Y = \{y_1, y_2, \ldots, y_M\}$ be the set of reconstruction or output values. Suppose the input is uniformly distributed in the interval $[-X_{max}, X_{max}]$. The rate of the quantizer is

$$R = \lceil \log_2 M \rceil \tag{8.6}$$

That is, R is the number of bits required to code M things — in this case, the M output levels.

The step size Δ is given by

$$\Delta = \frac{2X_{max}}{M} \tag{8.7}$$

since the entire range of input values is from $-X_{max}$ to X_{max}. For bounded input, the quantization error caused by the quantizer is referred to as *granular distortion*. If the quantizer replaces a whole range of values, from a maximum value to ∞, and similarly for negative values, that part of the distortion is called the *overload* distortion.

To get an overall figure for granular distortion, notice that decision boundaries b_i for a midrise quantizer are $[(i-1)\Delta, i\Delta], i = 1 .. M/2$, covering positive data X (and another half for negative X values). Output values y_i are the midpoints $i\Delta - \Delta/2, i = 1 .. M/2$,

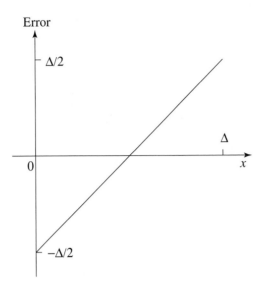

FIGURE 8.3: Quantization error of a uniformly distributed source.

again just considering positive data. The total distortion is twice the sum over the positive data, or

$$D_{gran} = 2 \sum_{i=1}^{\frac{M}{2}} \int_{(i-1)\Delta}^{i\Delta} \left(x - \frac{2i-1}{2}\Delta\right)^2 \frac{1}{2X_{max}} \, dx \qquad (8.8)$$

where we divide by the range of X to normalize to a value of at most 1.

Since the reconstruction values y_i are the midpoints of each interval, the quantization error must lie within the values $[-\frac{\Delta}{2}, \frac{\Delta}{2}]$. Figure 8.3 is a graph of quantization error for a uniformly distributed source. The quantization error in this case is also uniformly distributed. Therefore, the average squared error is the same as the variance σ_d^2 of the quantization error calculated from just the interval $[0, \Delta]$ with error values in $[-\frac{\Delta}{2}, \frac{\Delta}{2}]$. The error value at x is $e(x) = x - \Delta/2$, so the variance of errors is given by

$$
\begin{aligned}
\sigma_d^2 &= \frac{1}{\Delta} \int_0^\Delta (e(x) - \bar{e})^2 \, dx \\
&= \frac{1}{\Delta} \int_0^\Delta \left(x - \frac{\Delta}{2} - 0\right)^2 dx \qquad (8.9) \\
&= \frac{\Delta^2}{12}
\end{aligned}
$$

Similarly, the *signal* variance is $\sigma_x^2 = (2X_{max})^2/12$, so if the quantizer is n bits, $M = 2^n$, then from Eq. (8.2) we have

$$
\begin{aligned}
SQNR &= 10\log_{10}\left(\frac{\sigma_x^2}{\sigma_d^2}\right) \\
&= 10\log_{10}\left(\frac{(2X_{max})^2}{12}\cdot\frac{12}{\Delta^2}\right) \\
&= 10\log_{10}\left(\frac{(2X_{max})^2}{12}\cdot\frac{12}{\left(\frac{2X_{max}}{M}\right)^2}\right) \\
&= 10\log_{10} M^2 = 20\,n\,\log_{10} 2 \qquad (8.10) \\
&= 6.02\,n \;\; (dB) \qquad\qquad\qquad\quad (8.11)
\end{aligned}
$$

Hence, we have rederived the formula (6.3) derived more simply in Section 6.1. From Eq. (8.11), we have the important result that increasing one bit in the quantizer increases the signal-to-quantization noise ratio by 6.02 dB. More sophisticated estimates of D result from more sophisticated models of the probability distribution of errors.

8.4.2 Nonuniform Scalar Quantization

If the input source is not uniformly distributed, a uniform quantizer may be inefficient. Increasing the number of decision levels within the region where the source is densely distributed can effectively lower granular distortion. In addition, without having to increase the total number of decision levels, we can enlarge the region in which the source is sparsely distributed. Such *nonuniform quantizers* thus have nonuniformly defined decision boundaries.

There are two common approaches for nonuniform quantization: the Lloyd–Max quantizer and the companded quantizer, both introduced in Chapter 6.

Lloyd–Max Quantizer.*   For a uniform quantizer, the total distortion is equal to the granular distortion, as in Eq. (8.8). If the source distribution is not uniform, we must explicitly consider its probability distribution (*probability density function*) $f_X(x)$. Now we need the correct decision boundaries b_i and reconstruction values y_i, by solving for both simultaneously. To do so, we plug variables b_i, y_i into a total distortion measure

$$
D_{gran} = \sum_{j=1}^{M} \int_{b_{j-1}}^{b_j} (x - y_j)^2 \frac{1}{X_{max}} f_X(x)\,dx \qquad (8.12)
$$

Then we can minimize the total distortion by setting the derivative of Eq. (8.12) to zero. Differentiating with respect to y_j yields the set of reconstruction values

$$
y_j = \frac{\int_{b_{j-1}}^{b_j} x f_X(x)\,dx}{\int_{b_{j-1}}^{b_j} f_X(x)\,dx} \qquad (8.13)
$$

This says that the optimal reconstruction value is the weighted centroid of the x interval. Differentiating with respect to b_j and setting the result to zero yields

$$b_j = \frac{y_{j+1} + y_j}{2} \tag{8.14}$$

This gives a decision boundary b_j at the midpoint of two adjacent reconstruction values. Solving these two equations simultaneously is carried out by iteration. The result is termed the Lloyd–Max quantizer.

ALGORITHM 8.1   LLOYD–MAX QUANTIZATION

```
BEGIN
   Choose initial level set y₀
   i = 0
   Repeat
      Compute bᵢ using Equation 8.14
      i = i + 1
      Compute yᵢ using Equation 8.13
   Until |yᵢ − yᵢ₋₁| < ε
END
```

Starting with an initial guess of the optimal reconstruction levels, the algorithm above iteratively estimates the optimal boundaries, based on the current estimate of the reconstruction levels. It then updates the current estimate of the reconstruction levels, using the newly computed boundary information. The process is repeated until the reconstruction levels converge. For an example of the algorithm in operation, see Exercise 3.

Companded Quantizer.   In companded quantization, the input is mapped by a *compressor function G* and then quantized using a uniform quantizer. After transmission, the quantized values are mapped back using an *expander function G^{-1}*. The block diagram for the companding process is shown in Figure 8.4, where $\hat{X}$ is the quantized version of X. If the input source is bounded by x_{max}, then any nonuniform quantizer can be represented as a companded quantizer. The two commonly used companders are the μ-law and A-law companders (Section 6.1).

FIGURE 8.4: Companded quantization.

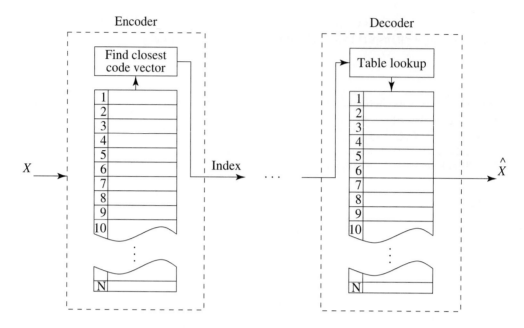

FIGURE 8.5: Basic vector quantization procedure.

8.4.3 Vector Quantization*

One of the fundamental ideas in Shannon's original work on information theory is that any compression system performs better if it operates on vectors or groups of samples rather than on individual symbols or samples. We can form vectors of input samples by concatenating a number of consecutive samples into a single vector. For example, an input vector might be a segment of a speech sample, a group of consecutive pixels in an image, or a chunk of data in any other format.

The idea behind *vector quantization* (VQ) is similar to that of scalar quantization but extended into multiple dimensions. Instead of representing values within an interval in one-dimensional space by a reconstruction value, as in scalar quantization, in VQ an n-component *code vector* represents vectors that lie within a region in n-dimensional space. A collection of these code vectors forms the *codebook* for the vector quantizer.

Since there is no implicit ordering of code vectors, as there is in the one-dimensional case, an index set is also needed to index into the codebook. Figure 8.5 shows the basic vector quantization procedure. In the diagram, the encoder finds the closest code vector to the input vector and outputs the associated index. On the decoder side, exactly the same codebook is used. When the coded index of the input vector is received, a simple table lookup is performed to determine the reconstruction vector.

Finding the appropriate codebook and searching for the closest code vector at the encoder end may require considerable computational resources. However, the decoder can execute quickly, since only a constant time operation is needed to obtain the reconstruction. Because of this property, VQ is attractive for systems with a lot of resources at the encoder end while the decoder has only limited resources, and the need is for quick execution time. Most multimedia applications fall into this category.

8.5   TRANSFORM CODING

From basic principles of information theory, we know that coding vectors is more efficient than coding scalars (see Section 7.4.2). To carry out such an intention, we need to group blocks of consecutive samples from the source input into vectors.

Let $\mathbf{X} = \{x_1, x_2, \ldots, x_k\}^T$ be a vector of samples. Whether our input data is an image, a piece of music, an audio or video clip, or even a piece of text, there is a good chance that a substantial amount of correlation is inherent among neighboring samples x_i. The rationale behind transform coding is that if $\mathbf{Y}$ is the result of a linear transform $\mathbf{T}$ of the input vector $\mathbf{X}$ in such a way that the components of $\mathbf{Y}$ are much less correlated, then $\mathbf{Y}$ can be coded more efficiently than $\mathbf{X}$.

For example, if most information in an RGB image is contained in a main axis, rotating so that this direction is the first component means that luminance can be compressed differently from color information. This will approximate the luminance channel in the eye.

In higher dimensions than three, if most information is accurately described by the first few components of a transformed vector, the remaining components can be coarsely quantized, or even set to zero, with little signal distortion. The more *decorrelated* — that is, the less effect one dimension has on another (the more orthogonal the axes), the more chance we have of dealing differently with the axes that store relatively minor amounts of information without affecting reasonably accurate reconstruction of the signal from its quantized or truncated transform coefficients.

Generally, the transform $\mathbf{T}$ itself does not compress any data. The compression comes from the processing and *quantization* of the components of $\mathbf{Y}$. In this section, we will study the Discrete Cosine Transform (DCT) as a tool to decorrelate the input signal. We will also examine the Karhunen–Loève Transform (KLT), which *optimally* decorrelates the components of the input $\mathbf{X}$.

8.5.1   Discrete Cosine Transform (DCT)

The Discrete Cosine Transform (DCT), a widely used transform coding technique, is able to perform decorrelation of the input signal in a data-independent manner. Because of this, it has gained tremendous popularity. We will examine the definition of the DCT and discuss some of its properties, in particular the relationship between it and the more familiar Discrete Fourier Transform (DFT).

Definition of DCT.   Let's start with the two-dimensional DCT. Given a function $f(i, j)$ over two integer variables i and j (a piece of an image), the 2D DCT transforms it into a new function $F(u, v)$, with integer u and v running over the same range as i and j. The general definition of the transform is

$$F(u, v) = \frac{2\,C(u)\,C(v)}{\sqrt{MN}} \sum_{i=0}^{M-1} \sum_{j=0}^{N-1} \cos\frac{(2i+1)u\pi}{2M} \cos\frac{(2j+1)v\pi}{2N} f(i, j) \qquad (8.15)$$

where $i, u = 0, 1, \ldots, M - 1$, $j, v = 0, 1, \ldots, N - 1$, and the constants $C(u)$ and $C(v)$ are determined by

$$C(\xi) = \begin{cases} \frac{\sqrt{2}}{2} & \text{if } \xi = 0, \\ 1 & \text{otherwise.} \end{cases} \tag{8.16}$$

In the JPEG image compression standard (see Chapter 9), an image block is defined to have dimension $M = N = 8$. Therefore, the definitions for the 2D DCT and its inverse (IDCT) in this case are as follows:

2D Discrete Cosine Transform (2D DCT).

$$F(u, v) = \frac{C(u)\,C(v)}{4} \sum_{i=0}^{7} \sum_{j=0}^{7} \cos \frac{(2i + 1)u\pi}{16} \cos \frac{(2j + 1)v\pi}{16} f(i, j), \tag{8.17}$$

where $i, j, u, v = 0, 1, \ldots, 7$, and the constants $C(u)$ and $C(v)$ are determined by Eq. (8.16).

2D Inverse Discrete Cosine Transform (2D IDCT).   The inverse function is almost the same, with the roles of $f(i, j)$ and $F(u, v)$ reversed, except that now $C(u)C(v)$ must stand inside the sums:

$$\tilde{f}(i, j) = \sum_{u=0}^{7} \sum_{v=0}^{7} \frac{C(u)\,C(v)}{4} \cos \frac{(2i + 1)u\pi}{16} \cos \frac{(2j + 1)v\pi}{16} F(u, v) \tag{8.18}$$

where $i, j, u, v = 0, 1, \ldots, 7$.

The 2D transforms are applicable to 2D signals, such as digital images. As shown below, the 1D version of the DCT and IDCT is similar to the 2D version.

1D Discrete Cosine Transform (1D DCT).

$$F(u) = \frac{C(u)}{2} \sum_{i=0}^{7} \cos \frac{(2i + 1)u\pi}{16} f(i), \tag{8.19}$$

where $i = 0, 1, \ldots, 7$, $u = 0, 1, \ldots, 7$.

1D Inverse Discrete Cosine Transform (1D-IDCT).

$$\tilde{f}(i) = \sum_{u=0}^{7} \frac{C(u)}{2} \cos \frac{(2i + 1)u\pi}{16} F(u), \tag{8.20}$$

where $i = 0, 1, \ldots, 7$, $u = 0, 1, \ldots, 7$.

One-Dimensional DCT.   Let's examine the DCT for a one-dimensional signal; almost all concepts are readily extensible to the 2D DCT.

An electrical signal with constant magnitude is known as a DC (direct current) signal. A common example is a battery that carries 1.5 or 9 volts DC. An electrical signal that changes its magnitude periodically at a certain frequency is known as an AC (alternating current) signal. A good example is the household electric power circuit, which carries electricity with sinusoidal waveform at 110 volts AC, 60 Hz (or 220 volts, 50 Hz in many other countries).

Most real signals are more complex. Speech signals or a row of gray-level intensities in a digital image are examples of such 1D signals. However, any signal can be expressed as a sum of multiple signals that are sine or cosine waveforms at various amplitudes and frequencies. This is known as Fourier analysis. The terms DC and AC, originating in electrical engineering, are carried over to describe these components of a signal (usually) composed of one DC and several AC components.

If a cosine function is used, the process of determining the amplitudes of the AC and DC components of the signal is called a *Cosine Transform*, and the integer indices make it a *Discrete Cosine Transform*. When $u = 0$, Eq. (8.19) yields the DC coefficient; when $u = 1$, or 2,..., up to 7, it yields the first or second, etc., up to the seventh AC coefficient.

Eq. (8.20) shows the *Inverse Discrete Cosine Transform*. This uses a sum of the products of the DC or AC coefficients and the cosine functions to reconstruct (recompose) the function $f(i)$. Since computing the DCT and IDCT involves some loss, $f(i)$ is now denoted by $\tilde{f}(i)$.

In short, the role of the DCT is to decompose the original signal into its DC and AC components; the role of the IDCT is to reconstruct (recompose) the signal. The DCT and IDCT use the same set of cosine functions; they are known as *basis functions*. Figure 8.6 shows the family of eight 1D DCT basis functions: $u = 0 .. 7$.

The DCT enables a new means of signal processing and analysis in the *frequency domain*. We mean to analyze blocks of eight pixels in an image, but we can begin by considering time-dependent signals, rather than space-dependent ones (since time-signal analysis is where the method originates).

Suppose $f(i)$ represents a signal that changes with time i (we will not be bothered here by the convention that time is usually denoted as t). The 1D DCT transforms $f(i)$, which is in the *time domain*, to $F(u)$, which is in the *frequency domain*. The coefficients $F(u)$ are known as the *frequency responses* and form the *frequency spectrum* of $f(i)$.

Let's use some examples to illustrate frequency responses.

EXAMPLE 8.1

The left side of Figure 8.7(a) shows a DC signal with a magnitude of 100, i.e., $f_1(i) = 100$. Since we are examining the *Discrete* Cosine Transform, the input signal is discrete, and its domain is [0, 7].

When $u = 0$, regardless of the i value, all the cosine terms in Eq. (8.19) become $\cos 0$, which equals 1. Taking into account that $C(0) = \sqrt{2}/2$, $F_1(0)$ is given by

$$
\begin{aligned}
F_1(0) &= \frac{\sqrt{2}}{2 \cdot 2} \cdot (1 \cdot 100 + 1 \cdot 100 + 1 \cdot 100 + 1 \cdot 100 \\
&\quad + 1 \cdot 100 + 1 \cdot 100 + 1 \cdot 100 + 1 \cdot 100) \\
&\approx 283
\end{aligned}
$$

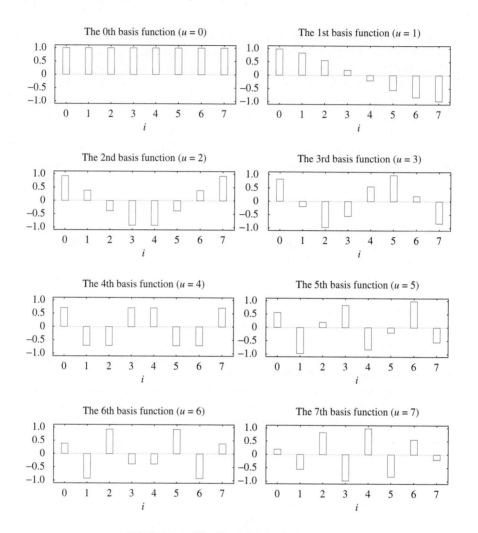

FIGURE 8.6: The 1D DCT basis functions.

When $u = 1$, $F_1(u)$ is as below. Because $\cos \frac{\pi}{16} = -\cos \frac{15\pi}{16}$, $\cos \frac{3\pi}{16} = -\cos \frac{13\pi}{16}$, etc. and $C(1) = 1$, we have

$$
\begin{aligned}
F_1(1) &= \frac{1}{2} \cdot (\cos \frac{\pi}{16} \cdot 100 + \cos \frac{3\pi}{16} \cdot 100 + \cos \frac{5\pi}{16} \cdot 100 + \cos \frac{7\pi}{16} \cdot 100 \\
&\quad + \cos \frac{9\pi}{16} \cdot 100 + \cos \frac{11\pi}{16} \cdot 100 + \cos \frac{13\pi}{16} \cdot 100 + \cos \frac{15\pi}{16} \cdot 100) \\
&= 0
\end{aligned}
$$

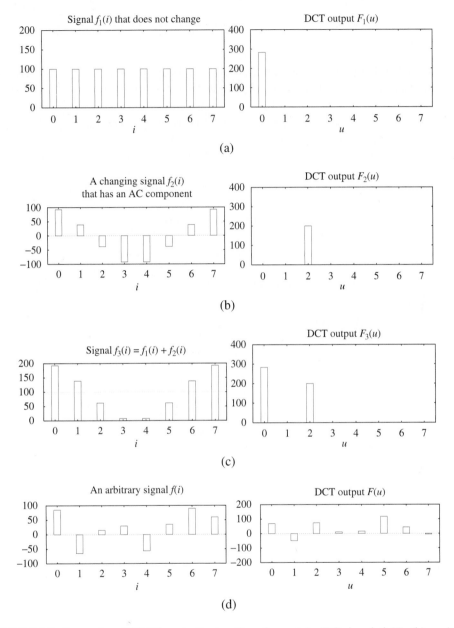

FIGURE 8.7: Examples of 1D Discrete Cosine Transform: (a) a DC signal $f_1(i)$; (b) an AC signal $f_2(i)$; (c) $f_3(i) = f_1(i) + f_2(i)$; and (d) an arbitrary signal $f(i)$.

Similarly, it can be shown that $F_1(2) = F_1(3) = \dots = F_1(7) = 0$. The 1D-DCT result $F_1(u)$ for this DC signal $f_1(i)$ is depicted on the right side of Figure 8.7(a) — only a DC (i.e., first) component of F is nonzero.

EXAMPLE 8.2

The left side of Figure 8.7(b) shows a discrete cosine signal $f_2(i)$. Incidentally (or, rather, purposely), it has the same frequency and phase as the second cosine basis function, and its amplitude is 100.

When $u = 0$, again, all the cosine terms in Eq. (8.19) equal 1. Because $\cos\frac{\pi}{8} = -\cos\frac{7\pi}{8}$, $\cos\frac{3\pi}{8} = -\cos\frac{5\pi}{8}$, and so on, we have

$$
\begin{aligned}
F_2(0) &= \frac{\sqrt{2}}{2 \cdot 2} \cdot 1 \cdot (100\cos\frac{\pi}{8} + 100\cos\frac{3\pi}{8} + 100\cos\frac{5\pi}{8} + 100\cos\frac{7\pi}{8} \\
&\quad + 100\cos\frac{9\pi}{8} + 100\cos\frac{11\pi}{8} + 100\cos\frac{13\pi}{8} + 100\cos\frac{15\pi}{8}) \\
&= 0
\end{aligned}
$$

To calculate $F_2(u)$, we first note that when $u = 2$, because $\cos\frac{3\pi}{8} = \sin\frac{\pi}{8}$, we have

$$
\cos^2\frac{\pi}{8} + \cos^2\frac{3\pi}{8} = \cos^2\frac{\pi}{8} + \sin^2\frac{\pi}{8} = 1
$$

Similarly,

$$
\begin{aligned}
\cos^2\frac{5\pi}{8} + \cos^2\frac{7\pi}{8} &= 1 \\
\cos^2\frac{9\pi}{8} + \cos^2\frac{11\pi}{8} &= 1 \\
\cos^2\frac{13\pi}{8} + \cos^2\frac{15\pi}{8} &= 1
\end{aligned}
$$

Then we end up with

$$
\begin{aligned}
F_2(2) &= \frac{1}{2} \cdot (\cos\frac{\pi}{8} \cdot \cos\frac{\pi}{8} + \cos\frac{3\pi}{8} \cdot \cos\frac{3\pi}{8} + \cos\frac{5\pi}{8} \cdot \cos\frac{5\pi}{8} \\
&\quad + \cos\frac{7\pi}{8} \cdot \cos\frac{7\pi}{8} + \cos\frac{9\pi}{8} \cdot \cos\frac{9\pi}{8} + \cos\frac{11\pi}{8} \cdot \cos\frac{11\pi}{8} \\
&\quad + \cos\frac{13\pi}{8} \cdot \cos\frac{13\pi}{8} + \cos\frac{15\pi}{8} \cdot \cos\frac{15\pi}{8}) \cdot 100 \\
&= \frac{1}{2} \cdot (1 + 1 + 1 + 1) \cdot 100 = 200
\end{aligned}
$$

We will not show the other derivations in detail. It turns out that $F_2(1) = F_2(3) = F_2(4) = \cdots = F_2(7) = 0$.

EXAMPLE 8.3

In the third row of Figure 8.7 the input signal to the DCT is now the sum of the previous two signals — that is, $f_3(i) = f_1(i) + f_2(i)$. The output $F(u)$ values are

$$F_3(0) = 283,$$
$$F_3(2) = 200,$$
$$F_3(1) = F_3(3) = F_3(4) = \cdots = F_3(7) = 0$$

Thus we discover that $F_3(u) = F_1(u) + F_2(u)$.

EXAMPLE 8.4

The fourth row of the figure shows an arbitrary (or at least relatively complex) input signal $f(i)$ and its DCT output $F(u)$:

$$f(i) \ (i = 0..7): \quad 85 \quad -65 \quad 15 \quad 30 \quad -56 \quad 35 \quad 90 \quad 60$$
$$F(u) \ (u = 0..7): \quad 69 \quad -49 \quad 74 \quad 11 \quad 16 \quad 117 \quad 44 \quad -5$$

Note that in this more general case, all the DCT coefficients $F(u)$ are nonzero and some are negative.

From the above examples, the characteristics of the DCT can be summarized as follows:

1. The DCT produces the frequency spectrum $F(u)$ corresponding to the spatial signal $f(i)$.

   In particular, the 0th DCT coefficient $F(0)$ is the DC component of the signal $f(i)$. Up to a constant factor (i.e., $\frac{1}{2} \cdot \frac{\sqrt{2}}{2} \cdot 8 = 2 \cdot \sqrt{2}$ in the 1D DCT and $\frac{1}{4} \cdot \frac{\sqrt{2}}{2} \cdot \frac{\sqrt{2}}{2} \cdot 64 = 8$ in the 2D DCT), $F(0)$ equals the average magnitude of the signal. In Figure 8.7(a), the average magnitude of the DC signal is obviously 100, and $F(0) = 2\sqrt{2} \times 100$; in Figure 8.7(b), the average magnitude of the AC signal is 0, and so is $F(0)$; in Figure 8.7(c), the average magnitude of $f_3(i)$ is apparently 100, and again we have $F(0) = 2\sqrt{2} \times 100$.

   The other seven DCT coefficients reflect the various changing (i.e., AC) components of the signal $f(i)$ at different frequencies. If we denote $F(1)$ as AC1, $F(2)$ as AC2, ..., $F(7)$ as AC7, then AC1 is the first AC component, which completes half a cycle as a cosine function over $[0, 7]$; AC2 completes a full cycle; AC3 completes one and one-half cycles; ..., and AC7, three and a half cycles. All these are, of course, due to the cosine basis functions, which are arranged in exactly this manner. In other words, the second basis function corresponds to AC1, the third corresponds to AC2, and so on. In the example in Figure 8.7(b), since the signal $f_2(i)$ and the third basis function have exactly the same cosine waveform, with identical frequency and phase, they will reach the maximum (positive) and minimum (negative) values synchronously. As a result, their products are always positive, and the sum of their products ($F_2(2)$ or AC2) is large. It turns out that all other AC coefficients are zero, since $f_2(i)$ and all the other basis functions happen to be orthogonal. (We will discuss orthogonality later in this chapter.)

It should be pointed out that the DCT coefficients can easily take on negative values. For DC, this occurs when the average of $f(i)$ is less than zero. (For an image, this never happens so the DC is nonnegative.) For AC, a special case occurs when $f(i)$ and some basis function have the same frequency but one of them happens to be half a cycle behind — this yields a negative coefficient, possibly with a large magnitude.

In general, signals will look more like the one in Figure 8.7(d). Then $f(i)$ will produce many nonzero AC components, with the ones toward AC7 indicating higher frequency content. A signal will have large (positive or negative) response in its high-frequency components only when it alternates rapidly within the small range [0, 7].

As an example, if AC7 is a large positive number, this indicates that the signal $f(i)$ has a component that alternates synchronously with the eighth basis function — three and half cycles. According to the Nyqist theorem, this is the highest frequency in the signal that can be sampled with eight discrete values without significant loss and aliasing.

2. The DCT is a *linear transform*.

In general, a transform $\mathcal{T}$ (or function) is *linear*, iff

$$\mathcal{T}(\alpha p + \beta q) = \alpha \mathcal{T}(p) + \beta \mathcal{T}(q), \tag{8.21}$$

where α and β are constants, and p and q are any functions, variables or constants. From the definition in Eq. (8.19), this property can readily be proven for the DCT, because it uses only simple arithmetic operations.

One-Dimensional Inverse DCT. Let's finish the example in Figure 8.7(d) by showing its inverse DCT (IDCT). Recall that $F(u)$ contains the following:

$$F(u) \ (u = 0..7): \quad 69 \quad -49 \quad 74 \quad 11 \quad 16 \quad 117 \quad 44 \quad -5$$

The 1D IDCT, as indicated in Eq. (8.20), can readily be implemented as a loop with eight iterations, as illustrated in Figure 8.8.

Iteration 0: $\tilde{f}(i) = \frac{C(0)}{2} \cdot \cos 0 \cdot F(0) = \frac{\sqrt{2}}{2 \cdot 2} \cdot 1 \cdot 69 \approx 24.3.$

Iteration 1: $\tilde{f}(i) = \frac{C(0)}{2} \cdot \cos 0 \cdot F(0) + \frac{C(1)}{2} \cdot \cos \frac{(2i+1)\pi}{16} \cdot F(1)$
$\approx 24.3 + \frac{1}{2} \cdot (-49) \cdot \cos \frac{(2i+1)\pi}{16} \approx 24.3 - 24.5 \cdot \cos \frac{(2i+1)\pi}{16}.$

Iteration 2: $\tilde{f}(i) = \frac{C(0)}{2} \cdot \cos 0 \cdot F(0) + \frac{C(1)}{2} \cdot \cos \frac{(2i+1)\pi}{16} \cdot F(1) + \frac{C(2)}{2} \cdot \cos \frac{(2i+1)\pi}{8} \cdot F(2)$
$\approx 24.3 - 24.5 \cdot \cos \frac{(2i+1)\pi}{16} + 37 \cdot \cos \frac{(2i+1)\pi}{8}.$

$\vdots$

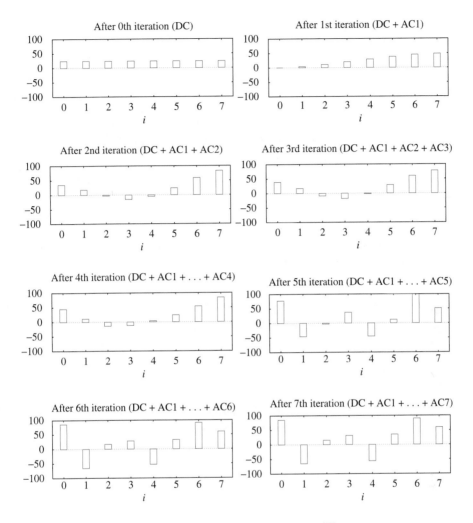

FIGURE 8.8: An example of 1D IDCT.

After iteration 0, $\tilde{f}(i)$ has a constant value of approximately 24.3, which is the recovery of the DC component in $f(i)$; after iteration 1, $\tilde{f}(i) \approx 24.3 - 24.5 \cdot \cos \frac{(2i+1)\pi}{16}$, which is the sum of the DC and first AC component; after iteration 2, $\tilde{f}(i)$ reflects the sum of DC and AC1 and AC2; and so on. As shown, the process of the sum-of-product in IDCT eventually reconstructs (recomposes) the function $f(i)$, which is approximately

$$\tilde{f}(i)\ (i = 0..7):\quad 85 \quad -65 \quad 15 \quad 30 \quad -56 \quad 35 \quad 90 \quad 60$$

As it happens, even though we went from integer to integer via intermediate *floats*, we recovered the signal exactly. This is not always true, but the answer is always close.

The Cosine Basis Functions   For a better decomposition, the basis functions should be *orthogonal*, so as to have the least redundancy amongst them.
Functions $B_p(i)$ and $B_q(i)$ are orthogonal if

$$\sum_i [B_p(i) \cdot B_q(i)] = 0 \qquad if \ p \neq q \tag{8.22}$$

Functions $B_p(i)$ and $B_q(i)$ are *orthonormal* if they are orthogonal and

$$\sum_i [B_p(i) \cdot B_q(i)] = 1 \qquad if \ p = q \tag{8.23}$$

The orthonormal property is desirable. With this property, the signal is not amplified during the transform. When the same basis function is used in both the transformation and its inverse (sometimes called *forward transform* and *backward transform*), we will get (approximately) the same signal back.
It can be shown that

$$\sum_{i=0}^{7} \left[\cos \frac{(2i+1) \cdot p\pi}{16} \cdot \cos \frac{(2i+1) \cdot q\pi}{16} \right] = 0 \qquad if \ p \neq q$$

$$\sum_{i=0}^{7} \left[\frac{C(p)}{2} \cos \frac{(2i+1) \cdot p\pi}{16} \cdot \frac{C(q)}{2} \cos \frac{(2i+1) \cdot q\pi}{16} \right] = 1 \qquad if \ p = q$$

The cosine basis functions in the DCT are indeed orthogonal. With the help of constants $C(p)$ and $C(q)$ they are also orthonormal. (Now we understand why constants $C(u)$ and $C(v)$ in the definitions of DCT and IDCT seemed to have taken some arbitrary values.)
Recall that because of the orthogonality, for $f_2(i)$ in Figure 8.7(b), only $F_2(2)$ (for $u = 2$) has a nonzero output whereas all other DCT coefficients are zero. This is desirable for some signal processing and analysis in the frequency domain, since we are now able to precisely identify the frequency components in the original signal.
The cosine basis functions are analogous to the basis vectors $\vec{x}, \vec{y}, \vec{z}$ for the 3D Cartesian space, or the so-called *3D vector space*. The vectors are orthonormal, because

$$\begin{aligned}
\vec{x} \cdot \vec{y} &= (1,0,0) \cdot (0,1,0) = 0 \\
\vec{x} \cdot \vec{z} &= (1,0,0) \cdot (0,0,1) = 0 \\
\vec{y} \cdot \vec{z} &= (0,1,0) \cdot (0,0,1) = 0 \\
\vec{x} \cdot \vec{x} &= (1,0,0) \cdot (1,0,0) = 1 \\
\vec{y} \cdot \vec{y} &= (1,0,0) \cdot (1,0,0) = 1 \\
\vec{z} \cdot \vec{z} &= (1,0,0) \cdot (1,0,0) = 1
\end{aligned}$$

Any point $P = (x_p, y_p, z_p)$ can be represented by a vector $\vec{OP} = (x_p, y_p, z_p)$, where O is the origin, which can in turn be decomposed into $x_p \cdot \vec{x} + y_p \cdot \vec{y} + z_p \cdot \vec{z}$.

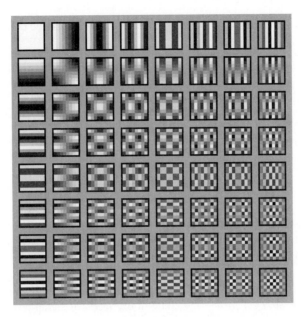

FIGURE 8.9: Graphical illustration of 8×8 2D DCT basis.

If we view the sum-of-products operation in Eq. (8.19) as the dot product of one of the discrete cosine basis functions (for a specified u) and the signal $f(i)$, then the analogy between the DCT and the Cartesian projection is remarkable. Namely, to get the x-coordinate of point P, we simply project P onto the x axis. Mathematically, this is equivalent to a dot product $\vec{x} \cdot \vec{OP} = x_p$. Obviously, the same goes for obtaining y_p and z_p.

Now, compare this to the example in Figure 8.7(b), for a point $P = (0, 5, 0)$ in the Cartesian space. Only its projection onto the y axis is $y_p = 5$ and its projections onto the x and z axes are both 0.

2D Basis Functions.   For two-dimensional DCT functions, we use the basis shown as 8×8 *images*. These are depicted in Figure 8.9, where white indicates positive values and black indicates negative. To obtain DCT coefficients, we essentially just form the inner product of each of these 64 basis images with an 8×8 block from an original image. Notice that now we are talking about an original signal indexed by space, not time. We do this for each 8×8 image block. The 64 products we calculate make up an 8×8 *spatial frequency* image $F(u, v)$.

2D Separable Basis.   Of course, for speed, most software implementations use fixed point arithmetic to calculate the DCT transform. Just as there is a mathematically derived Fast Fourier Transform, there is also a Fast DCT. Some fast implementations approximate coefficients so that all multiplies are shifts and adds. Moreover, a much simpler mechanism is used to produce 2D DCT coefficients — factorization into two 1D DCT transforms.

When the block size is 8, the 2D DCT can be *separated* into a sequence of two 1D DCT steps. First, we calculate an intermediate function $G(i, v)$ by performing a 1D DCT on each column — in this way, we have gone over to frequency space for the columns, but not for the rows:

$$G(i, v) = \frac{1}{2}C(v) \sum_{j=0}^{7} \cos \frac{(2j+1)v\pi}{16} f(i, j) \tag{8.24}$$

Then we calculate another 1D DCT, this time replacing the row dimension by its frequency counterpart:

$$F(u, v) = \frac{1}{2}C(u) \sum_{i=0}^{7} \cos \frac{(2i+1)u\pi}{16} G(i, v) \tag{8.25}$$

This is possible because the 2D DCT basis functions are *separable* (multiply separate functions of i and j). It is straightforward to see that this simple change saves many arithmetic steps. The number of iterations required is reduced from 8×8 to $8 + 8$.

Comparison of DCT and DFT. The discrete cosine transform [4] is a close counterpart to the *Discrete Fourier Transform (DFT)*, and in the world of signal processing, the latter is likely the more common. We have started off with the DCT instead because it is simpler and is also much used in multimedia. Nevertheless, we should not entirely ignore the DFT.

For a continuous signal, we define the continuous Fourier transform $\mathcal{F}$ as follows:

$$\mathcal{F}(\omega) = \int_{-\infty}^{\infty} f(t)e^{-i\omega t} \, dt \tag{8.26}$$

Using Euler's formula, we have

$$e^{ix} = \cos(x) + i \sin(x) \tag{8.27}$$

Thus, the continuous Fourier transform is composed of an infinite sum of sine and cosine terms. Because digital computers require us to discretize the input signal, we define a DFT that operates on eight samples of the input signal $\{f_0, f_1, \ldots, f_7\}$ as

$$F_\omega = \sum_{x=0}^{7} f_x \cdot e^{-\frac{2\pi i \omega x}{8}} \tag{8.28}$$

Writing the sine and cosine terms explicitly, we have

$$F_\omega = \sum_{x=0}^{7} f_x \cos\left(\frac{2\pi \omega x}{8}\right) - i \sum_{x=0}^{7} f_x \sin\left(\frac{2\pi \omega x}{8}\right) \tag{8.29}$$

Even without giving an explicit definition of the DCT, we can guess that the DCT is likely a transform that involves only the real part of the DFT. The intuition behind the formulation of the DCT that allows it to use only the cosine basis functions of the DFT is that we can cancel out the imaginary part of the DFT by making a symmetric copy of the original input signal.

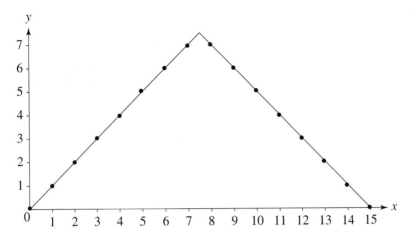

FIGURE 8.10: Symmetric extension of the ramp function.

This works because sine is an odd function; thus, the contributions from the sine terms cancel each other out when the signal is symmetrically extended. Therefore, the DCT of eight input samples corresponds to the DFT of 16 samples made up of the original eight input samples and a symmetric copy of these, as in Figure 8.10.

With the symmetric extension, the DCT is now working on a triangular wave, whereas the DFT tries to code the repeated ramp. Because the DFT is trying to model the artificial discontinuity created between each copy of the samples of the ramp function, a lot of high-frequency components are needed. (Refer to [4] for a thorough discussion and comparison of DCT and DFT.)

Table 8.1 shows the calculated DCT and DFT coefficients. We can see that more energy is concentrated in the first few coefficients in the DCT than in the DFT. If we try to approximate

TABLE 8.1: DCT and DFT coefficients of the ramp function

Ramp	DCT	DFT
0	9.90	28.00
1	−6.44	−4.00
2	0.00	9.66
3	−0.67	−4.00
4	0.00	4.00
5	−0.20	−4.00
6	0.00	1.66
7	−0.51	−4.00

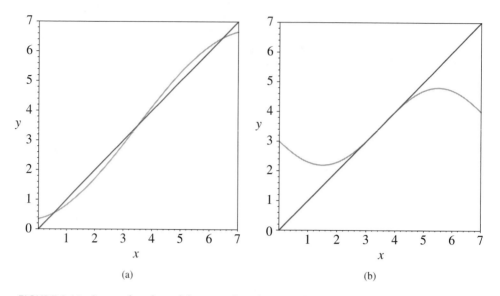

FIGURE 8.11: Approximation of the ramp function: (a) three-term DCT approximation; (b) three-term DFT approximation.

the original ramp function using only three terms of both the DCT and DFT, we notice that the DCT approximation is much closer. Figure 8.11 shows the comparison.

8.5.2   Karhunen–Loève Transform*

The Karhunen–Loève Transform (KLT) is a reversible linear transform that exploits the statistical properties of the vector representation. Its primary property is that it optimally decorrelates the input. To do so, it fits an n-dimensional ellipsoid around the (mean-subtracted) data. The main ellipsoid axis is the major direction of change in the data.

Think of a cigar that has unfortunately been stepped on. Cigar data consists of a cloud of points in 3-space giving the coordinates of positions of measured points in the cigar. The long axis of the cigar will be identified by a statistical program as the first KLT axis. The second most important axis is the horizontal axis across the squashed cigar, perpendicular to the first axis. The third axis is orthogonal to both and is in the vertical, thin direction. A KLT component program carries out just this analysis.

To understand the optimality of the KLT, consider the autocorrelation matrix $\mathbf{R_X}$ of the input vector $\mathbf{X}$, defined as

$$\mathbf{R_X} = E[\mathbf{XX}^T] \tag{8.30}$$

$$= \begin{bmatrix} R_X(1,1) & R_X(1,2) & \cdots & R_X(1,k) \\ R_X(2,1) & R_X(1,1) & \cdots & R_X(2,k-1) \\ \vdots & \vdots & \ddots & \vdots \\ R_X(k,1) & R_X(k-1,1) & \cdots & R_X(1,1) \end{bmatrix} \tag{8.31}$$

where $R_X(t, s) = E[X_t X_s]$ is the autocorrelation function. Our goal is to find a transform **T** such that the components of the output **Y** are uncorrelated — that is, $E[Y_t Y_s] = 0$, if $t \neq s$. Thus, the autocorrelation matrix of **Y** takes on the form of a positive diagonal matrix.

Since any autocorrelation matrix is symmetric and nonnegative definite, there are k orthogonal eigenvectors $\mathbf{u}_1, \mathbf{u}_2, \ldots, \mathbf{u}_k$ and k corresponding real and nonnegative eigenvalues $\lambda_1 \geq \lambda_2 \geq \cdots \geq \lambda_k \geq 0$. We define the Karhunen-Loève transform as

$$\mathbf{T} = [\mathbf{u}_1, \mathbf{u}_2, \cdots, \mathbf{u}_k]^T \tag{8.32}$$

Then, the autocorrelation matrix of **Y** becomes

$$\begin{aligned}
\mathbf{R_Y} &= E[\mathbf{YY}^T] & (8.33) \\
&= E[\mathbf{TXX}^T\mathbf{T}] & (8.34) \\
&= \mathbf{TR_XT}^T & (8.35) \\
&= \begin{bmatrix} \lambda_1 & 0 & \cdots & 0 \\ 0 & \lambda_2 & \cdots & 0 \\ 0 & \vdots & \ddots & 0 \\ 0 & 0 & \cdots & \lambda_k \end{bmatrix} & (8.36)
\end{aligned}$$

Clearly, we have the required autocorrelation matrix for **Y**. Therefore, the KLT is optimal, in the sense that it completely decorrelates the input. In addition, since the KLT depends on the computation of the autocorrelation matrix of the input vector, it is data dependent: it has to be computed for every dataset.

EXAMPLE 8.5

To illustrate the mechanics of the KLT, consider the four 3D input vectors $\mathbf{x}_1 = (4, 4, 5)$, $\mathbf{x}_2 = (3, 2, 5)$, $\mathbf{x}_3 = (5, 7, 6)$, and $\mathbf{x}_4 = (6, 7, 7)$. To find the required transform, we must first estimate the autocorrelation matrix of the input. The mean of the four input vectors is

$$\mathbf{m}_x = \frac{1}{4} \begin{bmatrix} 18 \\ 20 \\ 23 \end{bmatrix}$$

We can estimate the autocorrelation matrix using the formula

$$\mathbf{R_X} = \frac{1}{M} \sum_{i=1}^{n} \mathbf{x}_i \mathbf{x}_i^T - \mathbf{m}_x \mathbf{m}_x^T \tag{8.37}$$

where n is the number of input vectors. From this equation, we obtain

$$\mathbf{R_X} = \begin{bmatrix} 1.25 & 2.25 & 0.88 \\ 2.25 & 4.50 & 1.50 \\ 0.88 & 1.50 & 0.69 \end{bmatrix}$$

The eigenvalues of $\mathbf{R_X}$ are $\lambda_1 = 6.1963$, $\lambda_2 = 0.2147$, and $\lambda_3 = 0.0264$. Clearly, the first component is by far the most important. The corresponding eigenvectors are

$$\mathbf{u}_1 = \begin{bmatrix} 0.4385 \\ 0.8471 \\ 0.3003 \end{bmatrix} \quad \mathbf{u}_2 = \begin{bmatrix} 0.4460 \\ -0.4952 \\ 0.7456 \end{bmatrix} \quad \mathbf{u}_3 = \begin{bmatrix} -0.7803 \\ 0.1929 \\ 0.5949 \end{bmatrix}$$

Therefore, the KLT is given by the matrix

$$\mathbf{T} = \begin{bmatrix} 0.4385 & 0.8471 & 0.3003 \\ 0.4460 & -0.4952 & 0.7456 \\ -0.7803 & 0.1929 & 0.5949 \end{bmatrix}$$

Subtracting the mean vector from each input vector and applying the KLT, we have

$$\mathbf{y}_1 = \begin{bmatrix} -1.2916 \\ -0.2870 \\ -0.2490 \end{bmatrix} \quad \mathbf{y}_2 = \begin{bmatrix} -3.4242 \\ 0.2573 \\ 0.1453 \end{bmatrix}$$

$$\mathbf{y}_3 = \begin{bmatrix} 1.9885 \\ -0.5809 \\ 0.1445 \end{bmatrix} \quad \mathbf{y}_4 = \begin{bmatrix} 2.7273 \\ 0.6107 \\ -0.0408 \end{bmatrix}$$

Since the rows of $\mathbf{T}$ are orthonormal vectors, the inverse transform is just the transpose: $\mathbf{T}^{-1} = \mathbf{T}^T$. We can obtain the original vectors from the transform coefficients using the inverse relation

$$\mathbf{x} = \mathbf{T}^T \mathbf{y} + \mathbf{m}_x \tag{8.38}$$

In terms of the transform coefficients $\mathbf{y}_i$, the magnitude of the first few components is usually considerably larger than that of the other components. In general, after the KLT, most of the "energy" of the transform coefficients is concentrated within the first few components. This is the *energy compaction* property of the KLT.

For an input vector $\mathbf{x}$ with n components, if we coarsely quantize the output vector $\mathbf{y}$ by setting its last k components to zero, calling the resulting vector $\hat{\mathbf{y}}$, the KLT minimizes the mean squared error between the original vector and its reconstruction.

8.6 WAVELET-BASED CODING

8.6.1 Introduction

Decomposing the input signal into its constituents allows us to apply coding techniques suitable for each constituent, to improve compression performance. Consider again a time-dependent signal $f(t)$ (it is best to base discussion on continuous functions to start with). The traditional method of signal decomposition is the Fourier transform. Above, in our discussion of the DCT, we considered a special cosine-based transform. If we carry out analysis based on both sine and cosine, then a concise notation assembles the results into a function $\mathcal{F}(\omega)$, a complex-valued function of real-valued frequency ω given in Eq. (8.26). Such decomposition results in very fine resolution in the *frequency* domain. However, since a sinusoid is theoretically infinite in extent in time, such a decomposition gives no *temporal* resolution.

Another method of decomposition that has gained a great deal of popularity in recent years is the *wavelet transform*. It seeks to represents a signal with good resolution in *both* time and frequency, by using a set of basis functions called wavelets.

There are two types of wavelet transforms: the *Continuous Wavelet Transform* (CWT) and the *Discrete Wavelet Transform* (DWT). We assume that the CWT is applied to the large class of functions $f(x)$ that are square integrable on the real line — that is, $\int [f(x)]^2 \, dx < \infty$. In mathematics, this is written as $f(x) \in \mathbf{L}^2(R)$.

The other kind of wavelet transform, the DWT, operates on discrete samples of the input signal. The DWT resembles other discrete linear transforms, such as the DFT or the DCT, and is very useful for image processing and compression.

Before we begin a discussion of the theory of wavelets, let's develop an intuition about this approach by going through an example using the simplest wavelet transform, the so-called *Haar Wavelet Transform*, to form averages and differences of a sequence of float values.

If we repeatedly take averages and differences and keep results for every step, we effectively create a *multiresolution analysis* of the sequence. For images, this would be equivalent to creating smaller and smaller summary images, one-quarter the size for each step, and keeping track of differences from the average as well. Mentally stacking the full-size image, the quarter-size image, the sixteenth size image, and so on, creates a *pyramid*. The full set, along with difference images, is the multiresolution decomposition.

EXAMPLE 8.6   A Simple Wavelet Transform

The objective of the wavelet transform is to decompose the input signal, for compression purposes, into components that are easier to deal with, have special interpretations, or have some components that can be thresholded away. Furthermore, we want to be able to at least approximately reconstruct the original signal, given these components. Suppose we are given the following input sequence:

$$\{x_{n,i}\} = \{10, 13, 25, 26, 29, 21, 7, 15\} \qquad (8.39)$$

Here, $i \in [0..7]$ indexes "pixels", and n stands for the level of a *pyramid* we are on. At the top, $n = 3$ for this sequence, and we shall form three more sequences, for $n = 2, 1,$ and 0. At each level, less information will be retained in the beginning elements of the transformed signal sequence. When we reach pyramid level $n = 0$, we end up with the sequence average stored in the first element. The remaining elements store detail information.

Consider the transform that replaces the original sequence with its pairwise *average* $x_{n-1,i}$ and *difference* $d_{n-1,i}$, defined as follows:

$$x_{n-1,i} = \frac{x_{n,2i} + x_{n,2i+1}}{2} \qquad (8.40)$$

$$d_{n-1,i} = \frac{x_{n,2i} - x_{n,2i+1}}{2} \qquad (8.41)$$

Notice that the averages and differences are applied only on consecutive *pairs* of input sequences whose first element has an even index. Therefore, the number of elements in each set $\{x_{n-1,i}\}$ and $\{d_{n-1,i}\}$ is exactly half the number of elements in the original sequence. We can form a new sequence having length equal to that of the original sequence by concatenating the two sequences $\{x_{n-1,i}\}$ and $\{d_{n-1,i}\}$. The resulting sequence is thus

$$\{x_{n-1,i}, d_{n-1,i}\} = \{11.5, 25.5, 25, 11, -1.5, -0.5, 4, -4\} \tag{8.42}$$

where we are now at level $n - 1 = 2$. This sequence has exactly the same number of elements as the input sequence — the transform did not increase the amount of data. Since the first half of the above sequence contains averages from the original sequence, we can view it as a coarser approximation to the original signal.

The second half of this sequence can be viewed as the details or approximation errors of the first half. Most of the values in the detail sequence are much smaller than those of the original sequence. Thus, most of the energy is effectively concentrated in the first half. Therefore, we can potentially store $\{d_{n-1,i}\}$ using fewer bits.

It is easily verified that the original sequence can be reconstructed from the transformed sequence, using the relations

$$
\begin{aligned}
x_{n,2i} &= x_{n-1,i} + d_{n-1,i} \\
x_{n,2i+1} &= x_{n-1,i} - d_{n-1,i}
\end{aligned}
\tag{8.43}
$$

This transform is the discrete Haar wavelet transform. Averaging and differencing can be carried out by applying a so-called *scaling function* and *wavelet function* along the signal. Figure 8.12 shows the Haar version of these functions.

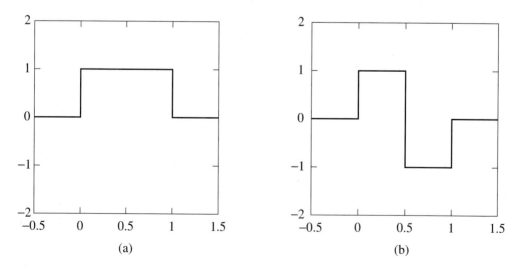

FIGURE 8.12: Haar Wavelet Transform: (a) scaling function; (b) wavelet function.

We can further apply the same transform to $\{x_{n-1,i}\}$, to obtain another level of approximation $x_{n-2,i}$ and detail $d_{n-2,i}$:

$$\{x_{n-2,i}, d_{n-2,i}, d_{n-1,i}\} = \{18.5, 18, -7, 7, -1.5, -0.5, 4, -4\} \qquad (8.44)$$

This is the essential idea of multiresolution analysis. We can now study the input signal in three different scales, along with the details needed to go from one scale to another. This process can continue n times, until only one element is left in the approximation sequence. In this case, $n = 3$, and the final sequence is given below:

$$\{x_{n-3,i}, d_{n-3,i}, d_{n-2,i}, d_{n-1,i}\} = \{18.25, 0.25, -7, 7, -1.5, -0.5, 4, -4\} \qquad (8.45)$$

Now we realize that n was 3 because only three resolution changes were available until we reached the final form.

The value 18.25, corresponding to the coarsest approximation to the original signal, is the average of all the elements in the original sequence. From this example, it is easy to see that the cost of computing this transform is proportional to the number of elements N in the input sequence — that is, $O(N)$.

Extending the one-dimensional Haar wavelet transform into two dimensions is relatively easy: we simply apply the one-dimensional transform to the rows and columns of the two-dimensional input separately. We will demonstrate the two-dimensional Haar transform applied to the 8×8 input image shown in Figure 8.13.

EXAMPLE 8.7   2D Haar Transform

This example of the 2D Haar transform not only serves to illustrate how the wavelet transform is applied to two-dimensional inputs but also points out useful interpretations of the

0	0	0	0	0	0	0	0
0	0	0	0	0	0	0	0
0	0	63	127	127	63	0	0
0	0	127	255	255	127	0	0
0	0	127	255	255	127	0	0
0	0	63	127	127	63	0	0
0	0	0	0	0	0	0	0
0	0	0	0	0	0	0	0

(a)

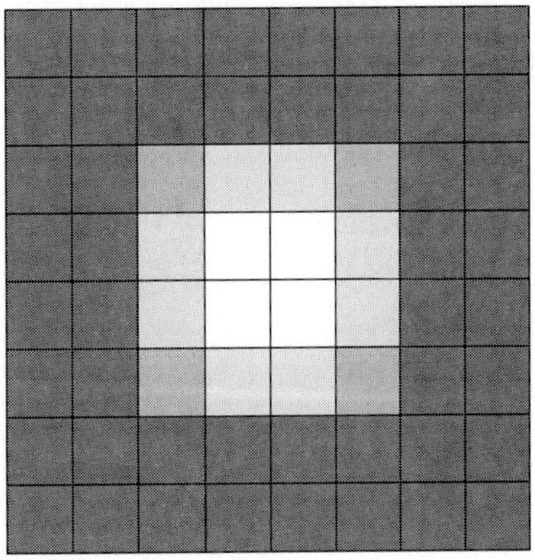

(b)

FIGURE 8.13: Input image for the 2D Haar Wavelet Transform: (a) pixel values; (b) an 8×8 image.

0	0	0	0	0	0	0	0
0	0	0	0	0	0	0	0
0	95	95	0	0	−32	32	0
0	191	191	0	0	−64	64	0
0	191	191	0	0	−64	64	0
0	95	95	0	0	−32	32	0
0	0	0	0	0	0	0	0
0	0	0	0	0	0	0	0

FIGURE 8.14: Intermediate output of the 2D Haar Wavelet Transform.

transformed coefficients. However, it is intended only to provide the reader with an intuitive feeling of the kinds of operations involved in performing a general 2D wavelet transform. Subsequent sections provide more detailed description of the forward and inverse 2D wavelet transform algorithms, as well as a more elaborate example using a more complex wavelet.

2D Haar Wavelet Transform. We begin by applying a one-dimensional Haar wavelet transform to each row of the input. The first and last two rows of the input are trivial. After performing the averaging and differencing operations on the remaining rows, we obtain the intermediate output shown in Figure 8.14.

We continue by applying the same 1D Haar transform to each column of the intermediate output. This step completes one level of the 2D Haar transform. Figure 8.15 gives the resulting coefficients.

We can naturally divide the result into four quadrants. The upper left quadrant contains the averaged coefficients from both the horizontal and vertical passes. Therefore, it can be

0	0	0	0	0	0	0	0
0	143	143	0	0	−48	48	0
0	143	143	0	0	−48	48	0
0	0	0	0	0	0	0	0
0	0	0	0	0	0	0	0
0	−48	−48	0	0	16	−16	0
0	48	48	0	0	−16	16	0
0	0	0	0	0	0	0	0

FIGURE 8.15: Output of the first level of the 2D Haar Wavelet Transform.

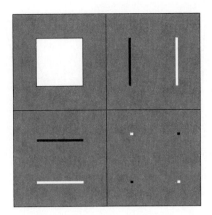

FIGURE 8.16: A simple graphical illustration of the Wavelet Transform.

viewed as a low-pass-filtered version of the original image, in the sense that higher-frequency edge information is lost, while low-spatial-frequency smooth information is retained.

The upper right quadrant contains the vertical averages of the horizontal differences and can be interpreted as information about the *vertical edges* within the original image. Similarly, the lower left quadrant contains the vertical differences of the horizontal averages and represents the *horizontal edges* in the original image. The lower right quadrant contains the differences from both the horizontal and vertical passes. The coefficients in this quadrant represent *diagonal edges*.

These interpretations are shown more clearly as images in Figure 8.16, where bright pixels code positive and dark pixels code negative image values.

The inverse of the 2D Haar transform can be calculated by first inverting the columns using Eq. (8.43), and then inverting the resulting rows.

8.6.2 Continuous Wavelet Transform*

We noted that the motivation for the use of wavelets is to provide a set of basis functions that decompose a signal in time over parameters in the frequency domain and the time domain simultaneously. A Fourier transform aims to pin down only the frequency content of a signal, in terms of spatially varying rather than time varying signals. What wavelets aim to do is pin down the frequency content at different parts of the image.

For example, one part of the image may be "busy" with texture and thus high-frequency content, while another part may be smooth, with little high-frequency content. Naturally, one can think of obvious ways to consider frequencies for localized areas of an image: divide an image into parts and fire away with Fourier analysis. The time-sequence version of that idea is called the *Short-Term* (or *Windowed*) *Fourier Transform*. And other ideas have also arisen. However, it turns out that wavelets, a much newer development, have neater characteristics.

To further motivate the subject, we should consider the *Heisenberg uncertainty principle*, from physics. In the context of signal processing, this says that there is a tradeoff between accuracy in pinning down a function's frequency, and its extent in time. We cannot do both

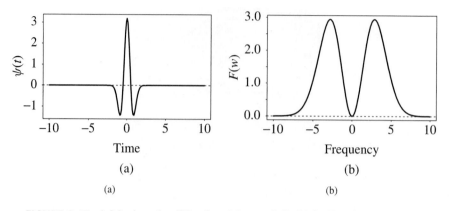

FIGURE 8.17: A Mexican-hat Wavelet: (a) $\sigma = 0.5$; (b) its Fourier transform.

accurately, in general, and still have a useful basis function. For example, a sine wave is exact in terms of its frequency but infinite in extent.

As an example of a function that dies away quickly and also has limited frequency content, suppose we start with a Gaussian function,

$$f(t) = \frac{1}{\sigma\sqrt{2\pi}} e^{\frac{-t^2}{2\sigma^2}} \tag{8.46}$$

The parameter σ expresses the *scale* of the Gaussian (bell-shaped) function.

The second derivative of this function, called $\psi(t)$, looks like a Mexican hat, as in Figure 8.17(a). Clearly, the function $\psi(t)$ is limited in time. Its equation is as follows:

$$\psi(t) = \frac{1}{\sigma^3\sqrt{2\pi}} \left[e^{\frac{-t^2}{2\sigma^2}} \left(\frac{t^2}{\sigma^2} - 1 \right) \right] \tag{8.47}$$

We can explore the frequency content of function $\psi(t)$ by taking its Fourier transform. This turns out to be given by

$$\mathcal{F}(\omega) = \omega^2 e^{-\frac{\sigma^2\omega^2}{2}} \tag{8.48}$$

Figure 8.17(b) displays this function: the candidate wavelet (8.47) is indeed limited in frequency as well.

In general, a wavelet is a function $\psi \in \mathbf{L}^2(R)$ with a zero average,

$$\int_{-\infty}^{+\infty} \psi(t)\, dt = 0 \tag{8.49}$$

that satisfies some conditions that ensure it can be utilized in a multiresolution decomposition. The conditions ensure that we can use the decomposition for zooming in locally in some part of an image, much as we might be interested in closer or farther views of some neighborhood in a map.

The constraint (8.49) is called the *admissibility condition* for wavelets. A function that sums to zero must oscillate around zero. Also, from (8.26), we see that the DC value, the Fourier transform of $\psi(t)$ for $\omega = 0$, is zero. Another way to state this is that the 0th moment M_0 of $\psi(t)$ is zero. The pth moment is defined as

$$M_p = \int_{-\infty}^{\infty} t^p \psi(t)\, dt \tag{8.50}$$

The function ψ is normalized with $\|\psi\| = 1$ and centered in the neighborhood of $t = 0$. We can obtain a *family* of wavelet functions by scaling and translating the *mother wavelet* ψ as follows:

$$\psi_{s,u}(t) = \frac{1}{\sqrt{s}} \psi\left(\frac{t-u}{s}\right) \tag{8.51}$$

If $\psi(t)$ is normalized, so is $\psi_{s,u}(t)$.

The *Continuous Wavelet Transform* (CWT) of $f \in \mathbf{L}^2(R)$ at time u and scale s is defined as

$$\mathcal{W}(f, s, u) = \int_{-\infty}^{+\infty} f(t) \psi_{s,u}(t)\, dt \tag{8.52}$$

The CWT of a 1D signal is a 2D function — a function of both *scale s* and *shift u*.

A very important issue is that, in contradistinction to (8.26), where the Fourier analysis function is stipulated to be the sinusoid, here (8.52) does not state what $\psi(t)$ actually is! Instead, we create a set of rules such functions must obey and then invent useful functions that obey these rules — different functions for different uses.

Just as we defined the DCT in terms of products of a function with a set of basis functions, here the transform $\mathcal{W}$ is written in terms of inner products with basis functions that are a scaled and shifted version of the mother wavelet $\psi(t)$.

The mother wavelet $\psi(t)$ is a *wave*, since it must be an oscillatory function. Why is it wave*let*? The spatial-frequency analyzer parameter in (8.52) is s, the scale. We choose some scale s and see how much content the signal has around that scale. To make the function decay rapidly, away from the chosen s, we have to choose a mother wavelet $\psi(t)$ that decays as fast as some power of s.

It is actually easy to show, from (8.52), that if all moments of $\psi(t)$ up to the nth are zero (or quite small, practically speaking), then the CWT coefficient $\mathcal{W}(f, s, u)$ has a Taylor expansion around $u = 0$ that is of order s^{n+2} (see Exercise 9). This is the localization in frequency we desire in a good mother wavelet.

We derive wavelet coefficients by applying wavelets at different scales over many locations of the signal. Excitingly, if we shrink the wavelets down small enough that they cover a part of the function $f(t)$ that is a polynomial of degree n or less, the coefficient for that wavelet and all smaller ones will be zero. The condition that the wavelet should have vanishing moments up to some order is one way of characterizing mathematical *regularity conditions* on the mother wavelet.

The inverse of the continuous wavelet transform is:

$$f(t) = \frac{1}{C_\psi} \int_{0}^{+\infty} \int_{-\infty}^{+\infty} \mathcal{W}(f, s, u) \frac{1}{\sqrt{s}} \psi\left(\frac{t-u}{s}\right) \frac{1}{s^2}\, du\, ds \tag{8.53}$$

where

$$C_\psi = \int_0^{+\infty} \frac{|\Psi(\omega)|^2}{\omega} \, d\omega < +\infty \tag{8.54}$$

and $\Psi(\omega)$ is the Fourier transform of $\psi(t)$. Eq. (8.54) is another phrasing of the admissibility condition.

The trouble with the CWT is that (8.52) is nasty: most wavelets are not analytic but result simply from numerical calculations. The resulting infinite set of scaled and shifted functions is not necessary for the analysis of *sampled* functions, such as the ones arise in image processing. For this reason, we apply the ideas that pertain to the CWT to the discrete domain.

8.6.3   Discrete Wavelet Transform*

Discrete wavelets are again formed from a mother wavelet, but with scale and shift in discrete steps.

Multiresolution Analysis and the Discrete Wavelet Transform.   The connection between wavelets in the continuous time domain and *filter banks* in the discrete time domain is multiresolution analysis; we discuss the DWT within this framework. Mallat [5] showed that it is possible to construct wavelets ψ such that the dilated and translated family

$$\left\{ \psi_{j,n}(t) = \frac{1}{\sqrt{2^j}} \, \psi\left(\frac{t - 2^j n}{2^j}\right) \right\}_{(j,n)\in\mathbf{Z}^2} \tag{8.55}$$

is an *orthonormal basis* of $\mathbf{L}^2(R)$, where $\mathbf{Z}$ represents the set of integers. This is known as "dyadic" scaling and translation and corresponds to the notion of zooming out in a map by factors of 2. (If we draw a cosine function $\cos(t)$ from time 0 to 2π and then draw $\cos(t/2)$, we see that while $\cos(t)$ goes over a whole cycle, $\cos(t/2)$ has only a half cycle: the function $\cos(2^{-1}t)$ is a *wider* function and thus is at a broader scale.)

Note that we change the scale of translations along with the overall scale 2^j, so as to keep movement in the lower-resolution image in proportion. Notice also that the notation used says that a larger index j corresponds to a coarser version of the image.

Multiresolution analysis provides the tool to *adapt signal resolution to only relevant details* for a particular task. The *octave decomposition* introduced by Mallat [6] initially decomposes a signal into an approximation component and a detail component. The approximation component is then recursively decomposed into approximation and detail at successively coarser scales. Wavelets are set up such that the approximation at resolution 2^{-j} contains all the necessary information to compute an approximation at coarser resolution $2^{-(j+1)}$.

Wavelets are used to characterize detail information. The averaging information is formally determined by a kind of dual to the mother wavelet, called the *scaling function* $\phi(t)$.

The main idea in the theory of wavelets is that at a particular level of resolution j, the set of *translates* indexed by n form a basis at that level. Interestingly, the set of translates forming the basis at the $j + 1$ next level, a coarser level, can all be written as a sum of weights times the level-j basis. The scaling function is chosen such that the coefficients of its translates are all necessarily bounded (less than infinite).

The scaling function, along with its translates, forms a basis at the coarser level $j+1$ (say 3, or the 1/8 level) but not at level j (say 2, or the 1/4 level). Instead, at level j the set of translates of the scaling function ϕ *along with the set of translates of the mother wavelet ϕ* do form a basis. We are left with the situation that the scaling function describes smooth, or approximation, information and the wavelet describes what is left over — detail information.

Since the set of translates of the scaling function ϕ at a coarser level can be written exactly as a weighted sum of the translates at a finer level, the scaling function must satisfy the so-called *dilation equation* [7]:

$$\phi(t) = \sum_{n \in \mathbf{Z}} \sqrt{2} h_0[n] \phi(2t - n) \tag{8.56}$$

The square brackets come from the theory of *filters*, and their use is carried over here. The dilation equation is a recipe for finding a function that can be built from a sum of copies of itself that are first scaled, translated, and dilated. Equation (8.56) expresses a condition that a function must satisfy to be a scaling function and at the same time forms a definition of the *scaling vector h_0*.

Not only is the scaling function expressible as a sum of translates, but as well the *wavelet* at the coarser level is also expressible as such:

$$\psi(t) = \sum_{n \in \mathbf{Z}} \sqrt{2} h_1[n] \phi(2t - n) \tag{8.57}$$

Below, we'll show that the set of coefficients h_1 for the wavelet can in fact be derived from the scaling function ones h_0 [Eq. (8.59) below], so we also have that the wavelet can be derived from the scaling function, once we have one. The equation reads

$$\psi(t) = \sum_{n \in \mathbf{Z}} (-1)^n h_0[1 - n] \phi(2t - n) \tag{8.58}$$

So the condition on a wavelet is similar to that on the scaling function, Eq. (8.56), and in fact uses the same coefficients, only in the opposite order and with alternating signs.

Clearly, for efficiency, we would like the sums in (8.56) and (8.57) to be as few as possible, so we choose wavelets that have as few vector entries h_0 and h_1 as possible. The effect of the scaling function is a kind of smoothing, or filtering, operation on a signal. Therefore it acts as a low-pass filter, screening out high-frequency content. The vector values $h_0[n]$ are called the low-pass filter *impulse response* coefficients, since they describe the effect of the filtering operation on a signal consisting of a single spike with magnitude unity (an impulse) at time $t = 0$. A complete discrete signal is made of a set of such spikes, shifted in time from 0 and weighted by the magnitudes of the discrete samples.

Hence, to specify a DWT, only the discrete low-pass filter impulse response $h_0[n]$ is needed. These specify the approximation filtering, given by the scaling function. The

TABLE 8.2: Orthogonal wavelet filters

Wavelet	Number of taps	Start index	Coefficients
Haar	2	0	[0.707, 0.707]
Daubechies 4	4	0	[0.483, 0.837, 0.224, −0.129]
Daubechies 6	6	0	[0.332, 0.807, 0.460, −0.135, −0.085, 0.0352]
Daubechies 8	8	0	[0.230, 0.715, 0.631, −0.028, −0.187, 0.031, 0.033, −0.011]

discrete *high-pass* impulse response $h_1[n]$, describing the details using the wavelet function, can be derived from $h_0[n]$ using the following equation:

$$h_1[n] = (-1)^n h_0[1 - n] \tag{8.59}$$

The number of coefficients in the impulse response is called the number of *taps* in the filter. If $h_0[n]$ has only a finite number of nonzero entries, the resulting wavelet is said to have *compact support*. Additional constraints, such as orthonormality and regularity, can be imposed on the coefficients $h_0[n]$. The vectors $h_0[n]$ and $h_1[n]$ are called the low-pass and high-pass *analysis* filters.

To *reconstruct* the original input, an inverse operation is needed. The inverse filters are called *synthesis* filters. For orthonormal wavelets, the forward transform and its inverse are transposes of each other, and the analysis filters are identical to the synthesis filters.

Without orthogonality, the wavelets for analysis and synthesis are called *biorthogonal*, a weaker condition. In this case, the synthesis filters are not identical to the analysis filters. We denote them as $\tilde{h}_0[n]$ and $\tilde{h}_1[n]$. To specify a biorthogonal wavelet transform, we require both $h_0[n]$ and $\tilde{h}_0[n]$. As before, we can compute the discrete high-pass filters in terms of sums of the low-pass ones:

$$h_1[n] = (-1)^n \tilde{h}_0[1 - n] \tag{8.60}$$
$$\tilde{h}_1[n] = (-1)^n h_0[1 - n] \tag{8.61}$$

Tables 8.2 and 8.3 (cf. [8]) give some commonly used orthogonal and biorthogonal wavelet filters. The "start index" columns in these tables refer to the starting value of the index n used in Eqs. (8.60) and (8.61).

Figure 8.18 shows a block diagram for the 1D dyadic wavelet transform. Here, $x[n]$ is the discrete sampled signal. The box $\boxed{\downarrow 2}$ means subsampling by taking every second element, and the box $\boxed{\uparrow 2}$ means upsampling by replication. The reconstruction phase yields series $y[n]$.

TABLE 8.3: Biorthogonal wavelet filters

Wavelet	Filter	Number of taps	Start index	Coefficients
Antonini 9/7	$h_0[n]$	9	−4	[0.038, −0.024, −0.111, 0.377, 0.853, 0.377, −0.111, −0.024, 0.038]
	$\tilde{h}_0[n]$	7	−3	[−0.065, −0.041, 0.418, 0.788, 0.418, −0.041, −0.065]
Villa 10/18	$h_0[n]$	10	−4	[0.029, 0.0000824, −0.158, 0.077, 0.759, 0.759, 0.077, −0.158, 0.0000824, 0.029]
	$\tilde{h}_0[n]$	18	−8	[0.000954, −0.00000273, −0.009, −0.003, 0.031, −0.014, −0.086, 0.163, 0.623, 0.623, 0.163, −0.086, −0.014, 0.031, −0.003, −0.009, −0.00000273, 0.000954]
Brislawn	$h_0[n]$	10	−4	[0.027, −0.032, −0.241, 0.054, 0.900, 0.900, 0.054, −0.241, −0.032, 0.027]
	$\tilde{h}_0[n]$	10	−4	[0.020, 0.024, −0.023, 0.146, 0.541, 0.541, 0.146, −0.023, 0.024, 0.020]

For analysis, at each level we transform the series $x[n]$ into another series of the same length, in which the first half of the elements is approximation information and the second half consists of detail information. For an N-tap filter, this is simply the series

$$\{x[n]\} \rightarrow y[n] = \left\{ \sum_j x[j]h_0[n-j] ; \sum_j x[j]h_1[n-j] \right\} \tag{8.62}$$

where for each half, the odd-numbered results are discarded. The summation over shifted coefficients in (8.62) is referred to as a *convolution*.

2D Discrete Wavelet Transform.   The extension of the wavelet transform to two dimensions is quite straightforward. A two-dimensional scaling function is said to be *separable* if it can be factored into a product of two one-dimensional scaling functions. That is,

$$\phi(x, y) = \phi(x)\phi(y) \tag{8.63}$$

For simplicity, only separable wavelets are considered in this section. Furthermore, let's assume that the width and height of the input image are powers of 2.

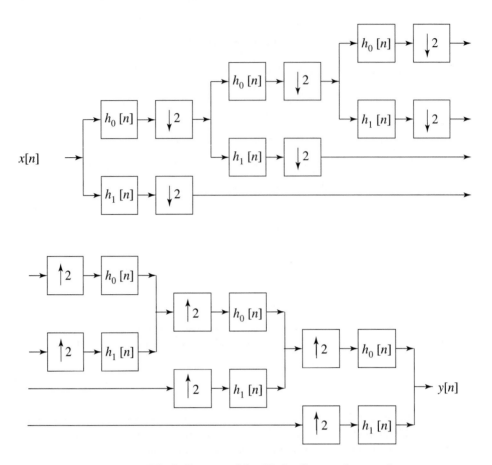

FIGURE 8.18: Block diagram of the 1D dyadic wavelet transform.

For an N by N input image, the two-dimensional DWT proceeds as follows:

1. Convolve each row of the image with $h_0[n]$ and $h_1[n]$, discard the odd-numbered columns of the resulting arrays, and concatenate them to form a transformed row.
2. After all rows have been transformed, convolve each column of the result with $h_0[n]$ and $h_1[n]$. Again discard the odd-numbered rows and concatenate the result.

After the above two steps, one stage of the DWT is complete. The transformed image now contains four subbands LL, HL, LH, and HH, standing for low-low, high-low, and so on, as Figure 8.19(a) shows. As in the one-dimensional transform, the LL subband can be further decomposed to yield yet another level of decomposition. This process can be continued until the desired number of decomposition levels is reached or the LL component only has a single element left. A two level decomposition is shown in Figure 8.19(b).

The inverse transform simply reverses the steps of the forward transform.

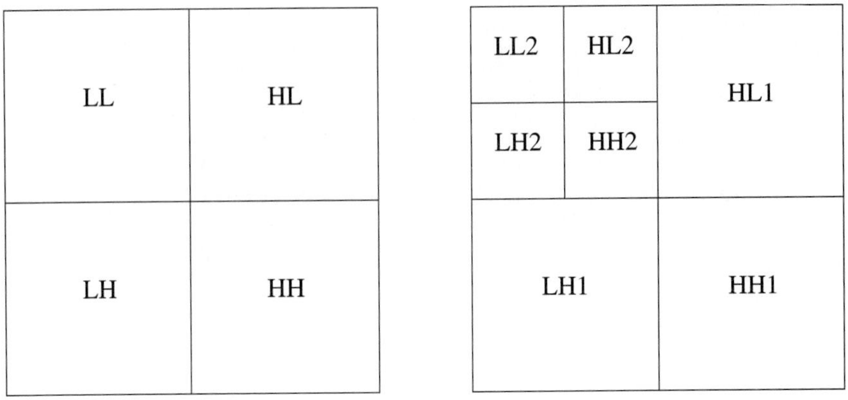

FIGURE 8.19: The two-dimensional discrete wavelet transform: (a) one-level transform; (b) two-level transform.

1. For each stage of the transformed image, starting with the last, separate each column into low-pass and high-pass coefficients. Upsample each of the low-pass and high-pass arrays by inserting a zero after each coefficient.

2. Convolve the low-pass coefficients with $h_0[n]$ and high-pass coefficients with $h_1[n]$ and add the two resulting arrays.

3. After all columns have been processed, separate each row into low-pass and high-pass coefficients and upsample each of the two arrays by inserting a zero after each coefficient.

4. Convolve the low-pass coefficients with $h_0[n]$ and high-pass coefficients with $h_1[n]$ and add the two resulting arrays.

If biorthogonal filters are used for the forward transform, we must replace the $h_0[n]$ and $h_1[n]$ above with $\tilde{h}_0[n]$ and $\tilde{h}_1[n]$ in the inverse transform.

EXAMPLE 8.8

The input image is a subsampled version of the image Lena, as shown in Figure 8.20. The size of the input is 16×16. The filter used in the example is the Antonini 9/7 filter set given in Table 8.3.

Before we begin, we need to compute the analysis and synthesis high-pass filters using Eqs. (8.60) and (8.61). The resulting filter coefficients are

$$
\begin{aligned}
h_1[n] &= [-0.065, 0.041, 0.418, -0.788, 0.418, 0.041, -0.065] \\
\tilde{h}_1[n] &= [-0.038, -0.024, 0.111, 0.377, -0.853, 0.377, 0.111, -0.024, -0.038]
\end{aligned}
$$

$$(8.64)$$

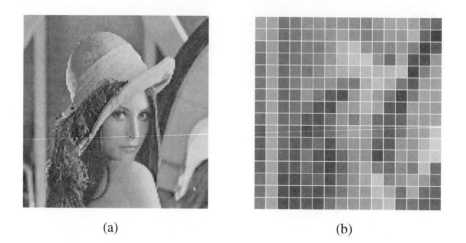

(a)   (b)

FIGURE 8.20: Lena: (a) original 128×128 image; (b) 16×16 subsampled image.

The input image in numerical form is

$$I_{00}(x, y) =$$

$$
\begin{bmatrix}
158 & 170 & 97 & 104 & 123 & 130 & 133 & 125 & 132 & 127 & 112 & 158 & 159 & 144 & 116 & 91 \\
164 & 153 & 91 & 99 & 124 & 152 & 131 & 160 & 189 & 116 & 106 & 145 & 140 & 143 & 227 & 53 \\
116 & 149 & 90 & 101 & 118 & 118 & 131 & 152 & 202 & 211 & 84 & 154 & 127 & 146 & 58 & 58 \\
95 & 145 & 88 & 105 & 188 & 123 & 117 & 182 & 185 & 204 & 203 & 154 & 153 & 229 & 46 & 147 \\
101 & 156 & 89 & 100 & 165 & 113 & 148 & 170 & 163 & 186 & 144 & 194 & 208 & 39 & 113 & 159 \\
103 & 153 & 94 & 103 & 203 & 136 & 146 & 92 & 66 & 192 & 188 & 103 & 178 & 47 & 167 & 159 \\
102 & 146 & 106 & 99 & 99 & 121 & 39 & 60 & 164 & 175 & 198 & 46 & 56 & 56 & 156 & 156 \\
99 & 146 & 95 & 97 & 144 & 61 & 103 & 107 & 108 & 111 & 192 & 62 & 65 & 128 & 153 & 154 \\
99 & 140 & 103 & 109 & 103 & 124 & 54 & 81 & 172 & 137 & 178 & 54 & 43 & 159 & 149 & 174 \\
84 & 133 & 107 & 84 & 149 & 43 & 158 & 95 & 151 & 120 & 183 & 46 & 30 & 147 & 142 & 201 \\
58 & 153 & 110 & 41 & 94 & 213 & 71 & 73 & 140 & 103 & 138 & 83 & 152 & 143 & 128 & 207 \\
56 & 141 & 108 & 58 & 92 & 51 & 55 & 61 & 88 & 166 & 58 & 103 & 146 & 150 & 116 & 211 \\
89 & 115 & 188 & 47 & 113 & 104 & 56 & 67 & 128 & 155 & 187 & 71 & 153 & 134 & 203 & 95 \\
35 & 99 & 151 & 67 & 35 & 88 & 88 & 128 & 140 & 142 & 176 & 213 & 144 & 128 & 214 & 100 \\
89 & 98 & 97 & 51 & 49 & 101 & 47 & 90 & 136 & 136 & 157 & 205 & 106 & 43 & 54 & 76 \\
44 & 105 & 69 & 69 & 68 & 53 & 110 & 127 & 134 & 146 & 159 & 184 & 109 & 121 & 72 & 113
\end{bmatrix}
$$

I represents the pixel values. The first subscript of I indicates the current stage of the transform, while the second subscript indicates the current step within a stage. We start by convolving the first row with both $h_0[n]$ and $h_1[n]$ and discarding the values with odd-numbered index. The results of these two operations are

$$(I_{00}(:, 0) * h_0[n]) \downarrow 2 = [245, 156, 171, 183, 184, 173, 228, 160]$$
$$(I_{00}(:, 0) * h_1[n]) \downarrow 2 = [-30, 3, 0, 7, -5, -16, -3, 16]$$

where the colon in the first index position indicates that we are showing a whole row. If you like, you can verify these operations using MATLAB's conv function.

Next, we form the transformed output row by concatenating the resulting coefficients. The first row of the transformed image is then

$$[245, 156, 171, 183, 184, 173, 228, 160, -30, 3, 0, 7, -5, -16, -3, 16]$$

Similar to the simple one-dimensional Haar transform examples, most of the energy is now concentrated on the first half of the transformed image. We continue the same process for the remaining rows and obtain the following result:

$$I_{11}(x, y) =$$

245	156	171	183	184	173	228	160	−30	3	0	7	−5	−16	−3	16
239	141	181	197	242	158	202	229	−17	5	−20	3	26	−27	27	141
195	147	163	177	288	173	209	106	−34	2	2	19	−50	−35	−38	−1
180	139	226	177	274	267	247	163	−45	29	24	−29	−2	30	−101	−78
191	145	197	198	247	230	239	143	−49	22	36	−11	−26	−14	101	−54
192	145	237	184	135	253	169	192	−47	38	36	4	−58	66	94	−4
176	159	156	77	204	232	51	196	−31	9	−48	30	11	58	29	4
179	148	162	129	146	213	92	217	−39	18	50	−10	33	51	−23	8
169	159	163	97	204	202	85	234	−29	1	−42	23	37	41	−56	−5
155	153	149	159	176	204	65	236	−32	32	85	39	38	44	−54	−31
145	148	158	164	157	188	215	−55	59	−110	28	26	48	−1	−64
134	152	102	70	153	126	199	207	−47	38	13	10	−76	3	−7	−76
127	203	130	94	171	218	171	228	12	88	−27	15	1	76	24	85
70	188	63	144	191	257	215	232	−5	24	−28	−9	19	−46	36	91
129	124	87	96	177	236	162	77	−2	20	−48	1	17	−56	30	−24
103	115	85	142	188	234	184	132	−37	0	27	−4	5	−35	−22	−33

We now go on and apply the filters to the columns of the above resulting image. As before, we apply both $h_0[n]$ and $h_1[n]$ to each column and discard the odd indexed results:

$$(I_{11}(0, :) * h_0[n]) \downarrow 2 = [353, 280, 269, 256, 240, 206, 160, 153]^T$$
$$(I_{11}(0, :) * h_1[n]) \downarrow 2 = [-12, 10, -7, -4, 2, -1, 43, 16]^T$$

Concatenating the above results into a single column and applying the same procedure to each of the remaining columns, we arrive at the final transformed image:

$$I_{12}(x, y) =$$

353	212	251	272	281	234	308	289	−33	6	−15	5	24	−29	38	120
280	203	254	250	402	269	297	207	−45	11	−2	9	−31	−26	−74	23
269	202	312	280	316	353	337	227	−70	43	56	−23	−41	21	82	−81
256	217	247	155	236	328	114	283	−52	27	−14	23	−2	90	49	12
240	221	226	172	264	294	113	330	−41	14	31	23	57	60	−78	−3
206	204	201	192	230	219	232	300	−76	67	−53	40	4	46	−18	−107
160	275	150	135	244	294	267	331	−2	90	−17	10	−24	49	29	89
153	189	113	173	260	342	256	176	−20	18	−38	−4	24	−75	25	−5
−12	7	−9	−13	−6	11	12	−69	−10	−1	14	6	−38	3	−45	−99
10	3	−31	16	−1	−51	−10	−30	2	−12	0	24	−32	−45	109	42
−7	5	−44	−35	67	−10	−17	−15	3	−15	−28	0	41	−30	−18	−19
−4	9	−1	−37	41	6	−33	2	9	−12	−67	31	−7	3	2	0
2	−3	9	−25	2	−25	60	−8	−11	−4	−123	−12	−6	−4	14	−12
−1	22	32	46	10	48	−11	20	19	32	−59	9	70	50	16	73
43	−18	32	−40	−13	−23	−37	−61	8	22	2	13	−12	43	−8	−45
16	2	−6	−32	−7	5	−13	−50	24	7	−61	2	11	−33	43	1

This completes one stage of the Discrete Wavelet Transform. We can perform another stage by applying the same transform procedure to the upper left 8×8 DC image of $I_{12}(x, y)$. The resulting two-stage transformed image is

$$I_{22}(x, y) =$$

558	451	608	532	75	26	94	25	−33	6	−15	5	24	−29	38	120
463	511	627	566	66	68	−43	68	−45	11	−2	9	−31	−26	−74	23
464	401	478	416	14	84	−97	−229	−70	43	56	−23	−41	21	82	−81
422	335	477	553	−88	46	−31	−6	−52	27	−14	23	−2	90	49	12
14	33	−56	42	22	−43	−36	1	−41	14	31	23	57	60	−78	−3
−13	36	54	52	12	−21	51	70	−76	67	−53	40	4	46	−18	−107
25	−20	25	−7	−35	35	−56	−55	−2	90	−17	10	−24	49	29	89
46	37	−51	51	−44	26	39	−74	−20	18	−38	−4	24	−75	25	−5
−12	7	−9	−13	−6	11	12	−69	−10	−1	14	6	−38	3	−45	−99
10	3	−31	16	−1	−51	−10	−30	2	−12	0	24	−32	−45	109	42
−7	5	−44	−35	67	−10	−17	−15	3	−15	−28	0	41	−30	−18	−19
−4	9	−1	−37	41	6	−33	2	9	−12	−67	31	−7	3	2	0
2	−3	9	−25	2	−25	60	−8	−11	−4	−123	−12	−6	−4	14	−12
−1	22	32	46	10	48	−11	20	19	32	−59	9	70	50	16	73
43	−18	32	−40	−13	−23	−37	−61	8	22	2	13	−12	43	−8	−45
16	2	−6	−32	−7	5	−13	−50	24	7	−61	2	11	−33	43	1

Notice that I_{12} corresponds to the subband diagram shown in Figure 8.19(a), and I_{22} corresponds to Figure 8.19(b). At this point, we may apply *different levels of quantization* to each subband according to some preferred bit allocation algorithm, given a desired bitrate. *This is the basis for a simple wavelet-based compression algorithm.* However, since in this example we are illustrating the mechanics of the DWT, here we will simply bypass the quantization step and perform an inverse transform to reconstruct the input image.

We refer to the top left 8×8 block of values as the innermost stage in correspondence with Figure 8.19. Starting with the innermost stage, we extract the first column and separate the low-pass and high-pass coefficients. The low-pass coefficient is simply the first half of the column, and the high-pass coefficients are the second half. Then we upsample them by appending a zero after each coefficient. The two resulting arrays are

$$\vec{a} = [558, 0, 463, 0, 464, 0, 422, 0]^T$$
$$\vec{b} = [14, 0, -13, 0, 25, 0, 46, 0]^T$$

Since we are using biorthogonal filters, we convolve $\vec{a}$ and $\vec{b}$ with $\tilde{h}_0[n]$ and $\tilde{h}_1[n]$ respectively. The results of the two convolutions are then added to form a single 8×1 array. The resulting column is

$$[414, 354, 323, 338, 333, 294, 324, 260]^T$$

All columns in the innermost stage are processed in this manner. The resulting image is

$$I'_{21}(x, y) =$$

```
414  337  382  403   70  -16   48   12  -33    6  -15    5   24  -29   38  120
354  322  490  368   39   59   63   55  -45   11   -2    9  -31  -26  -74   23
323  395  450  442   62   25  -26   90  -70   43   56  -23  -41   21   82  -81
338  298  346  296   23   77 -117 -131  -52   27  -14   23   -2   90   49   12
333  286  364  298    4   67  -75 -176  -41   14   31   23   57   60  -78   -3
294  279  308  350   -2   17   12  -53  -76   67  -53   40    4   46  -18 -107
324  240  326  412  -96   54  -25  -45   -2   90  -17   10  -24   49   29   89
260  189  382  359  -47   14  -63   69  -20   18  -38   -4   24  -75   25   -5
-12    7   -9  -13   -6   11   12  -69  -10   -1   14    6  -38    3  -45  -99
 10    3  -31   16   -1  -51  -10  -30    2  -12    0   24  -32  -45  109   42
 -7    5  -44  -35   67  -10  -17  -15    3  -15  -28    0   41  -30  -18  -19
 -4    9   -1  -37   41    6  -33    2    9  -12  -67   31   -7    3    2    0
  2   -3    9  -25    2  -25   60   -8  -11   -4 -123  -12   -6   -4   14  -12
 -1   22   32   46   10   48  -11   20   19   32  -59    9   70   50   16   73
 43  -18   32  -40  -13  -23  -37  -61    8   22    2   13  -12   43   -8  -45
 16    2   -6  -32   -7    5  -13  -50   24    7  -61    2   11  -33   43    1
```

We are now ready to process the rows. For each row of the upper left 8×8 sub-image, we again separate them into low-pass and high-pass coefficients. Then we upsample both by adding a zero after each coefficient. The results are convolved with the appropriate $\tilde{h}_0[n]$ and $\tilde{h}_1[n]$ filters. After these steps are completed for all rows, we have

$$I'_{12}(x, y) =$$

```
353  212  251  272  281  234  308  289  -33    6  -15    5   24  -29   38  120
280  203  254  250  402  269  297  207  -45   11   -2    9  -31  -26  -74   23
269  202  312  280  316  353  337  227  -70   43   56  -23  -41   21   82  -81
256  217  247  155  236  328  114  283  -52   27  -14   23   -2   90   49   12
240  221  226  172  264  294  113  330  -41   14   31   23   57   60  -78   -3
206  204  201  192  230  219  232  300  -76   67  -53   40    4   46  -18 -107
160  275  150  135  244  294  267  331   -2   90  -17   10  -24   49   29   89
153  189  113  173  260  342  256  176  -20   18  -38   -4   24  -75   25   -5
-12    7   -9  -13   -6   11   12  -69  -10   -1   14    6  -38    3  -45  -99
 10    3  -31   16   -1  -51  -10  -30    2  -12    0   24  -32  -45  109   42
 -7    5  -44  -35   67  -10  -17  -15    3  -15  -28    0   41  -30  -18  -19
 -4    9   -1  -37   41    6  -33    2    9  -12  -67   31   -7    3    2    0
  2   -3    9  -25    2  -25   60   -8  -11   -4 -123  -12   -6   -4   14  -12
 -1   22   32   46   10   48  -11   20   19   32  -59    9   70   50   16   73
 43  -18   32  -40  -13  -23  -37  -61    8   22    2   13  -12   43   -8  -45
 16    2   -6  -32   -7    5  -13  -50   24    7  -61    2   11  -33   43    1
```

We then repeat the same inverse transform procedure on $I'_{12}(x, y)$, to obtain $I'_{00}(x, y)$. Notice that $I'_{00}(x, y)$ is not exactly the same as $I_{00}(x, y)$, but the difference is small. These small differences are caused by round-off errors during the forward and inverse transform, and truncation errors when converting from floating point numbers to integer grayscale values. Figure 8.21 shows a three-level image decomposition using the Haar wavelet.

$$I'_{00}(x, y) =$$

$$
\begin{bmatrix}
158 & 170 & 97 & 103 & 122 & 129 & 132 & 125 & 132 & 126 & 111 & 157 & 159 & 144 & 116 & 91 \\
164 & 152 & 90 & 98 & 123 & 151 & 131 & 159 & 188 & 115 & 106 & 145 & 140 & 143 & 227 & 52 \\
115 & 148 & 89 & 100 & 117 & 118 & 131 & 151 & 201 & 210 & 84 & 154 & 127 & 146 & 58 & 58 \\
94 & 144 & 88 & 104 & 187 & 123 & 117 & 181 & 184 & 203 & 202 & 153 & 152 & 228 & 45 & 146 \\
100 & 155 & 88 & 99 & 164 & 112 & 147 & 169 & 163 & 186 & 143 & 193 & 207 & 38 & 112 & 158 \\
103 & 153 & 93 & 102 & 203 & 135 & 145 & 91 & 66 & 192 & 188 & 103 & 177 & 46 & 166 & 158 \\
102 & 146 & 106 & 99 & 99 & 121 & 39 & 60 & 164 & 175 & 198 & 46 & 56 & 56 & 156 & 156 \\
99 & 146 & 95 & 97 & 143 & 60 & 102 & 106 & 107 & 110 & 191 & 61 & 65 & 128 & 153 & 154 \\
98 & 139 & 102 & 109 & 103 & 123 & 53 & 80 & 171 & 136 & 177 & 53 & 43 & 158 & 148 & 173 \\
84 & 133 & 107 & 84 & 148 & 42 & 157 & 94 & 150 & 119 & 182 & 45 & 29 & 146 & 141 & 200 \\
57 & 152 & 109 & 41 & 93 & 213 & 70 & 72 & 139 & 102 & 137 & 82 & 151 & 143 & 128 & 207 \\
56 & 141 & 108 & 58 & 91 & 50 & 54 & 60 & 87 & 165 & 57 & 102 & 146 & 149 & 116 & 211 \\
89 & 114 & 187 & 46 & 113 & 104 & 55 & 66 & 127 & 154 & 186 & 71 & 153 & 134 & 203 & 94 \\
35 & 99 & 150 & 66 & 34 & 88 & 88 & 127 & 140 & 141 & 175 & 212 & 144 & 128 & 213 & 100 \\
88 & 97 & 96 & 50 & 49 & 101 & 47 & 90 & 136 & 136 & 156 & 204 & 105 & 43 & 54 & 76 \\
43 & 104 & 69 & 69 & 68 & 53 & 110 & 127 & 134 & 145 & 158 & 183 & 109 & 121 & 72 & 113
\end{bmatrix}
$$

Wavelet-Based Reduction Program. Keeping only the lowest-frequency content amounts to an even simpler wavelet-based image zooming-out reduction algorithm. Program `wavelet_reduction.c` on the book's web site gives a simple illustration of this principle, limited to just the scaling function and analysis filter to scale down an image some number of times (three, say) using wavelet-based analysis. The program operates on the Unix-based PGM (portable graymap) file format and uses the Antonini 9/7 biorthogonal filter in Table 8.3.

8.7 WAVELET PACKETS

Wavelet packets can be viewed as a generalization of wavelets. They were first introduced by Coifman, Meyer, Quake, and Wickerhauser [9] as a family of orthonormal bases for discrete functions of $\mathbf{R}^N$. A complete subband decomposition can be viewed as a decomposition of the input signal, using an analysis tree of depth $\log N$.

In the usual dyadic wavelet decomposition, only the low-pass-filtered subband is recursively decomposed and thus can be represented by a logarithmic tree structure. However, a wavelet packet decomposition allows the decomposition to be represented by any pruned subtree of the full tree topology. Therefore, this representation of the decomposition topology is isomorphic to all permissible subband topologies [10]. The leaf nodes of each pruned subtree represent one permissible orthonormal basis.

The wavelet packet decomposition offers a number of attractive properties, including

- Flexibility, since a best wavelet basis in the sense of some cost metric can be found within a large library of permissible bases

- Favorable localization of wavelet packets in both frequency and space.

- Low computational requirement for wavelet packet decomposition, because each decomposition can be computed in the order of $N \log N$ using fast filter banks.

Wavelet packets are currently being applied to solve various practical problems such as image compression, signal de-noising, fingerprint identification, and so on.

FIGURE 8.21: Haar wavelet decomposition. *Courtesy of Steve Kilthau.*

8.8   EMBEDDED ZEROTREE OF WAVELET COEFFICIENTS

So far, we have described a wavelet-based scheme for image decomposition. However, aside from referring to the idea of quantizing away small coefficients, we have not really addressed how to code the wavelet transform values — how to form a bitstream. This problem is precisely what is dealt with in terms of a new data structure, the Embedded Zerotree.

The *Embedded Zerotree Wavelet* (EZW) algorithm introduced by Shapiro [11] is an effective and computationally efficient technique in image coding. This work has inspired a number of refinements to the initial EZW algorithm, the most notable being Said and Pearlman's *Set Partitioning in Hierarchical Trees* (SPIHT) algorithm [12] and Taubman's *Embedded Block Coding with Optimized Truncation* (EBCOT) algorithm [13], which is adopted into the JPEG2000 standard.

The EZW algorithm addresses two problems: obtaining the best image quality for a given bitrate and accomplishing this task in an embedded fashion. An *embedded* code is one that contains all lower-rate codes "embedded" at the beginning of the bitstream. The bits are effectively ordered by importance in the bitstream. An embedded code allows the encoder to terminate the encoding at any point and thus meet any target bitrate exactly. Similarly, a decoder can cease to decode at any point and produce reconstructions corresponding to all lower-rate encodings.

To achieve this goal, the EZW algorithm takes advantage of an important aspect of low-bitrate image coding. When conventional coding methods are used to achieve low bitrates, using scalar quantization followed by entropy coding, say, the most likely symbol, after quantization, is zero. It turns out that a large fraction of the bit budget is spent encoding the *significance map*, which flags whether input samples (in the case of the 2D discrete wavelet transform, the transform coefficients) have a zero or nonzero quantized value. The EZW algorithm exploits this observation to turn any significant improvement in encoding the significance map into a corresponding gain in compression efficiency. The EZW algorithm consists of two central components: the zerotree data structure and the method of successive approximation quantization.

8.8.1 The Zerotree Data Structure

The coding of the significance map is achieved using a new data structure called the *zerotree*. A wavelet coefficient x is said to be *insignificant* with respect to a given threshold T if $|x| < T$. The zerotree operates under the hypothesis that if a wavelet coefficient at a coarse scale is insignificant with respect to a given threshold T, all wavelet coefficients of the same orientation in the same spatial location at finer scales are likely to be insignificant with respect to T. Using the hierarchical wavelet decomposition presented in Chapter 8, we can relate every coefficient at a given scale to a set of coefficients at the next finer scale of similar orientation.

Figure 8.22 provides a pictorial representation of the zerotree on a three-stage wavelet decomposition. The coefficient at the coarse scale is called the *parent* while all corresponding coefficients are the next finer scale of the same spatial location and similar orientation are called *children*. For a given parent, the set of all coefficients at all finer scales are called *descendants*. Similarly, for a given child, the set of all coefficients at all coarser scales are called *ancestors*.

The scanning of the coefficients is performed in such a way that no child node is scanned before its parent. Figure 8.23 depicts the scanning pattern for a three-level wavelet decomposition.

Given a threshold T, a coefficient x is an element of the zerotree if it is insignificant and all its descendants are insignificant as well. An element of a zerotree is a *zerotree root* if it is not the descendant of a previously found zerotree root. The significance map is coded using the zerotree with a four-symbol alphabet. The four symbols are

- **The zerotree root**. The root of the zerotree is encoded with a special symbol indicating that the insignificance of the coefficients at finer scales is completely predictable.

- **Isolated zero**. The coefficient is insignificant but has some significant descendants.

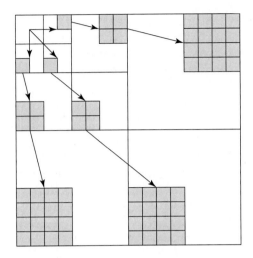

FIGURE 8.22: Parent–child relationship in a zerotree.

- **Positive significance**. The coefficient is significant with a positive value.

- **Negative significance**. The coefficient is significant with a negative value.

The cost of encoding the significance map is substantially reduced by employing the zerotree. The zerotree works by exploiting self-similarity on the transform coefficients. The underlying justification for the success of the zerotree is that even though the image has been transformed using a decorrelating transform, the occurrences of insignificant coefficients are not independent events.

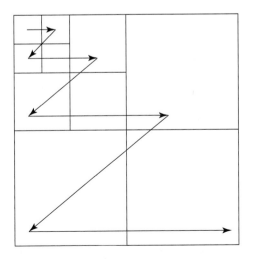

FIGURE 8.23: EZW scanning order.

In addition, the zerotree coding technique is based on the observation that it is much easier to predict insignificance than to predict significant details across scales. This technique focuses on reducing the cost of encoding the significance map so that more bits will be available to encode the expensive significant coefficients.

8.8.2 Successive Approximation Quantization

Embedded coding in the EZW coder is achieved using a method called *Successive Approximation Quantization* (SAQ). One motivation for developing this method is to produce an embedded code that provides a coarse-to-fine, multiprecision logarithmic representation of the scale space corresponding to the wavelet-transformed image. Another motivation is to take further advantage of the efficient encoding of the significance map using the zerotree data structure, by allowing it to encode more significance maps.

The SAQ method sequentially applies a sequence of thresholds $T_0, \ldots, T_{N-1}$ to determine the significance of each coefficient. The thresholds are chosen such that $T_i = T_{i-1}/2$. The initial threshold T_0 is chosen so that $|x_j| < 2T_0$ for all transform coefficients x_j. A *dominant list* and a *subordinate list* are maintained during the encoding and decoding process. The dominant list contains the coordinates of the coefficients that have not yet been found to be significant in the same relative order as the initial scan.

Using the scan ordering shown in Figure 8.23, all coefficients in a given subband appear on the initial dominant list prior to coefficients in the next subband. The subordinate list contains the magnitudes of the coefficients that have been found to be significant. Each list is scanned only once for each threshold.

During a dominant pass, coefficients having their coordinates on the dominant list implies that they are not yet significant. These coefficients are compared to the threshold T_i to determine their significance. If a coefficient is found to be significant, its magnitude is appended to the subordinate list, and the coefficient in the wavelet transform array is set to zero to enable the possibility of a zerotree occurring on future dominant passes at smaller thresholds. The resulting significance map is zerotree-coded.

The dominant pass is followed by a subordinate pass. All coefficients on the subordinate list are scanned, and their magnitude, as it is made available to the decoder, is refined to an additional bit of precision. Effectively, the width of the uncertainty interval for the true magnitude of the coefficients is cut in half. For each magnitude on the subordinate list, the refinement can be encoded using a binary alphabet with a 1 indicating that the true value falls in the upper half of the uncertainty interval and a 0 indicating that it falls in the lower half. The string of symbols from this binary alphabet is then entropy-coded. After the subordinate pass, the magnitudes on the subordinate list are sorted in decreasing order to the extent that the decoder can perform the same sort.

The process continues to alternate between the two passes, with the threshold halved before each dominant pass. The encoding stops when some target stopping criterion has been met.

8.8.3 EZW Example

The following example demonstrates the concept of zerotree coding and successive approximation quantization. Shapiro [11] presents an example of EZW coding in his paper for an

57	−37	39	−20	3	7	9	10
−29	30	17	33	8	2	1	6
14	6	15	13	9	−4	2	3
10	19	−7	9	−7	14	12	−9
12	15	33	20	−2	3	1	0
0	7	2	4	4	−1	1	1
4	1	10	3	2	0	1	0
5	6	0	0	3	1	2	1

FIGURE 8.24: Coefficients of a three-stage wavelet transform used as input to the EZW algorithm.

8×8 three-level wavelet transform. However, unlike the example given by Shapiro, we will complete the encoding and decoding process and show the output bitstream up to the point just before entropy coding.

Figure 8.24 shows the coefficients of a three-stage wavelet transform that we attempt to code using the EZW algorithm. We will use the symbols p, n, t, and z to denote positive significance, negative significance, zerotree root, and isolated zero respectively.

Since the largest coefficient is 57, we will choose the initial threshold T_0 to be 32. At the beginning, the dominant list contains the coordinates of all the coefficients. We begin scanning in the order shown in Figure 8.23 and determine the significance of the coefficients. The following is the list of coefficients visited, in the order of the scan:

$$\{57, -37, -29, 30, 39, -20, 17, 33, 14, 6, 10, 19, 3, 7, 8, 2, 2, 3, 12, -9, 33, 20, 2, 4\}$$

With respect to the threshold $T_0 = 32$, it is easy to see that the coefficients 57 and −37 are significant. Thus, we output a p and an n to represent them. The coefficient −29 is insignificant but contains a significant descendant, 33, in LH1. Therefore, it is coded as z. The coefficient 30 is also insignificant, and all its descendants are insignificant with respect to the current threshold, so it is coded as t.

Since we have already determined the insignificance of 30 and all its descendants, the scan will bypass them, and no additional symbols will be generated. Continuing in this manner, the dominant pass outputs the following symbols:

$$D_0 : pnztpttptzttpttt$$

Five coefficients are found to be significant: 57, −37, 39, 33, and another 33. Since we know that no coefficients are greater than $2T_0 = 64$, and the threshold used in the first dominant pass is 32, the uncertainty interval is thus $[32, 64)$. Therefore, we know that the value of significant coefficients lie somewhere inside this uncertainty interval.

The subordinate pass following the dominant pass refines the magnitude of these coefficients by indicating whether they lie in the first half or the second half of the uncertainty interval. The output is 0 if the values lie in $[32, 48)$ and 1 for values within $[48, 64)$. According to the order of the scan, the subordinate pass outputs the following bits:

$$S_0 : 10000$$

Now the dominant list contains the coordinates of all the coefficients except those found to be significant, and the subordinate list contains the values $\{57, 37, 39, 33, 33\}$. After the subordinate pass is completed, we attempt to rearrange the values in the subordinate list such that larger coefficients appear before smaller ones, with the constraint that the decoder is able do exactly the same.

Since the subordinate pass halves the uncertainty interval, the decoder is able to distinguish values from $[32, 48)$ and $[48, 64)$. Since 39 and 37 are not distinguishable in the decoder, their order will not be changed. Therefore, the subordinate list remains the same after the reordering operation.

Before we move on to the second round of dominant and subordinate passes, we need to set the values of the significant coefficients to 0 in the wavelet transform array so that they do not prevent the emergence of a new zerotree.

The new threshold for a second dominant pass is $T_1 = 16$. Using the same procedure as above, the dominant pass outputs the following symbols. Note that the coefficients in the dominant list will not be scanned.

$$D_1 : zznptnpttztptttttttttttttttptttttt \tag{8.65}$$

The subordinate list is now $\{57, 37, 39, 33, 33, 29, 30, 20, 17, 19, 20\}$. The subordinate pass that follows will halve each of the three current uncertainty intervals $[48, 64)$, $[32, 48)$, and $[16, 32)$. The subordinate pass outputs the following bits:

$$S_1 : 10000110000$$

Now we set the value of the coefficients found to be significant to 0 in the wavelet transform array.

The output of the subsequent dominant and subordinate passes is shown below:

$$D_2 : \quad zzzzzzzzptpzpptnttptpptt ptttptt pnppttttttptttttttttttttttt$$
$$S_2 : \quad 01100111001101100000110110$$
$$D_3 : \quad zzzzzzztzpztztnttpttttttptnnttttptttt pptppttptttttt$$
$$S_3 : \quad 001000100011101001100010011111101100010$$
$$D_4 : \quad zzzzzttztztzztzzpttppptttt pttpttnptt ptpttt pt$$
$$S_4 : \quad 1111101001101011000001011101101100010010010101010$$
$$D_5 : \quad zzzztztttt ztzzzztt ptt pttttt npt ppttt ppttp$$

Since the length of the uncertainty interval in the last pass is 1, the last subordinate pass is unnecessary.

On the decoder side, suppose we received information only from the first dominant and subordinate passes. We can reconstruct a lossy version of the transform coefficients by

56	−40	40	0	0	0	0	0
0	0	0	40	0	0	0	0
0	0	0	0	0	0	0	0
0	0	0	0	0	0	0	0
0	0	40	0	0	0	0	0
0	0	0	0	0	0	0	0
0	0	0	0	0	0	0	0
0	0	0	0	0	0	0	0

FIGURE 8.25: Reconstructed transform coefficients from the first dominant and subordinate passes.

reversing the encoding process. From the symbols in D_0 we can obtain the position of the significant coefficients. Then, using the bits decoded from S_0, we can reconstruct the value of these coefficients using the center of the uncertainty interval. Figure 8.25 shows the resulting reconstruction.

It is evident that we can stop the decoding process at any point to reconstruct a coarser representation of the original input coefficients. Figure 8.26 shows the reconstruction if the decoder received only D_0, S_0, D_1, S_1, D_2, and only the first 10 bits of S_2. The coefficients that were not refined during the last subordinate pass appear as if they were quantized using a coarser quantizer than those that were.

In fact, the reconstruction value used for these coefficients is the center of the uncertainty interval from the previous pass. The heavily shaded coefficients in the figure are those that were refined, while the lightly shaded coefficients are those that were not refined. As a result, it is not easy to see where the decoding process ended, and this eliminates much of the visual artifact contained in the reconstruction.

8.9   SET PARTITIONING IN HIERARCHICAL TREES (SPIHT)

SPIHT is a revolutionary extension of the EZW algorithm. Based on EZW's underlying principles of partial ordering of transformed coefficients, ordered bitplane transmission of refinement bits, and the exploitation of self-similarity in the transformed wavelet image, the SPIHT algorithm significantly improves the performance of its predecessor by changing the ways subsets of coefficients are partitioned and refinement information is conveyed.

A unique property of the SPIHT bitstream is its compactness. The resulting bitstream from the SPIHT algorithm is so compact that passing it through an entropy coder would produce only marginal gain in compression at the expense of much more computation. Therefore, a fast SPIHT coder can be implemented without any entropy coder or possibly just a simple patent-free Huffman coder.

Another signature of the SPIHT algorithm is that no ordering information is explicitly transmitted to the decoder. Instead, the decoder reproduces the execution path of the encoder

58	−38	38	−22	0	0	12	12
−30	30	18	34	12	0	0	0
12	0	12	12	12	0	0	0
12	20	0	12	0	12	12	−12
12	12	34	22	0	0	0	0
0	0	0	0	0	0	0	0
0	0	12	0	0	0	0	0
0	0	0	0	0	0	0	0

FIGURE 8.26: Reconstructed transform coefficients from D_0, S_0, D_1, S_1, D_2, and the first 10 bits of S_2.

and recovers the ordering information. A desirable side effect of this is that the encoder and decoder have similar execution times, which is rarely the case for other coding methods. Said and Pearlman [12] gives a full description of this algorithm.

8.10 FURTHER EXPLORATION

Sayood [14] deals extensively with the subject of lossy data compression in a well-organized and easy-to-understand manner.

Gersho and Gray [15] cover quantization, especially vector quantization, comprehensivly. In addition to the basic theory, this book provides a nearly exhaustive description of available VQ methods.

Gonzales and Woods [7] discuss mathematical transforms and image compression, including straightforward explanations for a wide range of algorithms in the context of image processing.

The mathematical foundation for the development of many lossy data compression algorithms is the study of *stochastic processes*. Stark and Woods [16] is an excellent textbook on this subject.

Finally, Mallat [5] is a book on wavelets, emphasizing theory.

Links included in the Further Exploration directory of the text web site for this chapter are

- An online, graphics-based demonstration of the wavelet transform. Two programs are included, one to demonstrate the 1D wavelet transform and the other for 2D image compression. In the 1D program, you simply draw the curve to be transformed.

- The Theory of Data Compression web page, which introduces basic theories behind both lossless and lossy data compression. Shannon's original 1948 paper on information theory can be downloaded from this site as well.

- The FAQ for the `comp.compression` and `comp.compression.research` groups. This FAQ answers most of the commonly asked questions about wavelet theory and data compression in general.

- A set of slides for scalar quantization and vector quantization, from the information theory course offered at Delft University.

- A link to an excellent article *"Image Compression — from DCT to Wavelets: A Review"*.

- Links to documentation and source code related to quantization.

8.11   EXERCISES

1. Assume we have an unbounded source we wish to quantize using an M-bit midtread uniform quantizer. Derive an expression for the total distortion if the step size is 1.

2. Suppose the domain of a uniform quantizer is $[-b_M, b_M]$. We define the loading fraction as

$$\gamma = \frac{b_M}{\sigma}$$

where σ is the standard deviation of the source. Write a simple program to quantize a Gaussian distributed source having zero mean and unit variance using a 4-bit uniform quantizer. Plot the SNR against the loading fraction and estimate the optimal step size that incurs the least amount of distortion from the graph.

3. * Suppose the input source is Gaussian-distributed with zero mean and unit variance — that is, the probability density function is defined as

$$f_X(x) = \frac{1}{\sqrt{2\pi}} e^{-\frac{x^2}{2}} \tag{8.66}$$

We wish to find a four-level Lloyd–Max quantizer. Let $\mathbf{y}_i = [y_i^0, \dots, y_i^3]$ and $\mathbf{b}_i = [b_i^0, \dots, b_i^3]$. The initial reconstruction levels are set to $\mathbf{y}_0 = [-2, -1, 1, 2]$. This source is unbounded, so the outer two boundaries are $+\infty$ and $-\infty$.

Follow the Lloyd–Max algorithm in this chapter: the other boundary values are calculated as the midpoints of the reconstruction values. We now have $\mathbf{b}_0 = [-\infty, -1.5, 0, 1.5, \infty]$. Continue one more iteration for $i = 1$, using Eq. (8.13) and find $y_0^1, y_1^1, y_2^1, y_3^1$, using numerical integration. Also calculate the squared error of the difference between $\mathbf{y}_1$ and $\mathbf{y}_0$.

Iteration is repeated until the squared error between successive estimates of the reconstruction levels is below some predefined threshold ϵ. Write a small program to implement the Lloyd–Max quantizer described above.

4. If the block size for a 2D DCT transform is 8×8, and we use only the DC components to create a thumbnail image, what fraction of the original pixels would we be using?

5. When the block size is 8, the definition of the DCT is given in Eq. (8.17).

FIGURE 8.27: Sphere shaded by a light.

(a) If an 8×8 grayscale image is in the range $0 .. 255$, what is the largest value a DCT coefficient could be, and for what input image? (Also, state *all* the DCT coefficient values for that image.)

(b) If we first subtract the value 128 from the whole image and then carry out the DCT, what is the exact effect on the DCT value $F[2, 3]$?

(c) Why would we carry out that subtraction? Does the subtraction affect the number of bits we need to code the image?

(d) Would it be possible to invert that subtraction, in the IDCT? If so, how?

6. We could use a similar DCT scheme for *video streams* by using a 3D version of DCT. Suppose one color component of a video has pixels f_{ijk} at position (i, j) and time k. How could we define its 3D DCT transform?

7. Suppose a uniformly colored sphere is illuminated and has shading varying smoothly across its surface, as in Figure 8.27.

(a) What would you expect the DCT coefficients for its image to look like?

(b) What would be the effect on the DCT coefficients of having a checkerboard of colors on the surface of the sphere?

(c) For the uniformly colored sphere again, describe the DCT values for a block that straddles the top edge of the sphere, where it meets the black background.

(d) Describe the DCT values for a block that straddles the left edge of the sphere.

8. The Haar wavelet has a scaling function which is defined as follows:

$$\phi(t) = \begin{cases} 1 & 0 \le t \le 1 \\ 0 & \text{otherwise} \end{cases} \tag{8.67}$$

and its scaling vector is $h_0[0] = h_0[1] = 1/\sqrt{2}$.

(a) Draw the scaling function, then verify that its dilated translates $\phi(2t)$ and $\phi(2t - 1)$ satisfy the dilation equation (8.56). Draw the combination of these functions that makes up the full function $\phi(t)$.

(b) Derive the wavelet vector $h_1[0]$, $h_1[1]$ from Eq. (8.59) and then derive and draw the Haar wavelet function $\psi(t)$ from Eq. (8.57).

9. Suppose the mother wavelet $\psi(t)$ has vanishing moments M_p up to and including M_n. Expand $f(t)$ in a Taylor series around $t = 0$, up to the nth derivative of f [i.e., up to leftover error of order $O(n+1)$]. Evaluate the summation of integrals produced by substituting the Taylor series into (8.52) and show that the result is of order $O(s^{n+2})$.

10. The program `wavelet_compression.c` on this book's web site is in fact simple to implement as a MATLAB function (or similar fourth-generation language). The advantage in doing so is that the `imread` function can input image formats of a great many types, and `imwrite` can output as desired. Using the given program as a template, construct a MATLAB program for wavelet-based image reduction, with perhaps the number of wavelet levels being a function parameter.

11. It is interesting to find the Fourier transform of functions, and this is easy if you have available a symbolic manipulation system such as MAPLE. In that language, you can just invoke the `fourier` function and view the answer directly! As an example, try the following code fragment:

```
with('inttrans');
f := 1;
F := fourier(f,t,w);
```

The answer should be $2\pi\,\delta(w)$. Let's try a Gaussian:

```
f := exp(-t^2);
F := fourier(f,t,w);
```

Now the answer should be $\sqrt{\pi}e^{(-w^2/4)}$: the Fourier transform of a Gaussian is simply another Gaussian.

12. Suppose we define the wavelet function

$$\psi(t) = exp(-t^{1/4})\sin(t^4), \quad t \geq 0 \qquad (8.68)$$

This function oscillates about the value 0. Use a plotting package to convince yourself that the function has a zero moment M_p for any value of p.

13. Implement both a DCT-based and a wavelet-based image coder. Design your user interface so that the compressed results from both coders can be seen side by side for visual comparison. The PSNR for each coded image should also be shown, for quantitative comparisons.

Include a slider bar that controls the target bitrate for both coders. As you change the target bitrate, each coder should compress the input image in real time and show the compressed results immediately on your user interface.

Discuss both qualitative and quantitative compression results observed from your program at target bitrates of 4 bpp, 1 bpp, and 0.25 bpp.

14. Write a simple program or refer to the sample DCT program `dct_1D.c` in the book's web site to verify the results in Example 8.2 of the 1D DCT example in this chapter.

8.12 REFERENCES

1 A. György, "On the Theoretical Limits of Lossy Source Coding," Tudományos Diákkör (TDK) Conference [Hungarian Scientific Student's Conference] at Technical University of Budapest, 1998. http://www.szit.bme.hu/~gya/mixed.ps.

2 S. Arimoto, "An Algorithm for Calculating the Capacity of an Arbitrary Discrete Memoryless Channel," *IEEE Transactions on Information Theory*, 18: 14–20, 1972.

3 R. Blahut, "Computation of Channel Capacity and Rate-Distortion Functions," *IEEE Transactions on Information Theory*, 18: 460–473, 1972.

4 J.F. Blinn, "What's the Deal with the DCT?" *IEEE Computer Graphics and Applications*, 13(4): 78–83, 1993.

5 S. Mallat, *A Wavelet Tour of Signal Processing*, San Diego: Academic Press, 1998.

6 S. Mallat, "A Theory for Multiresolution Signal Decomposition: The Wavelet Representation," *IEEE Transactions on Pattern Analysis and Machine Intelligence*, 11: 674–693, 1989.

7 R.C. Gonzalez and R.E. Woods, *Digital Image Processing*, 2nd ed., Upper Saddle River, NJ: Prentice Hall, 2002.

8 B.E. Usevitch, "A Tutorial on Modern Lossy Wavelet Image Compression: Foundations of JPEG 2000," *IEEE Signal Processing Magazine*, 18(5): 22–35, 2001.

9 R. Coifman, Y. Meyer, S. Quake, and V. Wickerhauser, "Signal Processing and Compression with Wavelet Packets," Numerical Algorithms Research Group, Yale University, 1990.

10 K. Ramachandran and M. Vetterli, "Best Wavelet Packet Basis in a Rate-Distortion Sense," *IEEE Transactions on Image Processing*, 2: 160–173, 1993.

11 J. Shapiro, "Embedded Image Coding using Zerotrees of Wavelet Coefficients," *IEEE Transactions on Signal Processing*, 41(12): 3445–3462, 1993.

12 A. Said and W.A. Pearlman, "A New, Fast, and Efficient Image Codec Based on Set Partitioning in Hierarchical Trees," *IEEE Transactions on Circuits and Systems for Video Technology*, 6(3): 243–250, 1996.

13 D. Taubman, "High Performance Scalable Image Compression with EBCOT," *IEEE Transactions on Image Processing*, 9(7): 1158–1170, 2000.

14 K. Sayood, *Introduction to Data Compression*, 2nd ed., San Francisco: Morgan Kaufmann, 2000.

15 A. Gersho and R.M. Gray, *Vector Quantization and Signal Compression*, Boston: Kluwer Academic Publishers, 1992.

16 H. Stark and J.W. Woods, *Probability and Random Processes with Application to Signal Processing*, 3rd ed., Upper Saddle River, NJ: Prentice Hall, 2001.

CHAPTER 9

Image Compression Standards

Recent years have seen an explosion in the availability of digital images, because of the increase in numbers of digital imaging devices, such as scanners and digital cameras. The need to efficiently process and store images in digital form has motivated the development of many image compression *standards* for various applications and needs. In general, standards have greater longevity than particular programs or devices and therefore warrant careful study. In this chapter, we examine some current standards and demonstrate how topics presented in Chapters 7 and 8 are applied in practice.

We first explore the standard JPEG definition, used in most images on the web, then go on to look at the wavelet-based JPEG2000 standard. Two other standards, JPEG-LS — aimed particularly at a lossless JPEG, outside the main JPEG standard — and JBIG, for bilevel image compression, are included for completeness.

9.1 THE JPEG STANDARD

JPEG is an image compression standard developed by the *Joint Photographic Experts Group*. It was formally accepted as an international standard in 1992 [1].

JPEG consists of a number of steps, each of which contributes to compression. We'll look at the motivation behind these steps, then take apart the algorithm piece by piece.

9.1.1 Main Steps in JPEG Image Compression

As we know, unlike one-dimensional audio signals, a digital image $f(i, j)$ is not defined over the time domain. Instead, it is defined over a *spatial domain* — that is, an image is a function of the two dimensions i and j (or, conventionally, x and y). The 2D DCT is used as one step in JPEG, to yield a frequency response that is a function $F(u, v)$ in the *spatial frequency domain*, indexed by two integers u and v.

JPEG is a lossy image compression method. The effectiveness of the DCT transform coding method in JPEG relies on three major observations:

> **Observation 1.** Useful image contents change relatively slowly across the image — that is, it is unusual for intensity values to vary widely several times in a small area — for example, in an 8×8 image block. Spatial frequency indicates how many times pixel values change across an image block. The DCT formalizes this notion with a measure of how much the image contents change in relation to the number of cycles of a cosine wave per block.

> **Observation 2.** Psychophysical experiments suggest that humans are much less likely to notice the loss of very high-spatial-frequency components than lower-frequency components.

YIQ or YUV

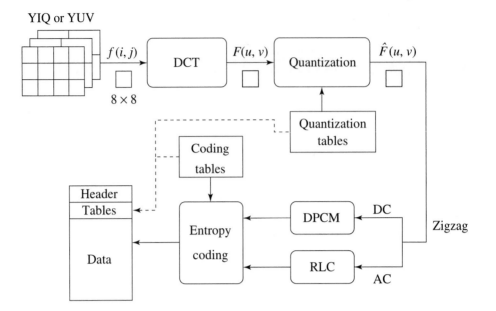

FIGURE 9.1: Block diagram for JPEG encoder.

JPEG's approach to the use of DCT is basically to reduce high-frequency contents and then efficiently code the result into a bitstring. The term *spatial redundancy* indicates that much of the information in an image is repeated: if a pixel is red, then its neighbor is likely red also. Because of Observation 2 above, the DCT coefficients for the lowest frequencies are most important. Therefore, as frequency gets higher, it becomes less important to represent the DCT coefficient accurately. It may even be safely set to zero without losing much perceivable image information.

Clearly, a string of zeros can be represented efficiently as the length of such a run of zeros, and compression of bits required is possible. Since we end up using fewer numbers to represent the pixels in blocks, by removing some location-dependent information, we have effectively removed spatial redundancy.

JPEG works for both color and grayscale images. In the case of color images, such as YIQ or YUV, the encoder works on each component separately, using the same routines. If the source image is in a different color format, the encoder performs a color-space conversion to YIQ or YUV. As discussed in Chapter 5, the chrominance images (I, Q or U, V) are *subsampled*: JPEG uses the 4:2:0 scheme, making use of another observation about vision:

> **Observation 3.** Visual acuity (accuracy in distinguishing closely spaced lines) is much greater for gray ("black and white") than for color. We simply cannot see much change in color if it occurs in close proximity — think of the blobby ink used in comic books. This works simply because our eye sees the black lines best, and our brain just pushes the color into place. In fact, ordinary broadcast TV makes use of this phenomenon to transmit much less color information than gray information.

When the JPEG image is needed for viewing, the three compressed component images can be decoded independently and eventually combined. For the color channels, each pixel must be first enlarged to cover a 2×2 block. Without loss of generality, we will simply use one of them — for example, the Y image, in the description of the compression algorithm below.

Figure 9.1 shows a block diagram for a JPEG encoder. If we reverse the arrows in the figure, we basically obtain a JPEG decoder. The JPEG encoder consists of the following main steps:

- Transform RGB to YIQ or YUV and subsample color

- Perform DCT on image blocks

- Apply Quantization

- Perform Zigzag ordering and run-length encoding

- Perform Entropy coding

DCT on Image Blocks.   Each image is divided into 8×8 blocks. The 2D DCT (Equation 8.17) is applied to each block image $f(i, j)$, with output being the DCT coefficients $F(u, v)$ for each block. The choice of a small block size in JPEG is a compromise reached by the committee: a number larger than 8 would have made accuracy at low frequencies better, but using 8 makes the DCT (and IDCT) computation very fast.

Using blocks at all, however, has the effect of isolating each block from its neighboring context. This is why JPEG images look choppy ("blocky") when the user specifies a high *compression ratio* — we can see these blocks. (And in fact removing such "blocking artifacts" is an important concern of researchers.)

To calculate a particular $F(u, v)$, we select the basis image in Figure 8.9 that corresponds to the appropriate u and v and use it in Equation 8.17 to derive one of the frequency responses $F(u, v)$.

Quantization.   The quantization step in JPEG is aimed at reducing the total number of bits needed for a compressed image [2]. It consists of simply dividing each entry in the frequency space block by an integer, then rounding:

$$\hat{F}(u, v) = \text{round}\left(\frac{F(u, v)}{Q(u, v)}\right) \tag{9.1}$$

Here, $F(u, v)$ represents a DCT coefficient, $Q(u, v)$ is a *quantization matrix* entry, and $\hat{F}(u, v)$ represents the *quantized DCT coefficients* JPEG will use in the succeeding entropy coding.

The default values in the 8×8 quantization matrix $Q(u, v)$ are listed in Tables 9.1 and 9.2 for luminance and chrominance images, respectively. These numbers resulted from psychophysical studies, with the goal of maximizing the compression ratio while minimizing perceptual losses in JPEG images. The following should be apparent:

TABLE 9.1: The luminance quantization table.

16	11	10	16	24	40	51	61
12	12	14	19	26	58	60	55
14	13	16	24	40	57	69	56
14	17	22	29	51	87	80	62
18	22	37	56	68	109	103	77
24	35	55	64	81	104	113	92
49	64	78	87	103	121	120	101
72	92	95	98	112	100	103	99

TABLE 9.2: The chrominance quantization table.

17	18	24	47	99	99	99	99
18	21	26	66	99	99	99	99
24	26	56	99	99	99	99	99
47	66	99	99	99	99	99	99
99	99	99	99	99	99	99	99
99	99	99	99	99	99	99	99
99	99	99	99	99	99	99	99
99	99	99	99	99	99	99	99

- Since the numbers in $Q(u, v)$ are relatively large, the magnitude and variance of $\hat{F}(u, v)$ are significantly smaller than those of $F(u, v)$. We'll see later that $\hat{F}(u, v)$ can be coded with many fewer bits. *The quantization step is the main source for loss in JPEG compression.*

- The entries of $Q(u, v)$ tend to have larger values toward the lower right corner. This aims to introduce more loss at the higher spatial frequencies — a practice supported by Observations 1 and 2.

We can handily change the compression ratio simply by multiplicatively *scaling* the numbers in the $Q(u, v)$ matrix. In fact, the *quality factor*, a user choice offered in every JPEG implementation, is essentially linearly tied to the scaling factor. JPEG also allows custom quantization tables to be specified and put in the header; it is interesting to use low-constant or high-constant values such as $Q \equiv 2$ or $Q \equiv 100$ to observe the basic effects of Q on visual artifacts.

Figures 9.2 and 9.3 show some results of JPEG image coding and decoding on the test image *Lena*. Only the luminance image (Y) is shown. Also, the lossless coding steps

An 8 × 8 block from the Y image of 'Lena'

200	202	189	188	189	175	175	175		515	65	−12	4	1	2	−8	5
200	203	198	188	189	182	178	175		−16	3	2	0	0	−11	−2	3
203	200	200	195	200	187	185	175		−12	6	11	−1	3	0	1	−2
200	200	200	200	197	187	187	187		−8	3	−4	2	−2	−3	−5	−2
200	205	200	200	195	188	187	175		0	−2	7	−5	4	0	−1	−4
200	200	200	200	200	190	187	175		0	−3	−1	0	4	1	−1	0
205	200	199	200	191	187	187	175		3	−2	−3	3	3	−1	−1	−3
210	200	200	200	188	185	187	186		−2	5	−2	4	−2	2	−3	0

$$f(i, j) \qquad\qquad F(u, v)$$

32	6	−1	0	0	0	0	0		512	66	−10	0	0	0	0	0
−1	0	0	0	0	0	0	0		−12	0	0	0	0	0	0	0
−1	0	1	0	0	0	0	0		−14	0	16	0	0	0	0	0
−1	0	0	0	0	0	0	0		−14	0	0	0	0	0	0	0
0	0	0	0	0	0	0	0		0	0	0	0	0	0	0	0
0	0	0	0	0	0	0	0		0	0	0	0	0	0	0	0
0	0	0	0	0	0	0	0		0	0	0	0	0	0	0	0
0	0	0	0	0	0	0	0		0	0	0	0	0	0	0	0

$$\hat{F}(u, v) \qquad\qquad \tilde{F}(u, v)$$

199	196	191	186	182	178	177	176		1	6	−2	2	7	−3	−2	−1
201	199	196	192	188	183	180	178		−1	4	2	−4	1	−1	−2	−3
203	203	202	200	195	189	183	180		0	−3	−2	−5	5	−2	2	−5
202	203	204	203	198	191	183	179		−2	−3	−4	−3	−1	−4	4	8
200	201	202	201	196	189	182	177		0	4	−2	−1	−1	−1	5	−2
200	200	199	197	192	186	181	177		0	0	1	3	8	4	6	−2
204	202	199	195	190	186	183	181		1	−2	0	5	1	1	4	−6
207	204	200	194	190	187	185	184		3	−4	0	6	−2	−2	2	2

$$\tilde{f}(i, j) \qquad\qquad \epsilon(i, j) = f(i, j) - \tilde{f}(i, j)$$

FIGURE 9.2: JPEG compression for a smooth image block.

Another 8 × 8 block from the Y image of 'Lena'

70	70	100	70	87	87	150	187
85	100	96	79	87	154	87	113
100	85	116	79	70	87	86	196
136	69	87	200	79	71	117	96
161	70	87	200	103	71	96	113
161	123	147	133	113	113	85	161
146	147	175	100	103	103	163	187
156	146	189	70	113	161	163	197

$$f(i,j)$$

−80	−40	89	−73	44	32	53	−3
−135	−59	−26	6	14	−3	−13	−28
47	−76	66	−3	−108	−78	33	59
−2	10	−18	0	33	11	−21	1
−1	−9	−22	8	32	65	−36	−1
5	−20	28	−46	3	24	−30	24
6	−20	37	−28	12	−35	33	17
−5	−23	33	−30	17	−5	−4	20

$$F(u,v)$$

−5	−4	9	−5	2	1	1	0
−11	−5	−2	0	1	0	0	−1
3	−6	4	0	−3	−1	0	1
0	1	−1	0	1	0	0	0
0	0	−1	0	0	1	0	0
0	−1	1	−1	0	0	0	0
0	0	0	0	0	0	0	0
0	0	0	0	0	0	0	0

$$\hat{F}(u,v)$$

−80	−44	90	−80	48	40	51	0
−132	−60	−28	0	26	0	0	−55
42	−78	64	0	−120	−57	0	56
0	17	−22	0	51	0	0	0
0	0	−37	0	0	109	0	0
0	−35	55	−64	0	0	0	0
0	0	0	0	0	0	0	0
0	0	0	0	0	0	0	0

$$\tilde{F}(u,v)$$

70	60	106	94	62	103	146	176
85	101	85	75	102	127	93	144
98	99	92	102	74	98	89	167
132	53	111	180	55	70	106	145
173	57	114	207	111	89	84	90
164	123	131	135	133	92	85	162
141	159	169	73	106	101	149	224
150	141	195	79	107	147	210	153

$$\tilde{f}(i,j)$$

0	10	−6	−24	25	−16	4	11
0	−1	11	4	−15	27	−6	−31
2	−14	24	−23	−4	−11	−3	29
4	16	−24	20	24	1	11	−49
−12	13	−27	−7	−8	−18	12	23
−3	0	16	−2	−20	21	0	−1
5	−12	6	27	−3	−2	14	−37
6	5	−6	−9	6	14	−47	44

$$\epsilon(i,j) = f(i,j) - \tilde{f}(i,j)$$

FIGURE 9.3: JPEG compression for a textured image block.

after quantization are not shown, since they do not affect the quality/loss of the JPEG images. These results show the effect of compression and decompression applied to a relatively smooth block in the image and a more textured (higher-frequency-content) block, respectively.

Suppose $f(i, j)$ represents one of the 8×8 blocks extracted from the image, $F(u, v)$ the DCT coefficients, and $\hat{F}(u, v)$ the quantized DCT coefficients. Let $\tilde{F}(u, v)$ denote the de-quantized DCT coefficients, determined by simply multiplying by $Q(u, v)$, and let $\tilde{f}(i, j)$ be the reconstructed image block. To illustrate the quality of the JPEG compression, especially the loss, the error $\epsilon(i, j) = f(i, j) - \tilde{f}(i, j)$ is shown in the last row in Figures 9.2 and 9.3.

In Figure 9.2, an image block (indicated by a black box in the image) is chosen at the area where the luminance values change smoothly. Actually, the left side of the block is brighter, and the right side is slightly darker. As expected, except for the DC and the first few AC components, representing low spatial frequencies, most of the DCT coefficients $F(u, v)$ have small magnitudes. This is because the pixel values in this block contain few high-spatial-frequency changes.

An explanation of a small implementation detail is in order. The range of 8-bit luminance values $f(i, j)$ is $[0, 255]$. In the JPEG implementation, each Y value is first reduced by 128 by simply subtracting.

The idea here is to turn the Y component into a zero-mean image, the same as the chrominance images. As a result, we do not waste any bits coding the mean value. (Think of an 8×8 block with intensity values ranging from 120 to 135.) Using $f(i, j) - 128$ in place of $f(i, j)$ will not affect the output of the AC coefficients — it alters only the DC coefficient.

In Figure 9.3, the image block chosen has rapidly changing luminance. Hence, many more AC components have large magnitudes (including those toward the lower right corner, where u and v are large). Notice that the error $\epsilon(i, j)$ is also larger now than in Figure 9.2 — JPEG does introduce more loss if the image has quickly changing details.

Preparation for Entropy Coding.   We have so far seen two of the main steps in JPEG compression: DCT and quantization. The remaining small steps shown in the block diagram in Figure 9.1 all lead up to *entropy coding* of the quantized DCT coefficients. These additional data compression steps are lossless. Interestingly, the DC and AC coefficients are treated quite differently before entropy coding: run-length encoding on ACs versus DPCM on DCs.

Run-Length Coding (RLC) on AC Coefficients.   Notice in Figure 9.2 the many zeros in $\hat{F}(u, v)$ after quantization is applied. *Run-length Coding (RLC)* (or *Run-length Encoding, RLE*) is therefore useful in turning the $\hat{F}(u, v)$ values into sets {*#-zeros-to-skip, next non-zero value*}. RLC is even more effective when we use an addressing scheme, making it most likely to hit a long run of zeros: a *zigzag scan* turns the 8×8 matrix $\hat{F}(u, v)$ into a *64-vector*, as Figure 9.4 illustrates. After all, most image blocks tend to have small high-spatial-frequency components, which are zeroed out by quantization. Hence the zigzag

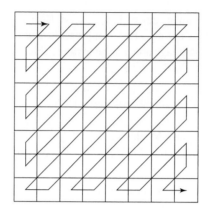

FIGURE 9.4: Zigzag scan in JPEG.

scan order has a good chance of concatenating long runs of zeros. For example, $\hat{F}(u, v)$ in Figure 9.2 will be turned into

$$(32, 6, -1, -1, 0, -1, 0, 0, 0, -1, 0, 0, 1, 0, 0, \dots, 0)$$

with three runs of zeros in the middle and a run of 51 zeros at the end.

The RLC step replaces values by a pair (RUNLENGTH, VALUE) for each run of zeros in the AC coefficients of $\hat{F}$, where RUNLENGTH is the number of zeros in the run and VALUE is the next nonzero coefficient. To further save bits, a special pair (0,0) indicates the end-of-block after the last nonzero AC coefficient is reached. In the above example, not considering the first (DC) component, we will thus have

$$(0, 6)(0, -1)(0, -1)(1, -1)(3, -1)(2, 1)(0, 0)$$

Differential Pulse Code Modulation (DPCM) on DC Coefficients. The DC coefficients are coded separately from the AC ones. Each 8×8 image block has only one DC coefficient. The values of the DC coefficients for various blocks could be large and different, because the DC value reflects the average intensity of each block, but consistent with Observation 1 above, the DC coefficient is unlikely to change drastically within a short distance. This makes DPCM an ideal scheme for coding the DC coefficients.

If the DC coefficients for the first five image blocks are 150, 155, 149, 152, 144, DPCM would produce 150, 5, −6, 3, −8, assuming the predictor for the ith block is simply $d_i = DC_{i+1} - DC_i$, and $d_0 = DC_0$. We expect DPCM codes to generally have smaller magnitude and variance, which is beneficial for the next *entropy coding* step.

It is worth noting that unlike the run-length coding of the AC coefficients, which is performed on each individual block, DPCM for the DC coefficients in JPEG is carried out on the entire image at once.

TABLE 9.3: Baseline entropy coding details — size category.

SIZE	AMPLITUDE
1	$-1, 1$
2	$3, -2, 2, 3$
3	$-7 .. -4, 4 .. 7$
4	$-15 .. -8, 8 .. 15$
.	.
.	.
.	.
10	$-1023 .. -512, 512 .. 1023$

Entropy Coding   The DC and AC coefficients finally undergo an entropy coding step. Below, we will discuss only the basic (or *baseline*[1]) entropy coding method, which uses Huffman coding and supports only 8-bit pixels in the original images (or color image components).

Let's examine the two entropy coding schemes, using a variant of Huffman coding for DCs and a slightly different scheme for ACs.

Huffman Coding of DC Coefficients   Each DPCM-coded DC coefficient is represented by a pair of symbols (SIZE, AMPLITUDE), where SIZE indicates how many bits are needed for representing the coefficient and AMPLITUDE contains the actual bits.

Table 9.3 illustrates the size category for the different possible amplitudes. Notice that DPCM values could require more than 8 bits and could be negative values. The one's-complement scheme is used for negative numbers — that is, binary code 10 for 2, 01 for -2; 11 for 3, 00 for -3; and so on. In the example we are using, codes 150, 5, -6, 3, -8 will be turned into

$$(8, 10010110), (3, 101), (3, 001), (2, 11), (4, 0111)$$

In the JPEG implementation, SIZE is Huffman coded and is hence a variable-length code. In other words, SIZE 2 might be represented as a single bit (0 or 1) if it appeared most frequently. In general, smaller SIZEs occur much more often — the entropy of SIZE is low. Hence, deployment of Huffman coding brings additional compression. After encoding, a custom Huffman table can be stored in the JPEG image header; otherwise, a default Huffman table is used.

On the other hand, AMPLITUDE is not Huffman coded. Since its value can change widely, Huffman coding has no appreciable benefit.

---

[1] The JPEG standard allows both Huffman coding and Arithmetic coding; both are entropy coding methods. It also supports both 8-bit and 12-bit pixel lengths.

Huffman Coding of AC Coefficients.   Recall we said that the AC coefficients are run-length coded and are represented by pairs of numbers (RUNLENGTH, VALUE). However, in an actual JPEG implementation, VALUE is further represented by SIZE and AMPLITUDE, as for the DCs. To save bits, RUNLENGTH and SIZE are allocated only 4 bits each and squeezed into a single byte — let's call this *Symbol 1*. *Symbol 2* is the AMPLITUDE value; its number of bits is indicated by SIZE:

Symbol 1: (RUNLENGTH, SIZE)

Symbol 2: (AMPLITUDE)

The 4-bit RUNLENGTH can represent only zero-runs of length 0 to 15. Occasionally, the zero-run length exceeds 15; then a special extension code, (15, 0), is used for Symbol 1. In the worst case, three consecutive (15, 0) extensions are needed before a normal terminating Symbol 1, whose RUNLENGTH will then complete the actual runlength. As in DC, Symbol 1 is Huffman coded, whereas Symbol 2 is not.

9.1.2   JPEG Modes

The JPEG standard supports numerous modes (variations). Some of the commonly used ones are:

- Sequential Mode
- Progressive Mode
- Hierarchical Mode
- Lossless Mode

Sequential Mode.   This is the default JPEG mode. Each gray-level image or color image component is encoded in a single left-to-right, top-to-bottom scan. We implicitly assumed this mode in the discussions so far. The "Motion JPEG" video codec uses Baseline Sequential JPEG, applied to each image frame in the video.

Progressive Mode.   Progressive JPEG delivers low-quality versions of the image quickly, followed by higher-quality passes, and has become widely supported in web browsers. Such multiple scans of images are of course most useful when the speed of the communication line is low. In Progressive Mode, the first few scans carry only a few bits and deliver a rough picture of what is to follow. After each additional scan, more data is received, and image quality is gradually enhanced. The advantage is that the user-end has a choice whether to continue receiving image data after the first scan(s).

Progressive JPEG can be realized in one of the following two ways. The main steps (DCT, quantization, etc.) are identical to those in Sequential Mode.

Spectral selection: This scheme takes advantage of the *spectral* (spatial frequency spectrum) characteristics of the DCT coefficients: the higher AC components provide only detail information.

Scan 1: Encode DC and first few AC components, e.g., AC1, AC2.

Scan 2: Encode a few more AC components, e.g., AC3, AC4, AC5.

$\vdots$

Scan k: Encode the last few ACs, e.g., AC61, AC62, AC63.

Successive approximation: Instead of gradually encoding spectral bands, all DCT coefficients are encoded simultaneously, but with their most significant bits (MSBs) first.

Scan 1: Encode the first few MSBs, e.g., Bits 7, 6, 5, and 4.

Scan 2: Encode a few more less-significant bits, e.g., Bit 3.

$\vdots$

Scan m: Encode the least significant bit (LSB), Bit 0.

Hierarchical Mode.   As its name suggests, Hierarchical JPEG encodes the image in a hierarchy of several different resolutions. The encoded image at the lowest resolution is basically a compressed low-pass-filtered image, whereas the images at successively higher resolutions provide additional details (differences from the lower-resolution images). Similar to Progressive JPEG, Hierarchical JPEG images can be transmitted in multiple passes with progressively improving quality.

Figure 9.5 illustrates a three-level hierarchical JPEG encoder and decoder (separated by the dashed line in the figure).

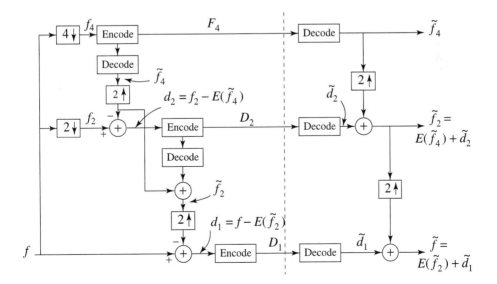

FIGURE 9.5: Block diagram for Hierarchical JPEG.

ALGORITHM 9.1   THREE-LEVEL HIERARCHICAL JPEG ENCODER

1. **Reduction of image resolution.** Reduce resolution of the input image f (e.g., 512×512) by a factor of 2 in each dimension to obtain f_2 (e.g., 256×256). Repeat this to obtain f_4 (e.g., 128×128).

2. **Compress low-resolution image f_4.** Encode f_4 using any other JPEG method (e.g., Sequential, Progressive) to obtain F_4.

3. **Compress difference image d_2.**

    (a) Decode F_4 to obtain $\tilde{f}_4$. Use any interpolation method to expand $\tilde{f}_4$ to be of the same resolution as f_2 and call it $E(\tilde{f}_4)$.

    (b) Encode difference $d_2 = f_2 - E(\tilde{f}_4)$ using any other JPEG method (e.g., Sequential, Progressive) to generate D_2.

4. **Compress difference image d_1.**

    (a) Decode D_2 to obtain $\tilde{d}_2$; add it to $E(\tilde{f}_4)$ to get $\tilde{f}_2 = E(\tilde{f}_4) + \tilde{d}_2$, which is a version of f_2 after compression and decompression.

    (b) Encode difference $d_1 = f - E(\tilde{f}_2)$ using any other JPEG method (e.g., Sequential, Progressive) to generate D_1.

ALGORITHM 9.2   THREE-LEVEL HIERARCHICAL JPEG DECODER

1. **Decompress the encoded low-resolution image F_4.** Decode F_4 using the same JPEG method as in the encoder, to obtain $\tilde{f}_4$.

2. **Restore image $\tilde{f}_2$ at the intermediate resolution.** Use $E(\tilde{f}_4) + \tilde{d}_2$ to obtain $\tilde{f}_2$.

3. **Restore image $\tilde{f}$ at the original resolution.** Use $E(\tilde{f}_2) + \tilde{d}_1$ to obtain $\tilde{f}$.

It should be pointed out that at step 3 in the encoder, the difference d_2 is not taken as $f_2 - E(f_4)$ but as $f_2 - E(\tilde{f}_4)$. Employing $\tilde{f}_4$ has its overhead, since an additional decoding step must be introduced on the encoder side, as shown in the figure.

So, is it necessary? It is, because the *decoder* never has a chance to see the original f_4. The restoration step in the decoder uses $\tilde{f}_4$ to obtain $\tilde{f}_2 = E(\tilde{f}_4) + \tilde{d}_2$. Since $\tilde{f}_4 \neq f_4$ when a lossy JPEG method is used in compressing f_4, the encoder must use $\tilde{f}_4$ in $d_2 = f_2 - E(\tilde{f}_4)$ to avoid unnecessary error at decoding time. This kind of decoder-encoder step is typical in many compression schemes. In fact, we have seen it in Section 6.3.5. It is present simply because the decoder has access only to encoded, not original, values.

Similarly, at step 4 in the encoder, d_1 uses the difference between f and $E(\tilde{f}_2)$, not $E(f_2)$.

Lossless Mode   Lossless JPEG is a very special case of JPEG which indeed has no loss in its image quality. As discussed in Chapter 7, however, it employs only a simple differential coding method, involving no transform coding. It is rarely used, since its compression ratio is very low compared to other, lossy modes. On the other hand, it meets a special need, and the newly developed JPEG-LS standard is specifically aimed at lossless image compression (see Section 9.3).

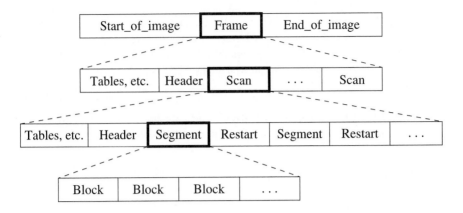

FIGURE 9.6: JPEG bitstream.

9.1.3   A Glance at the JPEG Bitstream

Figure 9.6 provides a hierarchical view of the organization of the bitstream for JPEG images. Here, a *frame* is a picture, a *scan* is a pass through the pixels (e.g., the red component), a *segment* is a group of blocks, and a *block* consists of 8×8 pixels. Examples of some header information are:

- **Frame header**

  - Bits per pixel
  - (Width, height) of image
  - Number of components
  - Unique ID (for each component)
  - Horizontal/vertical sampling factors (for each component)
  - Quantization table to use (for each component)

- **Scan header**

  - Number of components in scan
  - Component ID (for each component)
  - Huffman/Arithmetic coding table (for each component)

9.2   THE JPEG2000 STANDARD

The JPEG standard is no doubt the most successful and popular image format to date. The main reason for its success is the quality of its output for relatively good compression ratio. However, in anticipating the needs and requirements of next-generation imagery applications, the JPEG committee has defined a new standard: JPEG2000.

The new JPEG2000 standard [3] aims to provide not only a better rate-distortion tradeoff and improved subjective image quality but also additional functionalities the current JPEG standard lacks. In particular, the JPEG2000 standard addresses the following problems [4]:

- **Low-bitrate compression.** The current JPEG standard offers excellent rate-distortion performance at medium and high bitrates. However, at bitrates below 0.25 bpp, subjective distortion becomes unacceptable. This is important if we hope to receive images on our web-enabled ubiquitous devices, such as web-aware wristwatches, and so on.

- **Lossless and lossy compression.** Currently, no standard can provide superior lossless compression and lossy compression in a single bitstream.

- **Large images.** The new standard will allow image resolutions greater than $64\,k \times 64\,k$ without tiling. It can handle image sizes up to $2^{32} - 1$.

- **Single decompression architecture.** The current JPEG standard has 44 modes, many of which are application-specific and not used by the majority of JPEG decoders.

- **Transmission in noisy environments.** The new standard will provide improved error resilience for transmission in noisy environments such as wireless networks and the Internet.

- **Progressive transmission.** The new standard provides seamless quality and resolution scalability from low to high bitrates. The target bitrate and reconstruction resolution need not be known at the time of compression.

- **Region-of-interest coding.** The new standard permits specifying *Regions of Interest* (*ROI*), which can be coded with better quality than the rest of the image. We might, for example, like to code the face of someone making a presentation with more quality than the surrounding furniture.

- **Computer-generated imagery.** The current JPEG standard is optimized for natural imagery and does not perform well on computer-generated imagery.

- **Compound documents.** The new standard offers metadata mechanisms for incorporating additional non-image data as part of the file. This might be useful for including text along with imagery, as one important example.

In addition, JPEG2000 is able to handle up to 256 channels of information, whereas the current JPEG standard is able to handle only three color channels. Such huge quantities of data are routinely produced in satellite imagery.

Consequently, JPEG2000 is designed to address a variety of applications, such as the Internet, color facsimile, printing, scanning, digital photography, remote sensing, mobile applications, medical imagery, digital library, e-commerce, and so on. The method looks ahead and provides the power to carry out remote browsing of large compressed images.

The JPEG2000 standard operates in two coding modes: DCT-based and wavelet-based. The DCT-based coding mode is offered for backward compatibility with the current JPEG standard and implements baseline JPEG. All the new functionalities and improved performance reside in the wavelet-based mode.

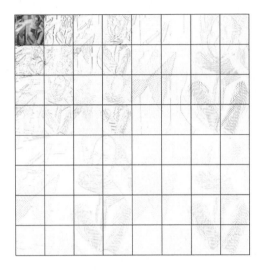

FIGURE 9.7: Code block structure of EBCOT.

9.2.1 Main Steps of JPEG2000 Image Compression*

The main compression method used in JPEG2000 is the *(Embedded Block Coding with Optimized Truncation) algorithm (EBCOT)*, designed by Taubman [5]. In addition to providing excellent compression efficiency, EBCOT produces a bitstream with a number of desirable features, including quality and resolution scalability and *random access.*

The basic idea of EBCOT is the partition of each subband LL, LH, HL, HH produced by the wavelet transform into small blocks called *code blocks.* Each code block is coded independently, in such a way that no information for any other block is used.

A separate, scalable bitstream is generated for each code block. With its block-based coding scheme, the EBCOT algorithm has improved error resilience. The EBCOT algorithm consists of three steps:

1. Block coding and bitstream generation
2. Postcompression rate distortion (PCRD) optimization
3. Layer formation and representation

Block Coding and Bitstream Generation.   Each subband generated for the 2D discrete wavelet transform is first partitioned into small code blocks of size 32×32 or 64×64. Then the EBCOT algorithm generates a highly scalable bitstream for each code block B_i. The bitstream associated with B_i may be independently truncated to any member of a predetermined collection of different lengths R_i^n, with associated distortion D_i^n.

For each code block B_i (see Figure 9.7), let $s_i[\mathbf{k}] = s_i[k_1, k_2]$ be the two-dimensional sequence of small code blocks of subband samples, with k_1 and k_2 the row and column index. (With this definition, the horizontal high-pass subband HL must be transposed so that k_1 and k_2 will have meaning consistent with the other subbands. This transposition

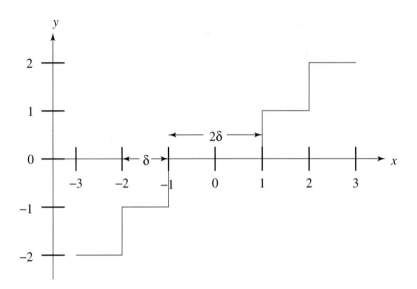

FIGURE 9.8: Dead zone quantizer. The length of the dead zone is 2δ. Values inside the dead zone are quantized to 0.

means that the HL subband can be treated in the same way as the LH, HH, and LL subbands and use the same context model.)

The algorithm uses a *dead zone* quantizer shown in Figure 9.8 — a double-length region straddling 0. Let $\chi_i[\mathbf{k}] \in \{-1, 1\}$ be the sign of $s_i[\mathbf{k}]$ and let $v_i[\mathbf{k}]$ be the quantized magnitude. Explicitly, we have

$$v_i[\mathbf{k}] = \frac{\|s_i[\mathbf{k}]\|}{\delta_{\beta_i}} \tag{9.2}$$

where δ_{β_i} is the step size for subband β_i, which contains code block B_i. Let $v_i^p[\mathbf{k}]$ be the pth bit in the binary representation of $v_i[\mathbf{k}]$, where $p = 0$ corresponds to the least significant bit, and let p_i^{max} be the maximum value of p such that $v_i^{p_i^{max}}[\mathbf{k}] \neq 0$ for at least one sample in the code block.

The encoding process is similar to that of a bitplane coder, in which the most significant bit $v_i^{p_i^{max}}[\mathbf{k}]$ is coded first for all samples in the code block, followed by the next most significant bit $v_i^{p_i^{(max-1)}}[\mathbf{k}]$, and so on, until all bitplanes have been coded. In this way, if the bitstream is truncated, then some samples in the code block may be missing one or more least-significant bits. This is equivalent to having used a coarser dead zone quantizer for these samples.

In addition, it is important to exploit the previously encoded information about a particular sample and its neighboring samples. This is done in EBCOT by defining a binary valued state variable $\sigma_i[\mathbf{k}]$, which is initially 0 but changes to 1 when the relevant sample's first nonzero bitplane $v_i^p[\mathbf{k}] = 1$ is encoded. This binary state variable is referred to as the *significance* of a sample.

Section 8.8 introduces the zerotree data structure as a way of efficiently coding the bitstream for wavelet coefficients. The underlying observation behind the zerotree data structure is that significant samples tend to be clustered, so that it is often possible to dispose of a large number of samples by coding a single binary symbol.

EBCOT takes advantage of this observation; however, with efficiency in mind, it exploits the clustering assumption only down to relatively large sub-blocks of size 16×16. As a result, each code block is further partitioned into a two-dimensional sequence of sub-blocks $B_i[\mathbf{j}]$. For each bitplane, explicit information is first encoded that identifies sub-blocks containing one or more significant samples. The other sub-blocks are bypassed in the remaining coding phases for that bitplane.

Let $\sigma^p(B_i[\mathbf{j}])$ be the significance of sub-block $B_i[\mathbf{j}]$ in bitplane p. The significance map is coded using a quad tree. The tree is constructed by identifying the sub-blocks with leaf nodes — that is, $B_i^0[\mathbf{j}] = B_i[\mathbf{j}]$. The higher levels are built using recursion: $B_i^t[\mathbf{j}] = \cup_{\mathbf{z} \in \{0,1\}^2} B_i^{t-1}[2\mathbf{j} + \mathbf{z}]$, $0 \leq t \leq T$. The root of the tree represents the entire code-block: $B_i^T[\mathbf{0}] = \cup_{\mathbf{j}} B_i[\mathbf{j}]$.

The significance of the code block is identified one quad level at a time, starting from the root at $t = T$ and working toward the leaves at $t = 0$. The significance values are then sent to an arithmetic coder for entropy coding. Significance values that are *redundant* are skipped. A value is taken as redundant if any of the following conditions is met:

- The parent is insignificant.

- The current quad was already significant in the previous bitplane.

- This is the last quad visited among those that share the same significant parent, and the other siblings are insignificant.

EBCOT uses four different coding primitives to code new information for a single sample in a bitplane p, as follows:

- **Zero coding.** This is used to code $v_i^p[\mathbf{k}]$, given that the quantized sample satisfies $v_i[\mathbf{k}] < 2^{p+1}$. Because the sample statistics are measured to be approximately Markovian, the significance of the current sample depends on the values of its eight immediate neighbors. The significance of these neighbors can be classified into three categories:

  - **Horizontal.** $h_i[\mathbf{k}] = \sum_{z \in \{1,-1\}} \sigma_i[k_1 + z, k_2]$, with $0 \leq h_i[\mathbf{k}] \leq 2$
  - **Vertical.** $v_i[\mathbf{k}] = \sum_{z \in \{1,-1\}} \sigma_i[k_1, k_2 + z]$, with $0 \leq v_i[\mathbf{k}] \leq 2$
  - **Diagonal.** $d_i[\mathbf{k}] = \sum_{z_1, z_2 \in \{1,-1\}} \sigma_i[k_1 + z_1, k_2 + z_2]$, with $0 \leq d_i[\mathbf{k}] \leq 4$

  The neighbors outside the code block are considered to be insignificant, but note that sub-blocks are not at all independent. The 256 possible neighborhood configurations are reduced to the nine distinct context assignments listed in Table 9.4.

- **Run-length coding.** The run-length coding primitive is aimed at producing runs of the 1-bit significance values, as a prelude for the arithmetic coding engine. When a

TABLE 9.4: Context assignment for the zero coding primitive.

Label	LL, LH and HL subbands			HH subband	
	$h_i[\mathbf{k}]$	$v_i[\mathbf{k}]$	$d_i[\mathbf{k}]$	$d_i[\mathbf{k}]$	$h_i[\mathbf{k}] + v_i[\mathbf{k}]$
0	0	0	0	0	0
1	0	0	1	0	1
2	0	0	> 1	0	> 1
3	0	1	x	1	0
4	0	2	x	1	1
5	1	0	0	1	> 1
6	1	0	> 0	2	0
7	1	> 0	x	2	> 0
8	2	x	x	> 2	x

horizontal run of insignificant samples having insignificant neighbors is found, it is invoked instead of the zero coding primitive. Each of the following four conditions must be met for the run-length coding primitive to be invoked:

- – Four consecutive samples must be insignificant.
- – The samples must have insignificant neighbors.
- – The samples must be within the same sub-block.
- – The horizontal index k_1 of the first sample must be even.

The last two conditions are simply for efficiency. When four symbols satisfy these conditions, one special bit is encoded instead, to identify whether any sample in the group is significant in the current bitplane (using a separate context model). If any of the four samples becomes significant, the index of the first such sample is sent as a 2-bit quantity.

- **Sign coding.** The sign coding primitive is invoked at most once for each sample, immediately after the sample makes a transition from being insignificant to significant during a zero coding or run-length coding operation. Since it has four horizontal and vertical neighbors, each of which may be insignificant, positive, or negative, there are $3^4 = 81$ different context configurations. However, exploiting both horizontal and vertical symmetry and assuming that the conditional distribution of $\chi_i[\mathbf{k}]$, given any neighborhood configuration, is the same as that of $-\chi_i[\mathbf{k}]$, the number of contexts is reduced to 5.

Let $\bar{h}_i[\mathbf{k}]$ be 0 if both horizontal neighbors are insignificant, 1 if at least one horizontal neighbor is positive, or -1 if at least one horizontal neighbor is negative (and $\bar{v}_i[\mathbf{k}]$ is

TABLE 9.5: Context assignments for the sign coding primitive.

Label	$\hat{\chi}_i[\mathbf{k}]$	$\bar{h}_i[\mathbf{k}]$	$\bar{v}_i[\mathbf{k}]$
4	1	1	1
3	1	0	1
2	1	−1	1
1	−1	1	0
0	1	0	0
1	1	−1	0
2	−1	1	−1
3	−1	0	−1
4	−1	−1	−1

defined similarly). Let $\hat{\chi}_i[\mathbf{k}]$ be the sign prediction. The binary symbol coded using the relevant context is $\chi_i[\mathbf{k}] \cdot \hat{\chi}_i[\mathbf{k}]$. Table 9.5 lists these context assignments.

- **Magnitude refinement.** This primitive is used to code the value of $v_i^p[\mathbf{k}]$, given that $v_i[\mathbf{k}] \geq 2^{p+1}$. Only three context models are used for the magnitude refinement primitive. A second state variable $\tilde{\sigma}_i[\mathbf{k}]$ is introduced that changes from 0 to 1 after the magnitude refinement primitive is first applied to $s_i[\mathbf{k}]$. The context models depend on the value of this state variable: $v_i^p[\mathbf{k}]$ is coded with context 0 if $\tilde{\sigma}[\mathbf{k}] = h_i[\mathbf{k}] = v_i[\mathbf{k}] = 0$, with context 1 if $\tilde{\sigma}_i[\mathbf{k}] = 0$ and $h_i[\mathbf{k}] + v_i[\mathbf{k}] \neq 0$, and with context 2 if $\tilde{\sigma}_i[\mathbf{k}] = 1$.

To ensure that each code block has a finely embedded bitstream, the coding of each bitplane p proceeds in four distinct passes, $(\mathcal{P}_1^p)$ to $(\mathcal{P}_4^p)$:

- **Forward-significance-propagation pass $(\mathcal{P}_1^p)$.** The sub-block samples are visited in scanline order. Insignificant samples and samples that do not satisfy the neighborhood requirement are skipped. For the LH, HL, and LL subbands, the neighborhood requirement is that at least one of the horizontal neighbors has to be significant. For the HH subband, the neighborhood requirement is that at least one of the four diagonal neighbors must be significant.

For significant samples that pass the neighborhood requirement, the zero coding and run-length coding primitives are invoked as appropriate, to determine whether the sample first becomes significant in bitplane p. If so, the sign coding primitive is invoked to encode the sign. This is called the forward-significance-propagation pass, because a sample that has been found to be significant helps in the new significance determination steps that propagate in the direction of the scan.

$S^{p_i}_{max}$	$P^{p_i}_{4}{}^{max}$	$P^{p_i}_{1}{}^{max-1}$	$P^{p_i}_{2}{}^{max-1}$	$P^{p_i}_{3}{}^{max-1}$	$S^{p_i}{}^{max-1}$	$P^{p_i}_{4}{}^{max-1}$	$\cdots$	P^0_1	P^0_2	P^0_3	S^0	P^0_4

FIGURE 9.9: Appearance of coding passes and quad-tree codes in each block's embedded bitstream.

- **Reverse-significance-propagation pass ($\mathcal{P}^{\mathbf{p}}_{\mathbf{2}}$).** This pass is identical to $\mathcal{P}^p_1$, except that it proceeds in the reverse order. The neighborhood requirement is relaxed to include samples that have at least one significant neighbor in any direction.

- **Magnitude refinement pass ($\mathcal{P}^{\mathbf{p}}_{\mathbf{3}}$).** This pass encodes samples that are already significant but that have not been coded in the previous two passes. Such samples are processed with the magnitude refinement primitive.

- **Normalization pass ($\mathcal{P}^{\mathbf{p}}_{\mathbf{4}}$).** The value $v^p_i[\mathbf{k}]$ of all samples not considered in the previous three coding passes is coded using the sign coding and run-length coding primitives, as appropriate. If a sample is found to be significant, its sign is immediately coded using the sign coding primitive.

Figure 9.9 shows the layout of coding passes and quad-tree codes in each block's embedded bitstream. S^p denotes the quad-tree code identifying the significant sub-blocks in bitplane p. Notice that for any bitplane p, S^p appears just before the final coding pass $\mathcal{P}^p_4$, not the initial coding pass $\mathcal{P}^p_1$. This implies that sub-blocks that become significant for the first time in bitplane p are ignored until the final pass.

Post Compression Rate-Distortion Optimization.   After all the subband samples have been compressed, a *post compression rate distortion (PCRD)* step is performed. The goal of PCRD is to produce an optimal truncation of each code block's independent bitstream such that distortion is minimized, subject to the bit-rate constraint. For each truncated embedded bitstream of code block B_i having rate $R^{n_i}_i$, the overall distortion of the reconstructed image is (assuming distortion is additive)

$$D = \sum_i D^{n_i}_i \tag{9.3}$$

where $D^{n_i}_i$ is the distortion from code block B_i having truncation point n_i. For each code block B_i, distortion is computed by

$$D^n_i = w^2_{b_i} \sum_{\mathbf{k} \in B_i} (\hat{s}^n_i[\mathbf{k}] - s_i[\mathbf{k}])^2 \tag{9.4}$$

where $s_i[\mathbf{k}]$ is the 2D sequence of subband samples in code block B_i and $\hat{s}^n_i[\mathbf{k}]$ is the quantized representation of these samples associated with truncation point n. The value $w^2_{b_i}$ is the L_2 norm of the wavelet basis function for the subband b_i that contains code block B_i.

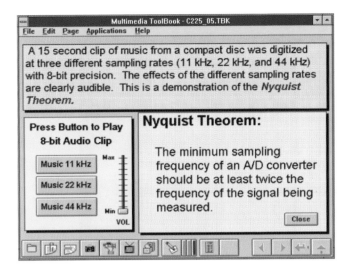

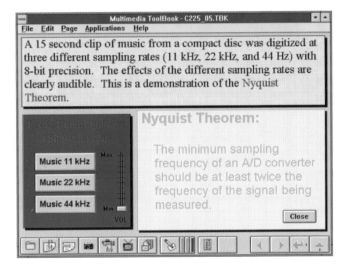

▲ FIGURE 2.4: Colors and fonts. *Courtesy of Ron Vetter.*

▶FIGURE 2.6: Color wheel.

(a) (b)

(c) (d)

▲ **FIGURE 3.5:** High-resolution color and separate R, G, B color channel images. (a) example of 24-bit color image `forestfire.bmp`. (b, c, d) R, G, and B color channels for this image.

▲ **FIGURE 3.7:** Example of 8-bit color image.

▲ **FIGURE 3.17:** JPEG image with low quality specified by user.

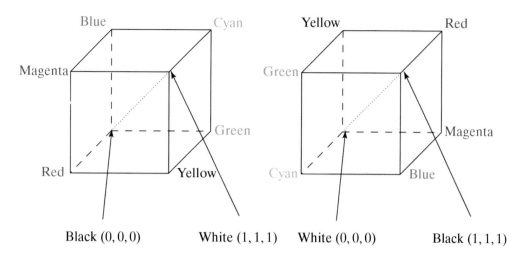

Black (0, 0, 0)   White (1, 1, 1)   White (0, 0, 0)   Black (1, 1, 1)

The RGB Cube   The CMY Cube

▲ FIGURE 4.15: RGB and CMY color cubes.

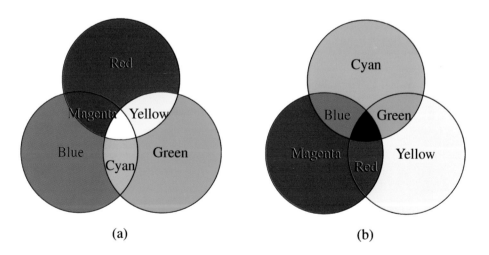

(a)   (b)

▲ FIGURE 4.16: Additive and subtractive color: (a) RGB is used to specify additive color; (b) CMY is used to specify subtractive color.

(a)

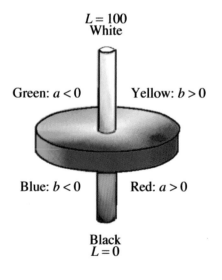

(b)   (c)   (d)

▲ FIGURE 4.18: $Y'UV$ decomposition of color image. Top image (a) is original color image; (b) is Y'; (c) is U; (d) is V.

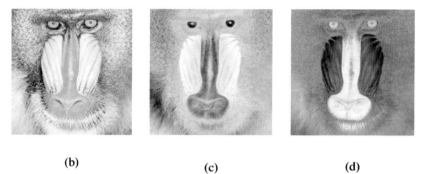

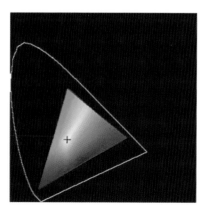

▲ FIGURE 4.14: CIELAB model.   ▲ FIGURE 4.21: SMPTE Monitor gamut.

▲ FIGURE 9.13: Comparison of JPEG and JPEG2000; (a) Original image; (b) JPEG (left) and JPEG2000 (right) images compressed at 0.75 bpp; (c) JPEG (left) and JPEG2000 (right) images compressed at 0.25 bpp.

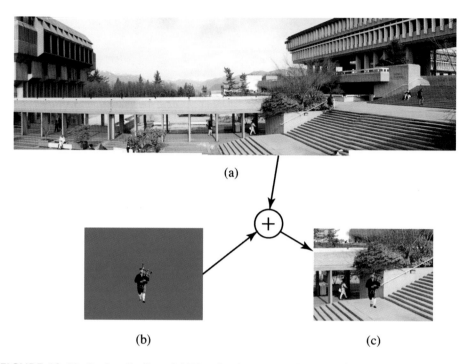

(a)

(b)   (c)

▲ FIGURE 12.10: Sprite Coding. (a) The the foreground object (piper) in a blue-screen image; (b) the foreground object (piper) in a bluescreen image; (c) the composed video scene. *Piper image courtesy of Simon Fraser University Pipe Band.*

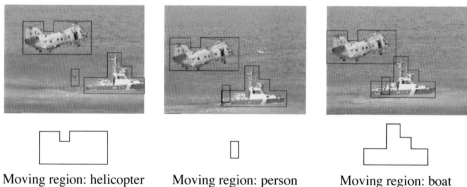

Moving region: helicopter   Moving region: person   Moving region: boat

▲ FIGURE 12.19: MPEG-7 Video segments.

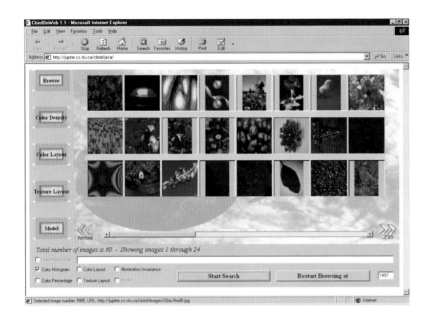

▲ **FIGURE 18.3:** Search by color histogram results. *Some thumbnail images are from the Corel Gallery and are copyright Corel. All rights reserved.*

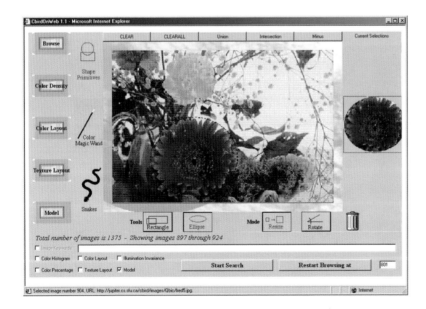

▲ **FIGURE 18.8:** C-BIRD interface showing object selection using an ellipse primitive. *Image is from the Corel Gallery and is copyright Corel. All rights reserved.*

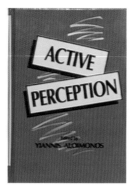

(a)

◀ FIGURE 18.10: Model and target images. (a) Sample model image; (b) sample database image containing the model book. *Active Perception textbook cover courtesy Lawrence Erlbaum Associates, Inc.*

(b)

▶ FIGURE 18.13: Color locales. (a) Color locales for the model image; (b) color locales for a database image.

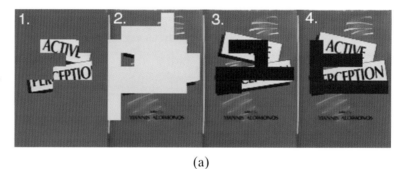

(a)

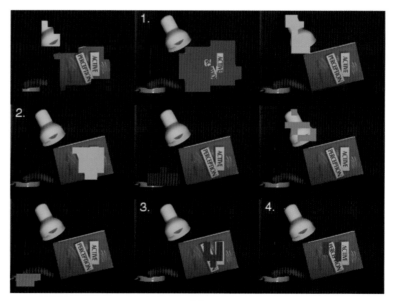

(b)

The optimal selection of truncation points n_i can be formulated into a minimization problem subject to the following constraint:

$$R = \sum_i R_i^{n_i} \leq R^{max} \tag{9.5}$$

where R^{max} is the available bit rate. For some λ, any set of truncation points $\{n_i^{\lambda}\}$ that minimizes

$$(D(\lambda) + \lambda R(\lambda)) = \sum_i \left(D_i^{n_i^{\lambda}} + \lambda R_i^{n_i^{\lambda}} \right) \tag{9.6}$$

is optimal in the rate-distortion sense. Thus, finding the set of truncation points that minimizes Equation (9.6) with total rate $R(\lambda) = R^{max}$ would yield the solution to the entire optimization problem.

Since the set of truncation points is discrete, it is generally not possible to find a value of λ for which $R(\lambda)$ is exactly equal to R^{max}. However, since the EBCOT algorithm uses relatively small code blocks, each of which has many truncation points, it is sufficient to find the smallest value of λ such that $R(\lambda) \leq R^{max}$.

It is easy to see that each code block B_i can be minimized independently. Let $\mathcal{N}_i$ be the set of feasible truncation points and let $j_1 < j_2 < \cdots$ be an enumeration of these feasible truncation points having corresponding distortion-rate slopes given by the ratios

$$S_i^{j_k} = \frac{\Delta D_i^{j_k}}{\Delta R_i^{j_k}} \tag{9.7}$$

where $\Delta R_i^{j_k} = R_i^{j_k} - R_i^{j_{k-1}}$ and $\Delta D_i^{j_k} = D_i^{j_k} - D_i^{j_{k-1}}$. It is evident that the slopes are strictly decreasing, since the operational distortion-rate curve is convex and strictly decreasing. The minimization problem for a fixed value of λ is simply the trivial selection

$$n_i^{\lambda} = \max \left\{ j_k \in \mathcal{N}_i | S_i^{j_k} > \lambda \right\} \tag{9.8}$$

The optimal value λ^* can be found using a simple bisection method operating on the distortion-rate curve. A detailed description of this method can be found in [6].

Layer Formation and Representation.   The EBCOT algorithm offers both resolution and quality scalability, as opposed to other well-known scalable image compression algorithms such as EZW and SPIHT, which offer only quality scalability. This functionality is achieved using a layered bitstream organization and a two-tiered coding strategy.

The final bitstream EBCOT produces is composed of a collection of quality layers. The quality layer $\mathcal{Q}_1$ contains the initial $R_i^{n_i^1}$ bytes of each code block B_i and the other layers $\mathcal{Q}_q$ contain the incremental contribution $L_i^q = R_i^{n_i^q} - R_i^{n_i^{q-1}} \geq 0$ from code block B_i. The quantity n_i^q is the truncation point corresponding to the rate distortion threshold λ_q selected for the qth quality layer. Figure 9.10 illustrates the layered bitstream (after [5]).

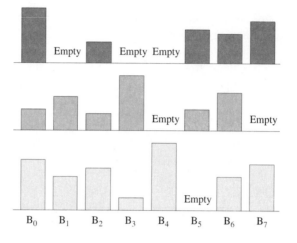

FIGURE 9.10: Three quality layers with eight blocks each.

Along with these incremental contributions, auxiliary information such as the length L_i^q, the number of new coding passes $N_i^q = n_i^q - n_i^{q-1}$, the value p_i^{max} when B_i makes its first nonempty contribution to quality layer $\mathcal{Q}_q$, and the index q_i of the quality layer to which B_i first makes a nonempty contribution must be explicitly stored. This auxiliary information is compressed in the second-tier coding engine. Hence, in this two-tiered architecture, the first tier produces the embedded block bitstreams, while the second encodes the block contributions to each quality layer.

The focus of this subsection is the second-tier processing of the auxiliary information accompanying each quality layer. The second-tier coding engine handles carefully the two quantities that exhibit substantial interblock redundancy. These two quantities are p_i^{max} and the index q_i of the quality layer to which B_i first makes a nonempty contribution.

The quantity q_i is coded using a separate embedded quad-tree code within each subband. Let $B_i^0 = B_i$ be the leaves and B_i^T be the root of the tree that represents the entire subband. Let $q_i^t = \min\{q_j | B_j \subset B_i^t\}$ be the index of the first layer in which any code block in quad B_i^t makes a nonempty contribution. A single bit identifies whether $q_i^t > q$ for each quad at each level t, with redundant quads omitted. A quad is redundant if either $q_i^t < q - 1$ or $q_j^{t+1} > q$ for some parent quad B_j^{t+1}.

The other redundant quantity to consider is p_i^{max}. It is clear that p_i^{max} is irrelevant until the coding of the quality layer $\mathcal{Q}_q$. Thus, any unnecessary information concerning p_i^{max} need not be sent until we are ready to encode $\mathcal{Q}_q$. EBCOT does this using a modified embedded quadtree driven from the leaves rather than from the root.

Let B_i^t be the elements of the quad tree structure built on top of the code blocks B_i from any subband, and let $p_i^{max,t} = \max\{p_j^{max} | B_j \subset B_i^t\}$. In addition, let $B_{i_{l_t}}$ be the ancestor of quads from which B_i descends and let P be a value guaranteed to be larger than p_i^{max} for any code block B_i. When code block B_i first contributes to the bitstream in quality layer $\mathcal{Q}_q$, the value of $p_i^{max} = p_{i_0}^{max,0}$ is coded using the following algorithm:

- For $p = P - 1, P - 2, \ldots, 0$

  - Send binary digits to identify whether $p_{i_t}^{max,t} < p$. The redundant bits are skipped.

  - If $p_i^{max} = p$, then stop.

The redundant bits are those corresponding to the condition $p_{i_t}^{max,t} < p$ that can be inferred either from ancestors such that $p_{i_{t+1}}^{max,t+1} < p$ or from the partial quad-tree code used to identify p_j^{max} for a different code block B_j.

9.2.2   Adapting EBCOT to JPEG2000

JPEG2000 uses the EBCOT algorithm as its primary coding method. However, the algorithm is slightly modified to enhance compression efficiency and reduce computational complexity.

To further enhance compression efficiency, as opposed to initializing the entropy coder using equiprobable states for all contexts, the JPEG2000 standard makes an assumption of highly skewed distributions for some contexts, to reduce the model adaptation cost for typical images. Several small adjustments are made to the original algorithm to further reduce its execution time.

First, a low-complexity arithmetic coder that avoids multiplications and divisions, known as the MQ coder [7], replaces the usual arithmetic coder used in the original algorithm. Furthermore, JPEG2000 does not transpose the HL subband's code blocks. Instead, the corresponding entries in the zero coding context assignment map are transposed.

To ensure a consistent scan direction, JPEG2000 combines the forward- and reverse-significance-propagation passes into a single forward-significance-propagation pass with a neighborhood requirement equal to that of the original reverse pass. In addition, reducing the sub-block size to 4×4 from the original 16×16 eliminates the need to explicitly code sub-block significance. The resulting probability distribution for these small sub-blocks is highly skewed, so the coder behaves as if all sub-blocks are significant.

The cumulative effect of these modifications is an increase of about 40% in software execution speed, with an average loss of about 0.15dB relative to the original algorithm.

9.2.3   Region-of-Interest Coding

A significant feature of the new JPEG2000 standard is the ability to perform region-of-interest (ROI) coding [8]. Here, particular regions of the image may be coded with better quality than the rest of the image or the background. The method is called MAXSHIFT, a scaling-based method that scales up the coefficients in the ROI so that they are placed into higher bitplanes. During the embedded coding process, the resulting bits are placed in front of the non-ROI part of the image. Therefore, given a reduced bitrate, the ROI will be decoded and refined before the rest of the image. As a result of these mechanisms, the ROI will have much better quality than the background.

(a)

(b)

(c)

(d)

FIGURE 9.11: Region of interest (ROI) coding of an image with increasing bit-rate using a circularly shaped ROI: (a) 0.4 bpp; (b) 0.5 bpp; (c) 0.6 bpp; (d) 0.7 bpp.

One thing to note is that regardless of scaling, full decoding of the bitstream will result in reconstruction of the entire image with the highest fidelity available. Figure 9.11 demonstrates the effect of region-of-interest coding as the target bitrate of the sample image is increased.

9.2.4   Comparison of JPEG and JPEG2000 Performance

After studying the internals of the JPEG2000 compression algorithm, a natural question that comes to mind is, how well does JPEG2000 perform compared to other well-known standards, in particular JPEG? Many comparisons have been made between JPEG and other well-known standards, so here we compare JPEG2000 only to the popular JPEG.

Various criteria, such as computational complexity, error resilience, compression efficiency, and so on, have been used to evaluate the performance of systems. Since our main focus is on the compression aspect of the JPEG2000 standard, here we simply compare compression efficiency. (Interested readers can refer to [9] and [10] for comparisons using other criteria.)

Given a fixed bitrate, let's compare quality of compressed images quantitatively by the PSNR: for color images, the PSNR is calculated based on the average of the mean square error of all the RGB components. Also, we visually show results for both JPEG2000 and JPEG compressed images, so that you can make your own qualitative assessment. We perform a comparison for three categories of images: natural, computer-generated, and medical, using three images from each category. The test images used are shown on the textbook web site in the Further Exploration section for this chapter.

For each image, we compress using JPEG and JPEG2000, at four bitrates: 0.25 bpp, 0.5 bpp, 0.75 bpp, and 1.0 bpp. Figure 9.12 shows plots of the average PSNR of the images in each category against bitrate. We see that JPEG2000 substantially outperforms JPEG in all categories.

For a qualitative comparison of the compression results, let's choose a single image and show decompressed output for the two algorithms using a low bitrate (0.75 bpp) and the lowest bitrate (0.25 bpp). From the results in Figure 9.13, it should be obvious that images compressed using JPEG2000 show significantly fewer visual artifacts.

9.3   THE JPEG-LS STANDARD

Generally, we would likely apply a lossless compression scheme to images that are critical in some sense, say medical images of a brain, or perhaps images that are difficult or costly to acquire. A scheme in competition with the lossless mode provided in JPEG2000 is the JPEG-LS standard, specifically aimed at lossless encoding [11]. The main advantage of JPEG-LS over JPEG2000 is that JPEG-LS is based on a low-complexity algorithm. JPEG-LS is part of a larger ISO effort aimed at better compression of medical images.

JPEG-LS is in fact the current ISO/ITU standard for lossless or "near lossless" compression of continuous-tone images. The core algorithm in JPEG-LS is called *LOw COmplexity LOssless COmpression for Images* (*LOCO-I*), proposed by Hewlett-Packard [11]. The design of this algorithm is motivated by the observation that complexity reduction is often more important overall than any small increase in compression offered by more complex algorithms.

LOCO-I exploits a concept called *context modeling*. The idea of context modeling is to take advantage of the structure in the input source — conditional probabilities of what pixel values follow from each other in the image. This extra knowledge is called the *context*. If the input source contains substantial structure, as is usually the case, we could potentially compress it using fewer bits than the 0th-order entropy.

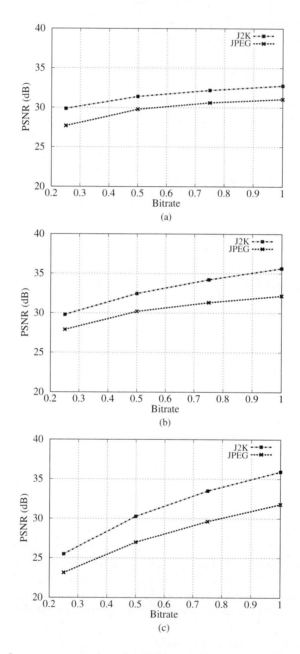

FIGURE 9.12: Performance comparison for JPEG and JPEG2000 on different image types: (a) Natural images; (b) Computer generated images; (c) Medical images.

(a)

(b)

(c)

FIGURE 9.13: Comparison of JPEG and JPEG2000: (a) original image; (b) JPEG (*left*) and JPEG2000 (*right*) images compressed at 0.75 bpp; (c) JPEG (*left*) and JPEG2000 (*right*) images compressed at 0.25 bpp. (This figure also appears in the color insert section.)

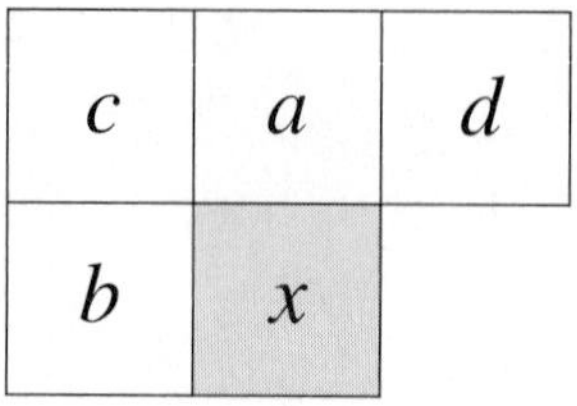

FIGURE 9.14: JPEG-LS context model.

As a simple example, suppose we have a binary source with $P(0) = 0.4$ and $P(1) = 0.6$. Then the 0th-order entropy $H(S) = -0.4 \log_2(0.4) - 0.6 \log_2(0.6) = 0.97$. Now suppose we also know that this source has the property that if the previous symbol is 0, the probability of the current symbol being 0 is 0.8, and if the previous symbol is 1, the probability of the current symbol being 0 is 0.1.

If we use the previous symbol as our *context*, we can divide the input symbols into two sets, corresponding to context 0 and context 1, respectively. Then the entropy of each of the two sets is

$$H(S_1) = -0.8 \log_2(0.8) - 0.2 \log_2(0.2) = 0.72$$
$$H(S_2) = -0.1 \log_2(0.1) - 0.9 \log_2(0.9) = 0.47$$

The average bit-rate for the entire source would be $0.4 \times 0.72 + 0.6 \times 0.47 = 0.57$, which is substantially less than the 0th-order entropy of the entire source in this case.

LOCO-I uses a context model shown in Figure 9.14. In raster scan order, the context pixels a, b, c, and d all appear before the current pixel x. Thus, this is called a *causal context*.

LOCO-I can be broken down into three components:

- **Prediction.** Predicting the value of the next sample x' using a causal template

- **Context determination.** Determining the context in which x' occurs

- **Residual coding.** Entropy coding of the prediction residual conditioned by the context of x'

9.3.1 Prediction

A better version of prediction can use an adaptive model based on a calculation of the local edge direction. However, because JPEG-LS is aimed at low complexity, the LOCO-I algorithm instead uses a fixed predictor that performs primitive tests to detect vertical and horizontal edges. The fixed predictor used by the algorithm is given as follows:

$$\hat{x}' = \begin{cases} \min(a, b) & c \geq \max(a, b) \\ \max(a, b) & c \leq \min(a, b) \\ a + b - c & \text{otherwise} \end{cases} \tag{9.9}$$

It is easy to see that this predictor switches between three simple predictors. It outputs a when there is a vertical edge to the left of the current location; it outputs b when there is a horizontal edge above the current location; and finally it outputs $a + b - c$ when the neighboring samples are relatively smooth.

9.3.2 Context Determination

The context model that conditions the current prediction error (the *residual*) is indexed using a three-component context vector $\mathbf{Q} = (q_1, q_2, q_3)$, whose components are

$$
\begin{aligned}
q_1 &= d - b \\
q_2 &= b - c \\
q_3 &= c - a
\end{aligned}
\tag{9.10}
$$

These differences represent the local gradient that captures the local smoothness or edge contents that surround the current sample. Because these differences can potentially take on a wide range of values, the underlying context model is huge, making the context-modeling approach impractical. To solve this problem, parameter reduction methods are needed.

An effective method is to quantize these differences so that they can be represented by a limited number of values. The components of $\mathbf{Q}$ are quantized using a quantizer with decision boundaries $-T, \cdots, -1, 0, 1, \cdots, T$. In JPEG-LS, $T = 4$. The context size is further reduced by replacing any context vector $\mathbf{Q}$ whose first element is negative by $-\mathbf{Q}$. Therefore, the number of different context states is $\frac{(2T+1)^3+1}{2} = 365$ in total. The vector $\mathbf{Q}$ is then mapped into an integer in $[0, 364]$.

9.3.3 Residual Coding

For any image, the prediction residual has a finite size, α. For a given prediction $\hat{x}$, the residual ε is in the range $-\hat{x} \le \varepsilon < \alpha - \hat{x}$. Since the value $\hat{x}$ can be generated by the decoder, the dynamic range of the residual ε can be reduced modulo α and mapped into a value between $-\lfloor \frac{\alpha}{2} \rfloor$ and $\lceil \frac{\alpha}{2} \rceil - 1$.

It can be shown that the error residuals follow a *two-sided geometric distribution* (TSGD). As a result, they are coded using adaptively selected codes based on *Golomb codes*, which are optimal for sequences with geometric distributions [12].

9.3.4 Near-Lossless Mode

The JPEG-LS standard also offers a near-lossless mode, in which the reconstructed samples deviate from the original by no more than an amount δ. The main lossless JPEG-LS mode can be considered a special case of the near-lossless mode with $\delta = 0$. Near-lossless compression is achieved using quantization: residuals are quantized using a uniform quantizer having intervals of length $2\delta + 1$. The quantized values of ε are given by

$$
Q(\varepsilon) = \mathrm{sign}(\varepsilon) \left\lfloor \frac{|\varepsilon| + \delta}{2\delta + 1} \right\rfloor
\tag{9.11}
$$

Since δ can take on only a small number of integer values, the division operation can be implemented efficiently using lookup tables. In near-lossless mode, the prediction and context determination step described previously are based on the quantized values only.

9.4 BILEVEL IMAGE COMPRESSION STANDARDS

As more and more documents are handled in electronic form, efficient methods for compressing bilevel images (those with only 1-bit, black-and-white pixels) are much in demand. A familiar example is fax images. Algorithms that take advantage of the binary nature of the image data often perform better than generic image-compression algorithms. Earlier facsimile standards, such as G3 and G4, use simple *models* of the structure of bilevel images. Each scanline in the image is treated as a run of black-and-white pixels. However, considering the neighboring pixels and the nature of data to be coded allows much more efficient algorithms to be constructed. This section examines the JBIG standard and its successor, JBIG2, as well as the underlying motivations and principles for these two standards.

9.4.1 The JBIG Standard

JBIG is the coding standard recommended by the Joint Bi-level Image Processing Group for binary images. This lossless compression standard is used primarily to code scanned images of printed or handwritten text, computer-generated text, and facsimile transmissions. It offers progressive encoding and decoding capability, in the sense that the resulting bitstream contains a set of progressively higher-resolution images. This standard can also be used to code grayscale and color images by coding each bitplane independently, but this is not the main objective.

The JBIG compression standard has three separate modes of operation: *progressive*, *progressive-compatible sequential*, and *single-progression sequential*. The progressive-compatible sequential mode uses a bitstream compatible with the progressive mode. The only difference is that the data is divided into *strips* in this mode.

The single-progression sequential mode has only a single lowest-resolution layer. Therefore, an entire image can be coded without any reference to other higher-resolution layers. Both these modes can be viewed as special cases of the progressive mode. Therefore, our discussion covers only the progressive mode.

The JBIG encoder can be decomposed into two components:

- Resolution-reduction and differential-layer encoder

- Lowest-resolution-layer encoder

The input image goes through a sequence of resolution-reduction and differential-layer encoders. Each is equivalent in functionality, except that their input images have different resolutions. Some implementations of the JBIG standard may choose to recursively use one such physical encoder. The lowest-resolution image is coded using the lowest-resolution-layer encoder. The design of this encoder is somewhat simpler than that of the resolution-reduction and differential-layer encoders, since the resolution-reduction and deterministic-prediction operations are not needed.

9.4.2 The JBIG2 Standard

While the JBIG standard offers both lossless and progressive (lossy to lossless) coding abilities, the lossy image produced by this standard has significantly lower quality than the original, because the lossy image contains at most only one-quarter of the number of pixels in the original image. By contrast, the JBIG2 standard is explicitly designed for lossy, lossless, and lossy to lossless image compression. The design goal for JBIG2 aims not only at providing superior lossless compression performance over existing standards but also at incorporating lossy compression at a much higher compression ratio, with as little visible degradation as possible.

A unique feature of JBIG2 is that it is both *quality progressive* and *content progressive*. By quality progressive, we mean that the bitstream behaves similarly to that of the JBIG standard, in which the image quality progresses from lower to higher (or possibly lossless) quality. On the other hand, content progressive allows different types of image data to be added progressively. The JBIG2 encoder decomposes the input bilevel image into regions of different attributes and codes each separately, using different coding methods.

As in other image compression standards, only the JBIG2 bitstream, and thus the decoder, is explicitly defined. As a result, any encoder that produces the correct bitstream is "compliant", regardless of the actions it actually takes. Another feature of JBIG2 that sets it apart from other image compression standards is that it is able to represent multiple pages of a document in a single file, enabling it to exploit interpage similarities.

For example, if a character appears on one page, it is likely to appear on other pages as well. Thus, using a dictionary-based technique, this character is coded only once instead of multiple times for every page on which it appears. This compression technique is somewhat analogous to video coding, which exploits interframe redundancy to increase compression efficiency.

JBIG2 offers content-progressive coding and superior compression performance through *model-based coding*, in which different models are constructed for different data types in an image, realizing additional coding gain.

Model-Based Coding.   The idea behind model-based coding is essentially the same as that of context-based coding. From the study of the latter, we know we can realize better compression performance by carefully designing a context template and accurately estimating the probability distribution for each context. Similarly, if we can separate the image content into different categories and derive a model specifically for each, we are much more likely to accurately model the behavior of the data and thus achieve higher compression ratio.

In the JBIG style of coding, adaptive and model templates capture the structure within the image. This model is general, in the sense that it applies to all kinds of data. However, being general implies that it does not explicitly deal with the structural differences between text and halftone data that comprise nearly all the contents of bilevel images. JBIG2 takes advantage of this by designing custom models for these data types.

The JBIG2 specification expects the encoder to first segment the input image into regions of different data types, in particular, text and halftone regions. Each region is then coded independently, according to its characteristics.

Text-Region Coding.

Each text region is further segmented into pixel blocks containing connected black pixels. These blocks correspond to characters that make up the content of this region. Then, instead of coding all pixels of each character, the bitmap of one representative instance of this character is coded and placed into a *dictionary*. For any character to be coded, the algorithm first tries to find a match with the characters in the dictionary. If one is found, then both a pointer to the corresponding entry in the dictionary and the position of the character on the page are coded. Otherwise, the pixel block is coded directly and added to the dictionary. This technique is referred to as *pattern matching and substitution* in the JBIG2 specification.

However, for *scanned* documents, it is unlikely that two instances of the same character will match pixel by pixel. In this case, JBIG2 allows the option of including refinement data to reproduce the original character on the page. The refinement data codes the current character using the pixels in the matching character *in the dictionary*. The encoder has the freedom to choose the refinement to be exact or lossy. This method is called *soft pattern matching*.

The numeric data, such as the index of matched character in the dictionary and the position of the characters on the page, are either bitwise or Huffman encoded. Each bitmap for the characters in the dictionary is coded using JBIG-based techniques.

Halftone-Region Coding

The JBIG2 standard suggests two methods for halftone image coding. The first is similar to the context-based arithmetic coding used in JBIG. The only difference is that the new standard allows the context template to include as many as 16 template pixels, four of which may be adaptive.

The second method is called *descreening*. This involves converting back to grayscale and coding the grayscale values. In this method, the bilevel region is divided into blocks of size $m_b \times n_b$. For an $m \times n$ bilevel region, the resulting grayscale image has dimension $m_g = \lfloor (m + (m_b - 1))/m_b \rfloor$ by $n_g = \lfloor (n + (n_b - 1))/n_b \rfloor$. The grayscale value is then computed to be the sum of the binary pixel values in the corresponding $m_b \times n_b$ block. The bitplanes of the grayscale image are coded using context-based arithmetic coding. The grayscale values are used as indices into a dictionary of halftone bitmap patterns. The decoder can use this value to index into this dictionary, to reconstruct the original halftone image.

Preprocessing and Postprocessing. JBIG2 allows the use of lossy compression but does not specify a method for doing so. From the decoder point of view, the decoded bit-stream is lossless with respect to the image encoded by the encoder, although not necessarily with respect to the original image. The encoder may modify the input image in a prepro-cessing step, to increase coding efficiency. The preprocessor usually tries to change the original image to lower the code length in a way that does not generally affect the image's appearance. Typically, it tries to remove noisy pixels and smooth out pixel blocks.

Postprocessing, another issue not addressed by the specification, can be especially useful for halftones, potentially producing more visually pleasing images. It is also helpful to tune the decoded image to a particular output device, such as a laser printer.

9.5 FURTHER EXPLORATION

The books by Pennebaker and Mitchell [1] and Taubman and Marcellin [3] provide good references for JPEG and JPEG2000, respectively. Bhaskaran and Konstantinides [2] provide detailed discussions of several image compression standards and the theory underlying them.

An easy-to-use JPEG demo, written in Java, is available for you to try, linked from this section of the text web site. Other useful links include

- Thumbnails for test images used for JPEG/JPEG2000 performance evaluation: natural images, computer-generated images, and medical images

- Many JPEG- and JPEG2000-related links

- Java and C implementations of JPEG2000 encoder and decoder

- A Java applet for JPEG and JPEG2000 comparison

- A simple explanation of context-based image compression

- The original research papers for LOCO-I

- The JPEG-LS public domain source code

- An introduction to JBIG and documentation and source code for JBIG and JBIG2

- A good resource for data compression compiled by Mark Nelson that includes libraries, documentation, and source code for JPEG, JPEG-2000, JPEG-LS, JBIG, etc.

9.6 EXERCISES

1. **(a)** JPEG uses the Discrete Cosine Transform (DCT) for image compression.

   i. What is the value of F(0, 0) if the image $f(i, j)$ is as below?

   ii. Which AC coefficient $|F(u, v)|$ is the largest for this $f(i, j)$? Why? Is this $F(u, v)$ positive or negative? Why?

20	20	20	20	20	20	20	20
20	20	20	20	20	20	20	20
80	80	80	80	80	80	80	80
80	80	80	80	80	80	80	80
140	140	140	140	140	140	140	140
140	140	140	140	140	140	140	140
200	200	200	200	200	200	200	200
200	200	200	200	200	200	200	200

   (b) Show in detail how a three-level hierarchical JPEG will encode the image above, assuming that

   i. The encoder and decoder at all three levels use Lossless JPEG.
   ii. *Reduction* simply averages each 2 × 2 block into a single pixel value.
   iii. *Expansion* duplicates the single pixel value four times.

2. In JPEG, the Discrete Cosine Ttransform is applied to 8×8 blocks in an image. For now, let's call it DCT-8. Generally, we can define a DCT-N to be applied to $N \times N$ blocks in an image. DCT-N is defined as:

$$F_N(u, v) = \frac{2C(u)C(v)}{N} \sum_{i=0}^{N-1} \sum_{j=0}^{N-1} \cos \frac{(2i+1)u\pi}{2N} \cos \frac{(2j+1)v\pi}{2N} f(i, j)$$

$$C(\xi) = \begin{cases} \frac{\sqrt{2}}{2} & \text{for } \xi = 0 \\ 1 & \text{otherwise} \end{cases}$$

Given $f(i, j)$ as below, show your work for deriving all pixel values of $F_2(u, v)$. (That is, show the result of applying DCT-2 to the image below.)

100	−100	100	−100	100	−100	100	−100
100	−100	100	−100	100	−100	100	−100
100	−100	100	−100	100	−100	100	−100
100	−100	100	−100	100	−100	100	−100
100	−100	100	−100	100	−100	100	−100
100	−100	100	−100	100	−100	100	−100
100	−100	100	−100	100	−100	100	−100
100	−100	100	−100	100	−100	100	−100

3. According to the DCT-N definition above, $F_N(1)$ and $F_N(N-1)$ are the AC coefficients representing the lowest and highest spatial frequencies, respectively.

   (a) It is known that $F_{16}(1)$ and $F_8(1)$ *do not* capture the same (lowest) frequency response in image filtering. Explain why.

   (b) Do $F_{16}(15)$ and $F_8(7)$ capture the same (highest) frequency response?

4. You are given a computer cartoon picture and a photograph. If you have a choice of using either JPEG compression or GIF, which compression would you apply for these two images? Justify your answer.

5. Suppose we view a decompressed 512×512 JPEG image but use only the *color* part of the stored image information, not the luminance part, to decompress. What does the 512×512 color image look like? Assume JPEG is compressed using a 4:2:0 scheme.

6. (a) How many principal modes does JPEG have? What are their names?

   (b) In the hierarchical model, explain briefly why we must include an encode/decode cycle on the coder side before transmitting difference images to the decode side.

   (c) What are the two methods used to decode only part of the information in a JPEG file, so that the image can be coarsely displayed quickly and iteratively increased in quality?

7. Could we use wavelet-based compression in ordinary JPEG? How?

8. We decide to create a new image-compression standard based on JPEG, for use with images that will be viewed by an alien species. What part of the JPEG workflow would we likely have to change?

9. Unlike EZW, EBCOT does not explicitly take advantage of the spatial relationships of wavelet coefficients. Instead, it uses the PCRD optimization approach. Discuss the rationale behind this approach.

10. Is the JPEG2000 bitstream SNR scalable? If so, explain how it is achieved using the EBCOT algorithm.

11. Implement transform coding, quantization, and hierarchical coding for the encoder and decoder of a three-level Hierarchical JPEG. Your code should include a (minimal) graphical user interface for the purpose of demonstrating your results. You do not need to implement the entropy (lossless) coding part; optionally, you may include any publicly available code for it.

9.7 REFERENCES

1 W.B. Pennebaker and J.L. Mitchell, *The JPEG Still Image Data Compression Standard*, New York: Van Nostrand Reinhold, 1993.

2 V. Bhaskaran and K. Konstantinides, *Image and Video Compression Standards: Algorithms and Architectures , 2nd ed.*, Boston: Kluwer Academic Publishers, 1997.

3 D.S. Taubman and M.W. Marcellin, *JPEG2000: Image Compression Fundamentals, Standards and Practice*, Norwell, MA: Kluwer Academic Publishers, 2002.

4 C. A. Christopoulos, "Tutorial on JPEG2000," In *Proc. of Int. Conf. on Image Processing*, 1999.

5 D. Taubman, "High Performance Scalable Image Compression with EBCOT," *IEEE Trans. Image Processing*, 9(7): 1158–1170, 2000.

6 K. Ramachandran and M. Vetterli, "Best Wavelet Packet Basis in a Rate-Distortion Sense," *IEEE Trans. Image Processing*, 2: 160–173, 1993.

7 I. Ueno, F. Ono, T. Yanagiya, T. Kimura, and M. Yoshida, *Proposal of the Arithmetic Coder for JPEG2000*, ISO/IEC JTC1/SC29/WG1 N1143, 1999.

8 A. N. Skodras, C. A. Christopoulos, and T. Ebrahimi, "JPEG2000: The Upcoming Still Image Compression Standard," In *11th Portuguese Conference on Pattern Recognition*, pp. 359–366, 2000.

9 D. Santa-Cruz and T. Ebrahimi, "A Study of JPEG2000 Still Image Coding Versus Other Standards," In *X European Signal Processing Conference*, pp. 673–676, 2000.

10 D. Santa-Cruz, T. Ebrahimi, J. Askelof, M. Larsson, and C. A. Christopoulos, *JPEG2000 Still Image Coding Versus Other Standards*, ISO/IEC JTC1/SC29/WG1 (ITU-T SG8), 2000.

11 M. Weinberger, G. Seroussi, and G. Sapiro, "The LOCO-I Lossless Image Compression Algorithm: Principles and Standardization into JPEG-LS," Technical Report HPL-98-193R1, Hewlett-Packard Technical Report HPL-98-193R1, 1998.

12 N. Merhav, G. Seroussi, and M. J. Weinberger, "Optimal Prefix Codes for Sources with Two-Sided Geometric Distributions," *IEEE Transactions on Information Theory*, 46(1): 121–135, 2000.

CHAPTER 10

Basic Video Compression Techniques

As discussed in Chapter 7, the volume of uncompressed video data could be extremely large. Even a modest CIF video with a picture resolution of only 352×288, if uncompressed, would carry more than 35 Mbps. In HDTV, the bitrate could easily exceed 1 Gbps. This poses challenges and problems for storage and network communications.

This chapter introduces some basic video compression techniques and illustrates them in standards H.261 and H.263 — two video compression standards aimed mostly at video-conferencing. The next two chapters further introduce several MPEG video compression standards and the latest, H.264.

10.1 INTRODUCTION TO VIDEO COMPRESSION

A video consists of a time-ordered sequence of frames — images. An obvious solution to video compression would be predictive coding based on previous frames. For example, suppose we simply created a predictor such that the prediction equals the previous frame. Then compression proceeds by subtracting images: instead of subtracting the image from itself (i.e., use a derivative), we subtract in time order and code the residual error.

And this works. Suppose most of the video is unchanging in time. Then we get a nice histogram peaked sharply at zero — a great reduction in terms of the entropy of the original video, just what we wish for.

However, it turns out that at acceptable cost, we can do even better by searching for just the right parts of the image to subtract from the previous frame. After all, our naive subtraction scheme will likely work well for a background of office furniture and sedentary university types, but wouldn't a football game have players zooming around the frame, producing large values when subtracted from the previously static green playing field?

So in the next section we examine how to do better. The idea of looking for the football player in the next frame is called *motion estimation*, and the concept of shifting pieces of the frame around so as to best subtract away the player is called *motion compensation*.

10.2 VIDEO COMPRESSION BASED ON MOTION COMPENSATION

The image compression techniques discussed in the previous chapters (e.g., JPEG and JPEG2000) exploit *spatial redundancy*, the phenomenon that picture contents often change relatively slowly across images, making a large suppression of higher spatial frequency components viable.

Reference frame   Target frame

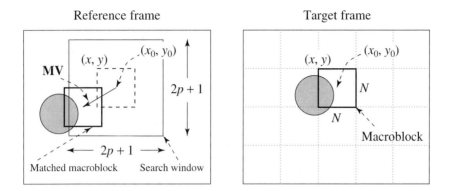

FIGURE 10.1: Macroblocks and motion vector in video compression: (a) reference frame; (b) target frame.

A video can be viewed as a sequence of images stacked in the *temporal* dimension. Since the frame rate of the video is often relatively high (e.g., $\geq$ 15 frames per second) and the camera parameters (focal length, position, viewing angle, etc.) usually do not change rapidly between frames, the contents of consecutive frames are usually similar, unless certain objects in the scene move extremely fast. In other words, the video has *temporal redundancy*.

Temporal redundancy is often significant and it is exploited, so that not every frame of the video needs to be coded independently as a new image. Instead, the difference between the current frame and other frame(s) in the sequence is coded. If redundancy between them is great enough, the difference images could consist mainly of small values and low entropy, which is good for compression.

As we mentioned, although a simplistic way of deriving the difference image is to subtract one image from the other (pixel by pixel), such an approach is ineffective in yielding a high compression ratio. Since the main cause of the difference between frames is camera and/or object motion, these motion generators can be "compensated" by detecting the displacement of corresponding pixels or regions in these frames and measuring their differences. Video compression algorithms that adopt this approach are said to be based on motion compensation (MC). The three main steps of these algorithms are:

1. Motion estimation (motion vector search)
2. Motion-compensation-based prediction
3. Derivation of the prediction error — the difference

For efficiency, each image is divided into *macroblocks* of size $N \times N$. By default, $N = 16$ for luminance images. For chrominance images, $N = 8$ if 4:2:0 chroma subsampling is adopted. Motion compensation is not performed at the pixel level, nor at the level of *video object*, as in later video standards (such as MPEG-4). Instead, it is at the macroblock level.

The current image frame is referred to as the *Target frame*. A match is sought between the macroblock under consideration in the Target frame and the most similar macroblock in previous and/or future frame(s) [referred to as *Reference frame(s)*]. In that sense, the Target macroblock is predicted from the Reference macroblock(s).

The displacement of the reference macroblock to the target macroblock is called a *motion vector* **MV**. Figure 10.1 shows the case of *forward prediction*, in which the Reference frame is taken to be a previous frame. If the Reference frame is a future frame, it is referred to as *backward prediction*. The *difference* of the two corresponding macroblocks is the prediction error.

For video compression based on motion compensation, after the first frame, only the motion vectors and difference macroblocks need be coded, since they are sufficient for the decoder to regenerate all macroblocks in subsequent frames.

We will return to the discussion of some common video compression standards after the following section, in which we discuss search algorithms for motion vectors.

10.3 SEARCH FOR MOTION VECTORS

The search for motion vectors $MV(u, v)$ as defined above is a matching problem, also called a *correspondence* problem [1]. Since MV search is computationally expensive, it is usually limited to a small immediate neighborhood. Horizontal and vertical displacements i and j are in the range $[-p, p]$, where p is a positive integer with a relatively small value. This makes a search window of size $(2p + 1) \times (2p + 1)$, as Figure 10.1 shows. The center of the macroblock (x_0, y_0) can be placed at each of the grid positions in the window.

For convenience, we use the upper left corner (x, y) as the origin of the macroblock in the Target frame. Let $C(x + k, y + l)$ be pixels in the macroblock in the Target (current) frame and $R(x + i + k, y + j + l)$ be pixels in the macroblock in the Reference frame, where k and l are indices for pixels in the macroblock and i and j are the horizontal and vertical displacements, respectively. The difference between the two macroblocks can then be measured by their *Mean Absolute Difference (MAD)*, defined as

$$MAD(i, j) = \frac{1}{N^2} \sum_{k=0}^{N-1} \sum_{l=0}^{N-1} |C(x + k, y + l) - R(x + i + k, y + j + l)|, \qquad (10.1)$$

where N is the size of the macroblock.

The goal of the search is to find a vector (i, j) as the motion vector $\mathbf{MV} = (u, v)$, such that $MAD(i, j)$ is minimum:

$$(u, v) = [(i, j) \mid MAD(i, j) \quad \text{is minimum}, \quad i \in [-p, p], j \in [-p, p]] \qquad (10.2)$$

We used the mean absolute difference in the above discussion. However, this measure is by no means the only possible choice. In fact, some encoders (e.g., H.263) will simply use the *Sum of Absolute Difference (SAD)*. Some other common error measures, such as the *Mean Square Error (MSE)*, would also be appropriate.

10.3.1 Sequential Search

The simplest method for finding motion vectors is to sequentially search the whole $(2p + 1) \times (2p+1)$ window in the Reference frame (also referred to as *full search*). A macroblock centered at each of the positions within the window is compared to the macroblock in the

Target frame, pixel by pixel, and their respective MAD is then derived using Equation (10.1). The vector (i, j) that offers the least MAD is designated the **MV** (u, v) for the macroblock in the Target frame.

PROCEDURE 10.1   **Motion-vector: sequential search**

BEGIN
$min\_MAD = LARGE\_NUMBER$;   /* Initialization */
for $i = -p$ to p
    for $j = -p$ to p
        {
            $cur\_MAD = MAD(i, j)$;
            if $cur\_MAD < min\_MAD$
                {
                    $min\_MAD = cur\_MAD$;
                    $u = i$;   /* Get the coordinates for **MV**. */
                    $v = j$;
                }
        }
END

Clearly, the sequential search method is very costly. From Equation (10.1), each pixel comparison requires three operations (subtraction, absolute value, addition). Thus the cost for obtaining a motion vector for a single macroblock is $(2p + 1) \cdot (2p + 1) \cdot N^2 \cdot 3 \Rightarrow O(p^2 N^2)$.

As an example, let's assume the video has a resolution of 720×480 and a frame rate of 30 fps; also, assume $p = 15$ and $N = 16$. The number of operations needed for each motion vector search is thus

$$(2p + 1)^2 \cdot N^2 \cdot 3 = 31^2 \times 16^2 \times 3.$$

Considering that a single image frame has $\frac{720 \times 480}{N \cdot N}$ macroblocks, and 30 frames each second, the total operations needed per second is

$$
\begin{aligned}
\text{OPS\_per\_second} &= (2p + 1)^2 \cdot N^2 \cdot 3 \cdot \frac{720 \times 480}{N \cdot N} \cdot 30 \\
&= 31^2 \times 16^2 \times 3 \times \frac{720 \times 480}{16 \times 16} \times 30 \approx 29.89 \times 10^9.
\end{aligned}
$$

This would certainly make real-time encoding of this video difficult.

10.3.2 2D Logarithmic Search

A cheaper version, suboptimal but still usually effective, is called *Logarithmic Search*. The procedure for a 2D Logarithmic Search of motion vectors takes several iterations and is akin to a binary search. As Figure 10.2 illustrates, only nine locations in the search window, marked "1," are initially used as seeds for a MAD-based search. After the one that yields

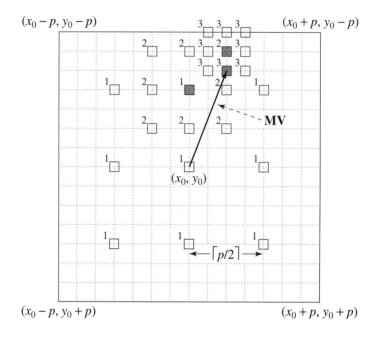

FIGURE 10.2: 2D Logarithmic search for motion vectors.

the minimum MAD is located, the center of the new search region is moved to it, and the stepsize (*offset*) is reduced to half. In the next iteration, the nine new locations are marked "2," and so on.[1] For the macroblock centered at (x_0, y_0) in the Target frame, the procedure is as follows:

PROCEDURE 10.2   Motion-vector: 2D-Logarithmic-search
BEGIN
offset $= \lceil \frac{p}{2} \rceil$;
Specify nine macroblocks within the search window in the Reference frame,
they are centered at (x_0, y_0) and separated by offset horizontally and/or vertically;
WHILE last $\neq$ TRUE
    {
        Find one of the nine specified macroblocks that yields minimum MAD;
        if offset $= 1$ then last $=$ TRUE;
        offset $= \lceil$ offset$/2 \rceil$;
        Form a search region with the new offset and new center found;
    }
END

Instead of sequentially comparing with $(2p+1)^2$ macroblocks from the Reference frame, the 2-D Logarithmic Search will compare with only $9 \cdot (\lceil \log_2 p \rceil + 1)$ macroblocks. In fact,

---

[1] The procedure is heuristic. It assumes a general continuity (monotonicity) of image contents — that they do not change randomly within the search window. Otherwise, the procedure might not find the best match.

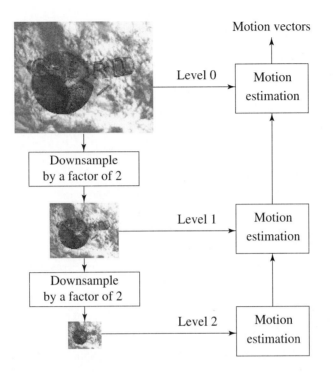

FIGURE 10.3: A three-level hierarchical search for motion vectors.

it would be $8 \cdot (\lceil \log_2 p \rceil + 1) + 1$, since the comparison that yielded the least MAD from the last iteration can be reused. Therefore, the complexity is dropped to $O(\log p \cdot N^2)$. Since p is usually of the same order of magnitude as N, the saving is substantial compared to $O(p^2 N^2)$.

Using the same example as in the previous subsection, the total operations per second drop to

$$
\begin{aligned}
\text{OPS\_per\_second} &= \left(8 \cdot (\lceil \log_2 p \rceil + 1) + 1\right) \cdot N^2 \cdot 3 \cdot \frac{720 \times 480}{N \cdot N} \cdot 30 \\
&= \left(8 \cdot \lceil \log_2 15 \rceil + 9\right) \times 16^2 \times 3 \times \frac{720 \times 480}{16 \times 16} \times 30 \\
&\approx 1.25 \times 10^9.
\end{aligned}
$$

10.3.3 Hierarchical Search

The search for motion vectors can benefit from a hierarchical (multiresolution) approach in which initial estimation of the motion vector can be obtained from images with a significantly reduced resolution. Figure 10.3 depicts a three-level hierarchical search in which the original image is at level 0, images at levels 1 and 2 are obtained by downsampling from the previous levels by a factor of 2, and the initial search is conducted at level 2. Since the size of the macroblock is smaller and p can also be proportionally reduced at this level, the number of operations required is greatly reduced (by a factor of 16 at this level).

The initial estimation of the motion vector is coarse because of the lack of image detail and resolution. It is then refined level by level toward level 0. Given the estimated motion vector (u^k, v^k) at level k, a 3×3 neighborhood centered at $(2 \cdot u^k, 2 \cdot v^k)$ at level $k - 1$ is searched for the refined motion vector. In other words, the refinement is such that at level $k - 1$, the motion vector (u^{k-1}, v^{k-1}) satisfies

$$(2u^k - 1 \leq u^{k-1} \leq 2u^k + 1, \quad 2v^k - 1 \leq v^{k-1} \leq 2v^k + 1),$$

and yields minimum MAD for the macroblock under examination.

Let (x_0^k, y_0^k) denote the center of the macroblock at level k in the Target frame. The procedure for hierarchical motion vector search for the macroblock centered at (x_0^0, y_0^0) in the Target frame can be outlined as follows:

PROCEDURE 10.3   Motion-vector: hierarchical-search

BEGIN

// Get macroblock center position at the lowest resolution level k, e.g., level 2.

$x_0^k = x_0^0/2^k; \quad y_0^k = y_0^0/2^k;$

Use Sequential (or 2D Logarithmic) search method to get initial estimated $\mathbf{MV}(u^k, v^k)$ at level k;

WHILE last $\neq$ TRUE

{

Find one of the nine macroblocks that yields minimum MAD
at level $k - 1$ centered at
$(2(x_0^k + u^k) - 1 \leq x \leq 2(x_0^k + u^k) + 1, \quad 2(y_0^k + v^k) - 1 \leq y \leq 2(y_0^k + v^k) + 1);$
if $k = 1$ then last = TRUE;
$k = k - 1;$
Assign (x_0^k, y_0^k) and (u^k, v^k) with the new center location and motion vector;

}

END

We will use the same example as in the previous sections to estimate the total operations needed each second for a three-level hierarchical search. For simplicity, the overhead for initially generating multiresolution target and reference frames will not be included, and it will be assumed that Sequential search is used at each level.

The total number of macroblocks processed each second is still $\frac{720 \times 480}{N \cdot N} \times 30$. However, the operations needed for each macroblock are reduced to

$$\left[\left(2 \left\lceil \frac{p}{4} \right\rceil + 1 \right)^2 \left(\frac{N}{4} \right)^2 + 9 \left(\frac{N}{2} \right)^2 + 9N^2 \right] \times 3.$$

TABLE 10.1: Comparison of computational cost of motion vector search methods according to the examples.

Search method	OPS_per_second for 720×480 at 30 fps	
	$p = 15$	$p = 7$
Sequential search	29.89×10^9	7.00×10^9
2D Logarithmic search	1.25×10^9	0.78×10^9
Three-level Hierarchical search	0.51×10^9	0.40×10^9

Hence,

$$
\begin{aligned}
\text{OPS\_per\_second} &= \left[\left(2 \left\lceil \frac{p}{4} \right\rceil + 1 \right)^2 \left(\frac{N}{4} \right)^2 + 9 \left(\frac{N}{2} \right)^2 + 9N^2 \right] \\
&\quad \times 3 \times \frac{720 \times 480}{N \cdot N} \times 30 \\
&= \left[\left(\frac{9}{4} \right)^2 + \frac{9}{4} + 9 \right] \times 16^2 \times 3 \times \frac{720 \times 480}{16 \times 16} \times 30 \\
&\approx 0.51 \times 10^9.
\end{aligned}
$$

Table 10.1 summarizes the comparison of the three motion vector search methods for a 720×480, 30 fps video when $p = 15$ and 7, respectively.

10.4 H.261

H.261 is an earlier digital video compression standard. Because its principle of motion-compensation–based compression is very much retained in all later video compression standards, we will start with a detailed discussion of H.261.

The International Telegraph and Telephone Consultative Committee (CCITT) initiated development of H.261 in 1988. The final recommendation was adopted by the International Telecommunication Union-Telecommunication standardization sector (ITU-T), formerly CCITT, in 1990 [2].

The standard was designed for videophone, videoconferencing, and other audiovisual services over ISDN telephone lines. Initially, it was intended to support multiples (from 1 to 5) of 384 kbps channels. In the end, however, the video codec supports bitrates of $p \times 64$ kbps, where p ranges from 1 to 30. Hence the standard was once known as $p * 64$, pronounced "p star 64". The standard requires the video encoders delay to be less than 150 msec, so that the video can be used for real-time, bidirectional video conferencing.

H.261 belongs to the following set of ITU recommendations for visual telephony systems:

- **H.221.** Frame structure for an audiovisual channel supporting 64 to 1,920 kbps

- **H.230.** Frame control signals for audiovisual systems

TABLE 10.2: Video formats supported by H.261.

Video format	Luminance image resolution	Chrominance image resolution	Bitrate (Mbps) (if 30 fps and uncompressed)	H.261 support
QCIF	176 × 144	88 × 72	9.1	Required
CIF	352 × 288	176 × 144	36.5	Optional

- **H.242.** Audiovisual communication protocols

- **H.261.** Video encoder/decoder for audiovisual services at $p \times 64$ kbps

- **H.320.** Narrowband audiovisual terminal equipment for $p \times 64$ kbps transmission

Table 10.2 lists the video formats supported by H.261. Chroma subsampling in H.261 is 4:2:0. Considering the relatively low bitrate in network communications at the time, support for CCIR 601 QCIF is specified as required, whereas support for CIF is optional.

Figure 10.4 illustrates a typical H.261 frame sequence. Two types of image frames are defined: intra-frames (*I-frames*) and inter-frames (*P-frames*).

I-frames are treated as independent images. Basically, a transform coding method similar to JPEG is applied within each I-frame, hence the name "intra".

P-frames are not independent. They are coded by a forward predictive coding method in which current macroblocks are predicted from similar macroblocks in the preceding I- or P-frame, and *differences* between the macroblocks are coded. *Temporal redundancy removal* is hence included in P-frame coding, whereas I-frame coding performs only *spatial redundancy removal*. It is important to remember that prediction from a previous P-frame is allowed (not just from a previous I-frame).

The interval between pairs of I-frames is a variable and is determined by the encoder. Usually, an ordinary digital video has a couple of I-frames per second. Motion vectors in H.261 are always measured in units of full pixels and have a limited range of ±15 pixels — that is, $p = 15$.

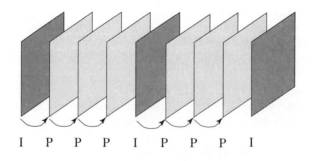

I   P   P   P   I   P   P   P   I

FIGURE 10.4: H.261 Frame sequence.

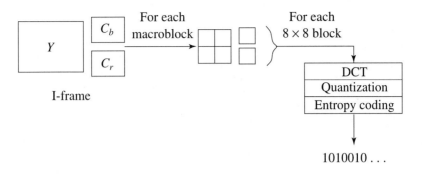

FIGURE 10.5: I-frame coding.

10.4.1 Intra-Frame (I-Frame) Coding

Macroblocks are of size 16×16 pixels for the Y frame of the original image. For Cb and Cr frames, they correspond to areas of 8×8, since 4:2:0 chroma subsampling is employed. Hence, a macroblock consists of four Y blocks, one Cb, and one Cr, 8×8 blocks.

For each 8×8 block, a DCT transform is applied. As in JPEG (discussed in detail in Chapter 9), the DCT coefficients go through a quantization stage. Afterwards, they are zigzag-scanned and eventually entropy-coded (as shown in Figure 10.5).

10.4.2 Inter-Frame (P-Frame) Predictive Coding

Figure 10.6 shows the H.261 P-frame coding scheme based on motion compensation. For each macroblock in the Target frame, a motion vector is allocated by one of the search methods discussed earlier. After the prediction, a *difference macroblock* is derived to measure the *prediction error*. It is also carried in the form of four Y blocks, one Cb, and one Cr block. Each of these 8×8 blocks goes through DCT, quantization, zigzag scan, and entropy coding. The motion vector is also coded.

Sometimes, a good match cannot be found — the prediction error exceeds a certain acceptable level. The macroblock itself is then encoded (treated as an intra macroblock) and in this case is termed a *non-motion-compensated macroblock*.

P-frame coding encodes the difference macroblock (not the Target macroblock itself). Since the difference macroblock usually has a much smaller entropy than the Target macroblock, a large *compression ratio* is attainable.

In fact, even the motion vector is not directly coded. Instead, the difference, **MVD**, between the motion vectors of the preceding macroblock and current macroblock is sent for entropy coding:

$$\mathbf{MVD} = \mathbf{MV}_{Preceding} - \mathbf{MV}_{Current} \tag{10.3}$$

10.4.3 Quantization in H.261

The quantization in H.261 does not use 8×8 quantization matrices, as in JPEG and MPEG. Instead, it uses a constant, called *step_size*, for all DCT coefficients within a macroblock.

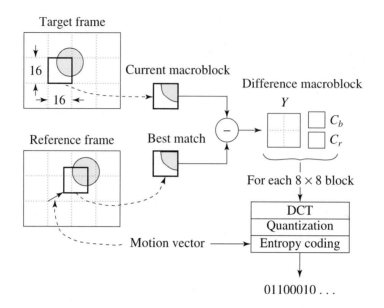

FIGURE 10.6: H.261 P-frame coding based on motion compensation.

According to the need (e.g., bitrate control of the video), *step_size* can take on any one of the 31 even values from 2 to 62. One exception, however, is made for the DC coefficient in intra mode, where a step_size of 8 is always used. If we use DCT and $QDCT$ to denote the DCT coefficients before and after quantization, then for DC coefficients in intra mode,

$$QDCT = \text{round}\left(\frac{DCT}{step\_size}\right) = \text{round}\left(\frac{DCT}{8}\right). \qquad (10.4)$$

For all other coefficients:

$$QDCT = \left\lfloor \frac{DCT}{step\_size} \right\rfloor = \left\lfloor \frac{DCT}{2 \times scale} \right\rfloor, \qquad (10.5)$$

where *scale* is an integer in the range of [1, 31].

The midtread quantizer, discussed in Section 8.4.1 typically uses a `round` operator. Equation (10.4) uses this type of quantizer. However, Equation (10.5) uses a `floor` operator and, as a result, leaves a center deadzone (as Figure 9.8 shows) in its quantization space, with a larger input range mapped to zero.

10.4.4 H.261 Encoder and Decoder

Figure 10.7 shows a relatively complete picture of how the H.261 encoder and decoder work. Here, Q and Q^{-1} stand for quantization and its inverse, respectively. Switching of the intra- and inter-frame modes can be readily implemented by a multiplexer. To avoid propagation of coding errors,

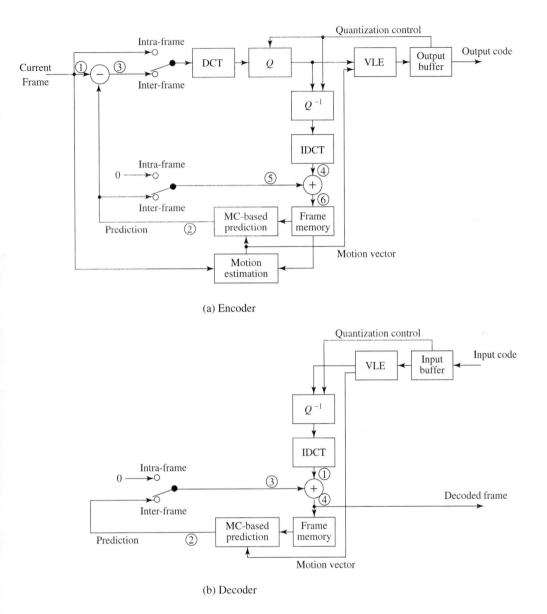

(a) Encoder

(b) Decoder

FIGURE 10.7: H.261: (a) encoder; (b) decoder.

- An I-frame is usually sent a couple of times in each second of the video.

- As discussed earlier (see DPCM in Section 6.3.5), decoded frames (not the original frames) are used as reference frames in motion estimation.

TABLE 10.3: Data flow at the observation points in H.261 encoder.

Current frame	Observation point					
	1	2	3	4	5	6
I	I			$\tilde{I}$	0	$\tilde{I}$
P_1	P_1	P_1'	D_1	$\tilde{D}_1$	P_1'	$\tilde{P}_1$
P_2	P_2	P_2'	D_2	$\tilde{D}_2$	P_2'	$\tilde{P}_2$

To illustrate the operational detail of the encoder and decoder, let's use a scenario where frames I, P_1, and P_2 are encoded and then decoded. The data that goes through the observation points, indicated by the circled numbers in Figure 10.7, is summarized in Tables 10.3 and 10.4. We will use I, P_1, P_2 for the original data, $\tilde{I}$, $\tilde{P}_1$, $\tilde{P}_2$ for the decoded data (usually a lossy version of the original), and P_1', P_2' for the predictions in the Inter-frame mode.

For the encoder, when the Current Frame is an Intra-frame, Point number 1 receives macroblocks from the I-frame, denoted I in Table 10.3. Each I undergoes DCT, Quantization, and Entropy Coding steps, and the result is sent to the Output Buffer, ready to be transmitted.

Meanwhile, the quantized DCT coefficients for I are also sent to Q^{-1} and IDCT and hence appear at Point 4 as $\tilde{I}$. Combined with a zero input from Point 5, the data at Point 6 remains as $\tilde{I}$ and this is stored in Frame Memory, waiting to be used for Motion Estimation and Motion-Compensation-based Prediction for the subsequent frame P_1.

Quantization Control serves as feedback — that is, when the Output Buffer is too full, the quantization step_size is increased, so as to reduce the size of the coded data. This is known as an *encoding rate control process*.

TABLE 10.4: Data flow at the observation points in H.261 decoder.

Current frame	Observation point			
	1	2	3	4
I	$\tilde{I}$		0	$\tilde{I}$
P_1	$\tilde{D}_1$	P_1'	P_1'	$\tilde{P}_1$
P_2	$\tilde{D}_2$	P_2'	P_2'	$\tilde{P}_2$

When the subsequent Current Frame P_1 arrives at Point 1, the Motion Estimation process is invoked to find the motion vector for the best matching macroblock in frame $\tilde{I}$ for each of the macroblocks in P_1. The estimated motion vector is sent to both Motion-Compensation-based Prediction and Variable-Length Encoding (VLE). The MC-based Prediction yields the best matching macroblock in P_1. This is denoted as P_1' appearing at Point 2.

At Point 3, the "prediction error" is obtained, which is $D_1 = P_1 - P_1'$. Now D_1 undergoes DCT, Quantization, and Entropy Coding, and the result is sent to the Output Buffer. As before, the DCT coefficients for D_1 are also sent to Q^{-1} and IDCT and appear at Point 4 as $\tilde{D}_1$.

Added to P_1' at Point 5, we have $\tilde{P}_1 = P_1' + \tilde{D}_1$ at Point 6. This is stored in Frame Memory, waiting to be used for Motion Estimation and Motion-Compensation-based Prediction for the subsequent frame P_2. The steps for encoding P_2 are similar to those for P_1, except that P_2 will be the Current Frame and P_1 becomes the Reference Frame.

For the decoder, the input code for frames will be decoded first by Entropy Decoding, Q^{-1}, and IDCT. For Intra-frame mode, the first decoded frame appears at Point 1 and then Point 4 as $\tilde{I}$. It is sent as the first output and at the same time stored in the Frame Memory.

Subsequently, the input code for Inter-frame P_1 is decoded, and prediction error $\tilde{D}_1$ is received at Point 1. Since the motion vector for the current macroblock is also entropy-decoded and sent to Motion-Compensation-based Prediction, the corresponding predicted macroblock P_1' can be located in frame $\tilde{I}$ and will appear at Points 2 and 3. Combined with $\tilde{D}_1$, we have $\tilde{P}_1 = P_1' + \tilde{D}_1$ at Point 4, and it is sent out as the decoded frame and also stored in the Frame Memory. Again, the steps for decoding P_2 are similar to those for P_1.

10.4.5   A Glance at the H.261 Video Bitstream Syntax

Let's take a brief look at the H.261 video bitstream syntax (see Figure 10.8). This consists of a hierarchy of four layers: *Picture*, *Group of Blocks* (*GOB*), *Macroblock*, and *Block*.

1. **Picture layer.** *Picture Start Code* (*PSC*) delineates boundaries between pictures. *Temporal Reference* (*TR*) provides a timestamp for the picture. Since temporal sub-sampling can sometimes be invoked such that some pictures will not be transmitted, it is important to have TR, to maintain synchronization with audio. *Picture Type* (*PType*) specifies, for example, whether it is a CIF or QCIF picture.

2. **GOB layer.** H.261 pictures are divided into regions of 11×3 macroblocks (i.e., regions of 176×48 pixels in luminance images), each of which is called a *Group of Blocks* (*GOB*). Figure 10.9 depicts the arrangement of GOBs in a CIF or QCIF luminance image. For instance, the CIF image has 2×6 GOBs, corresponding to its image resolution of 352×288 pixels.

   Each GOB has its *Start Code* (*GBSC*) and *Group number* (*GN*). The GBSC is unique and can be identified without decoding the entire variable-length code in the bitstream. In case a network error causes a bit error or the loss of some bits, H.261 video can be recovered and resynchronized at the next identifiable GOB, preventing the possible propagation of errors.

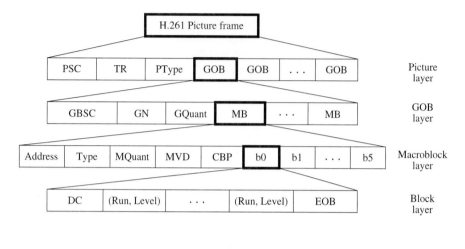

PSC	Picture Start Code		TR	Temporal Reference
PType	Picture Type		GOB	Group of Blocks
GBSC	GOB Start Code		GN	Group Number
GQuant	GOB Quantizer		MB	Macroblock
MQuant	MB Quantizer		MVD	Motion Vector Data
CBP	Coded Block Pattern		EOB	End of Block

FIGURE 10.8: Syntax of H.261 video bitstream.

GQuant indicates the quantizer to be used in the GOB, unless it is overridden by any subsequent *Macroblock Quantizer* (*MQuant*). GQuant and MQuant are referred to as *scale* in Equation (10.5).

3. **Macroblock layer.** Each *macroblock* (*MB*) has its own *Address*, indicating its position within the GOB, quantizer (MQuant), and six 8 × 8 image blocks (4 Y, 1 Cb, 1 Cr). *Type* denotes whether it is an Intra- or Inter-, motion-compensated or non-motion-compensated macroblock. *Motion Vector Data* (*MVD*) is obtained by taking the

GOB 0	GOB 1
GOB 2	GOB 3
GOB 4	GOB 5
GOB 6	GOB 7
GOB 8	GOB 9
GOB 10	GOB 11

CIF

GOB 0
GOB 1
GOB 2

QCIF

FIGURE 10.9: Arrangement of GOBs in H.261 luminance images.

difference between the motion vectors of the preceding and current macroblocks. Moreover, since some blocks in the macroblocks match well and some match poorly in Motion Estimation, a bitmask *Coded Block Pattern (CBP)* is used to indicate this information. Only well-matched blocks will have their coefficients transmitted.

4. **Block layer.** For each 8×8 block, the bitstream starts with *DC value*, followed by pairs of length of zero-run (*Run*) and the subsequent nonzero value (*Level*) for ACs, and finally the *End of Block (EOB)* code. The range of "Run" is $[0, 63]$. "Level" reflects quantized values — its range is $[-127, 127]$, and Level $\neq 0$.

10.5   H.263

H.263 is an improved video coding standard [3] for videoconferencing and other audio-visual services transmitted on Public Switched Telephone Networks (PSTN). It aims at low bitrate communications at bitrates of less than 64 kbps. It was adopted by the ITU-T Study Group 15 in 1995. Similar to H.261, it uses predictive coding for inter-frames, to reduce temporal redundancy, and transform coding for the remaining signal, to reduce spatial redundancy (for both intra-frames and difference macroblocks from inter-frame prediction) [3].

In addition to CIF and QCIF, H.263 supports sub-QCIF, 4CIF, and 16CIF. Table 10.5 summarizes video formats supported by H.263. If not compressed and assuming 30 fps, the bitrate for high-resolution videos (e.g., 16CIF) could be very high ($>$ 500 Mbps). For compressed video, the standard defines maximum bitrate per picture (BPPmaxKb), measured in units of 1,024 bits. In practice, a lower bit rate for compressed H.263 video can be achieved.

As in H.261, the H.263 standard also supports the notion of group of blocks. The difference is that GOBs in H.263 do not have a fixed size, and they always start and end at the left and right borders of the picture. As Figure 10.10 shows, each QCIF luminance image consists of 9 GOBs and each GOB has 11×1 MBs (176×16 pixels), whereas each 4CIF luminance image consists of 18 GOBs and each GOB has 44×2 MBs (704×32 pixels).

TABLE 10.5: Video formats supported by H.263.

Video format	Luminance image resolution	Chrominance image resolution	Bitrate (Mbps) (if 30 fps and uncompressed)	Bitrate (kbps) BPPmaxKb (compressed)
Sub-QCIF	128×96	64×48	4.4	64
QCIF	176×144	88×72	9.1	64
CIF	352×288	176×144	36.5	256
4CIF	704×576	352×288	146.0	512
16CIF	1408×1152	704×576	583.9	1024

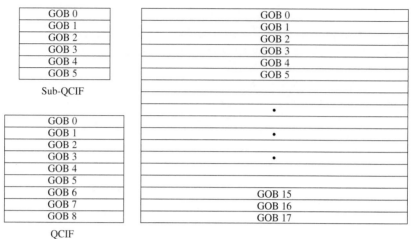

FIGURE 10.10: Arrangement of GOBs in H.263 luminance images.

10.5.1 Motion Compensation in H.263

The process of motion compensation in H.263 is similar to that of H.261. The motion vector (**MV**) is, however, not simply derived from the current macroblock. The horizontal and vertical components of the **MV** are predicted from the median values of the horizontal and vertical components, respectively, of **MV1**, **MV2**, **MV3** from the "previous", "above" and "above and right" macroblocks [see Figure 10.11(a)]. Namely, for the macroblock with **MV**(u, v),

$$
\begin{aligned}
u_p &= median(u_1, u_2, u_3), \\
v_p &= median(v_1, v_2, v_3).
\end{aligned}
\tag{10.6}
$$

Instead of coding the **MV**(u, v) itself, the error vector $(\delta u, \delta v)$ is coded, where $\delta u = u - u_p$ and $\delta v = v - v_p$. As shown in Figure 10.11(b), when the current MB is at the border of the picture or GOB, either $(0, 0)$ or **MV1** is used as the motion vector for the out-of-bound MB(s).

To improve the quality of motion compensation — that is, to reduce the prediction error — H.263 supports *half-pixel precision* as opposed to full-pixel precision only in H.261. The default range for both the horizontal and vertical components u and v of **MV**(u, v) is now $[-16, 15.5]$.

The pixel values needed at half-pixel positions are generated by a simple *bilinear inter-polation* method, as shown in Figure 10.12, where A, B, C, D and a, b, c, d are pixel values at full-pixel positions and half-pixel positions respectively, and " / " indicates division by truncation (also known as integer division).

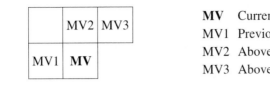

MV   Current motion vector
MV1   Previous motion vector
MV2   Above motion vector
MV3   Above and right motion vector

(a)

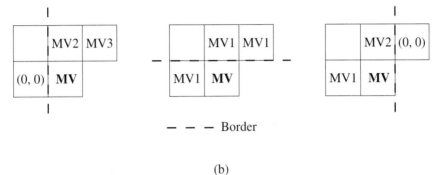

— — — Border

(b)

FIGURE 10.11: Prediction of motion vector in H.263: (a) predicted **MV** of the current macroblock is the median of (**MV1**, **MV2**, **MV3**); (b) special treatment of MVs when the current macroblock is at border of picture or GOB.

10.5.2 Optional H.263 Coding Modes

Besides its core coding algorithm, H.263 specifies many negotiable coding options in its various Annexes. Four of the common options are as follows:

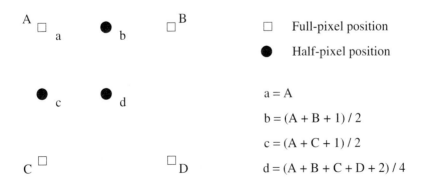

□   Full-pixel position
●   Half-pixel position

$a = A$

$b = (A + B + 1) / 2$

$c = (A + C + 1) / 2$

$d = (A + B + C + D + 2) / 4$

FIGURE 10.12: Half-pixel prediction by bilinear interpolation in H.263.

- **Unrestricted motion vector mode.** The pixels referenced are no longer restricted to within the boundary of the image. When the motion vector points outside the image boundary, the value of the boundary pixel geometrically closest to the referenced pixel is used. This is beneficial when image content is moving across the edge of the image, often caused by object and/or camera movements. This mode also allows an extension of the range of motion vectors. The maximum range of motion vectors is $[-31.5, 31.5]$, which enables efficient coding of fast-moving objects in videos.

- **Syntax-based arithmetic coding mode.** Like H.261, H.263 uses variable-length coding as a default coding method for the DCT coefficients. Variable-length coding implies that each symbol must be coded into a fixed, integral number of bits. By employing arithmetic coding, this restriction is removed, and a higher compression ratio can be achieved. Experiments show bitrate savings of 4% for inter-frames and 10% for intra-frames in this mode.

  As in H.261, the syntax of H.263 is structured as a hierarchy of four layers, each using a combination of fixed- and variable-length code. In the *syntax-based arithmetic coding* (*SAC*) mode, all variable-length coding operations are replaced with arithmetic coding operations. According to the syntax of each layer, the arithmetic encoder needs to code a different bitstream from various components. Since each of these bitstreams has a different distribution, H.263 specifies a model for each distribution, and the arithmetic coder switches the model on the fly, according to the syntax.

- **Advanced prediction mode.** In this mode, the macroblock size for motion compensation is reduced from 16 to 8. Four motion vectors (from each of the 8×8 blocks) are generated for each macroblock in the luminance image. Afterward, each pixel in the 8×8 luminance prediction block takes a weighted sum of three predicted values based on the motion vector of the current luminance block and two out of the four motion vectors from the neighboring blocks — that is, one from the block at the left or right side of the current luminance block and one from the block above or below. Although sending four motion vectors incurs some additional overhead, the use of this mode generally yields better prediction and hence considerable gain in compression.

- **PB-frames mode.** As shown by MPEG (detailed discussions in the next chapter), the introduction of a B-frame, which is predicted bidirectionally from both the previous frame and the future frame, can often improve the quality of prediction and hence the compression ratio without sacrificing picture quality. In H.263, a PB-frame consists of two pictures coded as one unit: one P-frame, predicted from the previous decoded I-frame or P-frame (or P-frame part of a PB-frame), and one B-frame, predicted from both the previous decoded I- or P-frame and the P-frame currently being decoded (Figure 10.13).

  The use of the PB-frames mode is indicated in *PTYPE*. Since the P- and B-frames are closely coupled in the PB-frame, the bidirectional motion vectors for the B-frame need not be independently generated. Instead, they can be temporally scaled and further enhanced from the forward motion vector of the P-frame [4] so as to reduce the bitrate overhead for the B-frame. PB-frames mode yields satisfactory results for

PB-frame

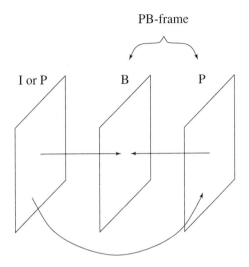

FIGURE 10.13: A PB-frame in H.263.

videos with moderate motion. Under large motions, PB-frames do not compress as well as B-frames. An improved mode has been developed in H.263 version 2.

10.5.3   H.263+ and H.263++

The second version of H.263, also known as H.263+ was approved in January 1998 by ITU-T Study Group 16. It is fully backward-compatible with the design of H.263 version 1.

The aim of H.263+ is to broaden the potential applications and offer additional flexibility in terms of custom source formats, different pixel aspect ratios, and clock frequencies. H.263+ includes numerous recommendations to improve code efficiency and error resilience [5]. It also provides 12 new negotiable modes, in addition to the four optional modes in H.263.

Since its development came after the standardization of MPEG-1 and 2, it is not surprising that it also adopts many aspects of the MPEG standards. Below, we mention only briefly some of these features and leave their detailed discussion to the next chapter, where we study the MPEG standards.

- The unrestricted motion vector mode is redefined under H.263+. It uses *Reversible Variable Length Coding (RVLC)* to encode the difference motion vectors. The RVLC encoder is able to minimize the impact of transmission error by allowing the decoder to decode from both forward and reverse directions. The range of motion vectors is extended again to $[-256, 256]$. Refer to [6, 7] for more detailed discussions on the construction of RVLC.

- A *slice* structure is used to replace GOB for additional flexibility. A slice can contain a variable number of macroblocks. The transmission order can be either sequential or arbitrary, and the shape of a slice is not required to be rectangular.

- H.263+ implements *Temporal*, *SNR*, and *Spatial scalabilities*. Scalability refers to the ability to handle various constraints, such as display resolution, bandwidth, and hardware capabilities. The enhancement layer for Temporal scalability increases perceptual quality by inserting B-frames between two P-frames.

  SNR scalability is achieved by using various quantizers of smaller and smaller step_size to encode additional enhancement layers into the bitstream. Thus, the decoder can decide how many enhancement layers to decode according to computational or network constraints. The concept of Spatial scalability is similar to that of SNR scalability. In this case, the enhancement layers provide increased spatial resolution.

- H.263+ supports improved PB-frames mode, in which the two motion vectors of the B-frame do not have to be derived from the forward motion vector of the P-frame, as in version 1. Instead, they can be generated independently, as in MPEG-1 and 2.

- Deblocking filters in the coding loop reduce blocking effects. The filter is applied to the edge boundaries of the four luminance and two chrominance blocks. The coefficient weights depend on the quantizer step_size for the block. This technique results in better prediction as well as a reduction in blocking artifacts.

The development of H.263 has continued beyond its second version, with the new extension known informally as H.263++ [8]. H.263++ includes the baseline coding methods of H.263 and additional recommendations for *enhanced reference picture selection* (*ERPS*), *data partition slice* (*DPS*), and additional supplemental enhancement information.

ERPS mode operates by managing a multiframe buffer for stored frames, enhancing coding efficiency and error resilience. DPS mode provides additional enhancement to error resilience by separating header and motion-vector data from DCT coefficient data in the bitstream and protects the motion-vector data by using a reversible code. The additional supplemental enhancement information provides the ability to add backward-compatible enhancements to an H.263 bitstream.

10.6 FURTHER EXPLORATION

Tekalp [9] and Poynton [10] set out the fundamentals of digital video processing. They provide a good overview of the mathematical foundations of the problems to be addressed in video.

The books by Bhaskaran and Konstantinides [11], Ghanbari [12], and Wang et al. [13] include good descriptions of video compression algorithms and present many interesting insights into this problem.

The Further Exploration section of the textbook web site for this chapter contains useful links to information on H.261 and H.263, including

- Tutorials and White Papers

- Software implementations

- An H263/H263+ library

- A Java H.263 decoder

10.7 EXERCISES

1. Thinking about my large collection of JPEG images (of my family taken in various locales), I decide to unify them and make them more accessible by simply combining them into a big H.261-compressed file. My reasoning is that I can simply use a viewer to step through the file, making a cohesive whole out of my collection. Comment on the utility of this idea, in terms of the compression ratio achievable for the set of images.

2. In block-based video coding, what takes more effort: compression or decompression? Briefly explain why.

3. An H.261 video has the three color channels Y, C_r, C_b. Should **MV**s be computed for each channel and then transmitted? Justify your answer. If not, which channel should be used for motion compensation?

4. Work out the following problem of 2D Logarithmic Search for motion vectors in detail (see Figure 10.14).

   The target (current) frame is a P-frame. The size of macroblocks is 4×4. The motion vector is **MV**$(\Delta x, \Delta y)$, in which $\Delta x \in [-p, p]$, $\Delta y \in [-p, p]$. In this question, assume $p \equiv 5$.

   The macroblock in question (darkened) in the frame has its upper left corner at (x_t, y_t). It contains 9 dark pixels, each with intensity value 10; the other 7 pixels are part of the background, which has a uniform intensity value of 100. The reference (previous) frame has 8 dark pixels.

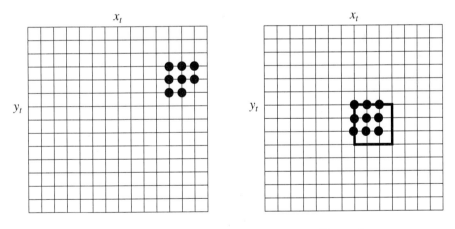

Reference frame   Target frame

● Pixel with intensity value 10

Other background (unmarked) pixels all have intensity value 100

FIGURE 10.14: 2D Logarithmic search for motion vectors.

(a) What is the best Δx, Δy, and Mean Absolute Error (MAE) for this macroblock?

(b) Show step by step how the 2D Logarithmic Search is performed, include the locations and passes of the search and all intermediate Δx, Δy, and MAEs.

5. The logarithmic **MV** search method is suboptimal, in that it relies on continuity in the residual frame.

(a) Explain why that assumption is necessary, and offer a justification for it.

(b) Give an example where this assumption fails.

(c) Does the hierarchical search method suffer from suboptimality too?

6. A video sequence is given to be encoded using H.263 in PB-mode, having a frame size of 4CIF, frame rate of 30 fps, and video length of 90 minutes. The following is known about the compression parameters: on average, two I-frames are encoded per second. The video at the required quality has an I-frame average compression ratio of 10:1, an average P-frame compression ratio twice as good as I-frame, and an average B-frame compression ratio twice as good as P-frame. Assuming the compression parameters include all necessary headers, calculate the encoded video size.

7. Assuming a search window of size $2p+1$, what is the complexity of motion estimation for a QCIF video in the advanced prediction mode of H.263, using

(a) The brute-force (sequential search) method?

(b) The 2D logarithmic method?

(c) The hierarchical method?

8. Discuss how the advanced prediction mode in H.263 achieves better compression.

9. In H.263 motion estimation, the *median* of the motion vectors from three preceding macroblocks (see Figure 10.11(a)) is used as a prediction for the current macroblock. It can be argued that the median may not necessarily reflect the best prediction. Describe some possible improvements on the current method.

10. H.263+ allows independent forward **MV**s for B-frames in a PB-frame. Compared to H.263 in PB-mode, what are the tradeoffs? What is the point in having PB joint coding if B-frames have independent motion vectors?

10.8   REFERENCES

1 D. Marr, *Vision*, San Francisco: W. H. Freeman, 1982.

2 *Video Codec for Audiovisual Services at $p \times 64$ kbit/s*, ITU-T Recommendation H.261, version 1 (Dec 1990), version 2 (Mar 1993).

3 *Video Coding for Low Bit Rate Communication*, ITU-T Recommendation H.263, version 1, (Nov 1995), version 2 (Feb 1998).

4 B.G. Haskell, A. Puri, and A. Netravali, *Digital Video: An Introduction to MPEG-2*, New York: Chapman & Hall, 1997.

5 G. Cote, B. Erol, and M. Gallant, "H.263+: Video Coding at Low Bit Rates," *IEEE Transactions on Circuits and Systems for Video Technology*, 8(7): 849–866, 1998.

6 Y. Takishima, M. Wada, and H. Murakami, "Reversible Variable Length Codes," *IEEE Transactions on Communications*, 43(2–4): 158–162, 1995.

7 C.W. Tsai and J.L. Wu "On Constructing the Huffman-Code-Based Reversible Variable-Length Codes," *IEEE Transactions on Communications*, 49(9): 1506–1509, 2001.

8 *Draft for H.263++ Annexes U, V, and W to Recommendation H.263*, International Telecommunication Union (ITU-T), 2000.

9 A.M. Tekalp, *Digital Video Processing*, Upper Saddle River, NJ: Prentice Hall PTR, 1995.

10 C.A. Poynton, *Digital Video and HDTV Algorithms and Interfaces*, San Francisco: Morgan Kaufmann, 2003.

11 V. Bhaskaran and K. Konstantinides, *Image and Video Compression Standards: Algorithms and Architectures*, 2nd ed., Boston: Kluwer Academic Publishers, 1997.

12 M. Ghanbari, *Video Coding: An Introduction to Standard Codecs*, London: Institue of Electrical Engineers, 1999.

13 Y. Wang, J. Ostermann, and Y.Q. Zhang, *Video Processing and Communications*, Upper Saddle River, NJ: Prentice Hall, 2002.

CHAPTER 11

MPEG Video Coding I — MPEG-1 and 2

11.1 OVERVIEW

The Moving Pictures Experts Group (MPEG) was established in 1988 [1, 2] to create a standard for delivery of digital video and audio. Membership grew from about 25 experts in 1988 to a community of more than 350, from about 200 companies and organizations [3, 4]. It is appropriately recognized that proprietary interests need to be maintained within the family of MPEG standards. This is accomplished by defining only a compressed bitstream that implicitly defines the decoder. The compression algorithms, and thus the encoders, are completely up to the manufacturers.

In this chapter, we will study some of the most important design issues of MPEG-1 and 2. The next chapter will cover some basics of the later standards, MPEG-4 and 7, which have somewhat different objectives.

11.2 MPEG-1

The MPEG-1 audio/video digital compression standard was approved by the International Organization for Standardization/International Electrotechnical Commission (ISO/IEC) MPEG group in November 1991 for *Coding of Moving Pictures and Associated Audio for Digital Storage Media at up to about 1.5 Mbit/s* [5]. Common digital storage media include compact discs (CDs) and video compact discs (VCDs). Out of the specified 1.5 Mbps, 1.2 Mbps is intended for coded video, and 256 kbps can be used for stereo audio. This yields a picture quality comparable to VHS cassettes and a sound quality equal to CD audio.

In general, MPEG-1 adopts the CCIR601 digital TV format, also known as *Source Input Format* (SIF). MPEG-1 supports only noninterlaced video. Normally, its picture resolution is 352×240 for NTSC video at 30 fps, or 352×288 for PAL video at 25 fps. It uses 4:2:0 chroma subsampling.

The MPEG-1 standard, also referred to as ISO/IEC 11172 [5], has five parts: 11172-1 Systems, 11172-2 Video, 11172-3 Audio, 11172-4 Conformance, and 11172-5 Software. Briefly, Systems takes care of, among many things, dividing output into packets of bitstreams, multiplexing, and synchronization of the video and audio streams. Conformance (or compliance) specifies the design of tests for verifying whether a bitstream or decoder complies with the standard. Software includes a complete software implementation of the MPEG-1 standard decoder and a sample software implementation of an encoder. We will

Previous frame   Target frame   Next frame

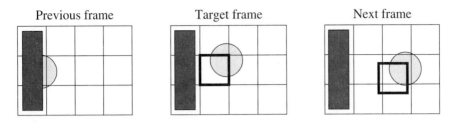

FIGURE 11.1: The need for bidirectional search.

examine the main features of MPEG-1 video coding and leave discussions of MPEG audio coding to Chapter 14.

11.2.1 Motion Compensation in MPEG-1

As discussed in the last chapter, motion-compensation-based video encoding in H.261 works as follows: In motion estimation, each macroblock of the target P-frame is assigned a best matching macroblock from the previously coded I- or P-frame. This is called a *prediction*. The difference between the macroblock and its matching macroblock is the *prediction error*, which is sent to DCT and its subsequent encoding steps.

Since the prediction is from a previous frame, it is called *forward prediction*. Due to unexpected movements and occlusions in real scenes, the target macroblock may not have a good matching entity in the previous frame. Figure 11.1 illustrates that the macroblock containing part of a ball in the target frame cannot find a good matching macroblock in the previous frame, because half of the ball was occluded by another object. However, a match can readily be obtained from the next frame.

MPEG introduces a third frame type — *B-frames* — and their accompanying bidirectional motion compensation. Figure 11.2 illustrates the motion-compensation-based B-frame coding idea. In addition to the forward prediction, a backward prediction is also performed, in which the matching macroblock is obtained from a future I- or P-frame in the video sequence. Consequently, each macroblock from a B-frame will specify up to *two* motion vectors, one from the forward and one from the backward prediction.

If matching in both directions is successful, two motion vectors will be sent, and the two corresponding matching macroblocks are averaged (indicated by "%" in the figure) before comparing to the target macroblock for generating the prediction error. If an acceptable match can be found in only one of the reference frames, only one motion vector and its corresponding macroblock will be used from either the forward or backward prediction.

Figure 11.3 illustrates a possible sequence of video frames. The actual frame pattern is determined at encoding time and is specified in the video's header. MPEG uses M to indicate the interval between a P-frame and its preceding I- or P-frame, and N to indicate the interval between two consecutive I-frames. In Figure 11.3, $M = 3, N = 9$. A special case is $M = 1$, when no B-frame is used.

Since the MPEG encoder and decoder cannot work for any macroblock from a B-frame without its succeeding P- or I-frame, the actual coding and transmission order (shown at the bottom of Figure 11.3) is different from the display order of the video (shown above).

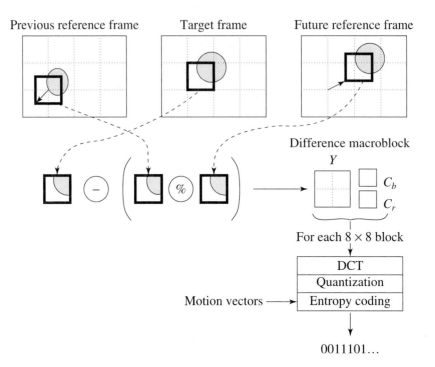

FIGURE 11.2: B-frame coding based on bidirectional motion compensation.

The inevitable delay and need for buffering become an important issue in real-time network transmission, especially in streaming MPEG video.

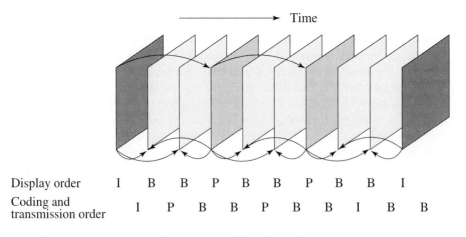

FIGURE 11.3: MPEG frame sequence.

TABLE 11.1: The MPEG-1 constrained parameter set.

Parameter	Value
Horizontal size of picture	≤ 768
Vertical size of picture	≤ 576
Number of macroblocks/picture	≤ 396
Number of macroblocks/second	$\leq 9,900$
Frame rate	≤ 30 fps
Bitrate	$\leq 1,856$ kbps

11.2.2   Other Major Differences from H.261

Beside introducing bidirectional motion compensation (the B-frames), MPEG-1 also differs from H.261 in the following aspects:

- **Source formats.** H.261 supports only CIF (352 × 288) and QCIF (176 × 144) source formats. MPEG-1 supports SIF (352 × 240 for NTSC, 352 × 288 for PAL). It also allows specification of other formats, as long as the *constrained parameter set* (*CPS*), shown in Table 11.1, is satisfied.

- **Slices.** Instead of GOBs, as in H.261, an MPEG-1 picture can be divided into one or more *slices* (Figure 11.4), which are more flexible than GOBs. They may contain variable numbers of macroblocks in a single picture and may also start and end anywhere, as long as they fill the whole picture. Each slice is coded independently.

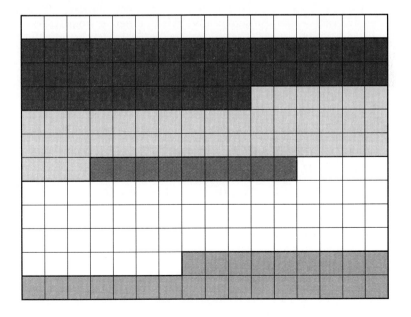

FIGURE 11.4: Slices in an MPEG-1 picture.

TABLE 11.2: Default quantization table (Q_1) for intra-coding.

8	16	19	22	26	27	29	34
16	16	22	24	27	29	34	37
19	22	26	27	29	34	34	38
22	22	26	27	29	34	37	40
22	26	27	29	32	35	40	48
26	27	29	32	35	40	48	58
26	27	29	34	38	46	56	69
27	29	35	38	46	56	69	83

For example, the slices can have different scale factors in the quantizer. This provides additional flexibility in bitrate control.

Moreover, the slice concept is important for error recovery, because each slice has a unique *slice_start_code*. A slice in MPEG is similar to the GOB in H.261 (and H.263): it is the lowest level in the MPEG layer hierarchy that can be fully recovered without decoding the entire set of variable-length codes in the bitstream.

- **Quantization.** MPEG-1 quantization uses different quantization tables for its intra- and inter-coding (Tables 11.2 and 11.3). The quantizer numbers for intra-coding (Table 11.2) vary within a macroblock. This is different from H.261, where all quantizer numbers for AC coefficients are constant within a macroblock.

  The *step_size[i, j]* value is now determined by the product of $Q[i, j]$ and *scale*, where Q_1 or Q_2 is one of the above quantization tables and *scale* is an integer in the

TABLE 11.3: Default quantization table (Q_2) for inter-coding.

16	16	16	16	16	16	16	16
16	16	16	16	16	16	16	16
16	16	16	16	16	16	16	16
16	16	16	16	16	16	16	16
16	16	16	16	16	16	16	16
16	16	16	16	16	16	16	16
16	16	16	16	16	16	16	16
16	16	16	16	16	16	16	16

range [1, 31]. Using DCT and $QDCT$ to denote the DCT coefficients before and after quantization, for DCT coefficients in intra-mode,

$$\text{QDCT}[i,\,j] = \text{round}\left(\frac{8 \times DCT[i,\,j]}{step\_size[i,\,j]}\right) = \text{round}\left(\frac{8 \times DCT[i,\,j]}{Q_1[i,\,j] \times scale}\right), \quad (11.1)$$

and for DCT coefficients in inter-mode,

$$\text{QDCT}[i,\,j] = \left\lfloor \frac{8 \times DCT[i,\,j]}{step\_size[i,\,j]} \right\rfloor = \left\lfloor \frac{8 \times DCT[i,\,j]}{Q_2[i,\,j] \times scale} \right\rfloor, \quad (11.2)$$

where Q_1 and Q_2 refer to Tables 11.2 and 11.3, respectively.

Again, a `round` operator is typically used in Equation (11.1) and hence leaves no dead zone, whereas a `floor` operator is used in Equation (11.2), leaving a center dead zone in its quantization space.

- To increase precision of the motion-compensation-based predictions and hence reduce prediction errors, MPEG-1 allows motion vectors to be of subpixel precision (1/2 pixel). The technique of bilinear interpolation discussed in Section 10.5.1 for H.263 can be used to generate the needed values at half-pixel locations.

- MPEG-1 supports larger gaps between I- and P-frames and consequently a much larger motion-vector search range. Compared to the maximum range of ± 15 pixels for motion vectors in H.261, MPEG-1 supports a range of $[-512, 511.5]$ for half-pixel precision and $[-1{,}024, 1{,}023]$ for full-pixel precision motion vectors. However, due to the practical limitation in its picture resolution, such a large maximum range might never be used.

- The MPEG-1 bitstream allows random access. This is accomplished by the *Group of Pictures (GOP)* layer, in which each GOP is time-coded. In addition, the first frame in any GOP is an I-frame, which eliminates the need to reference other frames. Thus, the GOP layer allows the decoder to seek a particular position within the bitstream and start decoding from there.

Table 11.4 lists typical sizes (in kilobytes) for all types of MPEG-1 frames. It can be seen that the typical size of compressed P-frames is significantly smaller than that of I-frames,

TABLE 11.4: Typical compression performance of MPEG-1 frames.

Type	Size	Compression
I	18 kB	7:1
P	6 kB	20:1
B	2.5 kB	50:1
Average	4.8 kB	27:1

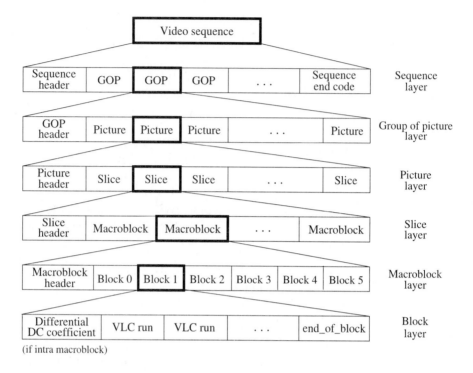

FIGURE 11.5: Layers of MPEG-1 video bitstream.

because inter-frame compression exploits temporal redundancy. Notably, B-frames are even smaller than P-frames, due partially to the advantage of bidirectional prediction. It is also because B-frames are often given the lowest priority in terms of preservation of quality; hence, a higher compression ratio can be assigned.

11.2.3 MPEG-1 Video Bitstream

Figure 11.5 depicts the six hierarchical layers for the bitstream of an MPEG-1 video.

1. **Sequence layer.** A video sequence consists of one or more groups of pictures (GOPs). It always starts with a sequence header. The header contains information about the picture, such as *horizontal_size* and *vertical_size*, *pixel_aspect_ratio*, *frame_rate*, *bit_rate*, *buffer_size*, *quantization_matrix*, and so on. Optional sequence headers between GOPs can indicate parameter changes.

2. **Group of Pictures (GOPs) layer.** A GOP contains one or more pictures, one of which must be an I-picture. The GOP header contains information such as *time_code* to indicate hour-minute-second-frame from the start of the sequence.

3. **Picture layer.** The three common MPEG-1 picture types are *I-picture* (intra-coding), *P-picture* (predictive coding), and *B-picture* (Bidirectional predictive coding), as dis-

TABLE 11.5: Profiles and Levels in MPEG-2.

Level	Simple profile	Main profile	SNR scalable profile	Spatially scalable profile	High profile	4:2:2 profile	Multiview profile
High		*			*		
High 1440		*		*	*		
Main	*	*	*		*	*	*
Low		*	*				

cussed above. There is also an uncommon type, *D-picture* (DC coded), in which only DC coefficients are retained. MPEG-1 does not allow mixing D-pictures with other types, which makes D-pictures impractical.

4. **Slice layer.** As mentioned earlier, MPEG-1 introduced the slice notion for bitrate control and for recovery and synchronization after lost or corrupted bits. Slices may have variable numbers of macroblocks in a single picture. The length and position of each slice are specified in the header.

5. **Macroblock layer.** Each macroblock consists of four Y blocks, one C_b block, and one C_r block. All blocks are 8×8.

6. **Block layer.** If the blocks are intra-coded, the differential DC coefficient (DPCM of DCs, as in JPEG) is sent first, followed by variable-length codes (VLC), for AC coefficients. Otherwise, DC and AC coefficients are both coded using the variable-length codes.

Mitchell et al. [6] provide detailed information on the headers in various MPEG-1 layers.

11.3   MPEG-2

Development of the MPEG-2 standard started in 1990. Unlike MPEG-1, which is basically a standard for storing and playing video on the CD of a single computer at a low bitrate (1.5 Mbps), MPEG-2 [7] is for higher-quality video at a bitrate of more than 4 Mbps. It was initially developed as a standard for digital broadcast TV.

In the late 1980s, *Advanced TV (ATV)* was envisioned, to broadcast HDTV via terrestrial networks. During the development of MPEG-2, digital ATV finally took precedence over various early attempts at analog solutions to HDTV. MPEG-2 has managed to meet the compression and bitrate requirements of digital TV/HDTV and in fact supersedes a separate standard, MPEG-3, initially thought necessary for HDTV.

The MPEG-2 audio/video compression standard, also referred to as ISO/IEC 13818 [8], was approved by the ISO/IEC Moving Picture Experts Group in November 1994. Similar to MPEG-1, it has parts for Systems, Video, Audio, Conformance, and Software, plus other aspects. MPEG-2 has gained wide acceptance beyond broadcasting digital TV over terrestrial, satellite, or cable networks. Among various applications such as Interactive TV, it is also adopted for *digital video discs* or *digital versatile discs* (DVDs).

TABLE 11.6: Four levels in the main profile of MPEG-2.

Level	Maximum resolution	Maximum fps	Maximum pixels/sec	Maximum coded data rate (Mbps)	Application
High	$1,920 \times 1,152$	60	62.7×10^6	80	Film production
High 1440	$1,440 \times 1,152$	60	47.0×10^6	60	Consumer HDTV
Main	720×576	30	10.4×10^6	15	Studio TV
Low	352×288	30	3.0×10^6	4	Consumer tape equivalent

MPEG-2 defined seven *profiles* aimed at different applications (e.g., low-delay videoconferencing, scalable video, HDTV). The profiles are *Simple, Main, SNR scalable, Spatially scalable, High, 4:2:2*, and *Multiview* (where two views would refer to stereoscopic video). Within each profile, up to four *levels* are defined. As Table 11.5 shows, not all profiles have four levels. For example, the Simple profile has only the Main level; whereas the High profile does not have the Low level.

Table 11.6 lists the four levels in the Main profile, with the maximum amount of data and targeted applications. For example, the High level supports a high picture resolution of $1,920 \times 1,152$, a maximum frame rate of 60 fps, maximum pixel rate of 62.7×10^6 per second, and a maximum data rate after coding of 80 Mbps. The Low level is targeted at SIF video; hence, it provides backward compatibility with MPEG-1. The Main level is for CCIR601 video, whereas High 1440 and High levels are aimed at European HDTV and North American HDTV, respectively.

The DVD video specification allows only four display resolutions: $720 \times 480, 704 \times 480$, 352×480, and 352×240. Hence, the DVD video standard uses only a restricted form of the MPEG-2 Main profile at the Main and Low levels.

11.3.1 Supporting Interlaced Video

MPEG-1 supports only noninterlaced (progressive) video. Since MPEG-2 is adopted by digital broadcast TV, it must also support interlaced video, because this is one of the options for digital broadcast TV and HDTV.

As mentioned earlier, in interlaced video, each frame consists of two fields, referred to as the *top-field* and the *bottom-field*. In a *frame-picture*, all scanlines from both fields are interleaved to form a single frame. This is then divided into 16×16 macroblocks and coded using motion compensation. On the other hand, if each field is treated as a separate picture, then it is called *field-picture*. As Figure 11.6(a) shows, each frame-picture can be split into two field-pictures. The figure shows 16 scanlines from a frame-picture on the left, as opposed to 8 scanlines in each of the two field portions of a field-picture on the right.

We see that, in terms of display area on the monitor/TV, each 16-column $\times$ 16-row macroblock in the field-picture corresponds to a 16×32 block area in the frame-picture, whereas each 16×16 macroblock in the frame-picture corresponds to a 16×8 block area

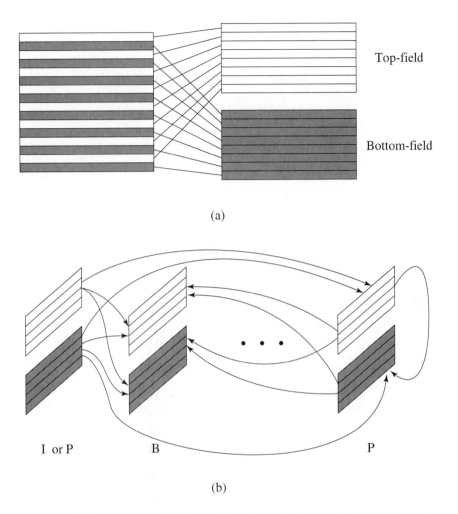

(a)

(b)

FIGURE 11.6: Field pictures and field-prediction for field-pictures in MPEG-2: (a) frame-picture versus field-pictures; (b) field prediction for field-pictures.

in the field-picture. As shown below, this observation will become an important factor in developing different modes of predictions for motion-compensation-based video coding.

Five Modes of Predictions   MPEG-2 defines *frame prediction* and *field prediction* as well as five different prediction modes, suitable for a wide range of applications where the requirement for the accuracy and speed of motion compensation vary.

1. **Frame prediction for frame-pictures.** This is identical to MPEG-1 motion-compensation-based prediction methods in both P-frames and B-frames. Frame prediction works well for videos containing only slow and moderate object and camera motions.

2. **Field prediction for field-pictures.** [See Figure 11.6(b).] This mode uses a macroblock size of 16×16 from field-pictures. For P-field-pictures (the rightmost ones shown in the figure), predictions are made from the two most recently encoded fields. Macroblocks in the top-field picture are forward-predicted from the top-field or bottom-field pictures of the preceding I- or P-frame. Macroblocks in the bottom-field picture are predicted from the top-field picture of the same frame or the bottom-field picture of the preceding I- or P-frame.

   For B-field-pictures, both forward and backward predictions are made from field-pictures of preceding and succeeding I- or P-frames. No regulation requires that field "parity" be maintained — that is, the top-field and bottom-field pictures can be predicted from either the top or bottom fields of the reference pictures.

3. **Field prediction for frame-pictures.** This mode treats the top-field and bottom-field of a frame-picture separately. Accordingly, each 16×16 macroblock from the target frame-picture is split into two 16×8 parts, each coming from one field. Field prediction is carried out for these 16×8 parts in a manner similar to that shown in Figure 11.6(b). Besides the smaller block size, the only difference is that the bottom-field will not be predicted from the top-field of the same frame, since we are dealing with frame-pictures now.

   For example, for P-frame-pictures, the bottom 16×8 part will instead be predicted from either field from the preceding I- or P-frame. Two motion vectors are thus generated for each 16×16 macroblock in the P-frame-picture. Similarly, up to four motion vectors can be generated for each macroblock in the B-frame-picture.

4. **16×8 MC for field-pictures.** Each 16×16 macroblock from the target field-picture is now split into top and bottom 16×8 halves — that is, the first eight rows and the next eight rows. Field prediction is performed on each half. As a result, two motion vectors will be generated for each 16×16 macroblock in the P-field-picture and up to four motion vectors for each macroblock in the B-field-picture. This mode is good for finer motion compensation when motion is rapid and irregular.

5. **Dual-prime for P-pictures.** This is the only mode that can be used for either frame-pictures or field-pictures. At first, field prediction from each previous field with the same parity (top or bottom) is made. Each motion vector **MV** is then used to derive a calculated motion vector **CV** in the field with the opposite parity, taking into account the temporal scaling and vertical shift between lines in the top and bottom fields. In this way, the pair **MV** and **CV** yields two preliminary predictions for each macroblock. Their prediction errors are averaged and used as the final prediction error. This mode is aimed at mimicking B-picture prediction for P-pictures without adopting backward prediction (and hence less encoding delay).

Alternate Scan and Field_DCT   *Alternate Scan* and *Field_DCT* are techniques aimed at improving the effectiveness of DCT on prediction errors. They are applicable only to frame-pictures in interlaced videos.

After frame prediction in frame-pictures, the prediction error is sent to DCT, where each block is of size 8×8. Due to the nature of interlaced video, the consecutive rows in these

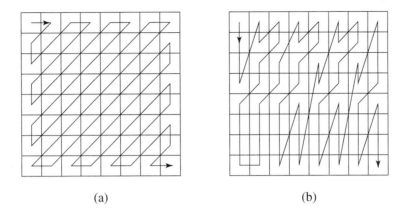

FIGURE 11.7: (a) Zigzag (progressive) and (b) alternate (interlaced) scans of DCT coefficients for videos in MPEG-2.

blocks are from different fields; hence, there is less correlation between them than between the alternate rows. This suggests that the DCT coefficients at low vertical spatial frequencies tend to have reduced magnitudes, compared to the ones in noninterlaced video.

Based on the above analysis, an alternate scan is introduced. It may be applied on a picture-by-picture basis in MPEG-2 as an alternative to a zigzag scan. As Figure 11.7(a) indicates, zigzag scan assumes that in noninterlaced video, the DCT coefficients at the upper left corner of the block often have larger magnitudes. Alternate scan (Figure 11.7(b)) recognizes that in interlaced video, the vertically higher spatial frequency components may have larger magnitudes and thus allows them to be scanned earlier in the sequence. Experiments have shown [7] that alternate scan can improve the PSNR by up to 0.3 dB over zigzag scan and is most effective for videos with fast motion.

In MPEG-2, Field_DCT can address the same issue. Before applying DCT, rows in the macroblock of frame-pictures can be reordered, so that the first eight rows are from the top-field and the last eight are from the bottom-field. This restores the higher spatial redundancy (and correlation) between consecutive rows. The reordering will be reversed after the IDCT. Field_DCT is not applicable to chrominance images, where each macroblock has only 8×8 pixels.

11.3.2 MPEG-2 Scalabilities

As in JPEG2000, *scalability* is also an important issue for MPEG-2. Since MPEG-2 is designed for a variety of applications, including digital TV and HDTV, the video will often be transmitted over networks with very different characteristics. Therefore it is necessary to have a single coded bitstream that is *scalable* to various bitrates.

MPEG-2 *scalable coding* is also known as *layered coding*, in which a base layer and one or more enhancement layers can be defined. The base layer can be independently encoded, transmitted, and decoded, to obtain basic video quality. The encoding and decoding of the enhancement layer, however, depends on the base layer or the previous enhancement layer. Often, only one enhancement layer is employed, which is called two-layer scalable coding.

Scalable coding is suitable for MPEG-2 video transmitted over networks with following characteristics.

- **Very different bitrates.** If the link speed is slow (such as a 56 kbps modem line), only the bitstream from the base layer will be sent. Otherwise, bitstreams from one or more enhancement layers will also be sent, to achieve improved video quality.

- **Variable-bitrate (VBR) channels.** When the bitrate of the channel deteriorates, bitstreams from fewer or no enhancement layers will be transmitted, and vice versa.

- **Noisy connections.** The base layer can be better protected or sent via channels known to be less noisy.

Moreover, scalable coding is ideal for progressive transmission: bitstreams from the base layer are sent first, to give users a fast and basic view of the video, followed by gradually increased data and improved quality. This can be useful for delivering compatible digital TV (ATV) and HDTV.

MPEG-2 supports the following scalabilities:

- **SNR scalability.** The enhancement layer provides higher SNR.

- **Spatial scalability.** The enhancement layer provides higher spatial resolution.

- **Temporal scalability.** The enhancement layer facilitates higher frame rate.

- **Hybrid scalability.** This combines any two of the above three scalabilities.

- **Data partitioning.** Quantized DCT coefficients are split into partitions.

SNR Scalability   Figure 11.8 illustrates how SNR scalability works in the MPEG-2 encoder and decoder.

The MPEG-2 SNR scalable encoder generates output bitstreams `Bits_base` and `Bits_enhance` at two layers. At the base layer, a coarse quantization of the DCT coefficients is employed, which results in fewer bits and a relatively low-quality video. After variable-length coding, the bitstream is called `Bits_base`.

The coarsely quantized DCT coefficients are then inversely quantized (Q^{-1}) and fed to the enhancement layer, to be compared with the original DCT coefficient. Their difference is finely quantized to generate a *DCT coefficient refinement*, which, after variable-length coding, becomes the bitstream called `Bits_enhance`. The inversely quantized coarse and refined DCT coefficients are added back, and after inverse DCT (IDCT), they are used for motion-compensated prediction for the next frame. Since the enhancement/refinement over the base layer improves the signal-to-noise-ratio, this type of scalability is called *SNR scalability*.

If, for some reason (e.g., the breakdown of some network channel), `Bits_enhance` from the enhancement layer cannot be obtained, the above scalable scheme can still work using `Bits_base` only. In that case, the input from the inverse quantizer (Q^{-1}) of the enhancement layer simply has to be treated as zero.

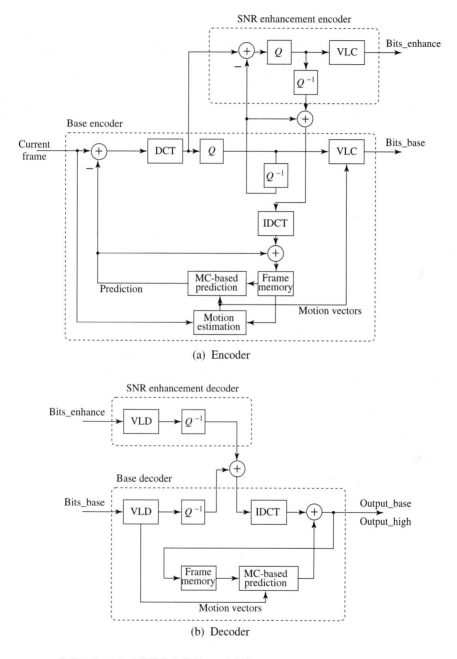

(a) Encoder

(b) Decoder

FIGURE 11.8: MPEG-2 SNR scalability: (a) encoder; (b) decoder.

The decoder (Figure 11.8(b)) operates in reverse order to the encoder. Both `Bits_base` and `Bits_enhance` are variable-length decoded (VLD) and inversely quantized (Q^{-1}) before they are added together to restore the DCT coefficients. The remaining steps are the same as in any motion-compensation-based video decoder. If both bitstreams (`Bits_base` and `Bits_enhance`) are used, the output video is `Output_high` with enhanced quality. If only `Bits_base` is used, the output video `Output_base` is of basic quality.

Spatial Scalability The base and enhancement layers for MPEG-2 spatial scalability are not as tightly coupled as in SNR scalability; hence, this type of scalability is somewhat less complicated. We will not show the details of both encoder and decoder, as we did above, but will explain only the encoding process, using high-level diagrams.

The base layer is designed to generate a bitstream of reduced-resolution pictures. Combining them with the enhancement layer produces pictures at the original resolution. As Figure 11.9(a) shows, the original video data is spatially decimated by a factor of 2 and sent to the base layer encoder. After the normal coding steps of motion compensation, DCT on prediction errors, quantization, and entropy coding, the output bitstream is `Bits_base`.

As Figure 11.9(b) indicates, the predicted macroblock from the base layer is now spatially interpolated to get to resolution 16×16. This is then combined with the normal, temporally predicted macroblock from the enhancement layer itself, to form the prediction macroblock for the purpose of motion compensation in this layered coding. The spatial interpolation here adopts *bilinear interpolation*, as discussed before.

The combination of macroblocks uses a simple weight table, where the value of the weight w is in the range of [0, 1.0]. If $w = 0$, no consideration is given to the predicted macroblock from the base layer. If $w = 1$, the prediction is entirely from the base layer. Normally, both predicted macroblocks are linearly combined, using the weights w and $1-w$, respectively. To achieve minimum prediction errors, MPEG-2 encoders have an analyzer to choose different w values from the weight table on a macroblock basis.

Temporal Scalability Temporally scalable coding has both the base and enhancement layers of video at a reduced temporal rate (frame rate). The reduced frame rates for the layers are often the same; however, they could also be different. Pictures from the base layer and enhancement layer(s) have the same spatial resolution as in the input video. When combined, they restore the video to its original temporal rate.

Figure 11.10 illustrates the MPEG-2 implementation of temporal scalability. The input video is temporally demultiplexed into two pieces, each carrying half the original frame rate. As before, the base layer encoder carries out the normal single-layer coding procedures for its own input video and yields the output bitstream `Bits_base`.

The prediction of matching macroblocks at the enhancement layer can be obtained in two ways [7]: *Interlayer motion-compensated prediction* or *combined motion-compensated prediction and interlayer motion-compensated prediction.*

- **Interlayer motion-compensated prediction.** [Figure 11.10(b).] The macroblocks of B-frames for motion compensation at the enhancement layer are predicted from the preceding and succeeding frames (either I-, P-, or B-) at the base layer, so as to exploit the possible inter-layer redundancy in motion compensation.

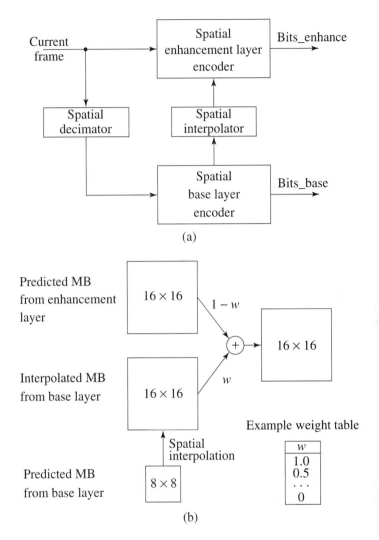

FIGURE 11.9: Encoder for MPEG-2 Spatial scalability: (a) block diagram; (b) combining temporal and spatial predictions for encoding at enhancement layer.

- **Combined motion-compensation prediction and interlayer motion-compensation prediction.** [Figure 11.10(c).] This further combines the advantages of the ordinary forward prediction and the above interlayer prediction. Macroblocks of B-frames at the enhancement layer are forward-predicted from the preceding frame at its own layer and "backward"-predicted from the preceding (or, alternatively, succeeding) frame at the base layer. At the first frame, the P-frame at the enhancement layer adopts only forward prediction from the I-frame at the base layer.

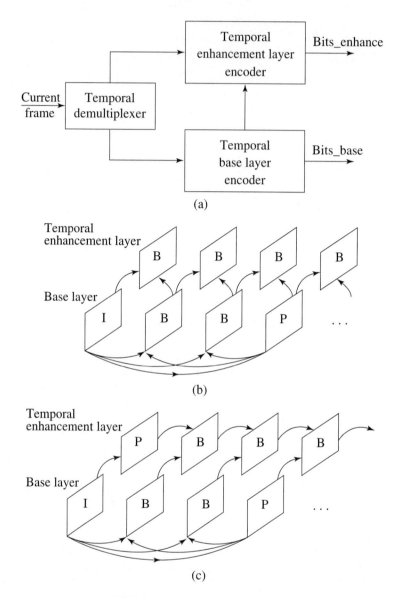

FIGURE 11.10: Encoder for MPEG-2 temporal scalability: (a) block diagram; (b) inter-layer motion-compensated prediction; (c) combined motion-compensated prediction and interlayer motion-compensated prediction.

Hybrid Scalability   Any two of the above three scalabilities can be combined to form hybrid scalability. These combinations are

- Spatial and temporal hybrid scalability

- SNR and spatial hybrid scalability

- SNR and temporal hybrid scalability

Usually, a three-layer hybrid coder will be adopted, consisting of base layer, enhancement layer 1, and enhancement layer 2.

For example, for Spatial and temporal hybrid scalability, the base layer and enhancement layer 1 will provide spatial scalability, and enhancement layers 1 and 2 will provide temporal scalability, in which enhancement layer 1 is effectively serving as a base layer.

For the encoder, the incoming video data is first temporally demultiplexed into two streams: one to enhancement layer 2; the other to enhancement layer 1 and the base layer (after further spatial decimation for the base layer).

The encoder generates three output bitstreams: (a) `Bits_base` from the base layer, (b) spatially enhanced `Bits_enhance1` from enhancement layer 1, and (c) spatially and temporally enhanced `Bits_enhance2` from enhancement layer 2.

The implementations of the other two hybrid scalabilities are similar and are left as exercises.

Data Partitioning   The compressed video stream is divided into two partitions. The base partition contains lower-frequency DCT coefficients, and the enhancement partition contains high-frequency DCT coefficients. Although the partitions are sometimes also referred to as layers (base layer and enhancement layer), strictly speaking, data partitioning does not conduct the same type of layered coding, since a single stream of video data is simply divided up and does not depend further on the base partition in generating the enhancement partition. Nevertheless, data partitioning can be useful for transmission over noisy channels and for progressive transmission.

11.3.3   Other Major Differences from MPEG-1

- **Better resilience to bit errors.** Since MPEG-2 video will often be transmitted on various networks, some of them noisy and unreliable, bit errors are inevitable. To cope with this, MPEG-2 systems have two types of streams: *Program* and *Transport*. The Program stream is similar to the Systems stream in MPEG-1; hence, it also facilitates backward compatibility with MPEG-1.

  The Transport stream aims at providing error resilience and the ability to include multiple programs with independent time bases in a single stream, for asynchronous multiplexing and network transmission. Instead of using long, variable-length packets, as in MPEG-1 and in the MPEG-2 Program stream, it uses fixed-length (188-byte) packets. It also has a new header syntax, for better error checking and correction.

- **Support of 4:2:2 and 4:4:4 chroma subsampling.** In addition to 4:2:0 chroma subsampling, as in H.261 and MPEG-1, MPEG-2 also allows 4:2:2 and 4:4:4, to increase color quality. As discussed in Chapter 5, each chrominance picture in 4:2:2 is horizontally subsampled by a factor of 2, whereas 4:4:4 is a special case, where no chroma subsampling actually takes place.

TABLE 11.7: Possible nonlinear scale in MPEG-2.

i	1	2	3	4	5	6	7	8	9	10	11	12	13	14	15	16
$scale_i$	1	2	3	4	5	6	7	8	10	12	14	16	18	20	22	24
i	17	18	19	20	21	22	23	24	25	26	27	28	29	30	31	
$scale_i$	28	32	36	40	44	48	52	56	64	72	80	88	96	104	112	

- **Nonlinear quantization.** Quantization in MPEG-2 is similar to that in MPEG-1. Its *step_size* is also determined by the product of $Q[i, j]$ and *scale*, where Q is one of the default quantization tables for intra- or inter- coding. Two types of scales are allowed. For the first, *scale* is the same as in MPEG-1, in which it is an integer in the range of [1, 31] and $scale_i = i$. For the second type, however, a nonlinear relationship exists — that is, $scale_i \neq i$. The ith scale value can be looked up in Table 11.7.

- **More restricted slice structure.** MPEG-1 allows slices to cross macroblock row boundaries. As a result, an entire picture can be a single slice. MPEG-2 slices must start and end in the same macroblock row. In other words, the left edge of a picture always starts a new slice, and the longest slice in MPEG-2 can have only one row of macroblocks.

- **More flexible video formats.** According to the standard, MPEG-2 picture sizes can be as large as $16\,k \times 16\,k$ pixels. In reality, MPEG-2 is used mainly to support various picture resolutions as defined by DVD, ATV, and HDTV.

Similar to H.261, H.263, and MPEG-1, MPEG-2 specifies only its bitstream syntax and the decoder. This leaves much room for future improvement, especially on the encoder side. The MPEG-2 video-stream syntax is more complex than that of MPEG-1, and good references for it can be found in [8, 7].

11.4 FURTHER EXPLORATION

The books by Mitchell et al. [6] and Haskell et al. [7] provide pertinent details regarding MPEG-1 and 2. The article by Haskell et al. [9] discusses digital video coding standards in general.

The textbook web site's Further Exploration section for this chapter gives URLs for various resources, including: the MPEG home page, FAQ page, and overviews and working documents of the MPEG-1 and MPEG-2 standards.

11.5 EXERCISES

1. As we know, MPEG video compression uses I-, P-, and B-frames. However, the earlier H.261 standard does not use B-frames. Describe a situation in which video compression would not be as effective without B-frames. (Your answer should be different from the one in Figure 11.1.)

2. Suggest an explanation for the reason the default quantization table Q_2 for inter-frames is all constant, as opposed to the default quantization table Q_1 of intra-frames.

3. What are some of the enhancements of MPEG-2, compared with MPEG-1? Why hasn't the MPEG-2 standard superseded the MPEG-1 standard?

4. B-frames provide obvious coding advantages, such as increase in SNR at low bitrates and bandwidth savings. What are some of the disadvantages of B-frames?

5. The MPEG-1 standard introduced B-frames, and the motion-vector search range has accordingly been increased from $[-15, 15]$ in H.261 to $[-512, 511.5]$. Why was this necessary? Calculate the number of B-frames between consecutive P-frames that would justify this increase.

6. Redraw Figure 11.8 of the MPEG-2 two-layer SNR scalability encoder and decoder to include a second enhancement layer.

7. Draw block diagrams for an MPEG-2 encoder and decoder for (a) SNR and spatial hybrid scalability, (b) SNR and temporal hybrid scalability.

8. Why aren't B-frames used as reference frames for motion compensation? Suppose there is a mode where any frame type can be specified as a reference frame. Discuss the tradeoffs of using reference B-frames instead of P-frames in a video sequence (i.e., eliminating P-frames completely).

9. Suggest a method for using motion compensation in the enhancement layer of an SNR-scalable MPEG-2 bitstream. Why isn't that recommended in the MPEG-2 standard?

10. Write a program to implement the SNR scalability in MPEG-2. Your program should be able to work on any macroblock using any quantization *step_sizes* and should output both `Bits_base` and `Bits_enhance` bitstreams. The variable-length coding step can be omitted.

11.6 REFERENCES

1 L. Chiariglione, "The Development of an Integrated Audiovisual Coding Standard: MPEG," *Proceedings of the IEEE*, 83: 151–157, 1995.

2 L. Chiariglione, "Impact of MPEG Standards on Multimedia Industry," *Proceedings of the IEEE*, 86(6): 1222–1227, 1998.

3 R. Schafer and T. Sikora, "Digital Video Coding Standards and Their Role in Video Communications," *Proceedings of the IEEE*, 83(6): 907–924, 1995.

4 D.J. LeGall, "MPEG: A Video Compression Standard for Multimedia Applications," *Communications of the ACM*, 34(4): 46–58, 1991.

5 *Information Technology — Coding of Moving Pictures and Associated Audio for Digital Storage Media at up to about 1.5 Mbit/s*, International Standard: ISO/IEC 11172, Parts 1–5, 1992.

6 J.L. Mitchell, W.B. Pennebaker, C.E. Fogg, and D.J. LeGall, *MPEG Video Compression Standard*, New York: Chapman & Hall, 1996.

7 B.G. Haskell, A. Puri, and A. Netravali, *Digital Video: An Introduction to MPEG-2*, New York: Chapman & Hall, 1997.

8 *Information Technology — Generic Coding of Moving Pictures and Associated Audio Information*, International Standard: ISO/IEC 13818, Parts 1–10, 1994.

9 B.G. Haskell, et al., "Image and Video Coding: Emerging Standards and Beyond," *IEEE Transactions on Circuits and Systems for Video Technology*, 8(7): 814–837, 1998.

CHAPTER 12

MPEG Video Coding II — MPEG-4, 7, and Beyond

12.1 OVERVIEW OF MPEG-4

MPEG-1 and -2 employ *frame-based* coding techniques, in which each rectangular video frame is treated as a unit for compression. Their main concern is high compression ratio and satisfactory quality of video under such compression techniques. MPEG-4 is a newer standard [1]. Besides compression, it pays great attention to user interactivities. This allows a larger number of users to create and communicate their multimedia presentations and applications on new infrastructures, such as the Internet, the World Wide Web (WWW), and mobile/wireless networks. MPEG-4 departs from its predecessors in adopting a new *object-based coding* approach — *media objects* are now entities for MPEG-4 coding. Media objects (also known as *audio and visual objects*) can be either *natural* or *synthetic*; that is to say, they may be captured by a videocamera or created by computer programs.

Object-based coding not only has the potential of offering higher compression ratio but is also beneficial for digital video composition, manipulation, indexing, and retrieval. Figure 12.1 illustrates how MPEG-4 videos can be composed and manipulated by simple operations such as insertion/deletion, translation/rotation, scaling, and so on, on the visual objects.

MPEG-4 (version 1) was finalized in October 1998 and became an international standard in early 1999, referred to as ISO/IEC 14496 [2]. An improved version (version 2) was finalized in December 1999 and acquired International Standard status in 2000. Similar to the previous MPEG standards, its first five parts are Systems, Video, Audio, Conformance, and Software. Its sixth part, *Delivery Multimedia Integration Framework* (DMIF), is new, and we will discuss it in more detail in Chapter 16, where we discuss multimedia network communications and applications.

Originally targeted at low-bitrate communication (4.8 to 64 kbps for mobile applications and up to 2 Mbps for other applications), the bitrate for MPEG-4 video now covers a large range, between 5 kbps and 10 Mbps.

As the *Reference Models* in Figure 12.2(a) show, an MPEG-1 system simply delivers audio and video data from its storage and does not allow any user interactivity. MPEG-2 added an Interaction component [indicated by dashed lines in Figure 12.2(a)] and thus permits limited user interactions in applications such as networked video and Interactive TV. MPEG-4 [Figure 12.2(b)] is an entirely new standard for (a) composing media objects to create desirable audiovisual scenes, (b) multiplexing and synchronizing the bitstreams for

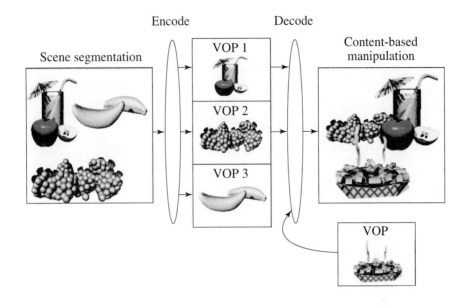

FIGURE 12.1: Composition and manipulation of MPEG-4 videos (VOP = Video Object Plane).

these media data entities so that they can be transmitted with guaranteed Quality of Service (QoS), and (c) interacting with the audiovisual scene at the receiving end. MPEG-4 provides a toolbox of advanced coding modules and algorithms for audio and video compression.

MPEG-4 defines *BInary Format for Scenes* (BIFS) [3] that facilitates the composition of media objects into a scene. BIFS is often represented by a scene graph, in which the nodes describe audiovisual primitives and their attributes and the graph structure enables a description of spatial and temporal relationships of objects in the scene. BIFS is an enhancement of Virtual Reality Modeling Language (VRML). In particular, it emphasizes timing and synchronization of objects, which were lacking in the original VRML design. In addition to BIFS, MPEG-4 (version 2) provides a programming environment, *MPEG-J* [4], in which Java applications (called *MPEGlets*) can access Java packages and APIs so as to enhance end users' interactivities.

The hierarchical structure of MPEG-4 visual bitstreams is very different from that of MPEG-1 and 2 in that it is very much video-object-oriented. Figure 12.3 illustrates five levels of the hierarchical description of a scene in MPEG-4 visual bitstreams. In general, each *Video-object Sequence* (VS) will have one or more *Video Objects* (VOs), each VO will have one or more *Video Object Layers* (VOLs), and so on. Syntactically, all five levels have a unique start code in the bitstream, to enable random access.

1. **Video-object Sequence (VS)**. VS delivers the complete MPEG-4 visual scene, which may contain 2D or 3D natural or synthetic objects.

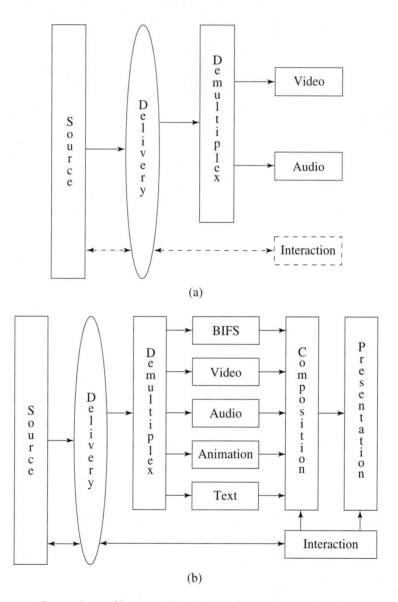

FIGURE 12.2: Comparison of interactivities in MPEG standards: (a) reference models in MPEG-1 and 2 (interaction in dashed lines supported only by MPEG-2); (b) MPEG-4 reference model.

2. **Video Object (VO)**. VO is a particular object in the scene, which can be of arbitrary (nonrectangular) shape, corresponding to an object or background of the scene.

3. **Video Object Layer (VOL)**. VOL facilitates a way to support (multilayered) scalable coding. A VO can have multiple VOLs under scalable coding or a single VOL under

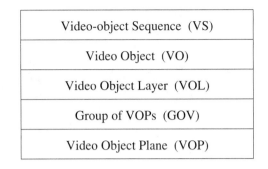

FIGURE 12.3: Video-object-oriented hierarchical description of a scene in MPEG-4 visual bitstreams.

nonscalable coding. As a special case, MPEG-4 also supports a special type of VOL with a shorter header. This provides bitstream compatibility with the baseline H.263 [5].

4. **Group of Video Object Planes (GOV)**. GOV groups video object planes. It is an optional level.

5. **Video Object Plane (VOP)**. A VOP is a snapshot of a VO at a particular moment, reflecting the VO's shape, texture, and motion parameters at that instant. In general, a VOP is an image of arbitrary shape. A degenerate case in MPEG-4 video coding occurs when the entire rectangular video frame is treated as a VOP. In this case, it is equivalent to MPEG-1 and 2. MPEG-4 allows overlapped VOPs — that is, a VOP can partially occlude another VOP in a scene.

12.2   OBJECT-BASED VISUAL CODING IN MPEG-4

MPEG-4 encodes/decodes each VOP separately (instead of considering the whole frame). Hence, its object-based visual coding is also known as *VOP-based coding*. Our discussion will start with coding for natural objects (more details can be found in [6, 7]). Section 12.3 describes synthetic object coding.

12.2.1   VOP-Based Coding vs. Frame-Based Coding

MPEG-1 and 2 do not support the VOP concept, hence, their coding method is referred to as *frame-based*. Since each frame is divided into many macroblocks from which motion-compensation-based coding is conducted, it is also known as *block-based coding*. Figure 12.4(a) shows three frames from a video sequence with a vehicle moving toward the left and a pedestrian walking in the opposite direction. Figure 12.4(b) shows the typical block-based coding in which the motion vector (**MV**) is obtained for one of the macroblocks.

MPEG-1 and 2 visual coding are concerned only with *compression ratio* and do not consider the existence of visual objects. Therefore, the motion vectors generated may be inconsistent with the object's motion and would not be useful for object-based video analysis and indexing.

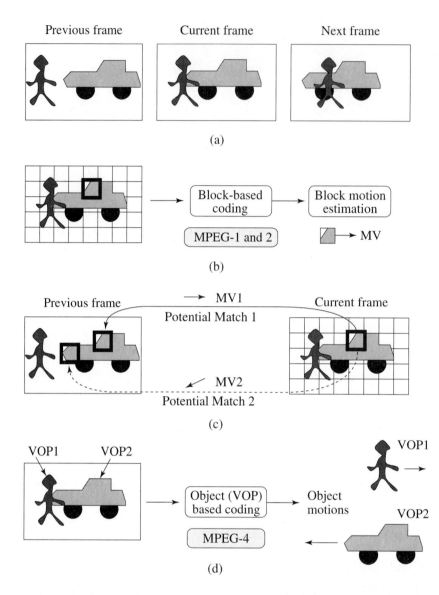

FIGURE 12.4: Comparison between block-based coding and object-based coding: (a) a video sequence; (b) MPEG-1 and 2 block-based coding; (c) two potential matches in MPEG-1 and 2; (d) object-based coding in MPEG-4.

Figure 12.4(c) illustrates a possible example in which both potential matches yield small prediction errors. If Potential Match 2 yields a (slightly) smaller prediction error than Potential Match 1, **MV**2 will be chosen as the motion vector for the macroblocks in the block-based coding approach, although only **MV**1 is consistent with the vehicle's direction of motion.

Object-based coding in MPEG-4 is aimed at solving this problem, in addition to improving compression. Figure 12.4(d) shows each VOP is of arbitrary shape and will ideally obtain a unique motion vector consistent with the object's motion.

MPEG-4 VOP-based coding also employs the motion compensation technique. An Intra-frame-coded VOP is called an *I-VOP*. Inter-frame-coded VOPs are called *P-VOP*s if only forward prediction is employed or *B-VOP*s if bidirectional predictions are employed. The new difficulty here is that the VOPs may have arbitrary shapes. Therefore, in addition to their texture, their shape information must now be coded.

It is worth noting that *texture* here actually refers to the visual content, that is the gray level and chroma values of the pixels in the VOP. MPEG-1 and 2 do not code shape information, since all frames are rectangular, but they do code the values of the pixels in the frame. In MPEG-1 and 2, this coding was not explicitly referred to as texture coding. The term "texture" comes from computer graphics and shows how this discipline has entered the video coding world with MPEG-4.

Below, we start with a discussion of motion-compensation-based coding for VOPs, followed by introductions to *texture coding*, *shape coding*, *static texture coding*, *sprite coding*, and *global motion compensation*.

12.2.2 Motion Compensation

This section addresses issues of VOP-based motion compensation in MPEG-4. Since I-VOP coding is relatively straightforward, our discussions will concentrate on coding for P-VOP and/or B-VOP unless I-VOP is explicitly mentioned.

As before, motion-compensation-based VOP coding in MPEG-4 again involves three steps: motion estimation, motion-compensation-based prediction, and coding of the prediction error. To facilitate motion compensation, each VOP is divided into many macroblocks, as in previous frame-based methods. Macroblocks are by default 16×16 in luminance images and 8×8 in chrominance images and are treated specially when they straddle the boundary of an arbitrarily shaped VOP.

MPEG-4 defines a rectangular *bounding box* for each VOP. Its left and top bounds are the left and top bounds of the VOP, which in turn specify the shifted origin for the VOP from the original $(0, 0)$ for the video frame in the absolute (frame) coordinate system (see Figure 12.5). Both horizontal and vertical dimensions of the bounding box must be multiples of 16 in the luminance image. Therefore, the box is usually slightly larger than a conventional bounding box.

Macroblocks entirely within the VOP are referred to as *interior macroblocks*. As is apparent from Figure 12.5, many of the macroblocks straddle the boundary of the VOP and are called *boundary macroblocks*.

Motion compensation for interior macroblocks is carried out in the same manner as in MPEG-1 and 2. However, boundary macroblocks could be difficult to match in motion

Video frame

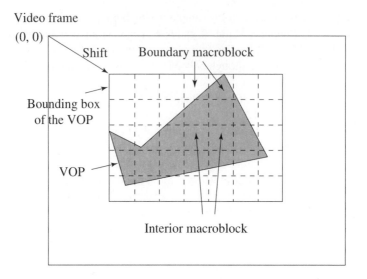

FIGURE 12.5: Bounding box and boundary macroblocks of VOP.

estimation, since VOPs often have arbitrary (nonrectangular) shape, and their shape may change from one instant in the video to another. To help match every pixel in the target VOP and meet the mandatory requirement of rectangular blocks in transform coding (e.g., DCT), a preprocessing step of *padding* is applied to the reference VOPs prior to motion estimation.

Only pixels within the VOP of the current (target) VOP are considered for matching in motion compensation, and padding takes place only in the reference VOPs.

For quality, some better extrapolation method than padding could have been developed. Padding was adopted in MPEG-4 largely due to its simplicity and speed.

The first two steps of motion compensation are: padding, and motion vector coding.

Padding. For all boundary macroblocks in the reference VOP, *horizontal repetitive padding* is invoked first, followed by *vertical repetitive padding* (Figure 12.6). Afterward, for all *exterior macroblocks* that are outside of the VOP but adjacent to one or more boundary macroblocks, *extended padding* is applied.

The horizontal repetitive padding algorithm examines each row in the boundary macroblocks in the reference VOP. Each boundary pixel is replicated to the left and/or right to

FIGURE 12.6: A sequence of paddings for reference VOPs in MPEG-4.

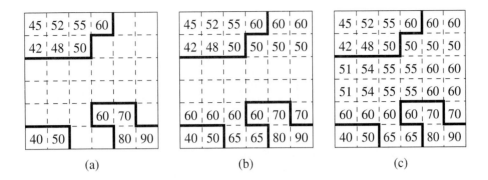

FIGURE 12.7: An example of repetitive padding in a boundary macroblock of a reference VOP: (a) original pixels within the VOP; (b) after horizontal repetitive padding; (c) followed by vertical repetitive padding.

fill in the values for the interval of pixels outside the VOP in the macroblock. If the interval is bounded by two boundary pixels, their average is adopted.

ALGORITHM 12.1 HORIZONTAL REPETITIVE PADDING

begin

for all rows in Boundary macroblocks in the Reference VOP

if ∃ (boundary pixel) in the row

for all *interval* outside of VOP

if *interval* is bounded by only one boundary pixel b

assign the value of b to all pixels in *interval*

else   // *interval* is bounded by two boundary pixels b_1 and b_2

assign the value of $(b_1 + b_2)/2$ to all pixels in *interval*

end

The subsequent vertical repetitive padding algorithm works similarly. It examines each column, and the newly padded pixels by the preceding horizontal padding process are treated as pixels inside the VOP for the purpose of this vertical padding.

EXAMPLE 12.1

Figure 12.7 illustrates an example of repetitive padding in a boundary macroblock of a reference VOP. Figure 12.7(a) shows the luminance (or chrominance) intensity values of pixels in the VOP, with the VOP's boundary shown as darkened lines. For simplicity, the macroblock's resolution is reduced to 6×6 in this example, although its actual macroblock size is 16×16 in luminance images and 8×8 in chrominance images.

1. **Horizontal repetitive padding** [Figure 12.7(b)]

   Row 0. The rightmost pixel of the VOP is the only boundary pixel. Its intensity value, 60, is used repetitively as the value of the pixels outside the VOP.

Row 1. Similarly, the rightmost pixel of the VOP is the only boundary pixel. Its intensity value, 50, is used repetitively as the pixel value outside of the VOP.

Rows 2 and 3. No horizontal padding, since no boundary pixels exist.

Row 4. There exist two intervals outside the VOP, each bounded by a single boundary pixel. Their intensity values, 60 and 70, are used as the pixel values of the two intervals, respectively.

Row 5. A single interval outside the VOP is bounded by a pair of boundary pixels of the VOP. The average of their intensity values, $(50 + 80)/2 = 65$, is used repetitively as the value of the pixels between them.

2. **Vertical repetitive padding** [Figure 12.7(c)]

Column 0. A single interval is bounded by a pair of boundary pixels of the VOP. One is 42 in the VOP; the other is 60, which just arose from horizontal padding. The average of their intensity values, $(42 + 60)/2 = 51$, is repetitively used as the value of the pixels between them.

Columns 1, 2, 3, 4 and 5. These columns are padded similarly to Column 0.

Extended Padding   Macroblocks entirely outside the VOP are *exterior* macroblocks. Exterior macroblocks immediately next to boundary macroblocks are filled by replicating the values of the border pixels of the boundary macroblock. We note that boundary macroblocks are by now fully padded, so all their horizontal and vertical border pixels have defined values. If an exterior macroblock has more than one boundary macroblock as its immediate neighbor, the boundary macroblock to use for extended padding follows a priority list: left, top, right, and bottom.

Later versions of MPEG-4 allow some average values of these macroblocks to be used. This extended padding process can be repeated to fill in all exterior macroblocks within the rectangular bounding box of the VOP.

Motion Vector Coding.   Each macroblock from the target VOP will find a best matching macroblock from the reference VOP through the following motion estimation procedure.

Let $C(x+k, y+l)$ be pixels of the macroblock in the target VOP, and $R(x+i+k, y+j+l)$ be pixels of the macroblock in the reference VOP. Similar to MAD in Eq. (10.1), a *Sum of Absolute Difference* (SAD) for measuring the difference between the two macroblocks can be defined as

$$SAD(i, j) = \sum_{k=0}^{N-1}\sum_{l=0}^{N-1} |C(x + k, y + l) - R(x + i + k, y + j + l)| \cdot Map(x + k, y + l)$$

where N is the size of the macroblock. $Map(p, q) = 1$ when $C(p, q)$ is a pixel within the target VOP; otherwise, $Map(p, q) = 0$. The vector (i, j) that yields the minimum SAD is adopted as the motion vector $\mathbf{MV}(u, v)$:

$$(u, v) = \{ (i, j) \mid SAD(i, j) \text{ is minimum}, \ i \in [-p, p], \ j \in [-p, p] \} \quad (12.1)$$

where p is the maximal allowable magnitude for u and v.

For motion compensation, the *motion vector* **MV** is coded. As in H.263 (see Figure 10.11), the motion vector of the target macroblock is not simply taken as the **MV**. Instead, **MV** is predicted from three neighboring macroblocks. The prediction error for the motion vector is then variable-length coded.

Following are some of the advanced motion compensation techniques adopted similar to the ones in H.263 (see Section 10.5).

- Four motion vectors (each from an 8×8 block) can be generated for each macroblock in the luminance component of a VOP.

- Motion vectors can have subpixel precision. At half-pixel precision, the range of motion vectors is $[-2,048, 2,047]$. MPEG-4 also allows quarter-pixel precision in the luminance component of a VOP.

- Unrestricted motion vectors are allowed: **MV** can point beyond the boundaries of the reference VOP. When a pixel outside the VOP is referenced, its value is still defined, due to padding.

12.2.3   Texture Coding

Texture refers to gray level (or chroma) variations and/or patterns in the VOP. Texture coding in MPEG-4 can be based either on DCT or *shape-Adaptive DCT* (SA-DCT).

Texture Coding Based on DCT.   In I-VOP, the gray (or chroma) values of the pixels in each macroblock of the VOP are directly coded, using the DCT followed by VLC, which is similar to what is done in JPEG for still pictures. P-VOP and B-VOP use motion-compensation-based coding, hence, it is the prediction error that is sent to DCT and VLC. The following discussion will be focused on motion-compensation-based texture coding for P-VOP and B-VOP.

Coding for Interior macroblocks, each 16×16 in the luminance VOP and 8×8 in the chrominance VOP, is similar to the conventional motion-compensation-based coding in H.261, H.263, and MPEG-1 and 2. Prediction errors from the six 8×8 blocks of each macroblock are obtained after the conventional motion estimation step. These are sent to a DCT routine to obtain six 8×8 blocks of DCT coefficients.

For boundary macroblocks, areas outside the VOP in the reference VOP are padded using repetitive padding, as described above. After motion compensation, texture prediction errors within the target VOP are obtained. For portions of the boundary macroblocks in the target VOP outside the VOP, zeros are padded to the block sent to DCT, since ideally, prediction errors would be near zero inside the VOP. Whereas repetitive padding and extended padding were for better matching in motion compensation, this additional zero padding is for better DCT results in texture coding.

The quantization $step\_size$ for the DC component is 8. For the AC coefficients, one of the following two methods can be employed:

- The H.263 method, in which all coefficients receive the same quantizer controlled by a single parameter, and different macroblocks can have different quantizers.

- The MPEG-2 method, in which DCT coefficients in the same macroblock can have different quantizers and are further controlled by the *step_size* parameter.

Shape-Adaptive DCT (SA-DCT)-Based Coding for Boundary Macroblocks. SA-DCT [8] is another texture coding method for boundary macroblocks. Due to its effectiveness, SA-DCT has been adopted for coding boundary macroblocks in MPEG-4 version 2.

1D DCT-N is a variation of the 1D DCT described earlier [Eqs. (8.19) and (8.20)], in that N elements are used in the transform instead of a fixed $N = 8$. (For short, we will denote the 1D DCT-N transform by DCT-N in this section.)

Eqs. (12.2) and (12.3) describe the DCT-N transform and its inverse, IDCT-N.

1D Discrete Cosine Transform-N (DCT-N)

$$F(u) = \sqrt{\frac{2}{N}} C(u) \sum_{i=0}^{N-1} \cos \frac{(2i+1)u\pi}{2N} f(i) \tag{12.2}$$

1D Inverse Discrete Cosine Transform-N (IDCT-N)

$$\tilde{f}(i) = \sum_{u=0}^{N-1} \sqrt{\frac{2}{N}} C(u) \cos \frac{(2i+1)u\pi}{2N} F(u) \tag{12.3}$$

where $i = 0, 1, \ldots, N - 1$, $u = 0, 1, \ldots, N - 1$, and

$$C(u) = \begin{cases} \frac{\sqrt{2}}{2} & \text{if } u = 0, \\ 1 & \text{otherwise} \end{cases}$$

SA-DCT is a 2D DCT and is computed as a separable 2D transform in two iterations of DCT-N. Figure 12.8 illustrates the process of texture coding for boundary macroblocks using SA-DCT. The transform is applied to each of the 8×8 blocks in the boundary macroblock.

Figure 12.8(a) shows one of the 8×8 blocks of a boundary macroblock, where pixels inside the macroblock, denoted $f(x, y)$, are shown gray. The gray pixels are first shifted upward to obtain $f'(x, y)$, as Figure 12.8(b) shows. In the first iteration, DCT-N is applied to each column of $f'(x, y)$, with N determined by the number of gray pixels in the column. Hence, we use DCT-2, DCT-3, DCT-5, and so on. The resulting DCT-N coefficients are denoted by $F'(x, v)$, as Figure 12.8(c) shows, where the dark dots indicate the DC coefficients of the DCT-Ns. The elements of $F'(x, v)$ are then shifted to the left to obtain $F''(x, v)$ in Figure 12.8(d).

In the second iteration, DCT-N is applied to each row of $F''(x, v)$ to obtain $G(u, v)$ (Figure 12.8(e)), in which the single dark dot indicates the DC coefficient $G(0, 0)$ of the 2D SA-DCT.

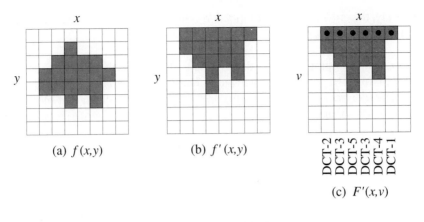

(a) $f(x,y)$ (b) $f'(x,y)$

(c) $F'(x,v)$

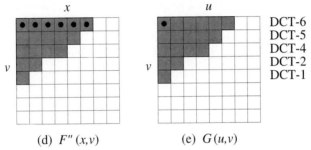

(d) $F''(x,v)$ (e) $G(u,v)$

FIGURE 12.8: Texture coding for boundary macroblocks using the Shape Adaptive DCT (SA-DCT).

Some coding considerations:

- The total number of DCT coefficients in $G(u, v)$ is equal to the number of gray pixels inside the 8×8 block of the boundary macroblock, which is less than 8×8. Hence, the method is *shape adaptive* and is more efficient to compute.

- At decoding time, since the array elements must be shifted back properly after each iteration of IDCT-Ns, a binary mask of the original shape is required to decode the texture information coded by SA-DCT. The binary mask is the same as the *binary alpha map* described below.

12.2.4 Shape Coding

Unlike in MPEG-1 and 2, MPEG-4 must code the shape of the VOP, since shape is one of the intrinsic features of visual objects.

MPEG-4 supports two types of shape information: *binary* and *grayscale*. Binary shape information can be in the form of a binary map (also known as a *binary alpha map*) that is of the same size as the VOP's rectangular bounding box. A value of 1 (opaque) or 0 (transparent) in the bitmap indicates whether the pixel is inside or outside the VOP.

Alternatively, the grayscale shape information actually refers to the shape's *transparency*, with gray values ranging from 0 (transparent) to 255 (opaque).

Binary Shape Coding   To encode the binary alpha map more efficiently, the map is divided into 16×16 blocks, also known as *Binary Alpha Blocks* (BAB). If a BAB is entirely opaque or transparent, it is easy to code, and no special technique of shape coding is necessary. It is the boundary BABs that contain the contour and hence the shape information for the VOP. They are the subject of binary shape coding.

Various contour-based and bitmap-based (or area-based) algorithms have been studied and compared for coding boundary BABs [9]. Two of the finalists were both bitmap-based. One was the *Modified Modified READ* (MMR) *algorithm*, which was also an optional enhancement in the fax Group 3 (G3) standard [10] and the mandatory compression method in the Group 4 (G4) standard [11]. The other finalist was *Context-based Arithmetic Encoding* (CAE), which was initially developed for JBIG [12]. CAE was finally chosen as the binary shape-coding method for MPEG-4 because of its simplicity and compression efficiency.

MMR is basically a series of simplifications of the *Relative Element Address Designate* (READ) algorithm. The basic idea behind the READ algorithm is to code the current line relative to the pixel locations in the previously coded line. The algorithm starts by identifying five pixel locations in the previous and current lines:

- a_0: the last pixel value known to both the encoder and decoder

- a_1: the transition pixel to the right of a_0

- a_2: the second transition pixel to the right of a_0

- b_1: the first transition pixel whose color is opposite to a_0 in the previously coded line

- b_2: the first transition pixel to the right of b_1 on the previously coded line

READ works by examining the relative positions of these pixels. At any time, both the encoder and decoder know the position of a_0, b_1, and b_2, while the positions a_1 and a_2 are known only in the encoder.

Three coding modes are used:

- If the run lengths on the previous and the current lines are similar, the distance between a_1 and b_1 should be much smaller than the distance between a_0 and a_1. Thus, the *vertical mode* encodes the current run length as $a_1 - b_1$.

- If the previous line has no similar run length, the current run length is coded using one-dimensional run-length coding. This is called the *horizontal mode*.

- If $a_0 \leq b_1 < b_2 < a_1$, we can simply transmit a codeword indicating it is in *pass mode* and advance a_0 to the position under b_2, and continue the coding process.

Some simplifications can be made to the READ algorithm for practical implementation. For example, if $\|a_1 - b_1\| < 3$, then it is enough to indicate that we can apply the vertical

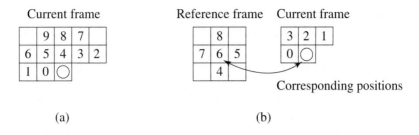

FIGURE 12.9: Contexts in CAE for binary shape coding in MPEG-4. ○ indicates the current pixel, and digits indicate the other pixels in the neighborhood: (a) intra-CAE; (b) inter-CAE.

mode. Also, to prevent error propagation, a k-factor is defined, such that every k lines must contain at least one line coded using conventional run-length coding. These modifications constitute the *Modified READ* algorithm used in the G3 standard. The Modified Modified READ (MMR) algorithm simply removes the restrictions imposed by the k-factor.

For Context-based Arithmetic Encoding, Figure 12.9 illustrates the "context" for a pixel in the boundary BAB. In intra-CAE mode, when only the target alpha map is involved (Figure 12.9(a)), ten neighboring pixels (numbered from 0 to 9) in the same alpha map form the context. The ten binary numbers associated with these pixels can offer up to $2^{10} = 1{,}024$ possible contexts.

Now, it is apparent that certain contexts (e.g., all 1s or all 0s) appear more frequently than others. With some prior statistics, a probability table can be built to indicate the probability of occurrence for each of the 1,024 contexts.

Recall that Arithmetic coding (Chapter 7) is capable of encoding a sequence of probabilistic symbols with a single number. Now, each pixel can look up the table to find a probability value for its context. CAE simply scans the 16×16 pixels in each BAB sequentially and applies Arithmetic coding to eventually derive a single floating-point number for the BAB.

Inter-CAE mode is a natural extension of intra-CAE: it involves both the target and reference alpha maps. For each boundary macroblock in the target frame, a process of motion estimation (in integer precision) and compensation is invoked first to locate the matching macroblock in the reference frame. This establishes the corresponding positions for each pixel in the boundary BAB.

Figure 12.9(b) shows the context of each pixel includes four neighboring pixels from the target alpha map and five pixels from the reference alpha map. According to its context, each pixel in the boundary BAB is assigned one of the $2^9 = 512$ probabilities. Afterward, the CAE algorithm is applied.

The 16×16 binary map originally contains 256 bits of information. Compressing it to a single floating number achieves a substantial saving.

The above CAE method is *lossless*! The MPEG-4 group also examined some simple lossy versions of the above shape-coding method. For example, the binary alpha map can be simply subsampled by a factor of 2 or 4 before arithmetic coding. The tradeoff is, of course, the deterioration of the shape.

Grayscale Shape Coding The term *grayscale shape coding* in MPEG-4 could be misleading, because the true shape information is coded in the binary alpha map. Grayscale here is used to describe the *transparency* of the shape, not the texture!

In addition to the bitplanes for RGB frame buffers, raster graphics uses extra bitplanes for an *alpha map*, which can be used to describe the transparency of the graphical object. When the alpha map has more than one bitplane, multiple levels of transparency can be introduced — for example, 0 for transparent, 255 for opaque, and any number in between for various degrees of intermediate transparency. The term grayscale is used for transparency coding in MPEG-4 simply because the transparency number happens to be in the range of 0 to 255 — the same as conventional 8-bit grayscale intensities.

Grayscale shape coding in MPEG-4 employs the same technique as in the texture coding described above. It uses the alpha map and block-based motion compensation and encodes prediction errors by DCT. The boundary macroblocks need padding, as before, since not all pixels are in the VOP.

Coding of the transparency information (grayscale shape coding) is lossy, as opposed to coding of the binary shape information, which is by default lossless.

12.2.5 Static Texture Coding

MPEG-4 uses wavelet coding for the texture of static objects. This is particularly applicable when the texture is used for mapping onto 3D surfaces.

As introduced in Chapter 8, wavelet coding can recursively decompose an image into *subbands* of multiple frequencies. The Embedded Zerotree Wavelet (EZW) algorithm [13] provides a compact representation by exploiting the potentially large number of insignificant coefficients in the subbands.

The coding of subbands in MPEG-4 static texture coding is conducted as follows:

- The subbands with the lowest frequency are coded using DPCM. Prediction of each coefficient is based on three neighbors.

- Coding of other subbands is based on a multiscale zerotree wavelet coding method.

The multiscale zerotree has a *parent–child relation* (PCR) *tree* for each coefficient in the lowest frequency subband. As a result, the location information of all coefficients is better tracked.

In addition to the original magnitude of the coefficients, the degree of quantization affects the data rate. If the magnitude of a coefficient is zero after quantization, it is considered insignificant. At first, a large quantizer is used; only the most significant coefficients are selected and subsequently coded using arithmetic coding. The difference between the quantized and the original coefficients is kept in residual subbands, which will be coded in the next iteration in which a smaller quantizer is employed. The process can continue for additional iterations; hence, it is very scalable.

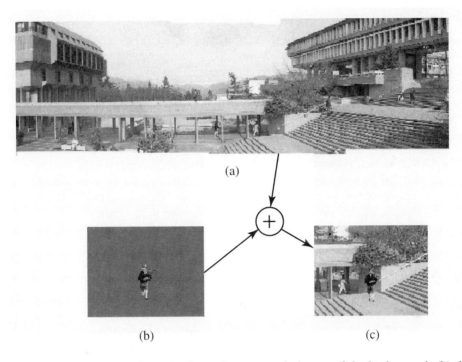

FIGURE 12.10: Sprite coding: (a) the sprite panoramic image of the background; (b) the foreground object (piper) in a bluescreen image; (c) the composed video scene. (This figure also appears in the color insert section.) *Piper image courtesy of Simon Fraser University Pipe Band.*

12.2.6 Sprite Coding

Video photography often involves camera movements such as pan, tilt, zoom in/out, and so on. Often, the main objective is to track and examine foreground (moving) objects. Under these circumstances, the background can be treated as a static image. This creates a new VO type, the *sprite* — a graphic image that can freely move around within a larger graphic image or set of images.

To separate the foreground object from the background, we introduce the notion of a *sprite panorama* — a still image that describes the static background over a sequence of video frames. It can be generated using image "stitching" and warping techniques [14]. The large sprite panoramic image can be encoded and sent to the decoder only once, at the beginning of the video sequence. When the decoder receives separately coded foreground objects and parameters describing the camera movements thus far, it can efficiently reconstruct the scene.

Figure 12.10(a) shows a sprite that is a panoramic image stitched from a sequence of video frames. By combining the sprite background with the piper in the bluescreen image (Figure 12.10(b)), the new video scene (Figure 12.10(c)) can readily be decoded with the aid of the sprite code and the additional pan/tilt and zoom parameters. Clearly, foreground objects can either be from the original video scene or newly created to realize flexible object-based composition of MPEG-4 videos.

12.2.7 Global Motion Compensation

Common camera motions, such as pan, tilt, rotation, and zoom (so-called *global* motions, since they apply to every block), often cause rapid content change between successive video frames. Traditional block-based motion compensation would result in a large number of significant motion vectors. Also, these types of camera motions cannot all be described using the translational motion model employed by block-based motion compensation. *Global motion compensation (GMC)* is designed to solve this problem. There are four major components:

- **Global motion estimation**. Global motion estimation computes the motion of the current image with respect to the sprite. By "global" is meant overall change due to camera change — zooming in, panning to the side, and so on. It is computed by minimizing the sum of square differences between the sprite S and the global motion-compensated image I'.

$$E = \sum_{i=1}^{N} (S(x_i, y_i) - I'(x_i', y_i'))^2. \tag{12.4}$$

  The idea here is that if the background (possibly stitched) image is a sprite $S(x_i, y_i)$, we expect the new frame to consist mainly of the same background, altered by these global camera motions. To further constrain the global motion estimation problem, the motion over the whole image is parameterized by a perspective motion model using eight parameters, defined as

$$x_i' = \frac{a_0 + a_1 x_i + a_2 y_i}{a_6 x_i + a_7 y_i + 1},$$

$$y_i' = \frac{a_3 + a_4 x_i + a_5 y_i}{a_6 x_i + a_7 y_i + 1}. \tag{12.5}$$

  This resulting constrained minimization problem can be solved using a gradient descent-based method [15].

- **Warping and blending**. Once the motion parameters are computed, the background images are warped to align with respect to the sprite. The coordinates of the warped image are computed using Eq. (12.5). Afterward, the warped image is blended into the current sprite to produce the new sprite. This can be done using simple averaging or some form of weighted averaging.

- **Motion trajectory coding**. Instead of directly transmitting the motion parameters, we encode only the displacements of reference points. This is called *trajectory coding* [15]. Points at the corners of the VOP bounding box are used as reference points, and their corresponding points in the sprite are calculated. The difference between these two entities is coded and transmitted as differential motion vectors.

- **Choice of local motion compensation (LMC) or GMC**. Finally, a decision has to be made whether to use GMC or LMC. For this purpose, we can apply GMC to the moving background and LMC to the foreground. Heuristically (and with much

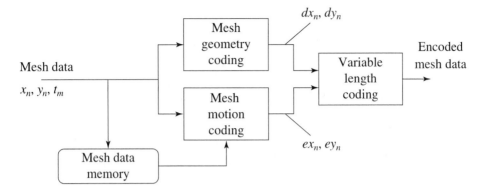

FIGURE 12.11: 2D Mesh Object Plane (MOP) encoding process.

detail skipped), if $SAD_{GMC} < SAD_{LMC}$, then use GMC to generate the predicted reference VOP. Otherwise, use LMC as before.

12.3   SYNTHETIC OBJECT CODING IN MPEG-4

The number of objects in videos that are created by computer graphics and animation software is increasing. These are denoted *synthetic objects* and can often be presented together with natural objects and scenes in games, TV ads and programs, and animation or feature films.

In this section, we briefly discuss *2D mesh-based* and *3D model-based* coding and animation methods for synthetic objects. Beek, Petajan, and Ostermann [16] provide a more detailed survey of this subject.

12.3.1   2D Mesh Object Coding

A *2D mesh* is a tessellation (or partition) of a 2D planar region using polygonal patches. The vertices of the polygons are referred to as *nodes* of the mesh. The most popular meshes are *triangular meshes*, where all polygons are triangles. The MPEG-4 standard makes use of two types of 2D mesh: *uniform mesh* and *Delaunay mesh* [17]. Both are triangular meshes that can be used to model natural video objects as well as synthetic animated objects.

Since the triangulation structure (the edges between nodes) is known and can be readily regenerated by the decoder, it is not coded explicitly in the bitstream. Hence, 2D mesh object coding is compact. All coordinate values of the mesh are coded in half-pixel precision.

Each 2D mesh is treated as a *mesh object plane* (MOP). Figure 12.11 illustrates the encoding process for 2D MOPs. Coding can be divided into *geometry coding* and *motion coding*. As shown, the input data is the x and y coordinates of all the nodes and the triangles (t_m) in the mesh. The output data is the displacements (dx_n, dy_n) and the prediction errors of the motion (ex_n, ey_n), both of which are explained below.

2D Mesh Geometry Coding   MPEG-4 allows four types of uniform meshes with different triangulation structures. Figure 12.12 shows such meshes with 4×5 mesh nodes. Each uniform mesh can be specified by five parameters: the first two specify the number of

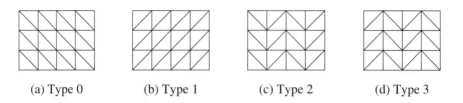

| (a) Type 0 | (b) Type 1 | (c) Type 2 | (d) Type 3 |

FIGURE 12.12: Four types of uniform meshes: (a) type 0; (b) type 1; (c) type 2; (d) type3.

nodes in each row and column respectively; the next two specify the horizontal and vertical size of each rectangle (containing two triangles) respectively; and the last specifies the type of the uniform mesh.

Uniform meshes are simple and are especially good for representing 2D rectangular objects (e.g., the entire video frame). When used for objects of arbitrary shape, they are applied to (overlaid on) the bounding boxes of the VOPs, which incurs some inefficiency.

A Delaunay mesh is a better object-based mesh representation for arbitrary-shaped 2D objects.

Definiton 1: If $\mathcal{D}$ is a Delaunay triangulation, then any of its triangles $t_n = (P_i, P_j, P_k) \in \mathcal{D}$ satisfies the property that the circumcircle of t_n does not contain in its interior any other node point P_l.

A Delaunay mesh for a video object can be obtained in the following steps:

1. **Select boundary nodes of the mesh**. A polygon is used to approximate the boundary of the object. The polygon vertices are the *boundary nodes* of the Delaunay mesh. A possible heuristic is to select boundary points with high curvatures as boundary nodes.

2. **Choose interior nodes**. Feature points within the object's boundary such as edge points or corners, can be chosen as interior nodes for the mesh.

3. **Perform Delaunay triangulation.** A *constrained Delaunay triangulation* is performed on the boundary and interior nodes, with the polygonal boundary used as a constraint. The triangulation will use line segments connecting consecutive boundary nodes as edges and form triangles only within the boundary.

Constrained Delaunay Triangulation. Interior edges are first added to form new triangles. The algorithm will examine each interior edge to make sure it is *locally Delaunay*. Given two triangles (P_i, P_j, P_k) and (P_j, P_k, P_l) sharing an edge $\overline{jk}$, if (P_i, P_j, P_k) contains P_l or (P_j, P_k, P_l) contains P_i in the interior of its circumcircle, then $\overline{jk}$ is not locally Delaunay and will be replaced by a new edge $\overline{il}$.

If P_l falls exactly on the circumcircle of (P_i, P_j, P_k) (and accordingly, P_i also falls exactly on the circumcircle of (P_j, P_k, P_l)), then $\overline{jk}$ will be viewed as locally Delaunay only if P_i or P_l has the largest x coordinate among the four nodes.

Figure 12.13(a) and (b) show the set of Delaunay mesh nodes and the result of the constrained Delaunay triangulation. If the total number of nodes is N, and $N = N_b + N_i$ where N_b and N_i denote the number of boundary nodes and interior nodes respectively, then

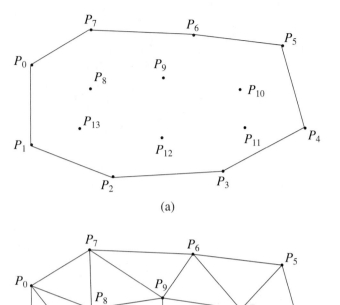

(a)

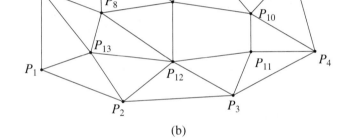

(b)

FIGURE 12.13: Delaunay mesh: (a) boundary nodes (P_0 to P_7) and interior nodes (P_8 to P_{13}); (b) triangular mesh obtained by constrained Delaunay triangulation.

the total number of triangles in the Delaunay mesh is $N_b + 2N_i - 2$. In the above figure, this sum is $8 + 2 \times 6 - 2 = 18$.

Unlike a uniform mesh, the node locations in a Delaunay mesh are irregular; hence, they must be coded. By convention of MPEG-4, the location (x_0, y_0) of the top left boundary node[1] is coded first, followed by the other boundary points counterclockwise [see Figure 12.13(a)] or clockwise. Afterward, the locations of the interior nodes are coded in any order.

Except for the first location (x_0, y_0), all subsequent coordinates are coded differentially — that is, for $n \geq 1$,

$$dx_n = x_n - x_{n-1}, \qquad dy_n = y_n - y_{n-1}, \qquad (12.6)$$

and afterward, dx_n, dy_n are variable-length coded.

---

[1] The top left boundary node is defined as the one that has the minimum $x + y$ coordinate value. If more than one boundary node has the same $x + y$, the one with the minimum y is chosen.

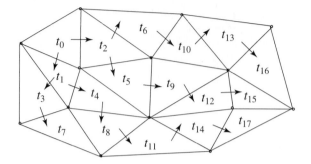

FIGURE 12.14: A breadth-first order of MOP triangles for 2D mesh motion coding.

2D Mesh Motion Coding.   The motion of each MOP triangle in either a uniform or Delaunay mesh is described by the motion vectors of its three vertex nodes. A new mesh structure can be created only in the intra-frame, and its triangular topology will not alter in the subsequent inter-frames. This enforces one-to-one mapping in 2D mesh motion estimation.

For any MOP triangle (P_i, P_j, P_k), if the motion vectors for P_i and P_j are known to be $\mathbf{MV_i}$ and $\mathbf{MV_j}$, then a prediction $\mathbf{Pred_k}$ will be made for the motion vector of P_k, rounded to a half-pixel precision:

$$\mathbf{Pred_k} = 0.5 \cdot (\mathbf{MV_i} + \mathbf{MV_j}). \qquad (12.7)$$

The prediction error $\mathbf{e_k}$ is coded as

$$\mathbf{e_k} = \mathbf{MV_k} - \mathbf{Pred_k}. \qquad (12.8)$$

Once the three motion vectors of the first MOP triangle t_0 are coded, at least one neighboring MOP triangle will share an edge with t_0, and the motion vector for its third vertex node can be coded, and so on.

The estimation of motion vectors will start at the *initial triangle* t_0, which is the triangle that contains the top left boundary node and the boundary node next to it, clockwise. Motion vectors for all other nodes in the MOP are coded differentially, according to Eq. (12.8). A breadth-first order is established for traversing the MOP triangles in the 2D mesh motion coding process.

Figure 12.14 shows how a spanning tree can be generated to obtain the breadth-first order of the triangles. As shown, the initial triangle t_0 has two neighboring triangles t_1 and t_2, which are not visited yet. They become child nodes of t_0 in the spanning tree.

Triangles t_1 and t_2, in turn, have their unvisited neighboring triangles (and hence child nodes) t_3, t_4, and t_5, t_6, respectively. The traverse order so far is t_0, t_1, t_2, t_3, t_4, t_5, in a breadth-first fashion. One level down the spanning tree, t_3 has only one child node t_7, since the other neighbor t_1 is already visited; t_4 has only one child node t_8; and so on.

2D Object Animation   The above mesh motion coding established a one-to-one mapping between the mesh triangles in the reference MOP and the target MOP. It generated motion vectors for all node points in the 2D mesh. Mesh-based texture mapping is now used to generate the texture for the new animated surface by warping [14] the texture of each triangle in the reference MOP onto the corresponding triangle in the target MOP. This facilitates the animation of 2D synthetic video objects.

For triangular meshes, a common mapping function for the warping is the *affine transform*, since it maps a line to a line and can guarantee that a triangle is mapped to a triangle. It will be shown below that given the six vertices of the two matching triangles, the parameters for the affine transform can be obtained, so that the transform can be applied to all points within the target triangle for texture mapping.

Given a point $\mathbf{P} = (x, y)$ on a 2D plane, a *linear transform* can be specified, such that

$$[x' \ y'] = [x \ y] \begin{bmatrix} a_{11} & a_{12} \\ a_{21} & a_{22} \end{bmatrix} \tag{12.9}$$

A transform T is linear if $T(\alpha \mathbf{X} + \beta \mathbf{Y}) = \alpha T(\mathbf{X}) + \beta T(\mathbf{Y})$, where α and β are scalars. The above linear transform is suitable for geometric operations such as rotation and scaling but not to translation, since addition of a constant vector is not possible.

Definiton 2: A transform A is an *affine transform* if and only if there exists a vector $\mathbf{C}$ and a linear transform T such that $A(\mathbf{X}) = T(\mathbf{X}) + \mathbf{C}$.

If the point (x, y) is represented as $[x, y, 1]$ in the homogeneous coordinate system commonly used in graphics [18], then an *affine transform* that transforms $[x, y, 1]$ to $[x', y', 1]$ is defined as:

$$[x' \ y' \ 1] = [x \ y \ 1] \begin{bmatrix} a_{11} & a_{12} & 0 \\ a_{21} & a_{22} & 0 \\ a_{31} & a_{32} & 1 \end{bmatrix}. \tag{12.10}$$

It realizes the following mapping:

$$x' = a_{11}x + a_{21}y + a_{31} \tag{12.11}$$
$$y' = a_{12}x + a_{22}y + a_{32} \tag{12.12}$$

and has at most 6 degrees of freedom represented by the parameters $a_{11}, a_{21}, a_{31}, a_{12}, a_{22}, a_{32}$.

The following 3×3 matrices are the affine transforms for translating by (T_x, T_y), rotating counterclockwise by θ, and scaling by factors S_x and S_y:

$$\begin{bmatrix} 1 & 0 & 0 \\ 0 & 1 & 0 \\ T_x & T_y & 1 \end{bmatrix}, \quad \begin{bmatrix} \cos\theta & \sin\theta & 0 \\ -\sin\theta & \cos\theta & 0 \\ 0 & 0 & 1 \end{bmatrix}, \quad \begin{bmatrix} S_x & 0 & 0 \\ 0 & S_y & 0 \\ 0 & 0 & 1 \end{bmatrix}$$

The following are the affine transforms for sheering along the x-axis and y-axis, respectively:

$$\begin{bmatrix} 1 & 0 & 0 \\ H_x & 1 & 0 \\ 0 & 0 & 1 \end{bmatrix}, \quad \begin{bmatrix} 1 & H_y & 0 \\ 0 & 1 & 0 \\ 0 & 0 & 1 \end{bmatrix}$$

where H_x and H_y are constants determining the degree of sheering.

The above simple affine transforms can be combined (by matrix multiplications) to yield composite affine transforms — for example, for a translation followed by a rotation, or a sheering followed by other transforms.

It can be proven (see Exercise 7) that any composite transform thus generated will have exactly the same matrix form and will have at most 6 degrees of freedom, specified by a_{11}, a_{21}, a_{31}, a_{12}, a_{22}, a_{32}.

If the triangle in the target MOP is

$$(\mathbf{P_0}, \mathbf{P_1}, \mathbf{P_2}) = ((x_0, y_0), (x_1, y_1), (x_2, y_2))$$

and the matching triangle in the reference MOP is

$$(\mathbf{P'_0}, \mathbf{P'_1}, \mathbf{P'_2}) = ((x'_0, y'_0), (x'_1, y'_1), (x'_2, y'_2)),$$

then the mapping between the two triangles can be uniquely defined by the following:

$$\begin{bmatrix} x'_0 & y'_0 & 1 \\ x'_1 & y'_1 & 1 \\ x'_2 & y'_2 & 1 \end{bmatrix} = \begin{bmatrix} x_0 & y_0 & 1 \\ x_1 & y_1 & 1 \\ x_2 & y_2 & 1 \end{bmatrix} \begin{bmatrix} a_{11} & a_{12} & 0 \\ a_{21} & a_{22} & 0 \\ a_{31} & a_{32} & 1 \end{bmatrix} \quad (12.13)$$

Eq. (12.13) contains six linear equations (three for x's and three for y's) required to resolve the six unknown coefficients a_{11}, a_{21}, a_{31}, a_{12}, a_{22}, a_{32}. Let Eq. (12.13) be stated as $\mathbf{X'} = \mathbf{X}A$. Then it is known that $A = \mathbf{X}^{-1}\mathbf{X'}$, with inverse matrix given by $\mathbf{X}^{-1} = adj(\mathbf{X})/det(\mathbf{X})$, where $adj(\mathbf{X})$ is the adjoint of $\mathbf{X}$ and $det(\mathbf{X})$ is the determinant. Therefore,

$$\begin{bmatrix} a_{11} & a_{12} & 0 \\ a_{21} & a_{22} & 0 \\ a_{31} & a_{32} & 1 \end{bmatrix} = \begin{bmatrix} x_0 & y_0 & 1 \\ x_1 & y_1 & 1 \\ x_2 & y_2 & 1 \end{bmatrix}^{-1} \begin{bmatrix} x'_0 & y'_0 & 1 \\ x'_1 & y'_1 & 1 \\ x'_2 & y'_2 & 1 \end{bmatrix}$$

$$= \frac{1}{det(\mathbf{X})} \begin{bmatrix} y_1 - y_2 & y_2 - y_0 & y_0 - y_1 \\ x_2 - x_1 & x_0 - x_2 & x_1 - x_0 \\ x_1 y_2 - x_2 y_1 & x_2 y_0 - x_0 y_2 & x_0 y_1 - x_1 y_0 \end{bmatrix} \begin{bmatrix} x'_0 & y'_0 & 1 \\ x'_1 & y'_1 & 1 \\ x'_2 & y'_2 & 1 \end{bmatrix} \quad (12.14)$$

where $det(\mathbf{X}) = x_0(y_1 - y_2) - y_0(x_1 - x_2) + (x_1 y_2 - x_2 y_1)$.

Since the three vertices of the mesh triangle are never colinear points, it is ensured that $\mathbf{X}$ is not singular — that is, $det(\mathbf{X}) \neq 0$. Therefore Eq. (12.14) always has a unique solution.

The above affine transform is piecewise — that is, each triangle can have its own affine transform. It works well only when the object is mildly deformed during the animation sequence. Figure 12.15(a) shows a Delaunay mesh with a simple word mapped onto it. Figure 12.15(b) shows the warped word in a subsequent MOP in the animated sequence after an affine transform.

12.3.2 3D Model-based Coding

Because of the frequent appearances of human faces and bodies in videos, MPEG-4 has defined special 3D models for *face objects* and *body objects*. Some of the potential applications for these new video objects include teleconferencing, human–computer interfaces, games, and e-commerce. In the past, 3D wireframe models and their animations have been

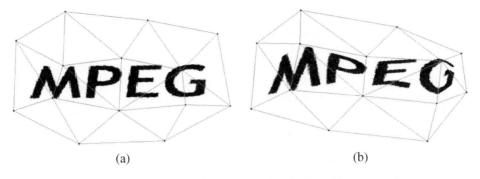

(a)   (b)

FIGURE 12.15: Mesh-based texture mapping for 2D object animation.

studied for 3D object animation [19]. MPEG-4 goes beyond wireframes, so that the surfaces of the face or body objects can be shaded or texture-mapped.

Face Object Coding and Animation.   Face models for individual faces could either be created manually or generated automatically through computer vision and pattern recognition techniques. However, the former is cumbersome and nevertheless inadequate, and the latter has yet to be achieved reliably.

MPEG-4 has adopted a generic default face model, developed by the Virtual Reality Modeling Language (VRML) Consortium [20]. *Face Animation Parameters (FAPs)* can be specified to achieve desirable animations — deviations from the original "neutral" face. In addition, *Face Definition Parameters (FDPs)* can be specified to better describe individual faces. Figure 12.16 shows the feature points for FDPs. Feature points that can be affected by animation (FAPs) are shown as solid circles; and those that are not affected are shown as empty circles.

Sixty-eight FAPs are defined [16]: FAP 1 is for visemes and FAP 2 for facial expressions.

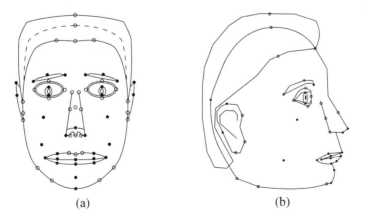

(a)   (b)

FIGURE 12.16: Feature points for face definition parameters (FDPs). (Feature points for teeth and tongue are not shown.)

Visemes code highly realistic lip motions by modeling the speaker's current mouth position. All other FAPs are for possible movements of head, jaw, lip, eyelid, eyeball, eyebrow, pupil, chin, cheek, tongue, nose, ear, and so on.

For example, expressions include *neutral, joy, sadness, anger, fear, disgust and surprise.* Each is expressed by a set of features — sadness for example, by slightly closed eyes, relaxed mouth, and upward-bent inner eyebrows. FAPs for movement include *head_pitch, head_yaw, head_roll, open_jaw, thrust_jaw, shift_jaw, push_bottom_lip, push_top_lip,* and so on.

For compression, the FAPs are coded using predictive coding. Predictions for FAPs in the target frame are made based on FAPs in the previous frame, and prediction errors are then coded using arithmetic coding. DCT can also be employed to improve the compression ratio, although it is considered more computationally expensive. FAPs are also quantized, with different quantization step sizes employed to explore the fact that certain FAPs (e.g., open_jaw) need less precision than others (e.g., push_top_lip).

Body Object Coding and Animation.   MPEG-4 Version 2 introduced *body objects,* which are a natural extension to face objects.

Working with the Humanoid Animation (H-Anim) Group in the VRML Consortium, MPEG adopted a generic virtual human body with default posture. The default is standing, with feet pointing to the front, arms at the sides, with palms facing inward. There are 296 *Body Animation Parameters* (BAPs). When applied to any MPEG-4-compliant generic body, they will produce the same animation.

A large number of BAPs describe joint angles connecting different body parts, including the spine, shoulder, clavicle, elbow, wrist, finger, hip, knee, ankle, and toe. This yields 186 degrees of freedom to the body, 25 to each hand alone. Furthermore, some body movements can be specified in multiple levels of detail. For example, five different levels, supporting 9, 24, 42, 60, and 72 degrees of freedom can be used for the spine, depending on the complexity of the animation.

For specific bodies, *Body Definition Parameters* (BDPs) can be specified for body dimensions, body surface geometry, and, optionally, texture. Body surface geometry uses a *3D polygon mesh* representation, consisting of a set of polygonal planar surfaces in 3D space [18]. The 3D mesh representation is popular in computer graphics for surface modeling. Coupled with texture mapping, it can deliver good (photorealistic) renderings.

The coding of BAPs is similar to that of FAPs: quantization and predictive coding are used, and the prediction errors are further compressed by arithmetic coding.

12.4 MPEG-4 OBJECT TYPES, PROFILES AND LEVELS

Like MPEG-2, MPEG-4 defines many Profiles and Levels for various applications. The standardization of profiles and levels in MPEG-4 serves two main purposes: ensuring interoperability between implementations and allowing testing of conformance to the standard. MPEG-4 not only specified Visual profiles (Part 2 [2]) and Audio profiles (Part 3 [2]) but also Graphics profiles, Scene description profiles, and one Object descriptor profile in its Systems part (Part 1 [2]). We will briefly describe the Visual profiles in this section.

Since MPEG-4 scenes often contain more than one video object, the concept of *object*

TABLE 12.1: Tools for MPEG-4 natural visual object types.

	Object types					
Tools	Simple	Core	Main	Simple scalable	N-bit	Scalable still texture
Basic MC-based tools	*	*	*	*	*	
B-VOP		*	*	*	*	
Binary shape coding		*	*		*	
Gray-level shape coding			*			
Sprite			*			
Interlace			*			
Temporal scalability (P-VOP)		*	*		*	
Spatial and temporal scalability (rectangular VOP)				*		
N-bit					*	
Scalable still texture						*
Error resilience	*	*	*	*	*	

type is introduced, to define the tools needed to create video objects and the ways they can be combined in a scene. Table 12.1 shows the various tools applicable to the MPEG-4 natural visual object types.[2] For example, for object type "core", only five tools are used. Tools such as "gray-level shape coding", "sprite", "interlace", and so on, will not be used.

Table 12.2 shows these object types in MPEG-4 visual profiles. Main profile, for example, supports only object types "simple", "core", "main", and "scalable still texture".

Table 12.3 lists the levels supported by the three most commonly used Visual profiles: simple, core, and main. For example, although CIF (352×288) is supported in four different levels (levels 2 and 3 in simple profile, level 2 in Core profile, and level 1 in Main profile), very different bitrates and maximum numbers of objects are specified. Hence, different qualities for CIF videos would be expected.

12.5   MPEG-4 PART10/H.264

The Joint Video Team (JVT) of ISO/IEC MPEG and ITU-T VCEG (Video Coding Experts Group) developed the H.264 video compression standard, which was scheduled to be completed by March 2003. It was formerly known by its working title "H.26L." Preliminary studies using software based on this new standard suggests that H.264 offers up to 50% better compression than MPEG-2 and up to 30% better than H.263+ and MPEG-4 advanced simple profile.

---

[2]We have not listed the MPEG-4 synthetic visual object types, which include animated 2D mesh, simple face, simple body, and so on.

TABLE 12.2: MPEG-4 Natural Visual Object Types and Profiles

Object types	Profiles					
	Simple	Core	Main	Simple Scalable	N-bit	Scalable Texture
Simple	*	*	*	*	*	
Core		*	*		*	
Main			*			
Simple scalable				*		
N-bit					*	
Scalable still texture			*			*

TABLE 12.3: MPEG-4 Levels in Simple, Core, and Main Visual Profiles

Profile	Level	Typical picture size	Bitrate (bits/sec)	Max number of objects
Simple	1	176 × 144 (QCIF)	64 k	4
	2	352 × 288 (CIF)	128 k	4
	3	352 × 288 (CIF)	384 k	4
Core	1	176 × 144 (QCIF)	384 k	4
	2	352 × 288 (CIF)	2 M	16
Main	1	352 × 288 (CIF)	2 M	16
	2	720 × 576 (CCIR601)	15 M	32
	3	1920 × 1080 (HDTV)	38.4 M	32

The outcome of this work is actually two identical standards: ISO MPEG-4 Part 10 and ITU-T H.264. With its superior compression performance over MPEG-2, H.264 is currently one of the leading candidates to carry HDTV video content on many potential applications. The following sections give a brief overview of this new standard in accordance with [21].

12.5.1 Core Features

Similar to the previous ITU-T H.263+, H.264 specifies a block-based, motion-compensated transform hybrid decoder with five major blocks:

- Entropy decoding

- Motion compensation or intra-prediction

- Inverse scan, quantization, and transform of residual pixels

- Reconstruction

- In-loop deblocking filter on reconstructed pixels

Each picture can again be separated into macroblocks (16×16 blocks), and arbitrary-sized slices can group multiple macroblocks into self-contained units.

VLC-Based Entropy Decoding.   Two entropy methods are used in the variable-length entropy decoder: Unified-VLC (UVLC) and Context Adaptive VLC (CAVLC). UVLC uses simple exponential Golomb codes to decode header data, motion vectors, and other nonresidual data, while the more complex CAVLC decodes residual coefficients.

In CAVLC, multiple VLC tables are predefined for each data type (runs, levels, etc.), and predefined rules predict the optimal VLC table based on the context (previously decoded symbols). CAVLC allows multiple statistical models to be used for each data type and improves entropy coding efficiently over existing fixed VLC, such as in H.263+.

Motion Compensation (P-Prediction).   Inter-frame motion compensation in H.264 is similar to H.263+ but more sophisticated. Instead of limiting motion-compensation block size to either 16×16 or 8×8, as in H.263+, H.264 uses a tree-structured motion segmentation down to 4×4 block size (16×16, 16×8, 8×16, 8×8, 8×4, 4×8, 4×4). This allows much more accurate motion compensation of moving objects.

Furthermore, motion vectors in H.264 can be up to sample accuracy. A six-tap sink filter is used for half-pixel interpolation, to preserve high frequency. Simple averaging is used for quarter-pixel interpolation, which provides not only more accurate motion but also a lower-pass filter than the half-pixel. Multiple reference frames are also a standard feature in H.264, so that the ability to choose a different reference frame for each macroblock is available in all profiles.

Intra-Prediction (I-Prediction).   H.264 exploits much more spatial prediction than in previous video standards such as H.263+. Intra- coded macroblocks are all predicted using neighboring reconstructed pixels (using both intra- and inter- coded reconstructed pixels). Similar to motion compensation, different block sizes can be chosen for each intra- coded macroblock (16×16 or 4×4). There are nine prediction modes for 4×4 blocks (where each 4×4 block in a macroblock can have a different prediction mode) and four prediction modes for 16×16 blocks. This sophisticated intra-prediction is powerful as it drastically reduces the amount of data to be transmitted when temporal prediction fails.

Transform, Scan, Quantization.   Given the powerful and accurate P- and I- prediction schemes in H.264, it is recognized that the spatial correlation in residual pixels is typically very low. Hence, a simple integer-precision 4×4 DCT is sufficient to compact the energy. The integer arithmetic allows exact inverse transform on all processors and eliminates encoder/decoder mismatch problems in previous transform-based codecs. H.264 also provides a quantization scheme with nonlinear *step-size*s to obtain accurate rate control at both the high and low ends of the quantization scale.

In-Loop Deblocking Filters. H.264 specifies a sophisticated signal-adaptive deblocking filter in which a set of filters is applied on 4×4 block edges. Filter length, strength, and type (deblocking/smoothing) vary, depending on macroblock coding parameters (intra- or inter- coded, motion-vector differences, reference-frame differences, coefficients coded) and spatial activity (edge detection), so that blocking artifacts are eliminated without distorting visual features. The H.264 deblocking filter is important in increasing the subjective quality of the standard.

12.5.2 Baseline Profile Features

The Baseline profile of H.264 is intended for real-time conversational applications, such as videoconferencing. It contains all the core coding tools of H.264 discussed above and the following additional error-resilience tools, to allow for error-prone carriers such as IP and wireless networks:

- **Arbitrary slice order (ASO).** The decoding order of slices within a picture may not follow monotonic increasing order. This allows decoding of out-of-order packets in a packet-switched network thus reducing latency.

- **Flexible macroblock order (FMO).** Macroblocks can be decoded in any order, such as checkerboard patterns, not just raster scan order. This is useful on error-prone networks, so that loss of a slice results in loss of macroblocks scattered in the picture, which can easily be masked from human eyes. This feature can also help reduce jitter and latency, as the decoder may decide not to wait for late slices and still be able to produce acceptable pictures.

- **Redundant slices**. Redundant copies of the slices can be decoded, to further improve error resilience.

12.5.3 Main Profile Features

The Main profile defined by H.264 represents non-low-delay applications such as broadcasting and stored-medium. The Main profile contains all Baseline profile features (except ASO, FMO, and redundant slices) plus the following non-low-delay and higher complexity features, for maximum compression efficiency:

- **B slices**. The bi-prediction mode in H.264 has been made more flexible than in existing standards. Bi-predicted pictures can also be used as reference frames. Two reference frames for each macroblock can be in any temporal direction, as long as they are available in the reference frame buffer. Hence, in addition to the normal forward + backward bi-prediction, it is legal to have backward + backward or forward + forward prediction as well.

- **Context Adaptive Binary Arithmetic Coding (CABAC)**. This coding mode replaces VLC-based entropy coding with binary arithmetic coding that uses a different adaptive statistics model for different data types and contexts.

- **Weighted Prediction**. Global weights (multiplier and an offset) for modifying the motion-compensated prediction samples can be specified for each slice, to predict lighting changes and other global effects, such as fading.

12.5.4   Extended Profile Features

The eXtended profile (or profile X) is designed for the new video streaming applications. This profile allows non-low-delay features, bitstream switching features, and also more error-resilience tools. It includes all Baseline profile features plus the following:

- B slices

- Weighted prediction

- **Slice data partitioning**. This partitions slice data with different importance into separate sequences (header information, residual information) so that more important data can be transmitted on more reliable channels.

- **SP and SI slice types**. These are slices that contain special temporal prediction modes, to allow bitstream switching, fast forward/backward, and random access.

The vastly improved H.264 core features, together with new coding tools offer significant improvement in compression ratio, error resiliency, and subjective quality over existing ITU-T and MPEG standards.

12.6   MPEG-7

As more and more multimedia content becomes an integral part of various applications, effective and efficient retrieval becomes a primary concern. In October 1996, the MPEG group therefore took on the development of another major standard, MPEG-7, following on MPEG-1, 2, and 4.

One common ground between MPEG-4 and MPEG-7 is the focus on audiovisual *objects*. The main objective of MPEG-7 [22] is to serve the need of audiovisual content-based retrieval (or audiovisual object retrieval) in applications such as digital libraries. Nevertheless, it is certainly not limited to retrieval — it is applicable to any multimedia applications involving the generation (*content creation*) and usage (*content consumption*) of multimedia data.

MPEG-7 became an international standard in September 2001. Its formal name is *Multimedia Content Description Interface*, documented in ISO/IEC 15938 [23]. The standard's seven parts are Systems, Description Definition Language, Visual, Audio, Multimedia Description Schemes, Reference Software, and Conformance.

MPEG-7 supports a variety of multimedia applications. Its data may include still pictures, graphics, 3D models, audio, speech, video, and composition information (how to combine these elements). These MPEG-7 data elements can be represented in textual or binary format, or both. Part 1 (Systems) specifies the syntax of *Binary format for MPEG-7* (BiM) data. Part 2 (Description Definition Language) specifies the syntax of the textual format which adopts XML Schema as its language of choice. A bidirectional lossless mapping is defined between the textual and binary representations.

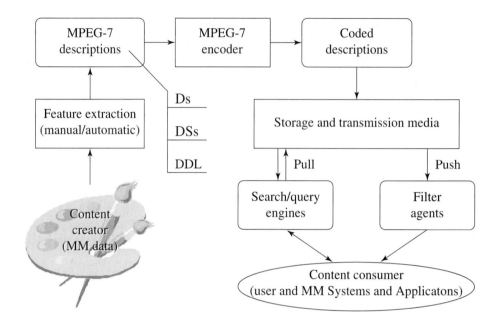

FIGURE 12.17: Possible Applications using MPEG-7.

Figure 12.17 illustrates some possible applications that will benefit from MPEG-7. As shown, features are extracted and used to instantiate MPEG-7 *descriptions*. They are then coded by the MPEG-7 encoder and sent to the *storage and transmission media*. Various search and query engines issue search and browsing requests, which constitute the *pull* activities of the Internet, whereas the agents filter out numerous materials *pushed* onto the *terminal* — users and/or computer systems and applications that consume the data.

For multimedia content description, MPEG-7 has developed *Descriptors* (D), *Description Schemes* (DS), and a *Description Definition Language* (DDL). Following are some of the important terms:

- **Feature**. A characteristic of the data

- **Descriptor (D)**. A definition (syntax and semantics) of the feature

- **Description Scheme (DS)**. Specification of the structure and relationship between Ds and DSs (see [24])

- **Description**.   A set of instantiated Ds and DSs that describes the structural and conceptual information of the content, storage and usage of the content, and so on

- **Description Definition Language (DDL)**. Syntactic rules to express and combine DSs and Ds (see [25])

It is made clear [23] that the scope of MPEG-7 is to standardize the Ds, DSs and DDL for descriptions. The mechanism and process of producing and consuming the descriptions are beyond the scope of MPEG-7. These are left open for industry innovation and competition and, more importantly, for the arrival of ever-improving new technologies.

Similar to the Simulation Model (SM) in MPEG-1 video, the Test Model (TM) in MPEG-2 video, and the Verification Models (VMs) in MPEG-4 (video, audio, SNHC, and systems), MPEG-7 names its working model the *Experimentation Model (XM)* — an alphabetical pun! XM provides descriptions of various tools for evaluating the Ds, DSs and DDL, so that experiments and verifications can be conducted and compared by multiple independent parties all over the world. The first set of such experiments is called the *core experiments*.

12.6.1 Descriptor (D)

MPEG-7 descriptors are designed to describe both low-level features, such as color, texture, shape, and motion, and high-level features of semantic objects, such as events and abstract concepts. As mentioned above, methods and processes for automatic and even semiautomatic feature extraction are not part of the standard. Despite the efforts and progress in the fields of image and video processing, computer vision, and pattern recognition, automatic and reliable feature extraction is not expected in the near future, especially at the high level.

The descriptors are chosen based on a comparison of their performance, efficiency, and size. Low-level visual descriptors for basic visual features [26] include

- **Color**

    - **Color space**. (a) RGB, (b) YCbCr, (c) HSV (hue, saturation, value) [18], (d) HMMD (HueMaxMinDiff) [27], (e) 3D color space derivable by a 3×3 matrix from RGB, (f) monochrome

    - **Color quantization**. (a) Linear, (b) nonlinear, (c) lookup tables

    - **Dominant colors**. A small number of representative colors in each region or image. These are useful for image retrieval based on color similarity

    - **Scalable color**. A color histogram in HSV color space. It is encoded by a Haar transform and hence is scalable

    - **Color layout**. Spatial distribution of colors for color-layout-based retrieval

    - **Color structure**. The frequency of a *color structuring element* describes both the color content and its structure in the image. The color structure element is composed of several image samples in a local neighborhood that have the same color

    - **Group of Frames/Group of Pictures (GoF/GoP) color**. Similar to the scalable color, except this is applied to a video segment or a group of still images. An aggregated color histogram is obtained by the application of *average, median*, or *intersection* operations to the respective bins of all color histograms in the GoF/GoP and is then sent to the Haar transform

- **Texture**

    - **Homogeneous texture**. Uses orientation and scale-tuned Gabor filters [28] that quantitatively represent regions of homogeneous texture. The advantage of

Gabor filters is that they provide simultaneous optimal resolution in both space and spatial-frequency domains [29]. Also, they are bandpass filters that conform to the human visual profile. A filter bank consisting of 30 Gabor filters, at five different scales and six different directions for each scale, is used to extract the texture descriptor

- **Texture browsing**. Describes the *regularity*, *coarseness*, and *directionality* of edges used to represent and browse homogeneous textures [30]. Again, Gabor filters are used

- **Edge histogram**. Represents the spatial distribution of four directional ($0°$, $45°$, $90°$, $135°$) edges and one nondirectional edge. Images are divided into small subimages, and an edge histogram with five bins is generated for each subimage

- **Shape**

  - **Region-based shape**. A set of *Angular Radial Transform* (ART) [31] coefficients is used to describe an object's shape. An object can consist of one or more regions, with possibly some holes in the object. ART transform is a 2D complex transform defined in terms of polar coordinates on a unit disc. ART basis functions are separable along the angular and radial dimensions. Thirty-six basis functions, 12 angular and three radial, are used to extract the shape descriptor

  - **Contour-based shape**. Uses a *curvature scale space* (CSS) representation [32] that is invariant to scale and rotation, and robust to nonrigid motion and partial occlusion of the shape

  - **3D shape**. Describes 3D mesh models and *shape index* [33]. The histogram of the shape indices over the entire mesh is used as the descriptor

- **Motion**

  - **Camera motion**. Fixed, pan, tilt, roll, dolly, track, boom. (See Fig 12.18 and [34].)

  - **Object motion trajectory**. A list of keypoints (x, y, z, t). Optional interpolation functions are used to specify the acceleration along the path. (See [34].)

  - **Parametric object motion**. The basic model is the 2D affine model for translation, rotation, scaling, sheering, and the combination of these. A planar perspective model and quadratic model can be used for perspective distortion and more complex movements

  - **Motion activity**. Provides descriptions such as the intensity, pace, mood, and so on, of the video — for example, "scoring in a hockey game" or "interviewing a person"

- **Localization**

  - **Region locator**. Specifies the localization of regions in images with a box or a polygon

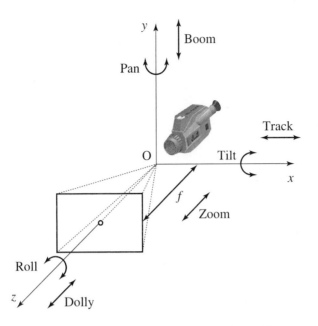

FIGURE 12.18: Camera motions: pan, tilt, roll, dolly, track, and boom. (Camera has an effective focal length of f. It is shown initially at the origin, pointing to the direction of z-axis.)

- **Spatiotemporal locator**. Describes spatiotemporal regions in video sequences. Uses one or more sets of descriptors of regions and their motions

- **Others**

    - **Face recognition**. A normalized face image is represented as a 1D vector, then projected onto a set of 49 basis vectors, representing all possible face vectors

12.6.2 Description Scheme (DS)

This section provides a brief overview of MPEG-7 Description Schemes (DSs) in the areas of Basic elements, Content management, Content description, Navigation and access, Content organization, and User interaction.

- **Basic elements**

    - **Datatypes and mathematical structures**. Vectors, matrices, histograms, and so on

    - **Constructs**. Links media files and localizing segments, regions, and so on

    - **Schema tools**. Includes root elements (starting elements of MPEG-7 XML documents and descriptions), top-level elements (organizing DSs for specific content-oriented descriptions), and package tools (grouping related DS components of a description into packages)

- **Content Management**

  – **Media Description**. Involves a single DS, the *MediaInformation* DS, composed of a *MediaIdentification* D and one or more *Media Profile* Ds that contain information such as coding method, transcoding hints, storage and delivery formats, and so on

  – **Creation and Production Description**. Includes information about creation (title, creators, creation location, date, etc.), classification (genre, language, parental guidance, etc.), and related materials

  – **Content Usage Description**. Various DSs to provide information about usage rights, usage record, availability, and finance (cost of production, income from content use)

- **Content Description**

  – **Structural Description**. A *Segment* DS describes structural aspects of the content. A *segment* is a section of an audiovisual object. The relationship among segments is often represented as a *segment tree*. When the relationship is not purely hierarchical, a *segment graph* is used

  The *Segment* DS can be implemented as a class object. It has five subclasses: *Audiovisual segment DS*, *Audio segment DS*, *Still region DS*, *Moving region DS*, and *Video segment DS*. The subclass DSs can recursively have their own subclasses

  A Still region DS, for example, can be used to describe an image in terms of its creation (title, creator, date), usage (copyright), media (file format), textual annotation, color histogram, and possibly texture descriptors, and so on. The initial region (image, in this case) can be further decomposed into several regions, which can in turn have their own DSs.

  Figure 12.19 shows a Video segment for a marine rescue mission, in which a person was lowered onto a boat from a helicopter. Three moving regions are inside the Video segment. A segment graph can be constructed to include such structural descriptions as composition of the video frame (helicopter, person, boat) spatial relationship and motion (above, on, close-to, move-toward, etc.) of the regions

  – **Conceptual Description**. This involves higher-level (nonstructural) description of the content, such as *Event* DS for basketball game or Lakers ballgame, *Object* DS for John or person, *State* DS for semantic properties at a given time or location, and *Concept* DS for abstract notations such as "freedom" or "mystery". As for Segment DSs, the concept DSs can also be organized in a tree or graph

- **Navigation and access**

  – **Summaries**. These provide a video summary for quick browsing and navigation of the content, usually by presenting only the keyframes. The following DSs are supported: *Summarization* DS, *HierarchicalSummary* DS, *HighlightLevel* DS,

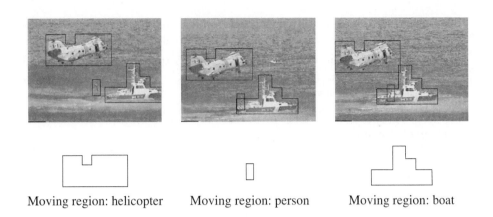

Moving region: helicopter   Moving region: person   Moving region: boat

FIGURE 12.19: MPEG-7 video segment. (This figure also appears in the color insert section.)

SequentialSummary DS. Hierarchical summaries provide a keyframe hierarchy of multiple levels, whereas sequential summaries often provide a slide show or audiovisual skim, possibly with synchronized audio and text

Figure 12.20 illustrates a summary for a video of a "dragon-boat" parade and race in a park. The summary is organized in a three-level hierarchy. Each video segment at each level is depicted by a keyframe of thumb-nail size

- **Partitions and Decompositions**. This refers to *view* partitions and decompositions. The *View partitions* (specified by *View* DSs) describe different space and frequency views of the audiovisual data, such as a spatial view (this could be a spatial segment of an image), temporal view (as in a temporal segment of a video), frequency view (as in a wavelet subband of an image), or resolution view (as in a thumbnail image), and so on. The *View decompositions* DSs

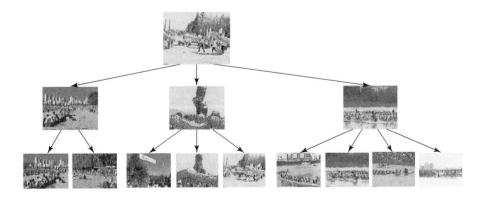

FIGURE 12.20: A video summary.

specify different tree or graph decompositions for organizing the views of the audiovisual data, such as a SpaceTree DS (a quad-tree image decomposition)

- **Variations of the Content**. A *Variation* DS specifies a variation from the original data in image resolution, frame rate, color reduction, compression, and so on. It can be used by servers to adapt audiovisual data delivery to network and terminal characteristics for a given Quality of Service (QoS)

- **Content Organization**

  - **Collections**. The *CollectionStructure* DS groups audiovisual contents into clusters. It specifies common properties of the cluster elements and relationships among the clusters.

  - **Models**. *Model* DSs include a Probability model DS, Analytic model DS, and Classifier DS that extract the models and statistics of the attributes and features of the collections.

- **User Interaction**

  - **UserPreference**. DSs describe user preferences in the consumption of audiovisual contents, such as content types, browsing modes, privacy characteristics, and whether preferences can be altered by an agent that analyzes user behavior.

12.6.3   Description Definition Language (DDL)

MPEG-7 adopted the XML Schema Language initially developed by the WWW Consortium (W3C) as its Description Definition Language (DDL). Since XML Schema Language was not designed specifically for audiovisual contents, some extensions are made to it. Without the details, the MPEG-7 DDL has the following components:

- **XML Schema structure components**

  - The Schema — the wrapper around definitions and declarations
  - Primary structural components, such as simple and complex type definitions, and attribute and element declarations
  - Secondary structural components, such as attribute group definitions, identity-constraint definitions, group definitions, and notation declarations
  - "Helper" components, such as annotations, particles, and wildcards

- **XML Schema datatype components**

  - Primitive and derived data types
  - Mechanisms for the user to derive new data types
  - Type checking better than XML 1.0

- **MPEG-7 Extensions**

  - Array and matrix data types

- Multiple media types, including audio, video, and audiovisual presentations
- Enumerated data types for `MimeType`, `CountryCode`, `RegionCode`, `CurrencyCode`, and `CharacterSetCode`
- *Intellectual Property Management and Protection* (IPMP) for Ds and DSs

12.7 MPEG-21

As we stepped into the new century (and millennium), multimedia had seen its ubiquitous use in almost all areas. An ever-increasing number of *content creators* and *content consumers* emerge daily in society. However, there is no uniform way to define, identify, describe, manage, and protect multimedia data as yet.

The development of the newest standard, *MPEG-21: Multimedia Framework* [35], started in June 2000. To quote from its draft Technical Report,

> "The *vision* for MPEG-21 is to define a multimedia framework to enable transparent and augmented use of multimedia resources across a wide range of networks and devices used by different communities."

The seven key elements in MPEG-21 are

- **Digital item declaration**, to establish a uniform and flexible abstraction and interoperable schema for declaring digital items.

- **Digital item identification and description**, to establish a framework for standardized identification and description of digital items, regardless of their origin, type, or granularity.

- **Content management and usage**, to provide an interface and protocol that facilitate management and use (searching, caching, archiving, distributing, etc.) of the content.

- **Intellectual property management and protection (IPMP)**, to enable contents to be reliably managed and protected.

- **Terminals and networks**, to provide interoperable and transparent access to content with Quality of Service (QoS) across a wide range of networks and terminals.

- **Content representation**, to represent content in an adequate way to pursuing the objective of MPEG-21, namely "content anytime anywhere".

- **Event reporting**, to establish metrics and interfaces for reporting *events* (user interactions), so as to understand performance and alternatives.

Most of the nine parts of MPEG-21 will become international standards by 2003. The development of MPEG-21 involved collaborative work with numerous other international organizations and standards bodies including W3C, Multiservice Switching Forum (MSF), Society of Motion Picture and Television Engineers (SMPTE), and Digital Audio Visual Council (DAVIC). The objective of the standard appears ambitious. It remains to be seen how effective and influential it will be compared to MPEG's earlier (extremely) successful standards.

12.8 FURTHER EXPLORATION

The books by Puri and Chen [3] and Pereira and Ebrahimi [36] provide an excellent collection of chapters with pertinent details of MPEG-4. An entire book edited by Manjunath, Salembier, and Sikora [37] is devoted to MPEG-7.

The Further Exploration section of the text web site for this chapter provides links to

- The MPEG home page

- The MPEG FAQ page

- Overviews, tutorials, and working documents of MPEG-4

- Tutorials on MPEG-4 Part 10/H.264

- Overviews of MPEG-7 and working documents for MPEG-21

- Documentation for XML schemas that form the basis of MPEG-7 DDL

12.9 EXERCISES

1. MPEG-4 motion compensation is supposed to be VOP-based. At the end, the VOP is still divided into macroblocks (interior macroblock, boundary macroblock, etc.) for motion compensation.

   (a) What are the potential problems of the current implementation? How can they be improved?
   (b) Can there be true VOP-based motion compensation? How would it compare to the current implementation?

2. MPEG-1, 2, and 4 are all known as decoder standards. The compression algorithms, hence the details of the encoder, are left open for future improvement and development. For MPEG-4, the major issue of *video object segmentation* — how to obtain the VOPs — is left unspecified.

   (a) Propose some of your own approaches to video object segmentation.
   (b) What are the potential problems of your approach?

3. Why was padding introduced in MPEG-4 VOP-based coding? Name some potential problems of padding.

4. Motion vectors can have subpixel precision. In particular, MPEG-4 allows quarter-pixel precision in the luminance VOPs. Describe an algorithm that will realize this precision.

5. As a programming project, compute the SA-DCT for the following 8×8 block:

$$
\begin{array}{cccccccc}
0 & 0 & 0 & 0 & 16 & 0 & 0 & 0 \\
4 & 0 & 8 & 16 & 32 & 16 & 8 & 0 \\
4 & 0 & 16 & 32 & 64 & 32 & 16 & 0 \\
0 & 0 & 32 & 64 & 128 & 64 & 32 & 0 \\
4 & 0 & 0 & 32 & 64 & 32 & 0 & 0 \\
0 & 16 & 0 & 0 & 32 & 0 & 0 & 0 \\
0 & 0 & 0 & 0 & 16 & 0 & 0 & 0 \\
0 & 0 & 0 & 0 & 0 & 0 & 0 & 0
\end{array}
$$

6. What is the computational cost of SA-DCT, compared to ordinary DCT? Assume the video object is a 4×4 square in the middle of an 8×8 block.

7. Affine transforms can be combined to yield a composite affine transform. Prove that the composite transform will have exactly the same form of matrix (with $[0\ 0\ 1]^T$ as the last column) and at most 6 degrees of freedom, specified by the parameters a_{11}, a_{21}, a_{31}, a_{12}, a_{22}, a_{32}.

8. Mesh-based motion coding works relatively well for 2D animation and face animation. What are the main problems when it is applied to body animation?

9. How does MPEG-4 perform VOP-based motion compensation? Outline the necessary steps and draw a block diagram illustrating the data flow.

10. What is the major motivation behind the development of MPEG-7? Give three examples of real-world applications that may benefit from MPEG-7.

11. Two of the main shape descriptors in MPEG-7 are "region-based" and "contour-based". There are, of course, numerous ways of describing the shape of regions and contours.

   (a) What would be your favorite shape descriptor?

   (b) How would it compare to ART and CSS in MPEG-7?

12.10 REFERENCES

1 T. Sikora, "The MPEG-4 Video Standard Verification Model," *IEEE Transactions on Circuits and Systems for Video Technology*, Special issue on MPEG-4, 7(1): 19–31, 1997.

2 *Information technology — Generic Coding of Audio-Visual Objects*, International Standard: ISO/IEC 14496, Parts 1–6, 1998.

3 A. Puri and T. Chen, eds.. *Multimedia Systems, Standards, and Networks*, New York: Marcel Dekker, 2000.

4 G. Fernando, et al., "Java in MPEG-4 (MPEG-J)," in *Multimedia, Systems, Standards, and Networks*, A. Puri and T. Chen, eds., New York: Marcel Dekker, 2000, p. 449–460.

5 *Video Coding for Low Bit Rate Communication*, ITU-T Recommendation H.263, Version 1, Nov. 1995, Version 2, Feb. 1998.

6 A. Puri, et al., "MPEG-4 Natural Video Coding — Part I," in *Multimedia, Systems, Standards, and Networks*, A. Puri and T. Chen, eds., New York: Marcel Dekker, 2000, p 205–244.

7 T. Ebrahimi, F. Dufaux, and Y. Nakaya, "MPEG-4 Natural Video Coding — Part II," in *Multimedia, Systems, Standards, and Networks*, A. Puri and T. Chen, eds., New York: Marcel Dekker, 2000, p. 245–269.

8 P. Kauff, et al., "Functional Coding of Video Using a Shape-Adaptive DCT Algorithm and an Object-Based Motion Prediction Toolbox," *IEEE Transactions on Circuits and Systems for Video Technology*, Special issue on MPEG-4, 7(1): 181–196, 1997.

9 J. Ostermann, E.S. Jang, J. Shin, and T. Chen, "Coding of Arbitrarily Shaped Video Objects in MPEG-4," in *Proceedings of the International Conference on Image Processing (ICIP '97)*, 1997.

10 *Standardization of Group 3 Facsimile Apparatus for Document Transmission*, ITU-T Recommendation T.4, 1980.

11 *Facsimile Coding Schemes and Coding Control Functions for Group 4 Facsimile Apparatus*, ITU-T Recommendation T.6, 1984.

12 *Information Technology — Coded Representation of Picture and Audio Information — Progressive Bi-Level Image Compression*, International Standard: ISO/IEC 11544, also ITU-T Recommendation T.82, 1992.

13 J.M. Shapiro, "Embedded Image Coding Using Zerotrees of Wavelet Coefficients," *IEEE Transactions on Signal Processing*, 41(12): 3445–3462, 1993.

14 G. Wolberg, *Digital Image Warping*, Los Alamitos, CA: Computer Society Press, 1990.

15 M.C. Lee, et al., "A Layered Video Object Coding System Using Sprite and Affine Motion Model," *IEEE Transactions on Circuits and Systems for Video Technology*, 7(1): 130–145, 1997.

16 P. van Beek, "MPEG-4 Synthetic Video," in *Multimedia, Systems, Standards, and Networks*, A. Puri and T. Chen, eds., New York: Marcel Dekker, 2000, pp. 299–330.

17 A.M. Tekalp, P. van Beek, C. Toklu, and B. Gunsel, "2D Mesh-Based Visual Object Representation for Interactive Synthetic/Natural Digital Video," *Proceedings of the IEEE*, 86: 1029–1051, 1998.

18 J.D. Foley, A. van Dam, S.K. Feiner, and J.F. Hughes, *Computer Graphics: Principles and Practice*, 2nd ed., Reading, MA: Addison-Wesley, 1990.

19 A. Watt and M. Watt, *Advanced Animation and Rendering Techniques*. Reading MA: Addison-Wesley, 1999.

20 *Information Technology — The Virtual Reality Modeling Language — Part 1: Functional Specification and UTF-8 Encoding*, International Standard: ISO/IEC 14772-1, 1997.

21 T. Wiegand, "JVT-F100: Study of Final Committee Draft of Joint Video Specification (ITU-T Rec. H.264 — ISO/IEC 14496-10 AVC), Draft 1d," in *Sixth Meeting of JVT of ISO/IEC MPEG and ITU-T VCEG*, 2002.

22 S.F. Chang, T. Sikora, and A. Puri, "Overview of the MPEG-7 Standard," *IEEE Transactions on Circuits and Systems for Video Technology*, Special issue on MPEG-7, 11(6): 688–695, 2001.

23 *Information Technology — Multimedia Content Description Interface*, International Standard: ISO/IEC 15938, Parts 1–6, 2001.

24 P. Salembier and J. R. Smith, "MPEG-7 Multimedia Description Schemes," *IEEE Transactions on Circuits Systems for Video Technology*, 11(6): 748–759, 2001.

25 J. Hunter and F. Nack, "An Overview of the MPEG-7 Description Definition Language (DDL) Proposals," *Signal Processing: Image Communication*, 16(1-2): 271–293, 2001.

26 T. Sikora, "The MPEG-7 Visual Standard for Content Description — An Overview," *IEEE Transactions on Circuits and Systems for Video Technology*, Special issue on MPEG-7, 11(6): 696–702, 2001.

27 B.S. Manjunath, J.-R. Ohm, V.V. Vasudevan, and A. Yamada, "Color and Texture Descriptors," *IEEE Transactions on Circuits Systems for Video Technology*, 11: 703–715, 2001.

28 B.S. Manjunath, G.M. Haley, and W.Y. Ma, "Multiband Techniques for Texture Classification and Segmentation," in *Handbook of Image and Video Processing*, A. Bovik, ed., San Diego: Academic Press, 2000, pp. 367–381.

29 T. P. Weldon, W. E. Higgins, and D. F. Dunn, "Efficient Gabor Filter Design for Texture Segmentation," *Pattern Recognition*, 29(12): 2005-2016, 1996.

30 P. Wu, B.S. Manjunath, S. Newsam, and H.D. Shin, "A Texture Descriptor for Browsing and Similarity Retrieval," *Signal Processing: Image Communication*, 16(1-2): 33–43, 2000.

31 P. Salembier and J. Smith, "Overview of MPEG-7 Multimedia Description Schemes and Schema Tools," in *Introduction to MPEG-7: Multimedia Content Description Interface*, B.S. Manjunath, P. Salembier, and T. Sikora, eds., New York: Wiley, 2002, Chapter 6.

32 F. Mokhtarian and A.K. Mackworth, "A Theory of Multiscale, Curvature-Based Shape Representation for Planar Curves," *IEEE Transsctions on Pattern Analysis and Machine Intelligence*,14(8): 789–805, 1992.

33 J.J. Koenderink and A.J. van Doorn, "Surface Shape and Curvature Scales," *Image and Vision Computing*, 10: 557–565, 1992.

34 S. Jeannin, et al., "Motion Descriptor for Content-Based Video Representation," *Signal Processing: Image Communication*, 16(1-2): 59–85, 2000.

35 *Information Technology – Multimedia Framework*, International Standard: ISO/IEC 21000, Parts 1–9, 2003.

36 F. Pereira and T. Ebrahimi, *The MPEG-4 Book*, Upper Saddle River, NJ: Prentice Hall, 2002.

37 B.S. Manjunath, P. Salembier, and T. Sikora, eds., *Introduction to MPEG-7: Multimedia Content Description Interface*, New York: Wiley, 2002.

CHAPTER 13

Basic Audio Compression Techniques

Compression of audio information is somewhat special in multimedia systems. Some of the techniques used are familiar, while others are new. In this chapter, we take a look at basic audio compression techniques applied to speech compression, setting out a general introduction to a large topic with a long history. More extensive information can be found in the References and Further Exploration sections at the end of the chapter.

In the next chapter, we consider the set of tools developed for general audio compression under the aegis of the Motion Picture Experts Group, MPEG. Since this is generally of high interest to readers focusing on multimedia, we treat that subject in greater detail.

To begin with, let us recall some of the issues covered in Chapter 6 on digital audio in multimedia, such as, the μ-law for companding audio signals. This is usually combined with a simple technique that exploits the temporal redundancy present in audio signals. We saw in Chapter 10, on video compression, that differences in signals between the present and a past time could very effectively reduce the size of signal values and, importantly, concentrate the histogram of pixel values (differences, now) into a much smaller range. The result of reducing the variance of values is that the entropy is greatly reduced, and subsequent Huffman coding can produce a greatly compressed bitstream.

The same applies here. Recall from Chapter 6 that quantized sampled output is called Pulse Code Modulation, or PCM. The differences version is called DPCM, and the adaptive version is called ADPCM. Variants that take into account speech properties follow from these.

In this chapter, we look at ADPCM, Vocoders, and more general Speech Compression: LPC, CELP, MBE, and MELP.

13.1 ADPCM IN SPEECH CODING

13.1.1 ADPCM

ADPCM forms the heart of the ITU's speech compression standards G.721, G.723, G.726, and G.727. (See the Further Exploration section for code for these standards.) The differences among these standards involve the bitrate and some details of the algorithm. The default input is μ-law-coded PCM 16-bit samples. Speech performance for ADPCM is such that the perceived quality of speech at 32 kbps is only slightly poorer than with the standard 64 kbps PCM transmission and is better than DPCM.

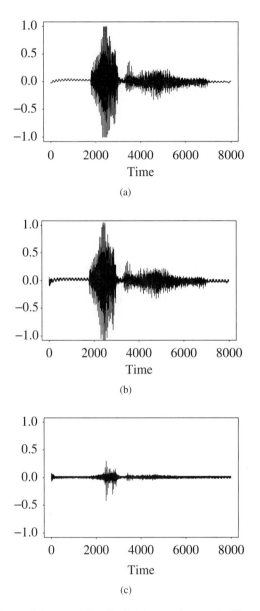

FIGURE 13.1: Waveform of the word "audio:" (a) speech sample, linear PCM at 8 kHz and 16 bits per sample; (b) speech sample, restored from G.721-compressed audio at 4 bits per sample; (c): difference signal between (a) and (b).

Figure 13.1 shows a 1-second speech sample of a voice speaking the word "audio." In Figure 13.1(a), the audio signal is stored as linear PCM (as opposed to the default μ-law PCM) recorded at 8,000 samples per second, with 16 bits per sample. After compression

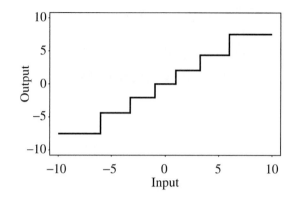

FIGURE 13.2: G.726 quantizer.

with ADPCM using standard G.721, the signal appears as in Figure 13.1(b). Figure 13.1(c) shows the difference between the actual and reconstructed, compressed signals. Although differences are apparent electronically between the two, the compressed and original signals are *perceptually* very similar.

13.2 G.726 ADPCM

ITU G.726 supersedes ITU standards G.721 and G.723. It provides another version of G.711, including companding, at a lower bitrate. G.726 can encode 13- or 14-bit PCM samples or 8-bit μ-law or A-law encoded data into 2-, 3-, 4-, or 5-bit codewords. It can be used in speech transmission over digital networks, videoconferencing, and ISDN communications.

The G.726 standard works by adapting a *fixed* quantizer in a simple way. The different sizes of codewords used amount to bitrates of 16 kbps, 24 kbps, 32 kbps, or 40 kbps, at an 8 kHz sampling rate. The standard defines a multiplier constant α that will change for every difference value e_n, depending on the current scale of signals. Define a scaled difference signal f_n as follows:

$$
\begin{aligned}
e_n &= s_n - \hat{s}_n \\
f_n &= e_n / \alpha
\end{aligned}
\tag{13.1}
$$

where $\hat{s}_n$ is the predicted signal value. f_n is then fed into the quantizer for quantization. The quantizer is as displayed in Figure 13.2. Here, the input value is defined as a ratio of a difference with the factor α.

By changing the value of α, the quantizer can adapt to change in the range of the difference signal. The quantizer is a nonuniform midtread quantizer, so it includes the value zero. The quantizer is *backward adaptive*.

A backward-adaptive quantizer works in principle by noticing if too many values are quantized to values far from zero (which would happen if the quantizer step size in f were too small) or if too many values fell close to zero too much of the time (which would happen if the quantizer step size were too large).

In fact, an algorithm due to Jayant [1] allows us to adapt a backward quantizer step size after receiving just one output! The Jayant quantizer simply expands the step size if the quantized input is in the outer levels of the quantizer and reduces the step size if the input is near zero.

Suppose we have a uniform quantizer, so that every range to which we compare input values is of size Δ. For example, for a 3-bit quantizer, there are $k = 0 .. 7$ levels. For 3-bit G.726, only 7 levels are used, grouped around zero.

The Jayant quantizer assigns *multiplier values* M_k to each level, with values smaller than 1 for levels near zero and values larger than 1 for outer levels. The multiplier multiplies the step size for the next signal value. That way, outer values enlarge the step size and are likely to bring the next quantized value back to the middle of the available levels. Quantized values near the middle reduce the step size and are likely to bring the next quantized value closer to the outer levels.

So, for signal f_n, the quantizer step size Δ is changed according to the quantized value k, for the previous signal value f_{n-1}, by the simple formula

$$\Delta \leftarrow M_k \Delta \tag{13.2}$$

Since the *quantized* version of the signal is driving the change, this is indeed a backward-adaptive quantizer.

In G.726, how α is allowed to change depends on whether the audio signal is actually speech or is likely data that is simply using a voice band. In the former case, sample-to-sample differences can fluctuate a great deal, whereas in the latter case of data transmission, this is less true. To adjust to either situation, the factor α is adjusted using a formula with two pieces.

G.726 works as a backward-adaptive Jayant quantizer by using fixed quantizer steps based on the logarithm of the input difference signal, e_n divided by α. The divisor α is written in terms of its logarithm:

$$\beta \equiv \log_2 \alpha \tag{13.3}$$

Since we wish to distinguish between situations when difference values are usually small, and when they are large, α is divided into a so-called *locked* part, α_L, and an *unlocked* part, α_U. The idea is that the locked part is a scale factor for small difference values and changes slowly, whereas the unlocked part adapts quickly to larger differences. These correspond to log quantities β_L and β_U.

The logarithm value is written as a sum of two pieces,

$$\beta = A\beta_U + (1 - A)\beta_L \tag{13.4}$$

where A changes so that it is about 1 for speech, and about 0 for voice-band data. It is calculated based on the variance of the signal, keeping track of several past signal values.

The "unlocked" part adapts via the equation

$$\begin{aligned} \alpha_U &\leftarrow M_k \alpha_U \\ \beta_U &\leftarrow \log_2 M_k + \beta_U \end{aligned} \tag{13.5}$$

where M_k is a Jayant multiplier for the kth level. The locked part is slightly modified from the unlocked part, via

$$\beta_L \leftarrow (1 - B)\beta_L + B\beta_U \tag{13.6}$$

where B is a small number, say 2^{-6}.

The G.726 predictor is complicated: it uses a linear combination of six quantized differences and two reconstructed signal values from the previous six signal values f_n.

13.3 VOCODERS

The coders (encoding/decoding algorithms) we have studied so far could have been applied to any signals, not just speech. *Vocoders* are specifically voice coders. As such, they cannot be usefully applied when other analog signals, such as modem signals, are in use.

Vocoders are concerned with modeling speech, so that the salient features are captured in as few bits as possible. They use either a model of the speech waveform in time (*Linear Predictive Coding* (LPC) vocoding), or else break down the signal into frequency components and model these (channel vocoders and formant vocoders).

Incidentally, we likely all know that vocoder simulation of the voice is not wonderful yet — when the library calls you with your overdue notification, the automated voice is strangely lacking in zest.

13.3.1 Phase Insensitivity

Recall from Section 8.5 that we can break down a signal into its constituent frequencies by analyzing it using some variant of Fourier analysis. In principle, we can also reconstitute the signal from the frequency coefficients developed that way. But it turns out that a complete reconstituting of speech waveform is unnecessary, perceptually: all that is needed is for the amount of energy at any time to be about right, and the signal will sound about right.

"Phase" is a shift in the time argument, inside a function of time. Suppose we strike a piano key and generate a roughly sinusoidal sound $\cos(\omega t)$, with $\omega = 2\pi f$. If we wait sufficient time to generate a phase shift $\pi/2$ and then strike another key, with sound $\cos(2\omega t + \pi/2)$, we generate a waveform like the solid line in Figure 13.3. This waveform is the sum $\cos(\omega t) + \cos(2\omega t + \pi/2)$.

If we did not wait before striking the second note (1/4 msec, in Figure 13.3), our waveform would be $\cos(\omega t) + \cos(2\omega t)$. But perceptually, the two notes would sound the same, even though in actuality they would be shifted in phase.

Hence, if we can get the energy spectrum right — where we hear loudness and quiet — then we don't really have to worry about the exact waveform.

13.3.2 Channel Vocoder

Subband filtering is the process of applying a bank of band-pass filters to the analog signal, thus actually carrying out the frequency decomposition indicated in a Fourier analysis. *Subband coding* is the process of making use of the information derived from this filtering to achieve better compression.

For example, an older ITU recommendation, G.722, uses subband filtering of analog signals into just two bands: voice frequencies in 50 Hz to 3.5 kHz and 3.5 kHz to 7 kHz.

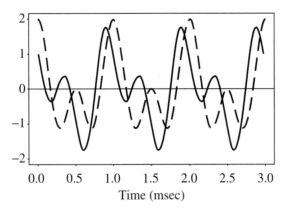

FIGURE 13.3: The solid line shows the superposition of two cosines, with a phase shift. The dashed line shows the same with no phase shift. The wave is very different, yet the sound is the same, perceptually.

Then the set of two signals is transmitted at 48 kbps for the low frequencies, where we can hear discrepancies well, and at only 16 kbps for the high frequencies.

Vocoders can operate at low bitrates, 1–2 kbps. To do so, a *channel vocoder* first applies a filter bank to separate out the different frequency components, as in Figure 13.4. However, as we saw above, only the energy is important, so first the waveform is "rectified" to its absolute value. The filter bank derives relative power levels for each frequency range. A subband coder would not rectify the signal and would use wider frequency bands.

A channel vocoder also analyzes the signal to determine the general pitch of the speech — low (bass), or high (tenor) — and also the *excitation* of the speech. Speech excitation is mainly concerned with whether a sound is *voiced* or *unvoiced*. A sound is unvoiced if its signal simply looks like noise: the sounds *s* and *f* are unvoiced. Sounds such as the vowels *a*, *e*, and *o* are voiced, and their waveform looks periodic. The *o* at the end of the word "audio" in Figure 13.1 is fairly periodic. During a vowel sound, air is forced through the vocal cords in a stream of regular, short puffs, occurring at the rate of 75–150 pulses per second for men and 150–250 per second for women.

Consonants can be voiced or unvoiced. For the nasal sounds of the letters *m* and *n*, the vocal cords vibrate, and air is exhaled through the nose rather than the mouth. These consonants are therefore voiced. The sounds *b*, *d*, and *g*, in which the mouth starts closed but then opens to the following vowel over a transition lasting a few milliseconds, are also voiced. The energy of voiced consonants is greater than that of unvoiced consonants but less than that of vowel sounds. Examples of unvoiced consonants include the sounds *sh*, *th*, and *h* when used at the front of a word.

A channel vocoder applies a vocal-tract transfer model to generate a vector of excitation parameters that describe a model of the sound. The vocoder also guesses whether the sound is voiced or unvoiced and, for voiced sounds, estimates the period (i.e., the sound's pitch). Figure 13.4 shows that the decoder also applies a vocal-tract model.

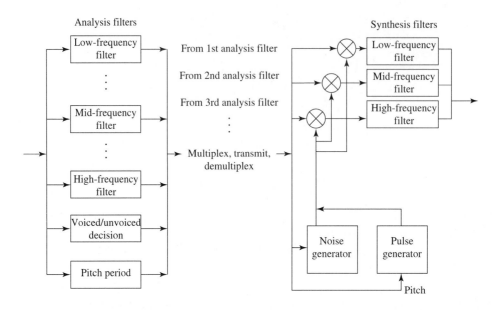

FIGURE 13.4: Channel vocoder.

Because voiced sounds can be approximated by sinusoids, a periodic pulse generator recreates voiced sounds. Since unvoiced sounds are noise-like, a pseudo-noise generator is applied, and all values are scaled by the energy estimates given by the band-pass filter set. A channel vocoder can achieve an intelligible but synthetic voice using 2,400 bps.

13.3.3   Formant Vocoder

It turns out that not all frequencies present in speech are equally represented. Instead, only certain frequencies show up strongly, and others are weak. This is a direct consequence of how speech sounds are formed, by resonance in only a few chambers of the mouth, throat, and nose. The important frequency peaks are called *formants* [2].

Figure 13.5 shows how this appears: only a few, usually just four or so, peaks of energy at certain frequencies are present. However, just where the peaks occur changes in time, as speech continues. For example, two different vowel sounds would activate different sets of formants — this reflects the different vocal tract configurations necessary to form each vowel. Usually, a small segment of speech is analyzed, say 10–40 msec, and formants are found. A *Formant Vocoder* works by encoding only the most important frequencies. Formant vocoders can produce reasonably intelligible speech at only 1,000 bps.

13.3.4   Linear Predictive Coding

LPC vocoders extract salient features of speech directly from the waveform rather than transforming the signal to the frequency domain. LPC coding uses a time-varying model of vocal-tract sound generated from a given excitation. What is transmitted is a set of parameters modeling the shape and excitation of the vocal tract, not actual signals or differences.

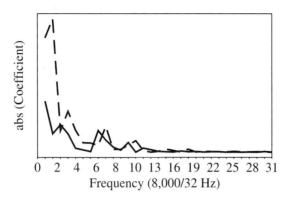

FIGURE 13.5: Formants are the salient frequency components present in a sample of speech. Here, the solid line shows frequencies present in the first 40 msec of the speech sample in Figure 6.15. The dashed line shows that while similar frequencies are still present one second later, they have shifted.

Since what is sent is an analysis of the sound rather than sound itself, the bitrate using LPC can be small. This is like using a simple descriptor such as MIDI to generate music: we send just the description parameters and let the sound generator do its best to create appropriate music. The difference is that as well as pitch, duration, and loudness variables, here we also send vocal tract excitation parameters.

After a block of digitized samples, called a *segment* or *frame*, is analyzed, the speech signal generated by the output vocal-tract model is calculated as a function of the current speech output plus a second term linear in previous model coefficients. This is how "linear" in the coder's name arises. The model is adaptive — the encoder side sends a new set of coefficients for each new segment.

The typical number of sets of previous coefficients used is $N = 10$ (the "model order" is 10), and such an LPC-10 [3] system typically uses a rate of 2.4 kbps. The model coefficients a_i act as predictor coefficients, multiplying previous speech output sample values.

LPC starts by deciding whether the current segment is voiced or unvoiced. For unvoiced speech, a wide-band noise generator is used to create sample values $f(n)$ that act as input to the vocal tract simulator. For voiced speech, a pulse-train generator creates values $f(n)$. Model parameters a_i are calculated by using a least-squares set of equations that minimize the difference between the actual speech and the speech generated by the vocal-tract model, excited by the noise or pulse-train generators that capture speech parameters.

If the output values generated are denoted $s(n)$, then for input values $f(n)$, the output depends on p previous *output* sample values, via

$$s(n) = \sum_{i=1}^{p} a_i s(n - i) + G f(n) \tag{13.7}$$

Here, G is known as the *gain* factor. Note that the coefficients a_i act as values in a linear predictor model. The pseudo-noise generator and pulse generator are as discussed above and depicted in Figure 13.4 in regard to the channel vocoder.

The speech encoder works in a blockwise fashion. The input digital speech signal is analyzed in some small, fixed-length segments, called speech frames. For the LPC speech coder, the frame length is usually selected as 22.5 msec, which corresponds to 180 samples for 8 kHz sampled digital speech. The speech encoder analyzes the speech frames to obtain the parameters such as LP coefficients a_i, $i = 1 .. p$, gain G, pitch P, and voiced/unvoiced decision U/V.

To calculate LP coefficients, we can solve the following minimization problem for a_j:

$$\min E\{[s(n) - \sum_{j=1}^{p} a_j s(n - j)]^2\} \tag{13.8}$$

By taking the derivative of a_i and setting it to zero, we get a set of p equations:

$$E\{[s(n) - \sum_{j=1}^{p} a_j s(n - j)]s(n - i)\} = 0, \qquad i = 1 .. p \tag{13.9}$$

Letting $\phi(i, j) = E\{s(n - i)s(n - j)\}$, we have

$$
\begin{bmatrix}
\phi(1, 1) & \phi(1, 2) & \cdots & \phi(1, p) \\
\phi(2, 1) & \phi(2, 2) & \cdots & \phi(2, p) \\
\vdots & \vdots & \ddots & \vdots \\
\phi(p, 1) & \phi(p, 2) & \cdots & \phi(p, p)
\end{bmatrix}
\begin{bmatrix}
a_1 \\
a_2 \\
\vdots \\
a_p
\end{bmatrix}
=
\begin{bmatrix}
\phi(0, 1) \\
\phi(0, 2) \\
\vdots \\
\phi(0, p)
\end{bmatrix}
\tag{13.10}
$$

The *autocorrelation method* is often used to calculate LP coefficients, where

$$\phi(i, j) = \sum_{n=p}^{N-1} s_w(n - i)s_w(n - j)/ \sum_{n=p}^{N-1} s_w^2(n) \qquad i = 0 \ldots p, \ j = 1 \ldots p \tag{13.11}$$

$s_w(n) = s(n+m)w(n)$ is the windowed speech frame starting from time m. Since $\phi(i, j)$ is determined only by $|i - j|$, we define $\phi(i, j) = R(|i - j|)$. Since we also have $R(0) \geq 0$, the matrix $\{\phi(i, j)\}$ is positive symmetric, and thus a fast scheme to calculate the LP coefficients is as follows.

PROCEDURE 13.1   LPC Coefficients

$E(0) = R(0), i = 1$
while $i \leq p$
    $k_i = [R(i) - \sum_{j=1}^{i-1} a_j^{i-1} R(i - j)]/E(i - 1)$
    $a_i^i = k_i$
    for $j = 1$ to $i - 1$
        $a_j^i = a_j^{i-1} - k_i a_{i-j}^{i-1}$
    $E(i) = (1 - k_i^2)E(i - 1)$
    $i \leftarrow i + 1$
for $j = 1$ to p
    $a_j = a_j^p$

After getting the LP coefficients, gain G can be calculated as

$$
\begin{aligned}
G &= E\{[s(n) - \sum_{j=1}^{p} a_j s(n - j)]^2\} \\
&= E\{[s(n) - \sum_{j=1}^{p} a_j s(n - j)]s(n)\} \qquad (13.12) \\
&= \phi(0,0) - \sum_{j=1}^{p} a_j \phi(0, j)
\end{aligned}
$$

For the autocorrelation scheme, $G = R(0) - \sum_{j=1}^{p} a_j R(j)$. Order-10 LP analysis is found to be enough for speech coding applications.

The pitch P of the current speech frame can be extracted by the correlation method by finding the index of the peak of

$$
v(i) = \sum_{n=m}^{N-1+m} s(n)s(n-i) \bigg/ [\sum_{n=m}^{N-1+m} s^2(n) \sum_{n=m}^{N-1+m} s^2(n-i)]^{1/2}
$$
$$
i \in [P_{\min}, P_{\max}] \qquad (13.13)
$$

The searching range $[P_{\min}, P_{\max}]$ is often selected as $[12, 140]$ for 8 kHz sampling speech. Denote P as the peak lag. If $v(P)$ is less than some given threshold, the current frame is classified as an unvoiced frame and will be reconstructed in the receiving end by stimulating with a white-noise sequence. Otherwise, the frame is determined as voiced and stimulated with a periodic waveform at the reconstruction stage. In practical LPC speech coders, the pitch estimation and U/V decision procedure are usually based on a dynamic programming scheme, so as to correct the often occurring errors of pitch doubling or halving in the single frame scheme.

In LPC-10, each segment is 180 samples, or 22.5 msec at 8 kHz. The speech parameters transmitted are the coefficients a_k; G, the gain factor; a voiced/unvoiced flag (1 bit); and the pitch period if the speech is voiced.

13.3.5 CELP

CELP, *Code Excited Linear Prediction* (sometimes *Codebook Excited*), is a more complex family of coders that attempts to mitigate the lack of quality of the simple LPC model by using a more complex description of the excitation. An entire set (a codebook) of excitation vectors is matched to the actual speech, and the index of the best match is sent to the receiver. This complexity increases the bitrate to 4,800–9,600 bps, typically.

In CELP, since all speech segments make use of the same set of templates from the template codebook, the resulting speech is perceived as much more natural than the two-mode excitation scheme in the LPC-10 coder. The quality achieved is considered sufficient for audio conferencing.

A low bitrate is required for conferencing, but the perceived quality of the speech must still be of an acceptable standard.

In CELP coders two kinds of prediction, Long Time Prediction (LTP) and Short Time Prediction (STP), are used to eliminate the redundancy in speech signals. STP is an analysis of *samples* — it attempts to predict the next sample from several previous ones. Here, redundancy is due to the fact that usually one sample will not change drastically from the next. LTP is based on the idea that in a *segment* of speech, or perhaps from segment to segment, especially for voiced sounds, a basic periodicity or pitch will cause a waveform that more or less repeats. We can reduce this redundancy by finding the pitch.

For concreteness, suppose we sample at 8,000 samples/sec and use a 10 msec frame, containing 80 samples. Then we can roughly expect a pitch that corresponds to an approximately repeating pattern every 12 to 140 samples or so. (Notice that the pitch may actually be longer than the chosen frame size.)

STP is based on a short-time LPC analysis, discussed in the last section. It is "short-time" in that the prediction involves only a few samples, not a whole frame or several frames. STP is also based on minimizing the residue error over the whole speech frame, but it captures the correlation over just a short range of samples (10 for order-10 LPC).

After STP, we can subtract signal minus prediction to arrive at a differential coding situation. However, even in a set of errors $e(n)$, the basic pitch of the sequence may still remain. This is estimated by means of LTP. That is, LTP is used to further eliminate the periodic redundancy inherent in the voiced speech signals. Essentially, STP captures the formant structure of the short-term speech spectrum, while LTP recovers the long-term correlation in the speech signal that represents the periodicity in speech.

Thus there are always two stages — and the order is in fact usually STP followed by LTP, since we always start off assuming zero error and then remove the pitch component. (If we use a closed-loop scheme, STP usually is done first). LTP proceeds using whole frames — or, more often, subframes equal to one quarter of a frame. Figure 13.6 shows these two stages.

LTP is often implemented as *adaptive codebook searching*. The "codeword" in the adaptive codebook is a shifted speech residue segment indexed by the lag τ corresponding to the current speech frame or subframe. The idea is to look in a codebook of waveforms to find one that matches the current subframe. We generally look in the codebook using a *normalized* subframe of speech, so as well as a speech segment match, we also obtain a scaling value (the *gain*). The gain corresponding to the codeword is denoted as g_0.

There are two types of codeword searching: *open-loop* and *closed-loop*. Open-loop adaptive codebook searching tries to minimize the long-term prediction error but not the perceptual weighted reconstructed speech error,

$$E(\tau) = \sum_{n=0}^{L-1} [s(n) - g_0 s(n - \tau)]^2 \tag{13.14}$$

By setting the partial derivative of g_0 to zero, $\partial E(\tau)/\partial g_0 = 0$, we get

$$g_0 = \frac{\sum_{n=0}^{L-1} s(n)s(n - \tau)}{\sum_{n=0}^{L-1} s^2(n - \tau)} \tag{13.15}$$

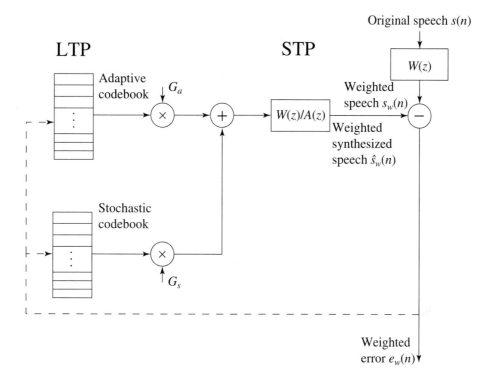

FIGURE 13.6: CELP analysis model with adaptive and stochastic codebooks.

and hence a minimum summed-error value

$$E_{\min}(\tau) = \sum_{n=0}^{L-1} s^2(n) - \frac{[\sum_{n=0}^{L-1} s(n)s(n-\tau)]^2}{\sum_{n=0}^{L-1} s^2(n-\tau)} \qquad (13.16)$$

Notice that the sample $s(n - \tau)$ could be in the previous frame.

Now, to obtain the optimum adaptive codebook index τ, we can carry out a search exclusively in a small range determined by the pitch period.

More often, CELP coders use a closed-loop search. Rather than simply considering sum-of-squares, speech is reconstructed, with perceptual error minimized via an adaptive codebook search. So in a closed-loop, adaptive codebook search, the best candidate in the adaptive codebook is selected to minimize the distortion of locally reconstructed speech. Parameters are found by minimizing a measure (usually the mean square) of the difference between the original and the reconstructed speech. Since this means that we are simultane-ously incorporating synthesis as well as analysis of the speech segment, this method is also called *analysis-by-synthesis*, or *A-B-S*.

The residue signal after STP based on LPC analysis and LTP based on adaptive code-word searching is like white noise and is encoded by codeword matching in the stochastic (random or probabilistic) codebook. This kind of sequential optimization of the adaptive codeword and stochastic codeword methods is used because jointly optimizing the adaptive and stochastic codewords is often too complex to meet real-time demands.

The decoding direction is just the reverse of the above process and works by combining the contribution from the two types of excitations.

DOD 4.8 KBPS CELP (FS1016)*.   DOD 4.8 kbps CELP [4] is an early CELP coder adopted as a U.S. federal standard to update the 2.4 kbps LPC-10e (FS1015) vocoder. This vocoder is now a basic benchmark to test other low-bitrate vocoders. FS1016 uses an 8 kHz sampling rate and 30 msec frame size. Each frame is further split into four 7.5 msec subframes. In FS1016, STP is based on an open-loop order-10 LPC analysis.

To improve coding efficiency, a fairly sophisticated type of transform coding is carried out. Then, quantization and compression are done in terms of the transform coefficients.

First, in this field it is common to use the *z-transform*. Here, z is a complex number and represents a kind of complex "frequency." If $z = e^{-2\pi i/N}$, then the discrete z-transform reduces to a discrete Fourier transform. The z-transform makes Fourier transforms look like polynomials. Now we can write the error in a prediction equation

$$e(n) = s(n) - \sum_{i=1}^{p} a_i s(n-i) \tag{13.17}$$

in the z domain as

$$E(z) = A(z)S(z) \tag{13.18}$$

where $E(z)$ is the z-transform of the error and $S(z)$ is the transform of the signal. The term $A(z)$ is the transfer function in the z domain, and equals

$$A(z) = 1 - \sum_{i=1}^{p} a_i z^{-i} \tag{13.19}$$

with the same coefficients a_i as appear in Equation (13.7). How speech is reconstructed, then, is via

$$S(z) = E(z)/A(z) \tag{13.20}$$

with the estimated error. For this reason, $A(z)$ is usually stated in terms of $1/A(z)$.

The idea of going to the z-transform domain is to convert the LP coefficients to *Line Spectrum Pair (LSP)* coefficients, which are given in this domain. The reason is that the LSP space has several good properties with respect to quantization. LSP representation has become standard and has been applied to nearly all the recent LPC-based speech coders, such as G.723.1, G.729, and MELP. To get LSP coefficients, we construct two polynomials

$$\begin{aligned} P(z) &= A(z) + z^{-(p+1)} A(z^{-1}) \\ Q(z) &= A(z) - z^{-(p+1)} A(z^{-1}) \end{aligned} \tag{13.21}$$

where p is the order of the LPC analysis and $A(z)$ is the transform function of the LP filter, with z the transform domain variable. The z-transform is just like the Fourier transform but with a complex "frequency."

The roots of these two polynomials are spaced around the unit circle in the z plane and have mirror symmetry with respect to the x-axis. Assume p is even and denote the phase angles of the roots of $P(z)$ and $Q(z)$ above the x axis as $\theta_1 < \theta_2 < \ldots < \theta_{p/2}$ and $\varphi_1 < \varphi_2 < \ldots < \varphi_{p/2}$, respectively. Then the vector $\{\cos(\theta_1), \cos(\varphi_1), \cos(\theta_2), \cos(\varphi_1) \ldots \cos(\theta_{p/2}), \cos(\varphi_{p/2})\}$ is the LSP coefficient vector, and vector $\{\theta_1, \varphi_1, \theta_2, \varphi_1 \ldots, \theta_{p/2}, \varphi_{p/2}\}$ is usually called *Line Spectrum Frequency*, or *LSF*. Based on the relationship $A(z) = [P(z) + Q(z)]/2$, we can reconstruct the LP coefficients at the decoder end from the LSP or LSF coefficients.

Adaptive codebook searching in FS1016 is via a closed-loop search based on perceptually weighted errors. As opposed to considering just the mean squared error, here errors are weighted so as to take human perception into account. In terms of the z-transform, it is found that the following multiplier does a good job:

$$W(z) = \frac{A(z)}{A(z/\gamma)} = \frac{1 - \sum_{i=1}^{p} a_i z^{-i}}{1 - \sum_{i=1}^{p} a_i \gamma^i z^{-i}} \quad 0 < \gamma < 1 \tag{13.22}$$

with a constant parameter γ.

The adaptive codebook has 256 codewords for 128 integer delays and 128 noninteger delays (with half-sample interval, for better resolution), the former ranging from 20 to 147. To reduce searching complexity, even subframes are searched in an interval relative to the previous odd subframe, and the difference is coded with 6 bits. The gain is nonuniformly scalar coded between -1 and 2 with 5 bits.

Stochastic codebook search is applied for each of the four subframes. The stochastic codebook of FS1016 is generated by clipping a unit variance Gaussian distribution random sequence to within a threshold of absolute value 1.2 and quantizing to three values -1, 0, and 1. The stochastic codebook has 512 codewords. The codewords are overlapped, and each is shifted by 2 with respect to the previous codeword. This kind of stochastic design is called an *Algebraic Codebook*. It has many variations and is widely applied in recent CELP coders.

Denoting the excitation vector as $v^{(i)}$, the periodic component obtained in the first stage is $v^{(0)}$. $v^{(1)}$ is the stochastic component search result in the second stage. In closed-loop searching, the reconstructed speech can be represented as

$$\widehat{s} = \widehat{s}_0 + (u + v^{(i)})H \tag{13.23}$$

where u is equal to zero at the first stage and $v^{(0)}$ at the second stage, and $\widehat{s}_0$ is the zero response of the LPC reconstructing filter. Matrix H is the truncated LPC reconstructing filter unit impulse-response matrix

$$H = \begin{bmatrix} h_0 & h_1 & h_2 & \cdots & h_{L-1} \\ 0 & h_0 & h_1 & \cdots & h_{L-2} \\ 0 & 0 & h_0 & \cdots & h_{L-3} \\ \vdots & \vdots & \vdots & \ddots & \vdots \\ 0 & 0 & 0 & 0 & h_0 \end{bmatrix} \tag{13.24}$$

where L is the length of the subframe (this simply represents a convolution). Similarly, defining W as the unit response matrix of the perceptual weighting filter, the perceptually weighted error of reconstructed speech is

$$e = (s - \widehat{s})W = e_0 - v^{(i)}HW \tag{13.25}$$

where $e_0 = (s - \widehat{s}_0)W - uHW$. The codebook searching process is to find a codeword $y^{(i)}$ in the codebook and corresponding $a^{(i)}$ such that $v^{(i)} = a^{(i)}y^{(i)}$ and ee^T is minimized. To make the problem tractable, adaptive and stochastic codebooks are searched sequentially. Denoting a quantized version by $\tilde{a}^{(i)} = Q[\hat{a}^{(i)}]$, then the criterion of codeword searching in the adaptive codebook or stochastic codebook is to minimize ee^T over all $y^{(i)}$ in terms of an expression in $\tilde{a}^{(i)}$, e_0, and $y^{(i)}$.

The decoder of the CELP codec is a reverse process of the encoder. Because of the unsymmetrical complexity property of vector quantization, the complexity in the decoder side is usually much lower.

G.723.1*.   G723.1 [5] is an ITU standard aimed at multimedia communication. It has been incorporated into H.324 for audio encoding in videoconference applications. G.723.1 is a dual-rate CELP-type speech coder that can work at bitrates of 5.3 kbps and 6.3 kbps.

G.723.1 uses many techniques similar to FS1016, discussed in the last section. The input speech is again 8 kHz, sampled in 16-bit linear PCM format. The speech frame size is also 30 msec and is further divided into four equal-sized subframes. Order-10 LPC coefficients are estimated in each subframe. LP coefficients are further converted to LSP vectors and quantized by predictive splitting VQ. LP coefficients are also used to form the perceptually weighted filter.

G.723.1 first uses an open-loop pitch estimator to get a coarse pitch estimation in a time interval of every two subframes. Closed-loop pitch searching is done in every speech subframe by searching the data in a range of the open-loop pitch. After LP filtering and removing the harmonic components by LTP, the stochastic residue is quantized by *Multi-pulse Maximum Likelihood Quantization (MP-MLQ)* for the 5.3 kbps coder or *Algebraic-Code-Excited Linear Prediction (ACELP)* for the 6.3 kbps coder, which has a slightly higher speech quality. These two modes can be switched at any boundary of the 30 msec speech frames.

In MP-MLQ, the contribution of the stochastic component is represented as a sequence of pulses

$$v(n) = \sum_{i=1}^{M} g_i \delta(n - m_i) \tag{13.26}$$

where M is the number of pulses and g_i is gain of the pulse at position m_i. The closed-loop search is done by minimizing

$$e(n) = r(n) - \sum_{i=1}^{M} g_i h(n - m_i) \tag{13.27}$$

where $r(n)$ is the speech component after perceptual weighting and eliminating the zero-response component and periodic component contributions. Based on methods similar to those presented in the last section, we can sequentially optimize the gain and position for each pulse. Say we first assume there is only one pulse and find the best gain and position. After removing the contribution from this pulse, we can get the next optimal pulse based on the same method. This process is done recursively until we get all M pulses.

The stochastic codebook structure for the ACELP model is different from FS1016. The following table shows the ACELP excitation codebook:

$$
\begin{array}{ll}
Sign & Positions \\
\pm 1 & 0,\ 8, 16, 24, 32, 40, 48,\ 56 \\
\pm 1 & 2, 10, 18, 26, 34, 42, 50,\ 58 \\
\pm 1 & 4, 12, 20, 28, 36, 44, 52, (60) \\
\pm 1 & 6, 14, 22, 30, 38, 46, 54, (62)
\end{array}
\tag{13.28}
$$

There are only four pulses. Each can be in eight positions, coded by three bits each. Also, the sign of the pulse takes one bit, and another bit is to shift all possible positions to odd. Thus, the index of a codeword has 17 bits. Because of the special structure of the algebraic codebook, a fast algorithm exists for efficient codeword searching.

Besides the CELP coder we discussed above, there are many other CELP-type codecs, developed mainly for wireless communication systems. The basic concepts of these coders are similar, except for different implementation details on parameter analysis and codebook structuring.

Some examples include the 12.2 kbps GSM *Enhanced Full Rate* (*EFR*) algebraic CELP codec [6] and IS-641EFR [7], designed for the North American digital cellular IS-136 TDMA system. G.728 [8] is a low-delay CELP speech coder. G.729 [9] is another CELP based ITU standard aimed at toll-quality speech communications.

G.729 is a *Conjugate-Structure Algebraic-Code-Excited-Linear-Prediction* (*CS-ACELP*) codec. G.729 uses a 10 msec speech analysis frame and thus has lower delay than G.723.1, which uses a 30 msec speech frame. G.729 also has some inherent protection schemes to deal with packet loss in applications such as VoIP.

13.3.6 Hybrid Excitation Vocoders*

Hybrid Excitation Vocoders are another large class of speech coders. They are different from CELP, in which the excitation is represented as the contributions of the adaptive and stochastic codewords. Instead, hybrid excitation coders use model-based methods to introduce multi-model excitation.

MBE. The *Multi-Band Excitation* (*MBE*) [10] vocoder was developed by MIT's Lincoln Laboratory. The 4.15 kbps IMBE codec[11] has become the standard for IMMSAT. MBE is also a blockwise codec, in which a speech analysis is done in a speech frame unit of about 20 to 30 msec. In the analysis part of the MBE coder, a spectrum analysis such as FFT is first applied for the windowed speech in the current frame. The short-time speech spectrum is further divided into different spectrum bands. The bandwidth is usually an integer times the basic frequency that equals the inverse of the pitch. Each band is described as "voiced" or "unvoiced".

The parameters of the MBE coder thus include the spectrum envelope, pitch, unvoiced/voiced (U/V) decisions for different bands. Based on different bitrate demands, the phase of the spectrum can be parameterized or discarded. In the speech decoding process, voiced bands and unvoiced bands are synthesized by different schemes and combined to generate the final output.

MBE utilizes the analysis-by-synthesis scheme in parameter estimation. Parameters such as basic frequency, spectrum envelope, and subband U/V decisions are all done via closed-loop searching. The criteria of the closed-loop optimization are based on minimizing the perceptually weighted reconstructed speech error, which can be represented in the frequency domain as

$$\varepsilon = \frac{1}{2\pi} \int_{-\pi}^{+\pi} G(\omega)|S_w(\omega) - S_{wr}(\omega)|d\omega \tag{13.29}$$

where $S_w(\omega)$ and $S_{wr}(\omega)$ are the original speech short-time spectrum and reconstructed speech short-time spectrum, and $G(\omega)$ is the spectrum of the perceptual weighting filter.

Similar to the closed-loop searching scheme in CELP, a sequential optimization method is used to make the problem tractable. In the first step, all bands are assumed voiced bands, and the spectrum envelope and basic frequency are estimated. Rewriting the spectrum error with the all-voiced assumption, we have

$$\check{\varepsilon} = \sum_{m=-M}^{M} [\frac{1}{2\pi} \int_{\alpha_m}^{\beta_m} G(\omega)|S_w(\omega) - A_m E_{wr}(\omega)|^2 d\omega] \tag{13.30}$$

in which M is band number in $[0, \pi]$, A_m is the spectrum envelope of band m, $E_{wr}(\omega)$ is the short-time window spectrum, and $\alpha_m = (m - \frac{1}{2})\omega_0$, $\beta_m = (m + \frac{1}{2})\omega_0$. Setting $\partial\check{\varepsilon}/\partial A_m = 0$, we get

$$A_m = \frac{\int_{\alpha_m}^{\beta_m} G(\omega)S_w(\omega)E_{wr}^*(\omega)d\omega}{\int_{\alpha_m}^{\beta_m} G(\omega)|E_{wr}(\omega)|^2 d\omega} \tag{13.31}$$

The basic frequency is obtained at the same time by searching over a frequency interval to minimize $\check{\varepsilon}$. Based on the estimated spectrum envelope, an adaptive thresholding scheme tests the matching degree for each band. We label a band as voiced if there is a good matching; otherwise, we declare the band as unvoiced and re-estimate the envelope for the unvoiced band as

$$A_m = \frac{\int_{\alpha_m}^{\beta_m} G(\omega)|S_w(\omega)|d\omega}{\int_{\alpha_m}^{\beta_m} G(\omega)d\omega} \tag{13.32}$$

The decoder uses separate methods to synthesize unvoiced and voiced speech, based on the unvoiced and voiced bands. The two types of reconstructed components are then combined to generate synthesized speech. The final step is overlapping the sum of the synthesized speech in each frame to get the final output.

Multiband Excitation Linear Predictive (MELP).   The MELP speech codec is a new U.S. federal standard to replace the old LPC-10 (FS1015) standard, with the application focus on low-bitrate safety communications. At 2.4 kbps, MELP [12] has comparable speech quality to the 4.8 kbps DOD-CELP (FS1016) and good robustness in a noisy environment.

MELP is also based on LPC analysis. Different from the hard-decision voiced/unvoiced model adopted in LPC-10, MELP uses a multiband soft-decision model for the excitation signal. The LP residue is band-passed, and a voicing strength parameter is estimated for each band. The decoder can reconstruct the excitation signal by combining the periodic pulses and white noises, based on the voicing strength in each band. Speech can be then reconstructed by passing the excitation through the LPC synthesis filter.

Different from MBE, MELP divides the excitation into five fixed bands of 0–500, 500–1000, 1000–2000, 2000–3000, and 3000–4000 Hz. It estimates a voice degree parameter in each band based on the normalized correlation function of the speech signal and the smoothed, rectified signal in the non-DC band. Let $s_k(n)$ denote the speech signal in band k, and $u_k(n)$ denote the DC-removed smoothed rectified signal of $s_k(n)$. The correlation function is defined as

$$R_x(P) = \frac{\sum_{n=0}^{N-1} x(n)x(n+P)}{[\sum_{n=0}^{N-1} x^2(n) \sum_{n=0}^{N-1} x^2(n+P)]^{1/2}} \qquad (13.33)$$

where P is the pitch of the current frame, and N is the frame length. Then the voicing strength for band k is defined as $\max(R_{s_k}(P), R_{u_k}(P))$.

To further remove the buzziness of traditional LPC-10 speech coders for the voiced speech segment, MELP adopts a jittery voiced state to simulate the marginal voiced speech segments. The jittery state is indicated by an aperiodic flag. If the aperiodic flag is set in the analysis end, the receiver adds a random shifting component to the periodic pulse excitation. The shifting can be as big as $P/4$. The jittery state is determined by the peakiness of the full-wave rectified LP residue $e(n)$,

$$\text{peakiness} = \frac{[\frac{1}{N} \sum_{n=0}^{N-1} e(n)^2]^{1/2}}{\frac{1}{N} \sum_{n=0}^{N-1} |e(n)|} \qquad (13.34)$$

If peakiness is greater than some threshold, the speech frame is determined as jittered.

To better reconstruct the short time spectrum of the speech signal, the spectrum of the residue signal is not assumed to be flat, as it is in the LPC-10 speech coder. After normalizing the LP residue signal, MELP preserves the magnitudes corresponding to the first $min(10, P/4)$ basic frequency harmonics. Basic frequency is the inverse of the pitch period. The higher harmonics are discarded and assumed to be unity spectrum.

The 10-d magnitude vector is quantized by 8-bit vector quantization, using a perceptual weighted distance measure. Similar to most modern LPC quantization schemes, MELP also converts LPC parameters to LSF and uses four-stage vector quantization. The bits allocated for the four stages are 7, 6, 6, and 6, respectively. Apart from integral pitch estimation similar to LPC-10, MELP applies a fractional pitch refinement procedure to improve the accuracy of pitch estimation.

In the speech reconstruction process, MELP does not use a periodic pulse to represent the periodic excitation signal but uses a dispersed waveform. To disperse the pulses, a *finite impulse response (FIR)* filter is applied to the pulses. MELP also applies a perceptual weighting filter post-filter to the reconstructed speech so as to suppress the quantization noise and improve the subject's speech quality.

13.4 FURTHER EXPLORATION

A comprehensive introduction to speech coding can be found in Spanias's excellent article [13]. Sun Microsystems has made available the code for its implementation of standards G.711, G.721, and G.723, in C. The code can be found from the link in this section of the text web site, along with sample audio files. Since the code operates on raw 2-byte data, the link also gives simple MATLAB conversion code to read and write WAV and RAW data.

For audio, the court of final appeal is the ITU standards body itself. Standards promoted by such groups allow our modems to talk to each other, permit the development of mobile communications, and so on. The ITU, which sells standards, is linked to from the text web site.

More information on speech coding can be found in the speech FAQ file links. Links to LPC and CELP code are also included.

13.5 EXERCISES

1. In Section 13.3.1 we discuss phase insensitivity. Explain the meaning of the term "phase" in regard to individual frequency components in a composite signal.

2. Input a speech segment, using C or MATLAB, and verify that formants indeed exist — that any speech segment has only a few important frequencies. Also, verify that formants change as the interval of speech being examined changes.

    A simple approach to coding a frequency analyzer is to reuse the DCT coding ideas we have previously considered in Section 8.5. In one dimension, the DCT transform reads

$$F(u) = \sqrt{\frac{2}{N}} C(u) \sum_{i=0}^{N-1} \cos \frac{(2i+1)u\pi}{2N} f(i) \qquad (13.35)$$

where $i, u = 0, 1, \ldots, N-1$, and the constants $C(u)$ are given by

$$C(u) = \begin{cases} \frac{\sqrt{2}}{2} & \text{if } u = 0 \\ 1 & \text{otherwise} \end{cases} \qquad (13.36)$$

If we use the speech sample in Figure 6.15, then taking the one-dimensional DCT of the first, or last, 40 msec (i.e., 32 samples), we arrive at the absolute frequency components as in Figure 13.5.

3. Write code to read a WAV file. You will need the following set of definitions: a WAV file begins with a 44-byte header, in unsigned byte format. Some important parameter information is coded as follows:

   Byte[22 .. 23]   Number of channels
   Byte[24 .. 27]   Sampling rate
   Byte[34 .. 35]   Sampling bits
   Byte[40 .. 43]   Data length

4. Write a program to add fade in and fade out effects to sound clips (in WAV format). Specifications for the fades are as follows: The algorithm assumes a linear envelope; the fade-in duration is from 0% to 20% of the data samples; the fade-out duration is from 80% to 100% of the data samples.

   If you like, you can make your code able to handle both mono and stereo WAV files. If necessary, impose a limit on the size of the input file, say 16 megabytes.

5. In the text, we study an adaptive quantization scheme for ADPCM. We can also use an adaptive prediction scheme. We consider the case of one tap prediction, $\hat{s}(n) = a \cdot s(n-1)$. Show how to estimate the parameter a in an open-loop method. Estimate the SNR gain you can get, compared to the direct PCM method based on a uniform quantization scheme.

6. Linear prediction analysis can be used to estimate the shape of the envelope of the short-time spectrum. Given ten LP coefficients $a_1, \ldots, a_{10}$, how do we get the formant position and bandwidth?

7. Download and implement a CELP coder (see the textbook web site). Try out this speech coder on your own recorded sounds.

8. In quantizing LSP vectors in G.723.1, splitting vector quantization is used: if the dimensionality of LSP is 10, we can split the vector into three subvectors of length 3, 3, and 4 each and use vector quantization for the subvectors separately. Compare the codebook space complexity with and without split vector quantization. Give the codebook searching time complexity improvement by using splitting vector quantization.

9. Discuss the advantage of using an algebraic codebook in CELP coding.

10. The LPC-10 speech coder's quality deteriorates rapidly with strong background noise. Discuss why MELP works better in the same noisy conditions.

11. Give a simple time-domain method for pitch estimation based on the autocorrelation function. What problem will this simple scheme have when based on one speech frame? If we have three speech frames, including a previous frame and a future frame, how can we improve the estimation result?

12. On the receiver side, speech is usually generated based on two frames' parameters instead of one, to avoid abrupt transitions. Give two possible methods to obtain smooth transitions. Use the LPC codec to illustrate your idea.

13.6 REFERENCES

1 N.S. Jayant and P. Noll, *Digital Coding of Waveforms*, Englewood Cliffs, NJ: Prentice-Hall, 1984.

2 J.C. Bellamy, *Digital Telephony*, New York: Wiley, 2000.

3 Thomas E. Tremain, "The Government Standard Linear Predictive Coding Algorithm: LPC-10," *Speech Technology*, April 1982.

4 J.P. Campbell, Jr., T.E. Tremain, and V.C. Welch, "The DOD 4.8 kbps Standard (Proposed Federal Standard 1016)," In *Advances in Speech Coding*. Boston: Kluwer Academic Publishers, 1991.

5 *Dual Rate Speech Coder for Multimedia Communications Transmitting at 5.3 and 6.3 kbit/s*, ITU-T Recommendation G.723.1, March, 1996.

6 *GSM Enhanced Full Rate Speech Transcoding (GSM 06.60)*, ETSI Standards Documentation, EN 301 245, 1998.

7 *TDMA Cellular/PCS Radio Interface-Enhanced Full Rate Speech Codec*, TIA/EIA/IS-641 standard, 1996.

8 *Coding of Speech at 16 kbit/s Ising Low-Delay Code Excited Linear Programming*, ITU-T Recommendation G.728, 1992.

9 *Coding of Speech at 8 kbit/s Using Conjugate-Structure Algebraic-Code-Excited Linear-Prediction (CS-ACELP)*, ITU-T Recommendation G.729, 1996.

10 D. W. Griffin and J. S. Lim "Multi-Band Excitation Vocoder," *IEEE Transactions on Acoustics, Speech, and Signal Processing*, 36(8): 1223–1235, 1988.

11 "Inmarsat [International Mobile Satellite]-M Voice Codec, v2," *Inmarsat-M Specification*, Feb 1991.

12 A.V. McCree and T.P. Barnwell, "Mixed Excitation LPC Vocoder Model for Low Bit Rate Speech Coding," *IEEE Transactions on Speech and Audio Processing*, 3(4): 242–250, July 1995.

13 A. Spanias, "Speech Coding: A Tutorial Review," *Proceedings of the IEEE*, 82: 1541–1582, 1994.

CHAPTER 14

MPEG Audio Compression

Have you ever attended a dance and found that for quite some time afterward you couldn't hear much? You were dealing with a type of *temporal masking*!

Have you ever noticed that the person on the sound board at a dance basically cannot hear high frequencies anymore? Since many technicians have such hearing damage, some compensate by increasing the volume levels of the high frequencies, so they can hear them. If your hearing is not damaged, you experience this music mix as too piercing.

Moreover, if a very loud tone is produced, you also notice it is impossible to hear any sound nearby in the frequency spectrum — the band's singing may be drowned out by the lead guitar. If you've noticed this, you have experienced *frequency masking*!

MPEG audio uses this kind of perception phenomenon by simply giving up on the tones that can't be heard anyway. Using a curve of human hearing perceptual sensitivity, an MPEG audio codec makes decisions on when and to what degree frequency masking and temporal masking make some components of the music inaudible. It then controls the quantization process so that these components do not influence the output.

So far, in the previous chapter, we have concentrated on telephony applications — usually, LPC and CELP are tuned to speech parameters. In contrast, in this chapter, we consider compression methods applicable to general audio, such as music or perhaps broadcast digital TV. Instead of modeling speech, the method used is a *waveform* coding approach — one that attempts to make the decompressed amplitude-versus-time waveform as much as possible like the input signal.

A main technique used in evaluating audio content for possible compression makes use of a *psychoacoustic model* of hearing. The kind of coding carried out, then, is generally referred to as *perceptual coding*.

In this chapter, we look at how such considerations impact MPEG audio compression standards and examine in some detail at the following topics:

- Psychoacoustics

- MPEG-1 Audio Compression

- Later MPEG audio developments: MPEG-2, 4, 7, and 21

14.1 PSYCHOACOUSTICS

Recall that the range of human hearing is about 20 Hz to about 20 kHz (for people who have not gone to many dances). Sounds at higher frequencies are *ultrasonic*. However, the frequency range of the voice is typically only from about 500 Hz to 4 kHz. The dynamic range, the ratio of the maximum sound amplitude to the quietest sound humans can hear, is on the order of about 120 dB.

Recall that the decibel unit represents ratios of intensity on a logarithmic scale. The reference point for 0 dB is the threshold of human hearing — the quietest sound we can hear, measured at 1 kHz. Technically, this is a sound that creates a barely audible sound intensity of 10^{-12} Watt per square meter. Our range of magnitude perception is thus incredibly wide: the level at which the sensation of sound begins to give way to the sensation of pain is about 1 Watt/m^2, so we can perceive a ratio of 10^{12}!

The range of hearing actually depends on frequency. At a frequency of 2 kHz, the ear can readily respond to sound that is about 96 dB more powerful than the smallest perceivable sound at that frequency, or in other words a power ratio of 2^{32}. Table 6.1 lists some of the common sound levels in decibels.

14.1.1 Equal-Loudness Relations

Suppose we play two pure tones, sinusoidal sound waves, with the same amplitude but different frequencies. Typically, one may sound louder than the other. The reason is that the ear does not hear low or high frequencies as well as frequencies in the middle range. In particular, at normal sound volume levels, the ear is most sensitive to frequencies between 1 kHz and 5 kHz.

Fletcher-Munson Curves.   The Fletcher-Munson equal-loudness curves display the relationship between perceived loudness (*in phons*) for a given stimulus sound volume (*Sound Pressure Level*, in dB), as a function of frequency. Figure 14.1 shows the ear's perception of equal loudness. The abscissa (shown in a semi-log plot) is frequency, in kHz. The ordinate axis is sound pressure level — the actual loudness of the tone generated in an experiment. The curves show the loudness with which such tones are perceived by humans. The bottom curve shows what level of pure tone stimulus is required to produce the perception of a 10 dB sound.

All the curves are arranged so that the perceived loudness level gives the same loudness as for that loudness level of a pure tone at 1 kHz. Thus, the loudness level at the 1 kHz point is always equal to the dB level on the ordinate axis. The bottom curve, for example, is for 10 phons. All the tones on this curve will be perceived as loud as a 10 dB, 1,000 Hz tone. The figure shows more accurate curves, developed by Robinson and Dadson [1], than the Fletcher and Munson originals [2].

The idea is that a tone is produced at a certain frequency and *measured* loudness level, then a human rates the loudness as it is perceived. On the lowest curve shown, each pure tone between 20 Hz and 15 kHz would have to be produced at the volume level given by the ordinate for it to be perceived at a 10 dB loudness level [1]. The next curve shows what the magnitude would have to be for pure tones to each be perceived as being at 20 dB, and so on. The top curve is for perception at 90 dB.

For example, at 5,000 Hz, we perceive a tone to have a loudness level of 10 phons when the source is actually only 5 dB. Notice that at the dip at 4 kHz, we perceive the sound as being about 10 dB, when in fact the stimulation is only about 2 dB. To perceive the same

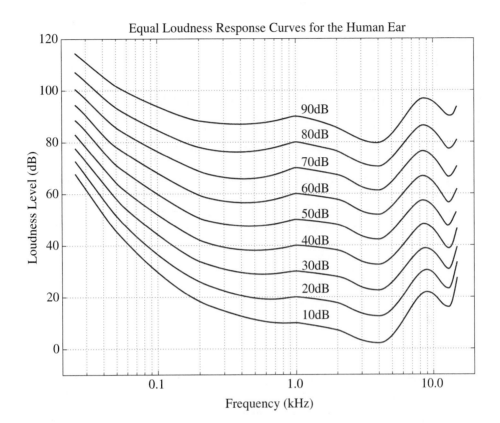

FIGURE 14.1: Fletcher-Munson equal loudness response curves for the human ear (remeasured by Robinson and Dadson).

effective 10 dB at 10 kHz, we would have to produce an absolute magnitude of 20 dB. The ear is clearly more sensitive in the range 2 kHz to 5 kHz and not nearly as sensitive in the range 6 kHz and above.

At the lower frequencies, if the source is at level 10 dB, a 1 kHz tone would also sound at 10 dB; however, a lower, 100 Hz tone must be at a level 30 dB — 20 dB higher than the 1 kHz tone! So we are not very sensitive to the lower frequencies. The explanation of this phenomenon is that the ear canal amplifies frequencies from 2.5 to 4 kHz.

Note that as the overall loudness increases, the curves flatten somewhat. We are approximately equally sensitive to low frequencies of a few hundred Hz if the sound level is loud enough. And we perceive most low frequencies better than high ones at high volume levels. Hence, at the dance, loud music sounds better than quiet music, because then we can actually hear low frequencies and not just high ones. (A "loudness" switch on some sound systems simply boosts the low frequencies as well as some high ones.) However, above 90 dB, people begin to become uncomfortable. A typical city subway operates at about 100 dB.

14.1.2   Frequency Masking

How does one tone interfere with another? At what level does one frequency drown out another? This question is answered by masking curves. Also, masking answers the question of how much noise we can tolerate before we cannot hear the actual music. Lossy audio data compression methods, such as MPEG Audio or Dolby Digital (AC-3) encoding, which is popular in movies, remove some sounds that are masked anyway, thus reducing the total amount of information.

The general situation in regard to masking is as follows:

- A lower tone can effectively mask (make us unable to hear) a higher tone.

- The reverse is not true. A higher tone does not mask a lower tone well. Tones can in fact mask lower-frequency sounds, but not as effectively as they mask higher-frequency ones.

- The greater the power in the masking tone, the wider its influence — the broader the range of frequencies it can mask.

- As a consequence, if two tones are widely separated in frequency, little masking occurs.

Threshold of Hearing.   Figure 14.2 shows a plot of the threshold of human hearing, for pure tones. To determine such a plot, a particular frequency tone is generated, say 1 kHz. Its volume is reduced to zero in a quiet room or using headphones, then turned up until the sound is just barely audible. Data points are generated for all audible frequencies in the same way.

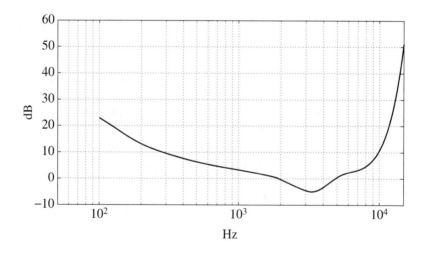

FIGURE 14.2: Threshold of human hearing, for pure tones.

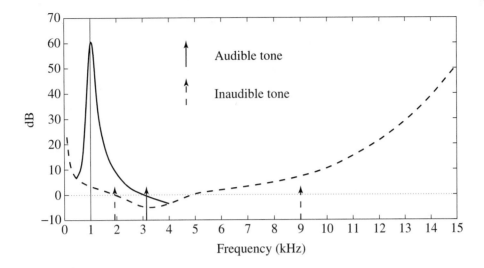

FIGURE 14.3: Effect on threshold of human hearing for a 1 kHz masking tone.

The point of the threshold of hearing curve is that if a sound is above the dB level shown — say it is above 2 dB for a 6 kHz tone — then the sound is audible. Otherwise, we cannot hear it. Turning up the 6 kHz tone so that it equals or surpasses the curve means we can then distinguish the sound.

An approximate formula exists for this curve, as follows [3]:

$$Threshold(f) = 3.64(f/1000)^{-0.8} - 6.5e^{-0.6(f/1000-3.3)^2} + 10^{-3}(f/1000)^4 \quad (14.1)$$

The threshold units are dB. Since the dB unit is a ratio, we do have to choose which frequency will be pinned to the origin, $(0, 0)$. In Equation (14.1), this frequency is 2,000 Hz: $Threshold(f) = 0$ at $f = 2$ kHz.

Frequency Masking Curves.   Frequency masking is studied by playing a particular pure tone, say 1 kHz again, at a loud volume and determining how this tone affects our ability to hear tones at nearby frequencies. To do so, we would generate a 1 kHz *masking tone* at a fixed sound level of 60 dB, then raise the level of a nearby tone, say 1.1 kHz, until it is just audible. The threshold in Figure 14.3 plots this audible level.

It is important to realize that this masking diagram holds only for a single masking tone: the plot changes if other masking tones are used. Figure 14.4 shows how this looks: the higher the frequency of the masking tone, the broader a range of influence it has.

If, for example, we play a 6 kHz tone in the presence of a 4 kHz masking tone, the masking tone has raised the threshold curve much higher. Therefore, at its neighbor frequency of 6 kHz, we must now surpass 30 dB to distinguish the 6 kHz tone.

The practical point is that if a signal can be decomposed into frequencies, then for frequencies that will be partially masked, only the audible part will be used to set quantization noise thresholds.

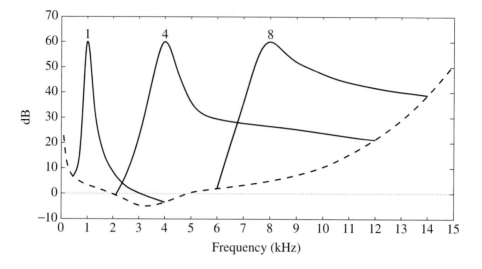

FIGURE 14.4: Effect of masking tones at three different frequencies.

Critical Bands. The human hearing range naturally divides into *critical bands*, with the property that the human auditory system cannot resolve sounds better than within about one critical band when other sounds are present. Hearing has a limited, frequency-dependent resolution. According to [4], "In a complex tone, the critical bandwidth corresponds to the smallest frequency difference between two partials such that each can still be heard separately. ... the critical bandwidth represents the ear's resolving power for simultaneous tones or partials."

At the low-frequency end, a critical band is less than 100 Hz wide, while for high frequencies, the width can be greater than 4 kHz. This indeed is yet another kind of *perceptual nonuniformity*.

Experiments indicate that the critical bandwidth remains approximately constant in width for masking frequencies below about 500 Hz — this width is about 100 Hz. However, for frequencies above 500 Hz, the critical bandwidth increases approximately linearly with frequency.

Generally, the audio frequency range for hearing can be partitioned into about 24 critical bands (25 are typically used for coding applications), as Table 14.1 shows.

Notwithstanding the *general* definition of a critical band, it turns out that our hearing apparatus actually is somewhat tuned to *certain* critical bands. Since hearing depends on physical structures in the inner ear, the frequencies at which these structures best resonate is important. Frequency masking is a result of the ear structures becoming "saturated" at the masking frequency and nearby frequencies.

Hence, the ear operates something like a set of band-pass filters, which each allows a limited range of frequencies through and blocks all others. Experiments that show this are based on the observation that a constant-volume sound will seem louder if it spans the boundary between two critical bands than it would were it contained entirely within one critical band [5]. In effect, the ear is not very discriminating *within* a critical band, because of masking.

TABLE 14.1: Critical bands and their bandwidths.

Band #	Lower bound (Hz)	Center (Hz)	Upper bound (Hz)	Bandwidth (Hz)
1	-	50	100	-
2	100	150	200	100
3	200	250	300	100
4	300	350	400	100
5	400	450	510	110
6	510	570	630	120
7	630	700	770	140
8	770	840	920	150
9	920	1000	1080	160
10	1080	1170	1270	190
11	1270	1370	1480	210
12	1480	1600	1720	240
13	1720	1850	2000	280
14	2000	2150	2320	320
15	2320	2500	2700	380
16	2700	2900	3150	450
17	3150	3400	3700	550
18	3700	4000	4400	700
19	4400	4800	5300	900
20	5300	5800	6400	1100
21	6400	7000	7700	1300
22	7700	8500	9500	1800
23	9500	10500	12000	2500
24	12000	13500	15500	3500
25	15500	18775	22050	6550

Bark Unit. Since the range of frequencies affected by masking is broader for higher frequencies, it is useful to define a new frequency unit such that, in terms of this new unit, each of the masking curves (the parts of Figure 14.4 above the threshold in quiet) have about the same width.

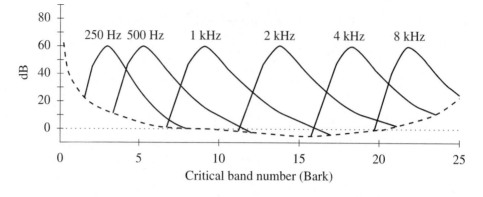

FIGURE 14.5: Effect of masking tones, expressed in Bark units.

The new unit defined is called the *Bark*, named after Heinrich Barkhausen (1881–1956), an early sound scientist. One Bark unit corresponds to the width of one critical band, for any masking frequency [6, 7]. Figure 14.5 displays critical bands, with the frequency (the abscissa) given in Bark units.

The conversion between a frequency f and its corresponding critical-band number b, expressed in Bark units, is as follows:

$$\text{Critical band number (Bark)} = \begin{cases} f/100, & \text{for } f < 500 \\ 9 + 4\log_2(f/1000), & \text{for } f \geq 500 \end{cases} \quad (14.2)$$

In terms of this new frequency measure, the critical-band number b equals 5 when $f = 500$ Hz. At double that frequency, for a masking frequency of 1 kHz, the Bark value goes up to 9. Another formula used for the Bark scale is as follows:

$$b = 13.0 \arctan(0.76 f) + 3.5 \arctan(f^2/56.25) \quad (14.3)$$

where f is in kHz and b is in Barks. The inverse equation gives the frequency (in kHz) corresponding to a particular Bark value b:

$$f = [(\exp(0.219 \times b)/352) + 0.1] \times b - 0.032 \times \exp[-0.15 \times (b - 5)^2] \quad (14.4)$$

Frequencies forming the boundaries between two critical bands are given by integer Bark values. The critical bandwidth (df) for a given center frequency f can also be approximated by [8]

$$df = 25 + 75 \times [1 + 1.4(f^2)]^{0.69} \quad (14.5)$$

where f is in kHz and df is in Hz.

The idea of the Bark unit is to define a more perceptually uniform unit of frequency, in that every critical band's width is roughly equal in terms of Barks.

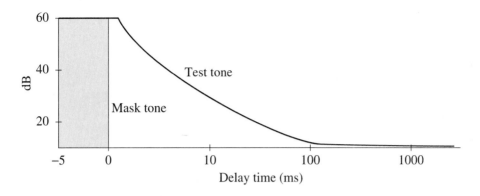

FIGURE 14.6: The louder the test tone, the shorter the amount of time required before the test tone is audible once the masking tone is removed.

14.1.3 Temporal Masking

Recall that after the dance it takes quite a while for our hearing to return to normal. Generally, any loud tone causes the hearing receptors in the inner ear (little hairlike structures called *cilia*) to become *saturated*, and they require time to recover. (Many other perceptual systems behave in this temporally slow fashion — for example, the receptors in the eye have this same kind of "capacitance" effect.)

To quantify this type of behavior, we can measure the time sensitivity of hearing by another masking experiment. Suppose we again play a masking tone at 1 kHz with a volume level of 60 dB, and a nearby tone at, say, 1.1 kHz with a volume level of 40 dB. Since the nearby test tone is masked, it cannot be heard. However, once the masking tone is turned off, we can again hear the 1.1 kHz tone, but only after a small amount of time. The experiment proceeds by stopping the test tone slightly after the masking tone is turned off, say 10 msec later.

The delay time is adjusted to the minimum amount of time such that the test tone can just be distinguished. In general, the louder the test tone, the less time it takes for our hearing to get over hearing the masking tone. Figure 14.6 shows this effect: it may take up to as much as 500 msec for us to discern a quiet test tone after a 60 dB masking tone has been played. Of course, this plot would change for different masking tone frequencies.

Test tones with frequencies near the masking tone are, of course, the most masked. Therefore, for a given masking tone, we have a two-dimensional temporal masking situation, as in Figure 14.7. The closer the frequency to the masking tone and the closer in time to when the masking tone is stopped, the greater likelihood that a test tone cannot be heard. The figure shows the total effect of both frequency and temporal masking.

The phenomenon of saturation also depends on just how long the masking tone has been applied. Figure 14.8 shows that for a masking tone played longer (200 msec) than another (100 msec), it takes longer before a test tone can be heard.

As well as being able to mask other signals that occur just after it sounds (*post-masking*), a particular signal can even mask sounds played just before the stronger signal (*pre-masking*).

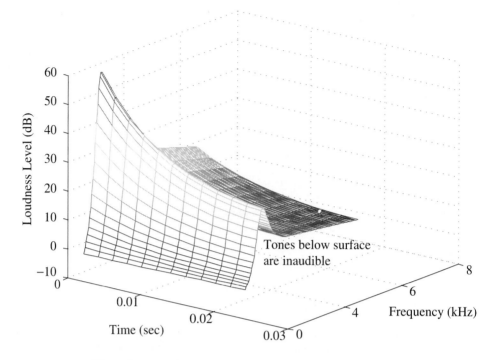

FIGURE 14.7: Effect of temporal masking depends on both time and closeness in frequency.

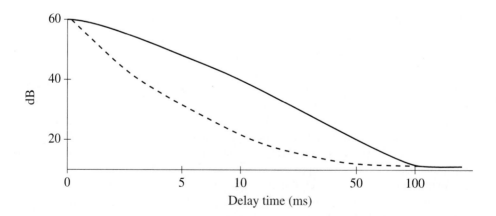

FIGURE 14.8: Effect of temporal masking also depends on the length of time the masking tone is applied. Solid curve: masking tone played for 200 msec; dashed curve: masking tone played for 100 msec.

Pre-masking has a much shorter effective interval (2-5 msec) in which it is operative than does post-masking (usually 50–200 msec).

MPEG audio compression takes advantage of these considerations in basically constructing a large, multidimensional lookup table. It uses this to transmit frequency components that are masked by frequency masking or temporal masking or both, using fewer bits.

14.2 MPEG AUDIO

MPEG Audio proceeds by first applying a filter bank to the input, to break the input into its frequency components. In parallel, it applies a psychoacoustic model to the data, and this model is used in a bit-allocation block. Then the number of bits allocated is used to quantize the information from the filter bank. The overall result is that quantization provides the compression, and bits are allocated where they are most needed to lower the quantization noise below an audible level.

14.2.1 MPEG Layers

MP3 is a popular audio compression standard. The "3" stands for Layer 3, and "MP" stands for the MPEG-1 standard. Recall that we looked at MPEG video compression in Chapter 11. However, the MPEG standard actually delineates three different aspects of multimedia: audio, video, and systems. MP3 forms part of the audio component of this first phase of MPEG. It was released in 1992 and resulted in the international standard ISO/IEC 11172-3, published in 1993.

MPEG audio sets out three downward-compatible *layers* of audio compression, each able to understand the lower layers. Each offers more complexity in the psychoacoustic model applied and correspondingly better compression for a given level of audio quality. However, an increase in complexity, and concomitantly in compression effectiveness, is accompanied by extra delay.

Layers 1 to 3 in MPEG Audio are compatible, because all layers include the same file header information.

Layer 1 quality can be quite good, provided a comparatively high bitrate is available. Digital Audio Tape typically uses Layer 1. Layer 2 has more complexity and was proposed for use in digital audio broadcasting. Layer 3 (MP3) is most complex and was originally aimed at audio transmission over ISDN lines. Each of the layers also uses a different frequency transform.

Most of the complexity increase is at the encoder rather than at the decoder side, and this accounts for the popularity of MP3 players. Layer 1 incorporates the simplest psychoacoustic model, and Layer 3 uses the most complex. The objective is a good tradeoff between quality and bitrate. "Quality" is defined in terms of listening test scores (the psychologists hold sway here), where a quality measure is defined by:

- 5.0 = "Transparent" — undetectable difference from original signal; equivalent to CD-quality audio at 14- to 16-bit PCM

- 4.0 = Perceptible difference, but not annoying

- 3.0 = Slightly annoying

- $2.0 =$ Annoying

- $1.0 =$ Very annoying

(Now that's scientific!) At 64 kbps per channel, Layer 2 scores between 2.1 and 2.6, and Layer 3 scores between 3.6 and 3.8. So Layer 3 provides a substantial improvement but is still not perfect by any means.

14.2.2   MPEG Audio Strategy

Compression is certainly called for, since even audio can take fairly substantial bandwidth: CD audio is sampled at 44.1 kHz and 16 bits/channel, so for two channels needs a bitrate of about 1.4 Mbps. MPEG-1 aims at about 1.5 Mbps overall, with 1.2 Mbps for video and 256 kbps for audio.

The MPEG approach to compression relies on quantization, of course, but also recognizes that the human auditory system is not accurate within the width of a critical band, both in terms of perceived loudness and audibility of a test frequency. The encoder employs a bank of filters that act to first analyze the frequency (*spectral*) components of the audio signal by calculating a frequency transform of a window of signal values. The bank of filters decomposes the signal into subbands. Layer 1 and Layer 2 codecs use a *quadrature-mirror filter* bank, while the Layer 3 codec adds a DCT. For the psychoacoustic model, a Fourier transform is used.

Then frequency masking can be brought to bear by using a psychoacoustic model to estimate the just noticeable noise level. In its quantization and coding stage, the encoder balances the masking behavior and the available number of bits by discarding inaudible frequencies and scaling quantization according to the sound level left over, above masking levels.

A sophisticated model would take into account the actual width of the critical bands centered at different frequencies. Within a critical band, our auditory system cannot finely resolve neighboring frequencies and instead tends to blur them. As mentioned earlier, audible frequencies are usually divided into 25 main critical bands, inspired by the auditory critical bands.

However, in keeping with design simplicity, the model adopts a *uniform width* for all frequency analysis filters, using 32 overlapping subbands [9, 10]. This means that at lower frequencies, each of the frequency analysis "subbands" covers the width of several critical bands of the auditory system, whereas at higher frequencies this is not so, since a critical band's width is less than 100 Hz at the low end and more than 4 kHz at the high end. For each frequency band, the sound level above the masking level dictates how many bits must be assigned to code signal values, so that quantization noise is kept below the masking level and hence cannot be heard.

In Layer 1, the psychoacoustic model uses only frequency masking. Bitrates range from 32 kbps (mono) to 448 kbps (stereo). Near-CD stereo quality is possible with a bitrate of 256–384 kbps. Layer 2 uses some temporal masking by accumulating more samples and examining temporal masking between the current block of samples and the ones just before and just after. Bitrates can be 32–192 kbps (mono) and 64–384 kbps (stereo). Stereo CD-audio quality requires a bitrate of about 192–256 kbps.

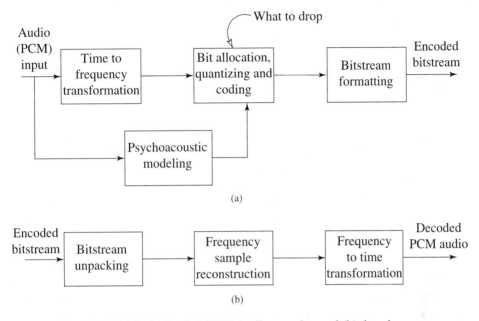

FIGURE 14.9: (a) Basic MPEG Audio encoder; and (b) decoder.

However, temporal masking is less important for compression than is frequency masking, which is why it is sometimes disregarded entirely in lower-complexity coders. Layer 3 is directed toward lower bitrate applications and uses a more sophisticated subband analysis, with nonuniform subband widths. It also adds nonuniform quantization and entropy coding. Bitrates are standardized at 32–320 kbps.

14.2.3   MPEG Audio Compression Algorithm

Basic Algorithm.   Figure 14.9 shows the basic MPEG audio compression algorithm. It proceeds by dividing the input into 32 frequency subbands, via a filter bank. This is a linear operation that takes as its input a set of 32 PCM samples, sampled in time, and produces as its output 32 frequency coefficients. If the sampling rate is f_s, say $f_s = 48$ ksps (kilosamples per second; i.e., 48 kHz), then by the Nyquist theorem, the maximum frequency mapped will be $f_s/2$. Thus the mapped bandwidth is divided into 32 equal-width segments, each of width $f_s/64$ (these segments overlap somewhat).

In the Layer 1 encoder, the sets of 32 PCM values are first assembled into a set of 12 groups of 32s. Hence, the coder has an inherent time lag, equal to the time to accumulate 384 (i.e., 12×32) samples. For example, if sampling proceeds at 32 kbps, then a time duration of 12 msec is required since each set of 32 samples is transmitted each millisecond. These sets of 12 samples, each of size 32, are called *segments*. The point of assembling them is to examine 12 sets of values at once in each of the 32 subbands, after frequency analysis has been carried out, then base quantization on just a summary figure for all 12 values.

Header	SBS format	SBS	Ancillary data

FIGURE 14.10: Example MPEG Audio frame.

The delay is actually somewhat longer than that required to accumulate 384 samples, since header information is also required. As well, *ancillary data*, such as multilingual data and surround-sound data, is allowed. Higher layers also allow more than 384 samples to be analyzed, so the format of the subband-samples (SBS) is also added, with a resulting *frame* of data, as in Figure 14.10. The header contains a synchronization code (twelve 1s — 111111111111), the sampling rate used, the bitrate, and stereo information. The frame format also contains room for so-called "ancillary" (extra) information. (In fact, an MPEG-1 audio decoder can at least partially decode an MPEG-2 audio bitstream, since the file header begins with an MPEG-1 header and places the MPEG-2 datastream into the MPEG-1 Ancillary Data location.)

MPEG Audio is set up to be able to handle stereo or mono channels, of course. A special *joint-stereo* mode produces a single stream by taking into account the redundancy between the two channels in stereo. This is the audio version of a composite video signal. It can also deal with *dual-monophonic* — two channels coded independently. This is useful for parallel treatment of audio — for example, two speech streams, one in English and one in Spanish.

Consider the 32×12 segment as a 32×12 matrix. The next stage of the algorithm is concerned with scale, so that proper quantization levels can be set. For each of the 32 subbands, the maximum amplitude of the 12 samples in that row of the array is found, which is the *scaling factor* for that subband. This maximum is then passed to the bit-allocation block of the algorithm, along with the SBS (subband samples). The key point of the bit-allocation block is to determine how to apportion the total number of code bits available for the quantization of subband signals to minimize the audibility of the quantization noise.

As we know, the psychoacoustic model is fairly complex — more than just a set of lookup tables (and in fact this model is not standardized in the specification — it forms part of the "art" content of an audio encoder and is one major reason all encoders are not the same). In Layer 1, a decision step is included to decide whether each frequency band is basically like a tone or like noise. From that decision and the scaling factor, a masking threshold is calculated for each band and compared with the threshold of hearing.

The model's output consists of a set of what are known as *signal-to-mask ratios* (*SMRs*) that flag frequency components with amplitude below the masking level. The SMR is the ratio of the short-term signal power within each frequency band to the minimum masking threshold for the subband. The SMR gives the amplitude resolution needed and therefore also controls the bit allocations that should be given to the subband. After determination of the SMR, the scaling factors discussed above are used to set quantization levels such that quantization error itself falls below the masking level. This ensures that more bits are used in regions where hearing is most sensitive. In sum, the coder uses fewer bits in critical bands when fewer can be used without making quantization noise audible.

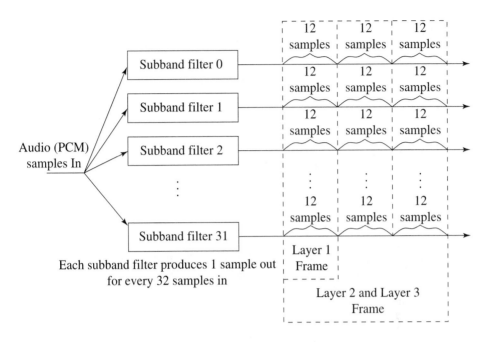

FIGURE 14.11: MPEG Audio frame sizes.

The scaling factor is first quantized, using 6 bits. The 12 values in each subband are then quantized. Using 4 bits, the bit allocations for each subband are transmitted, after an iterative bit allocation scheme is used. Then the data is transmitted, with appropriate bit depths for each subband. Altogether, the data consisting of the quantized scaling factor and the 12 codewords are grouped into a collection known as the Subband-Sample format.

On the decoder side, the values are de-quantized, and magnitudes of the 32 samples are reestablished. These are passed to a bank of *synthesis filters*, which reconstitute a set of 32 PCM samples. Note that the psychoacoustic model is not needed in the decoder.

Figure 14.11 shows how samples are organized. A Layer 2 or Layer 3 frame actually accumulates more than 12 samples for each subband: instead of 384 samples, a frame includes 1,152 samples.

Bit Allocation.   The bit-allocation algorithm is not part of the standard, and it can therefore be done in many possible ways. The aim is to ensure that all the quantization noise is below the masking thresholds. However, this is usually not the case for low bitrates. The psychoacoustic model is brought into play for such cases, to allocate more bits, from the number available, to the subbands where increased resolution will be most beneficial. One common scheme is as follows.

For each subband, the psychoacoustic model calculates the *Signal-to-Mask Ratio*, in dB. A lookup table in the MPEG Audio standard also provides an estimate of the SNR (signal-to-*noise* ratio), assuming quantization to a given number of quantizer levels.

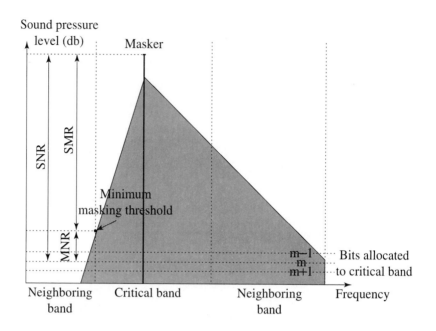

FIGURE 14.12: Mask-to-noise ratio and signal-to-mask ratio. A qualitative view of SNR, SMR and MNR, with one dominant masker and m bits allocated to a particular critical band.

Then the *Mask-to-Noise Ratio* (MNR) is defined as the difference

$$\text{MNR}_{\text{dB}} = \text{SNR}_{\text{dB}} - \text{SMR}_{\text{dB}} \tag{14.6}$$

as Figure 14.12 shows. The lowest MNR is determined, over all the subbands, and the number of code-bits allocated to this subband is incremented. Then a new estimate of the SNR is made, and the process iterates until no more bits are left to allocate.

Mask calculations are performed in parallel with subband filtering, as in Figure 14.13. The masking curve calculation requires an accurate frequency decomposition of the input signal, using a Discrete Fourier Transform (DFT). The frequency spectrum is usually calculated with a 1,024-point Fast Fourier Transform (FFT).

In Layer 1, 16 uniform quantizers are pre-calculated, and for each subband the quantizer giving the lowest distortion is chosen. The index of the quantizer is sent as 4 bits of side information for each subband. The maximum resolution of each quantizer is 15 bits.

Layer 2. Layer 2 of the MPEG-1 Audio codec includes small changes to effect bitrate reduction and quality improvement, at the price of an increase in complexity. The main difference in Layer 2 is that three groups of 12 samples are encoded in each frame, and temporal masking is brought into play, as well as frequency masking. One advantage is that if the scaling factor is similar for each of the three groups, a single scaling factor can be used for all three. But using three frames in the filter (before, current, and next), for a total of 1,152 samples per channel, approximates taking temporal masking into account.

PCM
audio signal

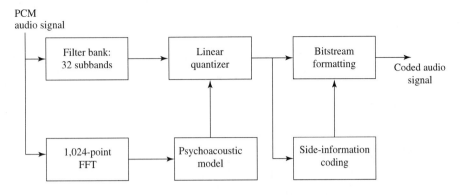

FIGURE 14.13: MPEG-1 Audio Layers 1 and 2.

As well, the psychoacoustic model does better at modeling slowly-changing sound if the time window used is longer. Bit allocation is applied to window lengths of 36 samples instead of 12, and resolution of the quantizers is increased from 15 bits to 16. To ensure that this greater accuracy does not mean poorer compression, the number of quantizers to choose from decreases for higher subbands.

Layer 3. Layer 3, or MP3, uses a bitrate similar to Layers 1 and 2 but produces substantially better audio quality, again at the price of increased complexity.

A filter bank similar to that used in Layer 2 is employed, except that now perceptual critical bands are more closely adhered to by using a set of filters with nonequal frequencies. This layer also takes into account stereo redundancy. It also uses a refinement of the Fourier transform: the *Modified Discrete Cosine Transform (MDCT)* addresses problems the DCT has at boundaries of the window used. The Discrete Fourier Transform can produce block edge effects. When such data is quantized and then transformed back to the time domain, the beginning and ending samples of a block may not be coordinated with the preceding and subsequent blocks, causing audible periodic noise.

The MDCT shown in Equation (14.7), removes such effects by overlapping frames by 50%.

$$F(u) = 2 \sum_{i=0}^{N-1} f(i) \cos\left[\frac{2\pi}{N}\left(i + \frac{N/2+1}{2}\right)(u+1/2)\right], u = 0, \dots, N/2 - 1 \quad (14.7)$$

The MDCT also gives better frequency resolution for the masking and bit allocation operations. Optionally, the window size can be reduced back to 12 samples from 36. Even so, since the window is 50% overlapped, a 12-sample window still includes an extra 6 samples. A size-36 window includes an extra 18 points. Since lower frequencies are more often tonelike rather than noiselike, they need not be analyzed as carefully, so a mixed mode is also available, with 36-point windows used for the lowest two frequency subbands and 12-point windows used for the rest.

PCM
audio signal

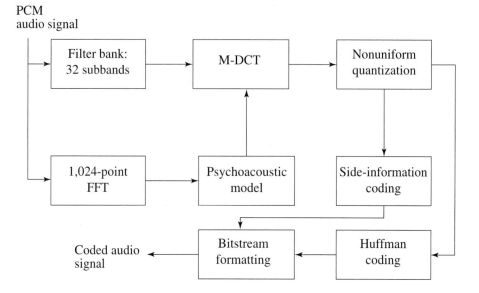

FIGURE 14.14: MPEG-1 Audio Layer 3.

As well, instead of assigning scaling factors to uniform-width subbands, MDCT coefficients are grouped in terms of the auditory system's actual critical bands, and scaling factors, called *scale factor bands*, are calculated from these.

More bits are saved by carrying out entropy coding and making use of nonuniform quantizers. And, finally, a different bit allocation scheme is used, with two parts. Firstly, a nested loop is used, with an inner loop that adjusts the shape of the quantizer, and an outer loop that then evaluates the distortion from that bit configuration. If the error ("distortion") is too high, the scale factor band is amplified. Second, a *bit reservoir* banks bits from frames that don't need them and allocates them to frames that do. Figure 14.14 shows a summary of MPEG Audio Layer 3 coding.

Table 14.2 shows various achievable MP3 compression ratios. In particular, CD-quality audio is achieved with compression ratios in the range of 12:1 to 8:1 (i.e., bitrates of 128 to 192 kbps).

14.2.4 MPEG-2 AAC (Advanced Audio Coding)

The MPEG-2 standard is widely employed, since it is the standard vehicle for DVDs, and it, too, has an audio component. The *MPEG-2 Advanced Audio Coding* (*AAC*) standard [11] was aimed at transparent sound reproduction for theaters. It can deliver this at 320 kbps for five channels, so that sound can be played from five directions: left, right, center, left-surround, and right-surround. So-called 5.1 channel systems also include a *low-frequency enhancement* (*LFE*) channel (a "woofer"). On the other hand, MPEG-2 AAC is also capable of delivering high-quality stereo sound at bitrates below 128 kbps. It is the audio coding

TABLE 14.2: MP3 compression performance.

Sound quality	Bandwidth	Mode	Compression ratio
Telephony	3.0 kHz	Mono	96:1
Better than shortwave	4.5 kHz	Mono	48:1
Better than AM radio	7.5 kHz	Mono	24:1
Similar to FM radio	11 kHz	Stereo	26:1 to 24:1
Near-CD	15 kHz	Stereo	16:1
CD	> 15 kHz	Stereo	14:1 to 12:1

technology for the *DVD-Audio Recordable* (*DVD-AR*) format and is also adopted by XM Radio, one of the two satellite radio services in North America.

MPEG-2 audio can support up to 48 channels, sampling rates between 8 kHz and 96 kHz, and bitrates up to 576 kbps per channel. Like MPEG-1, MPEG-2 supports three different "profiles", but with a different purpose. These are the *Main*, *Low Complexity* (*LC*), and the *Scalable Sampling Rate* (*SSR*). The LC profile requires less computation than the Main profile, but the SSR profile breaks up the signal so that different bitrates and sampling rates can be used by different decoders.

The three profiles follow mostly the same scheme, with a few modifications. First, an MDCT transform is carried out, either on a "long" window with 2,048 samples or a "short" window with 256 samples. The MDCT coefficients are then filtered by a *Temporal Noise Shaping* (*TNS*) tool, with the objective of reducing pre-masking effects and better encoding signals with stable pitch.

The MDCT coefficients are then grouped into 49 scale factor bands, approximately equivalent to a good-resolution version of the human acoustic system's critical bands. In parallel with the frequency transform, a psychoacoustic model similar to the one in MPEG-1 is carried out, to find masking thresholds.

The Main profile uses a predictor. Based on the previous two frames, and only for frequency coefficients up to 16 kHz, MPEG-2 subtracts a prediction from the frequency coefficients, provided this step will indeed reduce distortion. Quantization is governed by two rules: keep distortion below the masking threshold, and keep the average number of bits used per frame controlled, using a bit reservoir. Quantization uses scaling factors — which can be used to amplify some of the scale factor bands — and nonuniform quantization. MPEG-2 AAC also uses entropy coding for both scale factors and frequency coefficients.

Again, a nested loop is used for bit allocation. The inner loop adapts the nonlinear quantizer, then applies entropy coding to the quantized data. If the bit limit is reached for the current frame, the quantizer step size is increased to use fewer bits. The outer loop decides whether for each scale factor band the distortion is below the masking threshold. If a band is too distorted, it is amplified to increase the SNR of that band, at the price of using more bits.

In the SSR profile, a *Polyphase Quadrature Filter* (*PQF*) bank is used. The meaning of this phrase is that the signal is first split into four frequency bands of equal width, then an MDCT is applied. The point of the first step is that the decoder can decide to ignore one of the four frequency parts if the bitrate must be reduced.

14.2.5   MPEG-4 Audio

MPEG-4 audio integrates several different audio components into one standard: speech compression, perceptually based coders, text-to-speech, and MIDI. The primary general audio coder, MPEG-4 AAC [12], is similar to the MPEG-2 AAC standard, with some minor changes.

Perceptual Coders.   One change is to incorporate a *Perceptual Noise Substitution* module, which looks at scale factor bands above 4 kHz and includes a decision as to whether they are noiselike or tonelike. A noiselike scale factor band itself is not transmitted; instead, just its energy is transmitted, and the frequency coefficient is set to zero. The decoder then inserts noise with that energy.

Another modification is to include a *Bit-Sliced Arithmetic Coding* (*BSAC*) module. This is an algorithm for increasing bitrate scalability, by allowing the decoder side to be able to decode a 64 kbps stream using only a 16 kbps baseline output (and steps of 1 kbps from that minimum).

MPEG-4 audio also includes a second perceptual audio coder, a vector-quantization method entitled *Transform-domain Weighted Interleave Vector Quantization* (*TwinVQ*). This is aimed at low bitrates and allows the decoder to discard portions of the bitstream to implement both adjustable bitrate and sampling rate. The basic strategy of MPEG-4 audio is to allow decoders to apply as many or as few audio tools as bandwidth allows.

Structured Coders.   To have a low bitrate delivery option, MPEG-4 takes what is termed a *Synthetic/Natural Hybrid Coding* (*SNHC*) approach. The objective is to integrate both "natural" multimedia sequences, both video and audio, with those arising synthetically. In audio, the latter are termed *structured* audio. The idea is that for low bitrate operation, we can simply send a pointer to the audio model we are working with and then send audio model parameters.

In video, such a *model-based* approach might involve sending face-animation data rather than natural video frames of faces. In audio, we could send the information that English is being modeled, then send codes for the basesounds (phonemes) of English, along with other assembler-like codes specifying duration and pitch.

MPEG-4 takes a *toolbox* approach and allows specification of many such models. For example, *Text-To-Speech* (*TTS*) is an ultra-low bitrate method and actually works, provided we need not care what the speaker actually sounds like. Assuming we went on to derive Face Animation Parameters from such low bitrate information, we arrive directly at a very low bitrate videoconferencing system.

TABLE 14.3: Comparison of audio coding systems.

Codec	Bitrate kbps/channel	Complexity	Main application
Dolby AC-2	128–192	Low (encoder/decoder)	Point-to-point, cable
Dolby AC-3	32–640	Low (decoder)	HDTV, cable, DVD
Sony ATRAC	140	Low (encoder/decoder)	Minidisc

Another "tool" in structured audio is called *Structured Audio Orchestra Language* (*SAOL*, pronounced "sail"), which allows simple specification of sound synthesis, including special effects such as reverberation.

Overall, structured audio takes advantage of redundancies in music to greatly compress sound descriptions.

14.3   OTHER COMMERCIAL AUDIO CODECS

Table 14.3 summarizes the target bitrate range and main features of other modern general audio codecs. They bear many similarities to MPEG-2 audio codecs.

14.4   THE FUTURE: MPEG-7 AND MPEG-21

Recall that MPEG-4 is aimed at compression using objects. MPEG-4 audio has several interesting features, such as 3D localization of sound, integration of MIDI, text-to-speech, different codecs for different bitrates, and use of the sophisticated MPEG-2 AAC codec. However, newer MPEG standards are mainly aimed at "search": how can we find objects, assuming that multimedia is indeed coded in terms of objects?

The formulation of MPEG-21 [13] is an ongoing effort, aimed at driving a standardization effort for a *Multimedia Framework* from a consumer's perspective, particularly addressing interoperability. However, we can say something more specific about how MPEG-7 means to describe a structured model of audio [14], so as to promote ease of search for audio objects.

Officially called a method for *Multimedia Content Description Interface*, MPEG-7 provides a means of standardizing metadata for audiovisual multimedia sequences. MPEG-7 is meant to represent information about multimedia information.

The objective, in terms of audio, is to facilitate the representation and search for sound content, perhaps through the tune or other descriptors. Therefore, researchers are laboring to develop descriptors that efficiently describe, and can help find, specific audio in files. These might require human or automatic content analysis and might be aimed not just at low-level structures, such as melody, but at actually grasping information regarding structural and semantic content [15].

An example application supported by MPEG-7 is *automatic speech recognition* (*ASR*). Language understanding is also an objective for MPEG-7 "content". In theory, MPEG-7 would allow searching on spoken and visual events: "Find me the part where Hamlet says,

'To be or not to be.'" However, the objective of delineating a complete, structured audio model for MPEG-7 is by no means complete.

Nevertheless, low-level features are important. A recent summary of such work [16] sets out one set of such descriptors.

14.5 FURTHER EXPLORATION

Good reviews of MPEG Audio are contained in the articles [9, 17]. A comprehensive explication of natural audio coding in MPEG-4 appears in [18]. Structured audio is introduced in [19], and exhaustive articles on natural and structured audio in MPEG-4 appear in [20] and [21].

The Further Exploration section of the text web site for this chapter contains a number of useful links:

- Excellent collections of MPEG audio and MP3 links

- The MPEG audio FAQ

- An excellent reference by the Fraunhofer-Gesellschaft research institute, "MPEG 4 Audio Scalable Profile," on the subject of Tools for Large Step Scalability. This allows the decoder to decide how many tools to apply and at what complexity, based on available bandwidth.

14.6 EXERCISES

1. **(a)** What is the threshold of quiet, according to Equation (14.1), at 1,000 Hz? (Recall that this equation uses 2 kHz as the reference for the 0 dB level.)

   (b) Take the derivative of Equation (14.1) and set it equal to zero, to determine the frequency at which the curve is minimum. What frequency are we most sensitive to? Hint: One has to solve this numerically.

2. Loudness versus amplitude. Which is louder: a 1,000 Hz sound at 60 dB or a 100 Hz sound at 60 dB?

3. For the (newer versions of the) Fletcher-Munson curves, in Figure 14.1, the way this data is actually observed is by setting the y-axis value, the sound pressure level, and measuring a human's estimation of the effective perceived loudness. Given the set of observations, what must we do to turn these into the set of perceived loudness curves shown in the figure?

4. Two tones are played together. Suppose tone 1 is fixed, but tone 2 has a frequency that can vary. The *critical bandwidth* for tone 1 is the frequency range for tone 2 over which we hear *beats*, and a roughness in the sound. Beats are overtones at a lower frequency than the two close tones; they arise from the difference in frequencies of the two tones. The critical bandwidth is bounded by frequencies beyond which the two tones sound with two distinct pitches.

   (a) What would be a rough estimate of the critical bandwidth at 220 Hz?

   (b) Explain in words how you would set up an experiment to measure the critical bandwidth.

5. Search the web to discover what is meant by the following psychoacoustic phenomena:

  (a) Virtual pitch
  (b) Auditory scene analysis
  (c) Octave-related complex tones
  (d) Tri-tone paradox
  (e) Inharmonic complex tones

6. If the sampling rate f_s is 32 ksps, in MPEG Audio Layer 1, what is the width in frequency of each of the 32 subbands?

7. Given that the level of a *masking tone* at the 8th band is 60 dB, and 10 msec after it stops, the masking effect to the 9th band is 25 dB.

  (a) What would MP3 do if the original signal at the 9th band is at 40 dB?
  (b) What if the original signal is at 20 dB?
  (c) How many bits should be allocated to the 9th band in (a) and (b) above?

8. What does MPEG Layer 3 (MP3) audio do differently from Layer 1 to incorporate temporal masking?

9. Explain MP3 in a few paragraphs, for an audience of consumer-audio-equipment salespeople.

10. Implement MDCT, just for a single 36-sample signal, and compare the frequency results to those from DCT. For low-frequency sound, which does better at concentrating the energy in the first few coefficients?

11. Convert a CD-audio cut to MP3. Compare the audio quality of the original and the compressed version — can you hear the difference? (Many people cannot.)

12. For two stereo channels, we would like to be able to use the fact that the second channel behaves, usually, in a parallel fashion to the first, and apply information gleaned from the first channel to compression of the second. Discuss how you think this might proceed.

14.7 REFERENCES

1 D.W. Robinson and R.S. Dadson, "A Re-determination of the Equal-Loudness Eelations for Pure Tones," *British Journal of Applied Physics*, 7: 166–181, 1956.

2 H. Fletcher and W.A. Munson, "Loudness, Its Definition, Measurement and Calculation," *J. of the Acoustic Society of America*, 5: 82–107, 1933.

3 T. Painter and A. Spanias, "Perceptual Coding of Digital Audio," *Proceedings of the IEEE*, 88(4): 451–513, 2000.

4 B. Truax, *Handbook for Acoustic Ecology, 2nd ed.* Burnaby, BC, Canada: Cambridge Street Publishing, 1999.

5 D. O'Shaughnessy, *Speech Communications: Human and Machine*, Los Alamitos, CA: IEEE Press, 2000.

6   A.J.M. Houtsma, "Psychophysics and Modern Digital Audio Technology," *Philips Journal of Research*, 47: 3–14, 1992.

7   E. Zwicker and U. Tilmann, "Psychoacoustics: Matching Signals to the Final Receiver," *Journal of the Audio Engineering Society*, 39: 115–126, 1991.

8   D. Lubman, "Objective Metrics for Characterizing Automotive Interior Sound Quality," in *Inter-Noise '92*, 1067–1072.

9   D. Pan, "A Tutorial on MPEG/Audio Compression," *IEEE Multimedia*, 2(2): 60–74, 1995.

10   P. Noll, "MPEG Digital Audio Coding," *IEEE Signal Processing Magazine*, 14(5): 59–81, Sep. 1997.

11   *Information Technology — Generic Coding of Moving Pictures and Associated Audio Information, Part 7: Advanced Audio Coding (AAC)*, International Standard: ISO/IEC 13818-7, 1997.

12   *Information Technology — Coding of Audio-Visual Objects, Part 3: Audio*, International Standard: ISO/IEC 14496-3, 1998.

13   *Information Technology — Multimedia Framework*, International Standard: ISO/IEC 21000, Parts 1-7, 2003.

14   *Information Technology — Multimedia Content Description Interface, Part 4: Audio*, International Standard: ISO/IEC 15938-4, 2001.

15   A.T. Lindsay, S. Srinivasan, J.P.A. Charlesworth, P. N. Garner, and W. Kriechbaum, "Representation and Linking Mechanisms for Audio in MPEG-7," *Signal Processing: Image Communication*, 16: 193–209, 2000.

16   P. Philippe, "Low-Level Musical Descriptors for MPEG-7," *Signal Processing: Image Communication*, 16: 181–191, 2000.

17   S. Shlien, "Guide to MPEG-1 Audio Standard," *IEEE Transactions on Broadcasting*, 40: 206–218, 1994.

18   K. Brandenburg, O. Kunz, and A. Sugiyama, "MPEG-4 Natural Audio Coding," *Signal Processing: Image Communication*, 15: 423–444, 2000.

19   E.D. Scheirer, "Structured Audio and Effects Processing in the MPEG-4 Multimedia Standard," *Multimedia Systems*, 7: 11–22, 1999.

20   J.D. Johnston, S.R. Quackenbush, J. Herre, and B. Grill, "Review of MPEG-4 General Audio Coding," in *Multimedia Systems, Standards, and Networks*, ed. A. Puri and T. Chen, New York: Marcel Dekker, 2000, 131–155.

21   E.D. Scheirer, Y. Lee, and J.W. Yang, "Synthetic Audio and SNHC Audio in MPEG-4," in *Multimedia Systems, Standards, and Networks*, ed. A. Puri and T. Chen, New York: Marcel Dekker, 2000, 157–177.

MULTIMEDIA COMMUNICATION AND RETRIEVAL

Multimedia places great demands on networks and systems. This part examines several important multimedia networks and applications that are essential and challenging.

Multimedia Networks

With the ever-increasing bandwidth made available by breakthroughs in fiber optics, we are witnessing a convergence of telecommunication networks and computer and multimedia networks and a surge in mixed traffic types (Internet telephony, video-on-demand, etc.) through them. The technologies of multiplexing and scheduling are being constantly reexamined. Moreover, we are also witnessing an emergence of wireless networks (think about our cell phones and PDAs).

In Chapter 15, we look at basic issues and technologies for computer and multimedia networks, and in Chapter 16 we go on to consider multimedia network communications and applications. Chapter 17 provides a quick introduction to the basics of wireless networks and issues related to multimedia communication over these networks.

Content-Based Retrieval in Digital Libraries

Automated retrieval of syntactically and semantically useful contents from multimedia databases is crucial, especially when the contents have become so rich and the size of the databases has grown so rapidly. Chapter 18 looks at a particular application of multimedia database systems, examining the issues involved in content-based retrieval, storage, and browsing in digital libraries.

C H A P T E R   15

Computer and Multimedia Networks

Computer networks are essential to the modern computing environment we know and have come to rely upon. Multimedia networks share all major issues and technologies of computer networks. Moreover, the ever-growing needs for various multimedia communications have made networks one of the most active areas for research and development.

This chapter will start with a review of some common techniques and terminologies in computer and multimedia networks, followed by an introduction to various high-speed networks, since they are becoming a central part of most contemporary multimedia systems.

15.1 BASICS OF COMPUTER AND MULTIMEDIA NETWORKS

15.1.1 OSI Network Layers

It has long been recognized that network communication is a complex task that involves multiple levels of protocols. A multilayer protocol architecture was thus proposed by the International Organization for Standardization (ISO) in 1984, called *Open Systems Interconnection* (OSI), documented by ISO Standard 7498. The OSI Reference Model has the following network layers [1, 2]:

1. **Physical Layer**. Defines electrical and mechanical properties of the physical interface (e.g., signal level, specifications of the connectors, etc.); also specifies the functions and procedural sequences performed by circuits of the physical interface.

2. **Data Link Layer**. Specifies the ways to establish, maintain, and terminate a link, such as transmission and synchronization of data frames, error detection and correction, and access protocol to the Physical layer.

3. **Network layer**. Defines the routing of data from one end to the other across the network, such as circuit switching or packet switching. Provides services such as addressing, internetworking, error handling, congestion control, and sequencing of packets.

4. **Transport layer**. Provides end-to-end communication between *end systems* that support end-user applications or services. Supports either *connection-oriented* or *connectionless* protocols. Provides error recovery and flow control.

5. **Session layer**. Coordinates interaction between user applications on different hosts, manages sessions (connections), such as completion of long file transfers.

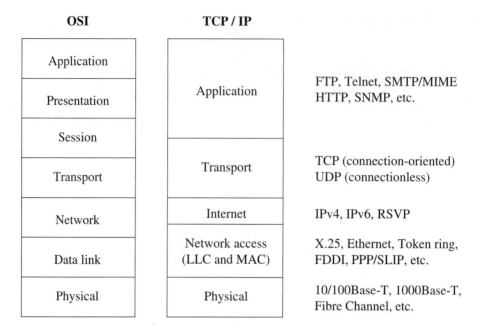

FIGURE 15.1: Comparison of OSI and TCP/IP protocol architectures and sample protocols.

6. **Presentation layer**. Deals with the syntax of transmitted data, such as conversion of different data formats and codes due to different conventions, compression, or encryption.

7. **Application layer**. Supports various application programs and protocols, such as FTP, Telnet, HTTP, SNMP, SMTP/MIME, and so on.

15.1.2   TCP/IP Protocols

The OSI protocol architecture, although instrumental in the development of computer networks, did not gain full acceptance, due largely to the competing and more practical TCP/IP set of protocols. TCP/IP protocols were developed before OSI and were funded mostly by the U.S. Department of Defense. They become the *de facto* standard after their adoption by the Internet.

Figure 15.1 compares the OSI and TCP/IP protocol architectures. It can be seen that TCP/IP reduced the total number of layers and basically merged the top three OSI layers into a single application layer. In fact, TCP/IP is even so flexible as to sometimes allow application layer protocols operating directly on IP.

Transport Layer: TCP and UDP.   TCP and UDP are two transport layer protocols used in TCP/IP to facilitate host-to-host (or peer-to-peer) communications.

1. **Transmission Control Protocol (TCP)**. TCP is *connection-oriented*: it provides reliable data transfer between pairs of communicating processes across the network. It handles the sending of application data to the destination process, regardless of datagram or packet size. However, TCP/IP is established for packet-switched networks only. Hence, there are no circuits, and data still have to be packetized.

   TCP relies on the IP layer for delivering the message to the destination computer specified by its IP address. It provides message packetizing, error detection, retransmission, packet resequencing, and multiplexing. Since a process running TCP/IP is required to be able to establish multiple network connections to a remote process, multiplexing is achieved by identifying connections using port numbers.

   For every TCP connection, both communicating computers allocate a buffer called a *window* to receive and send data. Flow control is established by only sending data in the window to the destination computer without overflowing its window. The maximum data that can be transmitted at a time is the size of the smaller window of the two computers.

   Each TCP datagram header contains the source and destination ports, sequence number, checksum, window field, acknowledgment number, and other fields.

   - The *source* and *destination ports* are needed for the source process to know where to deliver the message and for the destination process to know where to reply to the message (the address is specified in the IP layer).

   - As packets travel across the network, they can arrive out of order (by following different paths), be lost, or be duplicated. A *sequence number* reorders arriving packets and detects whether any are missing. The sequence number is actually the byte count of the first data byte of the packet rather than a serial number for the packet.

   - The *checksum* verifies with a high degree of certainty that the packet arrived undamaged, despite channel interference. If the calculated checksum for the received packet does not match the transmitted one, the packet is dropped.

   - The *window field* specifies how many bytes the current computer's buffer can receive. This is typically sent with acknowledgment packets.

   - *Acknowledgment* (ACK) packets have the *ACK number* specified — the number of bytes correctly received so far in sequence (corresponding to a sequence number of the first missing packet).

   The source process sends datagrams to the destination process up to the window number and waits for ACKs before sending any more data. The ACK packet will arrive with new window number information to indicate how much more data the destination buffer can receive. If ACK is not received in a small time interval, specified by *retransmission timeout* (RTO), the packet is resent from the local window buffer. TCP/IP does not specify congestion control mechanisms, yet every TCP/IP implementation should include it.

   Although TCP is reliable, the overhead of retransmission is often viewed as too high for many real-time multimedia applications, such as streaming video. These will typically use UDP.

2. **User Datagram Protocol (UDP).** UDP is *connectionless*: the message to be sent is a single datagram. If the message is too long or requires guaranteed delivery, it will have to be handled by the application layer. Essentially, the only thing UDP provides is multiplexing and error detection through a checksum. Although the UDP header does have fields to specify source and destination port numbers, the source port number is optional, since the destination computer is not expected to reply to the message (there is no acknowledgment).

   Although UDP data transmission is much faster than TCP, it is unreliable, especially in a congested network. The increasingly improving quality of fiber-optic networks minimizes packet loss. In most real-time multimedia applications (e.g., streaming video or audio), packets that arrive late are simply discarded. Although higher-level protocols can be used for retransmission, flow control, and congestion avoidance, more realistically *error concealment* must be explored for acceptable Quality of Service (QoS).

Network Layer: Internet Protocol (IP).   The IP layer provides two basic services: packet addressing and packet fragmentation. Point-to-point message transmission is readily supported within any *Local Area Networks* (LANs), and in fact, LANs usually support broadcast. However, when a message needs to be sent to a machine on a different LAN, an intermediate device is needed to forward the message. The IP protocol provides for a global addressing of computers across all interconnected networks, where every networked computer (or device) is assigned a globally unique IP address.

For an IP packet to be transmitted across different LANs or *Wide Area Networks* (WANs), *gateways* or *routers* are employed, which use *routing tables* to direct the messages according to destination *IP addresses*. A gateway is a computer that usually resides at the edge of the LAN and can send IP packets on both the LAN network interface and the WAN network interface to communicate with other interconnected computers not on the LAN. A router is a device that receives packets and routes them according to their destination address for the same type of network.

The IP layer also has to translate the destination IP address of incoming packets to the appropriate network address. In addition, routing tables identify for each destination IP the next best router IP through which the packet should travel. Since the best route can change depending on node availability, network congestion and other factors, routers have to communicate with each other to determine the best route for groups of IPs. The communication is done using *Internet Control Message Protocol* (ICMP).

IP is *connectionless*; it provides no end-to-end flow control. Every packet is treated separately and is not related to past or future packets. Hence, packets can be received out of order and can also be dropped or duplicated.

Packet fragmentation is performed when a packet has to travel over a network that accepts only packets of a smaller size. In that case, IP packets are split into the required smaller size, sent over the network to the next hop, and reassembled and resequenced there.

In its current version, IPv4 (IP version 4), IP addresses are 32-bit numbers, usually specified using *dotted decimal notation* (e.g., 128.77.149.63 = 10000000 01001101 10010101 00111111). The 32-bit addressing in principle allows $2^{32} \approx 4$ billion addresses, which seemed more than adequate. In reality, however, we could be running out of new IP addresses soon (projected in year 2008).

This is not only because of the proliferation of personal computers and wireless devices but also because IP addresses are assigned wastefully. For example, the IP address is of the form *(network number, host number)*. Under many network numbers, the percentage of used host numbers is relatively small, not to mention some inactive hosts that may still occupy their previously assigned addresses.

As a short-term solution to the shortage of IP address availability (due to limitations of service provider or cost), some LANs use *proxy servers* or *Network Address Translation* (NAT) devices that proxy servers implement (in addition to content caching and other features). The NAT device separates the LAN from the interconnected network and has only one IP address to handle the communication of all the computers on the LAN. Each computer on a LAN is assigned a local IP address that cannot be accessed from the interconnected network. The NAT device typically maintains a dynamic NAT table that translates communication ports used with its public IP address to the ports and local IP addresses of the communicating computers.

When a local computer sends an IP packet with the local address as the source, it goes through the NAT device, which changes the source IP address to the NAT device IP address that is global. When an IP packet arrives on some communication port to the NAT IP address, the destination address is changed to the local IP address according to the NAT table, and the packet is forwarded to the appropriate computer.

In January 1995, IPv6 (IP version 6) was recommended as the *next generation IP* (IPng) by the Internet Engineering Task Force (IETF) in its Request for Comments (RFC) 1752, "The Recommendation for the IP Next Generation Protocol". Among many improvements over IPv4, it adopts 128-bit addresses, allowing $2^{128} \approx 3.4 \times 10^{38}$ addresses [2]. This will certainly settle the problem of shortage of IP addresses for a long time (if not forever).

15.2 MULTIPLEXING TECHNOLOGIES

Modern communication links usually have high capacity. This became even more true after the introduction of fiber-optic networks. When the link capacity far exceeds any individual user's data rate, *multiplexing* must be introduced for users to share the capacity.

In this section, we examine the basic multiplexing technologies, followed by a survey on several modern networks, such as ISDN, SONET, and ADSL.

15.2.1 Basics of Multiplexing

1. **Frequency Division Multiplexing (FDM)**. In FDM, multiple *channels* are arranged according to their frequency. Analogously, radios and televisions are good examples of FDM — they share the limited bandwidth of broadcast bands in the air by dividing them into many channels. Nowadays, cable TV resembles an FDM data network even more closely, since it has similar transmission media. Ordinary voice channels and TV channels have conventional bandwidths of 4 kHz for voice, 6 MHz for NTSC TV, and 8 MHz for PAL or SECAM TV.

For FDM to work properly, analog signals must be *modulated* first, with a unique *carrier* frequency f_c for each channel. As a result, the signal occupies a bandwidth B_s centered at f_c. The receiver uses a band-pass filter tuned for the channel-of-interest to capture the signal, then uses a demodulator to decode it.

Basic modulation techniques include *Amplitude Modulation* (AM), *Frequency Modulation* (FM), and *Phase Modulation* (PM). A combination of Amplitude Modulation and Phase Modulation yields the *Quadrature Amplitude Modulation* (QAM) method [1, 2] used in many modern applications.

Digital data is often transmitted using analog signals. The classic example is a modem (modulator-demodulator) transmitting digital data on telephone networks. A carrier signal is modulated by the digital data before transmission, then demodulated upon its reception to recover the digital data. Basic modulation techniques are *Amplitude-Shift Keying (ASK)*, *Frequency-Shift Keying (FSK)*, and *Phase-Shift Keying (PSK)*. *QPSK (Quadrature Phase-Shift Keying)* is an advanced version of PSK that uses a phase shift of 90 degrees instead of 180 degrees [2]. As QAM, it can also combine phase with amplitude, so as to carry multiple bits on each subcarrier.

2. **Wavelength Division Multiplexing (WDM).** WDM is a variation of FDM that is especially useful for data transmission in optical fibers. In essence, light beams representing channels of different wavelengths are combined at the source and transmitted within the same fiber; they are split again at the receiver end. The combining and splitting of light beams is carried out by optical devices [e.g., *Add-Drop Multiplexer* (ADM)], which are highly reliable and more efficient than electronic circuits. Since the bandwidth of each fiber is very high (> 25 terahertz for each band), the capacity of WDM is tremendous — a huge number of channels can be multiplexed. As a result, the aggregate bitrate of fiber trunks can potentially reach dozens of terabits per second.

Two variations of WDM are

- **Dense WDM (DWDM),** which employs densely spaced wavelengths to allow a larger number of channels than WDM (e.g., more than 32).

- **Wideband WDM (WWDM),** which allows the transmission of color lights with a wider range of wavelengths (e.g., 1310 to 1557 nm for long reach and 850 nm for short reach) to achieve a larger capacity than WDM.

3. **Time Division Multiplexing (TDM).** As described above, FDM is more suitable for analog data and is less common in digital computer networks. TDM is a technology for directly multiplexing digital data. If the source data is analog, it must first be digitized and converted into Pulse Code Modulation (PCM) samples, as described in Chapter 6.

In TDM, multiplexing is performed along the time (t) dimension. Multiple buffers are used for m ($m > 1$) channels. A bit (or byte) will be taken from each buffer at one of the m cycled time slots until a frame is formed. The TDM frame will be transmitted and then demultiplexed after its reception.

The scheme described above is known as *Synchronous TDM*, in which each of the m buffers is scanned in turn and treated equally. If, at a given time slot, some sources

TABLE 15.1: Comparison of TDM Carrier Standards

Format	Number of channels	Data rate (Mbps)	Format	Number of channels	Data rate (Mbps)
T1	24	1.544	E1	32	2.048
T2	96	6.312	E2	128	8.448
T3	672	44.736	E3	512	34.368
T4	4032	274.176	E4	2048	139.264
			E5	8192	565.148

(accordingly buffers) do not have data to transmit, the slot is wasted. *Asynchronous TDM* (or *Statistical TDM*) gathers the statistics of the buffers in this regard. It will assign only k ($k < m$) time slots to scan the k buffers likely to have data to send. Asynchronous TDM has the potential for higher throughput, given the same carrier data rate. There is, however, an overhead, since now the source address must also be sent, along with the data, to have the frame demultiplexed correctly.

Traditionally, voice data over a telephone channel has a bandwidth of 4 kHz. According to the Nyquist theorem, 8,000 samples per second are required for a good digitization. This yields a time interval of 125 μsec for each sample. Each channel can transmit 8 bits per sample, producing a gross data rate (including data and control) for each voice channel of $8 \times 8{,}000 = 64$ kbps.

In North America and Japan, a T1 carrier[1] is basically a synchronous TDM of 24 voice channels (i.e., 24 time slots), of which 23 are used for data and the last one for synchronization. Each T1 frame contains $8 \times 24 = 192$ bits, plus one bit for framing [1, 2]. This yields a gross data rate of 193 bits per 125 μsec — that is, 193 bits/sample $\times$ 8,000 samples/sec $= 1.544$ Mbps.

Four T1 carriers can be further multiplexed to yield a T2. Note that T2 has a gross data rate of 6.312 Mbps, which is more than $4 \times 1.544 = 6.176$ Mbps, because more framing and control bits are needed. In a similar fashion, T3 and T4 are created.

Similar carrier formats have been defined by the ITU-T, with level 1 (E1) starting at 2.048 Mbps, in which each frame consists of 32 time slots: $8 \times 32 \times 8{,}000 = 2.048$ Mbps. Two slots are used for framing and synchronization; the other 30 are for data channels. The multiplexed number of channels quadruples at each of the next levels — E2, E3, and so on. Table 15.1 compares the data rates of both TDM carrier standards.

15.2.2   Integrated Services Digital Network (ISDN)

For over a century, *Plain Old Telephone Service* (POTS) was supported by the public circuit-switched telephone system for analog voice transmission. In 1980s, the ITU-T started to

---

[1] The format for the T1 carrier is called DS1, T2 is called DS2, and so on. Less strictly, these two notations (T and DS) are often used interchangeably.

develop ISDN to meet the needs of various digital services (e.g., caller ID, instant call setup, teleconferencing) in which digital data, voice, and sometimes video (e.g., in videoconferencing) can be transmitted.

By default, ISDN refers to *Narrowband ISDN*. The ITU-T has subsequently developed *Broadband ISDN* (B-ISDN). Its default switching technique is *Asynchronous Transfer Mode* (ATM) [3] which will be discussed later.

ISDN defines several types of full-duplex channels:

- **B (bearer)-channel**. 64 kbps each. B-channels are for data transmission. Mostly they are circuit-switched, but they can also support packet switching. If needed, one B-channel can be readily used to replace POTS.

- **D (delta)-channel**. 16 kbps or 64 kbps. D-channel takes care of call setup, call control (call forwarding, call waiting, etc.), and network maintenance. The advantage of having a separate D-channel is that control and maintenance can be done in realtime in D-channel while B-channels are transmitting data.

The following are the main specifications of ISDN:

- It adopts Synchronous TDM, in which the above channels are multiplexed.

- Two type of interfaces were available to users, depending on the data and subscription rates:

  - **Basic Rate Interface** provides two B-channels and one D-channel (at 16 kbps). The total of 144 kbps ($64 \times 2 + 16$) is multiplexed and transmitted over a 192 kbps link.

  - **Primary Rate Interface** provides 23 B-channels and one D-channel (at 64 kbps) in North America and Japan; 30 B-channels and two D-channels (at 64 kbps) in Europe. The 23B and 1D fit in T1 nicely, because T1 has 24 time slots and a data rate of 24 slots $\times$ 64 kbps/slot $\approx$ 1,544 kbps; whereas the 30B and 2D fit in E1, which has 32 time slots (30 of them available for user channels) and a data rate of $32 \times 64 = 2,048$ kbps.

Because of its relatively slow data rate and high cost, narrowband ISDN has generally failed to meet the requirement of data and multimedia networks. For home computer/Internet users, it has largely been replaced by Cable Modem and Asymmetric Digital Subscriber Line (ADSL) discussed below.

15.2.3   Synchronous Optical NETwork (SONET)

SONET is a standard initially developed by Bellcore for optical fibers that support data rates much beyond T3. Subsequent SONET standards are coordinated and approved by ANSI in ANSI T1.105, T1.106 and T1.107. SONET uses circuit switching and synchronous TDM.

TABLE 15.2: Equivalency of SONET and SDH

SONET electrical level	SONET optical level	SDH equivalent	Line rate (Mbps)	Payload rate (Mbps)
STS-1	OC-1	—	51.84	50.112
STS-3	OC-3	STM-1	155.52	150.336
STS-9	OC-9	STM-3	466.56	451.008
STS-12	OC-12	STM-4	622.08	601.344
STS-18	OC-18	STM-6	933.12	902.016
STS-24	OC-24	STM-8	1244.16	1202.688
STS-36	OC-36	STM-12	1866.24	1804.032
STS-48	OC-48	STM-16	2488.32	2405.376
STS-96	OC-96	STM-32	4976.64	4810.752
STS-192	OC-192	STM-64	9953.28	9621.504

In optical networks, electrical signals must be converted to optical signals for transmission and converted back after their reception. Accordingly, SONET uses the terms *Synchronous Transport Signal* (STS) for the electrical signals and *Optical Carrier* (OC) for the optical signals.

An STS-1 (OC-1) frame consists of 810 TDM bytes. It is transmitted in 125 μsec, — 8,000 frames per second, so the data rate is $810 \times 8 \times 8,000 = 51.84$ Mbps. All other STS-N (OC-N) signals are further multiplexing of STS-1 (OC-1) signals. For example, three STS-1 (OC-1) signals are multiplexed for each STS-3 (OC-3) at 155.52 Mbps.

Instead of SONET, ITU-T developed a similar standard, *Synchronous Digital Hierarchy* (SDH), using the technology of *Synchronous Transport Module* (STM). STM-1 is the lowest in SDH — it corresponds to STS-3 (OC-3) in SONET.

Table 15.2 lists the SONET electrical and optical levels and their SDH equivalents and data rates. Among all, OC-3 (STM-1), OC-12 (STM-4), OC-48 (STM-16), and OC-192 (STM-64) are the ones mostly used.

15.2.4 Asymmetric Digital Subscriber Line (ADSL)

ADSL is the telephone industry's answer to the *last mile* challenge — delivering fast network service to every home. It adopts a higher data rate downstream (from network to subscriber) and lower data rate upstream (from subscriber to network); hence, it is *asymmetric*.

ADSL makes use of existing telephone twisted-pair lines to transmit *Quadrature Amplitude Modulated* (QAM) digital signals. Instead of the conventional 4 kHz for audio signals on telephone wires, the signal bandwidth on ADSL lines is pushed to 1 MHz or higher.

ADSL uses FDM (Frequency Division Multiplexing) to multiplex three channels:

- The high speed (1.5 to 9 Mbps) downstream channel at the high end of the spectrum

TABLE 15.3: Maximum Distances for ADSL Using Twisted-Pair Copper Wire

Data Rate	Wire Size	Distance
1.544 Mbps	0.5 mm	5.5 km
1.544 Mbps	0.4 mm	4.6 km
6.1 Mbps	0.5 mm	3.7 km
6.1 Mbps	0.4 mm	2.7 km

- A medium speed (16 to 640 kbps) duplex channel

- A POTS channel at the low end (next to DC, 0–4 kHz) of the spectrum.[2]

The three channels can themselves be further divided into 4 kHz subchannels (e.g., 256 subchannels for the downstream channel, for a total of 1 MHz). The multiplexing scheme among these subchannels is also FDM.

Because signals (especially the higher-frequency signals near or at 1 MHz) attenuate quickly on twisted-pair lines, and noise increases with line length, the signal-to-noise ratio will drop to an unacceptable level after a certain distance. Not considering the effect of bridged taps, ADSL has the distance limitations shown in Table 15.3 when using only ordinary twisted-pair copper wires.

The key technology for ADSL is *Discrete Multi-Tone* (DMT). For better transmission in potentially noisy channels (either downstream or upstream), the DMT modem sends test signals to all subchannels first. It then calculates the signal-to-noise ratios, to dynamically determine the amount of data to be sent in each subchannel. The higher the SNR, the more data sent. Theoretically, 256 downstream subchannels, each capable of carrying over 60 kbps, will generate a data rate of more than 15 Mbps. In reality, DMT delivers 1.5 to 9 Mbps under current technology.

Table 15.4 offers a brief history of various digital subscriber lines (*xDSL*). DSL corresponds to the basic-rate ISDN service. HDSL was an effort to deliver the T1 (or E1) data rate within a low bandwidth (196 kHz) [2]. However, it requires two twisted pairs for 1.544 Mbps or three twisted pairs for 2.048 Mbps. SDSL provides the same service as HDSL on a single twisted-pair line. VDSL is a standard that is still actively evolving and forms the future of xDSL.

15.3 LAN AND WAN

Local Area Network (LAN) is restricted to a small geographical area, usually to a relatively small number of stations. *Wide Area Network* (WAN) refers to networks across cities and countries. Between LAN and WAN, the term *Metropolitan Area Network* (MAN) is sometimes also used.

---

[2]Alternatively, an ISDN channel can be supported in place of low- and medium-speed channels.

TABLE 15.4: History of Digital Subscriber Lines

Name	Meaning	Data rate	Mode
V.32 or V.34	Voice band modems	1.2 to 56 kbps	Duplex
DSL	Digital subscriber line	160 kbps	Duplex
HDSL	High data rate digital subscriber line	1.544 Mbps or 2.048 Mbps	Duplex
SDSL	Single line digital subscriber line	1.544 Mbps or 2.048 Mbps	Duplex
ADSL	Asymmetric digital subscriber line	1.5 to 9 Mbps 16 to 640 kbps	Down Up
VDSL	Very high data rate digital subscriber line	13 to 52 Mbps 1.5 to 2.3 Mbps	Down Up

15.3.1 Local Area Networks (LANs)

Most LANs use a broadcast technique. Without exception, they use a shared medium. Hence, medium access control is an important issue.

The IEEE 802 committee developed the IEEE 802 reference model for LANs. Since layer 3 and above in the OSI reference model are applicable to either LAN, MAN, or WAN, main developments of the IEEE 802 standards are on the lower layers — the Physical and the Data Link layers. In particular, the Data Link layer's functionality is enhanced, and the layer has been divided into two sublayers:

- **Medium Access Control (MAC) layer**. This layer assembles or disassembles frames upon transmission or reception, performs addressing and error correction, and regulates access control to a shared physical medium.

- **Logical Link Control (LLC) layer**. This layer performs flow and error control and MAC-layer addressing. It also acts as an interface to higher layers. LLC is above MAC in the hierarchy.

Following are some of the active IEEE 802 subcommittees and the areas they define:

- **802.1 (Higher Layer LAN Protocols)**. The relationship between the 802.X standards and the OSI reference model, the interconnection and management of the LANs

- **802.2 (LLC)**. The general standard for logical link control (LLC)

- **802.3 (Ethernet)**. Medium access control (CSMA/CD) and physical layer specifications for Ethernet

- **802.5 (Token Ring)**. Medium access control and physical layer specifications for token ring

- **802.9**. LAN interfaces at the medium access control and physical layers for integrated services

- **802.10 (Security)**. Interoperable LAN/MAN security for other IEEE 802 standards

- **802.11 (Wireless LAN)**. Medium access method and physical layer specifications for wireless LAN (WLAN)

- **802.14 (Cable-TV based broadband communication network)**. Standard protocol about two-way transmission of multimedia services over cable TV; e.g., Hybrid Fiber-Coax (HFC) cable modem and cable network

- **802.15 (Wireless PAN)**. Access method and physical layer specifications for *Wireless Personal Area Network* (WPAN). A Personal Area Network (PAN) supports coverages on the order of 10 meters

- **802.16 (Broadband wireless)**. Access method and physical layer specifications for broadband wireless networks

Ethernet. *Ethernet* is a packet-switched *bus* network, it is the most popular LAN to date. As of 1998, the coverage of Ethernets has reached 85% of networked computers. To send a message, the recipient's Ethernet address is attached to the message, and the message is sent to everyone on the bus. Only the designated station will receive the message, while others will ignore it.

The problem of medium access control for the network is solved by *Carrier Sense Multiple Access with Collision Detection* (CSMA/CD). The station that wishes to send a message must listen to the network (carrier sense) and wait until there is no traffic. Apparently, multiple stations could be waiting and then send their messages at the same time, causing a collision. During frame transmission, the station compares the signals received with the ones sent. If they are different, it detects a collision. Once a collision is detected, the station stops sending the frame, and the frame is retransmitted after a random delay.

A good transmission medium for Ethernet is coaxial cable (or optical fiber for newer generations). However, it is also possible to use twisted pair. Since these are simply telephone wires, in most cases they are already in office buildings or homes and do not need to be reinstalled.

Often a *star* LAN is used, in which each station is connected directly to a *hub*, which also helps cope with the potential of lower transmission quality. The hub is an active device and acts as a repeater. Every time it receives a signal from one station, it repeats, so other stations will hear. Logically, this is still a bus, although it is physically a star network.

The maximum data rate for ordinary Ethernet is 10 Mbps. For the 10 Mbps LAN, unshielded twisted pair was used in 10BASE-T within 100 meters, whereas optical fiber was used in 10BASE-F up to 2 kilometers.

Fast Ethernet (known as 100BASE-T) has a maximum data rate of 100 Mbps[3] and is entirely Ethernet-compatible. Indeed, it is common nowadays to mix 100BASE-T and 10BASE-T through a *switch* (instead of a hub) — that is, 100BASE-T link between server and 100BASE-T switch, and several 10BASE-T links between the switch and workstations. Since the switch is capable of handling multiple communications at the same time, all workstations can communicate up to a maximum data rate of 10 Mbps.

Token Ring.   Stations on a *token ring* are connected in a *ring* topology, as the name suggests. Data frames are transmitted in one direction around the ring and can be read by all stations. The ring structure can be merely *logical* when stations are actually (physically) connected to a hub, which repeats and relays the signal down the "ring".

A small frame, called a *token*, circulates while the ring is idle. To transmit, a station S must wait until the token arrives. The source station S then seizes the token and converts it to a front end of its data frame, which then travels on the ring and is received by the destination station. The data frame continues traveling on the ring until it comes back to station S, which releases it and puts it back onto the ring.

Access to the shared medium is regulated by allowing only one token; hence, collision is avoided. By default, the ring operates in a round-robin fashion. Every time a token is released, the next station gets the chance to take it, and so on. Optionally, a multiple priority scheme can also be used for access control — a station can transmit a frame at a given priority if it can grab a token with an equal or lower priority; otherwise, it makes a reservation and waits for its turn.

The data rates of the token rings were either 4 Mbps or 16 Mbps over shielded twisted pair. The 4 Mbps ring manipulates the token as described above. In the 16 Mbps ring, the token can be released as soon as the source station sends out the data frame. This increases ring usage by allowing more than one frame to travel on the ring simultaneously. New technology has enabled 100 Mbps token rings [2] and IEEE 802.5v was a feasibility study for Gigabit token ring in 1998.

Fiber Distributed Data Interface (FDDI).   *FDDI* is a successor of the original token ring [4]. Medium access control (MAC) of FDDI is similar to MAC in IEEE 802.5 described above for token rings.

FDDI has a dual-ring topology, with its primary ring for data transmission and secondary ring for fault tolerance [5]. If damage is detected in both rings, they can be joined to function as a single ring.

The bitrate of FDDI is 100 Mbps. Because of the relatively fast transmission speed, the source stations will simply *absorb* the token (instead of converting it as part of its data frame, as in the original token ring) before sending its data frame(s).

In FDDI, once a station captures a token, it is granted a time period and may send as many data frames as it can within the period. Also, the token will be released as soon as the frames are transmitted (early token release).

---

[3]Next generation Ethernets are *Gigabit Ethernet* and *10-Gigabit Ethernet*, which will be described later.

The FDDI network is allowed to spread over distances up to 100 km. It supports up to 500 stations, as long as the maximum distance of neighboring stations is less than 2 kilometers. Hence, FDDI is primarily used in LAN or MAN backbones.

FDDI supports both *synchronous* and *asynchronous* modes [5]. Synchronous mode enables bandwidth reservation and guaranteed data transmission up to the *synchronous capacity*. Asynchronous mode is similar to the token ring protocol. FDDI-2 supports an additional mode — *isochronous mode* [5], in which the network is time-sliced, with each machine getting a fixed piece. FDDI can thus provide isochronous services for delay-sensitive applications (such as audio and video) and synchronous and asynchronous services for others in the same network.

15.3.2 Wide Area Networks (WANs)

WAN usually refers to networks across cities and countries. Instead of broadcast, they invariably use some type of switching technologies.

Switching Technologies. The common types of switching technologies are *circuit switching* and *packet switching*. The latter also has its modern variants of *frame relay* and *cell relay*.

- **Circuit Switching**. The *public switched telephone network* (PSTN) is a good example of circuit switching, in which an end-to-end circuit (duplex, in this case) must be established that is dedicated for the duration of the connection at a guaranteed bandwidth. Although initially designed for voice communications, it can also be used for data transmission. Indeed, it is still the basis for narrowband ISDN, discussed in Section 15.2.2. To cope with multi-users and variable data rates, it adopts FDM or synchronous TDM multiplexing.

  Circuit switching is preferable if the user demands a connection and/or more or less constant data rates, as in certain constant-bitrate video communications. It is inefficient for general multimedia communication, especially for variable (sometimes bursty) data rates.

- **Packet Switching**. Packet switching is used for almost all data networks in which data rates tend to be variable and sometimes bursty. Before transmission, data is broken into small *packets*, usually 1,000 bytes or less. The header of each packet carries necessary control information, such as destination address, routing, and so on. X.25 was the most commonly used protocol for packet switching.

  Generally, two approaches are available to switch and route the packets: *datagram* and *virtual circuits*. In the former, each packet is treated independently as a datagram. No transfer route is predetermined prior to the transmission; hence, packets may be unknowingly lost or arrive in the wrong order. It is up to the receiving station to detect and recover the errors, as is the case with TCP/IP.

  In *virtual circuits*, a route is predetermined through *request* and *accept* by all nodes along the route. It is a "circuit" because the route is fixed (once negotiated) and used for the duration of the connection; nonetheless, it is "virtual" because the "circuit" is only logical and not dedicated, and packets from the same source to the same destination can be transferred through different "circuits". Sequencing (ordering the packets) is much easier in virtual circuits. Retransmission is usually requested upon detection of an error.

Packet switching becomes ineffective when the network is congested and becomes unreliable by severely delaying or losing a large number of packets.

- **Frame Relay**. Modern high-speed links have low error rate; in optical fiber, it can be down to the order of 10^{-12}. Many bits added to each packet for excessive error checking in ordinary packet switching (X.25) thus become unnecessary.

  As X.25, *frame relay* works at the data link control layer. Frame relay made the following major changes to X.25:

  - **Reduction of error checking**. No more acknowledgment, no more hop-to-hop flow control and error control. Optionally, end-to-end flow control and error control can be performed at a higher layer.

  - **Reduction of layers**. The multiplexing and switching virtual circuits are changed from layer 3 in X.25 to layer 2. Layer 3 of X.25 is eliminated.

  Frame relay is basically a cheaper version of packet switching, with minimal services. *Frames* have a length up to 1,600 bytes. When a bad frame is received, it will simply be discarded. The data rate for frame relay is thus much higher, in the range of T1 (1.5 Mbps) to T3 (44.7 Mbps).

- **Cell Relay (ATM)**. *Asynchronous transfer mode* adopts small and fixed-length (53 bytes) packets referred to as *cells*. Hence, ATM is also known as *cell relay*.

  As Figure 15.2 shows, the small packet size is beneficial in reducing latency in ATM networks. When the darkened packet arrives slightly behind another packet of a normal size (e.g., 1 kB) in Figure 15.2(a), it must wait for the completion of the other's transmission, causing *serialization delay*. When the packet (cell) size is small, as in Figure 15.2(b), much less waiting time is needed for the darkened cell to be sent. This turns out to significantly increase network throughput, which is especially beneficial for real-time multimedia applications. ATM is known to have the potential to deliver high data rates at hundreds (and thousands) of Mbps.

Figure 15.3 compares the above four switching technologies in terms of their bitrates and complexity. It can be seen that circuit switching is the least complex and offers a constant (fixed) data rate, while packet switching is the opposite.

15.3.3 Asynchronous Transfer Mode (ATM)

Ever since the 1980s, the dramatic increase in data communications and multimedia services (voice, video, etc.) has posed a major challenge to telecommunication networks. With the ever-expanding bandwidth through optical fiber, *broadband ISDN* (B-ISDN) became a reality. By 1990, the ITU-T (formerly CCITT) adopted synchronous optical network/synchronous digital hierarchy (SONET/SDH) as the base of B-ISDN. Since SONET

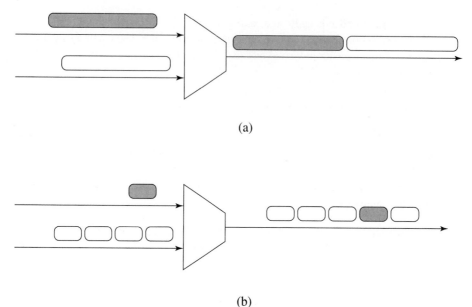

(a)

(b)

FIGURE 15.2: Latency: (a) serialization delay in a normal packet switching network; (b) lower latency in a cell network.

uses circuit switching technology and specifies only the transmission and multiplexing of data, a new standard for switching technology was desired.

ATM can provide high speed and low delay — its operational version has been scaled to 2.5 Gbps (OC-48). ATM is also flexible in supporting various technologies, such as Frame relay (bursty), IP Ethernet, xDSL, SONET/SDH, and wireless networks. Moreover, it is capable of guaranteeing predefined levels of Quality of Service (QoS). Hence, ATM was chosen as the switching technology for B-ISDN.

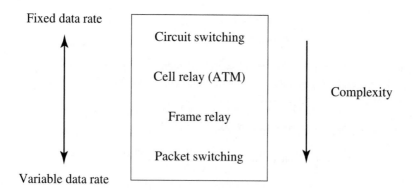

FIGURE 15.3: Comparison of different switching techniques.

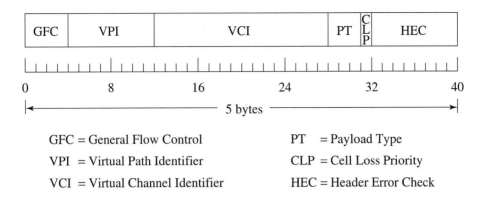

GFC = General Flow Control   PT   = Payload Type
VPI = Virtual Path Identifier   CLP = Cell Loss Priority
VCI = Virtual Channel Identifier   HEC = Header Error Check

FIGURE 15.4: ATM UNI cell header.

Initially, ATM was used for WANs, especially serving as backbones. Nowadays, it is also used in LAN applications.

The ATM Cell Structure.   ATM cells have a fixed format: their size is 53 bytes, of which the first 5 bytes are for the cell header, followed by 48 bytes of payload.

The ATM layer has two types of interfaces: *User-Network Interface* (UNI) is local, between a user and an ATM network, and *Network-Network Interface* (NNI) is between ATM switches.

Figure 15.4 illustrates the structure of an ATM UNI cell header. The header starts with a 4-bit general flow control (GFC) which controls traffic entering the network at the local user-network level. It is followed by an 8-bit Virtual Path Identifier (VPI) and 16-bit Virtual Channel Identifier (VCI) for selecting a particular virtual path and virtual circuit, respectively. The combination of VPI (8 bits) and VCI (16 bits) provides a unique routing indicator for the cell. As an analogy, VPI is like an area code (604), and VCI is like the following digits (555-1212) in a phone number.

The 3-bit payload type (PT) specifies whether the cell is for user data or management and maintenance, network congestion, and so on. For example, 000 indicates user data cell type 0, no congestion; 010 indicates user data cell type 0, congestion experienced. PT may be altered by the network, say from 000 to 010, to indicate that the network has become congested.

The 1-bit cell loss priority (CLP) allows the specification of a low-priority cell when CLP is set to 1. This provides a hint to the ATM switches about which cells to drop when the network is congested.

The 8-bit header error detection (HEC) checks errors only in the header (not in the payload). Since the rest of the header is only 32 bits long, this is a relatively long 8-bit field; it is used for both error checking and correction [2].

The NNI header is similar to the UNI header, except it does not have the 4-bit GFC. Instead, its VPI is increased to 12 bits.

ATM Layers and Sublayers.   Figure 15.5 illustrates the comparison between OSI layers and ATM layers and sublayers at *ATM Adaptation Layer* (AAL) and below. As

OSI   ATM

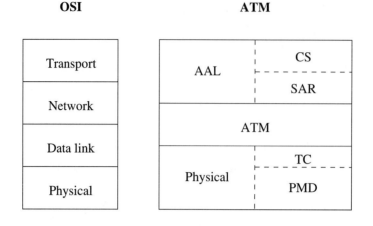

AAL = ATM Adaptation Layer

CS   = Convergence Sublayer

SAR = Segmentation and Reassembly

TC   = Transmission Convergence

PMD = Physical Medium Dependent

FIGURE 15.5: Comparison of OSI (layer 4 and below) and ATM layers.

shown, AAL corresponds to the OSI Transport layer and part of the Network layer. It consists of two sublayers: *convergence sublayer* (CS) and *segmentation and reassembly* (SAR). CS provides interface (convergence) to user applications. SAR is in charge of cell segmentation and reassembly.

The ATM layer corresponds to parts of the OSI Network and Data Link layers. Its main functions are flow control, management of virtual circuit and path, and cell multiplexing and demultiplexing. The ATM Physical layer consists of two sublayers: Transmission Convergence (TC) and Physical Medium Dependent (PMD). PMD corresponds to the OSI Physical layer, whereas TC does header error checking and packing/unpacking frames (cells). This makes the ATM Physical layer very different from the OSI Physical layer, where framing is left for the OSI Data Link layer.

15.3.4 Gigabit and 10-Gigabit Ethernets

Gigabit Ethernet became a standard (IEEE 802.3z) in 1998 [2]. It employs the same frame format and size as the previous Ethernets and is backward compatible with 10BASE-T and 100BASE-T. It is generally known as 1000BASE-T although it can be further classified as 1000BASE-LX, 1000BASE-SX, 1000BASE-CX, and 1000BASE-T when it uses various fiber or copper media. The maximum link distance under 1000BASE-LX is 5 kilometers for single-mode optical fiber (SM fiber), 550 meters for multi-mode fiber (*MM fiber*), and merely 25 meters for shielded twisted pair.

TABLE 15.5: Comparison of Fast, Gigabit, and 10-Gigabit Ethernets.

	Fast Ethernet (100BASE-T)	**Gigabit Ethernet** (1000BASE-T)	**10-Gigabit Ethernet**
Data rate	100 Mbps	1 Gbps	10 Gbps
Transmission mode	Full or half duplex	Full or halfduplex	Full duplex only
Access method	CSMA/CD	CSMA/CD	N/A (no collision)
Medium	Copper or fiber	Fiber or copper	Fiber only
Target distance	Up to 2 km (fiber) 200 m (copper)	Up to 5 km (SM fiber) 550 m (MM fiber) 25 m (copper)	Up to 40 km (SM fiber) 300 m (MM fiber)
Network Type	LAN	LAN/MAN	LAN/MAN/WAN
IEEE Standard Year	802.3u 1995	802.3z 1998	802.3ae 2002

Gigabit Ethernet adopts full-duplex modes for connections to and from switches and half-duplex modes for shared connections that use repeaters. Since collisions do occur frequently in half-duplex modes, Gigabit Ethernet uses standard Ethernet access method Carrier Sense Multiple Access with Collision Detection (CSMA/CD), as in its predecessors. Gigabit Ethernet has been rapidly replacing Fast Ethernet and FDDI, especially in network backbones. It has gone beyond LAN and found use in MANs.

10-Gigabit Ethernet was completed in 2002. It retains the main characteristics of Ethernet (bus, packet switching) and the same packet format as before. At a data rate of 10 Gbps, it functions only over optical fiber. Since it operates only under full duplex (switches and buffered distributors), it does not need CSMA/CD for collision detection.

10-Gigabit Ethernet is expected to finally enable the convergence of voice and data networks. It can be substantially cheaper than ATM. Its design encompasses all LAN, MAN, and WAN, and its carrying capacity is equivalent or superior to Fiber Channel, High Performance Parallel Interface (HIPPI), Ultra 320 or 640 SCSI, and ATM/SONET OC-192. The maximum link distance is increased to 40 kilometers for SM fiber (see Table 15.5). In fact, special care is taken for interoperability with SONET/SDH, so Ethernet packets can readily travel across SONET/SDH links.

Table 15.5 provides a brief comparison of Fast Ethernet, Gigabit Ethernet, and 10-Gigabit Ethernet.

15.4   ACCESS NETWORKS

An *access network* connects end users to the core network. It is also known as the "last mile" for delivering various multimedia services, which could include Internet access, telephony, and digital and analog TV services.

Beside ADSL, discussed earlier, some known options for access networks are:

- **Hybrid Fiber-Coax (HFC) Cable Network**. Optical fibers connect the core network with Optical Network Units (ONUs) in the neighborhood, each of which typically serves a few hundred homes. All end users are then served by a shared coaxial cable.

  Traditionally, analog cable TV was allocated a frequency range of 50–500 MHz, divided into 6 MHz channels for NTSC TV and 8 MHz channels in Europe. For HFC cable networks, the downstream is allocated a frequency range of 450–750 MHz, and upstream is allocated a range of 5–42 MHz. For the downstream, a cable modem acts as a tuner to capture the QAM modulated digital stream. The upstream uses Quadrature Phase-Shift Keying (QPSK) [2] modulation, because it is more robust in the noisy and congested frequency spectrum.

  A potential problem of HFC is the noise or interference on the shared coaxial cable. Privacy and security on the upstream channel are also a concern.

- **Fiber To The Curb (FTTC)**. Optical fibers connect the core network with ONUs at the curb. Each ONU is then connected to dozens of homes via twisted-pair copper or coaxial cable. For FTTC, a star topology is used at the ONUs, so the media to the end user are not shared — a much improved access network over HFC. Typical data rates are T1 to T3 in the downstream direction and up to 19.44 Mbps in the upstream direction.

- **Fiber To The Home (FTTH)**. Optical fibers connect the core network directly with a small group of homes, providing the highest bandwidth. For example, before reaching four homes, a 622 Mbps downstream can be split into four 155 Mbps downstreams by TDM. Since most homes have only twisted pairs and/or coaxial cables, the implementation cost of FTTH will be high.

- **Terrestrial Distribution**. Terrestrial broadcasting uses VHF and UHF spectra (approximately 40–800 MHz). Each channel occupies 8 MHz in Europe and 6 MHz in the U.S., and each transmission covers about 100 kilometers in diameter. AM and FM modulations are employed for analog videos, and *Coded Orthogonal Frequency Division Multiplexing* (COFDM) for digital videos. The standard is known as *Digital Video Broadcasting-Terrestrial* (DVB-T). Since the return channel (upstream) is not supported in terrestrial broadcasting, a separate POTS or N-ISDN link is recommended for the upstream in interactive applications.

- **Satellite Distribution**. Satellite broadcasting uses the Gigahertz spectrum. Each satellite covers an area of several thousand kilometers. For digital video, each satellite channel typically has a data rate of 38 Mbps, good for several *Digital Video Broadcasting* (DVB) channels. Its standard is Digital Video Broadcasting-Satellite (DVB-S). Similar to DVB-T, POTS or N-ISDN is proposed as a means of supporting upstream data in DVB-S.

TABLE 15.6: Speed of Common Peripheral Interfaces

Type	Data-rate	Type	Data-rate
Serial Port	115 kbps	Ultra2 SCSI	40 MB/s
Standard parallel port	115 kB/s	IEEE 1394 (FireWire, i.Link)	1.5–50 MB/s
USB	1.5 MB/s	USB 2	60 MB/s
ECP/EPP parallel port	3 MB/s	Wide Ultra2 SCSI (Fast 40)	80 MB/s
IDE	3.3–16.7 MB/s	Ultra3 SCSI	80 MB/s
SCSI-1	5 MB/s	Ultra ATA 133	133 MB/s
SCSI-2 (Fast SCSI, Fast narrow SCSI)	10 MB/s	Wide Ultra3 SCSI (Ultra 160 SCSI, Fast 80)	160 MB/s
Fast wide SCSI (Wide SCSI)	20 MB/s	HIPPI	100–200 MB/s
Ultra SCSI (SCSI-3, Ultra narrow SCSI)	20 MB/s	Ultra 320 SCSI	320 MB/s
EIDE	33 MB/s	Fiber Channel	100–400 MB/s
Wide Ultra SCSI (Fast 20)	40 MB/s	Ultra 640 SCSI	640 MB/s

USB	Universal Serial Bus	SCSI	Small Computer System Interface
ECP	Enhanced Capability Port	Narrow	8-bit data
EPP	Enhanced Parallel Port	Wide	16-bit data
IDE	Integrated Disk Electronics	HIPPI	High Performance Parallel Interface
EIDE	Enhanced IDE		

15.5   COMMON PERIPHERAL INTERFACES

For a comparison, Table 15.6 lists the speeds of various common peripheral interfaces for connecting I/O and other devices [hard disk, printer, CD-ROM, pointing devices (e.g., mouse), Personal Digital Assistant (PDA), digital camera, and so on].

15.6   FURTHER EXPLORATION

Good general discussions on computer networks and data communications are given in the books by Tanenbaum [1] and Stallings [2].

The Further Exploration section of the text web site for this chapter provides an extensive set of web resources for computer and multimedia networks including links to

- SONET FAQ, etc.

- xDSL introductions at the DSL Forum web site

- Introductions and White Papers on ATM

- FAQ and White Papers on 10 Gigabit Ethernet at the Alliance web site

- IEEE 802 standards

- IETF Request for Comments (RFC) for IPv6 (Internet Protocol, Version 6)

15.7 EXERCISES

1. What is the main difference between the OSI and TCP/IP reference models?

2. IPv6 is a newer IP protocol. What is its advantage over IPv4?

3. UDP does not provide end-to-end flow control, but TCP does. Explain how this is achieved using sequence numbers. Give an example where a packetized message sent using UDP is received incorrectly, but when using TCP it is received correctly under the same circumstances (without channel errors).

4. As a variation of FDM, WDM is used for multiplexing over fiber-optic channels. Compare WDM with FDM.

5. Both ISDN and ADSL deliver integrated network services, such as voice, video, and so on, to home users or small-office users. What are the advantages of ADSL over ISDN?

6. Several protocols, such as Ethernet, Token ring, and FDDI, are commonly used in LAN. Discuss the functionalities of these three technologies and differences among them.

7. Frame relay and Cell relay are variants of packet switching. Compare these two technologies.

8. What is the difference between switching and routing? Are routing algorithms specific to a switching technology?

9. How many sublayers are there in ATM? What are they?

10. In HFC cable networks, two modulation schemes are used for sending downstream and upstream data. Why should the upstream case be handled differently from downstream? Should we employ different multiplexing technologies as well?

15.8 REFERENCES

1 A.S. Tanenbaum, *Computer Networks*, 4th ed., Upper Saddle River, NJ: Prentice Hall PTR, 2003.

2 W. Stallings, *Data & Computer Communications*, 6th ed., Upper Saddle River, NJ: Prentice Hall, 2000.

3 W. Stallings, *ISDN and Broadband ISDN, with Frame Relay and ATM*, Upper Saddle River, NJ: Prentice Hall, 1999.

4 K. Tolly, "Introduction to FDDI," *Data Communications*, 22(11): 81–86, 1993.

5 R. Steinmetz and K. Nahrstedt, *Multimedia: Computing, Communications & Applications*, Upper Saddle River, NJ: Prentice Hall PTR, 1995.

CHAPTER 16

Multimedia Network Communications and Applications

Fundamentally, multimedia network communication and (traditional) computer network communication are similar, since they both deal with data communications. However, challenges in multimedia network communications arise because multimedia data (audio, video, etc.) are known as *continuous media*. They have the following characteristics:

- **Voluminous.** They demand high data rates, possibly dozens or hundreds of Mbps.

- **Real-Time and Interactive.** They demand low delay and synchronization between audio and video for "lip sync". In addition, applications such as videoconferencing and interactive multimedia require two-way traffic.

- **Sometimes Bursty.** Data rates fluctuate drastically — for example, in video-on-demand, no traffic most of the time but burst to high volume.

16.1 QUALITY OF MULTIMEDIA DATA TRANSMISSION

16.1.1 Quality of Service (QoS)

Quality of Service (QoS) for multimedia data transmission depends on many parameters. Some of the most important are:

- **Data Rate.** A measure of transmission speed, often in kilobits per second (kbps) or megabits per second (Mbps)

- **Latency (maximum frame/packet delay).** Maximum time needed from transmission to reception, often measured in milliseconds (msec). In voice communication, for example, when the round-trip delay exceeds 50 msec, *echo* becomes a noticeable problem; when the one-way delay is longer than 250 msec, *talker overlap* will occur, since each caller will talk without knowing the other is also talking.

- **Packet loss or error.** A measure (in percentage) of error rate of the packetized data transmission. Packets get lost or garbled, such as over the Internet. They may also be delivered late or in the wrong order. Since retransmission is often undesirable, a

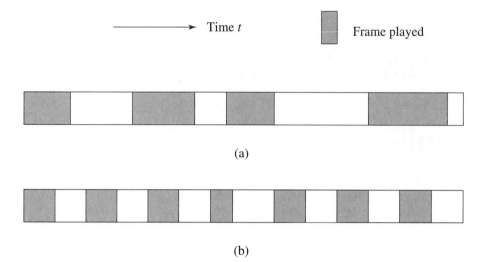

FIGURE 16.1: Jitters in frame playback: (a) high jitter; (b) low jitter.

simple error-recovery method for real-time multimedia is to replay the last packet, hoping the error is not noticeable.

In general, for uncompressed audio/video, the desirable packet loss is $< 10^{-2}$ (lose every hundredth packet, on average). When it approaches 10%, it becomes intolerable. For compressed multimedia and ordinary data, the desirable packet loss is less than 10^{-7} to 10^{-8}. Some prioritized delivery techniques, described in Section 16.1.3, can alleviate the impact of packet loss.

- **Jitter (*or* delay jitter).** A measure of smoothness of the audio/video playback. Technically, *jitter* is related to the variance of frame/packet delays. A large buffer (jitter buffer) can to hold enough frames to allow the frame with the longest delay to arrive, to reduce playback jitter. However, this increases the latency and may not be desirable in real-time and interactive applications. Figure 16.1 illustrates examples of high and low jitters in frame playbacks.

- **Sync skew.** A measure of multimedia data synchronization, often measured in milliseconds (msec). For a good *lip synchronization*, the limit of sync skew is ± 80 msec between audio and video. In general, ± 200 msec is still acceptable. For a video with speaker and voice the limit of sync skew is 120 msec if video precedes voice and 20 msec if voice precedes video. (The discrepancy is probably because we are used to have sound lagging image at a distance.)

Multimedia Service Classes   Based on the above measures, multimedia applications can be classified into the following types:

- **Real-Time (*also* Conversational).** Two-way traffic, low latency and jitter, possibly with prioritized delivery, such as voice telephony and video telephony

TABLE 16.1: Requirement on network bandwidth/bitrate.

Application	Speed requirement
Telephone	16 kbps
Audio conferencing	32 kbps
CD-quality audio	128–192 kbps
Digital music (QoS)	64–640 kbps
H. 261	64 kbps–2 Mbps
H. 263	< 64 kbps
DVI video	1.2–1.5 Mbps
MPEG-1 video	1.2–1.5 Mbps
MPEG-2 video	4–60 Mbps
HDTV (compressed)	> 20 Mbps
HDTV (uncompressed)	> 1 Gbps
MPEG-4 video-on-demand (QoS)	250–750 kbps
Videoconferencing (QoS)	384 kbps–2 Mbps

- **Priority data.** Two-way traffic, low loss and low latency, with prioritized delivery, such as e-commerce applications

- **Silver.** Moderate latency and jitter, strict ordering and sync. One-way traffic, such as streaming video; or two-way traffic (also *Interactive*), such as web surfing and Internet games

- **Best Effort** (*also* **Background**). No real-time requirement, such as downloading or transferring large files (movies)

- **Bronze.** No guarantees for transmission

Table 16.1 lists the general bandwidth/bit rate requirement for multimedia networks. Table 16.2 lists some specifications for tolerance to delay and jitter in digital audio and video of different qualities.

Perceived QoS.   Although QoS is commonly measured by the above technical parameters, QoS itself is a "collective effect of service performances that determine the degree of satisfaction of the user of that service," as defined by the International Telecommunications Union. In other words, it has everything to do with how the user *perceives* it.

In real-time multimedia, regularity is more important than latency (i.e., jitter and quality fluctuation are more annoying than slightly longer waiting); temporal correctness is more important than the sound and picture quality (i.e., ordering and synchronization of audio and video are of primary importance); and humans tend to focus on one subject at a time.

TABLE 16.2: Tolerance of latency and jitter in digital audio and video.

Application	Average latency tolerance (msec)	Average jitter tolerance (msec)
Low-end videoconference (64 kbps)	300	130
Compressed voice (16 kbps)	30	130
MPEG NTSC video (1.5 Mbps)	5	7
MPEG audio (256 kbps)	7	9
HDTV video (20 Mbps)	0.8	1

User focus is usually at the center of the screen, and it takes time to refocus, especially after a scene change.

Together with the perceptual nonuniformity we have studied in previous chapters, many issues of perception can be exploited in achieving the best perceived QoS in networked multimedia.

16.1.2   QoS for IP Protocols

QoS policies and technologies enable key metrics discussed in the previous section such as latency, packet loss, and jitter to be controlled by offering different levels of service to different packet streams or applications.

Frame relay routing protocol and ATM provide some levels of QoS, but currently most Internet applications are built on IP. IP is a "best-effort" communications technology and does not differentiate among different IP applications. Therefore it is hard to provide QoS over IP by current routing methods.

Abundant bandwidth improves QoS, but in complex networks, abundant bandwidth is unlikely to be available everywhere (in practice, many IP networks routinely use oversubscription). In particular, it is unlikely to be available in all the access links. Even if it is available everywhere, bandwidth alone can't resolve problems due to sudden peaks in traffic.

Differentiated Service (DiffServ) uses DiffServ code [Type of Service (TOS) octet in IPv4 packet and Traffic Class octet in IPv6 packet] to classify packets to enable their differentiated treatment. It is becoming more widely deployed in intradomain networks and enterprise networks, as it is simpler and scales well, although it is also applicable to end-to-end networks. DiffServ, in conjunction with other QoS techniques, is emerging as the de facto QoS technology. See IETF Request for Comments (RFC) 2998 for more information.

Multiple Protocol Label Switching (MPLS) facilitates the marriage of IP to OSI layer 2 technologies, such as ATM, by overlaying a protocol on top of IP. It introduces a 32-bit label and inserts one or more *shim* labels into the header of an IP packet in a backbone IP network. It thus creates tunnels, called *Label Switched Paths (LSP)*. By doing so, the backbone IP network becomes connection-oriented.

The two main advantages of MPLS are to support *Traffic Engineering* (*TE*), which is used essentially to control traffic flow, and *Virtual Private Networks* (*VPN*). Both TE and VPN help delivery of QoS for multimedia data. MPLS supports eight service classes. For more detail refer to RFC 3031.

DiffServ and MPLS can be used together to allow better control of both QoS performance per class and provision of bandwidth, retaining advantages of both MPLS and DiffServ.

16.1.3 Prioritized Delivery

When a high packet loss or error rate is detected in the event of network congestion, prioritized delivery of multimedia data can be used to alleviate the perceived deterioration.

- **Prioritization for types of media.** Transmission algorithms can provide prioritized delivery to different media — for example, giving higher priority to audio than to video — since loss of content in audio is often more noticeable than in video.

- **Prioritization for uncompressed audio.** PCM audio bitstreams can be broken into groups of every nth sample — prioritize and send k of the total of n groups ($k \leq n$) and ask the receiver to interpolate the lost groups if so desired. For example, if two out of four groups are lost, the effective sampling rate is 22.05 kHz instead of 44.1 kHz. Loss is perceived as change in sampling rate, not dropouts.

- **Prioritization for JPEG image.** The different *scans* in Progressive JPEG and different resolutions of the image in Hierarchical JPEG can be given different priorities, for example, highest priority for the scan with the DC and first few AC coefficients, and higher priority to lower-resolution components of the Hierarchical JPEG image.

- **Prioritization for compressed video.** Video prioritization algorithms can set priorities to minimize playback delay and jitter by giving the highest priority to reception of I-frames and the lowest priority to B-frames. In scalable video (such as MPEG-2 and 4) using layered coding, the base layer can be given higher priority than the enhancement layers.

16.2 MULTIMEDIA OVER IP

Due to the great popularity and availability of the Internet, various efforts have been made to make Multimedia over IP a reality, although it was known to be a challenge. This section will study some of the key issues, technologies, and protocols.

16.2.1 IP-Multicast

In network terminology, a *broadcast* message is sent to all nodes in the domain, a *unicast* message is sent to only one node, and a *multicast* message is sent to a set of specified nodes.[1]

IP-multicast enables multicast on the Internet. It is vital for applications such as mailing lists, bulletin boards, group file transfer, audio/video-on-demand, audio/videoconferencing, and so on. Steve Deering introduced IP-multicast technology in his 1988 Ph.D. dissertation.

---

[1] IPv6 also allows *anycast*, whereby the message is sent to any one of the specified nodes.

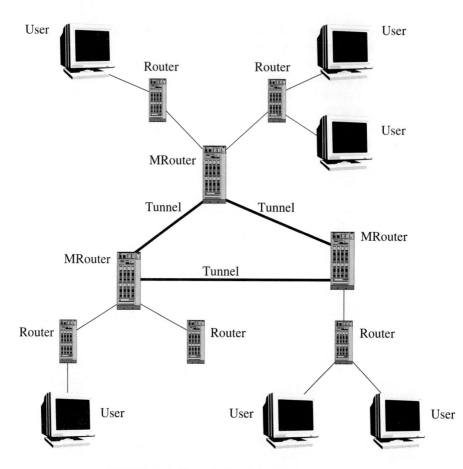

FIGURE 16.2: Tunnels for IP Multicast in MBone.

One of the first trials of IP-multicast was in March 1992, when the Internet Engineering Task Force (IETF) meeting in San Diego was broadcast (audio only) on the Internet.

MBone. The Internet *Multicast Backbone* (*MBone*) is based on IP-multicast technology [1]. Starting in the early 1990s, it has been used, for example, for audio and video conferencing on the Internet [2, 3]. Earlier applications include *vat* for audio conferencing, *vic* and *nv* for video conferencing. Other application tools include *wb* for whiteboards in shared workspace and *sdr* for maintaining session directories on MBone.

Since many routers do not support multicast, MBone uses a subnetwork of routers (*mrouters*) that support multicast to forward multicast packets. As Figure 16.2 shows, the mrouters (or so-called *islands*) are connected with *tunnels*. Multicast packets are encapsulated inside regular IP packets for "tunneling", so that they can be sent to the destination through the islands.

Recall that under IPv4, IP addresses are 32 bits. If the first 4 bits are 1110, the message is an IP-multicast message. It covers IP addresses ranging from 224.0.0.0 to 239.255.255.255.

IP-multicast has anonymous membership. The source host multicasts to one of the above IP-multicast addresses — it doesn't know who will receive. The host software maps IP-group addresses into a list of recipients. Then it either multicasts when there is hardware support (e.g., Ethernet and FDDI have hardware multicast) or sends multiple unicasts through the next node in the spanning tree.

One potential problem of multicasting is that too many packets will be traveling and alive in the network. Fortunately, IP packets have a *time-to-live* (*TTL*) field that limits the packet's lifetime. Each router decrements the TTL of the pass-by packet by at least one. The packet is discarded when its TTL is zero.

The IP-multicast method described above is based on UDP (not TCP), so as to avoid excessive acknowledgments from multiple receivers for every message. As a result, packets are delivered by "best effort", so reliability is limited.

Internet Group Management Protocol (IGMP).   *Internet Group Management Protocol (IGMP)* was designed to help the maintenance of multicast groups. Two special types of IGMP messages are used: `Query` and `Report`. `Query` messages are multicast by routers to all local hosts, to inquire about group membership. `Report` is used to respond to a query and to join groups.

On receiving a query, members wait for a random time before responding. If a member hears another response, it will not respond. Routers periodically query group membership, and declare themselves group members if they get a response to at least one query. If no responses occur after a while, they declare themselves nonmembers.

IGMP version 2 enforces a lower latency, so the membership is pruned more promptly after all members in the group leave.

Reliable Multicast Transport.   IETF RFC 2357 was an attempt to define criteria for evaluating reliable IP-multicast protocols.

As Almeroth [4] points out, MBone maintains a flat virtual topology and does not provide good route aggregation (at the peak time, MBone had approximately 10,000 routes). Hence, it is not scalable. Moreover, the original design is highly distributed (and simplistic). It assumes no central management, which results in ineffective tunnel management, that is, tunnels connecting islands are not optimally allocated. Sometimes multiple tunnels are created over a single physical link, causing congestion.

Paul et al. [5] presented the *Reliable Multicast Transport Protocol* (*RMTP*), which supports route aggregation and hierarchical routing.

Whetten and Taskale [6] provided an overview of *Reliable Multicast Transport Protocol II* (*RMTP II*) that supports *forward error control* (*FEC*) and is targeted for real-time delivery of multimedia data.

16.2.2   RTP (Real-time Transport Protocol)

The original Internet design provided "best-effort" service and was adequate for applications such as e-mail and FTP. However, it is not suitable for real-time multimedia applications. RTP is designed for the transport of real-time data, such as audio and video streams, often for audio- or videoconferencing. It is intended primarily for multicast, although it can also be applied to unicast. It was used, for example, in *nv* for MBone [3], Netscape LiveMedia, Microsoft Netmeeting, and Intel Videophone.

RTP usually runs on top of UDP, which provides efficient (but less reliable) connectionless datagram service. There are two main reasons for using UDP instead of TCP. First, TCP is a connection-oriented transport protocol; hence, it is more difficult to scale up in a multicast environment. Second, TCP achieves its reliability by retransmitting missing packets. As mentioned earlier, in multimedia data transmissions, the reliability issue is less important. Moreover, the late arrival of retransmitted data may not be usable in real-time applications anyway.

Since UDP will not guarantee that the data packets arrive in the original order (not to mention synchronization of multiple sources), RTP must create its own *timestamping* and *sequencing* mechanisms to ensure the ordering. RTP introduces the following additional parameters in the header of each packet [7]:

- **Payload type** indicates the media data type as well as its encoding scheme (e.g., PCM, H.261/H.263, MPEG 1, 2, and 4 audio/video, etc.) so the receiver knows how to decode it.

- **Timestamp** is the most important mechanism of RTP. The timestamp records the instant when the first octet of the packet is sampled; it is set by the sender. With the timestamps, the receiver can play the audio/video in proper timing order and synchronize multiple streams (e.g., audio and video) when necessary.

- **Sequence number** is to complement the function of timestamping. It is incremented by one for each RTP data packet sent, to ensure that the packets can be reconstructed in order by the receiver. This becomes necessary, for example, when all packets of a video frame sometimes receive the same timestamp, and timestamping alone becomes insufficient.

- **Synchronization source (SSRC) ID** identifies sources of multimedia data (e.g., audio, video). If the data come from the same source (translator, mixer), they will be given the same SSRC ID, so as to be synchronized.

- **Contributing Source (CSRC) ID** identifies the source of contributors, such as all speakers in an audio conference.

Figure 16.3 shows the RTP header format. The first 12 octets are of fixed format, followed by optional (0 or more) 32-bit Contributing Source (CSRC) IDs.

Bits 0 and 1 are for the version of RTP, bit 2 (P) for signaling a padded payload, bit 3 (X) for signaling an extension to the header, and bits 4 through 7 for a 4-bit CSRC count that indicates the number of CSRC IDs following the fixed part of the header.

Bit 8 (M) signals the first packet in an audio frame or last packet in a video frame, since an audio frame can be played out as soon as the first packet is received, whereas a video frame can be rendered only after the last packet is received. Bits 9 through 15 describe the payload type, Bits 16 through 31 are for sequence number, followed by a 32-bit timestamp and a 32-bit Synchronization Source (SSRC) ID.

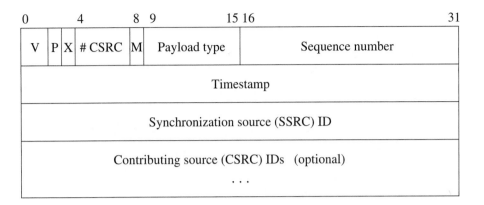

FIGURE 16.3: RTP packet header.

16.2.3   Real Time Control Protocol (RTCP)

RTCP is a companion protocol of RTP. It monitors QoS in providing feedback to the server (sender) on quality of data transmission and conveys information about the participants of a multiparty conference. RTCP also provides the necessary information for audio and video synchronization, even if they are sent through different packet streams.

The five types of RTCP packets are as below.

1. **Receiver report (RR)** provides quality feedback (number of last packet received, number of lost packets, jitter, timestamps for calculating round-trip delays).
2. **Sender report (SR)** provides information about the reception of RR, number of packets/bytes sent, and so on.
3. **Source description (SDES)** provides information about the source (e-mail address, phone number, full name of the participant).
4. **Bye** indicates the end of participation.
5. **Application specific functions (APP)** provides for future extension of new features.

RTP and RTCP packets are sent to the same IP address (multicast or unicast) but on different ports.

16.2.4   Resource ReSerVation Protocol (RSVP)

RSVP is a setup protocol for Internet resource reservation. Protocols such as RTP, described above, do not address the issue of QoS control. RSVP was thus developed [8] to guarantee desirable QoS, mostly for multicast, although it is also applicable to unicast.

A general communication model supported by RSVP consists of m senders and n receivers, possibly in various multicast groups (e.g., in Figure 16.4(a), $m = 2$, $n = 3$, and the trees for the two multicast groups are depicted by the arrows — solid and dashed lines, respectively). In the special case of broadcasting, $m = 1$; whereas in audio- or videoconferencing, each host acts as both sender and receiver in the session, that is, $m = n$.

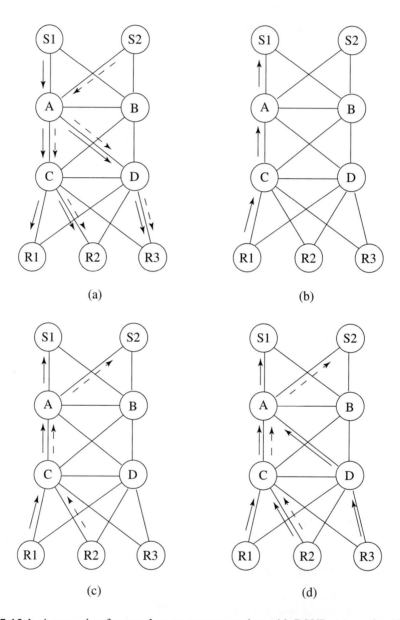

FIGURE 16.4: A scenario of network resource reservation with RSVP: (a) senders S1 and S2 send out their PATH messages to receivers R1, R2, and R3; (b) receiver R1 sends out RESV message to S1; (c) receiver R2 sends out RESV message to S2; (d) receivers R2 and R3 send out their RESV messages to S1.

The main challenges of RSVP are that many senders and receivers may compete for the limited network bandwidth, the receivers can be heterogeneous in demanding different contents with different QoS, and they can be dynamic by joining or quitting multicast groups at any time.

The most important messages of RSVP are `Path` and `Resv`. A `Path` message is initiated by the sender and travels towards the multicast (or unicast) destination addresses. It contains information about the sender and the path (e.g., the previous RSVP hop), so the receiver can find the reverse path to the sender for resource reservation. A `Resv` message is sent by a receiver that wishes to make a reservation.

- **RSVP is receiver-initiated.** A receiver (at a leaf of the multicast spanning tree) initiates the reservation request `Resv`, and the request travels back toward the sender but not necessarily all the way. A reservation will be merged with an existing reservation made by other receiver(s) for the same session as soon as they meet at a router. The merged reservation will accommodate the highest bandwidth requirement among all merged requests. The user-initiated scheme is highly scalable, and it meets users' heterogeneous needs.

- **RSVP creates only *soft state*.** The receiver host must maintain the soft state by periodically sending the same `Resv` message; otherwise, the state will time out. There is no distinction between the initial message and any subsequent refresh message. If there is any change in reservation, the state will automatically be updated according to the new reservation parameters in the refreshing message. Hence, the RSVP scheme is highly dynamic.

Figure 16.4 depicts a simple network with two senders (S1, S2), three receivers (R1, R2, and R3), and four routers (A, B, C, D). Figure 16.4(a) shows that S1 and S2 send `Path` messages along their paths to R1, R2, and R3. In (b) and (c), R1 and R2 send out `Resv` messages to S1 and S2, respectively, to make reservations for S1 and S2 resources. From C to A, two separate channels must be reserved since R1 and R2 requested different datastreams. In (d), R2 and R3 send out their `Resv` messages to S1, to make additional requests. R3's request was merged with R1's previous request at A, and R2's was merged with R1's at C.

Any possible variation of QoS that demands higher bandwidth can be dealt with by modifying the reservation state parameters.

16.2.5 Real-Time Streaming Protocol (RTSP)

Streaming Audio and Video.   In the early days, multimedia data was transmitted over the network (often with slow links) as a whole large file, which would be saved to a disk, then played back. Nowadays, more and more audio and video data is transmitted from a *stored media server* to the client in a datastream that is almost instantly decoded — *streaming audio* and *streaming video*.

Usually, the receiver will set aside buffer space to prefetch the incoming stream. As soon as the buffer is filled to a certain extent, the (usually) compressed data will be uncompressed and played back. Apparently, the buffer space needs to be sufficiently large to deal with the possible jitter and to produce continuous, smooth playback. On the other hand, too

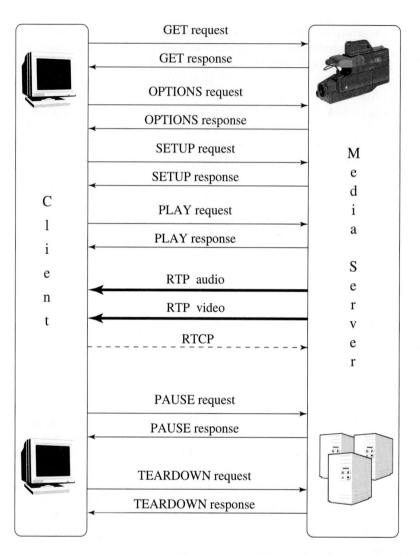

FIGURE 16.5: A possible scenario of RTSP operations.

large a buffer will introduce unnecessary initial delay, which is especially undesirable for interactive applications such as audio- or videoconferencing [9].

The RTSP Protocol. RTSP is for communication between a client and a stored media server. Figure 16.5 illustrates a possible scenario of four RTSP operations:

1. **Requesting presentation description.** The client issues a DESCRIBE request to the Stored Media Server to obtain the presentation description, such as, media types (audio, video, graphics, etc.), frame rate, resolution, codec, and so on, from the server.

2. **Session setup.** The client issues a `SETUP` to inform the server of the destination IP address, port number, protocols, and TTL (for multicast). The session is set up when the server returns a session ID.

3. **Requesting and receiving media.** After receiving a `PLAY`, the server starts to transmit streaming audio/video data, using RTP. It is followed by a `RECORD` or `PAUSE`. Other VCR commands, such as `FAST-FORWARD` and `REWIND` are also supported. During the session, the client periodically sends an RTCP packet to the server, to provide feedback information about the QoS received (as described in Section 16.2.3).

4. **Session closure.** `TEARDOWN` closes the session.

16.2.6   Internet Telephony

The *Public Switched Telephone Network* (PSTN) relies on copper wires carrying analog voice signals. It provides reliable and low-cost voice and facsimile services. In the eighties and nineties, modems were a popular means of "data over voice networks". In fact, they were predominant before the introduction of ADSL and cable modems.

As PCs and the Internet became readily available and more and more voice and data communications became digital (e.g., in ISDN), "voice over data networks," especially *Voice over IP* (*VoIP*) started to attract a great deal of interest in research and user communities. With ever-increasing network bandwidth and the ever-improving quality of multimedia data compression, *Internet telephony* [10] has become a reality. Increasingly, it is not restricted to voice (VoIP) — it is about integrated voice, video, and data services.

The main advantages of Internet telephony over *POTS*[2] are the following:

- It provides great flexibility and extensibility in accommodating integrated services such as voicemail, audio- and videoconferences, mobile phone, and so on.

- It uses packet switching, not circuit switching; hence, network usage is much more efficient (voice communication is bursty and VBR-encoded).

- With the technologies of multicast or multipoint communication, multiparty calls are not much more difficult than two-party calls.

- With advanced multimedia data-compression techniques, various degrees of QoS can be supported and dynamically adjusted according to the network traffic, an improvement over the "all or none" service in POTS.

- Good graphics user interfaces can be developed to show available features and services, monitor call status and progress, and so on.

As Figure 16.6 shows, the transport of real-time audio (and video) in Internet telephony is supported by RTP (whose control protocol is RTCP), as described in Section 16.2.2. Streaming media is handled by RTSP and Internet resource reservation is taken care of by RSVP.

Internet telephony is not simply a streaming media service over the Internet, because it requires a sophisticated signaling protocol. A streaming media server can be readily identified

---

[2] POTS refers to plain old telephone services that do not include new features such as call waiting, call forwarding, and so on.

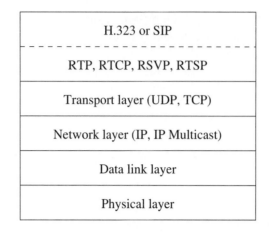

FIGURE 16.6: Network protocol structure for internet telephony.

by a URI (Universal Resource Identifier), whereas acceptance of a call via Internet telephony depends on the callee's current location, capability, availability, and desire to communicate.

The following are brief descriptions of the H.323 standard and one of the most commonly used signaling protocols, Session Initiation Protocol (SIP).

H.323.   H.323 [11, 12] is a standard for packet-based multimedia communication services over networks (LAN, Internet, wireless network, etc.) that do not provide a guaranteed QoS. It specifies signaling protocols and describes terminals, multipoint control units (for conferencing), and gateways for integrating Internet telephony with *General Switched Telephone Network (GSTN)*[3] data terminals.

The H.323 signaling process consists of two phases:

1. **Call setup.** The caller sends the *gatekeeper (GK)* a *Registration, Admission and Status (RAS) Admission Request (ARQ)* message, which contains the name and phone number of the callee. The GK may either grant permission or reject the request, with reasons such as "security violation" and "insufficient bandwidth".

2. **Capability exchange.** An H.245 control channel will be established, for which the first step is to exchange capabilities of both the caller and callee, such as whether it is audio, video, or data; compression and encryption, and so on.

H.323 provides mandatory support for audio and optional support for data and video. It is associated with a family of related software standards that deal with call control and data compression for Internet telephony. Following are some of the related standards:

Signaling and Control

- **H.225.** Call control protocol, including signaling, registration, admissions, packetization and synchronization of media streams

---

[3]GSTN is a synonym for PSTN (public switched telephone network).

- **H.245.** Control protocol for multimedia communications — for example, opening and closing channels for media streams, obtaining gateway between GSTN and Internet telephony

- **H.235.** Security and encryption for H.323 and other H.245-based multimedia terminals

Audio Codecs

- **G.711.** Codec for 3.1 kHz audio over 48, 56, or 64 kbps channels. G.711 describes Pulse Code Modulation for normal telephony

- **G.722.** Codec for 7 kHz audio over 48, 56, or 64 kbps channels

- **G.723.1.** Codec for 3.1 kHz audio over 5.3 or 6.3 kbps channels. (The VoIP Forum adopted G.723.1 as the codec for VoIP.)

- **G.728.** Codec for 3.1 kHz audio over 16 kbps channels

- **G.729, G.729a.** Codec for 3.1 kHz audio over 8 kbps channels. (The Frame Relay Forum adopted G.729 by as the codec for voice over frame relay.)

Video Codecs

- **H.261.** Codec for video at $p \times 64$ kbps ($p \geq 1$)

- **H.263.** Codec for low-bitrate video (< 64 kbps) over the GSTN

Related Standards

- **H.320.** The original standard for videoconferencing over ISDN networks

- **H.324.** An extension of H.320 for video conferencing over the GSTN

- **T.120.** Real-time data and conferencing control

Session Initiation Protocol (SIP) — A Signaling Protocol.   SIP [10] is an application-layer control protocol in charge of establishing and terminating sessions in Internet telephony. These sessions are not limited to VoIP communications — they also include multimedia conferences and multimedia distribution.

Similar to HTTP, SIP is a text-based protocol that is different from H.323. It is also a client-server protocol. A caller (the client) initiates a request, which a server processes and responds to. There are three types of servers. A *proxy server* and a *redirect server* forward call requests. The difference between the two is that the proxy server forwards the requests to the next-hop server, whereas the redirect server returns the address of the next-hop server to the client, so as to redirect the call toward the destination.

The third type is a *location server*, which finds current locations of users. Location servers usually communicate with the redirect or proxy servers. They may use finger,

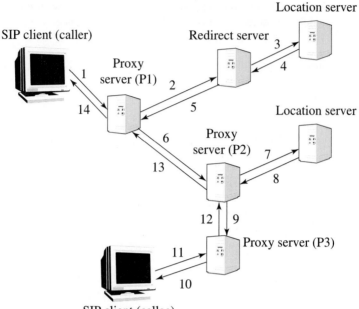

FIGURE 16.7: A possible scenario of SIP session initiation.

rwhois, *Lightweight Directory Access Protocol* (*LDAP*), or other multicast-based protocols to determine a user's address.

SIP can advertise its session using e-mail, news groups, web pages or directories, or *Session Announcement Protocol* (SAP) — a multicast protocol.

The *methods* (commands) for clients to invoke are

- INVITE — invites callee(s) to participate in a call.

- ACK — acknowledges the invitation.

- OPTIONS — inquires about media capabilities without setting up a call.

- CANCEL — terminates the invitation.

- BYE — terminates a call.

- REGISTER — sends user's location information to a registrar (a SIP server).

Figure 16.7 illustrates a possible scenario when a caller initiates a SIP session:

Step 1. Caller sends an INVITE john@home.ca to the local Proxy server P1.

Step 2. The proxy uses its Domain Name Service (DNS) to locate the server for john@home.ca and sends the request to it.

Steps 3, 4.   `john@home.ca` is not logged on the server. A request is sent to the nearby location server. John's current address, `john@work.ca`, is located.

Step 5.   Since the server is a redirect server, it returns the address `john@work.ca` to the proxy server P1.

Step 6.   Try the next proxy server P2 for `john@work.ca`.

Steps 7, 8.   P2 consults its location server and obtains John's local address, `john_doe@my.work.ca`.

Steps 9, 10.   The next-hop proxy server P3 is contacted, which in turn forwards the invitation to where the client (callee) is.

Steps 11–14.   John accepts the call at his current location (at work) and the acknowledgments are returned to the caller.

SIP can also use *Session Description Protocol* (SDP) to gather information about the callee's *media capabilities*.

Session Description Protocol (SDP).   As its name suggests, SDP describes multimedia sessions. As in SIP, SDP descriptions are in textual form. They include the number and types of media streams (audio, video, whiteboard session, etc.), destination address (unicast or multicast) for each stream, sending and receiving port numbers, and media formats (payload types). When initiating a call, the caller includes the SDP information in the `INVITE` message. The called party responds and sometimes revises the SDP information, according to its capability.

16.3   MULTIMEDIA OVER ATM NETWORKS

16.3.1   Video Bitrates over ATM

The ATM Forum supports various types of video bit-rates:

- **Constant Bitrate (CBR).** For example, for uncompressed video or CBR-coded video. As mentioned before, if the allocated bitrate of CBR is too low, cell loss and distortion of the video content are inevitable.

- **Variable Bit Rate (VBR).** The most commonly used video bitrate for compressed video. It can be further divided into *real-time Variable Bitrate* (*rt-VBR*) suitable for compressed video, and *non real-time Variable Bit Rate* (*nrt-VBR*) for specified QoS.

- **Available Bit Rate (ABR).** As in IP-based service, data transmission can be backed off or buffered due to congestion. Cell loss rate and minimum cell data rate can sometimes be specified.

- **Unspecified Bit Rate (UBR).** Provides no guarantee on any quality parameter.

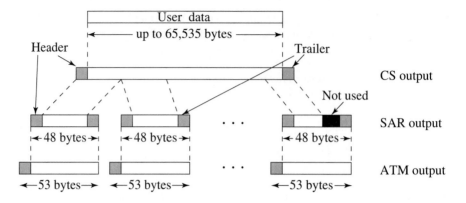

FIGURE 16.8: Headers and trailers added at the CS and SAR sublayers.

16.3.2   ATM Adaptation Layer (AAL)

AAL converts various formats of user data into ATM datastreams and vice versa. The following lists five types of AAL protocols:

- **AAL type 1** supports real-time, constant bitrate (CBR), connection-oriented data-streams.

- **AAL type 2** was intended for variable bitrate (VBR) compressed video and audio. However, the protocol never really materialized and is now inactive.

- **AAL types 3 and 4** were similar, and have since been combined into one type: AAL type 3/4. It supports variable bitrate (VBR) of either connection-oriented or connectionless general (non-real-time) data services.

- **AAL type 5** was the new protocol introduced for multimedia data transmission. It promises to support all classes of data and video services (from CBR to UBR, from rt-VBR to nrt-VBR). It is assumed that the layers above the AAL are connection-oriented and that the ATM layer beneath it has a low error rate.

As Figure 16.8 shows, headers and trailers are added to the original user data at the Convergence Sublayer (CS) and Segmentation And Reassembly (SAR) sublayer. They eventually form the 53-byte ATM cells with the 5-byte ATM header appended.

The existence of the five different types of AAL was due largely to history. In particular, all AAL types except AAL 5 were developed by the telecommunications industry and were generally unsuitable for interactive multimedia applications and services [13]. Table 16.3 provides a comparison among the three active AAL types, for example, comparing AAL 3/4 with AAL 5,

- AAL 3/4 has an overhead of designating 4 bytes for each SAR cell, whereas AAL 5 has none at this sublayer. Considering the numerous SAR cells, this is a substantial saving for AAL 5. It is of course possible only with modern, relatively error-free fiber-optic technology.

TABLE 16.3: Comparison of AAL types.

	AAL 1	AAL 3/4	AAL 5
CS header/trailer overhead	0 byte	8 bytes	8 bytes
SAR header/trailer overhead	1 or 2 bytes	4 bytes	0 byte
SAR payload	47 or 46 bytes	44 bytes	48 bytes
CS checksum	None	None	4 bytes
SAR checksum	None	10 bits	None

- As part of the SAR trailer, AAL 3/4 has a checksum field for error checking. To cut down the overhead, the checksum is only 10 bits long, which is unfortunately inadequate. AAL 5 does it at the CS and allocates 4 bytes for the checksum. Again, it is based on the assumption that bit-transmission error is rare. However, when AAL 5 does error checking, it has enough information from the long checksum.

By now, AAL 5 has superseded AAL 3/4. The ATM Forum agrees that beside CBR services that will use AAL 1, every other service will use AAL 5. For more details of the AALs, see Tanenbaum [13] and Stallings [14].

Table 16.4 summarizes the support for video transmission with and without ATM.

16.3.3   MPEG-2 Convergence to ATM

The ATM Forum has decided that MPEG-2 will be transported over AAL5. As mentioned in Section 11.3.3, by default, two MPEG-2 packets (each 188 bytes) from the transport stream (TS) will be mapped into one AAL-5 service data unit (SDU) [15].

When establishing a virtual channel connection, the following QoS parameters must be specified:

- Maximum cell transfer delay (latency)

TABLE 16.4: Support for digital video transmission.

Video requirement	Support in ATM	Support without ATM
Bandwidth	Scalable to several Gbps	Up to 100 Mbps
Latency and jitter	QoS support	RSVP
CBR or VBR	AAL 1, 2, 5, LAN emulation, circuit emulation, etc.	ISDN and ADSL
Multicasting	Multicast switch, or permanent virtual circuit	IP-multicast or protocol independent multicast (PIM)

- Maximum cell delay jitter

- Cell loss ratio (CLR)

- Cell error ratio (CER)

- Severely errored cell block ratio (SECBR)

An *audio-visual service-specific convergence sublayer* (*AVSSCS*) is also proposed, to enable transmitting video over AAL5 using ABR services.

16.3.4   Multicast over ATM

Compared to IP multicast, which is a "best-effort" service provided on top of UDP, multicast in ATM networks had several challenges [16, 17]:

- ATM is connection-oriented; hence, ATM multicasting must set up all multipoint connections.

- QoS in ATM must be negotiated at connection setup time and be known to all switches.

- It is difficult to support multipoint-to-point or multipoint-to-multipoint connections in ATM, because AAL 5 does not keep track of multiplexer number or sequence number. It cannot reassemble the data correctly at the receiver side if cells from different senders are interleaved at their reception.

    Scalable and efficient ATM multicast (*SEAM*) and *shared many-to-many ATM reservations* (*SMART*) are two approaches to multicasting over ATM [16]. The former uses a unique identifier and the latter a token scheme to avoid the ambiguity caused by cell interleaving.

16.4   TRANSPORT OF MPEG-4

The design of MPEG-4 was motivated by multimedia applications on the WWW. In particular, multimedia (text, graphics, audio, video, etc.) objects and scene descriptions (temporal and spatial relationships of the video objects) can be transmitted by the server and interpreted and reassembled at the client side, to drastically reduce multimedia data transmitted onto the WWW. This section briefly describes the *Delivery Multimedia Integration Framework* (*DMIF*) and the issue of MPEG-4 over IP.

16.4.1   DMIF in MPEG-4

DMIF is an interface between multimedia applications and their transport. It supports remote interactive network access (IP, ATM, PSTN, ISDN, or mobile), broadcast media (cable or satellite), and local media on disks.

The interface is transparent to the application, so a single application can run on different transport layers, as long as the right DMIF is instantiated.

Figure 16.9 shows the integration of delivery through three types of communication mediums. As shown, the local application interacts with a uniform *DMIF Application*

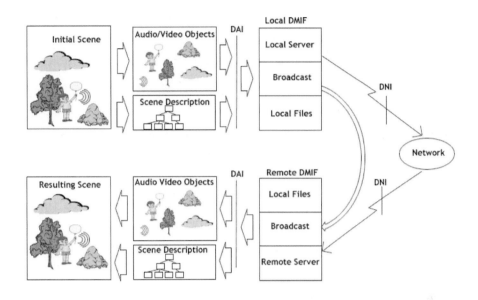

FIGURE 16.9: DMIF — the multimedia content delivery integration framework.

Interface (*DAI*), which translates the application's requests into specific protocol messages, to be transported through one of the three types of mediums.

When the delivery is through a network, the DMIF is unaware of the application. In fact, an additional *DMIF Network Interface* (*DNI*) is needed, to take care of their signaling messages for specific networks.

When delivering multimedia data, DMIF is similar to FTP. First, a SETUP session is established with the remote network site. Second, streams are selected and a STREAM request is sent to the DMIF peer, which returns a pointer to a separate connection where the streaming will take place. Third, the new connection is established, and data is streamed.

In the scenarios of Broadcast and Local storage, the application will know how the data is stored and delivered. Hence, this becomes part of the DMIF implementation.

DMIF has built-in QoS monitoring capability. It supports (a) continuous monitoring, (b) specific QoS queries, and (c) QoS violation notification.

16.4.2   MPEG-4 over IP

The specifications on MPEG-4 over IP networks are jointly developed by the MPEG and IETF as a framework in Part 8 of MPEG-4 (ISO/IEC 14496-8) and an Informative RFC in IETF.

MPEG-4 sessions can be carried over IP-based protocols such as RTP, RTSP, and HTTP. Details regarding RTP payload format are specified by IETF RFC 3016. In short, *generic RTP payload format* defines a mapping between logical MPEG-4 SL packets and RTP packets, and *FlexMux payload format* maps FlexMux packetized streams to RTP packets.

16.5   MEDIA-ON-DEMAND (MOD)

Media-on-Demand involves many fundamental multimedia network communication issues. In this section, we will briefly introduce Interactive TV, broadcast schemes for video-on-demand, and issues of buffer management.

16.5.1   Interactive TV (ITV) and Set-Top Box (STB)

Interactive TV (ITV) is a multimedia system based on the television sets in homes. It can support a growing number of activities, such as

- TV (basic, subscription, pay-per-view)

- Video-on-Demand (VOD)

- Information services (news, weather, magazines, sports events, etc.)

- Interactive entertainment (Internet games, etc.)

- E-commerce (online shopping, stock trading)

- Access to digital libraries and educational materials

A new development in Digital Video Broadcasting (DVB) is Multimedia Home Platform (DVB-MHP) which supports all the activities above as well as electronic program guide (EPG) for television.

The fundamental differences between ITV and conventional cable TV are first, that ITV invites user interactions; hence the need for two-way traffic — downstream (content provider to user) and upstream (user to content provider). Second, ITV is rich in information and multimedia content.

To perform the above functions, a Set-top Box (STB) is required, which generally has the following components, as Figure 16.10 shows:

- **Network interface and communication unit**, including tuner and demodulator (to extract the digital stream from analog channel), security devices, and a communication channel for basic navigation of WWW and digital libraries as well as services and maintenance

- **Processing unit**, including CPU, memory, and a special-purpose operating system for the STB

- **Audio/video unit**, including audio and video (MPEG-2 and 4) decoders, Digital Signal Processor (DSP), buffers, and D/A converters

- **Graphics unit**, supporting real-time 3D graphics for animation and games

- **Peripheral control unit**, controllers for disks, audio and video I/O devices (e.g., digital video cameras), CD/DVD reader and writer, and so on

Section 15.4 described various Access Networks and their comparative advantages and disadvantages in transmitting multimedia data efficiently and securely for ITV services.

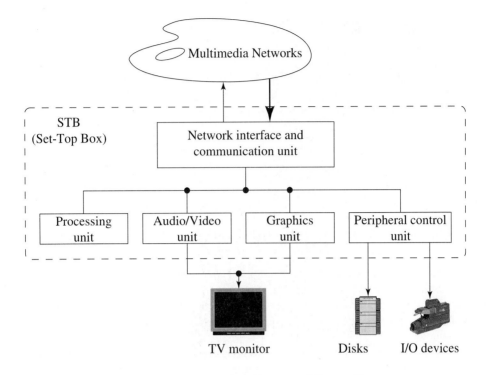

FIGURE 16.10: General architecture of Set-top Box.

16.5.2 Broadcast Schemes for Video-on-Demand

Among all possible Media-on-Demand services, the most popular is likely to be subscription to movies: over high-speed networks, customers can specify the movies they want and the time they want to view them. The statistics of such services suggest that most of the demand is usually concentrated on a few (10 to 20) popular movies (e.g., new releases and top-ten movies of the season). This makes it possible to multicast or broadcast these movies, since a number of clients can be put into the next group following their request.

An important quality measure of such MOD service is the waiting time (latency). We will define *access time* as the upper bound between the time of requesting the movie and the time of consuming the movie.

Given the potentially extremely high bandwidth of fiber-optic networks, it is conceivable that the entire movie can be fed to the client in a relatively short time if it has access to some high-speed network. The problem with this approach is the need for an unnecessarily large storage space at the client side.

Staggered Broadcasting.   For simplicity, we will assume all movies are encoded using constant-bitrate (CBR) encoding, are of the same length L (measured in time units), and will be played sequentially from beginning to end without interruption. The available high bandwidth W is divided by the playback rate b to yield the bandwidth ratio B. The bandwidth

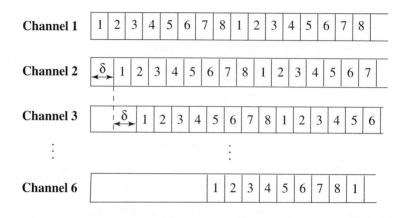

FIGURE 16.11: Staggered broadcasting with $M = 8$ movies and $K = 6$ channels.

of the server is usually divided up into K logical channels ($K \geq 1$).

Assuming the server broadcasts up to M movies ($M \geq 1$), all can be periodically broadcast on all these channels with the start-time of each movie staggered. This is therefore referred to as *Staggered broadcasting*. Figure 16.11 shows an example of Staggered broadcasting in which $M = 8$ and $K = 6$.

If the division of the bandwidth is equal among all K logical channels, then access time for any movie is $\delta = \frac{M \cdot L}{B}$. (Note: the access time is actually independent of the value of K.) In other words, access time will be reduced linearly with the increased network bandwidth.

Pyramid Broadcasting.   Viswanathan and Imielinski [18] proposed *Pyramid broadcasting*, in which movies are divided up into segments of increasing sizes. That is, $L_{i+1} = \alpha \cdot L_i$, where L_i is the size (length) of Segment S_i and $\alpha > 1$. Segment S_i will be periodically broadcast on Channel i. In other words, instead of staggering the movies on K channels, the segments are now staggered. Each channel is given the same bandwidth, and the larger segments are broadcast less frequently.

Since the available bandwidth is assumed to be significantly larger than the movie playback rate b (i.e., $B >> 1$), it is argued that the client can be playing a smaller Segment S_i and simultaneously be receiving a larger Segment S_{i+1}.

To guarantee continuous (noninterrupted) playback, the necessary condition is

$$playback\_time(S_i) \geq access\_time(S_{i+1}) \qquad (16.1)$$

The $playback\_time(S_i) = L_i$. Given the bandwidth allocated to each channel is $B/K \cdot b$, $access\_time(S_{i+1}) = \frac{L_{i+1} \cdot M}{B/K} = \frac{\alpha \cdot L_i \cdot M}{B/K}$, which yields

$$L_i \geq \frac{\alpha \cdot L_i \cdot M}{B/K} \qquad (16.2)$$

Consequently,

$$\alpha \leq \frac{B}{M \cdot K} \qquad (16.3)$$

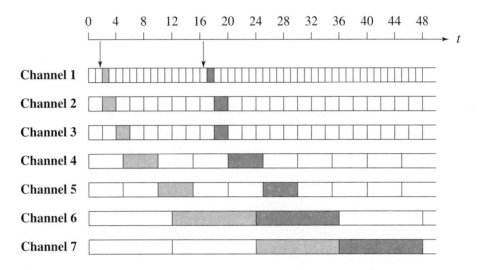

FIGURE 16.12: Skyscraper broadcasting with seven segments.

The size of S_1 determines access time for Pyramid broadcasting. By default, we set $\alpha = \frac{B}{M \cdot K}$ to yield the shortest access time. Access time drops exponentially with the increase in total bandwidth B, because α can be increased linearly.

A main drawback of the above scheme is the need for a large storage space on the client side, because the last two segments are typically 75–80% of the movie size. Instead of using a geometric series, *Skyscraper broadcasting* [19] uses {1, 2, 2, 5, 5, 12, 12, 25, 25, 52, 52, ... } as the series of segment sizes, to alleviate the demand on a large buffer.

Figure 16.12 shows an example of Skyscraper broadcasting with seven segments. As shown, two clients who made a request at time intervals (1, 2) and (16, 17), respectively, have their respective transmission schedules. At any given moment, no more than two segments need to be received.

Hu [20] described *Greedy Equal Bandwidth Broadcasting (GEBB)* in 2001. The segment sizes and their corresponding channel bandwidths are analyzed, with the objective of minimizing the total server bandwidth required to broadcast a specific video. Different from the above pyramid-based broadcasting schemes, GEBB operates in a "greedy" fashion. The client receives as much data as possible from all the channels immediately after "tuning in" to a video broadcast. The client ceases receiving a segment immediately before playing back the corresponding segment. Figure 16.13 illustrates GEBB. In this figure, all the bandwidths are equal.

The server bandwidth optimization problem can be formally stated as:

$$\text{minimize} \quad \sum_{i=1}^{K} B$$

$$\text{subject to} \quad B_i = \frac{S_i}{w + \sum_{j=1}^{i-1} S_j} \quad i = 1, 2, \ldots, K \quad (16.4)$$

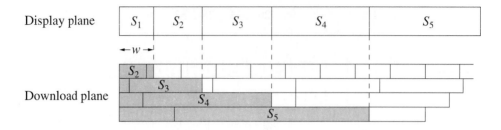

FIGURE 16.13: Illustration of GEBB. The shaded area represents data received and played back by the client.

where w is the wait time and the B_i is the bandwidth of Channel i. The condition represented by Equation (16.4) ensures that Segment S_i is completely received at the exact time when the playback of Segment S_{i-1} terminates. Thus, the segments are available exactly ontime for their playback.

The above nonlinear optimization problem is solved using the Lagrange multiplier method. The result is that the required bandwidth is minimized when the channel bandwidths are equal. The broadcasting bandwidth of each channel is

$$B_i = B_j = B^* \quad 1 \le i, j \le K \tag{16.5}$$

$$B^* = \left(\frac{S}{w}+1\right)^{\frac{1}{K}} - 1 \tag{16.6}$$

$$S_i = \left[\left(\frac{S}{w}+1\right)^{\frac{1}{K}}-1\right]\left(\frac{S}{w}+1\right)^{\frac{i-1}{K}} \tag{16.7}$$

The segment progression follows a geometrical sequence. $\left(\frac{S}{w}+1\right)^{\frac{1}{K}}$ is called the golden factor of video segmentation.

Harmonic Broadcasting.   Juhn and Tseng [21] invented Harmonic broadcasting in 1997, which adopts a different strategy. The size of all segments remains constant, whereas the bandwidth of channel i is $B_i = b/i$, where b is the movie's playback rate. In other words, the channel bandwidths follow the decreasing pattern $b, b/2, b/3, \dots b/K$. The total bandwidth allocated for delivering the movie is thus

$$B = \sum_{i=1}^{K} \frac{b}{i} = H_K \cdot b \tag{16.8}$$

where K is the total number of segments, and $H_K = \sum_{i=1}^{K} \frac{1}{i}$ is the *Harmonic number* of K.

Figure 16.14 shows an example of Harmonic broadcasting. After requesting the movie, the client is allowed to download and play the first occurrence of segment S_1 from channel 1. Meanwhile, the client will download all other segments from their respective channels.

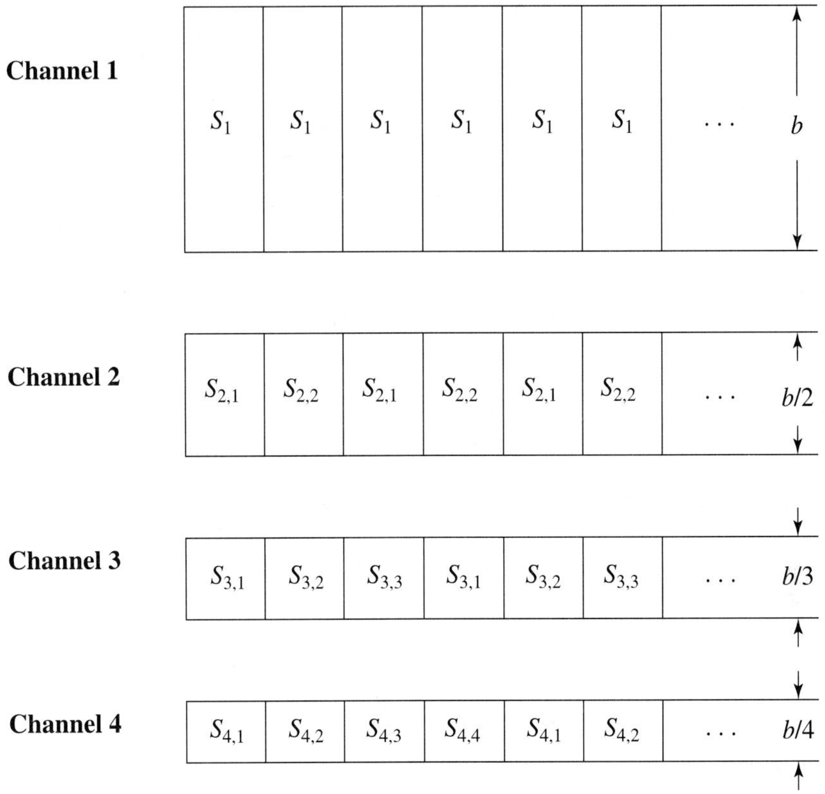

FIGURE 16.14: Harmonic broadcasting.

Take S_2 as an example: it consists of two halves, S_{21} and S_{22}. Since bandwidth B_2 is only $b/2$, during the playback time of S_1, one-half of S_2 (say S_{21}) will be downloaded (prefetched). It takes the entire playback time of S_2 to download the other half (say S_{22}), just as S_2 is finishing playback. Similarly, by this time, two-thirds of S_3 is already prefetched, so the remaining third of S_3 can be downloaded just in time for playback from channel 3, which has a bandwidth of only $b/3$, and so on.

The advantage of Harmonic broadcasting is that the Harmonic number grows slowly with K. For example, when $K = 30$, $H_K \approx 4$. If the movie is 120 minutes long, this yields small segments — only 4 minutes (120/30) each. Hence, the access time for Harmonic broadcasting is generally shorter than for Pyramid broadcasting, and the demand on total bandwidth (in this case $4b$) is modest. Juhn and Steng [21] show that the upper bound for the buffer size at the client side is 37% of the entire movie, which also compares favorably with the original pyramid broadcasting scheme.

However, the above Harmonic broadcasting scheme does not always work. For example, if the client starts to download at the second instance of S_1 in Figure 16.14, then by the time it finishes S_1, only the second half of S_2 — that is, S_{22} — is prefetched. The client will

Slot	1	2	3	4	5	6	7	8	9	10	11	12	13
Channel 1	S_1	S_1	S_1	S_1	S_1	S_1	S_1	S_1	S_1	S_1	S_1	S_1	S_1
Channel 2	S_2	S_4	S_2	S_5	S_2	S_4	S_2	S_5	S_2	S_4	S_2	S_5	S_2
Channel 3	S_3	S_6	S_8	S_3	S_7	S_9	S_3	S_6	S_8	S_3	S_7	S_9	S_3

FIGURE 16.15: First three channel-segment maps of Pagoda broadcasting.

not be able to simultaneously download and play S_{21} from channel 2, since the available bandwidth is only half the playback rate.

An obvious fix to the above problem is to ask the client to delay the playback of S_1 by one slot. The drawback of this delayed Harmonic broadcasting scheme is that it doubles the access time. Since 1997, several variants of the original method, such as *cautious harmonic broadcasting*, *quasi-harmonic broadcasting*, and *polyharmonic broadcasting*, have been proposed, all of which address the problem with added complexity.

Pagoda Broadcasting.   Harmonic broadcasting schemes broadcast videos using a large number of low-bandwidth streams, while Pyramid broadcasting schemes broadcast videos using a small number of high-bandwidth streams. The total required bandwidths of Pyramid broadcasting schemes are generally higher than those of Harmonic-based schemes. But managing a large number of independent datastreams for Harmonic broadcasting is likely to be daunting.

Paris, Carter, and Long [22, 23] proposed *Pagoda broadcasting* and its variant. They present a frequency broadcasting scheme that tries to combine the advantages of Harmonic and Pyramid schemes.

Figure 16.15 illustrates Pagoda broadcasting. It partitions each video into n fixed-size segments of duration $T = L/n$, where T is defined as a time slot. Then it broadcasts these segments at the consumption bandwidth b but with different periods. So the problem is to select the proper segment-to-channel mapping and the proper broadcasting period for each segment.

Compared to Pyramid and Harmonic broadcasting, Pagoda broadcasting is not bandwidth efficient for any given waiting time. It requires fewer segments compared to Harmonic broadcasting to achieve comparable waiting time requirements while requiring more segments than Pyramid broadcasting.

All the above protocols are based on the assumption that the videos are encoded using Constant Bit Rate (CBR). Some protocols were proposed to deal with VBR-encoded videos. For further study, readers are referred to [20, 24].

Stream Merging.   The above broadcast schemes are most effective when limited user interactions are expected — that is, once requested, clients will stay with the sequential access schedule and watch the movie in its entirety.

Stream merging is more adaptive to dynamic user interactions, which is achieved by dynamically combining multicast sessions [25]. It still makes the assumption that the client's receiving bandwidth is higher than the video playback rate. In fact, it is common

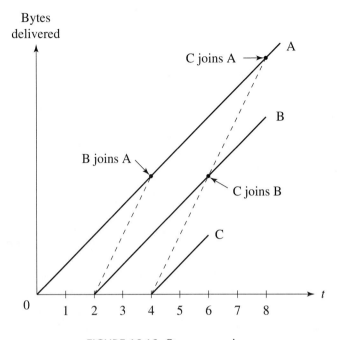

FIGURE 16.16: Stream merging.

to assume that the receiving bandwidth is at least twice the playback rate, so that the client can receive two streams at the same time.

The server will deliver a video stream as soon as it receives the request from a client. Meanwhile, the client is also given access to a second stream of the same video, which was initiated earlier by another client. At a certain point, the first stream becomes unnecessary, because all its contents have been prefetched from the second stream. At this time, the first stream will merge with (or "join") the second.

As Figure 16.16 shows, the "first stream" B starts at time $t = 2$. The solid line indicates the playback rate, and the dashed line indicates the receiving bandwidth, which is twice the playback rate. The client is allowed to prefetch from an earlier ("second") stream A, which was launched at $t = 0$. At $t = 4$, stream B joins A.

The technique of stream merging can be applied hierarchically — *Hierarchical multicast stream merging (HMSM)* [25]. As Figure 16.16 shows, stream C, which started at $t = 4$, would join B at $t = 6$, which in turn joined A. The original stream B would have been obsolete after $t = 4$, since it joined A. In this case, it will have to be retained until $t = 6$, when C joins A.

A variation of Stream merging is *piggybacking*, in which the playback rate of the streams is slightly and dynamically adjusted, to enable merging (piggybacking) of the streams.

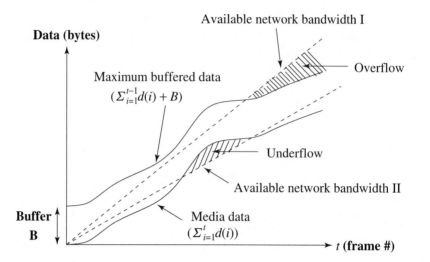

FIGURE 16.17: The data that a client can store in the buffer assists the smooth playback of the media when the media rate exceeds the available network bandwidth.

16.5.3 Buffer Management

Continuous media usually have expected *playback rates*, such as 30 fps for NTSC video and 25 fps for PAL. If the video is delivered through the network, then without work-ahead smoothing at playback time, the required network throughput must be higher than the video's peak bitrate for uninterrupted video playback.

As discussed earlier, most compressed media are VBR-coded. Usually, the more activities (motions in the video, changes in the speech or music), the higher the required bitrate. The mean bitrate for MPEG-1 is 1.5 Mbps and for MPEG-2 is ≥ 4 Mbps. Media that have VBR characteristics can have a low bitrate at one point and a much higher bitrate at another point. The peak bitrate can be much larger than the mean bitrate for the media and may not be supported by the network bandwidth available.

Although not popular nowadays, CBR coding is also an option — variable distortions can be introduced to maintain a constant bitrate. CBR coding is less efficient than VBR: to obtain comparable quality of coded media, the CBR bitrate is typically 15–30% higher than the mean VBR video bitrate (the average bitrate of the video).

To cope with the variable bitrate and network load fluctuation, buffers are usually employed at both sender and receiver ends [9]. A *prefetch buffer* is introduced at the client side (e.g., in the client's Set-top Box) to smooth the transmission rate (reducing the peak rate). If the size of frame t is $d(t)$, the buffer size is B, and the number of data bytes received so far (at play time for frame t) is $A(t)$, then for all $t \in 1, 2, \ldots, N$, it is required that

$$\sum_{i=1}^{t} d(i) \leq A(t) \leq \sum_{i=1}^{t-1} d(i) + B \tag{16.9}$$

When $A(t) < \sum_{i=1}^{t} d(i)$, we have inadequate network throughput and hence buffer *underflow* (or *starvation*), whereas when $A(t) > \sum_{i=1}^{t-1} d(i) + B$, we have excessive network throughput and buffer *overflow*. Both are harmful to smooth, continuous playback. In buffer underflow, no data is available to play, and in buffer overflow, media packets must be dropped.

Figure 16.17 illustrates the limits imposed by the media playback (consumption) data rate and the buffered data rate. (The transmission rates are the slopes of the curves.) At any time, data must be in the buffer for smooth playback, and the data transmitted must be more than the data consumed. If the network bandwidth available is as in Line II in the figure, at some point during playback, the data to be consumed will be greater than can be sent. The buffer will underflow, and playback will be interrupted. Also, at any point, the total amount of data transmitted must not exceed the total consumed plus the size of the buffer.

If the network available bandwidth is as in Line I and the media was sent as fast as possible without buffer considerations (as in normal file downloads), then toward the end of the video, the data received will be greater than the buffer can store at the time. The buffer will overflow and drop the extra packets. Then the server will have to retransmit the packets dropped, or these packets will be missing. Although, during overflow, some time is allowed for retransmission, this increases bandwidth requirements (and hence may cause underflow in the future). In many cases, such as broadcast, no back channel is available.

Techniques to maintain data in the prefetch buffer without overflowing or underflowing it are known as *transmission rate control* schemes. Two simple approaches are to prefetch video data to fill the buffer and try to transmit at the mean video bitrate, or to keep the buffer full without exceeding the available bandwidth. For video sections that require higher bandwidth than available, the transmission rate control schemes hope that the data already in the buffer and the available network bandwidth will enable smooth playback without buffer underflow.

An Optimal Plan for Transmission Rates.   Given knowledge about the data rate characteristics of the media stored on the server [26], it is possible to use the prefetch buffer more efficiently for the network. The media server can plan ahead for a transmission rate such that the media can be viewed without interruption and the reserved bandwidth minimized. Many transmission plans may minimize peak rate, but there is a unique plan that also minimizes rate variability — the variance of the transmission rate. Such a rate transmission plan is referred to as the *optimal work-ahead smoothing plan.*

Minimizing rate variability is important, since it implies the optimal rate plan is a set of piecewise, constant-rate-transmission segments. Basing the bandwidth reservation strategy on the current transmission rate rather than the peak rate allows some processing and network resources to be minimized and changes in bandwidth reservation to be less frequent. For discussion purposes, the following will refer to video media, although the technique could be extended for general media.

The video data rate can be analyzed frame by frame, although that might not be the best strategy, since inter-frames cannot be decoded by themselves and introduce a decoding delay anyhow. Additionally, the computational cost is high. Indeed, it is more practical to approximate the video data rate by considering the total data consumed by the time each I-frame should be displayed. The approximation could be made coarser by considering only the total data consumed at the first frame after a scene transition, assuming the movie datarate is constant in the same scene.

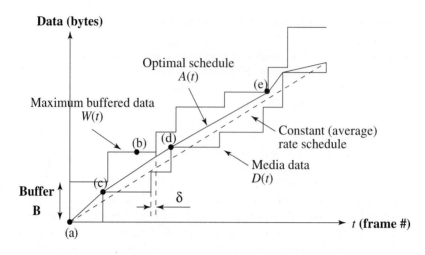

FIGURE 16.18: The optimal smoothing plan for a specific video and buffer size. In this case, it is not feasible to transmit at the constant (average) data rate.

As before, define $d(t)$ to be the size of frame t, where $t \in 1, 2, \ldots, N$, and N is the total number of frames in the video. Similarly, define $a(t)$ to be the amount of data transmitted by the video server during the playback time for frame t (for short, call it at time t). Let $D(t)$ be the total data consumed and $A(t)$ be the total data sent at time t. Formally:

$$D(t) = \sum_{i=1}^{t} d(i) \qquad (16.10)$$

$$A(t) = \sum_{i=1}^{t} a(i) \qquad (16.11)$$

Let the buffer size be B. Then at any time t, the maximum total amount of data that can be received without overflowing the buffer during the time $1..t$ is $W(t) = D(t-1) + B$. Now it is easy to state the conditions for a server transmission rate that avoids buffer overflow or underflow:

$$D(t) \leq A(t) \leq W(t) \qquad (16.12)$$

To avoid buffer overflow or underflow throughout the video's duration, Equation (16.12) has to hold for all $t \in 1, 2, \ldots, N$. Define S to be the server transmission schedule (or plan), i.e., $S = a(1), a(2), \ldots, a(N)$. S is called a *feasible transmission schedule* if for all t, S obeys Equation (16.12). Figure 16.18 illustrates the bounding curves $D(t)$ and $W(t)$ and shows that a constant (average)-bitrate transmission plan is not feasible for this video, because simply adopting the average bitrate would cause underflow.

When frame sizes $d(t)$ for all t are known ahead of transmission time, the server can plan ahead to generate an optimal transmission schedule that is feasible and minimize the peak transmission rate [26]. Additionally, the plan minimizes schedule variance, optimally trying to smooth the transmission as much as possible.

We can think of this technique as stretching a rubber band from $D(1)$ to $D(N)$ bounded by the curves defined by $D(t)$ and $W(t)$. The slope of the total-data-transmitted curve is the transmission data rate. Intuitively, we can minimize the slope (or the peak rate) if, whenever the transmission data rate has to change, it does so as early as possible in the transmission plan.

As an illustration, consider Figure 16.18. The server starts transmitting data when the prefetch buffer is at state (a). It determines that to avoid buffer underflow at point (c), the transmission rate has to be high enough to have enough data at point (c). However, at that rate, the buffer will overflow at point (b). Hence it is necessary to reduce the transmission rate somewhere between points (c) and (b).

The earliest such point (that minimizes transmission rate variability) is point (c). The rate is reduced to a lower constant bitrate until point (d), where the buffer is empty. After that, the rate must be further reduced (to lower than the average bitrate!) to avoid overflow until point (e), when the rate must finally be increased.

Consider any interval $[p, q]$ and let $B(t)$ represent the amount of data in the buffer at time t. Then the maximum constant data rate that can be used without overflowing the buffer is given by R_{max}:

$$R_{max} = \min_{p+1 \leq t \leq q} \frac{W(t) - (D(p) + B(p))}{t - p} \tag{16.13}$$

The minimum data rate that must be used over the same interval to avoid underflow is given by R_{min}:

$$R_{min} = \max_{p+1 \leq t \leq q} \frac{D(t) - (D(p) + B(p))}{t - p} \tag{16.14}$$

Naturally it is required that $R_{max} \geq R_{min}$, otherwise no constant bitrate transmission is feasible over interval $[p, q]$. The algorithm to construct the optimal transmission plan starts with interval $[p, q = p + 1]$ and keeps incrementing q, each time recalculating R_{max} and R_{min}. If R_{max} is to be increased, a rate segment is created with rate R_{max} over interval $[p, q_{max}]$, where q_{max} is the latest point at which the buffer is full (the latest point in interval $[p, q]$ where R_{max} is achieved).

Equivalently, if R_{min} is to be decreased, a rate segment is created with rate R_{min} over interval $[p, q_{min}]$, where q_{min} is the latest point at which the buffer is empty.

Planning transmission rates can readily consider maximum allowed network jitter. Suppose there is no delay in the receiving rate. Then at time t, $A(t)$ bytes of data were received, which must not exceed $W(t)$. Now suppose the network delay is at its worst — δ sec maximum delay. Video decoding will be delayed by δ seconds, so the prefetch buffer will not be freed. Hence the $D(t)$ curve needs to be modified to a $D(t - \delta)$ curve. Figure 16.18 depicts this. This situation provides protection against overflow or underflow in the plan for a given maximum delay jitter.

16.6   FURTHER EXPLORATION

For good general discussions on multimedia network communications see Steinmetz and Nahrstedt [27], Wu and Irwin [28], and Jeffay and Zhang [29]. Wang et al. [30] provide a good discussion on video processing and communications. For a discussion of ATM and MPEG-2, integrating digital video into broadband networks, see Orzessek and Sommer [15].

The Further Exploration section of the text web site for this chapter lists a good set of web resources for multimedia network communications such as

- ITU-T recommendations

- MBone sites

- RTP, RTSP, and SIP pages

- Introductions and White Papers on ATM

- Introductions and White Papers on DVB

An extensive list of RFCs from the IETF:

- Criteria for evaluating reliable multicast transport protocols

- Protocols for real-time transmission of multimedia data (RTP, RTSP, and RSVP)

- Protocols for VoIP (SIP, SDP, and SAP)

- Diffserv and MPLS

16.7   EXERCISES

1. Discuss at least two alternative methods for enabling QoS routing on packet-switched networks based on a QoS class specified for any multimedia packet (this would apply to any *store-and-forward* network).

2. Suggest a few additional priority delivery methods for specific multimedia applications that were not mentioned in Section 16.1.3.

3. When should RTP be used and when should RTSP be used? Is there an advantage in combining both protocols?

4. Consider again Figure 16.4, illustrating RSVP. In (d), receiver R3 decides to send an RSVP RESV message to S1. Assuming the figure specifies the complete state of the network, is the path reserved optimal for maximizing future network throughput? If not, what is the optimal path? Without modifying the RSVP protocol, suggest a scheme in which such a path will be discovered and chosen by the network nodes.

5. Browse the web to find current technologies designed for Internet telephony.

6. For Staggered broadcasting, if the division of the bandwidth is equal among all K logical channels ($K \geq 1$), show that access time is independent of the value of K.

7. Specify on Figure 16.17 the characteristics of *feasible* video transmission schedules. What is the *optimal transmission schedule*?

8. For the optimal work-ahead smoothing technique, how would you algorithmically determine at which point to change the planned transmission rate? What is the transmission rate?

9. Considering again the optimal work-ahead smoothing technique, it was suggested that instead of using every video frame, only frames at the beginning of statistically different compression video segments can be considered. How would you modify the algorithm (or video information) to support that?

10. *Unicast* transmission is when a server establishes a single communication channel with a specific client.

   (a) For video streaming, suggest a couple of methods for unicast video transmission, assuming the video is VBR encoded and client feedback is allowed.

   (b) Which one of your methods is better? Why?

11. *Multicast* transmission is when a server transmits a single multimedia stream to all listening multicast routers, and they forward it until a client receives the stream.

   (a) For VBR video streaming, suggest a couple of methods for multicast video transmission.

   (b) Which one of your methods is better? Why?

   Hint: Although a client may have a reverse channel for feedback, if all clients send feedback, it would cause congestion in the network.

16.8 REFERENCES

1 H. Eriksson, "MBONE: the Multicast Backbone," *Communications of the ACM*, 37(8): 54–60, 1994.

2 M.R. Macedonia and D.P. Brutzman, "MBone Provides Audio and Video across the Internet," *IEEE Computer*, 27(4): 30–36, 1994.

3 V. Kumar, *MBone: Interactive Multimedia on the Internet*, Indianapolis: New Riders, 1996.

4 K.C. Almeroth, "The Evolution of Multicast: from the MBone to Interdomain Multicast to Internet2 Deployment," *IEEE Network*, 14: 10–20, January/February 2000.

5 S. Paul, et al., "Reliable Multicast Transport Protocol (RMTP)," *IEEE Journal on Selected Areas in Communications*, 15(3): 407–421, 1997.

6 B. Whetten and G. Taskale, "An Overview of Reliable Multicast Transport Protocol II," *IEEE Network*, 14: 37–47, January/February 2000.

7 C. Liu, "Multimedia over IP: RSVP, RTP, RTCP, RTSP," In *Handbook of Emerging Communications Technologies: The Next Decade*, ed. R. Osso, Boca Raton, CRC Press, 2000, 29–46.

8 L. Zhang, et al., "RSVP: a New Resource ReSerVation Protocol," *IEEE Network*, 7(5): 8–19, 1993.

9 M. Krunz, "Bandwidth Allocation Strategies for Transporting Variable-Bit-Rate Video Traffic," *IEEE Communications Magazine*, 35(1): 40–46, 1999.

10 H. Schulzrinne and J. Rosenberg, "The IETF Internet Telephony Architecture and Protocols," *IEEE Network*, 13: 18–23, May/June 1999.

11 *Packet-based Multimedia Communications Systems*. ITU-T Recommendation H.323, November 2000 (earlier version September 1999).

12 J. Toga and J. Ott, "ITU-T Standardization Activities for Interactive Multimedia Communications on Packet-Based Networks: H.323 and Related Recommunications," *Computer Networks*, 31(3): 205–223, 1999.

13 A.S. Tanenbaum, *Computer Networks*, 4th ed., Upper Saddle River, NJ: Prentice Hall PTR, 2003.

14 W. Stallings, *Data & Computer Communications*, 6th ed., Upper Saddle River, NJ: Prentice Hall, 2000.

15 M. Orzessek and P. Sommer, *ATM & MPEG-2*, Upper Saddle River, NJ: Prentice Hall PTR, 1998.

16 U. Varshney, "Multicasting: Issues and Network Support," In *Multimedia Communications: Directions & Innovations*, ed. J.D. Gibson, San Diego: Academic Press, 2001, 297–310.

17 G. Armitage, "IP Multicast over ATM Metworks," *IEEE Journal on Selected Areas in Communications*, 15(3): 445–457, 1997.

18 S. Viswanathan and T. Imielinski, "Pyramid Broadcasting for Video on Demand Service," In *IEEE Conf. on Multimedia Computing and Networking*, 1995, 66–77.

19 K.A. Hua and S. Sheu, "Skyscraper Broadcasting: a New Broadcasting Scheme for Metropolitan Video-On-Demand Systems," In *Proceedings of the ACM SIGCOMM*, 1997, 89–100.

20 A. Hu, "Video-on-Demand Broadcasting Protocols: A Compreshensive Study," *Proceeding of IEEE IFCOM '01*, 2001, 508–517.

21 L. Juhn and L. Tseng, "Harmonic Broadcasting for Video-on-Demand Service," *IEEE Transactions on Broadcasting*, 43(3): 268–271, 1997.

22 J.F. Paris, S.W. Carter, and D.D.E. Long, "A Hybrid Broadcasting Protocol for Video on Demand," in *Proceeding of the 1999 Multimedia Computing and Networking Conference MMCN '99*, 1999, 317–326.

23 J.F. Paris, "A Simple Low-Bandwidth Broadcasting Protocol for Video-on-Demand," *Proceeding of the 7th International Conference on Computer Communications and Networks (IC3N '98)*, 1999, 690–697.

24 D. Saparilla, K. Ross, and M. Reisslein, "Periodic Broadcasting with VBR-Encoded Video," in *Proceeding of IEEE Infocom '99*, 1999, 464–471.

25 D. Eager, M. Vernon, and J. Zahorjan, "Minimizing Bandwidth Requirements for On-Demand Data Delivery," *IEEE Transactions on Knowledge and Data Engineering*, 13(5): 742–757, 2001.

26 J.D. Salehi, Z.L. Zhang, J.F. Kurose, and D. Towsley, "Supporting Stored Video: Reducing Rate Variability and End-to-End Resource Requirements through Optimal Smoothing," *ACM SIGMETRICS*, 24(1): 222–231, 1996.

27 R. Steinmetz and K. Nahrstedt, *Multimedia: Computing, Communications & Applications*, Upper Saddle River, NJ: Prentice Hall PTR, 1995.

28 C.H. Wu and J.D. Irwin, *Emerging Multimedia Computer Communication Technologies*. Upper Saddle River, NJ: Prentice Hall PTR, 1998.

29 K. Jeffay and H. Zhang, *Readings in Multimedia Computing and Networking*, San Francisco, CA: Morgan Kaufmann, 2002.

30 Y. Wang, J. Ostermann, and Y.Q. Zhang, *Video Processing and Communications*, Upper Saddle River, NJ: Prentice Hall, 2002.

CHAPTER 17

Wireless Networks

17.1 WIRELESS NETWORKS

The rapid developments in computer and communication technologies have made *ubiquitous computing* a reality. From cordless phones in the early days to cellular phones in the nineties and personal digital assistants (PDAs), PocketPCs, and videophones nowadays, wireless communication has been the core technology that enabled *personal communication services* (PCS), *personal communications network* (PCN) [1, 2], and *personal digital cellular* (PDC).

Geographically, wireless networks are often divided into *cells*. Each mobile phone in a cell contacts its *access point*, which serves as a gateway to the network. The access points themselves are connected through wired lines, or wireless networks or satellites that form the *core network*. When a mobile user moves out of the range of the initial access point, a *handoff* (or *handover*, as it is called in Europe) is required to maintain the communication.

In 1985, frequency bands at 902–928 MHz, 2.400–2.4835 GHz, and 5.725–5.850 GHz were assigned to Industrial, Scientific, and Medical applications by the FCC, hence the name *ISM bands*.

Traditionally, cell size is on the order of kilometers. The introduction of PCS, however, creates the need for a hierarchical cellular network in which several levels of cells can be defined:

- **picocell**. Each covers up to 100 meters; useful for wireless/cordless applications and devices (e.g., PDAs) in an office or home.

- **microcell**. Each covers up to 1,000 meters in cities or local areas, such as radio access payphones on the streets.

- **cell**. Each has up to 10,000 meters coverage; good for national or continental networks.

- **macrocell**. Provides worldwide coverage, such as satellite phones.

Fading is a common phenomenon in wireless (and especially mobile) communications, in which the received signal power (suddenly) drops. *Multipath fading* occurs when a signal reaches the receiver via multiple paths (some of them bouncing off buildings, hills, and other objects). Because they arrive at different times and phases, the multiple instances of the signal can cancel each other, causing the loss of signal or connection. The problem becomes more severe when higher data rates are explored.

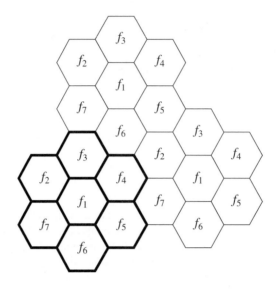

FIGURE 17.1: A possible geometric layout for an FDMA cellular system with a cluster size of seven hexagon cells.

17.1.1   Analog Wireless Networks

Earlier wireless communication networks were used mostly for voice communications, such as telephone and voice mail. First-generation (1G) cellular phones used analog technology and *Frequency Division Multiple Access* (FDMA), in which each user is assigned a separate frequency channel during the communication. Its standard was *Advanced Mobile Phone System* (AMPS) in North America, *Total Access Communication System* (TACS) and *Nordic Mobile Telephony* (NMT) in Europe and Asia. Digital data transmission users needed modems to access the network; the typical data rate was 9,600 bps.

AMPS, for example, operates at the 800–900 MHz frequency band. Each direction of the two-way communication is allocated 25 MHz, with *mobile station transmit* (MS transmit) in the band of 824 to 849 MHz and *base station transmit* (BS transmit) in the band of 869 to 894 MHz. Each of the 25 MHz bands is then divided up for two operator bands, A and B, giving each 12.5 MHz. FDMA further divides each of the 12.5 MHz operator bands into 416 channels, which results in each channel having a bandwidth of 30 KHz. The frequency of any MS transmit channel is always 45 MHz below the frequency of the corresponding BS transmit channel in communication.

Similarly, TACS operates at the 900 MHz frequency band. It carries up to 1,320 full-duplex channels, with a channel spacing of 25 KHz.

Figure 17.1 illustrates a possible geometric layout for an FDMA cellular system. (For clarity, cells from the first cluster are marked with thicker borders). A cluster of seven hexagon cells can be defined for the covered cellular area. As long as each cell in a cluster is assigned a unique set of frequency channels, interference from neighboring cells will be negligible.

The same set of frequency channels (denoted f_1 to f_7 in Figure 17.1) will be reused once in each cluster, following the illustrated symmetric pattern. The so called *reuse factor* is $K = 7$. In an AMPS system, for example, the maximum number of channels (including control channels) available in each cell is reduced to $416/K = 416/7 \approx 59$.

In this configuration, users in two different clusters using the same frequency f_n are guaranteed to be more than D apart geographically, where D is the diameter of the hexagonal cell. In a vacuum, electromagnetic radiation decays at a rate of D^{-2} over a distance D. However, in real physical spaces on the earth, the decay is consistently measured at a much faster rate of $D^{-3.5}$ to D^{-5}. This makes the FDMA scheme feasible for analog wireless communications, since interference by users of the same frequency channel from other groups becomes insignificant.

17.1.2   Digital Wireless Networks

Second-generation (2G) wireless networks use digital technology. Besides voice, digital data is increasingly transmitted for applications such as text messaging, streaming audio, and electronic publishing. In North America, the digital cellular networks adopted two competing technologies in 1993: *Time Division Multiple Access* (TDMA) and *Code Division Multiple Access* (CDMA). In Europe and Asia, *Global System for Mobile communications* (GSM) [1], which used TDMA, was introduced in 1992.

Below, we introduce TDMA and GSM first, followed by an introduction to *spread spectrum* and analysis of CDMA.

17.1.3   TDMA and GSM

As the name suggests, TDMA creates multiple channels in multiple time slots while allowing them to share the same carrier frequency. In practice, TDMA is always combined with FDMA — that is, the entire allocated spectrum is first divided into multiple carrier frequency channels, each of which is further divided in the time dimension by TDMA.

GSM was established by the *European Conference of Postal and Telecommunications Administrations* (CEPT) in 1982, with the objective of creating a standard for a mobile communication network capable of handling millions of subscribers and providing roaming services throughout Europe. It was designed to operate in the 900 MHz frequency range and was accordingly named GSM 900. Europe also supports GSM 1800, which is the original GSM standard modified to operate at the 1.8 GHz frequency range.

In North America, the GSM network uses frequencies at the range of 1.9 GHz (GSM 1900). However, the predominant use of TDMA technology is by operators using the TIA/EIA *IS-54B* and the *IS-136* standards. These standards are sometimes referred to as *digital-AMPS* or *D-AMPS*. IS-54B was superseded in 1996 by the newer IS-136 standard which employs *digital control channels* **DCCH** and other enhanced user services. IS-136 operates in the frequencies of 800 MHz and 1.9 GHz (the PCS frequency range), providing the same digital services in both. GSM and IS-136 combine TDMA with FDMA to use the allocated spectrum and provide easy backward compatibility with pure FDMA-mode (analog) mobile stations.

As Figure 17.2 shows, the uplink (mobile station to base station) of GSM 900 uses the 890–915 MHz band, and the downlink (base station to mobile station) uses 935–960 MHz.

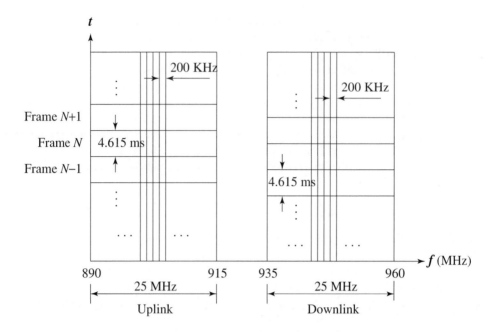

FIGURE 17.2: Frequency and time divisions in GSM.

In other words, each is allocated 25 MHz. The frequency division in GSM divides each 25 MHz into 124 carrier frequencies each with a separation of 200 KHz. The time division in GSM then divides each carrier frequency into *TDMA frames*; 26 TDMA frames are grouped into a *traffic channel* (TCH) of 120 msec that carries speech and data traffic.

Each TDMA frame is thus approximately 4.615 msec (i.e., 120/26 msec) and consists of eight time slots of length $4.615/8 \approx 0.577$ msec. Each mobile station is given unique time slots during which it can send and receive data. The send/receive does not occur at the same time slot; it is separated by three slots.

GSM provides a variety of data services. GSM users can send and receive data to users on POTS, ISDN, and packet-switched or circuit-switched public data networks. GSM also supports *Short Message Service* (SMS), in which text messages up to 160 characters can be delivered to (and from) mobile phones. One unique feature of GSM is the *subscriber identity module* (SIM), a smart card that carries the mobile user's personal number and enables ubiquitous access to GSM services.

By default, the GSM network is circuit switched, and its data rate is limited to 9.6 kbps. *General Packet Radio Service* (GPRS), developed in 1999, supports packet-switched data over wireless connections, so users are "always connected". It is also referred to as one of the 2.5G (between second- and third-generation) services. The theoretical maximum speed of GPRS is 171.2 kbps when all eight TDMA time slots are taken by a single user. In real implementations, single-user throughput reached 56 kbps in the year 2001. Apparently, when the network is shared by multiple users, the maximum data rate for each GPRS user will drop.

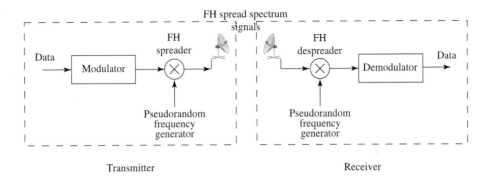

FIGURE 17.3: Transmitter and receiver of Frequency Hopping (FH) spread spectrum.

17.1.4 Spread Spectrum and CDMA

Spread spectrum is a technology in which the bandwidth of a signal is spread before transmission. In its appearance, the spread signal might be indistinguishable from background noise, so it has distinct advantages of being secure and robust against intentional interference (jamming).

Spread spectrum is applicable to digital as well as analog signals, because both can be modulated and "spread". The earlier generation of cordless phones and cellular phones, for example, used analog signals. However, it is the digital applications, in particular CDMA, that made the technology popular in various wireless data networks.

Following is a brief description of the two ways of implementing spread spectrum: *frequency hopping* and *direct sequence*.

Frequency Hopping.   Frequency hopping is the earlier method for spread spectrum. The technology of analog frequency hopping was invented by Hedy Lamarr, the actress [3], in 1940, during the World War II. Figure 17.3 illustrates the main components of the transmitter and receiver for frequency-hopping.

Initially, data (analog or digital) is modulated to generate some *baseband* signal centered at a base frequency f_b. Because of the relatively low data rate in current wireless applications, the bandwidth of the baseband B_b is generally narrow. For example, if the data rate is 9.6 kbps, then (depending on the modulating scheme) the bandwidth B_b would not be higher than $2 \times 9.6 = 19.2$ KHz. The pseudorandom frequency generator produces random frequencies f_r within a *wideband*[1] whose bandwidth is usually on the order of megahertz (MHz). At the Frequency-Hopping (FH) Spreader, f_r is modulated by the baseband signal to generate the Spread Spectrum Signal, which has the same shape as the baseband signal but a new center frequency

$$f_c = f_r + f_b. \tag{17.1}$$

---

[1] The choice of the frequency f_r is controlled by a random number generator. Because the algorithm is deterministic, it is not truly random but pseudorandom.

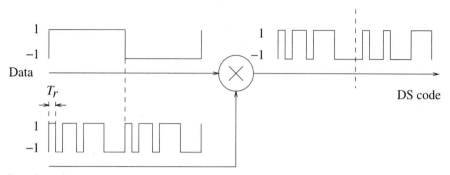

FIGURE 17.4: Spreading in Direct Sequence (DS) spread spectrum.

Since f_r changes randomly in the wideband, f_c of the resulting signal is "hopping" in the wideband accordingly.

At the receiver side, the process is reversed. As long as the same pseudorandom frequency generator is used, the signal is guaranteed to be properly despread and demodulated.

It is important to note that although the FH method uses a wideband spread spectrum, at any given moment during transmission, the FH signal occupies only a small portion of the band — that is, B_b.

The transmission of the FH spread spectrum signal is rather secure and robust against narrowband jamming attacks, since only a tiny portion of the FH signal can be received or jammed in any narrow band.

If the hopping rate is slower than the data rate, it is called *slow hopping* and is easier to realize. Slow hopping has been used in GSM and shown to help reducing multipath fading, since each TDMA frame with frequency hopping will likely be sent under a different carrier frequency. In *fast hopping*, the hopping rate is much faster than the data rate, which makes it more secure and effective in resisting narrowband interference.

Direct Sequence.   Occasionally, when the FH spread spectrum scheme is employed in a multiple-access environment, more than one signal can hop onto the same frequency and thus create undue interference. Although some form of TDMA can alleviate the problem, this still imposes a limitation on the maximum number of users.

A major breakthrough in wireless technology is the development and adoption of *Code Division Multiple Access* (CDMA). The foundation of CDMA is *Direct Sequence (DS) spread spectrum*. Unlike FDMA or frequency hopping, in which each user is supposed to occupy a unique frequency band at any moment, multiple CDMA users can make use of the same (and full) bandwidth of the shared wideband channel during the entire period of transmission! A common frequency band can also be allocated to multiple users in all cells — in other words, providing a reuse factor of $K = 1$. This has the potential to greatly increase the maximum number of users, as long as the interference from them is manageable.

As Figure 17.4 shows, for each CDMA transmitter a unique pseudo-noise sequence is fed to the Direct Sequence (DS) spreader. The pseudo-noise (also called *chip code* or *spreading*

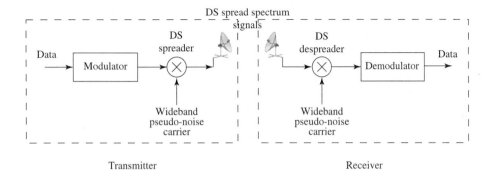

FIGURE 17.5: Transmitter and Receiver of Direct Sequence (DS) spread spectrum.

code) consists of a stream of narrow pulses called *chips*, with a bit width of T_r. Its bandwidth B_r is on the order of $1/T_r$. Because T_r is small, B_r is much wider than the bandwidth B_b of the narrowband signal.

The spreading code is multiplied with the input data. When the data bit is 1, the output DS code is identical to the spreading code, and when the data bit is -1, the output DS code is the inverted spreading code. As a result, the spectrum of the original narrowband data is spread, and the bandwidth of the DS signal is

$$B_{DS} = B_r. \tag{17.2}$$

The despreading process involves multiplying the DS code and the spreading sequence. As long as the same sequence is used as in the spreader, the resulting signal is the same as the original data. Figure 17.5 shows the implementation of the transmitter and receiver for the DS spread spectrum. An implementation detail slightly different from Figure 17.4 is that the DS spreader and despreader are actually analog devices. The data and spreading sequences are modulated into analog signals before being fed to the DS spreader.

There are two ways to implement CDMA multiple access: orthogonal codes or nonorthogonal codes. A mobile station is dynamically assigned a unique spreading code in the cell that is also being used by the base station to separate and despread its signal.

For orthogonal CDMA, the spreading codes in a cell are orthogonal to each other [4]. Most commonly, the Walsh–Hadamard codes are used, since they possess an important property called *orthogonal variable spreading factor* (OVSF). This states that OVSF codes of different lengths (i.e., different spreading factors) are still orthogonal. Orthogonality is desirable, since as long as the data is spread by orthogonal codes, it can be perfectly separated at the receiver end.

However, this property comes at a price: Walsh–Hadamard codes can have multiple autocorrelation peaks if the sequences are not synchronized, so external synchronization is necessary for the receiver to know where the beginning of the DS signal is. Synchronization is typically achieved by utilizing a *Global Positioning System* (GPS) in the base station. Another disadvantage is that orthogonal codes are concentrated around a small number of carrier frequencies and therefore have low spectral utilization.

Nonorthogonal codes are *Pseudo-random Noise* (PN) sequences. PN sequences need to have an average bit value of around 0.5 and a single autocorrelation peak at the start of the sequence. Thus, PN sequences are self-synchronizing and do not need external synchronization. A special PN sequence often used is the *Gold sequence*. Gold sequences have three cross-correlation peaks.

The DS spread spectrum makes use of the entire bandwidth of the wideband; hence, it is even more secure and robust against jamming. However, under multiple access, signals will still interfere with each other due to multipath fading, outer cell interference, and other factors. Below we provide a brief analysis of the viability of DS spread spectrum — that is, CDMA.

17.1.5   Analysis of CDMA

When FDMA or TDMA are used for a multiple-access system, bandwidth or time is divided up based on the worst case — that is, all users accessing the system simultaneously and all the time. This is of course hardly the case, especially for voice communications. CDMA allows users in the same channel to share the entire channel bandwidth. Since the effective noise is the sum of all other users' signals, it is based on the so called "average case" or "average interference". At the receiver, the DS input is recovered by correlating with the particular user's designated spreading code. Hence, as long as an adequate level of signal-to-noise ratio is maintained, the quality of the CDMA reception is guaranteed, and universal frequency reuse is achieved.

Let's denote the thermal noise of the receiver as N_T and the received signal power of each user as P_i. The interference to the source signal received at the base station is

$$N = N_T + \sum_{i=1}^{M-1} P_i$$

where M is the maximum number of users in a cell.

If we assume that the thermal noise N_T is negligible and the received P_i from each user is the same, then

$$N = (M - 1)P_i \qquad (17.3)$$

The received signal energy per bit E_b is the ratio of P_i over the date rate R (bps),

$$E_b = P_i/R, \qquad (17.4)$$

and the interference N_b is

$$N_b = N/W = (M - 1)P_i/W \qquad (17.5)$$

where W (Hz) is the bandwidth of the CDMA wideband signal carrier.

The signal-to-noise ratio (SNR) is thus

$$E_b/N_b = \frac{P_i/R}{(M - 1)P_i/W} = \frac{W/R}{M - 1} \qquad (17.6)$$

Rewriting Eq. (17.6), we have

$$M - 1 = \frac{W/R}{E_b/N_b}$$

or approximately

$$M \approx \frac{W/R}{E_b/N_b} \tag{17.7}$$

Equation (17.7) is an important result. It states that the capacity of the CDMA system — that is, the maximum number of users in a cell — is determined by two factors: W/R and E_b/N_b.

W/R is the ratio between the CDMA bandwidth W and user's data rate R. This is the *bandwidth spreading factor* or the *processing gain*. This is equivalent to the number of chips in the spreading sequence. Typically, it can be in the range 10^2 to 10^7.

E_b/N_b is the bit-level SNR. Depending on the QoS (error rate requirement) and the implementation (error-correction scheme, resistance to multipath fading, etc.), a digital demodulator can usually work well with a bit-level SNR in the range 3 to 9 dB.

As an example, let's assume the bit-level SNR to be a nominal 6 dB (from $10 \cdot \log E_b/N_b = 6$ dB); then $E_b/N_b \approx 4$. In the IS-95A standard, W = 1.25 MHz and R = 9.6 kbps. According to Eq. (17.7),

$$M \approx \frac{W/R}{E_b/N_b} \approx \frac{1,250/9.6}{4} \approx 32$$

This capacity of 32 seems to compare well with the AMPS system. When the reuse factor is $K = 7$, with a bandwidth of 1.25 MHz, the maximum number of AMPS channels allowed would be only $1{,}250/(30 \times 7) \approx 6$. However, the above CDMA analysis has assumed no interference from neighboring cells. If this were the case, AMPS could have adopted a reuse factor of $K = 1$; its maximum number of channels would have been $1{,}250/30 \approx 42$. So how does CDMA perform if the interference from neighboring cells is taken into consideration?

It turns out [5] that the received interference from all users in neighbor cells is merely about 60% of the interference from users within the cell. Hence, Eq. (17.7) can simply be modified to include a factor of 1.6 (i.e., 100% + 60%) to reflect the neighbor cell interference:

$$M \approx \frac{W/R}{1.6 \cdot E_b/N_b} \tag{17.8}$$

The above factor of 1.6 can also be called the *effective reuse factor*, because its role is similar to the reuse factor K in the FDMA systems. It should be apparent that CDMA offers a larger capacity than FDMA because of its better use of the whole bandwidth and the much smaller ($1.6 \ll 7$) reuse factor.

The above example now yields

$$M \approx \frac{1{,}250/9.6}{1.6 \times 4} \approx 22$$

— a capacity gain of 22/6 over AMPS.

Before concluding this brief analysis of CDMA, it must be pointed out that several major simplifications have been made above. Some contributed to enhanced performance, whereas others hampered performance. Viterbi [5] provided a thorough analysis of the principles of CDMA.

- We assumed that the received energy P_i from each user is equal. Otherwise, the "near-far" problem dominates, where the received signal from the "near user" is too strong and from the "far user" is too weak, and the whole system's performance will collapse. This requires a sophisticated power control on the transmitter. The modern CDMA power control updates power levels over 1,500 times per second to make sure the received P_i's are approximately the same.

- As a result of the tight power control required, CDMA networks have to implement soft handover. That is, when a mobile user crosses cell boundary, it has to communicate on at least two channels at once, one for each base station in range. It would use the lowest amount of power necessary for its signal to be received properly in at least one base station. This is done to minimize outer cell interference of the mobile.

- To reduce mutual interference, antennas are not omnidirectional. Instead, directional antennas are used, and collectively they are divided into *sectors*. In a three-way sectorized cell, AMPS capacity is reduced to $1{,}250/(30 \times 7 \times 3) \approx 2$. Remarkably, CDMA capacity is not susceptible to such sectorization. Therefore, its capacity gain over AMPS in sectored cells is even greater. In the above example, it is $22/2 \approx 11$.

- It was assumed that each user needs the full data rate all the time, which is false in many real applications. For example, voice applications use only 35–40% of the capacity. Effective *voice coding* can readily increase the network capacity by a factor of more than two.

17.1.6   3G Digital Wireless Networks

Third-generation (3G) wireless services feature various multimedia services, such as (low-rate) video over the Internet. Applications include wireless web surfing, video mail, continuous media on demand, mobile multimedia, mobile e-commerce, remote medical service, and so on. Unlike the current *Wireless LAN* (WLAN), which is by and large for indoor and private networks, 3G is mostly for public networks. While a large number of 2G wireless networks used both CDMA (such as IS-95A in North America) and TDMA (among them the most popular ones are GSM and IS-136), the 3G wireless networks will predominantly use *Wideband CDMA (WCDMA)*.

The 3G standardization process started in 1998, when the ITU called for *Radio Transmission Technology* (RTT) proposals for International Mobile Telecommunication-2000 (IMT-2000). Since then, the project has been known as 3G or universal mobile telecommunications system (UMTS). Regional standards bodies then adopted the IMT-2000 requirements, added their own, and developed proposals and their evaluations to submit to ITU (ITU-R for radio technologies).

Even as specifications were being developed in the regional standards bodies, which have members from many multinational corporations, it was noted that most bodies tend to adopt similar WCDMA technology. To achieve global standardization and more efficiently hold discussions about the same topic, the *Third Generation Partnership Project* (3GPP) was established in late 1998 to specify a global standard for WCDMA technology, which was named *Universal Terrestrial Radio Access* (UTRA). The standards bodies that joined to create the 3GPP forum are ARIB (Japan), ETSI (Europe), TTA (Korea), TTC (Japan), and T1 (North America). Later in 1999, CWTS (China) joined the group.

The 3GPP forum focused on WCDMA air interface, which is aimed at advancing GSM technology and is designed to interface with the GSM MAP core network. At the same time the Telecommunication Industry Association (TIA), with major industry support, had been developing the *cdma2000* air interface recommendation for ITU that is the evolution of the IS-95 standard and is designed to be used on ANSI-41 (or IS-41) core network.

As similar work was going on in Asia, following the 3GPP example, the standards organizations decided to form a second forum called *Third Generation Partnership Project 2* (3GPP2). The standards bodies that are members are ARIB (Japan), CWTS (China), TIA (North America), TTA (Korea), and TTC (Japan).

The 3GPP and 3GPP2 forums, despite having some similarities in WCDMA air interface proposals, still propose competing standards. However, in the interest of creating a global standard, the two forums are monitoring each other's progress and support recommendations by the operators harmonization group. The two forums have agreed to a harmonized standard referred to as *global 3G* (G3G) that will have three modes: Direct Spread (DS), Multi-Carrier (MC), and Time Division Duplex (TDD), where the DS and TDD modes are specified as in WCDMA by the 3GPP group, and the MC mode is, as in *cdma2000*, specified by 3GPP2. All air interfaces (all modes) can be used with both core networks. At the end of 1999, *ITU-R* released the *IMT-2000* specification that for the most part followed the harmonized standard recommendations for WCDMA.

The multimedia nature of the 3G wireless services calls for a rapid development of a new generation of handsets, where support for video, better software and user interface, and longer battery life will be key factors.

A migration (or evolution) path is specified for 2G wireless networks supporting digital communication over circuit-switched channels to 3G networks supporting high data rates over both circuit-switched and packet-switched channels. The evolution path has an intermediate step that is easier and cheaper to achieve (fewer changes to the network infrastructure) called 2.5G (2.5-generation), which is associated with enhanced data rates and packet data services (i.e., the addition of packet switching to 2G networks). Table 17.1 summarizes the 2G, 2.5G, and 3G standards that have been (or will be) developed using the IS-41 core networks (in North America) and GSM MAP core networks (in Europe, etc.).

TABLE 17.1: Evolution from 2G to 3G Wireless Networks

	ANSI-41 core network	**Peak data rate R**	**Carrier spectrum W**
2G	cdmaOne (IS-95A)	14.4 kbps	1.25 MHz
2.5G	cdmaOne (IS-95B)	115 kbps	1.25 MHz
3G	cdma2000 1X	307 kbps	1.25 MHz
3G	cdma2000 1xEV-DO	2.4 Mbps	1.25 MHz
3G	cdma2000 1xEV-DV	4.8 Mbps	1.25 MHz
3G	cdma2000 3X	> 2 Mbps	5 MHz
	GSM MAP core network	**Peak data rate R**	**Carrier spectrum W**
2G	GSM (TDMA)	14.4 kbps	1.25 MHz
2.5G	GPRS (TDMA)	170 kbps	1.25 MHz
3G	EDGE (TDMA)	384 kbps	1.25 MHz
3G	WCDMA	2 Mbps	5 MHz

The IS-95 Evolution. IS-95A and IS-95B, now known as *cdmaOne*, are based on the IS-41 core network and use narrowband CDMA air interface. As such, all development is geared toward extending the existing CDMA framework to 3G (wideband CDMA) with backward compatibility. This is seen as a major cost efficiency issue and therefore has major industry support, as well as quick adaptability. IS-95A is a 2G technology and has only circuit-switched channels with data rates up to 14.4 kbps. An extension to it is IS-95B (2.5G), which supports packet switching and achieves maximum rates of 115 kbps.

IMT-2000 MC mode, originally called cdma2000, can operate in all bands of the IMT spectrum (450, 700, 800, 900, 1700, 1800, 1900, and 2100 MHz). To ease the deployment of cdma2000, the evolution framework is divided into four stages, each is backward compatible with previous stages and cdmaOne.

The cdma2000 1X (or 1X RTT) specification, also known as the high rate packet data air interface specification, delivers enhanced services up to 307 kbps peak rate and 144 kbps on average. This air interface provides two to three times the data capacity of IS-95B. The 1X means that it occupies one times the channels for cdmaOne — 1.25 MHz carrier bandwidth per channel. As with the IS-95 air interface, the chip rate is 1.2288 Mcps (megachips per second).

The next step in cdma2000 deployment is cdma2000 1xEV (EV for EVolution), split into two phases. The air interface tries to support both ANSI-41 and GSM MAP networks, although priority is given to ANSI-41. The first phase is called 1xEV-DO (Data Only), supporting data transmission only at rates up to 2.4 Mbps. Voice communication is transmitted on a separate channel. Phase 2 is called 1xEV-DV (Data and Voice) and enhances the 1xEV interface to support voice communication as well. It promises an even higher data rate, up to 4.8 Mbps.

The last stage in the evolution to 3G is the recommended MC mode in IMT-2000. It is referred to as cdma2000 3X (or 3X RTT), since it uses a carrier spectrum of 5 MHz (3 × 1.25 MHz channels) to deliver a peak rate of at least 2–4 Mbps. The chip rate is also tripled to 3.686 Mcps.

Typical 3G data rates are 2 Mbps for stationary indoor applications, and 384 kbps and 128 kbps for slow- and fast-moving users, respectively.

The GSM Evolution.   The GSM radio access network (RAN) uses the GSM MAP core network. The IMT-2000 DS and TDD modes are based on the WCDMA technology developed for the GSM MAP network. GSM is TDMA-based and therefore less compatible with the WCDMA technology than IS-95. Hence the 3G WCDMA standard does not achieve backward compatibility with current-generation GSM networks. Moreover, each evolution toward 3G requires support for another mode of operation from mobile stations.

GSM is a 2G network providing only circuit-switched communication. *General Packet Radio Service* (GPRS) is a 2.5G enhancement that supports packet switching and higher date rates. As with CDMA2000 1X, EDGE (*Enhanced Data rates for Global Evolution* or *Enhanced Data GSM Environment*) supports up to triple the data rate of GSM and GPRS. EDGE is still a TDMA-based standard, defined mainly for GSM evolution to WCDMA. However it is defined in IMT-2000 as UWC-136 for Single Carrier Mode (IMT-SC) and, as such, is a 3G solution. It can achieve a data rate up to 384 kbps by new modulation and radio techniques, to optimize the use of available spectrum.

Eventually, the 3G technology (also referred to as 3GSM) will be adapted according to the WCDMA modes IMT-2000 recommendations. WCDMA has two modes of operation: Direct Sequence (DS) [also called Frequency Division Duplex (FDD)] and Time Division Duplex (TDD). FDD mode is used in the paired frequencies spectrum allocated where the uplink and downlink channels use different frequencies. However, for the unpaired frequencies, it is necessary to transmit both uplink and downlink channels at the same frequencies. This is achieved by using time slots, having the uplink use a different time slot than the downlink. It also requires a more complicated timing control in the mobile than in TDMA.

Key differences in WCDMA air interface from a narrowband CDMA air interface are

- To support bitrates up to 2 Mbps, a wider channel bandwidth is allocated. The WCDMA channel bandwidth is 5 MHz, as opposed to 1.25 MHz for IS-95 and other earlier standards.

- To effectively use the 5 MHz bandwidth, longer spreading codes at higher chip rates are necessary. The chip rate specified is 3.84 Mcps, as opposed to 1.2288 Mcps for IS-95.

- WCDMA supports variable bitrates, from 8 kbps up to 2 Mbps. This is achieved using variable-length spreading codes and time frames of 10 msec, at which the user data rate remains constant but can change from one frame to the other — hence *Bandwidth on Demand* (BoD).

- WCDMA base stations use asynchronous CDMA with Gold codes. This eliminates the need for a GPS in the base station for global time synchronization, as in IS-95 systems. Base stations can now be made smaller and less expensive and can be located indoors.

17.1.7 Wireless LAN (WLAN)

From the beginning, Wireless WAN (Wide Area Network) was popular, due to various voice and data applications. The increasing availability of laptop computers brought about keen interest in Wireless LANs (Local Area Networks). Moreover, the emergence lately of ubiquitous and pervasive computing [6] has created a new surge of interest in Wireless LANs (WLANs).

IEEE 802.11. IEEE 802.11 was the earlier standard for WLAN developed by the IEEE 802.11 working group. It specified Medium Access Control (MAC) and Physical (PHY) layers for wireless connectivity in a local area within a radius of several hundred feet. PHY supported both Frequency Hopping (FH) spread spectrum and Direct Sequence (DS) spread spectrum. The ISM frequency band used was 2.4 GHz. Moreover, (diffused) infrared light was also supported for indoor communications in the range of 10–20 meters.

WLAN can be used either as a replacement or an extension to the wired LAN. Similar to Ethernet, the basic access method of 802.11 is *Carrier Sense Multiple Access with Collision Avoidance* (CSMA/CA). The data rates supported by 802.11 were 1 Mbps and 2 Mbps.

The 802.11 standards also address the following important issues:

- **Security**. Enhanced *authentication* and *encryption*, since WLAN is even more susceptible to break-ins.

- **Power management**. Saves power during no transmission and handles *doze* and *awake*.

- **Roaming**. Permits acceptance of the basic message format by different access points.

IEEE 802.11b. IEEE 802.11b is an enhancement of 802.11. It still uses DS spread spectrum and operates in the 2.4 GHz band. With the aid of new technology, especially the Complementary Code Keying (CCK) modulation technique, it supports 5.5 and 11 Mbps in addition to the original 1 and 2 Mbps, and its functionality is comparable to Ethernet.

In North America, for example, the allocated spectrum for 802.11 and 802.11b is 2.400–2.4835 GHz. Regardless of the data rate (1, 2, 5.5, or 11 Mbps), the bandwidth of a DS spread spectrum channel is 20 MHz. Three nonoverlapped DS channels can be accommodated simultaneously, allowing a maximum of 3 access points in a local area.

IEEE 802.11b has gained public acceptance and is appearing in WLANs everywhere, including university campuses, airports, conference centers, and so on.

IEEE 802.11a. IEEE 802.11a operates in the 5 GHz band and supports data rates in the range of 6 to 54 Mbps. Instead of DS spread spectrum, it uses *Orthogonal Frequency Division Multiplexing* (OFDM). It allows 12 nonoverlapping channels, hence a maximum of 12 access points in a local area.

Because 802.11a operates in the higher frequency (5 GHz) band, it faces much less Radio Frequency (RF) interference, such as from cordless phones, than 802.11 and 802.11b. Coupled with the higher data rate, it has great potential for supporting various multimedia applications in a LAN environment.

High Performance Radio LAN (HIPERLAN/2) is the European sibling of IEEE 802.11a. It also operates in the 5 GHz band and is promised to deliver a data rate of up to 54 Mbps. Wesel [2] provides a good description of HIPERLAN.

IEEE 802.11g and others.   IEEE 802.11g, an extension of 802.11b, is an attempt to achieve data rates up to 54 Mbps in the 2.4 GHz band. As in 802.11a, OFDM will be used instead of DS spread spectrum. However, 802.11g still suffers from higher RF interference than does 802.11a, and as in 802.11b, has the limitation of three access points in a local area.

IEEE 802.11g is designed to be downward compatible with 802.11b, which brings a significant overhead for all 802.11b and 802.11g users on the 802.11g network.

Another half-dozen 802.11 standards are being developed that deal with various aspects of WLAN. The Further Exploration section of this chapter has WWW URLs for these standards. Notably, 802.11e deals with MAC enhancement for QoS, especially prioritized transmission for voice and video.

Bluetooth.   *Bluetooth* (named after the tenth-century king of Denmark Harold Bluetooth) is a new protocol intended for short-range (piconet) wireless communications. In particular, it can be used to replace cables connecting mobile and/or fixed computers and devices. It uses FH spread spectrum at the 2.4 GHz ISM band and a full-duplex signal that hops among 79 frequencies at 1 MHz intervals and at a rate of 1,600 hops per second. Bluetooth supports both circuit switching and packet switching. It supports up to three voice channels (each 64 kbps symmetric) and more than one data channel (each over 400 kbps symmetric).

The Bluetooth consortium web site (www.bluetooth.com) provides a detailed core specification and includes a description of the use of Wireless Application Protocol (WAP) in the Bluetooth environment. In the "briefcase trick", for example, the user's mobile phone will communicate with his/her laptop periodically, so e-mail can be reviewed from the handheld phone without opening the briefcase.

Some new Sony camcorders already have a built-in Bluetooth interface. This permits moving or still pictures to be sent to a PC or to the web directly (without a PC) through a mobile phone equipped with Bluetooth, at a speed of over 700 kbps, within a distance of 10 meters. Such camcorders can even be used to browse the WWW and send e-mail with JPEG or MPEG-1 attachments.

17.2   RADIO PROPAGATION MODELS

Radio transmission channels present much greater engineering difficulties than wired lines. In this section, we briefly present the most common radio channel models to gain insight into the cause of bit/frame errors and to classify the types of bit errors, the amount, and whether they are bursty.

Various effects cause radio signal degradation in the receiver side (other than noise). They can be classified as short-range and long-range effects. Accordingly, multipath fading models are available for small-scale fading channels, and path-loss models are available for long-range atmospheric attenuation channels.

For indoor channels, the radio signal power is generally lower, and there are more objects in a small place; some are moving. Hence, multipath fading is the main factor for signal degradation, and fading models are established. In such an environment, the transmitted signal is split into multiple paths going to the receiver, each path having its own attenuation, phase delay, and time delay.

Multipath models probabilistically state the received signal amplitude, which varies according to whether the signals superimposed at the receiver are added destructively or constructively. Signal fading occurs due to reflection, refraction, scattering, and diffraction (mainly from moving objects).

Outdoors there are also refraction, diffraction, and scattering effects, mostly caused by the ground and buildings. Long-range communication, however, is dominated by atmospheric attenuation. Depending on the frequency, radio waves can penetrate the ionosphere (> 3 GHz) and establish line-of-sight (LOS) communication, or for lower frequencies reflect off the ionosphere and the ground, or travel along the ionosphere to the receiver. Frequencies over 3 GHz (which are necessary for satellite transmissions to penetrate the ionosphere) experience gaseous attenuations, influenced primarily by oxygen and water (vapor and rain).

17.2.1 Multipath Fading

Fading models try to model the amplitude of the superimposed signal at the receiver. The *Doppler spread* of a signal is defined as the distribution of the signal power over the frequency spectrum (the signal is modulated at a specific frequency bandwidth). When the Doppler spread of the signal is small enough, the signal is coherent — that is, there is only one distinguishable signal at the receiver. This is typically the case for narrowband signals. However, when the signal is wideband, different frequencies of the signal have different fading paths, and a few distinguishable signal paths are observed at the receiver, separated in time. For narrowband signals, the most popular models are *Rayleigh fading* and *Rician fading*.

The Rayleigh model assumes an infinite number of signal paths with no line-of-sight (LOS) to the receiver for modeling the probability density function P_r of received signal amplitude r:

$$P_r(r) = \frac{r}{\sigma^2} \cdot e^{\frac{-r^2}{2\sigma^2}} \tag{17.9}$$

where σ is the standard deviation of the probability density function. Although the number of signal paths is typically not too large, the Rayleigh model does provide a good approximation when the number of paths is over 5.

A more general model that assumes a LOS is the Rician model. It defines a *K-factor* as a ratio of the signal power to the scattered power — that is, K is the factor by which the LOS signal is greater than the other paths. The Rician probability density function P_c is

$$P_c(r) = \frac{r}{\sigma^2} \cdot e^{\frac{-r^2}{2\sigma^2}-K} \cdot I_o(\frac{r}{\sigma}\sqrt{2K}), \quad \text{where } K = \frac{s^2}{2\sigma^2} \tag{17.10}$$

As before, r and σ are the signal amplitude and standard deviation respectively, and s is the LOS signal power. I_o is a modified Bessel function of the first kind with 0 order.

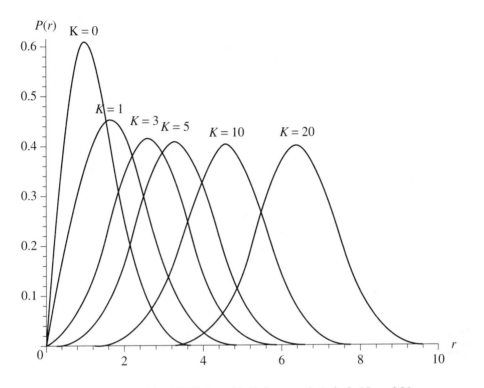

FIGURE 17.6: Rician PDF plot with K-factor = 0, 1, 3, 5, 10, and 20.

Note that when $s = 0$ ($K = 0$) there is no LOS, and the model thus reduces to a Rayleigh distribution. When $K = \infty$ the model reflects the *additive white Gaussian noise* (AWGN) conditions. Figure 17.6 shows the Rician probability density function for K-factors of 0, 1, 3, 5, 10, and 20, with standard deviation of $\sigma = 1.0$.

For a wideband signal, the fading paths are more empirically driven. One way is to model the amplitude as a summation over all the paths, each having randomized fading. The number of paths can be 7 for a closed-room environment (six walls and LOS) or a larger number for other environments. An alternative technique of modeling the channel fading is by measuring the channel impulse response.

A similar technique is utilized in CDMA systems, proposed in cdma2000 as well and added to WCDMA as part of the harmonization effort. A CDMA station (both mobile and base station) has *rake receivers*, which are multiple CDMA radio receivers tuned to signals with different phase and amplitude, to recompose the CDMA transmission that split to different distinguishable paths. The signal at each rake receiver is added up to achieve better SNR. To tune the rake receivers to the proper fading paths, CDMA systems have a special *pilot channel* that sends a well-known pilot signal, and the rake receivers are adjusted to recognize that symbol on each fading path.

17.2.2 Path Loss

For long-range communication, the signal loss is dominated by attenuation. The free-space attenuation model for LOS transmission is in inverse proportion to the square of distance (d^2) and is given by the Friis radiation equation

$$S_r = \frac{S_t G_t G_r \lambda^2}{(4\pi^2)d^2 L} \tag{17.11}$$

S_r and S_t are the received and transmitted signal power, G_r and G_t are the antenna gain factors, λ is the signal wavelength, and L is the receiver loss. It can be shown, however, that if we assume ground reflection, attenuation increases to be proportional to d^4.

Another popular medium-scale (urban city size) model is the Hata model, which is empirically derived based on Okumura path loss data in Tokyo. The basic form of the path loss equation in dB is given by

$$L = A + B \cdot log_{10}(d) + C. \tag{17.12}$$

Here, A is a function of the frequency and antenna heights, B is an environment function, and C is a function depending on the carrier frequency. Again, d is the distance from the transmitter to the receiver.

Satellite models are attenuated primarily by rain. Hence, meteorological rainfall density maps can be used to communicate with the region. Attenuation is computed according to the amount of rainfall in the area on the given date.

17.3 MULTIMEDIA OVER WIRELESS NETWORKS

We have studied the evolution of current 2G networks to future high-capacity 3G networks, but is there a demand for 3G networks? Multimedia over wireless will certainly need a higher bandwidth. Suggested multimedia applications range from web browsing, streaming video, videoconferencing, collaborative work, and slide-show presentations to enhanced roadside assistance and downloadable GPS maps for drivers.

In this section we are concerned mainly with sending video robustly over wireless channels, such as for a videoconferencing application. This application should be prominent on 3G handhelds, since it is a natural extension to voice communication.

Because wireless data transmissions incur the most data loss and distortion, error resilience and error correction become primary concerns. We have thus included some brief description of synchronization loss, error-resilient entropy coding, error concealment, and Forward Error Correction (FEC) in this section, although most of these techniques are also applicable to other networks.

A few characteristics of wireless handheld devices are worth keeping in mind when designing multimedia transmission, in particular video transmission. First, both the handheld size and battery life limit the processing power and memory of the device. Thus, encoding and decoding must have relatively low complexity. Of course, one advantage of the smaller device size is that lower-resolution videos are acceptable, which helps reduce processing time.

Second, due to memory constraints and reasons for the use of wireless devices, as well as billing procedures, real-time communication is likely to be required. Long delays before starting to see a video are either not possible or not acceptable.

Finally, wireless channels have much more interference than wired channels, with specific loss patterns depending on the environment conditions. The bitrate for wireless channels is also much more limited, although the 3G bitrates are more suitable for video. This implies that although a lot of bit protection must be applied, coding efficiency has to be maintained as well. Error-resilient coding is important.

3G standards specify that video shall be standard compliant. Moreover, most companies will concentrate on developing products using standards, in the interest of interoperability of mobiles and networks. The video standards reasonable for use over wireless channels are MPEG-4 and H.263 and its variants, since they have low bitrate requirements.

The 3GPP2 group has defined the following QoS parameters for wireless videoconferencing services [7]. The QoS parameters specified for the wireless part are more stringent than those required for end-to-end transmissions. The 3GPP QoS requirements for multimedia transmission are nearly identical [8].

- **Synchronization**. Video and audio should be synchronized to within 20 msec.

- **Throughput**. The minimum video bitrate to be supported is 32 kbps. Video rates of 128 kbps, 384 kbps, and above should be supported as well.

- **Delay**. The maximum end-to-end transmission delay is defined to be 400 msec.

- **Jitter**. The maximum delay jitter (maximum difference between the average delay and the 95th percentile of the delay distribution) is 200 msec.

- **Error rate**. The videoconferencing system should be able to tolerate a frame error rate of 10^{-2} or a bit error rate of 10^{-3} for circuit-switched transmission.

In the following, we discuss the vulnerability of a video sequence to bit errors and ways to improve resilience to errors.

17.3.1 Synchronization Loss

A video stream is either packetized and transmitted over a packet-switched channel or transmitted as a continuous bitstream over a circuit-switched channel. In either case, it is obvious that packet loss or bit error will reduce video quality. If a bit loss or packet loss is localized in the video in both space and time, the loss can still be acceptable, since a frame is displayed for a very short period, and a small error might go unnoticed.

However, digital video coding techniques involve variable-length codes, and frames are coded with different prediction and quantization levels. Unfortunately, when a packet containing variable bit-length data (such as DCT coefficients) is damaged, that error, if unconstrained, will propagate all the way throughout the stream. This is called *loss of decoder synchronization*. Even if the decoder can detect the error due to an invalid coded symbol or coefficients out of range, it still cannot establish the next point from which to start decoding [9].

As we have learned in Chapter 10 this complete bitstream loss does not happen for videos coded with standardized protocol layers. The Picture layer and the Group Of Blocks (GOB) layer or Slice headers have *synchronization markers* that enable decoder resynchronization. For example, the H.263 bitstream has four layers — the Picture layer, GOB layer, Macroblock layer, and Block layer. The Picture Layer starts with a unique 22-bit picture start code (PSC). The longest entropy-coded symbol possible is 13 bits, so the PSC serves as a synchronization marker as well. The GOB layer is provided for synchronization after a few blocks rather than the entire frame. The group of blocks start code (GBSC) is 17 bits long and also serves as a synchronization marker.[2] The macroblock and the Block layers do not contain unique start codes, as these are deemed high overhead.

ITU standards after H.261 (e.g., H.263, H.263+, etc.) support slice-structured mode instead of GOBs (H.263 Annex K), where slices group blocks together according to the block's coded bit length rather than the number of blocks. The objective is to space slice headers within a known distance of each other. That way, when a bitstream error looks like a synchronization marker, if the marker is not where the slice headers should be it is discarded, and no false resynchronization occurs.

Since slices need to group an integral number of macroblocks together, and macroblocks are coded using VLCs, it is not possible to have all slices the same size. However, there is a minimum distance after which the next scanned macroblock will be added to a new slice. We know that DC coefficients in macroblocks and motion vectors of macroblocks are differentially coded. Therefore, if a macroblock is damaged and the decoder locates the next synchronization marker, it might still not be able to decode the stream.

To alleviate the problem, slices also reset spatial prediction parameters; differential coding across slice boundaries is not permitted. The ISO MPEG standards (and H.264 as well) specify slices that are not required to be of similar bit length and so do not protect against false markers well.

Other than synchronization loss, we should note that errors in prediction reference frames cause much more damage to signal quality than errors in frames not used for prediction. That is, a frame error for an I-frame will deteriorate the quality of a video stream more than a frame error for a P- or B-frame. Similarly, if the video is scalable, an error at the base layer will deteriorate the quality of a video stream more than in enhancement layers.

MPEG-4 defines additional error-resilient tools that are useful for coding under noisy and wireless channel conditions. These are in addition to slice coding and Reversible Variable Length Codes (RVLCs) [10, 11]. To further help with synchronization, a data partitioning scheme will group and separate header information, motion vectors, and DCT coefficients into different packets and put synchronization markers between them. As we shall see later on, such a scheme is also beneficial to unequal protection Forward Error Correction (FEC) schemes.

---

[2]Synchronization markers are always larger than the minimum required, in case bit errors change bits to look like synchronization markers.

Additionally, an adaptive intra-frame refresh mode is allowed, where each macroblock can be coded independently of the frame as an inter- or intra- block according to its motion, to assist with error concealment. A faster-moving block will require more frequent refreshing — that is, be coded in intra- mode more often. Synchronization markers are easy to recognize and are particularly well suited to devices with limited processing power, such as cell phones and mobile devices.

For interactive applications, if a back channel is available to the encoder, a few additional error control techniques are available, classified as *sender-receiver feedback*. According to the bandwidth available at any moment, the receiver can ask the sender to lower or increase the video bitrate (transmission rate control), which combats packet loss due to congestion. If the stream is scalable, it can also ask for enhancement layers.

Additionally, Annex N of H.263+ specifies that the receiver can notice damage in a reference frame and request that the encoder use a different reference frame for prediction — a reference frame the decoder has reconstructed correctly.

The above techniques can be used in wireless real-time video applications such as video-conferencing, since wireless cell communication supports a back channel if necessary. However, it is obviously cheaper not to use one (it would reduce multiple-access interference in the uplink).

17.3.2 Error Resilient Entropy Coding

The main purpose of GOBs, slices, and synchronization markers is to reestablish decoder synchronization as soon as possible after an error. In Annex K of H.263+, slices achieve better resilience, since they impose further constraints on where the stream can be synchronized. However, another algorithm, called *Error Resilient Entropy Coding* (EREC), can achieve synchronization after every *single* macroblock, without any of the overhead of the slice headers or GOB headers. The algorithm is called EREC because it takes entropy-coded variable-length macroblocks and rearranges them in an error-resilient fashion. In addition, it can provide graceful degradation.

EREC takes a coded bitstream of a few blocks and rearranges them so that the beginning of all the blocks is a fixed distance apart. Although the blocks can be of any size and any media we wish to synchronize, the following description will refer to macroblocks in videos. The algorithm proceeds as in Figure 17.7.

Initially, EREC slots (rows) of fixed bit-length are allocated with total bit-length equal to (or exceeding) the total bit-length of all the macroblocks. The number of slots is equal to the number of macroblocks, except that the macroblocks have varying bit-length and the slots have a fixed bit-length (approximately equal to the average bit-length of all the macroblocks). As shown, the last EREC slot (row) is shorter when the total number of bits does not divide evenly by the number of slots.

Let k be the number of macroblocks which is equal to the number of slots, l be the total bit-length of all the macroblocks, $mbs[$ $]$ be the macroblocks, $slots[$ $]$ be the EREC slots, the procedure for encoding the macroblocks is shown below.

EREC slots   Macroblocks

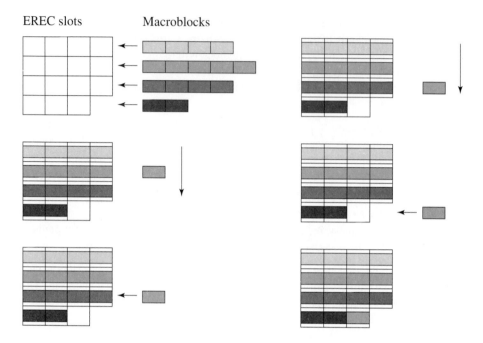

FIGURE 17.7: Example of macroblock encoding using EREC.

PROCEDURE 17.1   **EREC_Encode**
BEGIN
    $j = 0$;
    Repeat until $l = 0$
    {
        for $i = 0$ to $k - 1$
        {
            $m = (i + j) \bmod k$;
            // m is the macroblock number corresponding to slot i;
            Shift as many bits as possible (without overflow) from $mbs[i]$ into $slots[m]$;
            $sb =$ number of bits successfully shifted into $slots[m]$ (without overflow);
            $l = l - sb$;
        }
        $j = j + 1$;   // shift the macroblocks downwards
    }
END

The macroblocks are shifted into the corresponding slots until all the bits of the macroblock have been assigned or remaining bits of the macroblock don't fit into the slot. Then the macroblocks are shifted down, and this procedure repeats.

Macroblocks   EREC slots

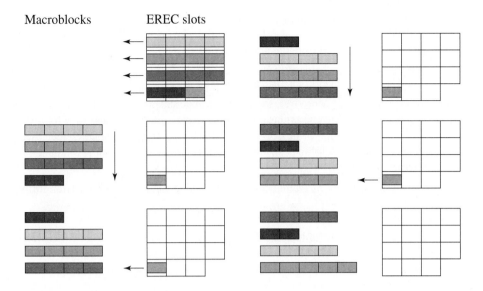

FIGURE 17.8: Example of macroblock decoding using EREC.

The decoder side works in reverse, with the additional requirement that it has to detect when a macroblock has been read in full. It accomplishes this by detecting the end of macroblock when all DCT coefficients have been decoded (or a block end code). Figure 17.8 shows an example of the decoding process for the macroblocks coded using EREC in Figure 17.7.

The transmission order of the data in the slots is row-major — that is, at first the data in slot 0 is sent, then slot 1, and so on, left to right. It is easy to see how this technique is resilient to errors. No matter where the damage is, even at the beginning of a macroblock, we still know where the next macroblock starts — it is a fixed distance from the previous one. In this case, no synchronization markers are used, so the GOB layer or slices are not necessary either (although we still might want to restrict spatial propagation of error).

When the macroblocks are coded using a data partitioning technique (such as the one for MPEG-4 described in the previous section) and also bitplane partitioning, an error in the bitstream will destroy less significant data while receiving the significant data. It is obvious that the chance for error propagation is greater for bits at the end of the slot than at the beginning. On average, this will also reduce visual deterioration over a nonpartitioned encoding. This achieves graceful degradation under worsening error conditions.

17.3.3 Error Concealment

Despite all the efforts to minimize occurrences of errors and their significance, errors can still be visually annoying. *Error concealment* techniques are thus introduced to approximate the lost data on the decoder side.

Many error concealment techniques apply either in the spatial, temporal, or frequency domain, or a combination of them. All the techniques use neighboring frames temporally or neighboring macroblocks spatially. The transport stream coder interleaves the video packets, so that in case of a burst packet loss, not all the errors will be at one place, and the missing data can be estimated from the neighborhood.

Error concealment is necessary for wireless video communication, since the error rates are higher than for wired channels and might even be higher than can be transmitted with appropriate bit protection. Moreover, the error rate fluctuates more often, depending on various mobility or weather conditions. Decoding errors due to missing or wrong data received are more noticeable on devices with limited resolution and small screen sizes. This is especially true if macroblock size remains large, to achieve encoding efficiency for lower wireless bitrates.

Following is a summary of techniques for error concealment. (See [12] for further details.)

1. **Dealing with lost macroblock(s)**. A simple and popular technique for concealment can be used when DCT blocks are damaged but the motion vectors are received correctly. The missing block coefficients are estimated from the reference frame, assuming no prediction errors. Since the goal of motion-compensated video is to minimize prediction errors, this is an appropriate assumption. The missing block is hence temporally masked using the block in the reference frame.

   We can achieve even better results if the video is scalable. In that case, we assume that the base layer is received correctly and that it contains the motion vectors and base layer coefficients that are most important. Then, for a lost macroblock at the enhancement layer, we use the motion vectors from the base layer, replace the DCT coefficients at the enhancement layer, and decode as usual from there. Since coefficients of less importance are estimated (such as higher-frequency coefficients), even if the estimation is not too accurate due to prediction errors, the concealment is more effective than in a nonscalable case.

   If motion vector information is damaged as well, this technique can be used only if the motion vectors are estimated using another concealment technique (to be discussed next). The estimation of the motion vector has to be good, or the visual quality of the video could be inauspicious. To apply this technique for intra-frames, some standards, such as MPEG-2, also allow the acquisition of motion vectors for intra-coded frames (i.e., treating them as intra- as well as inter-frames). These motion vectors are discarded if the block has no error.

2. **Combining temporal, spatial and frequency coherences**. Instead of just relying on the temporal coherence of motion vectors, we can combine it with spatial and frequency coherences. By having rules for estimating missing block coefficients using the received coefficients and neighboring blocks in the same frame, we can conceal errors for intra-frames and for frames with damaged motion vector information. Additionally, combining with prediction using motion vectors will give us a better approximation of the prediction error block.

   Missing block coefficients can be estimated spatially by minimizing the error of a smoothness function defined over the block and neighboring blocks. For simplicity, the smoothness function can be chosen as the sum of squared differences of pairwise neighboring pixels in the block. The function unknowns are the missing coefficients. In the case where motion information is available, prediction smoothness is added to the objective function for minimization, weighted as desired.

The simple smoothness measure defined above has the problem that it smoothes edges as well. We can attempt to do better by increasing the order of the smoothing criterion from linear to quadratic or cubic. This will increase the chances of having both edge reconstruction and smoothing along the edge direction. At a larger computational cost, we can use an edge-adaptive smoothing method, whereby the edge directions inside the block are first determined, and smoothing is not permitted across edges.

3. **Frequency smoothing for high-frequency coefficients**. Smoothing can be defined much more simply, to save on computational cost. Although the human visual system is more sensitive to low frequencies, it would be disturbing to see a checkerboard pattern where it does not belong. This will happen when a high-frequency coefficient is erroneously assigned a high value. The simplest remedy is to set high-frequency coefficients to 0 if they are damaged.

   If the frequencies of neighboring blocks are correlated, it is possible to estimate lost coefficients in the frequency domain directly. For each missing frequency coefficient in a block, we estimate its value using an interpolation of the same frequency coefficient values from the four neighboring blocks. This is applicable at higher frequencies only if the image has regular patterns. Unfortunately that is not usually the case for natural images, so most of the time the high coefficients are again set to 0. Temporal prediction error blocks are even less correlated at all frequencies, so this method applies only for intra-frames.

4. **Estimation of lost motion vectors**. Loss of motion vectors prevents decoding of an entire predicted block, so it is important to estimate motion vectors well. The easiest way to estimate lost motion vectors is to set them to 0. This works well only in the presence of very little motion. A better estimation is obtained by examining the motion vectors of reference macroblocks and of neighboring macroblocks. Assuming motion is also coherent, it is reasonable to take the motion vectors of the corresponding macroblock in the reference frame as the motion vectors for the damaged target block.

   Similarly, assuming objects with consistent motion fields occupy more than one macroblock, the motion vector for the damaged block can be approximated as an interpolation of the motion vectors of the surrounding blocks that were received correctly. Typical simple interpolation schemes are weighted-average and median. Also, the spatial estimation of the motion vector can be combined with the estimation from the reference frame using weighted sums.

17.3.4 Forward Error Correction (FEC)

Some data are vitally important for correct decoding. Missing DCT coefficients may be estimated or their effect visually concealed to some degree. However, some lost and improperly estimated data, such as picture coding mode, quantization level, or most data in higher layers of a video standard protocol stack, will cause catastrophic video decoding failure. In such cases, we would like to ensure "error-free" transmission. However, most channels, in particular wireless channels, are noisy, and to ensure correct transmission, we must provide adequate redundant retransmissions (when no back channel is available).

Forward Error Correction (FEC) is a technique that adds redundant data to a bitstream to recover some random bit errors in it. Ideally, the channel-packet error rate (or bit error rate) is estimated, and enough redundancy is added to make the probability of error after FEC recovery low.

The interval over which the packet error rate is estimated is chosen to be the smallest possible (to minimize latency and computation cost) that reliably estimates the frame loss probability. Naturally, when burst frame loss occurs, the estimation may no longer be adequate.

Frame errors are also called *erasures*, since the entire packet is dropped on an error. Videos have to be transmitted over a channel with limited bandwidth. Therefore, it is important to minimize redundancy, because it comes at the expense of bitrates available for video source coding. At the same time, enough redundancy is needed so that the video can maintain required QoS under the current channel error conditions. There is an optimal amount of redundancy that minimizes video distortion, given certain channel conditions.

FEC codes in general fall into two categories: *block codes* and *convolutional codes*. Block codes apply to a group of bits at once to generate redundancy. Convolutional codes apply to a string of bits one at a time and have memory that can store previous bits as well. The following presents both types of FEC codes in brief [13].

Block Codes.   Block codes [2] take as input k bits and append $r = n - k$ bits of FEC data, resulting in an n-bit-long string. These codes are referred to as (n, k) codes. The two types of block codes are *linear* and *cyclic*. All error correction codes operate by adding space between valid source strings. The space is measured using a *Hamming distance*, defined as the minimum number of bits between *any* coded strings that need to be changed so as to be identical to a second string.

To detect r errors, the Hamming distance has to at least equal r; otherwise, the corrupt string might seem valid again. This is not sufficient for correcting r errors however, since there is not enough distance among valid codes to choose a preferable correction. To correct r errors, the Hamming distance must be at least $2r$ [14, 15]. Linear codes are simple to compute but have higher coding overhead than cyclic codes.

Cyclic codes are stated in terms of generator polynomials of maximum degree equal to the number of source bits. The source bits are the coefficients of the polynomial, and redundancy is generated by multiplying with another polynomial. The code is cyclic, since the modulo operation in effect shifts the polynomial coefficients.

One of the most used classes of cyclic codes is the Bose–Chaudhuri–Hocquenghem (BCH) codes, since they apply to any binary string. The generator polynomial for BCH is given over GF(2) (the binary Galois field) and is the lowest-degree polynomial with roots of α^i, where α is a primitive element of the field (i.e., 2) and i goes over the range of 1 to twice the number of bits we wish to correct.

BCH codes can be encoded and decoded quickly using integer arithmetic, since they use Galois fields. H.261 and H.263 use BCH to allow for 18 parity bits every 493 source bits. Unfortunately, the 18 parity bits will correct at most two errors in the source. Thus, the packets are still vulnerable to burst bit errors or single-packet errors.

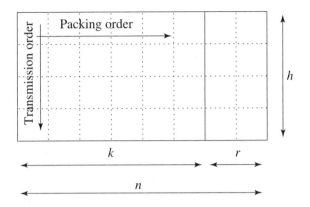

FIGURE 17.9: Interleaving scheme for redundancy codes. Packets or bits are stored in rows, and redundancy is generated in the last r columns. The sending order is by columns, top to bottom, then left to right.

An important subclass of BCH codes that applies to multiple packets is the Reed–Solomon (RS) codes. RS codes have a generator polynomial over $GF(2^m)$, with m being the packet size in bits. RS codes take a group of k source packets and output n packets with $r = n - k$ redundancy packets. Up to r lost packets can be recovered from n coded packets if we know the erasure points. Otherwise, as with all FEC codes, recovery can be applied only to half the number of packets (similarly, the number of bits), since error-point detection is now necessary as well.

In the RS codes, only $\lceil \frac{r}{2} \rceil$ packets can be recovered. Fortunately, in the packet FEC scenario the packets have headers that can contain a sequence number and CRC codes on the physical layer. In most cases, a packet with an error is dropped, and we can tell the location of the missing packet from the missing sequence number. RS codes are used in storage media such as CD-ROMs and in network multimedia transmissions that can have burst errors.

It is also possible to use packet interleaving to increase resilience to burst packet loss. As Figure 17.9 shows, the RS code is generated for each of the h rows of k source video packets. Then it is transmitted in column-major order, so that the first packet of each of the h rows is transmitted first, then the second, and so on. If a burst packet loss occurs, we can tolerate more than r erasures, since there is enough redundancy data. This scheme introduces additional delay but does not increase computational cost.

RS codes can be useful for transmission over packet networks. When there are burst packet losses, packet interleaving, and packet sequencing, it is possible to detect which packets were received incorrectly and recover them using the available redundancy. If the video has scalability, a better use of allocated bandwidth is to apply adequate FEC protection on the base layer, containing motion vectors and all header information required to decode video to the minimum QoS. The enhancement layers can receive either less protection or none at all, relying just on resilient coding and error concealment. Either way, the minimum QoS is already achieved.

A disadvantage of block codes is that they cannot be selectively applied to certain bits. It is difficult to protect higher-protocol-layer headers with more redundancy bits than for, say, DCT coefficients, if they are sent in the same transport packet (or even group of packets). On the other hand, convolutional codes can do this, which makes them more efficient for data in which unequal protection is advantageous, such as videos. Although convolutional codes are not as effective against burst packet loss, for wireless radio channels burst packet loss is not predominant (and not present in most propagation models).

Convolutional Codes.   Convolutional FEC codes are defined over generator polynomials as well [13]. They are computed by shifting k message bits into a coder that convolves them with the generator polynomial to generate n bits. The rate of such code is defined to be $\frac{k}{n}$. The shifting is necessary, since coding is achieved using memory (shift) registers. There can be more than k registers, in which case past bits also affect the redundancy code generated.

After producing the n bits, some redundancy bits can be deleted (or "punctured") to decrease the size of n, and increase the rate of the code. Such FEC schemes are known as *rate compatible punctured convolutional* (RCPC) codes. The higher the rate, the lower the bit protection will be, but also the less overhead on the bitrate. A Viterbi algorithm with soft decisions decodes the encoded bit stream, although *turbo codes* are gaining popularity.

RCPC codes provide an advantage over block codes for wireless (sections of the) network, since burst packet losses are not likely. RCPC puncturing is done after generation of parity information. Knowing the significance of the source bits for video quality, we can apply a different amount of puncturing and hence a different amount of error protection. Studies and simulations of wireless radio models have shown that applying unequal protection using RCPC according to bit significance information results in better video quality (up to 2 dB better) for the same allocated bitrate than videos protected using RS codes.

Simplistically, the Picture layer in a video protocol should get the highest protection, the macroblock layer that is more localized will get lower protection, and the DCT coefficients in the block layer can get little protection, or none at all. This could be extended further to scalable videos in similar ways.

The cdma2000 standard uses convolutional codes to protect transmitted bits for any data type, with different code rates for different transmission bitrates. If future 3G networks incorporate data-type-specific provisions and recognize the video standard chosen for transmission, they can adaptively apply transport coding of the video stream with enough unequal redundancy suitable to the channel conditions at the time and QoS requested.

17.3.5   Trends in Wireless Interactive Multimedia

The UMTS forum foresees that by 2010, the number of subscribers of wireless multimedia communication will exceed a billion worldwide, and such traffic will be worth over several hundred billion dollars to operators. Additionally, 3G will also speed the convergence of telecommunications, computers, multimedia content, and content providers to support enhanced services.

Most cellular networks around the world have already offered 2.5G services for a few years. Initial 3G services are also being offered globally, with cdma2000 1X service already commercially available in most countries.

Some of the present and future 3G applications are:

- *Multimedia Messaging Service (MMS)*, a new messaging protocol for multimedia data on mobile phones that incorporates audio, images, and other multimedia content, along with traditional text messages

- Mobile videophone, VoIP, and voice-activated network access

- Mobile Internet access, with streaming audio and video services

- Mobile intranet/extranet access, with secure access to corporate LANs, Virtual Private Networks (VPNs), and the Internet

- Customized infotainment service that provides access to personalized content anytime, anywhere, based on mobile portals

- Mobile online multiuser gaming

- Ubiquitous and pervasive computing [6], such as automobile telematics, where an automated navigation system equipped with GPS and voice recognition can interact with the driver to obviate reading maps while driving

The industry has long envisioned the convergence of IT, entertainment, and telecommunications. A major portion of the telecommunication field is dedicated to handheld wireless devices — the mobile stations (cell phones). At the same time, the computer industry has focused on creating handheld computers that can do at least some important tasks necessary for people on the go. Handheld computers are classified as Pocket PCs or PDAs.

Pocket PCs are typically larger, have a keyboard, and support most functions and programs of a desktop PC. PDAs do simpler tasks, such as storing event calendars and phone numbers. PDAs normally use a form of handwriting recognition for input, although some incorporate keyboards as well. PDA manufacturers are striving to support more PC-like functions and at the same time provide wireless packet services (including voice over IP), so that a PDA can be used as a phone as well as for wireless Internet connectivity.

As with all small portable computers, the Human Computer Interaction (HCI) problem is more significant than when using a desktop computer. Where there is no space for a keyboard, it is envisioned that command input will be accomplished through voice recognition.

Most of the new PDA products support image and video capture, MP3 playback, e-mail, and wireless protocols such as 802.11b and Bluetooth. Some also act as cell phones when connected to a GPRS or PCS network (e.g., the Handspring Treo). They have color screens and support web browsing and multimedia e-mail messaging. Some Bluetooth-enabled PDAs rely on Bluetooth-compatible cell phones to access mobile networks. However, as cell phones become more powerful and PDAs incorporate 802.11b interface cards, Bluetooth might become less viable.

As PDA manufacturers look to the future, they wish to support not only voice communication over wireless networks but also multimedia, such as video communication. Some PDAs incorporate advanced digital cameras with flash and zoom (e.g., the Sony CLIE). The encoding of video can be done using MPEG-4 or H.263, and the PDA could support multiple playback formats.

Cell phone manufacturers, for their part, are trying to incorporate more computer-like functionality, including the basic tasks supported by PDAs, web browsing, games, image and video capture, attachments to e-mail, streaming video, videoconferencing, and so on. Growth in demand is steady for interactive multimedia, in particular image and video communications. Most cell phone manufacturers and mobile service providers already support some kind of image or video communication, either in the form of e-mail attachments, video streaming, or even videoconferencing. Similarly to *Short-text Messaging Service* (SMS), the new messaging protocol *Multimedia Messaging Service* (MMS) is gaining support in the industry as an interim solution to the bandwidth limitation. New cell phones feature color displays and have built-in digital cameras. Most cell phones use integrated CMOS sensors, and some handsets even have two of them. By 2004, the number of camera sensors on mobile phones is estimated to exceed the number of digital cameras sold worldwide.

Cell phones have supported web browsing and e-mail functionality for a few years, but with packet services, Bluetooth, and MMS, they can support video streaming in various formats and MP3 playback. Some cell phones even include a touch screen that uses handwriting recognition and a stylus, as most PDAs do. Other cell phones are envisioned to be small enough to be wearable, instead of a wrist watch.

17.4   FURTHER EXPLORATION

Tanenbaum [14] has a good general discussion of wireless networks, and Wesel [2] offers some specifics about wireless communications networks. Viterbi [5] provides a solid analysis on spread spectrum and the foundation of CDMA. Wang et al. [16] give an in-depth discussion on error control in video communications.

The Further Exploration section of the text web site for this Chapter contains current web resources for wireless networks, including

- A survey on wireless networks and cellular phone technologies

- A report on GSM

- An introduction to GPRS

and links to

- NTIA for information on spectrum management

- Home pages of the CDMA Development Group, IMT-2000, UMTS, cdma2000 RTT, 3GPP, and so on

- Wireless LAN standards

We also show images of several PDAs and several modern cell phones.

17.5   EXERCISES

1. In implementations of TDMA systems such as GSM and IS-136, and to a lesser degree in networks based on CDMA, such as IS-95, an FDMA technology is still in use to divide the allocated carrier spectrum into smaller channels. Why is this necessary?

2. Discuss the difference between the way GSM/GPRS and WCDMA achieve variable bitrate transmissions.

3. We have seen a geometric layout for a cellular network in Figure 17.1. The figure assumes hexagonal cells and a symmetric plan (i.e., that the scheme for splitting the frequency spectrum over different cells is uniform). Also, the reuse factor is $K = 7$. Depending on cell sizes and radio interference, the reuse factor may need to be different. Still requiring hexagonal cells, can all possible reuse factors achieve a symmetric plan? Which ones can? Can you speculate on a formula for general possible reuse factors?

4. What is the spreading gain for IS-95? What is the spreading gain for WCDMA UTRA FDD mode, assuming all users want to transmit at maximum bitrate? What is the impact of the difference between the spreading gains?

5. When a cellular phone user travels across the cell boundary, a *handoff* (or handover) from one cell to the other is necessary. A hard (imperfect) handoff causes dropped calls.

   (a) CDMA (Direct Sequence) provides much better handoff performance than FDMA or Frequency Hopping (FH). Why?

   (b) Suggest an improvement to handoff so it can be softer.

6. In a CDMA cell, when a CDMA mobile station moves across a cell boundary, a *soft handoff* occurs. Moreover, cells are also split into sectors, and when a mobile station moves between sectors, a *softer handoff* occurs.

   (a) Provide arguments for why a softer handoff is necessary.

   (b) State at least one other difference between the two handoffs.

   Hint: During handoff in a CDMA system, the mobile stations can transmit at lower power levels than inside the cell.

7. Most of the schemes for channel allocation discussed in this chapter are fixed (or uniform) channel assignment schemes. It is possible to design a dynamic channel allocation scheme to improve the performance of a cell network. Suggest such a dynamic channel allocation scheme.

8. The 2.5G technologies are designed for packet-switching services. This provides data-on-demand connectivity without the need to establish a circuit first. This is advantageous for sporadic data bursts.

   (a) Suggest a method to implement multiple access control for TDMA packet services (such as GPRS).

   (b) Circuits are more efficient for longer data. Extend your suggested method so that the channel goes through a contention process only for the first packet transmitted.

   Hint: Add reservations to your scheme.

9. H.263+ and MPEG-4 use RVLCs, which allow decoding of a stream in both forward and backward directions from a synchronization marker. The RVLCs increase the bitrate of the encoding over regular entropy codes.

   (a) Why is this beneficial for transmissions over wireless channels?
   (b) What condition is necessary for it to be more efficient than FEC?

10. Why are RVLCs usually applied only to motion vectors? If you wanted to reduce the bitrate impact, what changes would you make?

17.6 REFERENCES

1 M. Rahnema, "Overview of GSM System and Protocol Architecture," *IEEE Communications Magazine*, 31(4): 92–100, 1993.

2 E.K. Wesel, *Wireless Multimedia Communications: Networking Video, Voice, and Data*, Reading, MA: Addison-Wesley, 1998.

3 F. Meeks, "The Sound of Lamarr," *Forbes*, May 14, 1990.

4 H. Holma and A. Toskala, eds., *WCDMA for UMTS: Radio Access for Third Generation Mobile Communications*, New York: Wiley 2001.

5 A.J. Viterbi, *CDMA: Principles of Spread Spectrum Communication*, Reading, MA: Addison-Wesley, 1995.

6 J. Burkhardt, et al., *Pervasive Computing: Technology and Architecture of Mobile Internet Applications*, Boston, MA: Addison Wesley, 2002.

7 Third Generation Partnership Project 2 (3GPP2), *Video Conferencing Services — Stage 1*, 3GGP2 Specifications, S.R0022, July 2000.

8 Third Generation Partnership Project (3GPP), *QoS for Speech and Multimedia Codec*, 3GPP Specifications, TR-26.912, March 2000.

9 K. N. Ngan, C. W. Yap, and K. T. Tan, *Video Coding For Wireless Communication Systems*, New York: Marcel Dekker, 2001.

10 Y. Takishima, M. Wada, and H. Murakami, "Reversible Variable Length Codes," *IEEE Transactions on Communications*, 43(2-4): 158–162, 1995.

11 C.W. Tsai and J.L. Wu, "On Constructing the Huffman-Code-Based Reversible Variable-Length Codes," *IEEE Transactions on Communications*, 49(9): 1506–1509, 2001.

12 Y. Wang and Q.F. Zhu, "Error Control and Concealment for Video Communication: A Review," *Proceedings of the IEEE*, 86(5): 974–997, 1998.

13 A. Houghton, *Error Coding For Engineers*, Norwell MA: Kluwer Academic Publishers, 2001.

14 A.S. Tanenbaum, *Computer Networks*, 4th ed., Upper Saddle River NJ: Prentice Hall PTR, 2003.

15 W. Stallings, *Data & Computer Communications*, 6th ed., Upper Saddle River, NJ: Prentice Hall, 2000.

16 Y. Wang, J. Ostermann, and Y. Q. Zhang, *Video Processing and Communications*, Upper Saddle River, NJ: Prentice Hall, 2002.

CHAPTER 18

Content-Based Retrieval in Digital Libraries

18.1 HOW SHOULD WE RETRIEVE IMAGES?

Consider the image in Figure 18.1 of a small portion of *The Garden of Delights* by Hieronymus Bosch (1453–1516), now in the Prado museum in Madrid. This is a famous painting, but we may be stumped in understanding the painter's intent. Therefore, if we are aiming at automatic retrieval of images, it should be unsurprising that encapsulating the semantics (meaning) in the image is an even more difficult challenge. A proper annotation of such an image certainly should include the descriptor "people". On the other hand, should this image be blocked by a "Net nanny" screening out "naked people" (as in [1])?

We know very well that most major web browsers have a web search button for multimedia content, as opposed to text. For Bosch's painting, a text-based search will very likely do the best job, should we wish to find this particular image. Yet we may be interested in fairly general searches, say for scenes with deep blue skies and orange sunsets. By pre-calculating some fundamental statistics about images stored in a database, we can usually find simple scenes such as these.

In its inception, retrieval from digital libraries began with ideas borrowed from traditional information retrieval disciplines (see, e.g., [2]). This line of inquiry continues. For example, in [3], images are classified into indoor or outdoor classes using basic information-retrieval techniques. For a training set of images and captions, the number of times each word appears in the document is divided by the number of times each word appears over all documents in a class. A similar measure is devised for statistical descriptors of the content of image segments, and the two information-retrieval-based measures are combined for an effective classification mechanism.

However, most multimedia retrieval schemes have moved toward an approach favoring multimedia content itself, without regard to or reliance upon accompanying textual information. Only recently has attention once more been placed on the deeper problem of addressing semantic content in images, once again making use of accompanying text. If data consists of statistical features built from objects in images and also of text associated with the images, each type of modality — text and image — provides semantic content omitted from the other. For example, an image of a red rose will not normally have the manually added keyword "red" since this is generally assumed. Hence, image features and associated words may disambiguate each other (see [4]).

FIGURE 18.1: How can we best characterize the information content of an image? *Courtesy of Museo del Prado.*

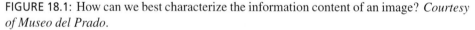

In this chapter, however, we shall focus only on the more standardized systems that make use of image features to retrieve images from databases or from the web. The types of features typically used are such statistical measures as the color histogram for an image. Consider an image that is colorful — say, a Santa Claus plus sled. The combination of bright red and flesh tones and browns might be enough of an image signature to allow us to at least find similar images in our own image database (of office Christmas parties).

Recall that a color histogram is typically a three-dimensional array that counts pixels with specific red, green, and blue values. The nice feature of such a structure is that is does not care about the orientation of the image (since we are simply counting pixel values, not their orientation) and is also fairly impervious to object occlusions. A seminal paper on this subject [5] launched a tidal wave of interest in such so-called "low-level" features for images.

Other simple features used are such descriptors as *color layout*, meaning a simple sketch of where in a checkerboard grid covering the image to look for blue skies and orange sunsets. Another feature used is *texture*, meaning some type of descriptor typically based on an edge image, formed by taking partial derivatives of the image itself — classifying edges according to closeness of spacing and orientation. An interesting version of this approach uses a histogram of such edge features. *Texture layout* can also be used. Search engines devised on these features are said to be *content-based*: the search is guided by image similarity measures based on the statistical content of each image.

Typically, we might be interested in looking for images similar to our current favorite Santa. A more industry-oriented application would typically be seeking a particular image of a postage stamp. Subject fields associated with image database search include art galleries and museums, fashion, interior design, remote sensing, geographic information systems, meteorology, trademark databases, criminology, and an increasing number of other areas.

A more difficult type of search involves looking for a particular *object* within images, which we can term a *search-by-object* model. This involves a much more complete catalog of image contents and is a much more difficult objective. Generally, users will base their searches on *search by association* [6], meaning a first cut search followed by refinement based on similarity to some of the query results. For general images representative of a kind of desired picture, a *category search* returns one element of the requested set, such as one or several trademarks in a database of such logos. Alternatively, the query may be based on a very specific image, such as a particular piece of art — a *target search*.

Another axis to bear in mind in understanding the many existing search systems is whether the domain being searched is narrow, such as the database of trademarks, or wide, such as a set of commercial stock photos.

For any system, we are up against the fundamental nature of machine systems that aim to replace human endeavors. The main obstacles are neatly summarized in what the authors of the summary in [6] term the *sensory gap* and the *semantic gap*:

> The sensory gap is the gap between the object in the world and the information in a (computational) description derived from a recording of that scene.

> The semantic gap is the lack of coincidence between the information that one can extract from the visual data and the interpretation that the same data have for a user in a given situation.

Image features record specifics about images, but the images themselves may elude description in such terms. And while we may certainly be able to describe images linguistically, the message in the image, the semantics, is difficult to capture for machine applications.

18.2 C-BIRD — A CASE STUDY

Let us consider the specifics of how image queries are carried out. To make the discussion concrete, we underpin our discussion by using the image database search engine devised by one of the authors of this text (see [7]). This system is called *Content-Based Image Retrieval from Digital libraries* (*C-BIRD*), an acronym devised from *content-based image retrieval*, or *CBIR*. (The URL for this search engine is given in the Further Exploration section for this chapter.)

FIGURE 18.2: C-BIRD image-search GUI.

18.2.1 C-BIRD GUI

Figure 18.2 shows the GUI for the C-BIRD system. The online image database can be browsed, or it can be searched using a selection of tools: text annotations, color histograms, illumination-invariant color histograms, color density, color layout, texture layout, and model-based search. Many of the images are keyframes from videos, and a video player is incorporated in the system.

Let's step through these options. Other systems, discussed in Section 18.3, have similar feature sets.

18.2.2 Color Histogram

In C-BIRD, features are precomputed for each image in the database. The most prevalent feature that is utilized in image database retrieval is the color histogram [5], a type of *global* image feature, that is, the image is not segmented; instead, every image region is treated equally.

A color histogram counts pixels with a given pixel value in red, green, and blue (RGB). For example, in pseudocode, for images with 8-bit values in each of R, G, B, we can fill a histogram that has 256^3 bins:

```
int hist[256][256][256];  // reset to 0
//image is an appropriate struct
//with byte fields red,green,blue

for i=0..(MAX_Y-1)
  for j=0..(MAX_X-1)
    {
      R = image[i][j].red;
      G = image[i][j].green;
      B = image[i][j].blue;
      hist[R][G][B]++;
    }
```

Usually, we do not use histograms with so many bins, in part because fewer bins tend to smooth out differences in similar but unequal images. We also wish to save storage space.

How image search proceeds is by matching the *feature vector* for the sample image, in this case the color histogram, with the feature vector for every — or at least many of — the images in the database.

C-BIRD calculates a color histogram for each target image as a preprocessing step, then references it in the database for each user query image. The histogram is defined coarsely, with bins quantized to 8 bits, with 3 bits for each of red and green and 2 for blue.

For example, Figure 18.3 shows that the user has selected a particular image — one with red flowers. The result obtained, from a database of some 5,000 images, is a set of 60 matching images. Most CBIR systems return as the result set either the top few matches or the match set with a similarity measure above a fixed threshold value. C-BIRD uses the latter approach and thus may return zero search results.

How matching proceeds in practice depends on what measure of similarity we adopt. The standard measure used for color histograms is called the *histogram intersection*. First, a color histogram $\mathbf{H}_i$ is generated for each image i in the database. We like to think of the histogram as a three-index array, but of course the machine thinks of it as a long vector — hence the term "feature vector" for any of these types of measures.

The histogram is *normalized*, so that its sum (now a `double`) equals unity. This normalization step is interesting: it effectively removes the *size* of the image. The reason is that if the image has, say, resolution 640×480, then the histogram entries sum to $307,200$. But if the image is only one-quarter that size, or 320×240, the sum is only $76,800$. Division by the total pixel count removes this difference. In fact, the normalized histograms can be viewed as *probability density functions (pdfs)*. The histogram is then stored in the database.

Now suppose we select a "model" image — the new image to match against all possible targets in the database. Its histogram $\mathbf{H}_m$ is intersected with all database image histograms $\mathbf{H}_i$, according to the equation [5]

$$intersection = \sum_{j=1}^{n} \min(\mathbf{H}_i^j, \mathbf{H}_m^j) \tag{18.1}$$

FIGURE 18.3: Search by color histogram results. (This figure also appears in the color insert section.) *Some thumbnail images are from the Corel Gallery and are copyright Corel. All rights reserved.*

where superscript j denotes histogram bin j, with each histogram having n bins. The closer the intersection value is to 1, the better the images match. This intersection value is fast to compute, but we should note that the intersection value is sensitive to color quantization.

18.2.3 Color Density

Figure 18.4 displays the scheme for showing color density. The user selects the percentage of the image having any particular color or set of colors, using a color picker and sliders. We can choose from either conjunction (ANDing) or disjunction (ORing) a simple color percentage specification. This is a coarse search method.

18.2.4 Color Layout

The user can set up a scheme of how colors should appear in the image, in terms of coarse blocks of color. The user has a choice of four grid sizes: $1 \times 1, 2 \times 2, 4 \times 4$ and 8×8. Search is specified on one of the grid sizes, and the grid can be filled with any RGB color value — or no color value at all, to indicate that the cell should not be considered. Every database image is partitioned into windows four times, once for each window size. A clustered color histogram is used inside each window, and the five most frequent colors are stored in the database. Each query cell position and size corresponds to the position and size of a window in the image. Figure 18.5 shows how this layout scheme is used.

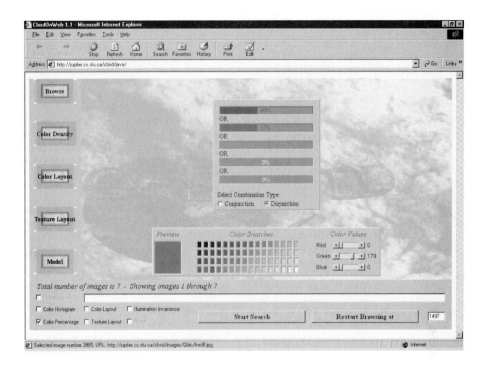

FIGURE 18.4: Color density query scheme.

18.2.5 Texture Layout

Similar to color layout search, this query allows the user to draw the desired texture distribution. Available textures are zero density texture, medium-density edges in four directions (0°, 45°, 90°, 135°) and combinations of them, and high-density texture in four directions and combinations of them. Texture matching is done by classifying textures according to directionality and density (or separation) and evaluating their correspondence to the texture distribution selected by the user in the texture block layout. Figure 18.6 shows how this layout scheme is used.

Texture Analysis Details

It is worthwhile considering some of the details for a texture-based content analysis aimed at image search. These details give a taste of typical techniques systems must employ to work in practical situations.

First, we create a texture histogram. A typical set of indices for comprehending texture is Tamura's [8]. Human perception studies show that "repetitiveness," "directionality," and "granularity" are the most relevant discriminatory factors in human textural perception [9]. Here, we use a two-dimensional texture histogram based on *directionality* ϕ and *edge separation* ξ, which is closely related to "repetitiveness". ϕ measures the edge orientations, and ξ measures the distances between parallel edges.

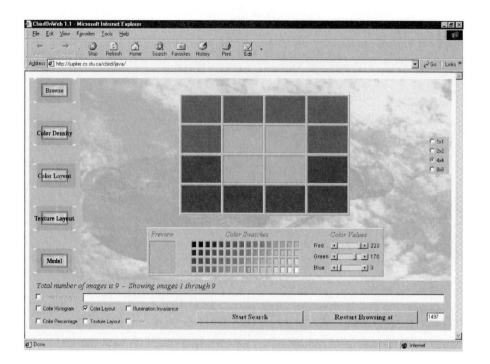

FIGURE 18.5: Color layout grid.

To extract an edge map, the image is first converted to luminance Y via $Y = 0.299R + 0.587G + 0.114B$. A *Sobel edge operator* [10] is applied to the Y-image by sliding the following 3×3 weighting matrices (*convolution masks*) over the image:

$$d_x : \begin{array}{|c|c|c|} \hline -1 & 0 & 1 \\ \hline -2 & 0 & 2 \\ \hline -1 & 0 & 1 \\ \hline \end{array} \qquad d_y : \begin{array}{|c|c|c|} \hline 1 & 2 & 1 \\ \hline 0 & 0 & 0 \\ \hline -1 & -2 & -1 \\ \hline \end{array} \qquad (18.2)$$

If we average around each pixel with these weights, we produce approximations to derivatives.

The edge magnitude D and the edge gradient ϕ are given by

$$D = \sqrt{d_x^2 + d_y^2}, \qquad \phi = \arctan \frac{d_y}{d_x} \qquad (18.3)$$

Next, the edges are thinned by suppressing all but maximum values. If a pixel i with edge gradient ϕ_i and edge magnitude D_i has a neighbor pixel j along the direction of ϕ_i with gradient $\phi_j \approx \phi_i$ and edge magnitude $D_j > D_i$, then pixel i is suppressed to 0.

To make a binary edge image, we set all pixels with D greater than a threshold value to 1 and all others to 0.

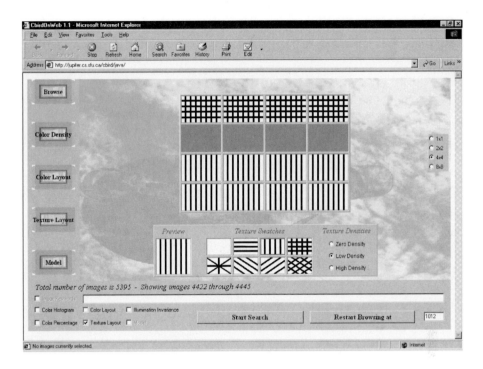

FIGURE 18.6: Texture layout grid.

For edge separation ξ, for each edge pixel i we measure the distance along its gradient ϕ_i to the nearest pixel j having $\phi_j \approx \phi_i$ within $15°$. If such a pixel j doesn't exist, the separation is considered infinite.

Having created edge directionality and edge separation maps, C-BIRD constructs a 2D texture histogram of ξ versus ϕ. The initial histogram size is 193×180, where separation value $\xi = 193$ is reserved for a separation of infinity (as well as any $\xi > 192$). The histogram size is then reduced by three for each dimension to size 65×60, where joined entries are summed together.

The histogram is "smoothed" by replacing each pixel with a weighted sum of its neighbors and is then reduced again to size 7×8, with separation value 7 reserved for infinity. At this stage, the texture histogram is also normalized by dividing by the number of pixels in the image segment.

18.2.6 Search by Illumination Invariance

Illumination change can dramatically alter the color measured by camera RGB sensors, from *pink* under daylight to *purple* under fluorescent lighting, for example.

To deal with illumination change from the query image to different database images, each color-channel band of each image is first normalized, then compressed to a 36-vector [11]. Normalizing each of the R, G, and B bands of an image serves as a simple yet effective guard against color changes when the lighting color changes. A two-dimensional color histogram

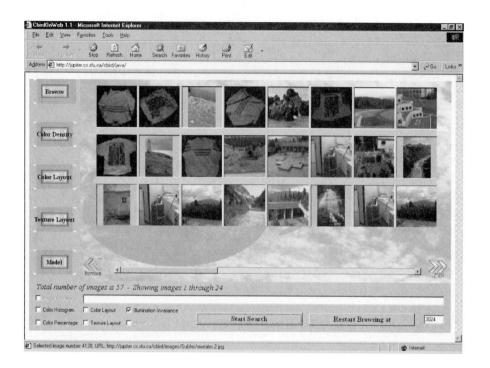

FIGURE 18.7: Search with illumination invariance. *Some thumbnail images are from the Corel Gallery and are copyright Corel. All rights reserved.*

is then created using the *chromaticity*, which is the set of band ratios $\{R, G\}/(R + G + B)$. Chromaticity is similar to the chrominance in video, in that it captures color information only, not luminance (or brightness).

A 128×128–bin 2D color histogram can then be treated as an image and compressed using a wavelet-based compression scheme [12]. To further reduce the number of vector components in a feature vector, the DCT coefficients for the smaller histogram are calculated and placed in zigzag order, then all but 36 components are dropped.

Matching is performed in the compressed domain by taking the Euclidean distance between two DCT-compressed 36-component feature vectors. (This illumination-invariant scheme and the object-model-based search described next are unique to C-BIRD.) Figure 18.7 shows the results of such a search.

Several of the above types of searches can be done at once by checking multiple checkboxes. This returns a reduced list of images, since the list is the conjunction of all resulting separate return lists for each method.

18.2.7   Search by Object Model

The most important search type C-BIRD supports is the model-based object search. The user picks a sample image and interactively selects a region for object searching. Objects photographed under different scene conditions are still effectively matched. This search type proceeds by the user selecting a thumbnail and clicking the Model tab to enter Object

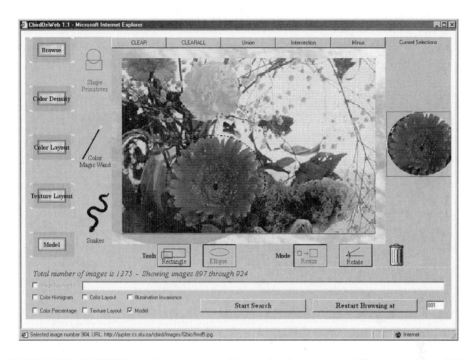

FIGURE 18.8: C-BIRD interface, showing object selection using an ellipse primitive. (This figure also appears in the color insert section.) *Image is from the Corel Gallery and is copyright Corel. All rights reserved.*

Selection mode. An object is then interactively selected as a portion of the image; this constitutes an object query by example.

Figure 18.8 shows a sample object selection. An image region can be selected using primitive shapes such as a rectangle or ellipse, a magic wand tool that is basically a seed-based flooding algorithm, an active contour (a "snake"), or a brush tool, where the painted region is selected. All the selections can be combined with each other using Boolean operations such as union, intersection, or exclusion.

Once the object region is defined to a user's satisfaction, it can be dragged to the right pane, showing all current selections. Multiple regions can be dragged to the selection pane, but only the active object in the selection pane will be searched on. The user can also control parameters such as flooding thresholds, brush size, and active contour curvature.

Details of the underlying mechanisms of this Search by Object Model are set out in [12] and introduced below as an example of a working system. Figure 18.9 shows a block diagram for how the algorithm proceeds. First, the user-selected model image is processed and its features are localized (details in the following sections). Color histogram intersection, based on the reduced chromaticity histogram described in Section 18.2.6 is then applied as a first "screen." Further steps estimate the pose (scale, translation, rotation) of the object inside a target image from the database. This is followed by verification by intersection of texture histograms and then a final check using an efficient version of a Generalized Hough Transform for shape verification.

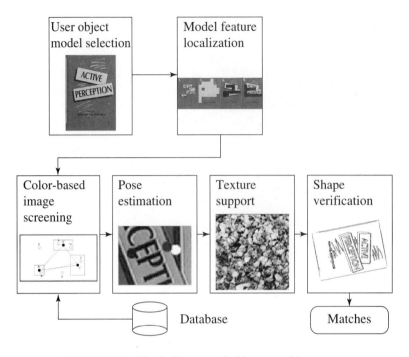

FIGURE 18.9: Block diagram of object matching steps.

A possible model image and one of the target images in the database might be as in Figure 18.10, where the scene in (b) was illuminated with a dim fluorescent light.

Locales in Feature Localization

The Search by Object Model introduced above — finding an object inside a target image — is a desirable yet difficult mechanism for querying multimedia data. An added difficulty is that objects can be photographed under different lighting conditions. Human vision has "color constancy" [13], an *invariant* processing, presumably, that allows us to see colors under different lighting as the *same*. For image indexing, it should be useful to determine only a *covariant* processing that changes along with changing light [12]. In that case, we could aim at also recovering the lighting change.

Since object-based search considers objects within an image, we should apply some sort of *segmentation* to look at regions of objects — say, patches that have about the same color. However, it has been found to be more useful to use a set of rough, possibly overlapping regions (called *locales* [7]) to express not a complete image segmentation but instead a coarser *feature localization*.

It is worthwhile looking in more detail at this locale-directed search method, which we describe along with the process of feature localization. Since we are interested in lighting change, we also look at a technique to compensate for illumination change, so as to carry out a color covariant search.

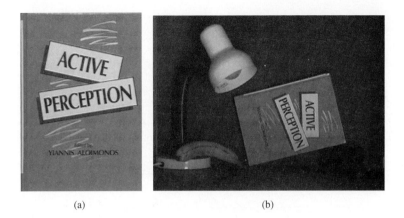

(a)   (b)

FIGURE 18.10: Model and target images: (a) sample model image; (b) sample database image containing the model book. (This figure also appears in the color insert sectin.) Active Perception *textbook cover courtesy Lawrence Erlbaum Associates, Inc.*

Feature Localization versus Image Segmentation

For image segmentation (cf. [14]): if R is a segmented region,

1. R is usually connected; all pixels in R are *connected* (8-connected or 4-connected).
2. $R_i \cap R_j = \phi, i \neq j$; regions are *disjoint*.
3. $\cup_{i=1}^{n} R_i = I$, where I is the entire image; the segmentation is *complete*.

Object retrieval algorithms based on image segmentation permit imprecise regions by allowing a tolerance on the region-matching measure. This accounts for small imprecision in the segmentation but not for over- or under-segmentation, which can be attributed to the pixel-level approach. This works only for simplified images, where object pixels have statistics that are position-invariant.

A coarse localization of image features based on proximity and compactness is likely to be a more effective and attainable process than image segmentation.

Definition: A *locale* $\mathcal{L}_f$ is a local enclosure of feature f.

A locale $\mathcal{L}_f$ uses blocks of pixels called *tiles* as its positioning units and has the following descriptors:

1. **Envelope L_f.** A set of tiles representing the locality of $\mathcal{L}_f$
2. **Geometric parameters.**

$$\text{Mass } M(\mathcal{L}_f) = \text{count of the pixels having feature } f,$$

$$\text{centroid } \mathbf{C}(\mathcal{L}_f) = \sum_{i=1}^{M(\mathcal{L}_f)} \mathbf{P}_i / M(\mathcal{L}_f), \quad \mathbf{P}_i = \text{position}$$

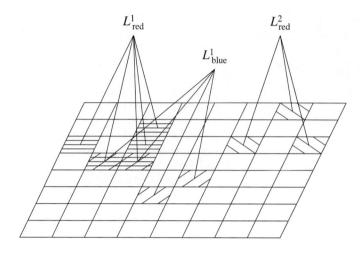

FIGURE 18.11: Locales for feature localization.

$$\text{and eccentricity } E(\mathcal{L}_f) \quad = \quad \sum_{i=1}^{M(\mathcal{L}_f)} \|\mathbf{P}_i - \mathbf{C}(\mathcal{L}_f)\|^2 / M(\mathcal{L}_f).$$

3. **Color, texture, and shape parameters of the locale.** For example, locale chromaticity, elongation, and locale texture histogram

Initially, an image is subdivided into square tiles (e.g., 8×8 or 16×16). While the pixel is the building unit for image segmentation, tile is the building unit for feature localization. Tiles group pixels with similar features within their extent and are said to have feature f if enough pixels in them have feature f (e.g., 10%).

Tiles are necessary for good estimation of initial object-level statistics and representation of multiple features *at the same location*. However, locale geometric parameters are measured in pixels, not tiles. This preserves feature granularity. Hence, feature localization is not merely a reduced-resolution variation on image segmentation.

After a feature localization process, the following can be true:

1. $\exists f : \mathcal{L}_f$ is *not connected.*
2. $\exists f \exists g : \mathcal{L}_f \cap \mathcal{L}_g \neq \phi, f \neq g$; locales are *non-disjoint.*
3. $\cup_f \mathcal{L}_f \neq I$, *non-completeness*; not all image pixels are represented.

Figure 18.11 shows a sketch of two locales for color red and one for color blue. The links represent an association with an envelope, which demonstrates that locales do not have to be connected, disjoint, or complete, yet colors are still localized.

Tile Classification

Before locales can be generated, tiles are first classified as having certain features, for example, red tiles, or red and blue tiles. Since color is most useful for CBIR and is invariant to translations, rotations, and scaling, we will start with color localization, although other features (texture, shape, motion, etc.) can certainly be localized similarly.

Dominant Color Enhancement

To localize on color, we first remove noise and blurring by restoring colors smoothed out during image acquisition. The image is converted from the RGB color space to a chromaticity-luminance color space. For a pixel with color (R, G, B), we define

$$I = R + G + B, r = R/I, g = G/I \qquad (18.4)$$

where the luminance I is separated from the chromaticity (r, g). Clearly, we can also use an approximately illumination-invariant version of color, as in Section 18.2.6.

Prior to classifying feature tiles, image pixels are classified as having either *dominant color* or *transitional color*. Pixels are classified dominant or transitional by examining their neighborhood.

Definition: *Dominant colors* are pixel colors that do not lie on a slope of color change in their pixel neighborhood. *Transitional colors* do.

If a pixel does not have sufficient number of neighbors with similar color values within a threshold, it is considered noise and is also classified as transitional. The uniformity of the dominant colors is enhanced by smoothing the dominant pixels only, using a 5×5 average filter, with the exception that only dominant pixels having similar color are averaged. Figure 18.12 shows how dominant color enhancement can clarify the target image in Figure 18.10 above.

Tile feature list

Tiles have a *tile feature list* of all the color features associated with the tile and their geometrical statistics. On the first pass, dominant pixels are added to the tile feature list. For each pixel added, if the color is close to a feature on the list within the luminance-chromaticity thresholds, the color and geometrical statistics for the feature are updated. Otherwise, a new color feature is added to the list. This feature list is referred to as the *dominant feature list*.

On the second pass, all transitional colors are added to the dominant feature list without modifying the color, but updating the geometrical statistics. To determine which dominant feature list node the transitional pixel should merge to, we examine the neighborhood of the transitional pixel and find the closest color that is well represented in the neighborhood. If an associated dominant color doesn't exist, it is necessary to create a second *transitional feature list* and add the transitional color to it.

The dominant color (r_i, g_i, I_i) taken on by a transitional pixel tp having color (r, g, I) satisfies the following minimization:

$$\min_{i=1}^{nc} \left\| \begin{pmatrix} r \\ g \end{pmatrix} - \begin{pmatrix} r_i \\ g_i \end{pmatrix} \right\| \Big/ F(r_i, g_i, I_i) \qquad (18.5)$$

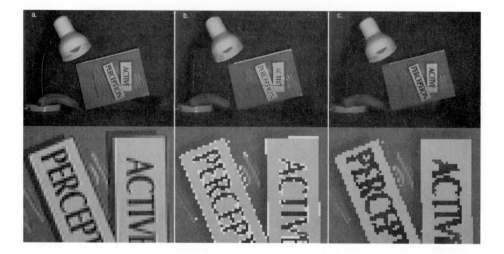

FIGURE 18.12: Smoothing using dominant colors: (a) original image not smoothed; (b) smoothed image with transitional colors shown in light gray; (c) smoothed image with transitional colors shown in the replacement dominant colors (if possible). Lower row shows detail images.

The parameter nc is the number of nonsimilar colors in the neighborhood of the tp. Similar colors are averaged to generate the (r_i, g_i, I_i) colors. $F(r_i, g_i, I_i)$ is the frequency of the ith average color, or in other words, the number of similar colors averaged to generate color i. The color that minimizes this equation is the best compromise for dominant color selection for tp in terms of color similarity and number of similar colors in the neighborhood. The neighborhood size was chosen to be 5×5 in our implementation.

When all pixels have been added to the tiles, the dominant and transitional color feature lists are merged. If a transitional list node is close in color to a dominant list node, the geometrical statistics for the merged node are updated, but only the color from the dominant list is preserved. Otherwise, the nodes from both lists are just concatenated onto the joint list.

Locale Generation

Locales are generated using a dynamic 4×4 overlapped pyramid linking procedure [15]. On each level, parent nodes compete for inclusion of child nodes in a fair competition. Image tiles are the bottom-level child nodes of the pyramid, and locales are generated for the entire image when the competition propagates to the top level. The top-level pyramid node has a list of color features with associated envelopes (collections of tiles) and geometrical statistics [12].

Competition on each level is initialized by using a 2×2 nonoverlapped linkage structure, where four child nodes are linked with a single parent node. The `LocalesInit` initialization proceeds as follows:

PROCEDURE 18.1   LocalesInit // Pseudo-code for link initialization

```
BEGIN
```
Let $c[n_x][n_y]$ be the 2D array of child nodes.
Let $p[n_{x/2}][n_{y/2}]$ be the 2D array of parent nodes.
For each child node $c[i][j]$ do
   Let $cn = c[i][j]$ and $pn = p[i/2][j/2]$.
   For each node cn_p in the feature list of cn do
      Find node pn_q in the feature list of pn that has similar color.
      If the merged eccentricity of cn_p and pn_q has $E < \tau$ then
         Merge cn_p and pn_q.
      If pn_q doesn't exist or $E >= \tau$ then
         Add cn_p to the start of the feature list of pn.
```
END
```

After the pyramid linkage initialization, the competition begins. Since a 4×4 overlapped pyramid structure is used, four parents compete for linkage with the child, one of which is already linked to it. This process is illustrated by the `EnvelopeGrowing` pseudo-code:

PROCEDURE 18.2   EnvelopeGrowing // Pseudo-code for locale generation

```
BEGIN
```
Let $c[n_x][n_y]$ be the 2D array of child nodes.
Let $p[n_{x/2}][n_{y/2}]$ be the 2D array of parent nodes.
Repeat until parent-child linkage does not change anymore
   For each child node $c[i][j]$ do
      Let $cn = c[i][j]$ and $pn \in p[\frac{i \pm 1}{2}][\frac{j \pm 1}{2}]$
      For each node cn_p in the feature list of cn do
         Find node pn_q in the feature lists of pn
         that has similar color and minimizes the distance
         $\|\mathbf{C}(cn_p) - \mathbf{C}(pn_q)\|$
         If the merged eccentricity of cn_p and pn_q has $E < \tau$ then
            Swap the linkage of cn_p to its parent to pn_q.
            Update the associated geometrical statistics.
In the parent feature list p remove empty nodes.
Go up a level in the pyramid and repeat the procedure.
```
END
```

Following the pyramidal linking, locales having small mass are removed, since small locales are not accurate enough and are probably either an insignificant part of an object or noise. To increase the efficiency of the search, locales are also sorted according to decreasing mass size.

The color update equation for parent locale j and child locale i at iteration $k + 1$ is

$$\left(r_j^{(k+1)}, g_j^{(k+1)}, I_j^{(k+1)} \right)^T = \frac{\left(r_j^{(k)}, g_j^{(k)}, I_j^{(k)} \right)^T M_j^{(k)} + \left(r_i^{(k)}, g_i^{(k)}, I_i^{(k)} \right)^T M_i^{(k)}}{M_j^{(k)} + M_i^{(k)}} \quad (18.6)$$

and the update equations for the geometrical statistics are

$$M_j^{(k+1)} = M_j^{(k)} + M_i^{(k)} \quad (18.7)$$

$$\mathbf{C}_j^{(k+1)} = \frac{\mathbf{C}_j^{(k)} M_j^{(k)} + \mathbf{C}_i^{(k)} M_i^{(k)}}{M_j^{(k+1)}} \quad (18.8)$$

$$E_j^{(k+1)} = \frac{(E_j^{(k)} + C_{x,j}^{(k)\,2} + C_{y,j}^{(k)\,2}) M_j^{(k)} + (E_i^{(k)} + C_{x,i}^{(k)\,2} + C_{y,i}^{(k)\,2}) M_i^{(k)}}{M_j^{(k+1)}}$$

$$- C_{x,j}^{(k+1)2} - C_{y,j}^{(k+1)2} \quad (18.9)$$

Figure 18.13 shows how color locales appear for sample model and target images.

Texture Analysis

Every *locale* is associated with a locale-based texture histogram as discussed in Section 18.2.5. Thus a *locale-dependent* threshold makes more sense in generating the edge map. The threshold is obtained by examining the histogram of the locale edge magnitudes. The texture histogram is smoothed using a Gaussian filter and subsampled to size 8×7, then normalized.

The locale-based texture is a more effective measure of texture than is a global one, since the locale-dependent thresholds can be adjusted adaptively. Figure 18.14 compares locale-based edge detection to global-threshold-based edge detection, as discussed in Section 18.2.5. The edge-maps shown demonstrate that for the lamp and the banana objects, some edge points are missing when using global thresholding, but most of them exist when using locale-based thresholding. To draw the locale-based edge-map, edge pixels generated for any locale are unioned together.

Object Modeling and Matching

Object models in C-BIRD consist of a set of localized features. As shown above, they provide a rich set of statistical measures for later matching. Moreover, their geometric relationships, such as the spatial arrangement of locales, are also extracted. They are best represented using vectors connecting centroids of the respective locales.

The object-search method recovers 2D rigid object translation, scale, and rotation, as well as illumination change (full details are given in [12]). C-BIRD also allows a combination search, where an object search can be combined with other, simpler search types. In that case, the searches are executed according to decreasing speed. Since object search is the most complex search available, it is executed last, and only on the search results passed on so far by the other search types.

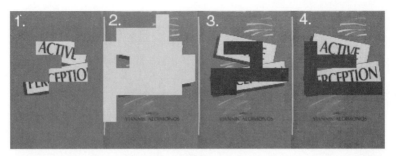

(a)

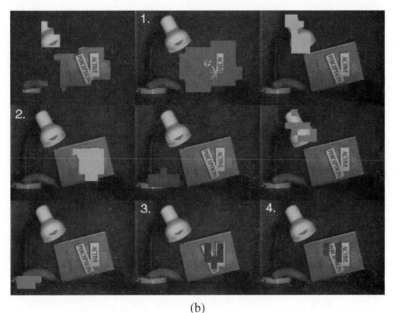

(b)

FIGURE 18.13: Color locales: (a) color locales for the model image; (b) color locales for a database image. (This figure also appears in the color insert section.)

The object image selected by the user is sent to the server for matching against the locales database. The localization of the submitted model object is considered the appropriate localization for the object, so that image locales need to be found that have a one-to-one correspondence with model locales. Such a correspondence is called an *assignment*.

A locale assignment has to pass several screening tests to verify an object match. Screening tests are applied in order of increasing complexity and dependence on previous tests. Figure 18.9 shows the sequence of steps during an object matching process: (a) user object model selection and model feature localization, (b) color-based screening test, (c) pose estimation, (d) texture support, and (e) shape verification.

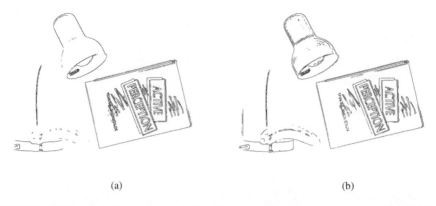

(a)   (b)

FIGURE 18.14: Global versus locale-based thresholds: (a) the edge map for the database image using a global threshold; (b) the edge map for the database image using a locale-based threshold.

The object match measure Q is formulated as follows:

$$Q = n \sum_{i=1}^{m} w_i Q_i \qquad (18.10)$$

where n is the number of locales in the assignment, m is the number of screening tests considered for the measure, Q_i is the fitness value of the assignment in screening test i, and w_i are weights that correspond to the importance of the fitness value of each screening test. The w_i can be arbitrary; they do not have to sum to 1. Care has to be taken to normalize the Q_i values to lie in the range $[0 .. 1]$, so that they all have the same numerical meaning.

Locales with higher mass (more pixels) statistically have a smaller percentage of localization error. The features are better defined, and small errors average out, so we have higher confidence in locales with large mass. Similarly, assignments with many model locales are preferable to few model locales, since the cumulative locale mass is larger and the errors average out.

We try to assign as many locales as possible first, then compute the match measure and check the error using a tight threshold. Locales are removed or changed in the assignment as necessary until a match is obtained. At that point, it is probably the best match measure possible, so it is unnecessary to try other assignments. In this case, all possible permutations of locale assignments do not have to checked.

In the worst case, when the object model is not present in the search image, we have to test all assignments to determine there is no match. The image locales in the database and the object model locales are sorted according to decreasing mass size.

Matching Steps

The screening tests applied to locales to generate assignments and validate them are:

- Color-based screening tests (step b):

- Illumination color covariant screening

- Chromaticity voting

- Elastic correlation

- Estimation of image object pose (step c)

- Texture support (step d)

- Shape verification (step e)

- Recovery of lighting change

The idea of color covariant matching is to realize that colors may change, from model to target, since the lighting may easily change. A diagonal model of lighting change states that the entire red channel responds to lighting change via an overall multiplicative change, as do the green and blue channels, each with their own multiplicative constant [11].

Locales *vote* on the correct lighting change, since each assignment of one model locale color to a target one implies a diagonal lighting shift. Many votes in the same cell of a voting space will imply a probable peak value for lighting change. Using the chromaticity voting scheme, all image locales are paired with all model locales to vote for lighting change values in a voting array.

We can evaluate the feasibility of having an assignment of image locales to model locales using the estimated chromaticity shift parameters by a type of *elastic correlation*. This computes the probability that there can be a correct assignment and returns the set of possible assignments. Having a candidate set of chromaticity shift parameters, each candidate is successively used to compute the elastic correlation measure. If the measure is high enough (higher than 80%, say), the possible assignments returned by the elastic correlation process are tested for object matching using pose estimation, texture support, and shape verification.

Figure 18.15 shows the elastic correlation process applied in the model chromaticity space $\Omega\{r', g'\}$: the model image has three locale colors at A′, B′ and C′. All the image locale colors, A, B, C, D, E, and F, are shifted to the model illuminant. Although the locales (A′, B′, C′) and (A, B, C) are supposed to be matching entities, they do not appear at exactly the same location. Instead of a rigid template matching (or correlation) method, we employ elastic correlation, in which the nodes A, B, C are allowed to be located in the vicinity of A′, B′, C′, respectively.

The pose estimation method (step (c)) uses geometrical relationships between locales for establishing pose parameters. For that reason, it has to be performed on a feasible locale assignment. Locale spatial relationships are represented by relationships between their centroids. The number of assigned locales is allowed to be as few as two, which is enough geometry information to drive estimation of a rigid body 2D displacement model with four parameters to recover: x, y translation, rotation **R**, and scale s [12].

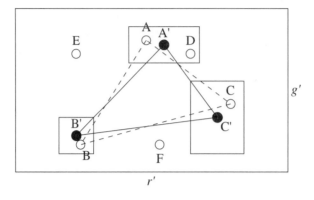

FIGURE 18.15: Elastic correlation in $\Omega\{r', g'\}$.

Results of pose estimation are both the best pose parameters for an assignment and the minimization objective value, which is an indication of how well the locales assignment fit using the rigid-body displacement model. If the error is within a small threshold, the pose estimate is accepted.

The texture-support screening test uses a variation of histogram intersection technique, where the texture histograms of locales in the assignment are intersected. If the intersection measure is higher than a threshold, the texture match is accepted.

The final match verification process (step (e)) is shape verification by the method of *Generalized Hough Transform* (*GHT*) [16]. The GHT is robust with respect to noise and occlusion [17]. Performing a full GHT search for all possible rotation, scale, and translation parameters is computationally expensive and inaccurate. Such a search is not feasible for large databases.

However, after performing pose estimation, we already know the pose parameters and can apply them to the model reference point to find the estimated reference point in the database image. Hence, the GHT search reduces to a mere confirmation that the number of votes in a small neighborhood around the reference point is indicative of a match. This GHT matching approach takes only a few seconds for a typical search. The reference point used is the model center, since it minimizes voting error caused by errors in edge gradient measurements.

Once we have shape verification, the image is reported as a match, and its match measure Q returned, if Q is large enough. After obtaining match measures Q_i for all images in the database, the Q_i measures are sorted according to decreasing value. The number of matches can further be restricted to the top k if necessary. An estimate of the correct illumination change follows from correct matches reported.

Figure 18.16(a) shows the GHT voting result for searching the pink book from one of the database images as in Figure 18.10(b). Darkness indicates the number of votes received, which in turn indicates the likelihood that the object is in the image and at that location. Figure 18.16(b) shows the reconstructed edge map for the book. Since the model edge map and the location, orientation, and scale of the object are known now, this reconstruction is entirely automated.

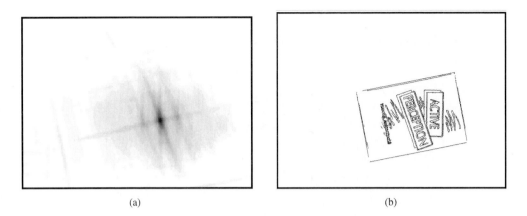

(a)   (b)

FIGURE 18.16: Using the GHT for shape verification: (a) GHT accumulator array image; (b) reconstruction of the detected object using the estimated pose and the GHT template (edge map).

Figure 18.17 shows some search results for the pink book in C-BIRD.

While C-BIRD is an experimental system, it does provide a proof in principle that the difficult task of search by object model is possible.

Video Locales

Definition: A *video locale* is a sequence of image feature locales that share similar features in the spatiotemporal domain of videos.

Like locales in images, video locales have their color, texture, and geometric properties. Moreover, they capture motion parameters, such as motion trajectory and speed, as well as temporal information, such as the lifespan of the video locale and its temporal relationships with respect to other video locales.

Since video proceeds in small time steps, we can also expect to develop new locales from ones already known from previous video frames more easily than simply starting from scratch in each frame [18].

Figure 18.18 shows that while speeding up the generation of locales substantially, little difference occurs in generating locales from each image (Intra-frame) and from predicting and then refining the locales (Inter-frame).

While we shall not go into the details of generating the video locales, suffice it to say that the inter-frame algorithm is always much faster than the intra-frame one. Moreover, video locales provide an effective means toward real-time video object segmentation and tracking [18].

18.3   SYNOPSIS OF CURRENT IMAGE SEARCH SYSTEMS

Some other current image search engines are mentioned here, along with URLs for each (more URLs and resources are in the Further Explorations section). The following is by no means a complete synopsis. Most of these engines are experimental, but all those included here are interesting in some way. Several include query features different from those outlined for C-BIRD.

(a)

(b)

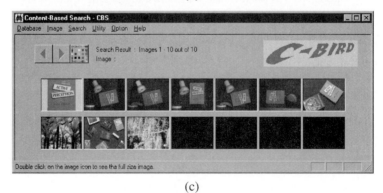

(c)

FIGURE 18.17: Search result for the pink book model with illumination change support: (a) search results using pose estimation only; (b) search results using pose estimation and texture support; (c) search results using GHT shape verification. *Some thumbnail images are from the Corel Gallery and are copyright Corel. All rights reserved.*

(a)   (b)   (c)

FIGURE 18.18: Intra-frame and Inter-frame video locales algorithm results: (a) original images; (b) intra-frame results; (c) inter-frame results.

18.3.1 QBIC

Query by Image Content (*QBIC*), developed by Niblack and colleagues [19] at IBM's Almaden Research Center in San Jose, is arguably the most famous search engine. Its URL is www.qbic.almaden.ibm.com.

One interesting feature in QBIC is the metric it uses for color histogram difference. Instead of simple histogram intersection, as in Equation (18.1), the metric recognizes that colors that are *similar*, such as red and orange, should not have a zero intersection. Instead, a color-distance matrix A is introduced, with elements

$$a_{ij} = (1 - d_{ij}/d_{max}) \tag{18.11}$$

Here, d_{ij} is defined as a three-dimensional color difference (using Euclidean distance, or any other likely distance — sum of absolute values, say).

Then a histogram-difference D^2 is defined as follows [20]:

$$D^2 = z^T A\, z \tag{18.12}$$

Vector z is a histogram-difference vector (for vectorized histograms). For example, the histogram-difference vectors z would be of length 256 if our two-dimensional chromaticity histograms were 16×16.

The striking feature of this metric is that it allows us to use simple differences of average three-dimensional color as a first screen, because the simpler metric is guaranteed to be a bound on the more complex one in Equation (18.12) [20].

QBIC has been developed further since its initial version and now forms an essential (and licensable) part of IBM's suite of Digital Library products. These aim at providing a complete media-collection management system.

An interesting development in the QBIC research effort at IBM is the attempt to include grayscale imagery in its domain [21], a difficult retrieval task. QBIC can combine other attributes with color-only-based searches — these can be textual annotations, such as captions, and texture. Texture, particularly, helps in graylevel image retrieval, since to some extent it captures structural information in an image. Database issues begin to dominate once the data set becomes very large, with careful control on cluster sizes and representatives for a tree-based indexing scheme.

18.3.2   UC Santa Barbara Search Engines

- **Alexandria Digital Library (ADL)** is a seasoned image search engine devised at the University of California, Santa Barbara. The ADL is presently concerned with geographical data: "spatial data on the web". The user can interact with a map and zoom into a map, then retrieve images as a query result type that pertain to the selected map area. This approach mitigates the fact that terabytes, perhaps, of data need to be stored for LANDSAT images, say. Instead, ADL uses a multiresolution approach that allows fast browsing by making use of image thumbnails. Multiresolution images means that it is possible to select a certain region within an image and zoom in on it. http://www.alexandria.ucsb.edu

- **NETRA** [22] is also part of the Alexandria Digital Library project. Now in its second generation as NETRA II, it emphasizes color image segmentation for object- or region- based search. http://maya.ece.ucsb.edu/Netra/

- **Perception-Based Image Retrieval (PBIR)** aims at a better version of learning and relevance feedback techniques with learning algorithms that try to get at the underlying query behind the user's choices in zeroing in on the right target. http://www.mmdb.ece.ucsb.edu/ demo/corelacm/

18.3.3   Berkeley Digital Library Project

The URL for this University of California, Berkeley, search engine is http://elib.cs.berkeley .edu. Text queries are supported, with search aimed at a particular commercial or other set of stock photos. The experimental version tries to include semantic information from text as a clue for image search.

18.3.4   Chabot

Chabot is an earlier system, also from UC Berkeley, that aims to include 500,000 digitized multiresolution images. Chabot uses the relational database management system POSTGRES to access these images and associated textual data. The system stores both text and color histogram data. Instead of color percentages, a "mostly red" type of simple query is acceptable. http://http.cs.berkeley.edu/ginger/chabot.html

18.3.5   Blobworld

Blobworld [23] was also developed at UC Berkeley. It attempts to capture the idea of objects by segmenting images into regions. To achieve a good segmentation, an *expectation maximization (EM)* algorithm derives the maximum likelihood for a good clustering in the feature space. Blobworld allows for both textual and content-based searching. The system has some degree of feedback, in that it displays the internal representation of the submitted image and the query results, so the user can better guide the algorithm. http://elib.cs.berkeley.edu/photos/blobworld

18.3.6   Columbia University Image Seekers

A team at Columbia University has developed the following search engines:

- **Content-Based Visual Query (CBVQ)**, developed by the ADVENT project at Columbia University, is the first of the series. (ADVENT stands for *All Digital Video Encoding, Networking and Transmission.*) It uses content-based image retrieval based on color, texture, and color composition. http://maya.ctr.columbia.edu:8088/cbvq

- **VisualSEEk** is a color-photograph retrieval system. Queries are by color layout, or by an image instance, such as the URL of a seed image, or by instances of prior matches. VisualSEEk supports queries based on the spatial relationships of visual features. http://www.ctr.columbia.edu/visualseek

- **SaFe**, an integrated spatial and feature image system, extracts regions from an image and compares the spatial arrangements of regions. http://disney.ctr.columbia.edu/safe

- **WebSEEk** collects images (and text) from the web. The emphasis is on making a searchable catalogue with such topics as animals, architecture, art, astronomy, cats, and so on. Relevance feedback is provided in the form of thumbnail images and motion icons. For video, a good form of feedback is also inclusion of small, short video sequences as animated GIF files. http://www.ctr.columbia.edu/webseek (includes a demo version)

18.3.7   Informedia

The Informedia Digital Video Library project at Carnegie Mellon University is now in its second generation, known as Informedia II. This centers on "video mining" and is funded by a consortium of government and corporate sponsors. http://informedia.cs.cmu.edu/

18.3.8   MetaSEEk

MetaSEEk is a meta-search engine, also developed at Columbia but under the auspices of their IMKA Intelligent Multimedia Knowledge Application Project. The idea is to query several other online image search engines, rank their performance for different classes of visual queries, and use them selectively for any particular search. http://ana.ctr.columbia.edu/metaseek/

18.3.9 Photobook and FourEyes

Photobook [24] was one of the earlier CBIR systems developed by the MIT Media Laboratory. It searches for three different types of image content (faces, 2-D shapes, and texture images) using three mechanisms. For the first two types, it creates an eigenfunction space — a set of "eigenimages". Then new images are described in terms of their coordinates in this basis. For textures, an image is treated as a sum of three orthogonal components in a decomposition denoted as *Wold* features [25].

With relevance feedback added, Photobook became FourEyes [26]. Not only does this system assign positive and negative weight changes for images, but given a similar query to one it has seen before, it can search faster than previously. http://vismod.www.media.mit.edu-/vismod/demos/photobook

18.3.10 MARS

MARS (Multimedia Analysis and Retrieval System) [27] was developed at the University of Illinois at Urbana-Champaign. The idea was to create a dynamic system of feature representations that could adapt to different applications and different users. Relevance feedback (see Section 18.4), with changes of weightings directed by the user, is the main tool used. www-db.ics.uci.edu/pages/research/mars.shtml

18.3.11 Virage

Visual Information Retrieval (Virage) [28] operates on objects within images. Image indexing is performed after several preprocessing operations, such as smoothing and contrast enhancement. The details of the feature vector are proprietary; however, it is known that the computation of each feature is made by not one but several methods, with a composite feature vector composed of the concatenation of these individual computations. http://www.virage.com/

18.3.12 Viper

Visual Information Processing for Enhanced Retrieval (VIPER) is an experimental system that concentrates on a user-guided shaping of finer and finer search constraints. This is referred to as relevance feedback. The system is developed by researchers at the University of Geneva. VIPER makes use of a huge set of approximately 80,000 potential image features, based on color and textures at different scales and in a hierarchical decomposition of the image at different scales. VIPER is distributed under the auspices of the open software distribution system GNU ("Gnu's Not Unix") under a General Public License. http://viper.unige.ch

18.3.13 Visual RetrievalWare

Visual RetrievalWare is an image search technology owned by Convera, Inc. It is built on techniques created for use by various government agencies for searching databases of standards documents. Its image version powers Yahoo's Image Surfer. Honeywell has licensed this technology as well. Honeywell x-rayed over one million of its products and plans to be able to index and search a database of these x-ray images. The features this software uses are color content, shape content, texture content, brightness structure, color structure, and aspect ratio. http://vrw.convera.com:8015/cst

18.4   RELEVANCE FEEDBACK

Relevance feedback is a powerful tool that has been brought to bear in recent CBIR systems is (see, e.g., [27]).   Briefly, the idea is to involve the user in a loop, whereby images retrieved are used in further rounds of convergence onto correct returns. The usual situation is that the user identifies images as good, bad, or don't care, and weighting systems are updated according to this user guidance. (Another approach is to *move the query toward positively marked content* [29]. An even more interesting idea is to move *every* data point in a disciplined way, by *warping* the space of feature points [30]. In the latter approach, the points themselves move along with the high-dimensional space being warped, much like raisins embedded in a volume of Jello that is being squeezed!)

18.4.1   MARS

In the MARS system [27], weights assigned to feature points are updated by user input. First, the MARS authors suppose that there are many features, $i = 1 .. I$ of them, such as color, texture, and so on. For each such feature, they further suppose that we can use multiple representations of each. For example, for color we may use color histograms, color layout, moments of color histograms, dominant colors, and so on. Suppose that, for each i, there are $j = 1 .. J_i$ such representations. Finally, for each representation j of feature i, suppose there is associated a set of $k = 1 .. K_{ij}$ components of a feature vector. So in the end, we have feature vector components r_{ijk}.

Each kind of feature i has importance, or weight, W_i, and weights W_{ij} are associated with each of the representations for the kind of feature i. Weights W_{ijk} are also associated with each component of each representation. Weights are meant to be *dynamic*, in that they change as further rounds of user feedback are incorporated.

Let $F = \{f_i\}$ be the whole set of features f_i. Let $R = \{r_{ij}\}$ be the set of representations for a given feature f_i. Then, again, just for the current feature i, suppose that $M = \{m_{ij}\}$ is a set of *similarity measures* used to determine how similar or dissimilar two representations are in set R. That is, different metrics should be used for different representations: a vector-based representation might use Mahalanobis distance for comparing feature vectors, while histogram intersection may be used for comparing color histograms. With set D being the raw image data, an entire expression of a relevance feedback algorithm is expressed as a model (D, F, R, M).

Then the retrieval process suggested in [29] is as follows:

1. Initialize weights as uniform values:

$$
\begin{aligned}
W_i &= 1/I \\
W_{ij} &= 1/J_i \\
W_{ijk} &= 1/K_{ij}
\end{aligned}
$$

Recall that I is the number of features in set F; J_i is the number of representations for feature f_i; and K_{ij} is the length of the representation vector r_{ij}.

2. A database image's similarity to the query is first defined in terms of components:

$$S(r_{ij}) = m_{ij}(r_{ij}, W_{ijk}).$$

Then each representation's similarity values are grouped as

$$S(f_i) = \sum_j W_{ij} S(r_{ij}).$$

3. Finally, the overall similarity S is defined as

$$S = \sum_i W_i S(f_i).$$

4. The top N images similar to query image Q are then returned.

5. Each of the retrieved images is marked by the user as highly relevant, relevant, no opinion, nonrelevant, or highly nonrelevant, according to his or her subjective opinion.

6. Weights are updated, and the process is repeated.

Similarities have to be normalized to get a meaningful set of images returned:

1. Since representations may have different scales, features are normalized, both offline (*intranormalization*), and online (*internormalization*).

2. Intranormalization: the idea here is the normalization of the r_{ijk} so as to place equal emphasis on each component within a representation vector r_{ij}. For *each component* k, find an average over all M images in the database, μ_k. Then replace that component by its normalized score in the usual fashion from statistics:

$$r_{ijk} \to \frac{r_{ijk} - \mu_k}{\sigma_k}.$$

3. Internormalization: here we look for equal emphasis for each similarity value $S(r_{ij})$ within the overall measure S. We find the mean μ_{ij} and standard deviation σ_{ij} over all database image *similarity measures S*.

4. Then, online, for any new query Q we replace the raw similarity between Q and a database image m by

$$S_{m,Q}(r_{ij}) \to \frac{S_{m,Q}(r_{ij}) - \mu_{ij}}{3\sigma_{ij}}.$$

Finally, the weight update process is as follows:

1. Scores of $\{3, 1, 0, -1, -3\}$ are assigned to user opinions "highly relevant" to "highly nonrelevant".

2. Weights are updated as

$$W_{ij} \to W_{ij} + Score$$

for images viewed by the user. Then weights are normalized by

$$W_{ij} \to \frac{W_{ij}}{\sum W_{ij}}.$$

3. The inverse of the standard deviation of feature r_{ijk} is assigned to the component weight W_{ijk}:

$$W_{ijk} = \frac{1}{\sigma_{ijk}}.$$

That is, the smaller the variance, the larger the weight.

4. Finally, these weights are also normalized:

$$W_{ijk} \rightarrow \frac{W_{ijk}}{\sum W_{ijk}}.$$

The basic advantage of putting the user into the loop by using relevance feedback is that this way, the user need not provide a completely accurate initial query. Relevance feedback establishes a more accurate link between low-level features and high-level concepts, somewhat closing the semantic gap. Of course, retrieval performance of CBIR systems is bettered this way.

18.4.2   iFind

An experimental system that explicitly uses relevance feedback in image retrieval is the Microsoft Research system *iFind* [31]. This approach attempts to get away from just low-level image features by addressing the semantic content in images. Images are associated with keywords, and a semantic net is built for image access based on these, integrated with low-level features. Keywords have links to images in the database, with weights assigned to each link. The degree of relevance, the weight, is updated on each relevance feedback round.

Clearly, an image can be associated with multiple keywords, each with a different degree of relevance. Where do the keywords come from? They can be generated manually or retrieved from the ALT HTML tag associated with an image, using a web crawler.

18.5   QUANTIFYING RESULTS

Generally speaking, some simple expression of the performance of image search engines is desirable.

In information retrieval theory, *precision* is the percentage of relevant documents retrieved compared to the number of all the documents retrieved, and *recall* is the percentage of relevant documents retrieved out of all relevant documents. Recall and precision are widely used for reporting retrieval performance for image retrieval systems as well. However, these measures are affected by the database size and the amount of similar information in the database. Also, they do not consider fuzzy matching or search result ordering.

In equation form, these quantities are defined as

$$Precision = \frac{Desired\ images\ returned}{All\ retrieved\ images}$$

$$Recall = \frac{Desired\ images\ returned}{All\ desired\ images} \tag{18.13}$$

In general, the more we relax thresholds and allow more images to be returned, the smaller the precision, but the larger the recall. The curve of precision versus recall is termed a *receiver operator characteristic* (*ROC*) curve. It plots the relationship between sensitivity and specificity over a range of parameters.

18.6   QUERYING ON VIDEOS

Video indexing can make use of *motion* as the salient feature of temporally changing images for various types of queries. We shall not examine video indexing in any detail here but refer the reader to the excellent survey in [32].

In brief, since temporality is the main difference between a video and just a collection of images, dealing with the time component is first and foremost in comprehending the indexing, browsing, search, and retrieval of video content. A direction taken by the QBIC group [21] is a new focus on storyboard generation for automatic understanding of video — the so-called "inverse Hollywood" problem. In production of a video, the writer and director start with a visual depiction of how the story proceeds. In a video understanding situation, we would ideally wish to regenerate this storyboard as the starting place for comprehending the video.

The first place to start, then, would be dividing the video into *shots*, where each shot consists roughly of the video frames between the on and off clicks of the Record button. However, transitions are often placed between shots — fade-in, fade-out, dissolve, wipe, and so on — so detection of shot boundaries may not be so simple as for abrupt changes.

Generally, since we are dealing with digital video, if at all possible we would like to avoid uncompressing MPEG files, say, to speed throughput. Therefore, researchers try to work on the compressed video. A simple approach to this idea is to uncompress just enough to recover the DC term, generating a thumbnail 64 times smaller than the original. Since we must consider P- and B-frames as well as I-frames, even generating a good approximation of the best DC image is itself a complicated problem.

Once DC frames are obtained from the whole video — or, even better, are obtained on the fly — many approaches have been used for finding shot boundaries. Features used have typically been color, texture, and motion vectors, although such concepts as trajectories traversed by objects have also been used [33].

Shots are grouped into *scenes*. A scene is a collection of shots that belong together and that are contiguous in time. Even higher-level semantics exist in so-called "film grammar" [34]. Semantic information such as the basic elements of the story may be obtainable. These are (at the coarsest level) the story's exposition, crisis, climax, and denouement.

Audio information is important for scene grouping. In a typical scene, the audio has no break within a scene, even though many shots may take place over the course of the scene. General timing information from movie creation may also be brought to bear.

Text may indeed be the most useful means of delineating shots and scenes, making use of closed-captioning information already available. However, relying on text is unreliable, since it may not exist, especially for legacy video.

Different schemes have been proposed for organizing and displaying storyboards reasonably succinctly. The most straightforward method is to display a two-dimensional array of *keyframes*. Just what constitutes a good keyframe has of course been subject to much debate. One approach might be to simply output one frame every few seconds. However, action has a tendency to occur between longer periods of inactive story. Therefore, some kind of clustering method is usually used, to represent a longer period of time that is more or less the same within the temporal period belonging to a single keyframe.

Some researchers have suggested using a graph-based method. Suppose we have a video of two talking heads, the interviewer and the interviewee. A sensible representation might be a digraph with directed arcs taking us from one person to the other, then back again. In this way, we can encapsulate much information about the video's structure and also have available the arsenal of tools developed for graph pruning and management.

Other "proxies" have also been developed for representing shots and scenes. A grouping of *sets* of keyframes may be more representative than just a sequence of keyframes, as may keyframes of variable sizes. Annotation by text or voice, of each set of keyframes in a "skimmed" video, may be required for sensible understanding of the underlying video.

A *mosaic* of several frames may be useful, wherein frames are combined into larger ones by matching features over a set of frames. This results in set of larger keyframes that are perhaps more representational of the video.

An even more radical approach to video representation involves selecting (or creating) a *single* frame that best represents the entire movie! This could be based on making sure that people are in the frame, that there is action, and so on. In [35], Dufaux proposes an algorithm that selects shots and keyframes based on measures of motion-activity (via frame difference), spatial activity (via entropy of the pixel value distribution), skin-color pixels, and face detection.

By taking into account skin color and faces, the algorithm increases the likelihood of the selected keyframe including people and portraits, such as close-ups of movie actors, thereby producing interesting keyframes. Skin color is learned using labeled image samples. Face detection is performed using a neural net.

Figure 18.19(a) shows a selection of frames from a video of beach activity (see [36]). Here, the keyframes in Figure 18.19(b) are selected based mainly on color information (but being careful with respect to the changes incurred by changing illumination conditions when videos are shot).

A more difficult problem arises when changes between shots are gradual and when colors are rather similar overall, as in Figure 18.20(a). The keyframes in Figure 18.20(b) are sufficient to show the development of the whole video sequence.

Other approaches attempt to deal with more profoundly human aspects of video, as opposed to lower-level visual or audio features. Much effort has gone into applying data mining or knowledge-base techniques to *classifying* videos into such categories as sports, news, and so on, and then subcategories such as football and basketball. Zhou and Kuo [37] give a good summary of attempts to provide intelligent systems for video analysis.

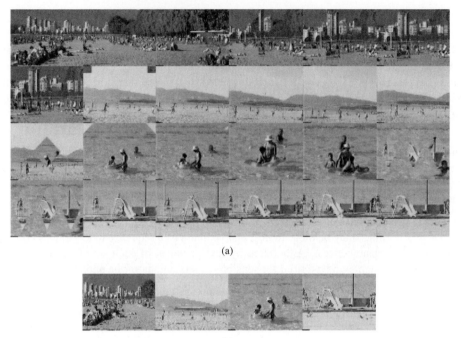

(a)

(b)

FIGURE 18.19: Digital video and associated keyframes, beach video: (a) frames from a digital video; (b) keyframes selected.

18.7 QUERYING ON OTHER FORMATS

Work on using audio or combining audio with video to better comprehend multimedia content is fascinating. Wang et al. [38] is a good introduction to using both audio and video cues. He et al. [39] offer an interesting effort to understand and navigate slides from lectures, based on the time spent on each slide and the speaker's intonation. Other interesting approaches include search-by-audio [40] and "query-by-humming" [41].

Other features researchers have looked at for indexing include indexing actions, concepts and feelings, facial expressions, and so on. Clearly, this field is a developing and growing one, particularly because of the advent of the MPEG-7 standard (see Chapter 12).

18.8 OUTLOOK FOR CONTENT-BASED RETRIEVAL

A recent overview [42] collecting the very latest ideas in content-based retrieval identified the following present and future trends: indexing, search, query, and retrieval of multimedia data based on

1. Video retrieval using video features: image color and object shape, video segmentation, video keyframes, scene analysis, structure of objects, motion vectors, optical flow (from computer vision), multispectral data, and so-called "signatures" that summarize the data

(a)

(b)

FIGURE 18.20: Garden video: (a) frames from a digital video; (b) keyframes selected.

2. Spatiotemporal queries, such as trajectories

3. Semantic features; syntactic descriptors

4. Relevance feedback, a well-known technique from information retrieval

5. Sound, especially spoken documents, such as using speaker information

6. Multimedia database techniques, such as using relational databases of images

7. Fusion of textual, visual, and speech cues

8. Automatic and instant video manipulation; user-enabled editing of multimedia databases

9. Multimedia security, hiding, and authentication techniques such as watermarking

This field is truly rich and meshes well with the outline direction of MPEG-7.

In another direction, researchers try to create a search profile to encompass most instances available, say all "animals". Then, for relational database searches, such search profiles are communicated via database queries. For searches using visual features, intelligent search engines learn a user's query concepts through active learning [43]. This type of endeavor is called "query-based learning".

Another approach focuses on comprehending how people view images as similar, on the basis of perception [44]. The function used in this approach is a type of "perceptual similarity measure" and is *learned* by finding the best set of features (color, texture, etc.) to capture "similarity" as defined via the groups of similar images identified.

18.9 FURTHER EXPLORATION

Good books [45, 46, 47, 48] are beginning to appear on the issues involved in CBIR.

Links to many useful content-based retrieval sites are collected in the Further Exploration section of the text web site for this chapter:

- A Java applet version of the C-BIRD system described in Section 18.2

- A demo of QBIC as an artwork server

- Demo versions of the Alexandria Digital Library, the Berkeley Digital Library Project, Photobook, Visual RetrievalWare, VIPER, and VisualSEEk

- A demo of MediaSite, now rebranded Sonic Foundary Media Systems. The Informedia project provided the search engine power for this commercially available system.

- A demo of the NETRA system. The idea is to select an image, then a particular segment within an image, and search on that model.

- A video describing the technology for the Virage system. Virage provides the search engine for AltaVista's Image Search

- The keyframe production method for Figures 18.19 and 18.20.

- And links to standard sets of digital images and videos, for testing retrieval and video segmentation programs

18.10 EXERCISES

1. What is the essence of *feature localization*? What are the pros and cons of this approach, as opposed to the traditional image segmentation method?

2. Show that the update equation (Equation 18.9) is correct — that is, the eccentricity $E_j^{(k+1)}$ for parent locale j at iteration $k + 1$ can be derived using the eccentricity, centroid, and mass information for the parent locale j and child locale i at iteration k. (Note: $C_{x,j}^{(k)}$ and $C_{y,j}^{(k)}$ are the x and y components of the centroid $\mathbf{C}_j^{(k)}$, respectively.)

3. Try the VIPER search engine, refining the search with relevance feedback for a few iterations. The demo mentions Gabor histograms and Gabor blocks. Read enough of the files associated with the site to determine the meaning of these terms, and write a short explanation of their use.

4. Try a few of the more experimental image search engines in the Further Exploration section above. Some are quite impressive, but most are fairly undependable when used on broad data domains.

5. Devise a text-annotation taxonomy (categorization) for image descriptions, starting your classification using the set of Yahoo! categories, say.

6. Examine several web site image captions. How useful would you say the textual data is as a cue for identifying image contents? (Typically, search systems use *word stemming*, for eliminating tense, case, and number from words — the word *stemming* becomes the word *stem*.)

7. Suggest at least three ways in which audio analysis can assist in video retrieval-system-related tasks.

8. Suppose a color histogram is defined coarsely, with bins quantized to 8 bits, with 3 bits for each red and green and 2 for blue. Set up an appropriate structure for such a histogram, and fill it from some image you read. Template Visual C++ code for reading an image is on the text web site, as `sampleCcode.zip` under "Sample Code".

9. Try creating a texture histogram as described in Section 18.2.5. You could try a small image and follow the steps given there, using MATLAB, say, for ease of visualization.

10. Describe how you may find an image containing some 2D "brick pattern" in an image database, assuming the color of the "brick" is yellow and the color of the "gaps" is blue. (Make sure you discuss the limitations of your method and the possible improvements.)

    (a) Use color only.

    (b) Use edge-based texture measures only.

    (c) Use color, texture, and shape.

11. The main difference between a static image and video is the availability of motion in the latter. One important part of CBR from video is motion estimation (e.g., the direction and speed of any movement). Describe how you could estimate the movement of an object in a video clip, say a car, if MPEG (instead of uncompressed) video is used.

12. Color is three-dimensional, as Newton pointed out. In general, we have made use of several different color spaces, all of which have some kind of brightness axis, plus two intrinsic-color axes.

    Let's use a *chromaticity* two-dimensional space, as defined in Equation (4.7). We'll use just the first two dimensions, $\{x, y\}$. Devise a 2D color histogram for a few images, and find their histogram intersections. Compare image similarity measures with those derived using a 3D color histogram, comparing over several different color resolutions. Is it worth keeping all three dimensions, generally?

13. Implement an image search engine using low-level image features such as color histogram, color moments, and texture. Construct an image database that contains at least 500 images from at least 10 different categories. Perform retrieval tasks using a single low-level feature as well as a combination of features. Which feature combination gives the best retrieval results, in terms of both precision and recall, for each category of images?

18.11 REFERENCES

1 M.M. Fleck, D.A. Forsyth, and C. Bregler, "Finding Naked People," in *European Congress on Computer Vision*, 1996, (2)593–602.

2 C.C. Chang and S.Y. Lee, "Retrieval of Similar Pictures on Pictorial Databases," *Pattern Recognition*, 24:675–680, 1991.

3 S. Paek, C.L. Sable, V. Hatzivassiloglou, A. Jaimes, B.H. Schiffman, S.F. Chang, and K.R. McKeown, "Integration of Visual and Text Based Approaches for the Content Labeling and Classification of Photographs," in *ACM SIGIR'99 Workshop on Multimedia Indexing and Retrieval*, 1999, 423–444.

4 K. Barnard and D.A. Forsyth, "Learning the Semantics of Words and Pictures," in *Proceedings of the International Conference on Computer Vision*, 2001, 2:408–415.

5 M.J. Swain and D.H. Ballard, "Color Indexing," *International Journal of Computer Vision*, 7(1):11–32, 1991.

6 A.W.M. Smeulders, M. Worring, S. Santini, A. Gupta, and R. Jain, "Content-Based Image Retrieval at the End of the Early Years" *IEEE Transactions on Pattern Analysis and Machine Intelligence*, 22:1349–1380, 2000.

7 Z.N. Li, O.R. Zaïane, and Z. Tauber, "Illumination Invariance and Object Model in Content-Based Image and Video Retrieval," *Journal of Visual Communication and Image Representation*, 10(3):219–244, 1999.

8 H. Tamura, S. Mori, and T. Yamawaki, "Texture Features Corresponding to Visual Perception," *IEEE Transactions on Systems, Man, and Cybernetics*, SMC-8(6):460–473, 1978.

9 A.R. Rao and G.L. Lohse, "Towards a Texture Naming System: Identifying Relevant Dimensions of Texture," in *IEEE Conference on Visualization*, 1993, 220–227.

10 R. Jain, R. Kasturi, and B.G. Schunck, *Machine Vision*. New York: McGraw-Hill, 1995.

11 M.S. Drew, J. Wei, and Z.N. Li, "Illumination-Invariant Image Retrieval and Video Segmentation," *Pattern Recognition*, 32:1369–1388, 1999.

12 M.S. Drew, Z.N. Li, and Z. Tauber, "Illumination Color Covariant Locale-Based Visual Object Retrieval," *Pattern Recognition*, 35(8):1687–1704, 2002.

13 B.V. Funt and G.D. Finlayson, "Color Constant Color Indexing," *IEEE Transactions on Pattern Analysis and Machine Intelligence*, 17:522–529, 1995.

14 D.H. Ballard and C.M. Brown, *Computer Vision*, Upper Saddle River, NJ: Prentice Hall, 1982.

15 T.H. Hong and A. Rosenfeld, "Compact Region Extraction Using Weighted Pixel Linking in a Pyramid," *IEEE Transactions on Pattern Analysis and Machine Intelligence*, 6:222–229, 1984.

16 D. Ballard, "Generalizing the Hough Transform to Detect Arbitrary Shapes," *Pattern Recognition*, 13(2):111–122, 1981.

17 P. Gvozdjak and Z.N. Li, "From Nomad to Explorer: Active Object Recognition on Mobile Robots," *Pattern Recognition*, 31(6):773–790, 1998.

18 J. Au, Z.N. Li, and M.S. Drew, "Object Segmentation and Tracking Using Video Locales," in *Proceedings of the International Conference on Pattern Recognition (ICPR 2002)*, 2002, 2:544–547.

19 M. Flickner, et al, "Query by Image and Video Content: The QBIC System," *IEEE Computer*, 28(9):23–32, 1995.

20 J. Hafner, H.S. Sawhney, W. Equitz, M. Flickner, and W. Niblack, "Efficient Color Histogram Indexing for Quadratic Form Distance Functions," *IEEE Transactions on Pattern Analysis and Machine Intelligence*, 17:729–736, 1995.

21 W. Niblack, Xiaoming Zhu, J.L. Hafner, T. Breuel, D. Ponceleon, D. Petkovic, M.D. Flickner, E. Upfal, S.I. Nin, S. Sull, B. Dom, Boon-Lock Yeo, A. Srinivasan, D. Zivkovic, and M. Penner, "Updates to the QBIC System," in *Storage and Retrieval for Image and Video Databases*, 1998, 150–161.

22 Y. Deng, D. Mukherjee, and B.S. Manjunath, "NETRA-V: Toward an Object-Based Video Representation," in *Storage and Retrieval for Image and Video Databases (SPIE)*, 1998, 202–215.

23 C. Carson, S. Belongie, H. Greenspan, and J. Malik, "Blobworld: Image Segmentation Using Expectation-Maximization and its Application to Image Querying," *IEEE Transactions on Pattern Analysis and Machine Intelligence*, 24(8):1026–1038, 2002.

24 A. Pentland, R. Picard, and S. Sclaroff, "Photobook: Content-Based Manipulation of Image Databases," in *Storage and Retrieval for Image and Video Databases (SPIE)*, 1994, 34–47.

25 F. Liu and R.W. Picard, "Periodicity, Directionality, and Randomness: Wold Features for Image Modeling and Retrieval," *IEEE Transactions on Pattern Analysis and Machine Intelligence*, 18:722–733, 1996.

26 R.W. Picard, T. P. Minka, and M. Szummer, "Modeling User Subjectivity in Image Libraries," in *IEEE International Conference on Image Processing*, 1996, 2:777–780.

27 Y. Rui, T. S. Huang, M. Ortega, and S. Mehrotra, "Relevance Feedback: A Power Tool for Interactive Content-Based Image Retrieval," *IEEE Transactions on Circuits and Systems for Video Technology*, 8(5):644–655, 1998.

28 A. Hampapur, A. Gupta, B. Horowitz, and C.F. Shu, "The Virage Image Search Engine: An Open Framework for Image Management," in *Storage and Retrieval for Image and Video Databases (SPIE)*, 1997, 188–198.

29 Y. Ishikawa, R. Subramanya, and C. Faloutsos, "Mindreader: Querying Databases through Multiple Examples," in *24th International Conference on Very Large Data Bases, VLDB*, 1998, 433–438.

30 H.Y. Bang and T. Chen, "Feature Space Warping: An Approach to Relevance Feedback," in *International Conference on Image Processing*, 2002, I:968–971.

31 Y. Lu, C. Hu, X. Zhu, H. Zhang, and Q. Yang, "A Unified Framework for Semantics and Feature Based Relevance Feedback in Image Retrieval Systems," in *Eighth ACM International Conference on Multimedia*, 2000, 31–37.

32 R. Brunelli, O. Mich, and C.M. Modena, "A Survey on the Automatic Indexing of Video Data," *Journal of Visual Communication and Image Representation*, 10:78–112, 1999.

33 S.F. Chang, et al., "VideoQ: An Automated Content Based Video Search System Using Visual Cues," in *Proceedings of ACM Multimedia 97*, 1997, 313–324.

34 D. Bordwell and K. Thompson, *Film Art: An Introduction*, New York: McGraw-Hill, 1993.

35 F. Dufaux, "Key Frame Selection to Represent a Video," in *International Conference on Image Processing*, 2000, 2:275–278.

36 M.S. Drew and J. Au, "Video Keyframe Production by Efficient Clustering of Compressed Chromaticity Signatures," In *ACM Multimedia 2000*, 2000, 365–368.

37 W. Zhou and C.C.J. Kuo, *Intelligent Systems for Video Understanding*, Upper Saddle River, NJ: Prentice-Hall PTR, 2002.

38 Y. Wang, Z. Liu, and J.C. Huang, "Multimedia Content Analysis Using Both Audio and Visual Clues," *IEEE Signal Processing Magazine*, 17:12–36, 2000.

39 L. He, E. Sanocki, A. Gupta, and J. Grudin, "Auto-Summarization of Audio-Video Presentations," in *ACM Multimedia*, 1999, 1:489–498.

40 E. Wold, T. Blum, D. Keislar, and J. Wheaton, "Content-Based Classification, Search, and Retrieval of Audio," *IEEE Multimedia*, 3:27–36, 1996.

41 N. Kosugi, Y. Nishihara, T. Sakata, M. Yamamuro, and K. Kushima, "A Practical Query-by-Humming System for a Large Music Database," in *ACM Multimedia*, 2000, 333–342.

42 S. Basu, A. Del Bimbo, A.H. Tewfik, and H. Zhang, "Special Issue on Multimedia Database," *IEEE Transactions on Multimedia*, 4(2):141–143, 2002.

43 I.J. Cox, M.L. Miller, T.P. Minka, T.V. Papathomas, and P.N. Yianilos, "The Bayesian Image Retrieval System, Pichunter: Theory, Implementation and Psychological Experiments," *IEEE Transactions on Image Processing*, 9(1):20–37, 2000.

44 B. Li, E. Chang, and C.T. Wu, "DPF — A Perceptual Distance Function for Image Retrieval," in *IEEE International Conference on Image Processing*, 2002, 2:597–600.

45 G. Lu, *Multimedia Database Management Systems*, Norwood, MA: Artech House Publishing, 1999.

46 A. Del Bimbo, *Visual Information Retrieval*, San Francisco: Morgan Kaufmann, 1999.

47 M. Lew, ed., *Principles of Visual Information Retrieval*, Berlin: Springer-Verlag, 2001.

48 V. Castelli and L.D. Bergman, eds., *Image Databases: Search and Retrieval of Digital Imagery*, New York: Wiley, 2002.

Index